Entrepreneurship and Small Business Management

A Volume in the Wiley Series
in Management and Administration

ENTREPRENEURSHIP AND SMALL BUSINESS MANAGEMENT

HANS SCHÖLLHAMMER
University of California, Los Angeles

ARTHUR H. KURILOFF
University of California, Los Angeles

JOHN WILEY & SONS
New York   Chichester   Brisbane   Toronto

Library of Congress Cataloging in Publication Data

Schöllhammer, Hans, 1933–
   Entrepreneurship and small business management.

   (Wiley series in management and administration)
   1. New business enterprises—Management.
2. Small business—Management. 3. Entrepreneur.
I. Kuriloff, Arthur H., joint author. II. Title.
HD69.N3S36   658.022   78-9443
ISBN 0-471-76260-1

Printed in the United States of America
10 9 8 7 6 5 4 3 2 1

HANS SCHÖLLHAMMER

Hans Schöllhammer is an Associate Professor in the Graduate School of Management, University of California, Los Angeles. He received his DBA degree from Indiana University and has taught at Columbia University, the Cranfield Institute of Technology, and the Institute for International Studies and Training. He has held management positions in industry and in recent years has been involved in consulting with new and small business ventures through the Small Business Institute of the Small Business Administration. Hans Schöllhammer has published books, monographs and articles treating international and comparative management issues.

ARTHUR H. KURILOFF

Arthur H. Kuriloff, Lecturer in the Graduate School of Management, University of California, Los Angeles, brings to his writing an extensive background in line management and in consulting with business organizations. He holds the BSME and MBA degrees.

He has started and managed three successful small companies and now owns and manages the fourth. His experience includes over twenty years in line management. He has served as a senior member on the professional staff of Cresap, McCormick and Paget, Inc. (New York office), management consultants. For the past ten years he has concentrated on the solution of problems in entrepreneurship and starting and running the small business.

Mr. Kuriloff has lectured extensively on management subjects before such organizations as the American Management Association and the Industrial Conference Board. He has conducted educational seminars for executives at many universities and colleges.

Arthur Kuriloff is the author of *Reality in Management*, McGraw-Hill Book Co., 1966, and of *Organizational Development for Survival*, A.M.A., 1972, and co-author of *How to Start Your Own Business—and Succeed*, McGraw-Hill, 1978. He has published numerous articles dealing with management principles and practice.

*To our venturesome students in
Entrepreneurship and Venture
Initiation, and Small Business
Management*

PREFACE

The economic development of a nation is sparked largely by its enterprising spirit. This characteristic emerges from the interplay of behavior and activity of a special segment of the population known as entrepreneurs.

If the nation's economy is not to stagnate under the ministrations of professionals, it must be continuously revitalized by the infusion of new energy, new ideas, and nuclei for economic growth. Entrepreneurs and their small businesses are of signal importance in this process of renewal.

The importance of small business is shown by the Bureau of Census figures at the close of the 1960s. The Internal Revenue Service reported tax returns for 1968 from 11,672,000 businesses including proprietorships, active partnerships, and corporations. Of these, about 90 percent employed fewer than 250 people, a size considered to be small business by the Small Business Administration. Slightly more than 50 percent of all businesses reported an annual income of less than $10,000; these are too small to meet the criteria of small business enterprise as discussed in this book. There remain about five and a half million small businesses that are in the category discussed here. That is about twice the number reported in 1945—a substantial increase. There is reason to assume that small businesses will continue to increase with the advance of technology and the desire of many young people to venture into their own endeavors.

Our purpose in preparing this book is to present in one place the theory, general principles, and practice required to initiate and manage a small business successfully. We have not attempted to cover entrepreneurship in general. We have concentrated rather on entrepreneurship as it applies to starting a small business and on management tailored to running it. We have tried to prepare budding enterprises to recognize and avoid the pitfalls of the new small business—and to do what is needed when it is needed to enhance their chances for success.

The material presented in this book has been drawn from academic sources and from the practices of entrepreneurs who have been eminently successful in founding their own businesses. The pedagogic approach has been tested and refined in programs covering seven years of experience in the Graduate School of Management at the University of California, Los Angeles.

We have aimed the book primarily at the university level. It should serve the needs of senior students and graduate students in schools of management and business administration. In addition, others who want to learn about starting and running a business should find much useful information in the text.

We have tried to avoid the customary assumption that the user of a management textbook is already in business and needs only to know how to manage it. Recognizing that no one can run a business until it has been started, we begin with the development and testing of the original idea for a product or service and consider the sequential steps that must be taken to interest and find capital. Then we examine the principles and practice of running the business.

We have attempted to offer an educational vehicle that will meet the changing values of our new breed of students. Our close contact with numbers of young college people in schools of management clearly substantiates what is common knowledge today, that many of these students seek work that incorporates values of social utility, ethicality, and humanistic quality. They want to follow their own stars by working for themselves or for smaller companies in which they have the opportunity for early responsibility. To meet these requirements, we have stressed the desirability of nonfrivolous products or services designed to serve the needs of customers in a substantial and ethical way.

The plan of the book is keyed to a rational, step-by-step procedure in starting a new business and running it effectively. The book is divided into three parts. The first deals with entrepreneurship, the second with small business management, and the third presents a series of complex, comprehensive cases in small business.

Part 1, on entrepreneurship, gives a brief historical survey of entrepreneurship, including a summary of more recent findings about the need for achievement and the possibility of strengthening it in the individual. Chapters 2 and 3 concentrate on ways to identify and analyze new venture opportunities in terms of market possibilities and market strategy. Chapter 4 discusses the legal considerations that must be met in starting a business and in protecting new venture ideas. Chapter 5 tells how to put it all together in the development of a comprehensive prospectus for the new business. The problems of financing the new venture are discussed in Chapter 6. These include estimating financial requirements, identifying sources of capital, and using capital substitutes.

Part 2 covers the more traditional requirements of successful management from the point of view of the small business organization. Chapter 7 treats short- and long-range planning needs of the small company, emphasizing the critical elements in which many small businesses have been notoriously weak. Chapter 8 addresses the special problem of organizing the small firm, including influence of size, the technology employed, the roles of personnel, and the roles of the formal and informal organizations. Personnel management in the small company is given special treatment in Chapter 9, which covers initial personnel planning, recruitment and selection, compensation policies and practices, and the issue of unionization. Chapter 10 suggests some simple ways for developing a management succession program and outlines procedures available to the small business for training and developing managers. Chapter 11 discusses marketing management in the small firm, considering strategy and tactics for developing the product: pricing and distribution, packaging and branding, advertising, market research and sales forecasting, and developing a marketing plan. Production and operations are covered in Chapter 12. The issues discussed include location, design, and layout of the small plant; intensive or extensive use of facilities; possibilities of the short workweek; recommendations for the conduct of research and development; and major issues in purchasing and production. Chapter 13 addresses management control methods including elements of planning and control; control through analysis of financial statements; fundamentals of production, inventory, and quality control; and the application of simple charting for control purposes. The methodology of organizational development as applicable to the small business is treated in Chapter 14. The discussion focuses on achieving organizational effectiveness through purposeful activity; included are structural and behavioral-oriented methods for developing viable management.

Part 3 contains a selected group of cases concentrating on initiating and managing small business. These cases highlight the instructional purposes of the book and are offered as a major pedagogic device for reinforcing the teaching of entrepreneurship and small business management.

Hans Schöllhammer
Arthur H. Kuriloff

CONTENTS

PART II Small Business Management   178

PART I

ENTREPRENEURSHIP AND STARTING A NEW BUSINESS

INTRODUCTION

In Part I of this book we assume that the reader has had no prior experience in launching a business venture. The presentation therefore concentrates on four key requirements that make a broad base for the entrepreneurial adventure: 1) know yourself; 2) know the business you want to enter; 3) know marketing; and, 4) know financial management.

KNOW YOURSELF

Not everyone is capable of starting and running a business successfully; statistically, those who have done so show entrepreneurial personalities. The entrepreneurial personality is characterized by special qualities that have been clearly isolated through research.[1] Quite logically then, persons contemplating becoming enterprisers in business would do well to check how closely their own characteristics match those found in successful entrepreneurs.

Too wide a difference might well suggest the inadvisability of entering the world of business as an owner. On the other hand, if the characteris-

---

[1]David C. McClelland and David G. Winter, *Motivating Economic Achievement*, New York: The Free Press, 1969, is a major reference summarizing the relationship of entrepreneurial personality to economic achievement. See particularly chapters 1, 7, 9, and 12 for treatment of policy for economic development and chapters 2, 4, 7, and 9–11 for treatment of motivation and methods for strengthening personal entrepreneurial drives.

tics of the prospective enterpriser match reasonably well those of successful entrepreneurs, this would give a reassuring go-ahead signal.

A third possibility remains. Prospective businesspersons may practice procedures designed to strengthen the basic entrepreneurial quality known as the *need for achievement*. They can use these procedures to increase their achieving drive.

Know yourself means examining oneself for entrepreneurial characteristics. The decision about proceeding with the business venture may then be made with some understanding of the fit between existing personal characteristics and those leading toward success in entrepreneurship.

KNOW THE BUSINESS

Persons who want to start a business should have a solid background in that specific business. The technical requirements of getting out the product or rendering the service should be understood in considerable detail before venturing into a business.

It is demanding enough to manage the myriad details of setting up an enterprise and getting it established without at the same time trying to learn the intricacies of an unfamiliar business—to acquire the know-how of its customs and practices. The novice would be wise to gain experience by finding a job in the specific business and working in it for a year or two before venturing. Gaining experience by working for someone else is a sure way to avoid the penalties in money and trauma that usually come with trying to learn a business while starting it.

KNOW MARKETING

Most small business failures, as reported by Dun & Bradstreet and others, result from lack of sales. The inability to generate sales can stem from many sources, but chief among them is the lack of knowledge of marketing. Small business owners do not need to be great experts in marketing theory, but they should understand how to identify their segment of the market, how to reach the potential customer, how to identify the needs of the potential customer and convert them into wants, how to set prices, and how to manage the total marketing task, including how to sell the product or service. The small business owner should have a practical grasp of these factors much as a good auto mechanic should know how to tune an engine without being concerned with the thermodynamic theory of the cycle upon which it operates.

The evaluation of market potential for an entrepreneurial idea is treated in Part I of this book. Some fundamental ways of analyzing significant variables in the marketing process are given in Part II, where marketing management from the point of view of an established small business is discussed.

KNOW FINANCIAL MANAGEMENT

The entrepreneur should know enough about the financial aspects of starting and building the small business to keep it alive and growing. That means understanding how to estimate capital requirements and how to make the financial projections needed for management planning and control.

The life blood of the small business, indeed any business, is cash flow and profit. It is not necessary for the owner to be a bookkeeper, but it is mandatory that the proprietor of the small business personally develop the fundamental financial short- and long-range plans and projections needed to manage cash flow and to produce profit. These plans allow the owner to develop a road map of the future. What is most important, this map permits making today's decisions with some inkling of the likely consequences. As George Steiner puts it: "Long-range planning deals with the futurity of current decisions. . . . The essence of long-range planning is a systematic identification of opportunities and threats that lie in the future which, in combination with other relevant data, provide a basis for a company's making current decisions to exploit the opportunities and avoid the threats."[2] Current decisions can best be made on the basis of short-range plans keyed approximately to carefully made long-range plans.

Small businesspersons who plan carefully in financial areas avoid the bear-traps of diminishing cash flow and vanishing profits. They improve their chances for profitable operations by making things happen the way they want them to. They tend to avoid the typical behavior of racing to handle one emergency after another. They are not reactive managers; they are *proactive* managers who meet the requirements for managerial competence.

REQUIREMENTS FOR MANAGERIAL COMPETENCE

The overall requirements for managerial competence include technical competence in the business, technical competence in managing an organization, and interpersonal competence.

---

[2]George A. Steiner, *Comprehensive Managerial Planning*, Oxford, Ohio: The Planning Executives Institute, 1972, p. 4.

Technical competence in managing a business suggests, in addition to knowing how to get out the product or service, the ability to isolate a sound business idea, to evaluate its possibilities, and to develop a course of action for putting it all together in an effective business plan.

Technical competence in managing an organization means an understanding of planning in all the functional areas and of organizing, staffing, directing, and controlling operations. Some features of these competencies are treated in Part I—those that are important in starting a business. Other components that play a major part in managing an ongoing business are treated in Part II.

Interpersonal competence means competence to manage relations with and among people in the company in such a way as to promote smooth and effective teamwork. Interpersonal competence may be seen in an organization whose members show the ability to identify those problems that are significantly impeding achievement, and who solve these problems so they stay solved without impairing the organization's ability to solve the next problem.[3]

Interpersonal competence emerges from sound teamwork in which members contribute from their special backgrounds and skills to organization problem solving and achievement. The entrepreneur should be skillful in welding individuals into a well-functioning team. Unfortunately, some entrepreneurs behave in ways that are poorly calculated to build teamwork and organizational effectiveness. These owners show authoritarian traits: aggressiveness, independence, toughness, and often conceit—traits that in moderation can certainly be beneficial, particularly in starting a business, but when carried to extreme can be harmful to the organization. The position we take in Part I, and develop in greater depth in Part II, is normative: we describe an ideal approach, based on what has been learned about managing a business in the last four decades.

Our objective in Part I is to work through the stages of entrepreneurship, beginning with identification of an intriguing idea for product or service to starting the small business. The Small Business Administration (SBA), a federal agency, has a number of definitions of small business. These vary from industry to industry, and can cover manufacturing companies, for example, with as many as 1500 employees. A small business, just starting, would likely have no more than a tiny fraction of that number of personnel. In Part I of this book we consider a small business to be one in which the proprietor can walk through the establishment and know each company member by name. Practical experience suggests that the small company fitting this definition would usually have not more than 150 people and that a starting venture would be

---

[3]Chris Argyris, *Organization and Innovation*, Homewood, Ill.: Richard D. Irwin, and The Dorsey Press, 1965, p. 4.

limited to a small handful at most. In the second part of this book, which treats the management of the ongoing business, other criteria take over for describing a company as small; these will be found in the introduction to Part II.

CHAPTER 1

The Nature of Entrepreneurship

The affluence of a nation may be judged by its ability to produce useful goods and services and to distribute them widely throughout the population. The question arises, what factors undergird the process of building economic wealth? Some countries, notably several in Western civilization, have built a wealthy economy, while others, even though they have comparable climates and resources in raw materials, have not achieved similar success. Historians and economists have not always agreed on the sources that stimulate the drive toward national wealth. One consistent theme appears in the literature on the wealth of nations, however; it points to a special class of individuals who have been the initiators of economic growth. These persons are known as *entrepreneurs*.

The natural habitat of entrepreneurs is small business. They are rarely found in giant industries. When a company grows beyond some critical size, its increasing complexity forces it to replace its venturesome founders with professional managers who are not usually noted for their inventive, risk-taking behavior. They are rather the guardians and conservators of the status quo.

Entrepreneurs, on the other hand, are quick to see possibilities for achievement. They are not blinded, as managers in large, staid organizations often are, by the ingrown culture in which they are embedded. Entrepreneurs do not suffer from the trained incapacity of the professional, to use Thorstein Veblen's ironic term.

New ideas for new products and services often originate in unexpected places. We see examples of this phenomenon everywhere. Credit cards were not invented by banks; instant photography was not originated by a large camera manufacturer; and the ever-present xerographic office copying machine was not created by a large office equipment manufacturer. These were the concepts of individuals who grasped an idea, developed it, and pursued its success doggedly with unflagging spirit. Although not every innovation is of such magnitude as these, the small entrepreneur makes many minor new contributions that collectively are highly important to the economy.

Entrepreneurs, in the modern sense, are the self-starters and doers who have organized and built successful enterprises since the Industrial Revolution. Those who wish to start their own business can benefit from studying the characteristics of entrepreneurship. Understanding the psychological profile of the entrepreneur, they can judge whether they fit the pattern and have a reasonable chance for success in starting a business of their own.

ENTREPRENEURSHIP IN HISTORICAL PERSPECTIVE

Every age has had its entrepreneurs; entrepreneurs in today's sense arose in England with the advent of the Industrial Revolution in the late eighteenth century. This was the era of the first practical prime movers and production machinery: the governed steam engine of James Watt, the commercial spinning jenny of Richard Arkwright, the rolling mill and steam lathe of John Wilkinson, and the automatic screw machine of Henry Maudslay. Men of this type were of enormous importance in the economic development of England. They were moved by a burning interest in applying the findings of science and in gaining massive increases in productive output through the use of new technology.

These early entrepreneurs were characterized by restlessness and abounding energy. Few had money, and none came from nobility. They emerged from the lower middle classes, driven by an impelling need to convert dreams and innovative ideas into actuality. Their major objectives were growth, enlargement of their organizations, and investment for its own sake. They believed in the worth of the work in which they were totally absorbed. They did not consider the wealth they accumulated of first importance. Their successes gave worth and dignity to their efforts; a sense of achievement was their prime reward.[1]

Innovation a Key Ingredient

The early English industrial entrepreneurs demonstrated a key ingredient of the enterprising personality—an innovative spirit. They were involved in developing inventions for commercial use and in applying new scientific discoveries to productive purposes. They ventured into areas of human endeavor where no one had ever been before. Their successes proved the worth of doing new and useful things or doing old things in newer and better ways. In their efforts, they set a basic value

---

[1]Robert L. Heilbroner, *The Making of Economic Society*, Englewood Cliffs, N.J.: Prentice-Hall, 1962, pp. 76–81.

for entrepreneurs who were to follow—that innovation must be the central characteristic of entrepreneurial endeavor. Creativity is the essence of the entrepreneurial act.

Joseph A. Schumpeter, the respected economist, placed special emphasis on the concept of innovation as being the criterion that distinguishes enterprise from other forms of endeavor. Those who lead enterprises he called entrepreneurs.[2] He further sharpened his definition by stating that nobody is an entrepreneur all the time; one behaves as an entrepreneur only when carrying out innovations.

Schumpeter added that what counts in entrepreneurship is getting things done. It is leadership not ownership that is important. In this regard, the entrepreneurial role is not risk bearing in a financial sense. Those who put up capital for the venture bear the risk. Entrepreneurs who invest capital, or part of it, of course assume risk in proportion to their share of the investment.

It should be pointed out that even if entrepreneurs do not bear risk in the financial sense, they are engaged by definition in a risky activity. This quality of uncertainty influences the environment in which they must seek funding. They customarily find the search for venture capital difficult and often disheartening for this reason.

Schumpeter made another point of great importance when he pointed out that entrepreneurial profit comes specifically from innovation. It is bound to be temporary and will inexorably diminish under the eroding forces of competition. The implication here is that no enterprise can rest on its laurels. Innovation must be a continual process if the enterprise is to achieve longevity. The history of business is full of examples of firms that died from failure to recognize the fleeting nature of their profits from initial successful innovation.

CHARACTERISTICS OF ENTREPRENEURS

The history of entrepreneurship indicates that entrepreneurs share common origins and common characteristics. As we have seen, the originators of industrial enterprise in England came from lower- and middle-class origins. In American history of the late nineteenth century enterprisers, Heilbroner points out that the average entrepreneur was the son of parents in comfortable financial circumstances, neither very wealthy nor very poor.[3] Schumpeter wrote that entrepreneurs do not form a social class but have their origins in all classes.[4] The latter portion

---

[2]Joseph A. Schumpeter, "The Enterpreneur as Innovator," *Readings in Management*, 2d ed., Ernest Dale, ed., New York: McGraw-Hill, 1970, p. 9.
[3]Heilbroner, *The Making of Economic Society*, pp. 76–81.
[4]Schumpeter, *The Entrepreneur as Innovator*, p. 9.

of this statement is subject to modification in the light of recent sociological research, which will be discussed below.

Entrepreneurs, as described by many writers who have studied their personal characteristics, seem to possess many similar traits. Among these are a high level of energy, a desire to become involved in innovative adventures, a willingness to assume personal responsibility for making events occur in preferred ways, and a desire for achievement for its own sake. To these Geoffrey Crowther has added an optimistic attitude and a belief in the future.[5]

In recent years, penetrating studies of the enterprising personality by David C. McClelland and his associates have led to a much clearer understanding of the characteristics of entrepreneurs than that given by historical reporting. The following paragraphs summarize McClelland's findings.[6]

The Need for Achievement Prime among the psychological drives that motivate the entrepreneur is a high need for achievement, usually identified as *n Ach*. This need can be defined as a want or drive within the person that motivates behavior toward accomplishment. Accomplishment, defined in an entrepreneurial context, is the fulfilling of a goal embodying a reasonable challenge to the individual's competence. A task seen as easy carries no challenge and is therefore not motivating.

Desire for Responsibility Entrepreneurs desire personal responsibility for accomplishment. They prefer to use their own resources in their own fashion in working toward goals and to be accountable personally for results. They will, however, perform well in a group as long as they can personally influence the results in some specific way.

Preference for Moderate Risks Entrepreneurs are not gamblers. They prefer to set goals that require a high level of performance, a level that they believe will demand exertion but that they are confident they can meet.

Perception of Probability of Success Confidence in ability to achieve success is a significant quality of entrepreneurial personalities. They study the facts that can be gathered and form judgments on them. When facts are not fully available, they fall back on their high level of self-confidence and proceed with the task.

Stimulation by Feedback Entrepreneurs want to know how they're

---

[5]Geoffrey Crowther, *The Wealth and Poverty of Nations*, Claremont, Calif.: Claremont College, 1957, p. 11.
[6]David C. McClelland, *The Achieving Society*, New York: Free Press, Collier-Macmillan, 1967.

doing, whether the feedback is good or bad. They are stimulated to higher levels of performance by learning how effective their efforts are as the task progresses.

Energetic Activity Entrepreneurs exhibit a much higher level of energy than the average person. They are active and mobile and are engaged a high proportion of the time in novel ways of getting the task done. They tend to be acutely aware of the passage of time. This awareness stimulates them to energetic engagement with their work.

Future Orientation Optimistically oriented toward the future, entrepreneurs plan and think ahead. They search for and anticipate possibilities that lie beyond the present.

Skill in Organizing Entrepreneurs show unusual skill in organizing both work and people for achieving goals. They are highly objective in choosing individuals for specific tasks. They will choose the expert over a friend for the sake of getting the job done efficiently.

Attitude toward Money To entrepreneurs, financial gain is second in importance to achievement. They value money, but not for itself. They view it rather as a concrete symbol of a challenging objective accomplished—a testimony to their competence.

Conclusions Reached by Other Researchers

Many other researchers have studied the characteristics of entrepreneurs. Some have looked into their origins and others into their psychological characteristics. The findings of these studies add to our understanding of the background and drives of many entrepreneurs, but all stress the importance of *n Ach*. Brief summaries of the conclusions of two typical studies are given in the following paragraphs.

Locus of Control Albert Shapero, professor of management in the Graduate School of Business at the University of Texas, reports studies showing that many persons who start new businesses are displaced persons in one way or another. Some are political refugees from foreign countries or the sons or daughters of in-migrants. Others are those who have lost their jobs through being fired or moved aside in a management shuffle. Whether from a burning desire to achieve independence or bitterness with their personal situations, these displaced persons risk setting up their own business.

There are in addition people who are influenced to try for independence by a friend or acquaintance who sells them on the possibilities in an entrepreneurial idea. Still others decide to venture on their own when they come to a clear decision point or discontinuity in their lives: they have just earned their college degree, or their children have left home for good.

Wanting to be independent, however, is not enough. Prospective entrepreneurs must be able to imagine themselves in the role. They must view the move into the strange new world of business as credible, as an act both imaginable and achievable.

Shapero's studies show that one important personality dimension of entrepreneurs is the degree to which they think they can affect the world around them.[7] In psychological words this is known as the *locus of control*. People who are *external* believe that the rewards in life come from forces outside themselves—luck, fate, or powerful others to whom they relate in some way. At the other end of the spectrum are people known as *internal* who believe they can influence events to their own good or detriment. They seek independence and autonomy and they rely on their own resources to achieve these ends. Most fit somewhere between these extremes. Very successful entrepreneurs tested for locus of control scored as high internals.

Characteristics of Successful Entrepreneurs In an attempt to reach a better understanding of the psychological characteristics of the successful entrepreneur, John A. Hornaday and John Aboud used objective tests.[8] This approach was aimed at avoiding projective tests similar to McClelland's, which can be administered and interpreted only by trained psychologists. Hornaday and Aboud sought an objective and structured procedure that nonpsychologists could administer successfully, one that might identify other entrepreneurial characteristics in addition to the admittedly important *n Ach*.

The subjects of the testing were a group of sixty entrepreneurs who had been in business from about eight to thirteen years. These entrepreneurs met the criteria set for the study: they were defined as successful because they had started a business where there was none before; they had at least eight employees; and they had been established for at least five years.

Three objective tests were used in the study: The Kuder Occupational Interest Survey, Form DD; Gordon's Survey of Inter-personal Values; and a questionnaire composed of three scales drawn from the Edwards Personal Preference Scale. In addition, the study used interviews based upon a standardized interview schedule and a five-point scale of personal self-estimates called the Self-Evaluation Scale.

---

[7]Albert Shapero, "The Displaced, Uncomfortable Entrepreneur," *Psychology Today*, November, 1975.

[8]John A. Hornaday and John Aboud, "Characteristics of Successful Entrepreneurs," in *Entrepreneurship and Venture Management*, Clifford M. Baumback and Joseph R. Mancuso, eds., Englewood Cliffs, N.J.: Prentice-Hall, 1975, pp. 11–21.

The results of the study showed that compared to the population at large, entrepreneurs are significantly higher on scales reflecting need for achievement, independence, and effectiveness of their leadership. They are low on scales reflecting need for support by others.

Studies such as these add some useful data to the work done by McClelland and his associates. But *n Ach* always seems to emerge as central to the requirements for successful entrepreneurship.

ENVIRONMENTAL CONDITIONING OF ENTREPRENEURS

The most critical factor in the psychological profile of entrepreneurs is the need for achievement, as we have indicated. The development of high *n Ach* is seen by McClelland and his associates to depend primarily on the family environment in which the individual has grown up.[9] The family environment reflects the values and expectations of the parents, which in turn materially influence the conditioning of the growing child.

Independence and Mastery

High *n Ach* is promoted when children are trained to take care of them-selves and encouraged to acquire competence in dealing with people and events in their lives, provided that such training does not occur too early or too late. Children pressed to be on their own too soon have usually been subjected to parental authoritarianism. When this happens, the offspring are told what to do and expected to obey. They are restricted in their ability to make their own choices and to develop the independence characteristic of high *n Ach*. This condition is typically found in lower-class families where the father tends to be authoritarian and the desire is to have the children take care of themselves as early as possible to relieve the financial burden on the family.

Children in predominantly middle- or upper-class families who are sheltered from the more demanding tasks of taking care of themselves and of independent action for too long a period also fail to acquire high *n Ach*. In general terms, the research suggests that children develop high *n Ach* when required to meet reasonably high standards of achievement somewhere between the ages of six and eight. This age span seems to be that in which the psychological set of high standards of achievement is successfully developed.

Supportive Family Climate

An important element in the development of high *n Ach* is a supportive family climate. Here children are given encouragement in their en-

---

[9]McClelland, *The Achieving Society*, chapter 9.

deavors. The parents set high, but attainable, standards of performance as a matter of course. They impose these standards covertly, without making an issue of them. The parents, especially the father, are nonauthoritarian. The offspring are permitted to achieve these standards without interference. The parents respond to youthful achievements with real pleasure, but not to the extent of being overly protective or indulgent. A moderate, supportive climate of this kind seems to be found primarily in middle-class families. It is not surprising then to find that entrepreneurs usually come from middle-class families.

DETERMINATION OF ENTREPRENEURIAL POTENTIAL

Launching a new business presents risks of various kinds. If those who wish to start a new business could assess their level of *n Ach,* they could gain confidence in their ability to succeed, or they could conclude that they should work for someone else. Although there is no known way to make such an assessment with absolute certainty, there are ways in which individuals may gauge personal qualifications for starting and managing a new business to success. The following characteristics of the successful high *n Ach* entrepreneur provide guides for self-analysis.

Innovative Ability Innovation requires searching for new opportunities. That may mean improving an existing product or service, creating a new product or service, or combining existing elements of products or services in newer and more useful ways.

Tolerance for Ambiguity Tolerating ambiguity implies an ability to deal with the unstructured and unpredictable. This characteristic is closely associated with the innovative process. Innovation stems from creativity in the here and now, which requires improvising in the present, relying on one's competence, and being totally absorbed in the process.[10] The creative person has the ability to build structure from an amorphous situation.

Desire to Achieve The desire to accomplish (*n Ach*) is a significant signal of entrepreneurial drive. This quality marks its possessors as energetic doers who will not rest until they have achieved the goals they have set for themselves.

Realistic Planning Ability Setting challenging but practicable goals is a sign of realistic planning. Goals so defined are in keeping with the

---

[10]Abraham H. Maslow, *Eupsychian Management*, Homewood, Ill.: Richard D. Irwin, Dorsey Press, 1965, p. 188.

entrepreneur's *n Ach*; they require the application of superior competence to meet their challenge. The entrepreneur derives a keen sense of achievement from accomplishment.

Goal-Oriented Leadership Entrepreneurs need purposeful activity. Their high *n Ach* motivates them to direct their own energy and that of their coworkers and subordinates toward sharply defined goals. All efforts within the organization are focused on its main objective under this goal-oriented leadership.

Objectivity The objective person guides entrepreneurial thinking and activities in a pragmatic way. Entrepreneurs gather the available facts, study them, and determine a course of action with a cool-headed regard for its practicability. They do not deceive themselves by wishful thinking. When there are insufficient facts to define the situation completely, they proceed with confidence in their own ability to overcome unforeseen obstacles. They take the risks in a calculating fashion.

Personal Responsibility Entrepreneurs assume personal responsibility as a matter of course. As self-initiating doers, they set goals for themselves and decide how to go about reaching them through their own competencies. They are individualists, do things in their own fashion, and hold themselves accountable for accomplishing what they set out to do.

Adaptability The adaptable person adjusts to changing circumstances. When entrepreneurs find themselves blocked because conditions differ from what they had expected, they do not give up. Rather, they assess the situation objectively, formulate a new plan that they believe will be effective in the new circumstances, and activate it. The need to adapt to changing conditions presents another kind of challenge that they rise to meet.

Ability as Organizer and Administrator Entrepreneurs show organizing and administrative ability in identifying and grouping talent for the sake of accomplishment. They respect competence and will choose a specialist to get a task done efficiently. They tend not to perform well in routine matters and do better, on the whole, to leave routine tasks to others. Their great strength as administrators lies in their ability to look ahead and to anticipate future possibilities.

METHODS OF SELF-ANALYSIS

Those thinking of going into business should take stock of their own needs, drives, and aspirations before taking the decisive step. The needs referred to here are those that would help individuals decide whether their personality fits the entrepreneurial role. Identification of these needs would tell them something about the motivational drives that impel their behavior—and something about their aspirations in life. With this kind of understanding, they would be better prepared to decide whether going into business for themselves would be a desirable act.

McClelland has settled upon three basic needs that influence the attainment of economic ends in one way or another. These are the need for achievement, n Ach; the need for affiliation, n Affil; and the need for power, n Pow.[11] The need for achievement has already been treated. The meaning of n Affil may best be described as the need to establish warm, friendly relations with others—the desire to be liked or accepted. In a different vein, n Pow describes the need to control the means of influencing others. Implied is the desire for dominance, for convincing others of the correctness or superiority of one's position.

It would be foolish to say that any individual possesses any one of these needs to the exclusion of the others. Most people have all three in lesser or greater degree. But of the three, n Ach has been shown by the research to be the key factor in motivating the entrepreneur and therefore it has direct economic consequences. The need for achievement, then, should be the focal point for self-assessment by those who would be business enterprisers.

Personal Achievement Analysis

One way in which individuals can gain insight into their needs is to review events that seem to them outstanding in their careers. Two kinds of experiences should be singled out: those remembered with exceptional satisfaction and those recalled with a great deal of dissatisfaction.

The person should examine the content of each episode with the aim of determining the sources of satisfaction in the one case, and dissatisfaction in the other. If the theme of the remembered event focuses on triumph over odds or the solution of a difficult problem through applied ingenuity, the need that was fulfilled would fall into the n Ach category. In the second category, n Affil would be shown if the satisfaction came from smoothing dissension in a working group or building cooperative relationships with peers. If the satisfaction reflected success in gaining ascendency in a group of peers through persuasion or politicking, the need could be classified as n Pow.

Individuals can uncover additional data by reviewing events that produced dissatisfaction in their careers. Examples are situations in which

---

[11]McClelland, *The Achieving Society*, chapter 9.

they were thwarted in efforts to assume responsibility for a task, difficulties stemming from unfairness of the boss toward self or others, or episodes that produced frustration in their quest for status.

Analysis of these data will help bring to light the kinds of needs that motivate individuals. Satisfaction with superior accomplishment, attaining a high standard of excellence, and demonstrating outstanding competence would be clear indication of *n Ach*.

The motivating effect of achievement has been shown in the work of Frederick Herzberg and his associates.[12] This finding is congruent with McClelland's conclusion that *n Ach* is the source of the motivational drive shown by the entrepreneurial personality. To put it simply, human beings with a high need to achieve are impelled toward achieving behavior. When the behavior produces success they experience great satisfaction from the achievement.

Testing for Entrepreneurial Characteristics

To this date there is no specific testing procedure that will precisely identify the *n Ach* level of an individual. The methods employed by McClelland are statistical and, although capable of producing reliable results for groups of various kinds, are too sensitive and too easily influenced by the social environment in which the tests are given to be used for individual selection of high *n Ach* persons.[13] Nevertheless, those considering going into business can gain much from understanding some of the key testing procedures, since they point to ways of strengthening individual *n Ach*.

The first experiments with *n Ach* involved a special version of thematic apperception tests. The researchers aimed to discover if these tests could be used to detect changes in motivation following deliberate attempts to heighten the subjects' motivation.[14] Subjects were aroused by being told that certain tasks they were to perform would indicate their level of intelligence and show how well qualified they were to assume positions of responsibility. Intelligence and leadership are both qualities highly regarded in American culture, and therefore the instructions were deemed capable of stimulating desire to perform well in the tasks.

After arousal in this fashion, the subjects were shown somewhat fuzzy pictures of scenes associated with work: a man poring over papers on his desk, for example, or two well-dressed executives engaged in a discussion about an architectural plan of some kind. Each picture was

---

[12]Frederick Herzberg, *Work and the Nature of Man*, Cleveland: World Publishing Co., 1966, chapters 7, 8.

[13]David C. McClelland, "Business Drive and National Achievement," *Harvard Business Review*, July–August, 1962, p. 103.

[14]Saul W. Gellerman, *Motivation and Productivity*, New York: American Management Association, 1963, pp. 122–23.

flashed on a screen for a few seconds. The subjects were requested to write a story about each, taking only five minutes for the writing. The stories reflected what the subjects might fantasize when in a state of heightened stimulation to perform well.

These stories were then compared with stories written by a control group who had not been aroused by special conditioning. The stories written under aroused conditions carried significantly more references to doing an excellent job, or meeting or wanting to meet high standards of performance. The experiments demonstrated a significant change in the direction of the subjects' thinking under aroused awareness, or achievement pressure.

The next stage of research was designed to see if some persons wrote stories containing achievement-related statements without prior arousal. If this occurred, it would seem reasonable to assume that such individuals demonstrated bias or concern for achievement. The number of incidents of this kind appearing in the stories could then be scored to indicate the individual's *n Ach*. It was subsequently found that those who scored high on *n Ach* under normal conditions would perform better in tasks when they were aroused than those whose *n Ach* scores were low under normal conditions. Further research showed an unmistakable linkage between high *n Ach* and entrepreneurial qualities.[15]

Following is an example of an actual story written by an advanced graduate student who had briefly observed a picture of a man seated at a desk littered with documents. The man seemed to be staring at a photograph of his wife and children at the far side of the desk.

> This man, a physicist, is involved in a very rushed and important job. The company for which he works is striving desperately to meet a schedule much too short for the work required. The pressure has been so great many tempers have been tried and interpersonal relationships of the employees sorely taxed. Dr. Jerome, pictured here, is taking a short break from the mass confusion—thinking how nice it would be to get away with his family and do some fishing.
>
> Realizing a company that creates such tensions is not a place to spend his life, he resolves to quit and take his family on an extended vacation as soon as this particular job is done. This decision came as such a relief to him that his mind clears, he finds a better way to do the job, solve the problem, than anyone imagined, and manages to instrument a procedure so the company makes its deadline with plenty to spare. Much to everyone's surprise, Dr. Jerome quits and sails off to the seashore with his beloved family in tow.

---

[15]McClelland, *The Achieving Society*, pp. 39–46.

This story indicates a combination of *n Ach* and *n Affil* with no evidence of *n Pow* when checked against the scoring criteria for these needs.

The criteria for achievement imagery include statements of a standard of excellence, often inferred from the use of such words as *good* or *better;* statements of unique accomplishment; or statements of a long-term goal, such as the desire for a successful career.

The criteria for affiliation imagery are statements reflecting desire to establish, maintain, or restore a positive emotional relationship with others; statements that one person likes another or wants to be liked, or takes action to mend a broken relationship; or statements that describe affiliative activities such as parties, bull sessions, or reunions.

Power imagery is indicated by statements showing emotional concern about getting or keeping control over the means of influencing others, those indicating that someone is actually doing something about getting or keeping such control, or those that describe an interpersonal relationship in which a superior has such control over a subordinate.

In the student's story, no statement falls into the category of *n Pow.* Achievement imagery is shown in the first two sentences by the indications of the importance of the task to be performed and the obstacle represented by the short time schedule for its accomplishment. Achievement imagery is evident in the second paragraph in which the protagonist, Dr. Jerome, finds a *"better* way to do the job," *"solve* the problem," "manages *to instrument* a procedure so the company *makes its deadline."*

Affiliative imagery is shown in the first paragraph by "thinking *how nice it would be to get away with his family."* In the second paragraph another example of affiliative imagery is "sails off to the seashore *with his beloved family* in tow."

An interesting feature of the story implies entrepreneurial motivation issuing from an undercurrent of affiliation imagery. Dr. Jerome clearly wants to work in a friendlier environment than that of the organization pictured. Realization of this desire triggers his decision to quit, a decisive plan—which he does after solving the company's problem, a decisive act. Both the planning and the action to attain a goal are indications of the achievement motive.

If we can take this story as typical of the student who wrote it, he would appear not to possess the very high level of *n Ach* associated with entrepreneurship, but he would have sufficient *n Ach* to motivate him to superior achievement in whatever professional field he might choose to enter.

Another kind of test involves games of skill in which participants have the opportunity to control the outcome to some extent and in which they can adjust performance through immediate feedback on the results of their efforts. One testing vehicle of this kind is the ring toss game.

Here participants are given the opportunity to decide at what distance they will stand from a peg to toss rings over it. The range may be from one to twenty feet, and the participants have four rings in each try. In the first two tries, the testees throw the rings from a position they have chosen, but at which they must stay for four tosses. That allows them to adjust their distance for the second try, according to their performance. In the third try, points are awarded for making two or more ringers. The farther back participants stand, the higher the number of points they can score. The fourth try reverses the point scoring: the closer participants stand to the peg, the larger the point score awarded for two ringers.

The game played under these rules discloses that people with high n Ach prefer situations of moderate risk in which they can control results through their own efforts. In the third try, they will stand at middle distance, where there is appreciable challenge accompanying reasonable chance for success with moderately high payoff. In the fourth round, high n Ach persons will again choose some middle distance from the peg, even though the rewards are much less. Their motivation to do so comes not from the chance for maximum reward, which is very high close to the peg, but from their feeling that playing next to the peg is not fun—there is no challenge to the game.

Other games offer the participants choices between allowing the outcome to be a matter of chance, as in rolling dice, or a matter over which they have some control through the exercise of personal effort and skill, as in throwing darts at a target. High n Ach people prefer the latter, where they can use their own skill rather than rely completely on chance.

Business games of various kinds are also used as means for disclosing high n Ach. These games seek to uncover the characteristics of high n Ach players—their setting of high but attainable goals, use of feedback to adjust their performance, preference for striving for goals through their own competencies rather than through chance, adaptability in the face of rapid change, and ability to organize in ill-defined situations.

Persons thinking of going into their own business would do well to look back over their own approaches to situations represented by games such as these. Do they prefer to take personal responsibility for the outcome rather than to rely on chance? Have they responded to feedback by trying harder, whether the data were good or bad? Have they altered course to accommodate change? Have their attitudes been objective in the face of adverse or fuzzy environmental factors? These kinds of questions can be answered through careful introspection. If the answers conform with the guidelines for entrepreneurial behavior as practiced by the high n Ach person, then the individual has some indications that augur well for success in a new business venture.

CAN *n ACH* BE DEVELOPED?

McClelland and his associates, in identifying and testing for *n Ach*, hit on the thought that it might be possible to strengthen or develop this characteristic. Knowing a great deal about the particular beliefs and actions associated with *n Ach*, they were able to design an educational program for developing *n Ach* in the individual.[16] Special training is concentrated in short intensive courses of ten days to two weeks duration. These courses are keyed to the concept of the self-fulfilling prophecy—creating a powerful belief in individuals that they have the ability to change through their own efforts.

The first stage in training helps persons gain awareness of their potential for acquisition of entrepreneurial characteristics. They are then required to write specific plans for personal change in the next two years. Later in the program they are asked to write detailed, specific plans for achieving their goals explaining what difficulties they expect to encounter, how they propose to hurdle them, and what their expectancies and personal emotional responses are likely to be at various points in the process. Individuals are coached to be specific, realistic, and practical in this planning. They are requested to evaluate their progress in meeting their goals every six months, in writing. This procedure keeps them focused on their goals and also gives them the feedback on performance that entrepreneurs find so valuable in guiding their efforts toward achievement.

The second stage of training focuses on the development of what McClelland terms the achievement syndrome. Individuals are taught to think, talk, act, and perceive others as does a person with high *n Ach*. They are taught how to write stories that score high in *n Ach* through learning how to think in terms of standards of excellence, innovative accomplishment, and setting long-term goals for achievement. They are coached to take positions of moderate risk in games where they can succeed through their own skill and continual feedback on performance. Through these means and through constant use of the language of achievement participants are conditioned to a new way of thinking. Their whole attitude is adjusted to see the world from an achieving point of view.

The third part of the program deals with cognitive supports. The purpose here is to help persons correlate the new way of thinking with their prior assumptions and ways of viewing the world. Participants are given support for the new concepts in three areas: the logical and scien-

---

[16]David C. McClelland, "Achievement Motivation Can Be Developed," *Harvard Business Review*, November–December, 1965

tific basis for associating *n Ach* with entrepreneurial success, their self-image, and understanding what is important to them in their lives. The rational basis for connecting *n Ach* with success in enterprise is presented through theory and data from research. Participants explore their self-concept through individual and group sessions. They attempt to answer the questions: Do I have high *n Ach*? If not, do I want to acquire high *n Ach*? Do I have more potent needs, such as *n Affil* or *n Pow*, that would make it difficult or unattractive for me to try to develop my *n Ach*? Individuals are then ready to decide whether or not they should prepare for an entrepreneurial career.

The final aspect of training concentrates on giving the participants emotional support in their effort to change themselves. They experience confirmation and essentiality in the helping relationship given by trainers and associates. Confirmation implies the knowledge that others experience them as they experience themselves; confirmation validates their perception of self and reinforces their self-confidence. Essentiality implies that the individuals are able to use their major abilities and to express their major needs; as they improve in doing both, feelings of essentiality increase.[17]

The whole pattern of training for developing *n Ach* conforms to one of the best ways known to help individuals increase their degree of self-acceptance, confirmation, and essentiality—that is, through generating conditions for psychological success. Chris Argyris has stated these conditions as the following:

• Individuals are able to define their own goals.
• The goals are related to their central needs, abilities, and values.
• The individual defines the paths to these goals.
• The achievement of the goals represents a realistic level of aspiration for the individual. A goal is realistic to the extent that its achievement represents a challenge or a risk that requires hitherto unused, untested abilities.[18]

The program for developing *n Ach*, as previously described, may be seen to fit this outline. The practical results attained by McClelland and his associates in helping individuals develop high levels of *n Ach* and subsequently achieve entrepreneurial success show that *n Ach* may be significantly heightened through appropriate training.

McClelland summarizes the results of several *n Ach* training programs as follows:

The courses have been given: to executives in a large American firm,

---

[17]Chris Argyris, *Intervention Theory and Method*, Reading, Mass.: Addison-Wesley, 1970, p. 39.
[18]Ibid.

and in several Mexican firms; to underachieving high school boys; and to businessmen in India from Bombay and from a small city–Kakinada in the state of Andhra Pradesh. In every instance save one (the Mexican case), it was possible to demonstrate statistically, some two years later, that men who took the course had done better (made more money, got promoted faster) than comparable men who did not take the course or who took some other management course.[19]

MANAGEMENT IN ENTREPRENEURSHIP

There are certain other important subjects besides *n Ach* that can be taught to budding enterprisers. These are systematic approaches to the identification of business opportunities, the analysis of risk, and the acquisition of managerial competence. These will be mentioned only briefly here, since they will be discussed in detail in later chapters.

Identifying Opportunities

As we have stated, entrepreneurship revolves around innovation. Innovation includes newer and better things to do and newer and better ways of doing them. But newer and better things to do implies providing useful goods or services—honest goods or services, soundly conceived to meet the needs or wants of society. Consumers must find satisfaction in that which the business offers them, or the business will fail.

The relationship between the enterprising businessperson and society can be healthy only when founded on ethical practice. Ethical practice proceeds from fundamentally sound managerial values and philosophy. These are the foundations upon which the identification and selection of business opportunities must rest. Identification of opportunities, selection of those appropriate to the strengths of business, the assessment of obstacles, and the development of ways to overcome them are all part of the fundamental business planning process.[20] Transactions between the business and that portion of society it serves must provide commensurate value for both in quality and equity. In this fashion opportunities can be evaluated and converted into the actuality of value: service to society and profit to the entrepreneur.

---

[19]David C. McClelland, "That Urge to Achieve," in *Think*, November–December, 1966, International Business Machines Corporation. McClelland reports in full detail on these and other cases of *n Ach* training in *Motivating Economic Achievement*, New York: Free Press, 1969.
[20]George A. Steiner, *Top Management Planning*, New York: Macmillan, 1969, pp. 32–33.

Analyzing Risk

We have indicated that the entrepreneurial personality prefers risk that is moderate and controllable through personal resources.[21] The entrepreneur, in other words, prefers to take calculated risks. Calculated risks in business are really decisions about spending money in the short or long run. Two key questions should be asked in analyzing a business risk: What is the likelihood of success? Will the return be worth the risk?

The following questions explore typical risks that should be analyzed before the business decision is made:

- How should we price our product?
- Should we make or buy this part?
- Should we sell through salesmen or sales representatives?
- Should we buy a carload of raw stock for inventory at a special low price or save our cash by buying small quantities at a higher price as we need the stock?
- When should we launch the advanced model of our product?
- Should we adopt the four-day workweek?

Both quantitative and qualitative techniques that the entrepreneur can use to help form judgments about taking such risks will be discussed later. These techniques help to limit the risk to the moderate level the entrepreneur prefers.

Acquiring Managerial Competence

The business world generally accepts the statement that management requires a combination of science and art. Insofar as management is an art, the skills may come from personal qualities resulting from early conditioning or learned through personally controlled experience. Insofar as it is scientific, those skills may be deliberately acquired through learning. One school of thought outlines the practice of management as planning, organizing, staffing, directing, and controlling.[22] Much of the managerial activity in these categories may be learned. These will be treated later from the special standpoint of managing the small business.

---

[21]Robert H. Brockhaus, "Risk Taking Propensity of Entrepreneurs," *Proceedings of the Academy of Management*, 1976, pp. 457–60. In this study, Brockhaus suggests that the risk-taking propensities of entrepreneurs may not be a distinguishing characteristic, because they do not differ significantly from about two-thirds of the population at large. The implication here is that they *do* differ from one-third of the population, which furnishes one modest indicator to add to the several important others that would-be enterprisers can use to assess their own characteristics.

[22]Harold Koontz and Cyril O'Donnell, *Principles of Management*, 5th ed., New York: McGraw-Hill, 1972.

REWARDS OF ENTREPRENEURSHIP

We have seen that the entrepreneurial personality is different from that of the average person. Entrepreneurs are not content with the more pedestrian life of those who work for others. They seek reward in the hurly-burly of their own business—reward that comes from intensely personal achievement. Their major reward comes from experiencing self-actualization in their special field.

Self-actualization, a term associated with the psychological writings of Abraham H. Maslow and others, implies the motivation to realize one's potentialities within the limits of reality.[23] Entrepreneurial activity by definition springs from the special qualities of enterprising persons—the rugged individuals of American folklore. Through their own initiative, using their own skills in their own fashion, they scale the heights of achievement. They learn and grow as they achieve. They find dignity and worth in their work, but most rewarding is the self-fulfillment that the work makes possible, the doing of a hard job well.

The second great reward experienced by successful entrepreneurs is a feeling of independence. They do what they think needs doing when they think it needs doing. They are their own persons in a psychological sense, and this trait gives them a feeling of freedom, of lack of constraints, that they value.

In another area, entrepreneurs gain the reward of social service. When successful, they are responsive to the needs of those segments of society with which their business engages: their investors, suppliers, bankers, subcontractors, work force, and customers. They provide economic good in the form of product or service; income for those who work for them; a share in the profits of the operation for their shareholders; and, when they manage well, continuity of existence ensuring their ability to make these contributions over the years. The rewards of social service are highly regarded by many entrepreneurs.[24]

COSTS OF ENTREPRENEURSHIP

If entrepreneurship has rewards, it also has costs. Entrepreneurs are not forty-hour-a-week persons; they punch no time clock and are not clock watchers. Many men and women who start their own businesses work

---

[23]Abraham H. Maslow, *Motivation and Personality*, New York: Harper & Brothers, 1954, pp. 91–92.

[24]In a discussion of the rewards and penalties attached to running one's own business, it was the consensus of eighteen successful entrepreneurs that social service is highly regarded. The discussion was held at the Graduate School of Management, University of California at Los Angeles, December 1971.

fourteen or fifteen hours a day, seven days a week. They are keenly aware of the swift passage of time and attempt to use every moment to positive advantage. An early British entrepreneur, Richard Arkwright, personified this model. As Heilbroner reports: "Richard Arkwright was a bundle of ceaseless energy in promoting his interests, jouncing about England over execrable roads in a post chaise driven by four horses, pursuing his correspondence as he traveled."[25]

One who puts so many waking hours into a narrowly channeled endeavor foregoes many important aspects of life as well as many of its amenities. Family relations often suffer. Many an entrepreneur has married a business only to lose spouse and family. The entrepreneur's social life is usually limited, revolving around those associated with the business. There is little time for music, literature, or art. Life is governed by the overweening demands of business, and personal lifestyle becomes ingrown and circumscribed. These are costs that the would-be entrepreneur should recognize, face, and be prepared to accept or alleviate.

SUMMARY: Factors in Entrepreneurial Success

We have seen that innovation is a major characteristic of successful business enterprise. It is this characteristic that distinguishes enterprise from many other forms of human endeavor and that produces profit for the enterpriser. To be continuously successful, entrepreneurs must be continuously creative. They must introduce improvements and new products or services from time to time to prevent the inroads of competition.

Entrepreneurs show a unique pattern of psychological traits. They are driven by a high need for achievement toward accomplishing tasks that challenge their competencies. They are inordinately energetic. They do not gamble. Rather they assess the situation and assume responsibility for success when they perceive a reasonable chance of achieving it through their own skill.

Entrepreneurs are future oriented. They are stimulated by feedback on their activity and will renew their efforts whether the signals show good or poor performance. They are skillful at organizing the resources they command. Their attitude toward money is somewhat cavalier; they value money more as a token of successful achievement than as wealth to be hoarded.

Entrepreneurs, by and large, emerge from middle-class origins.

---

[25]Heilbroner, *The Making of Economic Society*, p. 81.

Brought up in a supportive family climate, they gain mastery over their environment and achieve independence at a natural pace.

Testing for entrepreneurial potential has not yet reached a stage where individuals may rely on it as a sure predictor of success. Nevertheless, by introspective analysis of significant events in their careers, individuals may form some judgments that can help them decide whether or not to tackle their own business.

The need for achievement can be strengthened in the following ways:
- by conditioning oneself to think like an achiever
- by adopting the language of achievement and using it continuously
- by planning for the future and assessing one's level of achievement through timely feedback on performance
- by behaving in a confident, positive fashion

Successful management of enterprise rests on three basic factors: 1) identification of opportunities, 2) analysis of the risk attached to grasping opportunities, and 3) sound management practice in converting opportunities to reality and in running the business. The first depends upon awareness—continuous search for newer and better things to do and newer and better ways of doing things. The second and third come with personal growth through self-education in the principles and practice of management.

Entrepreneurial activities bring both rewards and costs. Rewards come from doing what one wishes, being one's own person. Costs include sacrifice of many amenities of life, social interaction, and the pleasures of family living.

SUGGESTED READINGS

Anyon, Jay G. *Entrepreneurial Dimensions of Management.* Wynnewood, Penn.: Livingston Publishing Co., 1973.

Liles, Patrick R. *New Business Ventures and the Entrepreneur.* Homewood, Ill.: Richard D. Irwin, 1974, pp. 1–15.

Mancuso, Joseph. *Fun and Guts: The Entrepreneur's Philosophy.* Reading, Mass.: Addison-Wesley, 1973.

McClelland, David C. "Achievement Motivation Can Be Developed." *Harvard Business Review*, November–December, 1965.

McClelland, David C., and Winter, David G. *Motivating Economic Achievement.* New York: Free Press, 1969.

Palmer, Michael. "The Application of Psychological Testing to Entrepreneurial Potential." *California Management Review* 13, Spring, 1971.

CHAPTER 2

Identifying
New Venture Opportunities

Many opportunities exist for identifying newer and better things to do and newer and better ways of doing things. Entrepreneurs are those persons who search for and see the opportunity latent in a novel idea, then work energetically to convert the opportunity to the reality of business.

Entrepreneurs are alert to the world around them. They are curious and store information that interests them in their memory. When an opportunity rewards their alertness, they seek approaches to combine what they have learned in unique ways to meet the challenge of the opportunity-laden idea.

Two kinds of awareness impel exploration for new venture opportunities: those reflecting external orientation and those reflecting internal orientation.

EXTERNAL ORIENTATION

Curiosity and interest in what is going on in the world stimulate external orientation. The enterprising person explores many sources of ideas. The following list gives a sense of the variety of sources available.

- Newspapers, trade journals, and professional publications tell about trends in social usage, changing customs, and developments in specific fields of activity.
- Specialty magazines address particular interests such as sports, camping, food, fashion, and hobbies.
- Trade shows, fairs, and exhibitions display new products and innovations in processes and services.

- Government agencies provide information on patents open to public use.
- Patent brokers furnish information on patents or patentable ideas that may be bought for commercial use.
- Consumer groups may be brought together for open discussion of a potential product or service. New and useful ideas can be generated in this way.
- In a going concern, the members of the company can be encouraged to propose concepts worthy of commercial development.

These represent many, but not all, of the external resources available for germinating ideas for new ventures. The entrepreneur can exploit these sources for ideas.

INTERNAL ORIENTATION

Internal orientation stimulates the use of personal resources to identify new venture opportunities. Every person stores knowledge over the years. This knowledge is composed of data of various kinds: ideas, concepts, principles, images, and facts—encyclopedic knowledge that may be drawn upon at will.

The entrepreneur, seeing a need and hitting upon an idea for filling it, goes through three stages in using internal resources. These are:

1. analysis of the concept until it is sharply defined, including outlining problems that need to be solved
2. search of the memory to find similarities and elements that seem related to the concept and its problems
3. recombining these elements in new and useful ways to solve the problems and make the basic concept practicable[1]

It is doubtful whether the person consciously follows this procedure, but understanding the general process helps in the search for innovative solutions. Certainly entrepreneurs are well equipped by virtue of their independent attitude and objectivity to gain benefit from conscious application of this approach.

The entrepreneur's objective attitude aids in solving problems. Too often we leap to answers before we have clearly identified the problem. Symptoms tend to take on the shape of the problem—and a solution posed prematurely does not solve a problem. What is required is a conscious withholding of the problem-solving attempt until the problem is sharply defined.

---

[1]An informative discussion of the creative process will be found in Milton Rokeach, "In Pursuit of the Creative Process," in Gary A. Steiner, ed., *The Creative Organization*, Chicago: University of Chicago Press, 1965, chapter 4.

The creative act demands extreme flexibility. The cautious objectivity of the adult should prevail during the analysis and statement of the problem. Searching for elements that may be combined to find an answer and trying and testing combinations of ideas is a process of synthesis that seems best accomplished by retreat to the uncritical simplicity and innocence of childhood. The critical faculties are held in abeyance until possible answers are formulated. At this point the adult once more takes over and subjects the proposed solution to careful scrutiny and critical analysis.[2]

The creative act frequently seems to short-circuit the process of synthesis. An innovative solution often occurs in an illuminating flash, when all necessary elements leap into place by themselves. As Edwin Land of Polaroid fame put it, "Invention is the sudden cessation of ignorance." Figure 2–1 gives a graphic depiction of the innovative process.

SOURCES OF IDEAS FOR NEW PRODUCTS OR SERVICES

Although there are many approaches to the search for ideas for new products or services, the process can be speeded by using a more or less orderly list of suggestions for stimulating thought. Careful use of the suggestions in the following paragraphs can aid materially in the quest for new ideas upon which a business can be founded.

Necessity the Mother of Invention

Invention or innovation sometimes follows from a clear perception of a need that should be filled. There are many examples of products or services that have been developed from such a perception. These range from simple to complex, from inexpensive to costly. The instances quoted here are relatively simple and are within the capability of a small business.

The double-headed nail, an early invention used for temporary wood frameworks, relieves the difficulty of extracting nails after the need for the structure has passed. This nail is driven in until the lower head embeds in the wood surface, leaving the second head about a quarter of an inch in the air. The nail may now be readily removed by inserting the claws of a hammer under the second head in one quick, easy motion. The double-headed nail has found ready acceptance in the construc-

---

[2]Abraham H. Maslow, *Toward a Psychology of Being*, New York: D. van Nostrand, 1962, chapter 10.

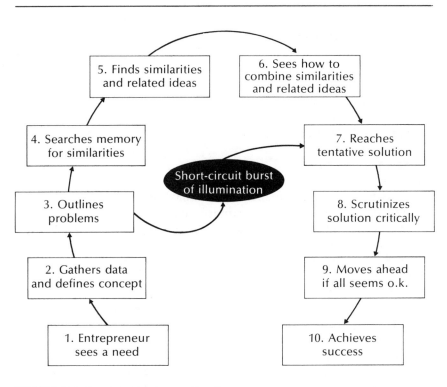

FIGURE 2–1. Steps in the Innovative Process

tion of temporary movie sets, bleachers, concrete forms, and similar structures.

An innovative method of irrigation has been developed in Israel where water is scarce, expensive, and relatively salty. Known as drip irrigation, the method uses equipment that drips water into the soil under trees in an orchard, keeping the soil moisture at a desired level at all times. The advantages of the drip method of irrigating include saving of one-third to one-half the water required by the more conventional sprinkler irrigation method, maintaining better health of trees with water of much higher salt content than ordinarily used with sprinklers, and achieving superior productivity of trees in a given time. Several small companies in the United States have been formed to manufacture drip irrigation equipment to the Israeli designs.

In a completely different field, a new product is an antifog liquid originally developed to keep the visors of astronauts' helmets clear in the cold of space. It is wiped on visors or lenses and prevents fogging caused by sudden change in temperature. This liquid, manufactured under license from NASA, was the basis for a new small business.

Hobbies or Personal Interests

Hobbies or personal interests can often spark new businesses. The following examples are typical and come directly from the experiences of entrepreneurs known personally to the authors.

A woman artist who traveled extensively in Mexico became interested in the native arts and crafts. She soon found herself collecting figurines and other craft objects for her own enjoyment. Her friends saw and admired her collection and suggested that they would like to buy similar Mexican handicraft objects. She thereupon developed sources of supply in Mexico and established a small importing business that grew and flourished.

Another woman became interested in baking pies. She pursued this hobby avidly and developed a handsome and tasty chocolate mousse pie. Her neighbors sampled the pie and asked her to bake some for their social affairs. The reputation of her pie spread and she soon found herself in the business of baking a hundred pies a week. Her chocolate mousse pies became so desired as to command a price of ten dollars apiece. She was offered fifty thousand dollars for her recipe, which she refused. She prefers to run a business that exceeds a hundred thousand dollars a year gross in sales at this writing.

An aircraft designer working for a large company in San Diego became interested in catamaran sailing vessels. He and his two sons built a small catamaran in which to sail for their own pleasure on the Pacific. He was asked to build a similar catamaran for a friend who had tried sailing his. That was the start of a successful small family business.

Watching Trends

Trends in fashion and custom provide a fruitful source of ideas for new ventures. Many opportunities exist for the alert observer to capitalize on trends by doing the appropriate thing at the right time.

A woman who set up a small "mod" youth clothing store at a beach resort found herself designing and making certain items of dress in the room at the back of the store. Her designs proved so popular with the youth trade that she eventually gave up the retail store and concentrated on manufacturing. She soon found it necessary to move into larger quarters as her business grew. Recently, after the third jump in growth, she sold the business and has retired on the proceeds.

In a similar vein, change in fashion has brought a demand for hand-crafted jewelry. One woman entrepreneur recognized this trend early and established relations with Navajo and Zuni craftsmen in the Southwest. She has developed a sizeable wholesale business in Indian handicraft.

The field of convenience foods has experienced tremendous growth in recent years and is still growing. One young man bought a small marginal Mexican food manufacturing concern, modernized it, and developed a new marketing strategy that helped the business increase its profitability and grow. He then engaged in an acquisition process, adding three other similar enterprises to his operation. He sought and found capable management for these plants. He plans to continue building in this fashion, expanding and growing carefully in this specific field of the convenience food business.

Observing Others' Deficiencies

A fertile field for new ideas for product or service lies in observing deficiencies in those currently available. This approach aims at improving performance or adding desirable features.

One example of such a case is the invention of a new kind of key and lock now on the market. The inventor realized that there would be a market for a key that would identify the person who held it and open the door only to that person. He designed a digitally coded electrical locking system in which key cards are made up to individual electric circuit paths. Each cardholder has a different pattern that identifies him individually and operates the electromagnetic lock. One million unique circuits are possible. The lock will not open to any other than the group of patterns for which it is coded. The lock may be fitted to sound an alarm if an attempt to force it is made or an improperly coded key card is inserted. In addition, the circuitry may be used to record the identity of the cardholder and the time of opening the lock. The inventor disposed of his patented design to a major lock manufacturer on a royalty basis after successful development and demonstration of the product.

The waterbed marks a departure from conventional bed design. Here the inventor sought a way to float the weight of the sleeper over the entire body, eliminating the pressure points that occur on the conventional mattress. The manufacture and distribution of waterbeds has become a fast-growing business.

In a completely different field, several small companies have been successful in developing techniques for the low-cost production of metal stampings. These companies provide a short-run, low-cost facility. Customers may economically fill needs for limited quantities of stampings that would be prohibitive in cost were they tooled in the conventional manner. Success in this business depends on special expertise in devising temporary tooling and very fast setup and handling techniques to reduce labor costs.

Why Isn't There a . . . ?

Opportunities for new business ventures sometimes come in answer to the question, "Why isn't there a gadget that will do thus and so?" Some examples of successful products designed to fill needs identified in this fashion include the following.

Observing his wife struggle to clean an old paint brush in which the paint had hardened, her enterprising husband asked himself, "Why isn't there a disposable paint brush?" He and a friend thereupon developed a disposable paint brush that consists of a plastic handle into which a polyurethane tapered brush is inserted. Upon completion of the painting task, the brush is discarded. They tested the market by making samples and demonstrating them in hardware and paint stores. They sold sufficient quantities to ascertain the worth of the idea, then sold the patent to a major company on a royalty basis.

Another product originated in response to the question, "Why isn't there a potable water dispenser at the faucet?" This led to the development and production of a small water purifier that attaches to the kitchen faucet.

The answer to "Why isn't there a plantable flower pot?" produced the compressed peat moss planter. It is no longer necessary to perform the delicate operation of removing a plant from its flower pot without disturbing the roots when transplanting.

Other Uses for Ordinary Things

Many commercial products come from the application of ordinary things to other uses than that for which they were intended. Examples range from changing the character and use of finished products to developing novel applications of waste materials. Some instances illustrate the wide range of possibilities for establishing a business in this way.

Driftwood picked up on the beach along the ocean and selected for interesting shape and weathered appearance provides the basis for a wholesale business. It is sold at retail by florists and nursery shops as decorative pieces to be used ornamentally in the home.

Douglas fir plywood, a common building material, has a unique characteristic that has been used to found a small business. Every sheet of fir plywood has a different grain pattern. Through a mechanical process that removes some of the soft grain, the pattern is accentuated. The unique pattern of the grain is highlighted by wiping a dark stain over a light background enamel. This product was called Etchedwood by its originators. They supplied special finishes with the product so that the home craftsman could install the sheets and achieve a high quality finish of professional appearance with little difficulty.

Electric generating plants using coal as a source of heat produce large quantities of fly ash, inert hard particles that deposit in the effluent passages and smokestacks. One entrepreneur has become a millionaire by collecting and selling this waste product by the carload. It is used to make aggregate for lightweight concrete and as a component of phonograph records and bricks, among other things.

The conversion of ordinary objects and materials to novel uses offers a great variety of possibilities for identifying new venture opportunities.

Spinoffs from Present Occupations

Many new companies are formed as spinoffs from existing businesses. Entrepreneurially inclined employees often see ways to improve products they are familiar with or conceive new ideas for products or services as a result of their exposure to their occupation. Engineers, scientists, and technicians lead in detecting new spinoff opportunities, although the enterprising personality may have almost any kind of background. The following are instances of businesses that were formed as spinoffs.

Two young partners, one an engineer and the other an engineering salesman, discovered an innovative way to test electronic printed circuit boards. The procedure produces a computerized printout identifying specifically any faulty component or solder joint on a given board. This is a service business that allows electronic manufacturers to test each board in a production run at a very small cost compared to older procedures, which depend upon the skill of an electronic technician. The business has grown very fast and is right on its projected plans for growth and profit after five years of operation.

A salesman for a sales representative company became aware of the need for a source that could supply small runs of insulating shells to the customer's required size and shape. Customers were manufacturers of electronic products. Several large manufacturers could supply high quantity production runs at low unit cost. But to tool for an experimental or pilot run of a few hundred parts was very expensive for their customers. The salesman founded a most successful small company by setting up a novel low-cost manufacturing procedure for filling the needs of this special segment of the market.

A typist for a large company augmented her income by typing manuscripts and business documents for individuals in her home at night and on weekends. Her clients discovered that she had an artistic bent and several asked her to lay out sales brochures and advertising displays for them. She soon found herself so occupied with this kind of work that she left her job to concentrate on her own business. She then saw the possibility of moving into the advertising agency field, which she has done successfully.

The step from a regular job to a business in a similar or allied field presents a logical and expeditious way to make the transition. One does not have to learn a completely new field but can start with the advantage of thorough knowledge of the technical aspects of the business. There are, of course, both practical and ethical considerations that should not be violated. Entrepreneurs who set themselves up in direct competition with their former employers must be careful to avoid questionable practices. They should not transgress on patents, for example, or carry away lists of customers. And to get into direct competition with an established firm is certainly not the easiest way to start a business. Fierce competitive pressure from an entrenched going concern is not likely to help a new business overcome the many other obstacles facing it.

PRODUCTS SUITABLE FOR THE SMALL FIRM

The new small business faces certain constraints that narrow its choice of product. It must match its product or process to its limited resources in money, manpower, and facilities. Otherwise it will probably not survive the difficult phases of starting and initial growth.

Prudence suggests a careful study of the intended product or service to see if it fits the pattern followed by many successful small businesses. The entrepreneur's ability to stay within the limitations imposed by resources in money, technical competencies, and facilities is enhanced by following this pattern, as are chances for success.[3]

The small firm does well to choose a segment of the market that allows it to use its small size as a significant advantage. This strategy tends to isolate it from the inroads of competition. One tested way to gain this advantage is to provide a product or service to larger concerns.

The product or service should be required in the completion or manufacture of the customer's own product. Many times this necessitates working closely with the customer in the development of the product. Particular importance should be placed in guiding the design from its inception to ensure ease of manufacturing in quantity and low cost. A close relationship must be maintained with the customer and requests for service must be responded to quickly. The small firm has the ability to move quickly. By exercising this ability, it can develop and cement a mutually beneficial relationship.

The product or process supplied to others should be too small in volume to interest the customer in installing a facility for producing it. If, in addition, the product or process requires special equipment or special skills that the small company has, it has a reasonable chance to protect itself from this kind of competition.

Another characteristic of the product or process that the small concern should seek is high value added. To be profitable, the return to the company for its sales must exceed all its costs. These typically include labor, materials, manufacturing expense, marketing expense, and administrative expense. The principal reason for the establishment of the small business is to add as much value as possible to the product or process through the application of its special competencies.

Another way of looking at this concept is that suggested by Peter Drucker, which he calls *contributed value*.[4] Contributed value measures the difference between the gross revenue received by a company for the sales of its product or service and what it spends for raw materials plus the services it must purchase. In other words, contributed value measures the effectiveness of the organization's total effort in converting its expertise into profit. It takes into account all the costs of all the operations of the business and the gross reward received for these efforts. Obviously, the smaller the cost of materials and the more expert the skills applied to increasing the worth of the raw material, the greater is the possibility for producing profit. The objective of the small company should therefore be to develop the highest practicable level of skills to apply to materials for the purpose of increasing the contributed value in the product it sells.

A final important consideration in the small business is the time span required for completion of its product or process. Small companies should seek products or projects that can be managed comfortably within their financial capacity. Lengthy projects make heavy demands on cash for salaries, materials, and services. A small company can see its cash dwindle to nothing if it is not careful to ensure inflow of money from sales on a continuing basis. Many a small company has gone bankrupt from lack of adequate cash flow. One danger to avoid is that of draining away the liquid resources of the company in projects where the payoff is in the future.

Examples of Businesses Meeting These Criteria

Some examples of small companies that have prospered by meeting the criteria outlined above have been mentioned previously in this chapter. These include the short-run metal stamping companies, the company set up to test printed circuit boards in a new and inexpensive way, and the company manufacturing insulating shells to customers' special designs. There are many other successful businesses that meet the criteria. They range from supplying tiny precision gear trains to manufacturers of miniature motor-driven devices to chemical micromachining of rare metal films to the specific designs of computer manufacturers. In services they cover a spectrum from the monitoring and adjustment of electroplating solutions for companies not finding it practicable to do it themselves to management development services aimed at teaching engineers and scientists how to write clear reports.

---

[4]Peter F. Drucker, *The Practice of Management*, New York: McGraw-Hill, 1954, p. 72.

The entrepreneur considering starting a business would build on the experience of others by searching out and identifying opportunities for supplying a product or service needed by larger organizations to complete their own products or services.

IMPORTANCE OF MARKETING ORIENTATION

The most frequent cause for small business failure, as reported by Dun & Bradstreet in their yearly *Failure Record*, is lack of sales; the second most frequent cause is competitive weakness. Both causes of failure reflect a naiveté on the part of the founders, stemming from ignorance about the overriding necessity for a marketing orientation in any business if it is to succeed.

Too often entrepreneurs conceive an idea for a new product or service and promptly become enamored with it. They concentrate on the development of the idea and on its conversion to actuality. They invest time, money, and energy in developing the idea without thought of identifying the customer and the customer's needs and willingness to buy. The entrepreneur's orientation is inward to personal ego needs and their satisfaction. This approach is usually disastrous. The result is often a product or service, perhaps cleverly worked out and produced, that few will buy.

Looking outward to the market can produce a far more profitable result. Here the entrepreneur's orientation is to the customer. The design of the product comes from finding out what the potential buyer really wants and is willing to pay for. The entrepreneur, once reasonably sure of the specifications to be met, then assesses the resources at hand to see if the necessary technical skills, equipment, and financial ability are available to produce the product at a profit. Prepared by careful objective study, the answer can be stated to a question fundamental to the success of any business: "What business are we truly in?" The entrepreneur avoids the dangers of *marketing myopia* by operating on a marketing strategy.[5]

Monopoly through Uniqueness

Innovation or invention gives monopoly, which may be a highly desirable quality in product or process. The uniqueness of product or process may permit rapid and profitable development of a special market. The small new company originating a product that captures the imagination of the customer can grow rapidly. But its management should remember

---

[5]Theodore Levitt, *Innovation in Marketing*, New York: McGraw-Hill, 1962, chapter 3.

that the advantages of uniqueness are transitory. Success, particularly when associated with high profit, induces competition—and with competition prices decline, and therefore so does profit.[6]

The ballpoint pen is a classic example of this phenomenon. Brought out as an improvement on the fountain pen after World War II, the ballpoint pen sold at retail for $15. In its original form, its operation left much to be desired, since it often skipped and was difficult to control. Inevitably competition arose, with much improved quality and sharply declining retail prices. Today ballpoint pens of superior performance can be bought for a few cents.

This pattern suggests the need for a continual search in a marketing-oriented mode for ways to extend the life of existing products and for the development of new products to take up the loss of profitability resulting from competition.

Product Improvements or Modifications for Profit

Newness in product or service is not necessarily mandatory in starting a business or in maintaining profitability of an existing business. Many ideas for new ventures lie in product improvement. Improvements are often keyed to meeting special requirements of specific customers. The modified product may then be found to have wider application to a class or group of customers with similar needs.

That newness of product is not mandatory to establishing a successful business is amply demonstrated by such franchise operations as the Baskin-Robbins ice cream stores. Baskin-Robbins' success rests on a marketing concept that adds novelty and fun to a long-accepted American dessert favorite, ice cream. Customers are attracted to gaily decorated clean stores where they have a wide choice of flavors to select from—many unusual—identified by deliberately chosen zany names.

In a completely different field, the Kelty backpack frame for hikers rose to eminence in a long-established field by improvements in design and the use of welded aluminum structure. Its light weight and comfortably body-contoured form enabled a substantial penetration of an existing market.

The electronic measuring instrument field is full of products modified to meet the special requirements of a customer, then discovered to have wide application in the business in which that customer is engaged. A typical instance is the digital voltmeter, which has been adapted to measure pressure at points remote from the instrument.

Products can very often create a widening of a market or the develop-

---

[6]Joseph A. Schumpeter, *Business Cycles: A Theoretical, Historical, and Statistical Analysis of the Capitalist Process*, vol. 1, New York: McGraw-Hill, 1939. An informative concept of the entrepreneur as innovator may be found on pp. 102–9.

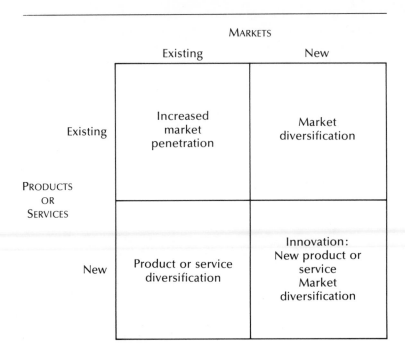

		MARKETS	
		Existing	New
PRODUCTS OR SERVICES	Existing	Increased market penetration	Market diversification
	New	Product or service diversification	Innovation: New product or service Market diversification

FIGURE 2–2. Product-Market Matrix

ment of a new market segment through the addition of features originally requested by one customer. A marketing-oriented sales force can stimulate growth of this kind by carefully observing the customer's operations. A special feature designed into an existing product may solve a customer's problem, then open a new segment of the market.

PRODUCT-MARKET MATRIX

After a small company has become established, study of its product-market matrix will suggest ways to enhance a specific market or expand into a new one. The matrix gives a way of cross-checking the possibilities of existing and new products (or services) against existing and new markets. The product-market matrix can be diagrammed as shown in Figure 2–2.

The matrix consists of four boxes. It reflects the scope of alternatives in a company's product-market strategies. As the upper left box shows, the firm can choose to emphasize the sale of an existing product in an already developed market. The emphasis is on increasing market penetration. The upper right box suggests the possibility of market diversification by finding new uses for the existing product. The lower left box indicates the possibility of further exploitation of an existing market by diversifying the product line and offering the additional products to the same customers. The lower right box implies the creation of wholly new markets for new products and represents another avenue to market diversification. This approach presents the greatest risk in the matrix and also the greatest chance for large profits.

Existing Product, Existing Market

We live in a turbulent world that changes at an increasingly rapid pace. Products are born, live, and die within shorter time spans than ever before in history. Today's product, marketing marvel though it may be, is surely headed for the scrap heap sooner or later. The search for new ideas for products to replace it must go on incessantly.

The environment in which the small company must stay alive changes continually under the impact of technical, social, and legislative forces. The character of markets changes in response. The small company necessarily specializes to meet the requirements of a particular market segment. But as its market changes, the demand for its products may dry up. The existing market tends to fade away. Unless the company innovates continually, it too will find itself fading away. The small company cannot depend indefinitely on its traditional market for existence. Innovation is mandatory for survival.

Existing Product, New Markets: Market Diversification

Market diversification offers the small company an opportunity to exploit its existing product line by finding new uses that open up a new market segment. Small changes or improvements in existing products may appeal to a new class of customer.

The digital thermometer, in which the temperature is displayed directly in numbers, offers a welcome improvement in this instrument. It is no longer necessary to read the top of a red line against a scale to find the room temperature. The temperature is shown directly in bold, clear numbers.

A firm that develops management training exercises brought out a self-administered test that allows managers to judge their individual management style. The firm found that many managers had trouble in following the directions given in the original edition. These required answering scores of forced-choice questions, performing some arithmetic, and tracing through a decision tree to arrive at the answers. By simplifying the format and providing guidelines, the test was made easy to follow, and its sales appeal was greatly heightened. Business has increased markedly since the change, with new customers being referred by old.

These examples illustrate ways of widening an existing market.

Change may be directed at features other than change in product itself. New packaging using color and clever art work can widen the appeal of the product. A more informative way of illustrating the carton, so the potential customer can see what the product inside is and understand its use better can also create a wider market. Again, redesign of the carton to make it easier to stack and stock can expand sales to wholesaler or retailer. Small changes can often improve sales by gaining wider acceptance for the product. Market diversification may be achieved through techniques such as these.

New Products for Existing Markets: Product Diversification

Another avenue for increasing the scope of the small business is the addition of new products for an existing market. Products may be true innovations or simply additions of products presently on the market but new to the company.

Major innovations in a field in which the company already operates can be a fruitful source of increased revenue. For example, a small company that manufactured bench-sized temperature testing chambers for laboratory use realized that temperature is not the only variable to be controlled in testing technical equipment or components. Many of its customers needed to control air pressure and humidity as well and were resorting to homemade expedients of various kinds for these purposes. The company designed and developed new products for pressure and humidity testing, using its special technical competencies to advantage. These sister products were sold primarily to their existing customers—a straightforward case of product diversification in a given general field.

A product similar or identical to one already on the market but new to the company offers the opportunity to increase revenue from existing customers. It is not uncommon for customers to request a firm with whom they have a good relationship to supply a product already on the market. As long as it makes good business sense and the product fits what the small company is doing, filling requests of this kind can be beneficial. A small specialty food producer in Southern California was requested by its major wholesaler to add tacos and enchiladas to its line of quick-frozen tortillas. The company increased its profits by adding these items to its product line.

Occasionally a small company may benefit by adding a product different from those in its line but already on the market in another country. It may arrange to import or produce the product itself. A mail-order house in the Southwest discovered a balance-type mail scale on the market in England but not ordinarily found in stationery stores in this country.

Although one version of a balance scale may be obtained here, these tend to be utilitarian in appearance; they operate on the displacement of a spring. The imported balance uses exact weights on a knife-edged pivoted lever and is more accurate. Handsomely designed and fabricated, the balance appeals to customers, primarily private parties, who value these attributes.

These instances represent product diversification in one way or another. They provide avenues for the small company to improve its revenues by adding new products for existing markets.

New Products for New Markets: Market Diversification

The final category in the product-market matrix concerns new products for new markets. This is the channel of greatest risk, but it can often bring large profits. The development of new products for new markets requires invention or at least considerable innovation. The small company must exercise its competencies and special managerial know-how, to which an element of good fortune must often be added, to bring the adventure to a successful outcome.

Opportunities abound for identifying new needs for new markets. Growth and change generate these needs, and filling a need in turn creates change that stimulates further growth. Table 2–1 suggests some typical interacting influences among growth, change, and needs.[7] As the table implies, the relationship of growth, change, and needs is circular in nature.

Alertness to the needs brought on by growth and change can trigger ideas leading to innovation or invention upon which a new business may be founded. Some diverse examples follow.

The need to develop instrumentation for monitoring and regulating the quality of water used in industrial processes led three partners to form a small company for this purpose. The company grew rapidly to 150 employees in four years. The three principals sold the company to a much larger firm that produces chemicals for water treatment and remained on as operating managers.

A small company in the chemical microetching service business saw the need for a very thin keyboard for hand-held miniature computers. They were able to apply their special know-how in the development of a proprietary design that gave the desired thinness and greatly improved electrical performance over any similar item on the market. They were literally swamped with orders, which gave them a year-and-a-half backlog for production of the keyboard. As a proof of their foresight,

---

[7]We are indebted to David Menkin of Menda Scientific Products, Inc., for the content of Table 2–1.

Typical Areas of Growth →	Areas of Change →	Typical Areas of Change →	New Needs	Typical New Needs →	Growth Areas
Population	Urban living Youth Markets Housing Privacy	Employment	Higher skills—more training Retraining Labor saving	Waste disposal	Creation of by-products New processing methods Recycling
Service industries	Travel Education Entertainment	Developing countries	Food supplements Know-how Training	More hygienic environment	Antismog devices Antipollution measures for water Sewage disposal
Personal income	Use of disposable income Swimming pools Second homes Recreation	Raw materials	Use of less scarce materials Synthetics Ecological preservation and renewal	Personal Safety	Burglar alarms Nonlethal personal protective weapons Safety devices Limited access devices
Life span	Health services Retirement facilities Activities for senior citizens			New sources of energy	Solar energy technology Geothermal energy technology
Knowledge	Continuing education Educational methods Information storage and retrieval Library methods			Energy saving devices	High efficiency fuel atomizer Engine knock sensor to increase fuel economy of automobiles

TABLE 2–1. RELATIONSHIP OF GROWTH, CHANGE, AND NEEDS

they estimated that the product would have a three-year life before competition reduced its profitability to a marginal level. They started immediately to develop other proprietary products to replace it at the proper time.

The needs arising from the evolving patterns of growth and change present many opportunities in a great variety of fields. These range from the simple and unsophisticated to complex, technical products and services.

Technological Change as a Source of New Products or Services

Innovations or inventions stemming from technological change offer great opportunities—coupled with high risks. Small companies with the requisite technical competence may be first in bringing out a new product by pursuing a rigorous policy of technical innovation. When combined with an intelligent marketing effort, the results can be spectacular.

The small electronics firm that originated the digital voltmeter opened a new market with this product and capitalized handsomely on its innovation for several years before competition caught up with it. No patents were involved; the design was a clever innovation based upon advancing technical knowledge. The company kept developing improved versions of the instrument through concentrated programs that took advantage of advanced design concepts and components. The engineering development absorbed substantial investment—but the payoff, too, was substantial.

A second path open to the small company is to follow the innovator as quickly as possible. This course requires exceptional skill in research and development to learn from the mistakes or deficiencies of the innovator and to bring a production prototype to fruition rapidly. If the product shows some significant improvement or even small features that give it a slight competitive edge over the leader, the company can make inroads into the market. And it can do so profitably if it keeps its pricing level up with that of the leader.

The electronics field is full of examples of this kind of follow-the-leader development. From components to computers, the innovative company finds competitors quickly challenging its position in the market. This situation is common in almost any field that can be named.[8] Some of the instances we have already quoted are typical: the hand-held miniature computer, electronic measuring instruments, waterbeds, and drip-irrigation systems have found the innovator dogged quickly by

---

[8]Frank T. Paine and William Naumes, *Strategy & Policy Formation*, Philadelphia: W. B. Saunders, 1974. See pp. 156–61 for a discussion of company strategy under different conditions of market-share growth.

intense competition from followers. Here some followers have done well; others have been unable to withstand the rigors of competition.

Some companies launch me-too products. These are very similar to those originated by the innovator. The company putting out me-too products aims to find some advantages in costs or manufacturing methods with the intent of cutting the price to the customer. This is a dangerous procedure as more than one company has discovered. Once the leading company has established a market, it is usually in a substantial position to ride out a price war. And it is only after the leader has a grip on the market that its position is likely to be challenged by me-too competitors. The leader can generally undercut a lower-priced competitor, maintain its position in the market because it has established good relations with its customers, and move ahead on the momentum it has generated until it has knocked the competitor out of the running. It can then either increase price or rely on increased volume, or both, to raise sales sufficiently above the break-even point to restore profitability. Making a me-too product because one thinks to sell it at a cheaper price than the originator is generally a questionable business practice; it often proves to be a dangerous pitfall.

PITFALLS IN SELECTING NEW VENTURE OPPORTUNITIES

The major reasons for the failure of the small new business may be charged to managerial incompetence.[9] Although managerial incompetence may show itself in any number of ways, major deficiencies seem to reflect lack of line experience, lack of managerial experience, and unbalanced experience. Unbalanced experience indicates inadequate background in marketing (including sales), finance, purchasing, and production in the case of the individual proprietor or of the partners who make up the management team. Too often the would-be enterpriser starts off wrongly through lack of experience, and the situation is made worse by lack of objectivity. Many pitfalls traceable to these lacks can be avoided by careful study and planning before the product or service is accepted for development and exploitation.

Lack of Objectivity

A serious fault too commonly seen in the novice entrepreneur is a lack of objectivity. Engineers and technically trained people are particularly prone to falling in love with their idea for product or service. They seem

---

[9]See "The Failure Record," a comprehensive study of business failures published yearly by the Business Economics Department of Dun & Bradstreet.

unaware of the mandatory need for the careful kind of scrutiny they would give to a design or project in the ordinary course of their professional work. Emotional attachment to an idea for a business venture can be disastrous. The way to avoid this pitfall is to subject the idea to rigorous study and investigation. Only after the idea has passed intensive research from a marketing feasibility and business standpoint, as detailed in following chapters, should the investment in time and money for its development be undertaken.

Lack of Familiarity with the Market

As we have indicated, most beginners in business do not appreciate the importance of a marketing approach in laying the foundation for their new ventures. They show a managerial short-sightedness attributable to ignorance.[10] When affected by this fuzzy outlook, managers tend to think of their companies as being involved in the production of a product rather than in a customer-satisfying activity. As a consequence, they do not know the market and have no basis for judging the potential acceptance of their product or service. Nor do they understand the life cycle that must be considered in introducing a new product or service.

No product is instantaneously profitable, nor does its success endure indefinitely. Managers must not only project the life cycle of the new product, they must also recognize that introducing the product at the right time is important to its success. Selecting the right time to bring out the product implies gaining a sense of the life cycle of the whole competitive field. Does the company want to be the innovator, first in the field, and accept the attendant risk? Or would it prefer to follow reasonably quickly behind the originating firm? Or, as a last resort of questionable soundness, does it want to risk the price-cutting approach by finding less expensive ways of making the product? Timing is critical in each approach. Action taken too soon or too late results in failure. But deciding on the right moment is a tricky business in the exercise of managerial judgment. Judgment can best be made on the basis of careful feasibility studies, which are covered in detail in the next chapter.

Inadequate Understanding of Technical Requirements

A pitfall to be avoided in selecting the idea for a new venture is lack of understanding of the technical requirements needed to make the product work as it is supposed to, or to produce the product itself. The development of a new product often involves the exploration of new techniques. A technical product may be pushing the forefront of knowl-

---

[10]Theodore Levitt, "Marketing Myopia," *Harvard Business Review*, July–August, 1960.

edge and may require overcoming large gaps in know-how. Failure to perceive the technical difficulties to be overcome in developing or producing a product can swamp the budding enterprise.

Even in apparently simple operations there can be unexpected difficulties. Learning how to run a fine paint stripe on decorative wall paneling proved a time-consuming and costly experience for one small company. Bringing the performance of a small, high-precision electric motor back to the performance of the prototypes cost another small company many thousands of dollars.

Selecting the best way to make a part can be a troublesome problem, and choosing an inadequate or improper method can be costly. A small company, newly formed to manufacture miniature precision gears, contracted to supply several hundred gear trains to a customer's specifications. The train involved one internal gear. The company found that it could not hold the required tolerances on this gear with the gear shaping machine it had in its shop. After a forced study of the problem, it found that the only practical way to make the gear was by broaching. This involved a lengthy and costly delay in having a broach designed and fabricated, and leasing and installing a broaching machine for cutting the gear teeth.

The enterpriser cannot be too thorough in studying the project under contemplation before venturing upon it. Carrying the product successfully through unexpected technical difficulties and pulling it through to smooth production sometimes poses time-consuming and costly problems.

Underestimating Financial Requirements

A common difficulty in the development of a new product is an overly optimistic estimate of the funds required to carry the project to completion. Sometimes venturers are naive, sometimes ignorant of costs, but too often they are victims of inadequate research and planning. Innovators and inventors are prone to underestimate development costs by wide margins. It is not uncommon to see estimates of less than half of what the project actually takes. Elements of cost are completely overlooked and the difficulties of the development work brushed aside without due consideration. One company well experienced in working with patent development automatically doubles the budget proposed by the inventor in its preliminary assessment of the idea. It then has its engineering department prepare a carefully researched development plan and budget for operational use.

A similar pitfall faces the introduction of a new service. Often overlooked are the costs of special equipment or for rigorous training of personnel before introducing the service. As a homely example, a small company entering the carpet cleaning business must budget for training its operators to ensure their skill before sending them into its customers' residences.

Successful franchise companies have learned through hard experience the importance of thoroughly training their new franchisees in both the skills of the business and in sound business practices before permitting them to open their doors. They know that the success of their business can be ensured only by having successful franchisees. Midas-International Corporation, as an instance, teaches its new franchisees not only how to install mufflers in their new Midas Muffler shops, but also how to keep adequate business records and how to manage credits effectively.

Inadequate preparation to meet the new service or product development can be avoided by thorough study and research of the basic problems and by setting aside a reserve fund to handle contingencies that undoubtedly will arise.

Lack of Product Differentiation

The product should have unique advantages if it is to be the foundation of a new small business. It should have special characteristics and originality in concept and design that draw the customer to it. It should give superior performance or service in at least some regards over similar products. Otherwise it becomes a me-too product of doubtful competitive merit.

Product differentiation flowing from originality in design and superior performance is the best way to assure an awareness of differences between the small company's product and those of competitors. Pricing becomes less of a problem when the customer sees the product as superior to its competitors.[11] The small company can then compete favorably by demonstrating that its product is better than others.

The product must not only perform as promised, it should also be able to pass another critical test: the potential customer must be able to recognize the purpose of the product by looking at it. The most cleverly designed product will find difficulty in the marketplace unless this criterion is met.

Menda Scientific Products, Inc., of California developed an original design for a baby oil dispenser. It consists of a small stainless steel container with a depressible cup-shaped element on its top. When this cup is pressed down, a small quantity of oil is pumped into it. The original concept was that the top would be pressed down with a small cotton ball, which would then pick up a quantity of baby oil. This proce-

---

[11]Levitt, *Innovation in Marketing*, p. 84.

dure would overcome the usually messy problem of pouring oil from a tilted bottle onto a cotton ball.

The first round of sales was made to local department stores willing to take on the new product. Unfortunately, potential customers were not able to identify the intended use of the product by looking at it. Faced with lack of sales, the company sought other markets for the product and other ways to sell it. It discovered a need of a similar kind in doctors' offices. Here the fluid is alcohol, employed in swabbing skin. The product was introduced by having medical equipment salesmen demonstrate its use to the doctor. Sales immediately followed. This product has been a staple in the company's product line for several years.

In searching for an idea for a new venture, the enterpriser should seek originality in concept. The product that is unique in a significant way gains the advantages of differentiation.

Inadequate Understanding of Legal Issues

Business is subject to many legal requirements, and legal devices can offer protection against several kinds of encroachment against business. Enterprisers should be familiar with both.

The forces of consumerism have become strong in recent years; the need to make the working place safe for those who work there is now subject to enforceable legal sanction. Products and services must be reliable and safe. Electrical equipment must be shockproof; childrens' toys must be free from hazard; and food products must meet medical standards of safety and hygiene.

Inventions may be protected by patent. However, the legal ramifications of this protection are intricate. The inventor should understand the major difficulties associated with patents before believing that a patent will give absolute protection. It would be wise for the originator of the patentable concept to consult competent counsel when considering this protection.

Other aspects of legal protection include copyrights, trademarks, and service marks. The small business owner may want to become familiar with these. Patents, copyrights, trademarks, and service marks are discussed in Chapter 4.

SUMMARY: Capturing Ideas for the New Venture

Entrepreneurs tap both external and internal resources in searching for new venture opportunities. They read widely and strive for original ideas by searching for newer and better things to do and newer and better ways to do things.

A marketing orientation underpins the success of small business. Entrepreneurs seeking success should work from the outside in, rather than from the inside out. They should clearly identify the potential customer's needs and tailor product or service to meet them. They should not so fall in love with their product or service as to hasten to produce it and expect the customer to buy it.

In an ongoing small business, the product-market matrix offers a framework for assessing business potential by cross-checking marketing possibilities of existing or new markets. Product diversification is required to exploit an existing market, and market diversification requires new markets for existing products or innovation of new products for new markets. The latter presents the highest risk and also the greatest possibility of high returns.

Entrepreneurs should avoid the more common pitfalls in launching a new venture. To tip the odds in their favor, they should:

1. Maintain an objective and searching attitude toward ideas for product or service.
2. Become thoroughly familiar with the situation of the market segment they expect to penetrate.
3. Understand in detail the technical requirements of product or process.
4. Explore thoroughly the financial requirements of development and production of product or process.
5. Know the legal constraints that apply to the intended product or service.
6. Ensure that the product or service offers unique advantages that in some way differentiate it from competition.
7. Protect the creative idea through patent, copyright, trademark, service mark.

SUGGESTED READINGS

Bond, Floyd A., ed. *Technological Change and Economic Growth.* Ann Arbor: University of Michigan, 1965.

Burns, Tom, and Stalker, G. M. *The Management of Innovation.* London: Tavistock Publications, 1961.

Cooper, Arnold C. "R & D is More Efficient in Small Companies." *Harvard Business Review* 42, May–June, 1964, pp. 75–83.

Haefele, John W. *Creativity and Innovation.* New York: Reinhold, 1962.

Moore, A. D. *Invention, Discovery, and Creativity.* Garden City, N.Y.: Doubleday, 1969.

Olken, H. "Spin-Offs: A Business Pay-Off." *California Management Review* 9, Winter, 1966, pp. 17–23.

Peters, Donald H., and Roberts, Edward B. "Unutilized Ideas in University Laboratories." *Academy of Management Journal*, June 1970, pp. 179–91.

Platt, J. R. "Strong Inference." *Science* 146, October 16, 1964, pp. 347–53.

Roberts, Edward B. "A Basic Study of Innovators: How to Keep and Capitalize on Their Talents." *Research Management* 11, July 1968, pp. 249–66.

Wright, R. A. "Key to Innovation: Loosening Reins on the Backyard Inventor." *The New York Times,* May 14, 1967.

CHAPTER 3

Evaluating New Venture Opportunities

A crucial task in starting a new enterprise is the analysis of its feasibility. The high costs of failure make it imperative to investigate comprehensively and systematically the strategic variables that determine the feasibility and ultimately the long-term profitability of a new venture opportunity. The budding enterpriser should realize that one strategic factor alone seldom shapes the ultimate success or failure of a new venture. In most situations a combination of several variables influences its potential success. These variables should be identified and investigated before the new idea is put into practice. The results of a feasibility analysis enable the entrepreneur to judge the potential of the business.

ESTABLISHING THE FEASIBILITY OF A NEW VENTURE

Every year many millions of dollars are spent in starting new enterprises. Many of these newly established businesses vanish within a year or two, and only a very few are eventually successful. One study, "Why New Products Fail," gives evidence that the factors underlying the failure of new ventures are in most cases within the control of the entrepreneur.[1] This study also lists as the major reasons for the failure of new ventures the following shortcomings:

---

[1] "Why New Products Fail," *The Conference Board Record,* October 1964, p. 11. Other analyses on the causes of failure of small businesses come to very similar conclusions. See for example, *The Failure Record Through 1965* and *The Business Failure Record 1974,* both published by Dun & Bradstreet, New York; David T. Stanley and Marjorie Girth, *Bankruptcy: Problems, Process, Reform,* Washington, D.C.: The Brookings Institution, 1971, pp. 110–12; John Argenti, *Corporate Collapse: The Causes and Symptoms,* New York: John Wiley & Sons, 1976.

- *Inadequate market knowledge.* This deficiency includes a lack of information about the demand potential for the product or service, the present and future size of the market, the market share that can realistically be expected, and appropriate distribution methods.
- *Faulty product performance.* Frequently new products do not perform properly because of hastily taken shortcuts in production development and product testing, or inadequate quality control.
- *Ineffective marketing and sales efforts.* Poor results often indicate inadequate or misdirected promotional efforts and a lack of appreciation of the problems involved in selling to, or servicing of, unfamiliar markets.
- *Inadequate awareness of competitive pressures.* New ventures often fail because the entrepreneur did not take into account the possible reactions of competitors, such as severe price cuts or special discounts to retailers.
- *Rapid product obsolescence.* The economic life of new products tends to get shorter; in many industries technological advances are so rapid as to make a new product obsolescent shortly after it is launched.
- *Poor timing for the start of the new venture.* Choosing the wrong time to launch a new venture often leads to commercial failure. A new product or service may be introduced before a real market interest or technological need for it exists, or it may be placed on the market too late, when consumer interest is waning.
- *Undercapitalization, unforeseen operating expenses, excessive investments in fixed assets, and related financial difficulties.* These financial problems are also among the major causes of new venture failures.

A comprehensive and sytematic feasibility analysis should identify these dangers, if they exist, and indicate ways of controlling them. The above list suggests those requirements that are important in the future success of a new venture: adequate market knowledge, a competitively superior product that performs its intended function well, a keen awareness of the competitive situation, an adequate financial base combined with appropriate investment strategies, and a good sense of timing in starting the new venture. These requirements can be fulfilled by competent management. The essence of a feasibility analysis for an intended new venture is thus to find reasonably conclusive answers to some very basic but also very difficult questions: What will it take to implement the new venture idea? Will it sell? What will it cost? Will it show a profit? The diagram of Figure 3–1 shows the key areas in analyzing and evaluating the feasibility of a new venture.

The purpose of this chapter is to show how to conduct an analysis and evaluation of each key area. A basic requirement is to break the analysis of each area into specific activities. Table 3–1 shows, in a summary form, the types of issues that should be investigated in each of the key areas.

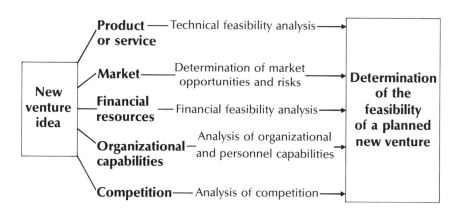

FIGURE 3–1. Key Areas in Assessing the Feasibility of a New Venture

The detail of the investigations will depend largely on the magnitude and complexity of the intended new venture; there is no standard format that can be used for every new venture. Figure 3–2 suggests the interrelatedness of the feasibility analyses for different areas.

Table 3–1 and Figure 3–2 show the broad scope of a systematic, comprehensive evaluation of an intended new venture. The analyses can proceed side by side, although in an interrelated fashion. For example, the interrelatedness of the market and technical aspects of a feasibility analysis may be seen in the flow chart of Figure 3–2. This chart assumes that the results at each stage of the investigation are essentially positive. They predict success and thus warrant proceeding with the next stage of the evaluation. In practice the results of some phases in the feasibility analysis of key areas may be inconclusive or negative, while others are positive. These danger signals should not be ignored. The entrepreneur should modify or change the original design and do some retesting. If the results become positive, it is safe to proceed with the next stage in the evaluative process. If the modifications still do not lead to positive results, the entrepreneur may well have to consider abandoning the idea.

The feasibility of a new venture is established in stages that represent critical decision points. For some ventures the feasibility study may require analysis of more areas than those shown in Figure 3–1 and additional steps to those of Table 3–1 and Figure 3–2. For other ventures the feasibility analyses may be less complex. It is, however, important to recognize that the assessment of an intended new venture must take into account all the critical factors that may affect its potential success. The rest of this chapter focuses separately on the five key areas of a

TABLE 3–1. SPECIFIC ACTIVITIES OF FEASIBILITY ANALYSES

Technical Feasibility Analysis	Market Feasibility Analysis	Financial Feasibility Analysis	Analysis of Organizational Capabilities	Competitive Analysis
Crucial technical specifications Design Durability Reliability Product safety Standardization *Engineering requirements* Machines Tools Instruments Work flow *Product development* Blueprints Models Prototypes *Product testing* Lab testing, field testing *Plant location issues* Desirable characteristics of plant site (proximity to suppliers, customers, environmental regulations) *Plant layout studies*	*Market potential* Identification of potential customers and their dominant characteristics (e.g., age, income level, buying habits) Potential market share (as affected by competitive situation) Potential sales volume Sales price projections *Market testing* Selection of test markets Actual market test Analysis of market test results *Marketing planning issues* Preferred channels of distribution, impact of promotional efforts, required distribution points (warehouses), packaging considerations price differentiation	*Required financial resources for:* fixed assets, current assets, necessary working capital *Available financial resources* *Required borrowing* Potential sources of funds *Cost of borrowing* *Repayment conditions* *Operating cost analysis* Fixed costs Variable costs *Projected cash flow* *Projected profitability*	*Personnel requirements* Required skills levels and other personal characteristics of potential employees *Managerial requirements* *Determination of individual responsibilities* *Determination of required organizational relationships* *Potential organization development* Competitive Analysis	*Existing competitors* Size, financial resources, market entrenchment *Potential reaction of competitors to newcomer* Price cutting, aggressive advertising, introduction of new products, etc. *Potential new competitors*

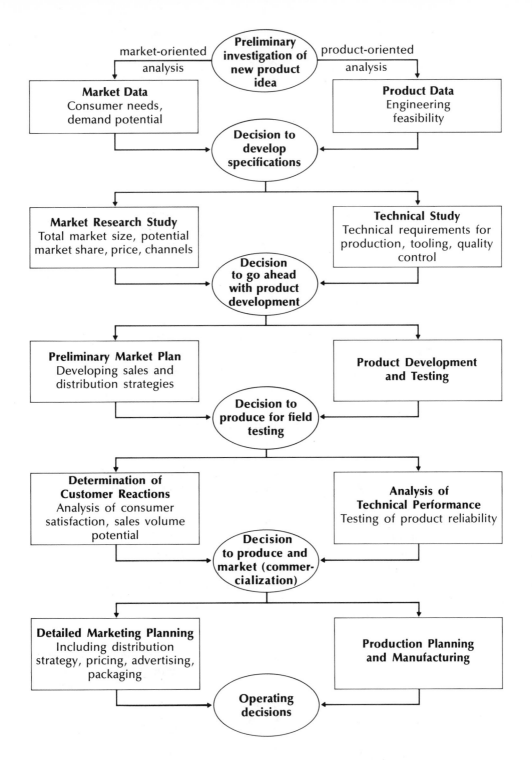

FIGURE 3–2. Interrelationship between Market and Technical Analyses

feasibility analysis: the product or service, the market, the financial re-sources, the organizational capabilities, and the competition.

TECHNICAL FEASIBILITY ANALYSIS

Every entrepreneurial idea—be it the production of a product or the provision of a service—has technical aspects that should be carefully analyzed before any effort toward implementation of the idea is under-taken. The two most important steps in this process are 1) identifying the critical technical specifications, and 2) testing the product or service to find out whether it meets performance specifications.

Identifying Critical Technical Specifications

The evaluation of a new venture idea should start with identifying the technical requirements that are market critical and thus mandatory to satisfying the expectations of potential customers. Although a wide range of requirements may be critical, the more important technical re-quirements are:

- functional design of the product and attractiveness in appearance
- flexibility, permitting ready modification of the external features of the product to meet customer demands or technological and com-petitive changes
- durability of the materials from which the product is made
- reliability, ensuring performance as expected under normal operat-ing conditions
- product safety, posing no potential dangers under normal operating conditions
- reasonable utility—an acceptable rate of obsolescence
- ease and low cost of maintenance
- standardization through elimination of unnecessary variety among potentially interchangeable parts
- ease of processing, or manufacture
- ease in handling and use.

This list shows the broad range of technical requirements that must be analyzed. The results of this investigation provide a basis for deciding whether a new venture idea is really feasible from a technical point of view. However, in conducting a technical analysis along these lines, the entrepreneur must realize from the outset that there are trade-offs be-tween technical excellence and associated cost, as Figure 3–3 illustrates.

An increase in the technical excellence (quality) of a product is usually associated with an increase in its cost of production. However, while

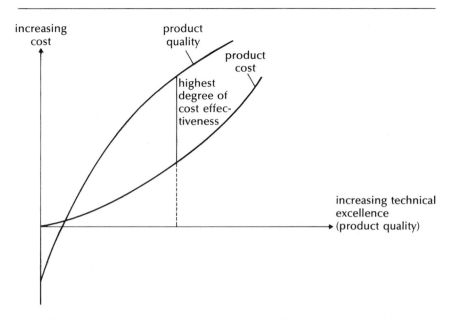

FIGURE 3–3. General Interrelationship between Product Quality and Product Cost (at a transitional point in the product's life cycle)

with increasing technical excellence of a product its production costs tend to rise at an increasing rate, its quality generally improves only at a decreasing rate. As Figure 3–3 shows the criterion for deciding on the optimum degree of quality of a product is the maximization of the cost effectiveness: to increase the technical excellence of the product to that level at which the marginal product quality equals marginal cost. This level is reached where the slopes of the product-quality and the product-cost curves are equal.

In addition to quality and cost relationships the entrepreneur must also consider the ultimate consumers and the value they place on alternative degrees of quality. For example, consumers may not be willing to pay for improvements in product quality commensurate with the necessary increases in production costs. Quality improvements, to the extent that they cause cost increases will require a price increase, which generally leads to a decrease in total market demand. However, there may be instances in which product quality above the maximum cost effectiveness (see Figure 3–3) will attract a new group of customers who are willing to pay a very high price that will yield a high profit. In such an exceptional case an entrepreneur may be well advised to exploit this market potential and to stress a product-market strategy sometimes called snob appeal. In the majority of new venture situations such an approach, however, will not work. In other words, the entrepreneur should avoid unnecessary gold plating when the market-demand situation does not justify it. In actual practice it may be difficult to determine the optimal level of product quality, but it is useful to keep the concept of these interrelationships as expressed in Figure 3–3 in mind when analyzing the technical feasibility of a new product.

Developing and Testing the Product

Product development and testing may include engineering studies, laboratory testing, evaluation of alternative materials, and the fabrication of various breadboard models and prototypes for field testing. At every stage the positive and negative results of the investigation must be carefully weighed and the necessary adjustments made. Figure 3–4 shows schematically the possible sequence for establishing the technical feasibility and the producibility of a new product.

The first step in establishing the technical feasibility of a new venture idea is identifying critical technical requirements and formulating performance specifications. At each subsequent step the results must be evaluated against these requirements and specifications. The entrepreneur who implements an idea in this manner establishes its technical feasibility and gains reasonable assurance that it will meet the requirements of potential customers.

ASSESSING MARKET OPPORTUNITIES

Assembling, screening, and analyzing relevant information about the market and the marketability of its product are basic in judging the potential success of an intended new venture. Three major aspects to this procedure are:

1. investigating market potential and identifying potential customers (or users)
2. analyzing the extent to which the new enterprise might exploit a potential market
3. determining the actual market opportunities and risks through market testing.

Analysis of Market Potential

Determining and evaluating the market potential of a planned new business venture should start with gathering market-relevant data about the potential customers, their purchasing motivations, buying habits, and the impact of changes in the product characteristics on the market poten-

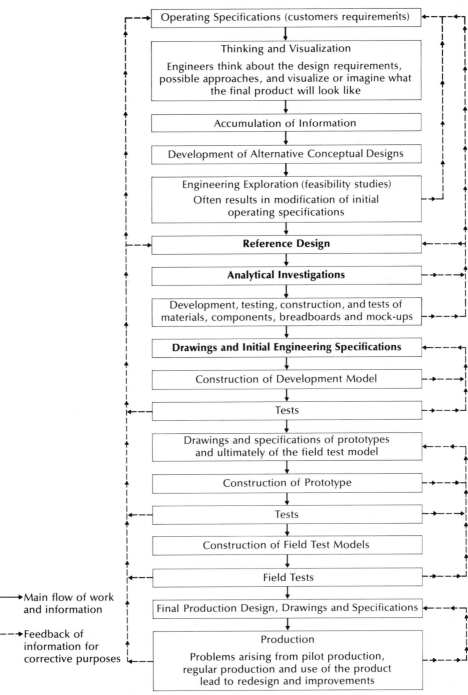

Operating Specifications (customers requirements)

| Thinking and Visualization |
| Engineers think about the design requirements, possible approaches, and visualize or imagine what the final product will look like |

| Accumulation of Information |

| Development of Alternative Conceptual Designs |

| Engineering Exploration (feasibility studies) |
| Often results in modification of initial operating specifications |

| **Reference Design** |

| **Analytical Investigations** |

| Development, testing, construction, and tests of materials, components, breadboards and mock-ups |

| **Drawings and Initial Engineering Specifications** |

| Construction of Development Model |

| Tests |

| Drawings and specifications of prototypes and ultimately of the field test model |

| Construction of Prototype |

| Tests |

| Construction of Field Test Models |

| Field Tests |

| Final Production Design, Drawings and Specifications |

| Production |
| Problems arising from pilot production, regular production and use of the product lead to redesign and improvements |

→ Main flow of work and information

--→ Feedback of information for corrective purposes

FIGURE 3–4. The Process of Product Development and Testing

Source: Delmar W. Karger and Robert G. Murdick, *Managing Engineering and Research*, New York: Industrial Press, 1963, p. 264

tial. This task can be challenging and perplexing, especially in a rapidly changing market. Researching the market potential of a new venture may involve subjective or personal judgments; it is therefore not always very scientific.

Entrepreneurs should, however, try to use a scientific approach; they should probe for objective information about potential customers, letting the chips fall where they may. Unfortunately, many budding entrepreneurs are so enamored of their new venture idea that they neglect to probe for the existence of a market or they conduct market research simply to validate their beliefs. In contrast, wise entrepreneurs spend considerable effort in identifying the actual market potential. They will guard against slanting the market research design through personal bias.

Identifying the Market Potential

The market potential is an expression of the maximum sales opportunities for a particular product or service during a stated period of time, for example, one year. An estimation of the market potential should ideally involve both the current demand for the product and a projection of future market trends. Although the literature recommends a variety of guidelines for identifying and estimating the market potential of a new venture, there is no one approach that is clearly superior to others.[2] In general it is advisable to follow three steps:

1. identify the specific end-users of the product or service
2. identify the major market segments, that is, relatively homogeneous customer categories
3. determine or estimate the potential volume of purchases within each market segment and the summation of all segments.

The first step, identifying potential customers or end-users, may in some cases be fairly easy, because the product makes it obvious who would want it. For example, the maker of electronic micro chips to be used solely in minicalculators has a clearly defined potential customer base. In other cases much investigation may be required to identify potential users. For example, a producer of electronic minicircuits with a wide range of applications may find it difficult to determine who the

---

[2]See for example Edgar A. Pessemier, *New Product Decisions: An Analytical Approach*, New York: McGraw-Hill, 1966, pp. 86–91; John Harris, "The New Product Profile Chart: Selecting and Appraising New Projects," in *New Products/New Profits*, edited by Elizabeth Marting, New York: American Management Association, 1964, pp. 113–31; John T. O'Meara, "Selecting Profitable Products," *Harvard Business Review*, January–February, 1961, pp. 83–89.

most promising customers might be. Answers to the following questions should be sought to identify potential users:

Who are the potential buyers of the product? In the case of a consumer product, what are the personal characteristics of the customers, such as age, sex, income level, educational background? In the case of an industrial product, what are the characteristics of the industry that may use this product, such as the size of the industry, number of firms, and geographical dispersion?

Where are the potential buyers located?

Why would customers want to buy this product? What are their buying habits? How often do they buy? What is the size of the average order?

What is the total monthly or annual demand for this product?

How cyclical is the demand?

What is the potential growth of this market?

Once the likely customers have been identified, the second step is to classify them into relatively homogeneous categories—each having similar, identifiable characteristics. Typical significant characteristics are the potential customers' physical location, their demographic characteristics, the channels of distribution by which they can best be reached, and the advertising media to which they seem to be most responsive. This categorization of potential users is critical because it later enables the new venture organization to select specific categories, or market segments, by matching its own capabilities against what is needed to attract and gain the loyalty of these customer groups.

The third step involves estimating the potential consumption of the new product or service by each market segment immediately and in future periods. This task is obviously the most crucial aspect in any attempt to determine the market potential of a new venture. One way to get information is to select a representative test market, a geographically limited market area in which the new product is actually marketed. From the results of this market test the total market potential may be estimated.

A less time consuming and less costly approach is to investigate relatively constant, measurable relationships—so-called ratios of usage—between the use of the new product and some statistical measure that is known or that can be reliably estimated. For example, the market potential of a new, optional antismog device for passenger automobiles is clearly related to new car production and the number of cars currently in use. For another more detailed approach to estimating market potential see the reading on this subject from The Conference Board, which is found in Appendix 1 at the end of this chapter.

These three steps indicate the complexity of estimating the market potential of a new product. But in spite of the difficulties, an attempt should be made to get a reasonably reliable appraisal of the market potential. The essential aim is to find out whether the market or some segment of it would be large enough to support the new entry. In addition, the entrepreneur ultimately needs to know the rate of penetration of the market that the new company might realistically achieve over a given period of time. The answer to this question depends, to a large extent, on the relative competitive situation. An analysis of the strengths and weaknesses of existing or new competitors is thus an indispensable part of a comprehensive feasibility analysis for a new venture. Information about the current market potential can also give some clues about the growth prospect of a given market. With this awareness the new company's short- and long-term potential sales volume, the attendant costs, and finally the profits that might be realized from a given level of sales, can be appraised.

Estimating Price (Cost)-Volume Relationships

Once the total market potential of a new product has been established by summing the potential volume of purchases per market segment, the impact of strategic factors such as pricing and promotion on the total volume of sales revenues must be considered. The entrepreneur will want to know, for example, how various price levels or differences in the amount of promotional support may affect the total volume of sales. The total volume of sales, in turn, will have an effect on the cost structure. Assuming certain economies of scale, unit costs would be reduced by increasing the total volume of output. However, a higher level of output may find a market only at lower prices. For this reason it is important to find out how much the prospective consumers are willing to pay for the new product or service. It must not be overlooked that the price should represent the value of the product in the mind of the consumer and not simply the sum of all costs plus a desired profit margin. The pricing strategy of a firm cannot ignore the customers' concept of value. The entrepreneur should therefore find out how specific customer groups will respond to specific prices. As a result of this investigation the new company may choose not to have a uniform pricing structure for its products. It may differentiate between a deluxe and an economy model or charge different prices to different types of customers by granting them quantity and functional discounts. The entrepreneur should set the relationship between price and volume of output only after careful study, for this determination can critically affect the profitability of the new business venture.

The theoretical concept describing the relationship between a given price level and the associated level of sales is known as the *price elasticity of demand*. It measures the sensitivity of buyers to price changes. If, for example, a relatively small reduction in price significantly stimulates unit sales, the price elasticity of demand is high. Conversely, if substantial changes in the price lead to only minor changes in unit sales, the demand is said to be inelastic. Although the effort may prove difficult, the entrepreneur should try to determine what the price elasticity for the new product may actually be, and thus to ascertain the sensitivity of the potential buyers to price changes.

The economies of scale should also be determined: How would the costs per unit of output change with a higher or lower level of production? To answer this question the entrepreneur should try to determine total costs for various levels of production and the resultant unit costs. This effort will also give some idea about the optimum size of the enterprise. The optimum size is defined as one that obtains, in a given state of technology, the lowest average unit cost of production and distribution. It may be that the entrepreneur does not command the financial resources to establish a business of the optimum size. However, a significant difference between the actual size of the firm and the ideal optimum size will probably increase the competitive pressures with which the firm will have to cope.

The estimates developed to this point should be modified by factors reflecting confidence in their reliability. Every quantity in the analyses of market potential and price and cost as a function of volume should be multiplied by a judgmentally determined coefficient. A coefficient of 1.0 would express perfect confidence, 0.9 a confidence of 90 percent, and so on, down to perhaps 0.6 as the least acceptable expression of confidence. The entrepreneur can decide on the basis of these results whether or not characteristics of the market pose an acceptable risk for the new venture.

The data obtained by analyzing the market potential and the impact of marketing strategy decisions should preferably be summarized in the form of a preliminary projected income statement as shown in Table 3–2.

TABLE 3–2. PROJECTED INCOME STATEMENT

	Calcuation	Periods* 1 2 3 4 $\cdots n$
(1) Potential unit sales		
(2) Average unit price		
(3) Potential sales revenue	(1) × (2)	
(4) Unit manufacturing costs		
(5) Cost of goods sold	(1) × (4)	
(6) Other costs		
(7) Profit before tax	(3) − (5 + 6)	
(8) Tax		
(9) Net profit (or loss)	(7) − (8)	

On the basis of an assessment of the market potential, the entrepreneur can project the physical volume of sales during future periods. Periods as short as feasible should be chosen to decrease the likelihood of financial danger. Multiplying the average unit price by the projected unit sales gives the projected sales revenue. Deducting from this figure the manufacturing, distribution, and other cost items, and the taxes to be paid, gives the projected net profit (or loss). That is the essential criterion for assessing the economic (market) feasibility of a prospective new venture.

Sources of Market Information

The preceding sections have dealt with categories of information that must be investigated to evaluate the existing and future market opportunities for a new venture. The purpose of this section is to describe major sources of information for such an analysis.

The entrepreneur will rarely find existing market data that relate directly to the new product or service. Two approaches may be taken to obtain desired data: 1) Conduct a survey that is specifically designed to gather information on a particular project. Information generated in this way is referred to as *primary data.* 2) Locate relevant data published by organizations such as the U.S. Bureau of the Census (for example, Census of Manufacturers), other government agencies, trade associations, chambers of commerce, and university bureaus of business research. Information of this kind is referred to as *secondary data.*

Gathering primary data is usually much more costly and time consuming than accumulating secondary data. Secondary data may have the drawback of not quite meeting the specific requirements of the entrepreneur. It is wise, however, to start by looking for secondary data. If the required information cannot be obtained in this way, a specifically designed market research study should be conducted.

As a first step in gathering and piecing together information for determining the market opportunities of a new venture, a *data matrix* should be prepared. This matrix should list all the desired informational inputs and the sources of information being checked. Table 3–3 suggests a format for such a matrix.

Statistical data published by the U.S. Department of Commerce are the most widely used source of secondary data in conducting a market feasibility analysis for a new venture idea. The monthly *Survey of Current Business* and various reports of the Bureau of the Census contain a wide range of statistical data that are often relevant in a market analysis. Similarly, publications by the Small Business Administration may contain useful information. Most industry and trade associations publish

---

*Depending upon the complexity of the new project, the selected period could be a week, a month, a quarter, or a year. The greater the complexity and the more variable the cyclical patterns, the shorter should be the period.

TABLE 3–3. DATA MATRIX FOR MARKET FEASIBILITY STUDY

Information Requirements	Sources of Information											
	Secondary Data						Primary Data					
	1	2	3	4	5	6	1	2	3	4	5	6

General economic trends
Various economic indicators such as new orders, housing starts, inventories, consumer spending

Market data
Customers; customer demand patterns (e.g., seasonal variations in demand; governmental regulations affecting demand, etc.)

Pricing data
Range of prices for the same, complementary and substitute products; base prices; discount structures, etc.

Channels of distribution
Wholesalers, retailers

Competitive data
Major competitors and their competitive strength

regular reports that give a great deal of market information. Another valuable source is the public records of the local city, county, or state governments. Local newspapers and private companies such as the Marketing Research Corporation of America can also provide data for assessing the market potential of some new ventures.

Obviously there are limitations to the use of secondary data. For example, the classifications used in tabulating statistical data may not fit the specific project under study, or the data may be too broad or already obsolete. However, since secondary data can generally be obtained faster and at less cost than primary data, one should find out first whether appropriate information can be obtained in this way. For the remainder of the required information, entrepreneurs will have to rely on primary sources. They can use do-it-yourself specific surveys or they can contract this task to a consulting firm. Specific surveys, which are usually rather costly, are designed to get information about market opportunities, customer preferences, and marketing requirements that cannot be obtained in any other way. Surveys can be conducted as personal and telephone interviews or by mailed questionnaires.

Personal Interviews Personal interviews with major prospective customers are particularly appropriate for gathering information about complex product concepts. Personal interviews promote market acceptance in two ways: they stimulate interest in the new product and they establish contacts with potential customers. To conduct a successful interview, the respondent must thoroughly understand the new venture idea. Drawings, diagrams, models, or prototypes are useful in explaining the new product. A standardized interviewing guide should be used to compare the results of several interviews.

Interviewing prospective customers individually can be a costly and time consuming method for gathering market information. The interviewer should save money and time by being wary of personal biases of the respondents, which can produce misleading data.

Telephone Interviews Telephone interviews can be used as a source of market information when the basic features of the new product are well defined and do not require a demonstration of its functions or performance. Appendix 2 to this chapter shows a guide for conducting a telephone survey.

Mail Surveys If a broadly based investigation of potential customers' receptiveness to a new product concept is desired, mail surveys can be used effectively. A mail survey should always include a detailed description of the product, a letter requesting the cooperation of the addressee, and a questionnaire to be answered and returned in a self-addressed stamped envelope.

With any of these methods of gathering information, close attention should be given to the selection of the sample of interviewees so that it is representative of potential buyers and large enough to ensure the statistical validity of the results.[3]

The Role of Market Testing

A systematic assessment of the market opportunities and an evaluation of the likely success of a new venture usually requires a market test. In

---

[3]For detailed discussions of the principles of sampling and the statistical validity of survey results see American Marketing Association, *Sampling in Marketing Research*, Chicago: 1958; William G. Cochran, *Sampling Techniques*, New York: John Wiley & Sons, 1963; Arthur E. Mace, *Sample-Size Determination*, New York: Reinhold, 1964; or D. Raj, *The Design of Sample Surveys*, New York: McGraw-Hill, 1972.

many new ventures a series of market tests may be necessary at successive steps of implementation. Market testing tends to be the ultimate research technique for reducing the risks inherent in a new venture and gauging its likely success.

Market testing requires that the new product be scrutinized and evaluated by potential buyers. Among the preferred methods are displaying the product at trade shows, selling it in a limited number of selected areas, and using test markets where the receptivity of prospective buyers may be closely observed and analyzed. A market test can give the following important information: 1) the likely sales volume and profitability when the new product is marketed on a larger scale, 2) an indication of the sales volume at different price levels, 3) an indication of the the soundness of the chosen market strategy, and 4) information about the key influences that would make people want to buy. Market testing also gives clues to opportunities in marketing, distribution, and servicing. The testing process may reveal unsuspected weaknesses or shortcomings that require drastic alteration or even scrapping of the new venture idea. In such a case, market testing becomes a means for limiting losses and liabilities.

The entrepreneur should be aware of the drawbacks as well as the advantages of market testing. The time consumed by the procedure may cause delay in the realization of the new venture idea. The new product or service may be prematurely exposed to competitors, which would give them time to organize a counter-strategy. Market testing can be relatively expensive. The small business owner should use ingenuity to mount an adequate market testing program without straining customarily limited financial resources.

As has been implied, market testing must be carefully planned to produce reliable results. The desired data should be sought only after clearly specifying the critical variables. Particular attention must be paid to the selection of test areas, length of the test period, and the techniques for gathering and analyzing the test data.

Importance of the Market Feasibility Study

Although the assessment of the market opportunities for a new venture tends to be a time consuming, complex task, it is the better part of wisdom for the entrepreneur to perform a market feasibility study rather than to plunge blindly into a new venture. The approaches presented here are aimed at giving early insights into the prospects for success or failure of the venture. Through a careful analysis of the market opportunities, the entrepreneur can gain not only information on the market feasibility of the new venture, but also the data on which to base decisions about the course of action most likely to bring success. As a concluding point, a market feasibility analysis is mandatory to uncovering the important data necessary to evaluate the financial prospects of a new venture.

FINANCIAL FEASIBILITY ANALYSIS

A financial feasibility analysis is basic to determining the financial resources required for a particular level of activity and the profits that can be expected. The financial requirements and the returns can vary considerably, depending upon the selection of alternatives that exist for most new ventures. For example, an entrepreneur may have the component parts of a new product manufactured in-house, which requires investment in production machinery and perhaps buildings. In contrast, manufacture of the new product may be subcontracted to outside suppliers; here the firm becomes essentially a warehousing and marketing operation with little investment in fixed assets. In this case the profit margin of the firm might prove smaller. However, the total return on invested capital could be higher than in the case of a fully integrated operation. This example, hinging on what is called a make-or-buy decision, shows the variability of the financial feasibility of a new venture. The break-even diagram of Figure 3–5 shows alternative A (buying from an outside source) with low fixed costs but relatively high variable costs and alternative B (making in-house) with high fixed costs but relatively low variable costs.

As this example shows, alternative A has a considerably lower break-even point and, up to a sales volume of less than about 138,000 units, higher total profits. If sales were more than 138,000 units, alternative B would yield a higher total profit. The main advantage of alternative A is, however, the low level of fixed investment, which may be a very important consideration for a new venture.

Another factor that can change the financial feasibility of an intended new venture is the scope of operation. Bringing a new product to actuality on a large scale may require a large fixed investment and perhaps relatively high unit costs. A small-scale operation, on the other hand, would require much less fixed investment. Although the unit cost in the latter case might be higher, concentrating the marketing effort on customers who can pay a higher price may still afford the small-scale operation a satisfactory return on its investment; the returns on the large-scale operation may be less than acceptable. These examples show that the financial feasibility of a new venture depends to a large extent on the alternatives chosen for starting it. One way of launching an entrepreneurial idea may turn out to be financially infeasible; an alternate approach may very well lead to financially acceptable results.

The analysis of the financial feasibility of a new venture requires prob-

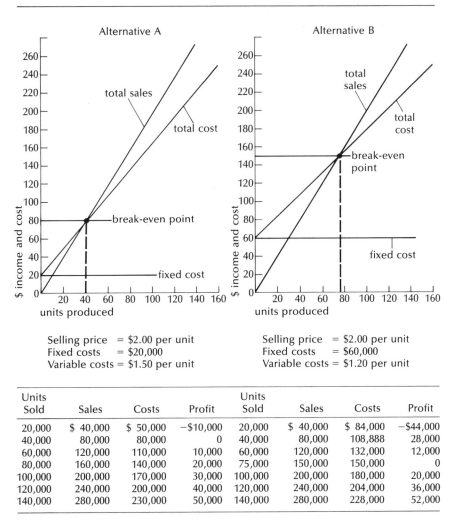

FIGURE 3–5. Break-Even Analyses with Different Fixed and Variable Costs

Units Sold	Sales	Costs	Profit	Units Sold	Sales	Costs	Profit
20,000	$ 40,000	$ 50,000	−$10,000	20,000	$ 40,000	$ 84,000	−$44,000
40,000	80,000	80,000	0	40,000	80,000	108,888	28,000
60,000	120,000	110,000	10,000	60,000	120,000	132,000	12,000
80,000	160,000	140,000	20,000	75,000	150,000	150,000	0
100,000	200,000	170,000	30,000	100,000	200,000	180,000	20,000
120,000	240,000	200,000	40,000	120,000	240,000	204,000	36,000
140,000	280,000	230,000	50,000	140,000	280,000	228,000	52,000

ing various alternatives for implementation. The analytical approach to this problem focuses on four essential steps:

1. Determining the total financial requirement by itemizing the operationally necessary funds.
2. Determining the available financial resources and their costs, which implies examining sources of funds and cost of capital.
3. Determining the future cash flow that can be expected from the operation by means of a cash flow analysis at relatively short intervals, preferably monthly.

4. Determining the expected return through a return-on-investment
analysis.

The Total Financial Requirement

The first step in a financial feasibility calculation is a detailed analysis of
all the financial obligations and pay-out requirements that the new venture would be expected to meet over the foreseeable future. This information can be accumulated and organized in a variety of ways. The
scheme shown in Table 3–4 is one guide for the development of a financial requirement statement. In a new venture it is imperative to project
the financial requirements—preferably on a month-by-month basis—as
far into the future as can be done with reasonable accuracy, as Table 3–4
shows.

The estimates for each category of expenditure should be as detailed
as possible for each period and should carefully take into account when
payments become due. In making these forecasts of the expected financial requirements it must always be kept in mind that environmental
dynamics such as price increases may raise start-up and operating expenditures considerably. Also, as the firm grows it is likely to require
more cash to cover investments in inventories and fixed assets and to
experience a lag in collecting increasingly larger receivables.

The most important variable that affects a firm's financing requirements is the projected volume of sales. Carelessly made, inaccurate sales
forecasts tend to magnify errors in the projected financial requirements.
A carefully made sales forecast therefore becomes the basis for projecting financial requirements. For this purpose it is useful to establish ratios
between a given level of sales and the required items of expenditure. For
example, it may be determined that the required fixed investments are
about 30 percent of sales. Because these relationships usually remain
fairly stable, they may be used for projecting financial requirements.

Consideration should be given to seasonal and other fluctuations in
sales. A somewhat more refined method of forecasting financial requirements would be to tie them not only to the amount of sales but also
to changes in other variables. These might include the level of advertising expenditures or macroeconomic variables such as changes in consumer disposable income. The relatively fixed relationships between the
behavior of the various expenditure categories and other significant variables should be determined with a reasonable degree of accuracy.

Financial requirements should be projected on a monthly, or even
weekly basis for at least the first year of operation of a new venture.
Banks asked for medium-term loans may request three-to-five-year projections of financial requirements, with figures on a quarterly schedule.
Although these forecasts pose a demanding task because a new venture

TABLE 3-4. FINANCIAL REQUIREMENTS STATEMENT

	Period 1	Period 2	Period n

Start-up expenses

Product (business) development expenses (expenditures associated with the conceptual development of the venture idea)

Legal expenses (expenditures for all legal matters including patent search and registration procedures)

Product testing expenses (expenditures associated with the development and testing of models and prototypes)

Expenditures for market opportunity analyses

Expenditures for other feasibility analyses

Miscellaneous business development and start-up expenditures (such as expenditures for materials, test equipment, and salaries and wages during the start-up phase)

Required fixed investments

Buildings

Equipment and machinery

Office equipment

Expenditures for the installation of equipment and machinery

Operating expenses

Material and other supplies

Wages, salaries

Marketing and promotion expenditures

General administrative expenditures

Rent

Interest payments

Repayments on loans

Insurance

Expenditures for utilities

Taxes

Contingency funds

Funds to cover expenditures caused by unforeseen developments or by changes in the venture implementation strategy

Total required payments per period

has no historical data, the importance of carefully working out these projections cannot be over-emphasized.

Available Financial Resources and Their Costs

The second essential step in the financial feasibility analysis is projecting the financial resources available and the funds that would be generated by operations. Since Chapter 6 deals extensively with financing new business ventures, treatment here will be brief.

In determining potentially available financial resources, one should distinguish between short-, intermediate-, and long-term sources of financing. Short-term sources of funds are generally those scheduled for repayment within one year. Two major sources are trade credit from suppliers, represented by accounts payable, and short-term loans from banks or other lending institutions. (Factoring, sale of accounts receivable, can also be considered as a source of short-term financing. Factoring tends to be expensive for the new firm and should not be considered in a financial feasibility analysis.) Trade credit from suppliers can help to finance purchases and credit sales to customers. If a firm's sales average $1,000 a day with an average collection period of 30 days, its accounts receivable on any given day would be approximately $30,000.. If the firm buys an average of $600 worth of supplies a day and the payment terms are 60 days, then the accounts payable would average about $36,000. The firm would get an effective net credit of $6,000. A new firm should make maximum use of trade credits from suppliers and try to minimize the time that its own funds are tied up in accounts receivable. Trade credit, it must be recognized, can be costly when discounts offered for cash or early payment are lost. However, a new firm may frequently have no other form of financing available and thus be forced to use it even at high cost.

The interest rates on short-term loans from commercial banks depend on the type of security the borrower can furnish and the general rate of interest current in the economy. Banks differ in their basic attitudes toward risk. As a result, the interest rate charged to a borrower may vary according to a particular bank's view of the risk. Banks also differ in the services and support they offer the borrower. A new venture should therefore always investigate carefully the various banks from which it can borrow.

Intermediate-term sources of finance are those available for one to three years, or in some cases up to five years. The major categories are term loans from commercial banks or insurance companies, sales contracts, and lease financing.

Term loans generally require fixed amortization payments according to a predetermined repayment schedule. They are usually secured in some way, as by a mortgage on production machinery. Term loans tend to have a variable interest rate. Standard practice is to stipulate a given percentage above the existing rediscount rate of the Federal Reserve Bank system or above the prime rate charged by leading banks. Conditional sales contracts are also a source of intermediate financing. They enable the buyer to purchase capital equipment that is paid for in installments over a specified period, during which the seller retains title to the equipment. Sale and leaseback agreements, by which a firm sells specified assets to a financial institution then immediately leases them back, are also a frequently used form of intermediate financing. Although the cost of leasing assets rather than owning them tends to be higher, sometimes the new firm may have little or no choice.

Long-term sources of finance are long-term loans from investment banks, equity that can be raised, and eventually reinvested earnings. The cost of long-term loans is, as in other loans, the interest rate that has to be paid. The cost of equity is more difficult to determine; it is essentially the rate of return on equity that the entrepreneur expects. Reinvested earnings should also be considered to cost at least the same rate as equity capital.

As this discussion shows, there is a wide range of potential sources of funds. In considering each source of funding, its specific costs, advantages, and disadvantages should be weighed. Since costs of funds vary, it is advisable to calculate the average cost of capital by estimating the proportion of total financing to be acquired by a given method and multiplying it by the cost of that method to get a weighted cost. The sum of the weighted costs then gives the average weighted cost of capital. Table 3–5 illustrates this process.

TABLE 3–5. CALCULATING THE AVERAGE COST OF CAPITAL

(1) Method of Financing	(2) Proportion (assumed)	(3) Cost (assumed)	(4) Weighted Cost [(2) × (3)]
Short-term debt	20	7%	1.40
Intermediate-term debt	10	8	0.80
Long-term debt	20	9	1.80
Equity	20	10	5.00
Weighted average cost of capital			9.00%

The average cost of capital can be used as a measure for judging the financial feasibility of a new venture by finding out whether there is a positive net present value when all anticipated cash flows are discounted at the average rate of cost of capital.

Anticipated Cash Flows

When projected sales, the associated financial requirements, and the available financial resources are known, it is possible to determine the anticipated cash flow and the ways in which a negative cash flow may be countered. Table 3–6 shows a breakdown of the information needed for cash flow planning.

As the table indicates, it is important to determine systematically, for a series of time periods, the anticipated operating inflows, outflows, and resultant net cash flow. Every business requires, in addition, a minimum cash balance to meet emergencies. A negative cash flow plus the desired minimum cash balance gives the amount that must be financed. The next step is to identify the sources of funds to meet the financial requirements at every period.

The net cash flow of a new venture tends to be highly negative in the beginning. Eventually it must turn positive and yield a profit if the venture is to be successful. A detailed cash flow and financial analysis along the lines shown in Table 3–6 is fundamental to assessing the feasibility of a new venture. The final step in this analysis is determining the return on investment the venture will yield.

Anticipated Return on Investment

The ultimate test of the feasibility of a new venture is whether it will yield a satisfactory return on the invested capital. One way of calculating the rate of return is to relate the average earnings expected over a given period of time either to the total amount of investment (return on investment) or the net worth of the organization (return on equity). Both ratios are then compared with the potential yield from alternative investment opportunities. The entrepreneur can judge from this comparison whether the expected return from a new venture would be acceptable.

A somewhat more sophisticated way of viewing the anticipated return is to calculate the present value of the expected net cash flow by using the cost of capital as a discount rate. Relating the sum of the discounted net cash flows to the total investment during the period under consideration yields a return on investment ratio that represents the present value of the anticipated profitability.

Still a third method for calculating a return on investment ratio is to use what is widely referred to as the Du Pont system of financial analysis. This approach establishes several financial ratios and shows how these ratios interact to determine the profitability of the investment. It is illustrated in Figure 3–6.

TABLE 3–6. CASH FLOW PLANNING

Cash Flow and Financing Transactions	Period . . . 1	Period . . . 2	Period n
(I) *Cash outflows*			
Start-up expenses			
.			
.			
Fixed investments			
.			
.			
Operating expenses			
.			
.			
Total cash outflow			
(II) *Cash inflows*			
Cash sales			
Accounts receivable			
Total operating inflows			
(III) *Net cash flow* [(II) − (I)]			
(IV) *Desired minimum cash balance*			
(V) *Total amount of funds required* [(III), if negative, + (IV)]			
(VI) *Sources of funds to meet financing requirements*			
Short-term			
Net trade credit			
Commercial loans			
Intermediate-term			
Term loans			
Conditional sales contracts			
Long-term			
Long-term loans			
Equity			
Total financing			

This method can be used for analyzing the financial situation for every period for which forecasts have been made. It is, in effect, a simple simulation model that shows how the return on investment will change in response to changes of other variables.

Projecting financial results of a planned venture requires certain assumptions about market and cost behavior. Every assumption reflects a degree of uncertainty and risk. To arrive at an explicit appreciation of the risk factor in a financial feasibility analysis one must indicate the degree of probability associated with each important variable, such as the expected market potential, the selling price, and the operating costs. For this purpose David Hertz has proposed a method that determines return on investment by examining nine key input factors and the likely range

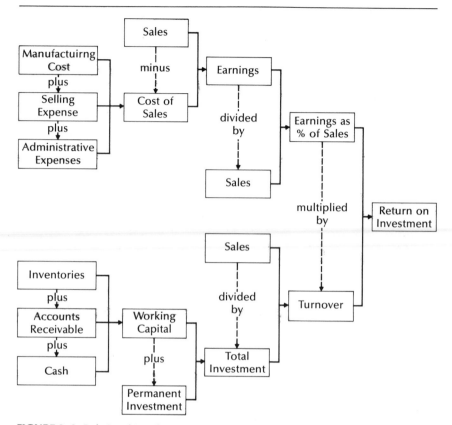

FIGURE 3–6. Relationship of Factors Affecting Return on Investment

of their values.[4] This method is much more sophisticated than those previously described. It requires a computer program to carry out the many calculations needed and presents some practical difficulties in specifying the range and probabilities of the key input factors. These requirements probably place it beyond the capacities of the new business. However, at a later stage of development of the enterprise it may prove advantageous as a powerful way to estimate the returns and financial feasibility of a planned venture. It is described briefly here.

In the Hertz method nine input factors are grouped into three categories: market analyses, investment analyses, and cost analyses as shown in Figure 3–7a. A low, middle (or best estimate), and high value are assigned to the individual variables in each category. The likelihood

[4]David B. Hertz, "Risk Analysis in Capital Investment," *Harvard Business Review*, January–February 1964, pp. 95–106; also David B. Hertz, *New Power for Management*, New York: McGraw-Hill, 1969, pp. 66–87.

(a)

Determine probability values for significant factors

Select—at random—sets of these factors according to the chances they have of turning up in the future

Determine rate of return for each combination

Repeat process to give a clear portrayal of investment risk

chances that rate will be achieved or exceeded

rate of return

(b) Input Factors

chances that value will be achieved

range of values

Market Size

e.v.*

Selling Price

Market Growth Rate

Share of Market

Investment Required

Residual Value of Investment

** Operating Costs

Fixed Costs

Useful Life of Facilities

*Expected value = average of all possible outcomes or the "one best estimate."
**(Related to production volume)

	Conventional "Cost Estimate" Approach	Range* of Estimated Values		
		Low	Med	High
Market analyses				
1. Market size (tons 000)	250	100	250	340
2. Selling prices ($/ton)	$510	$385	$510	$575
3. Market growth rate	3%	0%	3%	6%
4. Eventual share of market	12%	3%	12%	17%
Investment cost analyses				
5. Total investment required (millions)	$9.5	$7.0	$9.5	$10.5
6. Useful life of facilities (years)	10	5	10	15
7. Residual value at 10 years (millions)	$4.5	$3.5	$4.5	$5.0
Other costs				
8. Operating costs ($/ton)	$435	$370	$435	$545
9. Fixed costs ($1,000s)	$300	$250	$300	$375
Expected value of ROI %	25.2		14.6	

*Range figures represent approximately 1% to 99% probabilities. That is, there is only a 1 in 100 chance that the value actually achieved will be respectively greater or less than the range.

FIGURE 3–7. Return on Investment Analysis: a. Determining investment risk, b. Determining expected value of ROI

Source: David B. Hertz, *New Power for Management*, New York: McGraw-Hill, 1969, pp. 81, 83.

of the occurrence of various values within the range for each of the nine items listed is then estimated. The nine items as shown are 1) market size, 2) selling price, 3) market growth rate, 4) eventual share of market, 5) total investment required, 6) useful life of facilities, 7) residual value, 8) operating costs, and 9) fixed costs.

Next, one particular value is selected at random for each of the nine factors. The rate of return on investment is then calculated for the combination. This process is repeated until all sets of these factors have been exhausted. The result gives the range of the rates of return and the probability of achieving them for the totality of sets of input factors. Figure 3–7b outlines the process.

ASSESSING ORGANIZATIONAL CAPABILITIES

Every business enterprise requires people with various skills and talents to work cooperatively toward accomplishing a common organizational objective. Even though the new product may be superior and the financial resources ample, it is nevertheless people who are the organization's source of vitality; it is people whose activities bring its success. An accurate evaluation of the total personnel requirements and especially of the required managerial talent is an indispensable part of a feasibility analysis of a new venture.[5] This analysis requires that three questions be answered:

1. What personnel skills and talents are available and what organization structure, if any, already exists?
2. What kind of organization and what talents will be needed initially for the effective implementation of the new venture?
3. What skills and talents will be required once the new venture starts to succeed and grow?

The answers to these questions tell whether it would be possible to bring into the new organization the talents required to meet initial and later personnel needs. Experience has shown that it is important to distinguish between questions 2 and 3. The successful launching of a new venture requires the initiative and drive of an entrepreneur. Unfortunately this person frequently does not have the skill, or the patience, for managing routine day-to-day affairs of a business that has grown past some critical size. The entrepreneur should therefore be prepared to seek qualified help to perform the managerial and administrative tasks of a rapidly growing concern.

---

[5]The management of managerial resources is covered in detail in Chapter 14.

Determining Personnel Requirements and Designing the Initial Organization Structure

The first step in determining personnel needs is analyzing the anticipated workload and the various necessary activities. In the second step, these activities are grouped into sets of tasks that individuals can handle effectively. In the third step, the various tasks are categorized to form the basis of the structure of the organization.

Every organization has a unique set of activities. The outline in Table 3–7 gives a guide for categorizing these activities of the firm.

Once the total range of required activities and levels of skill have been identified, the various activities are grouped into tasks to be performed in individual positions. Then the required degree of professional competence, educational background, and other qualifications are specified for each position.

The interrelationships of the various positions, in a hierarchical order, can now be determined from the position descriptions. Particular attention should be paid to such aspects of organizational design as reasonable spans of management control and the delineation of line and staff functions.[6]

Comparing Personnel Needs and Availability

A comparison of needed personnel with the qualified persons available to the new venture determines the staffing requirements. The essential question to be answered is: How difficult would it be to attract and hire persons with the needed talents under the prevailing conditions of the new organization? These conditions include its lack of a "track record" and its financial limitations. To answer this question one must evaluate the new venture's need to hire from the outside. This evaluation should also take into account that personnel requirements may change *when the new venture grows and reaches some degree of maturity*. It is therefore important to allow for organizational flexibility from the outset.

The entrepreneur faces some problems in staffing the new business. The capabilities of people already available to the new firm tend to be overestimated and the difficulty of attracting new people with the skills needed tends to be underestimated. Qualified people who have clearly demonstrated their competence are not easily persuaded to join a new organization with an uncertain future. The entrepreneur may not realize that employees often do not have the same intense commitment to the enterprise as the owner. They may not wish to put in the long hours and weekend work that is a normal part of the entrepreneur's life. More

---

[6]The formal organization structure is designed on the basis of these interrelationships.

TABLE 3–7. ACTIVITY ANALYSIS

Activities	Required Level of Skill		
	High	Medium	Low
Managerial and supervisory			
Planning and budgeting			
Control			
General accounting			
Cost accounting			
Marketing and distribution			
Purchasing			
Engineering and maintenance			
Production			
Quality control			
Finance			
Personnel			
Legal, insurance matters			
Administrative			
Technical/Engineering			
Clerical			
Operative			

people may be needed to do the work of the organization than the personnel planning shows. For these reasons the personnel requirements for the new business should be estimated and planned with as much care as its financial requirements.

ANALYSIS OF THE COMPETITION

Practically all business enterprises in a market economy face intelligent competition. A new enterprise cannot survive unless it offers and maintains competitive advantages such as a superior product, better service, shorter delivery time, or a relatively lower price. These kinds of advantages are the reasons why customers buy from a particular firm. Many new enterprises pay too little attention to exploring and developing a competitive edge. This lack is one of the most important reasons for the failure of new enterprises. The feasibility studies for a new venture should therefore include an analysis of competitive pressures and of the actions competitors might take against it. This analysis should be done separately from the market feasibility analysis, although the issues are obviously interrelated.

Every business generally has to contend with two major types of competitive pressures: 1) direct competition from products or services very similar to its own that appeal to approximately the same market, and 2) indirect competition from substitutes. It is important to recognize both types of competitive pressures and to judge how their impact on the new venture may change over time.

A pragmatic approach to the analysis of competitive pressures focuses on three tasks:

1. identifying major potential competitors
2. identifying the various strategies and tactics the competitors can employ and their potential impact on the operation of the planned venture
3. identifying the specific competitive advantages the planned venture offers and developing a strategy based on the consistent emphasis of these advantages.

The results of this analysis should then be summarized in a manner similar to that shown in Table 3–8.

This analysis will reveal whether a planned new venture offers sufficient competitive advantages in its product or service to withstand the pressures from direct and indirect competitors. Generally it is not enough for a new venture merely to neutralize the competitors' stategic advantages. In order to survive the inevitably difficult initial period, the new venture must have a clear superiority through at least two major competitive strategies. In addition, the feasibility study for a new venture must also consider any new measures that competitors may intro-

TABLE 3–8. ANALYSIS OF COMPETITION

	Competitive Strength Measured on a Scale of 5 (high) to 1 (low) for:				
	Patents	Technology	Location	Service	Price
New Venture					
Direct Competition					
Company A					
Company B					
Indirect Competition					
Company X					
Company Y					

duce to meet its challenge. It should seek to uncover the weaknesses of its competition and strive continuously to improve its competitive edge.

SUMMARY: Guidelines to Evaluating New Venture Opportunities

A crucial task in starting a new business enterprise is the systematic analysis and evaluation of its feasibility. Feasibility analyses tend to be demanding and complex because they must treat not only future developments that are frequently uncertain, but also all the variables that potentially affect the success or failure of the venture. This chapter presented the several analyses that, taken together, provide a basis for estimating the feasibility of a new venture opportunity. A comprehensive feasibility study should analyze five major areas: 1) the technical, or engineering, aspects of the planned venture, 2) the market opportunities, 3) the required financial resources and the anticipated financial returns, 4) the necessary personnel and organizational capabilities, and 5) the competitive situation.

The major steps in a technical feasibility analysis involve identifying the critical specifications, investigating the product quality-cost relationships, and conducting several stages of product testing. An assessment of market opportunities requires identifying the market potential and the way this potential can best be achieved. Market testing is an important source of information for establishing the overall feasibility of a new venture. The financial feasibility analysis should include a projection of the financial requirements, a determination of the potentially available financial resources and their cost, and an analysis of expected cash flow and returns. An assessment of personnel requirements and organizational capabilities and an investigation of the competitive advantages of the firm's product or service conclude the systematic evaluation of the new venture.

APPENDIX 1: How One Company Calculates Total Market Potential for New Products

The following is a highly simplified illustration of the calculations commonly performed by the marketing research department of one company in estimating the total market potential for proposed new products. The proceudre is applied in the case of new products to be incorporated in other products whose total current and projected output is determined—in the absence of reliable published data—by surveys of companies manufacturing them. The new item may be either: (a) one that is new to the company but is already being marketed by others, or (b) one that is new to the market—possibly replacing one or more existing products, or being proposed as an added element or ingredient for use in the buyer's product.

First, the company's marketing research unit carries out investigations to determine:

- The degree to which the proposed product is (or would be) incorporated in each of the end products of which it will be a part. The mathematical expression of this is called the weighted average usage factor. An attempt is made to calculate the current and the probable future rate of usage of the product per unit of each end product.
- Current and projected output of each end product incorporating the proposed product.

WEIGHTED AVERAGE USAGE FACTOR

A key element in the company's approach is the calculation of a weighted average usage factor—the average amount of proposed prod-

This article is reprinted from *Evaluating New-Product Proposals*, New York: The Conference Board, Report No. 604, © 1973, pp. 12, 13. Used by permission.

uct [K] incorporated by all producers in a unit of end product [X].[1] This calculation is carried out in two steps which are illustrated in Table 1.

Step 1. The first step consists of multiplying, for each producer of end product [X], its reported market share of product [X] by its average usage rate of [K]. The company forms an estimate of the market share held by each producer of end product [X] by asking, during interviews with these producers, the following kinds of questions: "Leaving yourself out, who's who in this industry anyway? What share do they have?" The company has found through experience that by the time all producers have been interviewed, a market share profile emerges. The market share estimates thus developed are shown in column (2) of Table 1.

The company obtains data showing the average usage of [K] per unit of output of product [X] from the producers of [X] during interviews or, in instances where interviewing is considered to be impractical or unnecessary, by mail survey. The usage estimates thus obtained from each producer are shown in columns (3), (4), and (5) of Table 1.

A hypothetical example of the calculation of the weighted average usage factor of [K] for end product [X] is shown in columns (6), (7), and (8). In this example, three years (1960, 1965, and 1970) are used for illustrative purposes. In actual practice, however, an attempt is made to gather historical data for a series of years so that trends may be computed.

Step 2. The second step is a summation. Thus, for all producers in the example (companies X_1 through X_5) a computed average of 1.21 pounds of [K] was used per 100 pounds of product [X] in 1960, and 1.55 pounds in 1965. It is estimated that usage will increase to 1.70 pounds by 1970.

TOTAL USAGE

In order to estimate total usage of proposed product [K], the computed usage factors (development of which is shown in Table 1) are applied to historical, current, and future estimates of total output of the end products in which [K] is used. Continuing with the example, Table 2 shows for the years 1960, 1965, and 1970:

- *Weighted average usage of* [K] *in three end products:* [X], [Y], *and* [Z] *(column 2).* The weighted average usage of [K] per 100 pounds of

---

[1]If product [K] were not yet on the market, then the investigation would seek to determine the usage of product(s) which would be replaced by or used in conjunction with the new product [K].

TABLE 1. COMPUTATION OF WEIGHTED AVERAGE USAGE FACTOR FOR PROPOSED PRODUCT [K] IN END PRODUCT [X]

Manufacturers of End Product [X]		Reported Use of [K] (lbs of [K] per 100 lbs. of [X])			Weighted Average Use [K] Σ (Market Share × Use)		
		Actual		Estimated			
(1)	(2)	(3)	(4)	(5)	(6)	(7)	(8)
	Reported				1960	1965	1970
Company	Market Share	1960	1965	1970	(2) × (3)	(2) × (4)	(2) × (5)
X_1	50%	1.0	1.5	1.5	0.50	0.75	0.75
X_2	30	1.5	2.0	2.5	0.45	0.60	0.75
$X_3 \ldots X_5$	20	1.3	1.0	1.0	0.26	0.20	0.20
Weighted average usage of [K] per 100 lbs. of end product [X]					1.21	1.55	1.70

product [X] is taken from Table 1; usage of [K] in products [Y] and [Z] would have been similarly computed in that previous step; however, the calculations are not shown.

- *Estimated total output of end products [X], [Y], and [Z] (column 3).* Data showing total historical and current output of the end product may sometimes be derived from published sources. However, in the absence of published data, it may be necessary for the company to estimate historical and current—as well as future—output of the end products in which [K] will be incorporated. Such estimates may be based on information elicited from the end-product producers themselves. Since estimates of future total end-product output are likely to vary from respondent to respondent, an average estimate is calculated. Thus, the 1,500,000 pounds of output of end product [X] projected for the year 1970 represents an average or "most likely" estimate, and is based on the individual estimates elicited from producers $X_1 \ldots X_5$. In some cases, it has been found feasible to express estimated future output in terms of a range of possibilities.
- *Estimated total usage of [K] in end products [X], [Y], and [Z], respectively (column 4).* In some cases, estimates of future total usage are expressed in terms of a range.

An example of the actual calculation is shown below. Thus, in 1960 a total of 1,000,000 pounds of [X] were produced, requiring an average input of 1.21 pounds of [K] for every 100 pounds produced. Total esti-

TABLE 2. CALCULATION OF TOTAL USAGE OF PROPOSED PRODUCT [K] IN END PRODUCTS [X], [Y], and [Z]

(1) Year	(2) Weighted Average Usage Factor [K] (lbs. of [K] per 100 lbs. of End Product)	(3) Estimated Total Production of End Product (lbs.)	(4) Usage of [K] (lbs.)
End Product [X]			
1960	1.21	1,000,000	12,100
1965	1.55	1,250,000	19,375
1970	1.70	1,500,000	25,500
End Product [Y]			
1960	2.13	3,000,000	63,900
1965	2.13	2,500,000	53,250
1970	2.63	2,250,000	59,175
End Product [Z]			
1960	3.25	5,000,000	162,500
1965	3.15	6,000,000	189,000
1970	3.00	6,500,000	195,000

mated usage of [K] in the output of product [X] for that year was therefore 12,100 pounds.

$$\frac{1,000,000}{100} \times 1.21 = 12,100 \text{ lbs. } [K]$$

The final calculation is a summation, illustrated in Table 3. Thus, the grand total market for [K] is estimated in this example to be 238,500 pounds in 1960, 261,625 pounds in 1965, and 279,675 pounds in 1970.

TABLE 3. COMPUTED TOTAL MARKET FOR [K] (POUNDS)

End Product	1960	1965	1970
[X]	12,100	19,375	25,500
[Y]	63,900	53,250	59,175
[Z]	162,500	189,000	195,000
Estimated total usage of [K]	238,500	261,625	279,675

APPENDIX 2. Telephone Survey Questionnaires

MANUFACTURERS' SURVEY

Hello. My name is _____. I am a student at UCLA's Graduate School of Management and I'm conducting a research project for one of my classes. I'd like to ask you a few questions about the manufactuirng of light fixtures.

1. Do you manufacture table lamps? Yes _____ [Go to (5).] No _____ [Go to (2).]

2. Have you made them within the past 3 years? Yes _____ No _____

3. Do you intend to start making them within the next year? Yes _____ No _____

4. Why aren't you interested in producing table lamps? _____

5. What other types of light fixtures do you make?
   chandelier_____   floor lamps_____   industrial_____
   swag lamps_____   specialty _____   other _____

6. About what percentage of your yearly output is in each of these types of light fixtures? [Fill in percentages in (5).]

7. Which style of lamp is your best seller? Second? Third?
   First _____   Second _____   Third _____

8. What is the price range for each of your three best sellers?
   1._____   2._____   3._____
        range/average price   range/average price   range/average price

9. What is the average price within each range?

10. Which style or styles aren't selling very well?
    _____   _____   _____

11. In your opinion, which styles will sell best one year from now?
    _____   _____   _____

12. How do you sell your _____ lamps? Do you use
    your own salesmen _____   factory direct to consumer_____
    manufacturers' representatives_____   wholesalers _____
    factory direct to retailer _____   other _____

13. (If they use manufacturers' representatives:) Which manufacturers' representatives do you use?
    _____   _____   _____

14. How do you promote your _____ lamp line?
    catalogs_____   point-of-sale displays_____
    sales calls _____   media advertising_____

15. Which techniques of product promotion do you believe is the most effective? _____

16. In your estimation, what percentage of retail sales for your product line is made in each of the following types of retail outlets?

department stores _____   mass merchandisers_____
light specialty stores _____   furniture stores_____
discount department stores_____   hardware stores _____
drug stores_____   other _____

17. What is your company's approximate annual sales?

under $1 million _____ $5 to 10 million _____ $15 to 25 million _____
$1 to 5 million _____ $10 to 15 million _____ $25 to 50 million _____
                                            over $50 million _____

RECORD

Name of respondent _____

Position _____

Company_____

Date _____

Time of day _____

Comments:

RETAILERS' SURVEY

1. Which style of _____ lamps is your best seller? Second? Third?
   1._____   2._____   3._____

2. What is the price range for each of your three best sellers?
   1._____   2._____   3._____
      range/average price   range/average price   range/average price

3. What is the average selling price within each range? [Record answer in (2).]

4. Which style or styles aren't selling very well?
   _____   _____   _____

5. In your opinion, which styles will be best sellers one year from now?
   _____   _____   _____

6. Do you buy your _____ lamps directly from the manufacturer or do you buy them through wholesalers?
   direct purchase_____   wholesalers _____   both _____

7. From what type of sources do you receive information about manufacturers' lamp product lines?
   catalogs_____   salesmen_____
   manufacturers' representatives____   other _____

8. Which of these methods do you prefer?_____

9. (If they use manufacturers' representatives:) Which manufacturers' representatives do you use?
   _____   _____   _____

10. What is your estimate of your annual sales volume in _____ lamps?

under $1,000 _____   10,000 to 15,000_____
1,000 to 5,000_____   15,000 to 25,000_____
5,000 to 10,000_____   25,000 to 50,000_____
over 50,000 _____

SUGGESTED READINGS

Allen, Louis L. *Starting and Succeeding in Your Own Small Business.* New York: Grosset & Dunlap, 1968.

Baty, Gordon B. *Entrepreneurship —Playing to Win.* Reston, Va.: Reston Publishing Co., 1974.

Foster, Douglas W. *Planning for Products and Markets.* London: Longman, 1972.

Hawkins, C. J., and Pearce, D. W. *Capital Investment Appraisal.* London: Macmillan, 1971.

Matthews, Tony, and Mayers, Colin. *Developing a Small Firm.* London: British Broadcasting Corporation, 1968.

MacDonald, Morgan B. *Appraising the Market for New Industrial Products.* New York: National Industrial Conference Board, 1967.

Pessemier, Edgar A. *New Product Decisions.* New York: McGraw-Hill, 1966.

Reutlinger, Shlomo. *Techniques for Project Appraisal under Uncertainty.* Baltimore: The Johns Hopkins Press, 1970.

Scrase, Robert R., ed. *New Products: Concepts, Development, and Strategy.* Ann Arbor: Bureau of Business Research, The University of Michigan, 1967.

Summers, George W. *Financing and Initial Operations of New Firms.* Englewood Cliffs, N.J.: Prentice-Hall, 1962.

Twiss, Brian. *Managing Technological Innovation.* London: Longman, 1974.

CHAPTER 4

Selected Legal Aspects of Starting a Business

This chapter presents some important legal considerations that should be weighed in forming a new business. The entrepreneur should make careful decisions in these matters, for proper choices in the beginning can save much trouble and expense later. The material presented here is not intended to make the reader a legal expert in these matters, nor is it designed to cover completely the legal issues involved in starting a new business. It should, however, give the novice businessperson sufficient background to discuss legal needs intelligently with an attorney. Some of the more important consequences of selecting a legal organizational form are discussed, as is the attorney's role in providing guidance, counsel, and advocacy in the process.

The entrepreneur starting a business must make a basic decision about what legal structure the firm is to take. This structure should not be confused with the organizational structure normally used to show management roles and relationships on organization charts.

STRUCTURAL ALTERNATIVES

The laws of each of our fifty states provide several alternative legal forms of organization. From these the executive may select that best suited to meet the needs of the new venture. Several of these forms are discussed below.

This chapter was prepared by Edward Poll, Attorney at Law, Beverly Hills.

Sole Proprietorship

The sole proprietorship is perhaps the oldest form of organization used in modern society. Until recently sole proprietorships out numbered all other organizational forms.

The sole proprietorship is a business engaged in and conducted by an individual who usually retains legal ownership of all business assets in his or her own name. Employees may be hired as in other forms of business. The individual, however, remains the sole owner of all the assets of the venture.

The sole proprietorship, of all the forms of business structure, requires the least amount of documentation both at its inception and throughout its existence. Many of the formalities and fees that would be necessary in partnerships and corporations are avoided and continue to be less of a burden throughout the venture's existence. A list of typical expense items for various organization structures is presented in Table 4–1 on pages 110 and 111.

A primary advantage of a sole proprietorship is the ease with which decisions can be made. Only the sole proprietor makes essential business decisions. Figure 4–1 shows a typical chart of this organizational form.

This same advantage is often seen as a disadvantage. Standing alone, the proprietor's entire fortune—all wordly assets regardless of where or how held—is subject to lien for satisfaction of creditors' claims. No distinction is drawn between the sole proprietor and the business for federal tax reporting. The sole proprietor is permitted to deduct business expenses as in other organizational forms, but there is no separate and

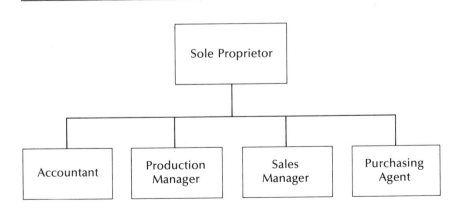

FIGURE 4–1. Typical Organization for the Small Company as a Sole Proprietorship

distinct income reporting unit. The sole proprietor files one federal tax return that incorporates both business and personal activities.

The sole proprietorship has become less common for a variety of reasons including the following: some states have, either by specific legislation or by interpretation of existing legislation, made provisions for the *closed corporation* discussed below; financing requirements tend to be greater than ever before, which requires expanded equity participation; and popularity has decreased because of greater awareness of legislation permitting the separation of personal affairs and assets from business affairs and liabilities.

Sole proprietorships obviously are suitable for many business ventures; the trend, however, is increasingly toward partnerships and corporations.

Partnership

The relationship known as partnership is a very personal one that requires the greatest care and respect, much as a marriage relationship does. Partnership has been defined by some as "an association of two or more persons to carry on a business, with a legal objective, for profit." The Uniform Partnership Act,[1] which has been adopted in part or in its entirety by most states, defines a partnership as "an association of two or more persons to carry on as co-owners a business for profit." Under old common law, only natural persons, that is, human beings, could be partners.

Some legal theoreticians still disagree about whether a partnership is a legal entity (an *artificial person* recognized by law as having rights, powers, and duties separate and distinct from those of the individual human beings composing such entity) or just an aggregate of persons acting in concert. Some states, and even the Internal Revenue Code, provide that a partnership is a separate and distinct entity for some purposes but not for others. The Uniform Partnership Act, a significant factor in making partnership laws of the various states similar, unfortunately did not resolve this disagreement. The distinction between *legal entity* and *aggregate* theories is important with respect to the ownership and conveyance of property, the continuity of the partnership upon the death of a partner or assignment of a partner's interest, the priority of creditors, the fiduciary duties of partners, and the joint and several liabilities of partners.

---

[1]The Uniform Partnership Act is a model partnership law developed for use on a national level by the National Conference of Commissioners on Uniform State Laws. Each state has specifically enacted legislation governing partnership activities. Many states have adopted the Uniform Partnership Act in its entirety; others have enacted variations of it.

A partnership relationship can be created only by contract, oral or written, between the parties. A person or legal entity must be capable of entering into contractual relationships to become a partner. Common law has been changed by many states. Some, for example, have recently given married women the power to enter into contracts, and therefore partnerships, without written consent of their husbands. Although the law has been changed, women are still confronted with special problems in dealing with creditors and lending institutions, who want the added security of their husbands' signatures.

The parties may seek to avoid drafting a written partnership agreement for various reasons. They may believe that problems incident to such an agreement are theoretical and time consuming. Therefore, to avoid "unnecessary expense," the parties may begin their business venture using the sketchiest of forms, perhaps purchased from a stationery store, or possibly even worse, self-created, as the basis for the partnership. Where no written agreement is entered into, the existence of a partnership may be shown by transactions, by conduct, or by declarations of the parties. Evidence considered critical to a determination of the existence of a partnership includes: an intention to be partners; co-ownership of, and a community of interest in, the business; and the sharing of profits and losses.

Full realization of the ramifications of the organizational form of a business, including the serious nature of each party's obligation to the venture, is essential to the continued viability of a new business. Expert advice should be sought rather than reliance on do-it-yourself forms. The agreements surrounding the organization of the new venture, particularly of a partnership agreement, provide the basis of the entire relationship between the parties until such time as they desire a change or until change is imposed by law.

Rights and Obligations of Partners The Uniform Partnership Act, or the applicable state law, determines the rights and obligations of the parties toward one another. These prescribed rights and obligations may be altered by agreement between the partners. Among the rights specifically given in the Uniform Partnership Act are the right of each partner to:

- share in the management and conduct of the business
- share equally in the profits of the firm
- receive repayment of contributions
- receive indemnification for payments made on behalf of the partnership
- receive interest on advances
- have access to the books and records of the partnership
- have formal accounting of partnership affairs

Among the obligations required of each partner are the obligations to:

- contribute toward losses sustained by the partnership
- work for the partnership without remuneration
- submit to majority vote when differences arise about the conduct of partnership affairs
- disclose to other partners any information pertaining to partnership affairs
- account to the partnership for all profits derived from any partnership transaction or from the use of partnership property

As may be seen from the above, major obligations of partners are the exercise of *good faith* and *integrity* in dealing with each other. The Uniform Partnership Act recognizes as a basic principle that each partner has a fiduciary obligation (founded in trust and confidence) to other partners.

Partners are required, as are members of a board of directors in a corporation, to make full disclosure of all material facts within their knowledge that in any way relate to partnership affairs. Further, partners must refrain from making false representations to other partners.

Although partners have stringent obligations controlling their conduct with respect to other partners, any partner dealing with unsuspecting ("innocent") third persons may bind the partnership and its property. In other words, within certain limits prescribed by the applicable state legislation, the Uniform Partnership Act, or the particular partnership agreement, each individual partner has the right and the power to sign contracts in the usual and ordinary course of business of the partnership. One partner may thereby impose obligations upon the remaining partners. Innocent third persons (good-faith purchasers) are protected by such legislation when dealing with partners who have apparent authority to bind the partnership.

Special rules and regulations may prevail about real property, the transfer of assets, or the conduct of business outside the usual course of affairs. In such cases signatures of all parties may be required.

Partners, as has been indicated, have the right to be reimbursed for fraudulent acts and to demand an accounting of any other partner's actions. Despite the apparent protection afforded by various legislative schemes, partners may find themselves unable to enforce their legal remedies against a partner who has defrauded them. For example, the defrauding partner may be judgment proof because of lack of assets with which to reimburse the partnership for misappropriated funds.

Persons admitted as partners into an existing partnership are generally held responsible for the obligations of the partnership arising even before their admission. It is as though they had been partners when such obligations were incurred. This rule is intended to eliminate or reduce the difficulties that arose under prior law when a new partner was admitted without liquidation of the previous debts of the partnership. For the protection of the new partners, an exception to this rule specifies that incoming partners' responsibility for pre-existing debts shall be limited only to the partnership property. In other words, new partners' personal assets are not liable for pre-existing debts of the old partnership. States still controlled by common law rules provide that an incoming partner is not liable for debts of the firm at the time of becoming a member of the firm, in the absence of an agreement to assume such liabilities. The theory that holds here is that the credit of the new partner never entered into the consideration of the creditors of the old partnership. As a consequence, those creditors should not receive additional security for payment of partnership debts at the expense of an innocent new partner.

Tax Implications Detailed treatment of the tax ramifications of a partnership is beyond the scope of this text. Nevertheless, it should be clear that the form of a business organization materially affects tax consequences. Following are some of the more important aspects of taxes associated with a partnership.

The federal income tax laws give partnerships a unique status. Partnerships are not taxable as such. The partnership files no tax return, but is required to file an information return (Form 1065), signed by one of the partners, reporting the items of gross income, deductions, and the names and distributive shares of its members. Partners are individually liable for their proportionate share of taxes resulting from partnership income.

The Internal Revenue Code of 1954 recognizes that a partnership is a separate income tax reporting unit (not income tax paying unit) that is required to compute its own income, distinct from that of the individual partners. Each partner in determining personal income tax liability, however, is required to take into account only the individual distributive share of various categories of partnership income, gain, loss, deduction, or credit.

A partner's interest in the totality of the partnership is considered a capital asset, which is separate and distinct from that partner's interest in specific assets. Unlike the assets of the partnership, which may include capital assets such as goodwill, fixtures, and equipment *and* non-capital assets such as raw material, finished goods inventory, and advertising brochures, a partnership interest is always considered a capital *asset.* The concept of the partnership interest as a capital asset is essential in determining the amount and character of a partner's gain or loss upon retirement, termination of the partnership, or upon the sale or other disposition of the partnership interest.

The 1954 Internal Revenue Code further specifically allows an individual partner, in computing personal net income, to deduct the individual share of the ordinary loss (excess of deductions over gross income of the partnership). This provision is particularly important in real estate partnerships. Depreciation is permitted as a deduction against gross income, oftentimes resulting in *paper losses* or net losses deductible by individual partners for tax purposes.

Unless the partnership agreement provides otherwise, gain and loss must be allocated among partners in accordance with their profit and loss ratios. In cases where some partners contribute capital and others contribute only services, partners frequently agree that losses shall be borne by those who contribute capital and not by others. In other cases the partners who contribute services usually bear losses only to the extent of their share of accumulated earnings. Even when the entire partnership loss is charged to one partner's account, a court has held that that partner is entitled to a deduction for the full loss. The other partner, who is not to bear any portion of such loss, is not entitled to a deduction. Tax consequences will generally follow the partnership agreement. Partners can by agreement alter and amend their initial partnership arrangement.

Under prior law, partners could defer inclusion of partnership income by the use of a partnership taxable year that differed from the taxable years of the partners. For example, if the taxable year of the partnership ended on January 31, and the partners were on a calendar year basis, the reporting of eleven months of partnership income would be postponed for a full taxable year. To restrict the postponement of the reporting of income, the Internal Revenue Code currently requires new partnerships to adopt a taxable year that coincides with the taxable year for the principal partners. This is usually the calendar year, unless the Commissioner of Internal Revenue is satisfied that a business purpose exists for the adoption of a different taxable year. The law further restricts members of partnerships from changing their taxable years to reduce the opportunity of shifting tax burdens between the partnership (entity theory) and its partners (aggregate theory).

Termination and Dissolution The termination of a partnership is significant for tax purposes for three reasons:

1. Termination closes the taxable year of the partnership; if the partner and partnership are on different taxable years, the partners may experience a bunching of partnership income.
2. Termination may prevent continued use of a favorable fiscal year arrangement for partnership activity; if the business activities are carried on by another partnership, the successor partnership will be regarded as a new partnership and required to obtain the consent of the Commissioner of Internal Revenue for the adoption of a taxable year different from that of the principal partners.

3. Termination of a partnership results in partnership properties being deemed to be distributed to partners.

Section 708 (b) of the 1954 Internal Revenue Code provides that a partnership shall be considered terminated in two cases: 1) where there is a cessation of partnership business activities; and 2) where there is a sale or exchange of an interest of 50 percent or more in capital and profits of the partnership within a twelve-month period. Provisions relating to partnership mergers and divisions may also affect the parties and therefore should be reviewed carefully.

Termination, for purposes other than taxation, is defined somewhat differently. For example, The Uniform Partnership Act defines termination in conjunction with dissolution. *Dissolution* refers to the change in the partnership relationship caused by any one partner's ceasing to be associated in the business. Dissolution is not, in and of itself, a termination of the partnership or a termination of the rights and powers of the various partners. Many of these rights and powers continue during the winding up process that follows dissolution. *Termination* is the culmination of the winding up process. In other words, termination occurs when all of the partnership affairs are concluded as the result of the liquidation and after expression of intent to cease carrying on the partnership business (dissolution). This definition contrasts with the definition of termination used by the Internal Revenue Code.

The following conditions may cause dissolution of partnership:

- expiration of a term certain (a specified period of time) or undertaking specified in the partnership agreement
- express will of any partner when no definite term of particular undertaking is otherwise specified
- express will of all partners, either before or after the expiration or conclusion of a term certain or undertaking specified
- expulsion of a partner in accordance with the provisions of the partnership agreement
- withdrawal, retirement, or death of a partner (except where a partnership agreement provides for the continuation of the partnership despite withdrawal, retirement, or death of a partner)
- sale or transfer of substantially all of the assets of a partnership
- bankruptcy of any partner or of the partnership

Unlike the corporation, the partnership is a very personal relationship. Regardless of the cause, when a change of partners occurs, the partnership will be dissolved in the eyes of the law except as may be otherwise provided by agreement.

Dissolution of a partnership does not release the partners from either the obligation to creditors or the obligation to act equitably toward one another. These duties remain until the affairs of the partnership are wound up and the partnership terminated. Further, dissolution operates only with respect to future transactions; as to everything past, the partnership and its partners (including the estate of a deceased partner) continue in their same relation and retain their same obligations until all pre-existing matters are concluded. The winding up or liquidation of partnership affairs includes the performance of existing contracts, collection of debts or claims due the firm, and payment of debts owed by the firm.

Dissolution of a partnership ends the general agency of partners growing out of their partnership relationship. Partners' implied power to act for the partnership in all matters, exclusive of liquidation matters, ceases. Even though former partners may presume to act for, and do act and contract for, the partnership as though there were no dissolution, no partnership liability attaches to other members of the former partnership so long as statutory procedures for dissolution are followed. This area is of concern to potential creditors.

The agreement between partners should provide for the amount and method of payment of a partner's interest upon disability, withdrawal, retirement, or death. Failure to so provide may well cause bitter controversy when dissolution occurs.

Limited Partnership The limited partnership is a particular form that can be set up to give the limited partners special tax advantages and shield them from liability. Although it is not often used for ordinary business enterprises, the limited partnership finds frequent use in real estate developments and some kinds of international ventures.

Establishing a limited partnership is essentially the same as setting up a standard form of general partnership. In some states a special notice must be filed with an authorized clerk or recorder in the county or district where the limited partnership has its principal office.

The limited partnership is composed of one or more general partners and one or more limited partners. The general partners manage the operation; the limited partners are investors only. The limited partners have limited liability. They may lose only the amount of their investment and their percentage of the assets of the firm. General partners, who manage the firm, have unlimited liability as in any ordinary partnership.

Limited partners may have no say in managing the affairs of the firm. If they violate this proscription, they automatically dissolve the limited status of the partnership and it reverts, in the eyes of the law, to a normal partnership in which the partners have unlimited liability for the debts of the firm.

If the assets of the limited partnership are sold, the limited partners usually have a controlling voice in approving the sale. The same is true in the transfer of the firm's assets.

The life of the limited partnership is stipulated in the original agreement and certificate filed with the appropriate public authority. A limited partner's interest may usually be transferred; sometimes the consent of the general partner is required for transfer. A general partner's interest is often not transferable without the unanimous consent of all other partners; sometimes this procedure is modified by some other condition agreed upon at formation of the limited partnership.

As with a general partnership, a limited partnership is not a taxable entity. The net income (or losses) are reportable on a partnership return but taxed at the individual partner's level. The tax treatment of limited partnerships has been a primary reason for adopting this form of organization. Without risking unlimited exposure, the limited partners are able to receive the tax benefits of noncash losses. This advantage can be particularly beneficial in real estate ventures where depreciation on a large project is a substantial "expense" item and is deductible by individual limited partners. If this entity were a corporation, the same benefits would not be passed along to the shareholders. The limited partner, usually in a high income bracket, receives the tax advantages of an individual but suffers none of the consequences of personal liability if the project fails.

Corporations

Although sole proprietorships and partnerships continue to play a vital role in the economic viability of the United States, new business executives in ever greater numbers choose the corporate form for their business. Despite conflicting considerations that must be weighed before the decision to incorporate is made, entrepreneurs in many cases today find the corporate form best suited to their needs, for both tax and nontax reasons.

A corporation is *an artificial being, an invisible entity,* whose creation is authorized by the legislature of each of the fifty states. Only those powers specifically enumerated by legislation are granted to a corporation.

Every corporation must adhere strictly to the legislative requirements of its state of incorporation. Because there are so many variances in requirements among the fifty states, both substantive and procedural, the following discussion relates to characteristics of corporations in general.

Limited Liability The single most important nontax factor prompting incorporation is the concept of *limited liability*. The liability of shareholders to creditors of the corporation is ordinarily limited to the amount of each shareholder's capital stock investment. Sole proprietors expose their entire net worth to their creditors for satisfaction of business debts. Partners have similar exposure; partners' liability is joint and several, which may place added strain on the partnership relationship. However, investors (shareholders) in a corporation successfully avoid this exposure; their liability to corporate creditors is limited to their investment in the corporation.

The value of the corporate *shield* in limiting the liability of owner-shareholders is less important in some circumstances than in others. For example, in many small businesses, owner-shareholders often have already committed most of their worldly goods to the business and have no additional net worth to protect. Also, lenders and suppliers to the small corporation may require the personal guarantee of the shareholders. Guarantees, however, are generally required only by principal lenders or suppliers. They believe the added exposure will increase the owner-shareholder's commitment to the venture and thereby the likelihood that the loan or extension of credit will be repaid. The personal guarantee provides additional security. Smaller and less sophisticated creditors do not normally need, nor would the entrepreneur grant, this additional protection.

Insurance of various kinds may further reduce the importance of the concept of limited liability. However, many businesses face major risks that are uninsurable, such as performance under the terms and conditions of specific contracts. In such cases the limited liability of corporate shareholders is particularly attractive.

Disgruntled creditors seeking enforcement of corporate obligations frequently try to use the so-called *alter ego* (other self) doctrine. This doctrine may be summarized as follows: the obligations of a corporation may be imputed to the owner-shareholder, which can occur where it appears that the corporation is influenced and governed by the shareholder to too great an extent. Interest and ownership are so closely tied together that the individuality or separateness of the person and of the corporation no longer exists. The fiction of a separate existence of the corporation would sanction a fraud or promote an injustice under these particular circumstances. The concept of the law is to prevent the use of the corporation, a state-sanctioned entity, to defraud innocent, good-faith creditors.

Application of this doctrine unfortunately cannot be reduced to a simple formula. In applying the theory of alter ego, what must be established is the unity of interest and ownership. This unity may be established by showing the commingling of personal and corporate funds, payment of personal expenses from corporate funds, disregard of the corporation as a separate entity in transactions and bookkeeping, failure to apply for a permit to issue stock, inadequate capitalization, and non-conformity to corporation laws in the holding of stockholders' and directors' meetings. This kind of evidence would influence any court's final determination. Each jurisdiction sanctioning the use of the alter ego doctrine emphasizes various factors that may not be relevant in other jurisdictions. The laws of the state of incorporation govern in each case.

Tax Implications The basic form of federal income tax for corporations is as follows: a regular tax of 22 percent is applicable to the entire annual corporate taxable income, plus a surtax of 26 percent on income in excess of $25,000. The $25,000 surtax exemption must be divided among several corporations if they are affiliated, that is, entitled to file a consolidated federal income tax return.

The capital structure of a large publicly held corporation is in most instances dictated by the necessity for public financing. In the case of a closely held corporation, on the other hand, the capital structure may be relatively unimportant from a nontax point of view. Therefore there may be considerable freedom to adopt a capitalization structure offering the greatest benefits.

For example, there are substantial tax benefits available from the simple device of having shareholders contribute a portion of the corporation's necessary capital in return for promissory notes or other evidence of indebtedness rather than stock. Interest paid on bona fide debt is deductible by the corporation; the repayment of a loan does not result in taxable income to the shareholder who has lent money to the corporation. A payment by the corporation as dividend income is not deductible by the corporation. Also a payment in return for shares will frequently be regarded as equivalent to a dividend. Dividends are taxable to the shareholder without being deductible by the corporation. Interest payments, as has been stated, are deductible by the corporation. Hence, tax planning is important in managing corporate finances.

For these reasons debt financing by shareholders should be given full consideration in every corporation that is to be closely held; the tax benefits available should be carefully weighed against whatever tax and nontax disadvantages may be involved. The disadvantages of fixed maturity, fixed interest-bearing obligations in a newly organized corporation, the corporation's need for credit from third persons and the effect on credit of debt owed to shareholders, and the need to retain earnings for growth will depend upon individual circumstances.

If it is decided to use some debt financing, the questions of *how much?* and *what kind?* arise. The wrong answers to these questions can spell complete loss of expected tax benefits. What is even worse, these may be replaced by liabilities for back taxes and interest.

A court may decide that the "debt" was in fact equity and that the payment of "interest" or "principal" was really the payment of dividends under one or any combination of the following conditions:

- if the amount of debt is unreasonably high compared to equity
- if there is no intention that the debt be paid when due
- if the debt is subordinated to other corporate obligations
- if the obligation to pay interest or principal is conditional upon profits

There is no exact line between what is debt and what is equity. If the debt is represented by a negotiable promissory note in the usual form, bears interest at a reasonable rate, has a fixed maturity date not more than twenty years from the date of issue, and can probably be paid when due, very little risk will be incurred. However, if by subsequent action the parties act as if there were no true debt, the courts will probably find that no debt exists.

A new corporation may elect to be taxed by calendar year or fiscal year. The corporation may adopt any taxable year without obtaining prior approval of the Internal Revenue Service; approval is required for any subsequent change. It is advisable to decide on a specific twelve-month accounting period at the outset and to report the same accounting period consistently on all forms filed by the corporation. The tax year is another device that may be used effectively in planning for taxation of the corporation and its shareholders.

Transferability of Ownership Interest Another element leading entrepreneurs to incorporate is the ease of transferability. The corporate form permits the ready transfer of ownership, wholly or in part, to other persons. Despite the need for approval from one or more state agencies, shares of corporate stock are generally far more easily transferred than are partnership interests. Formalities of transfer must be carefully observed.

However, many persons entering into a small or closely held corporation desire to restrict the transferability of shares. The obvious purpose of this restriction is to limit the admission of outsiders to the circle of shareholders. Restrictions on the transferability of stock may be provided in the charter or articles of incorporation, in the bylaws, or in a separate agreement among the shareholders. An agreement among shareholders providing for a right of first refusal or option to purchase is usually the most practical method of restricting stock transfers.

Board of Directors The management of a corporation, unlike proprietorships and partnerships, is vested legally in a board of directors. (See Figure 4–2 for a typical organization chart depicting the hierarchy of authority.) Each member of the board has a fiduciary duty to the corporation and its shareholders. Being fiduciaries, directors must act with the utmost good faith and are held accountable for any breaches of trust in their corporate dealings. A director may not use his position to secure for himself an advantage not common to all shareholders. Any private profit gained because of a director's official position must be turned over to the corporation.

The rigid common law rule prohibiting all dealings between a director and the corporation is no longer applicable. Today, a director may transact business with the corporation on many different levels. The general rule of law declares that a contract or other transaction between a corpo-

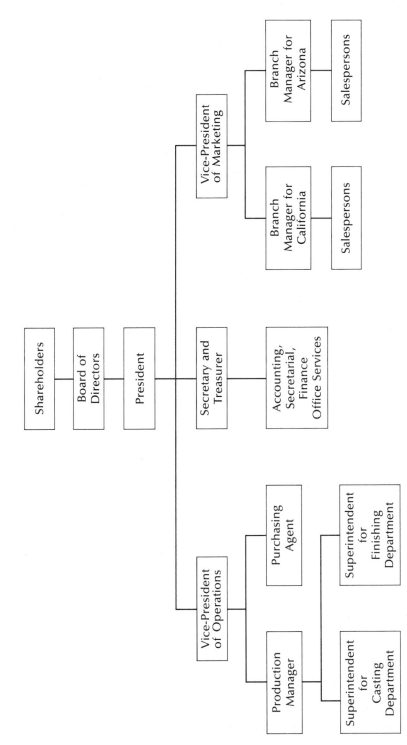

FIGURE 4–2. Typical Organization Chart for a Corporation

ration and its director is neither void nor voidable merely because the director has a financial interest in the transaction or because the director took part in consummating the transaction. However, directors must disclose their interest to the board of directors and the board must vote in favor of the transaction in good faith without counting the vote of the interested director. Despite approval of the board of directors, the contract or transaction must be just and reasonable at the time the contract or transaction is approved.

Some jurisdictions employ the corporate opportunity doctrine, which prevents a director or corporate officer from seizing opportunities in the company's line of business to the detriment of the corporation. In other words, directors and officers may be required to bring opportunities to the corporation before taking advantage of them for their personal gain. If directors violate their fiduciary duty in this respect, the corporation may claim for itself all benefits obtained by those directors or officers.

One very important consideration, too often given very little attention by incorporators, is the composition of the board of directors. A small, closely held corporation usually has on its board the principal shareholder, wife, or husband, or other relative, and perhaps one or two other persons. This membership may represent the best board available; nevertheless, such a board is too often assembled without thought. In selecting personnel for a board of directors several types of boards should be considered.

A *working* board, contrasted with a *titular* board, can be a significant source of advice for a new venture. Working directors may take on important responsibilities for the new corporation to the benefit of all concerned. At the very least they are always available for consultation. On the other hand, the venture may be such that a particular contact would be helpful to advance the interests of the corporation. The mere presence on the board of a prominent business executive, even if in name only, would help to make such contact.

Titular directors were more common in earlier times. Recent court decisions have imposed severe penalties on directors for losses legally attributable to their failure to perform diligently their functions as directors. Typical instances have been reliance on financial information prepared by management without independent analysis and failure to exercise independent business judgment. These incidents have made many business executives reluctant to join boards of directors in name only.

Boards may also be classified as *inside* or *outside*, depending upon whether the majority of directors are selected from within the ranks of the enterprise or from persons outside the company. Outside directors can use independent judgment to chart a course of action for the company. They are not concerned about losing their positions if they should disagree with the chief executive officer. Whatever the kind of board, only competent people should be elected to serve as directors.

Tax Treatment Corporations, like individuals, are treated as separate entities for federal income tax purposes. That is in contrast to partnerships, which are tax-reporting but not tax-paying entities. The doctrine of corporate entity has been repeatedly recognized by the courts and sanctioned by the Sixteenth Amendment. The separateness of the corporate entity will not be disregarded merely because there is only one shareholder. Further, the corporate entity will remain unaffected in spite of changes in stock ownership, corporate name, principal place of business, or type of business.

Only in extreme cases will the Internal Revenue Service seek to disregard the corporate entity and hold individual shareholders responsible for its income tax liability. Tax courts may "pierce the corporate fiction" in cases where the entity was in fact unreal or invalidly formed, where the alleged corporate action was a sham, or where a challenged transaction did not appreciably affect the taxpayer's beneficial interest except to reduce tax liability. Where there is a legitimate business purpose— where there is no fraud or sham—the corporate entity will be honored. Seldom has the evasion or avoidance of taxation been considered a business. A taxpayer has the right to decrease taxes or to avoid them by methods permitted by law. However, where avoidance or evasion of taxes has been the primary intention of the transaction, the means and forms used for its accomplishment are subject to very careful scrutiny.

The Special Case of Subchapter S Corporations Disregarding the corporate entity at the request of the Internal Revenue Service is the exception rather than the rule. Much more common is the setting aside of the corporate entity at the request of the shareholders of a corporation under rules and regulations commonly known as *Subchapter S* of the Internal Revenue Code of 1954. The effect is to have corporate income (and losses) bypass the corporation and be taxed to (or deducted by) the individual shareholders on a pro rata basis.

To qualify for the Subchapter S status, a business must qualify as a small business corporation. The requirements are: there must be only one class of stock; there must be no more than ten shareholders; each shareholder must be either a natural person or an estate (but not a corporation or a partnership). In addition, a Subchapter S corporation cannot be a member of an affiliated group of corporations.

The election of Subchapter S status must be made by a qualified corporation in the last month of the preceding taxable year or in the first month of the then current taxable year. Failure to file an election within the prescribed time period will result in a loss of the election for the current year. A new election will have to be filed at the proper time for the election to be effective in a future year.

The election must be consented to by all shareholders to be effective. An election is valid and continues to be effective unless voluntarily terminated. Termination of Subchapter S status may come about by transfer of stock to a new shareholder who fails to consent to the election, or by the corporation's ceasing to qualify as a small business corporation. The only penalty for terminating the election is the inability to renew the election within five years.

A Subchapter S corporation provides all the advantages of incorporation without the disadvantage of double taxation. The profits from the business are taxed only once and only at the personal tax rate of the individual shareholders.

Expenses of Incorporation An important factor in an entrepreneur's decision about adopting the corporate form is the cost of incorporation. A comparison of costs for various forms of organization is shown in Table 4–1.

The sole proprietorship requires the least legal involvement and is therefore the least expensive. A partnership implies a change from a state of being separate to a state of involvement with one or more other persons. To protect each party fully and to state accurately the understanding between the prospective partners, a partnership agreement should be drawn; legal fees will be incurred to obtain a properly drawn agreement.

Of all the forms of structural organization, incorporation may be the least expensive in the long run. Initially, however, incorporating may require the greatest expenditure. The primary expenses are:

- those payable at the time the charter or articles of incorporation are filed with the appropriate state government agency, which may include prepayment of state franchise tax or minimum state income tax
- attorney's fees
- miscellaneous charges and costs such as stock certificates, corporate seal, and minute book

These expenses can be amortized against corporate income over a period of time, usually not less than five years.

Corporate Jurisdiction A small, closely held corporation seldom gains anything by incorporating in a state other than that in which its principal operations are to be located, particularly if it is an intrastate business. Most states require the qualification of "foreign corporations" (corporations incorporated in other states) and payment of corporate income tax. Consequently, a corporation doing business in more than one state usually must comply with the formal requirements of more than one jurisdiction. Only when corporations are relatively large and owned by more than a few shareholders do considerations of incorporation in a state other than that of the principal place of operations become important.

Licenses and Permits Either immediately before or upon incorporation several specific acts must be performed. These include compliance with state and local requirements for buisness licenses. If the corporation anticipates engaging in the business of selling tangible personal property, local sales and use tax regulations must be consulted. Any required permits should be obtained before starting business.

A federal employer identification number must be obtained for use on federal tax returns, statements, and other documents. Application for the identification number may be gotten from the Internal Revenue Service or Social Security Administration. A corporation that is an employer ordinarily will have to withhold income tax and social security (FICA) tax from taxable wages paid to its employees. The employer must also pay a social security tax equal to the social security tax withheld from the employee's wages. Withheld income tax and social security taxes are generally deposited at an authorized commercial bank depository or a federal reserve bank, accompanied by Federal Tax Deposit Form 501. The deposits are made semimonthly, monthly, or quarterly, depending upon the amount of the tax; an Employer's Quarterly Federal Tax Return (IRS Form 941) must be filed on or before the end of the month following each calendar quarter. It should be observed that the officers or other persons charged by the corporation with the responsibility of withholding employee taxes may be personally liable for 100 percent penalty for failure to collect those taxes. Sanctions against such officers or persons responsible for collecting taxes are aggressively enforced.

A corporation, as employer, may be subject to the Federal Unemployment Tax. If this is the case, taxes are deposited with the Federal Tax Deposit Form 508 in a fashion similar to withholding taxes. An Unemployment Tax Return (IRS Form 940) must be filed and any balance due paid on or before January 31 of each year.

Workers' compensation laws, different in each state, should be consulted where appropriate. Generally the employer must either be insured against workers' compensation liability by an authorized insurer or obtain consent from the appropriate government agency to self-insure.

Other Forms of Organization

There are other forms of organization beside the three previously presented. They include joint ventures, real estate investment trusts, condominiums, and nonprofit corporations. These are, however, variations on a theme, mere adaptations of the three primary organizational structures presented here. These variations are used in special situations; legal advice should be sought before entering into a transaction using any of them.

TABLE 4–1. COMPARISON OF EXPENSES FOR VARIOUS LEGAL ORGANIZATIONAL STRUCTURES (STATE OF CALIFORNIA)

Expense	Sole Proprietorship	General Partnership	Limited Partnership	Corporation
Licenses and permits	Varies with local government imposing fees	Varies with local government imposing fees	Varies with local government imposing fees	Varies with local government imposing fees
Fictitious Business Name Statement	$10 for each fictitious name	$10 for each fictitious name	$10 for each fictitious name	$10 for each fictitious name
Attorney's fees	Varies with amount of work done; ordinarily less than for other organizational structures	Varies depending primarily on complexity of partnership agreement	Varies depending on complexity of partnership agreement and certificate and qualification of securities, if required	(see below)
Certificate of Limited Partnership recording fee	—	—	$2 plus $0.80 for each page after first page	
Articles of Incorporation filing fee	—	—	—	Graduated according to total value of shares; minimum of $33
Recording fee	—	—	—	$2
Copy fee to Secretary of State	—	—	—	$3 per copy, if required
Certification	—	—	—	$2 plus $0.80 per page, if Secretary of State prepares copies

TABLE 4–1. (continued)

Expense	Sole Proprietorship	General Partnership	Limited Partnership	Corporation
Recording fee to county clerk, county of principal place of business	—	—	—	$2 plus $0.80 per page after first page
Prepayment of minimum franchise (income) tax	—	—	—	$200
Attorney's fees for preparation of articles of incorporation, minutes of first meetings, and other initial documents	—	—	—	Varies, depending on complexity of corporate structure and work required for tax, securities, and other regulatory problems (range of $400–$1,000)
Qualification of securities, if not exempt	—	—	—	Fees of Department of Corporations vary depending on type of qualification and value of securities to be issued
Purchase of minute book, seal, and form stock certificates	—	—	—	Ordinarily under $50

PROTECTION OF IDEAS AND CONCEPTS

The entrepreneur who has originated a new and useful concept for a product or process should take precautionary steps to protect ownership of it. Ideas may be protected with patents, trademarks, service marks, and copyrights, as explained below.

Patents

Patents may be obtained on any "new, useful, and unobvious process (primarily industrial or technical); machine; manufacture; or composition of matter (generally chemical compounds, formulas, and the like); or any new, useful, and unobvious improvement thereof."[2] Patents may also be secured on any distinct and new variety of plant, other than tuber-propagated, that is asexually reproduced; and on any new and unobvious original and ornamental design for an article of manufacture.

It should be noted that ideas in themselves are not patentable; nor are methods of doing business, an inoperable device, or an improvement in a device that is obvious or the result of the application of mere mechanical skill.[3]

Patents are issued by the Commissioner of Patents, U.S. Department of Commerce. A patent gives the inventor the exclusive right to make, use, or sell the patent for a period of seventeen years in the United States, its territories and possessions. Design patents for ornamental devices are granted for three and one-half, seven, or fourteen years, as the applicant elects.[4]

Disclosure Document Program A desirable service offered the inventor by the U.S. Patent Office is the Disclosure Document Program. The inventor or the inventor's attorney or agent prepares and submits to the Commissioner of Patents a document intended to establish the priority of the invention. The Patent Office retains the document in its files for two years, then destroys it unless it is referred to in a separate letter in a related patent application filed within the two-year period.

The two-year period is not a period of grace during which the inventor can wait to file application for patent without possible loss of benefits. The inventor must usually establish diligence in completing the inven-

---

[2]*Know Your Patent Procedures*, Management Aids for Small Manufacturers, No. 49, Small Business Administration, 1969, pp. 1–2.

[3]A useful outline of patenting procedure is given in "Know Your Patenting Procedures," *Management Aids for Small Manufacturers*, No. 49, April 1973, available from the Small Business Administration.

[4]A booklet entitled *General Information Concerning Patents* may be had for the asking from the Patent Office, Washington, D.C. 20231.

tion or in filing application for patent after sending in the Disclosure Document.

The Disclosure Document is not a patent application, as has been indicated. It does not lessen the value of the conventional witnessed and notarized records as evidence of conception of an invention. The document is intended to furnish a more credible form of evidence of origination than that given by the widespread practice of sending a disclosure to oneself or another by registered mail.

The Disclosure Document should be clear, with a complete enough explanation of the manner and process of making and using the invention so a person with reasonable knowledge in the field could make and use it. The enterpriser would be wise to employ a qualified patent attorney or patent agent to help in the preparation and submission of the Disclosure Document. As in other matters relating to legal protection, the entrepreneur should choose an expert to handle unfamiliar complex procedures.

Trademarks and Service Marks

A trademark is a distinguishing name or symbol identifying a product used in commerce subject to regulation by Congress. An example of a description of a trademark is "design of a flying red horse." It can be protected against use by others for a period of twenty years by registration and may be renewed for an additional twenty years. Registration is a service provided by the Commissioner of Patents, U.S. Patent Office.

Most states also offer trademark registration and, in addition, service mark registration. The State of California Division of Business and Industry Development clarifies the descriptions of trademark and service marks as follows:

Trademark

A trademark is a word; a name, a symbol; a device; or a combination of these elements. ("Device" means generally a "design" or an "artistic figure.")

A trademark is used to identify an applicant's merchandise and to enable customers to recognize applicant's products and to distinguish them from the products of others.

A trademark should not be described ordinarily as a label. The word "label" is not included in the definition of a trademark. The trademark most usually consists of part of the matter printed on a label.

Not everything printed on a label or on a container is part of the trademark. Statements of ingredients, the name and address of a business, cautions, instructions for use: these are not part of the trademark. A trademark is the customer's recognition factor. It is intended to be something that will catch the customer's attention and enable him to buy again a product he previously bought and liked.

Service Mark

The description must be brief but accurate. Most service marks are very simple. For example, the words "The Fog Cutters" is a service mark identifying restaurant services.

A service mark is a word or words, or a design or designs, or combinations of a word or words and design or designs. A service mark is used to advertise services. The function of the service mark is to distinguish one person's services from the services of others. Prospective customers are made familiar with the service mark by the advertising thereof. If the services are excellent, the customer in theory will deal with the person using the service mark when he again needs the particular service.

The following are examples of services: banking services; real estate broker's services; motel services; entertainment services by a musical group.[5]

The enterpriser should take advantage of the commercial benefits of a distinctive trademark or service mark. These symbols help customers to identify products or services they have used and like. Recognition of the symbol stimulates repeat business.

Copyrights

The Copyright Office attached to the Library of Congress, Washington, D.C., offers protection to authors, composers, and artists from the pirating of their *literary* or *artistic* work. Copyrights, as with patents, trademarks, and service marks, provide a legal monopoly for the holder. The copyright protects a work from its creation for the life of the author plus 50 years.

The small business owner may wish to copyright published material pertinent to the business, including catalogs, catalog sheets, brochures, and instructions on how to use the product. To gain protection, the originating individual or company must first make a claim by imprinting a notice in the front of the piece. A standard form is the following: © Copyright, followed by the year of publication, and the name of the originating individual or company. (See also the copyright page of this book.) Application for copyright is made to the Copyright Office, Library of Congress after publication.

---

[5]*A Guide For Establishing a Business*, Division of Business & Industry Development, Sacramento: California State Department of Commerce, Figure 5, p. 8; Figure 7, p. 11, publication undated.

Marketable but Unpatentable Ideas

Occasionally entrepreneurs may develop an idea for an unpatentable product that could be profitable but is outside the scope of their own business. They may wish to make a deal with a firm capable of exploiting the idea. They face the problem of disclosing the idea to a suitable organization without losing the opportunity for financial gain. This course is hard to pursue successfully because most firms are chary of inventors or "idea" persons. In the rare instance it may be possible to come to a satisfactory arrangement—provided a binding contractual arrangement can be agreed upon.

As background, it should be understood that ideas become public property as soon as divulged. Disclosure should not be made, therefore, before agreement has been reached, as evidenced by a contract signed by both parties.

The Small Business Administration suggests the use of a letter, which when signed by both parties, becomes a contract. It should be prepared in duplicate so each party can have a copy. A typical letter is shown in Figure 4–3.

This contract binds the company to hold in confidence any features not already known to it. It may not make use of the idea without compensating the originator as mutually agreed upon. The company is also protected against any unwarranted claims.

A Concluding Note

The entrepreneur should be cautioned that in protecting the creative idea, whether through patent, trademark, service mark, copyright, or in the disclosure of a unique idea to another firm, it is wise to employ professional counsel. The best time to use legal counsel is in the beginning, to avoid entanglements. It is usually far less expensive—and far less traumatic—to avoid complication by proper procedure than to resolve a legal problem by lawsuit.

ATTORNEYS

Whether or not to seek the advice of an attorney is an important and sometimes difficult decision. Once the decision to use an attorney has been made, however, the entrepreneur must find a capable lawyer.

Each locality has a bar association that usually maintains a referral list of attorneys. The list is customarily divided into categories such as general practice, family relations, business and patents. Individuals may select an attorney from these lists. It may be advisable to talk with two or three before selecting one. Lawyers usually will not charge for the first exploratory visit, or if they do, will require only a nominal fee.

John Doe Company
123 Fourth Street
Anytown, U.S.A.

Gentlemen:

I have developed a new idea for the packaging of your product which I believe would greatly increase your sales and profits. The new method of packaging would not raise production costs.

If you are interested in details of the idea, I shall be glad to forward you complete information if you will kindly sign the enclosed agreement form. Promptly upon receipt of the signed form, I shall forward to you all information I have regarding the idea.

Sincerely, Robert Roe

AGREEMENT TO REVIEW IDEA

We, the undersigned, agree to receive in confidence full details about an idea for product packaging to be submitted for our consideration by Robert Roe.

It is further understood that we assume no responsibility whatever with respect to features which can be demonstrated to be already known to us. We also agree not to divulge any details of the idea submitted without permission of Robert Roe or to make use of any feature or information of which the said Robert Roe is the originator, without payment of compensation to be fixed by negotiation with the said Robert Roe or his lawful representative.

It is specifically understood that, in receiving the idea of Robert Roe, the idea is being received and will be reviewed in confidence and that, within a period of 30 days, we will report to said Robert Roe the results of our findings and will advise whether or not we are interested in negotiating for the purchase of the right to use said idea.

Company_____
Street and Number_____
City_____ State_____ Zip_____

Official to receive disclosures (please type)

_____ Title _____
Date _____ Signature _____
Accepted: _____
                          Robert Roe, Inventor

FIGURE 4–3. Suggested Contract for Submission and Review of Ideas

Source: "Small Business Profits from Unpatentable Ideas," *Management Aids for Small Manufacturers*, No. 53, Washington, D.C.: Small Business Administration, May 1974, p. 3.

The source most often used in finding a lawyer is reference from others. Friends, relatives, or neighbors may have been satisfied with a lawyer and will recommend that person's services. Local newspapers and law schools can also be sources of referral.

Role of Attorney

An attorney often has opportunities to influence business executives. The ultimate success or failure of a business has on occasion hinged on counsel provided management at a critical juncture. A lawyer knowledgeable in business planning, coordination, and control can be vitally helpful, particularly to small business managers, in giving counsel on the legal aspects of business affairs. An attorney who thinks constructively, from the point of view of management, markedly increases the value of the legal advice given. Counsel given without knowledge of business considerations may result in consequences that are disadvantageous or possibly disastrous. This is not to say that a lawyer should regularly give business advice, only that the lawyer should be aware of the possible consequences to the business. Similarly, the small business owner should realize that an attorney can be a valuable sounding board in analyzing and weighing business alternatives. Entrepreneurs should realize, however, that decisions affecting business affairs can be made ultimately only by themselves.

An attorney can play more than one role within an organization. For example, the attorney, in addition to being counsel for the corporation, may be a director, an officer, an employee, a stockholder, a creditor (bond or note holder), a trustee of pension or profit-sharing trust, and counsel to individual shareholders, directors, or officers.

Bringing an attorney into the life of the business venture has several advantages beyond the contribution made to the formation of the company. By being involved with the venture, the attorney is able to maintain up-to-date knowledge of the organization's affairs, operations, and financial status. Many facts that the entrepreneur may believe irrelevant or insignificant can be pertinent and important to an attorney. Knowledge of such facts makes it possible to practice *preventive law*. Preventive law anticipates potential problems and treats them before they become significant. The practice of preventive law also permits opportunities to be identified and seized.

As a practical matter, the more an attorney is consulted, the easier it is to get attention and commitment. A busy attorney is more inclined to pay attention to regular clients than to seek new clients. The more involved an attorney is in the specific business, the more knowledgeable the attorney is likely to be, requiring less time to gain understanding of a particular problem. Such prior knowledge can save time and money.

Compensation for the Attorney

Several methods are available for compensating an attorney. The method used depends largely on the type of work to be performed and the degree of involvement required.

An attorney may receive a retainer, payable annually, semiannually, quarterly, or monthly. A retainer normally covers legal advice of a routine and general nature. Retainers do not cover litigation or extraordinary services. However, most attorneys do bear in mind the retainer relationship when billing for extra services. Any retainer arrangement should be stated clearly in a letter to the client, which should be acknowledged. The letter of retainer should specify the duration of the agreement and the time for periodic review to determine whether the retainer fee continues to be equitable for both parties. A principal advantage of such a retainer arrangement is that the client generally will use the services of the attorney frequently. The client is more likely to appreciate the need for and to employ preventive law to avoid trouble.

Without a retainer, work done by an attorney is normally billed on an hourly basis; the client is charged for each hour of work performed. Bills are usually rendered at the end of the month. Attorney and client should always agree upon the hourly fee to be charged. It is, however, generally impossible for an attorney to state precisely what the total fee will be for a given task. Although an estimate may be given of the amount of time that a task will require, usually too many unknown factors prevent more than an approximation.

In certain cases an attorney may agree to work for a previously agreed upon sum, or in other cases for a contingent fee, which is a percentage of recovery. Simple incorporations are usually performed for a fixed fee; cases involving collection of debts are often taken by counsel for a percentage of the sum that may be recovered.

Fees should be discussed in the first meeting with the attorney. Too often clients are surprised and upset by the fees that are charged because they failed to raise the issue at the beginning of the relationship.

SUMMARY: Importance of Proper Legal Procedures

A number of preliminary considerations and legal decisions face the entrepreneur starting a new business venture. Selecting an attorney should be among the first decisions made. The entrepreneur should then decide *with* the attorney what structural form to employ for the venture. The attorney's role in this process should not be merely that of a mechanical scrivener. Rather the attorney should counsel and assist the client in making the best possible choice in light of all the relevant facts. This choice will affect the rights, obligations, and liabilities of the owners of the business, as well as tax matters. The advice of a capable attorney at the outset can help the entrepreneur avoid expensive and time-consuming legal problems.

An attorney is also needed to advise the firm when patents, trademarks, service marks, copyrights, and disclosures of unpatentable ideas to another firm are involved. Whenever a unique idea is to be protected, it is wise to employ professional counsel to handle the complex procedures.

Perhaps the role of the attorney most useful to the entrepreneur is that of general adviser on the legal aspects of business matters. If the attorney has an ongoing relationship with the firm and is informed about the life of the business, it is possible to practice preventive law. This kind of legal advice can help the business to avoid potential legal tangles and seize opportunities that only an attorney could identify.

SUGGESTED READINGS

"Advising California Business Enterprises." *Continuing Education of the Bar*. Berkeley: University of California Extension, 1958.

"Advising Small Corporate Clients." Paper presented by The Joint Committee on Continuing Legal Education of the Virginia Bar Association and Virginia State Bar, Richmond, Va., 1972.

American Jurisprudence 2d edition, vols. 18 and 19, *Corporations*, vols. 59 and 60, *Partnership*. San Francisco: Bancroft Whitney Co., 1971.

Herwitz, David. *Business Planning*. Brooklyn, N.Y.: Foundation Press, 1966.

Kleinman, Seymour. *Fundamentals of Business Law*. Chicago: Callaghan & Co., 1973.

Liles, Patrick R. *New Business Ventures and the Entrepreneur*. Homewood, Ill.: Richard D. Irwin, 1974, pp. 75–101.

Lusk, Harold F.; Hewitt, Charles M.; Donnell, John D.; and Barnes, A. James. *Business Law, Principles and Cases*, 3d U.C.C. edition. Homewood, Ill.: Richard D. Irwin, 1974.

Mertens, Jacob, Jr. *The Law of Federal Income Taxation*. Chicago: Callaghan & Company, 1967, chapters 28 and 38.

"Organizing Corporations in California," *California Continuing Education of the Bar*. Berkeley: University of California Extension, 1973.

Paust, Jordan L., and Rupp, Robert D. *Business Law*, 2d edition. St. Paul, Minn.: West Publishing Co., 1974.

Tax Choices in Organizing a Business. Chicago: Commerce Clearing House, 1973.

U.S. Master Tax Guide. Chicago: Commerce Clearing House, 1973.

CHAPTER 5

Putting It All Together: Preparing the Prospectus for a New Venture

Assuming that the study and practical research detailed in the previous chapters have been done, in essence the strategic planning for the new venture, the aspiring enterpriser is now ready to put it all together. The most practical way to integrate the data accumulated to this point is to develop a business prospectus—a comprehensive plan for the new business. The prospectus should be carefully prepared in every detail, and it should be in writing. With a written prospectus, missing information or gaps in the data become visible, and the overall plan may be checked for logical integrity and sequence.

The prospectus is a planning document in which critical aspects of the proposed business are projected from assumptions. It is a wise procedure therefore to repeat the planning process several times, varying the assumptions from optimistic to pessimistic until the final document represents a best effort at a reasonable representation of actuality.

The prospectus is the basic document that the entrepreneur will use to interest and attract capital. If the planning process has been iterated and reiterated with a variety of assumptions, the entrepreneur will be so well prepared as to be able to answer with confidence any question posed by a prospective investor.

The material that follows is based upon the outline for a prospectus for a new business shown in Figure 5–1. Although there are a number of versions in the literature, this outline has stood the test of practice. It has been used on many occasions to prepare plans that have successfully interested investors in funding a new business. The next chapter presents a variation of this approach designed particularly to interest venture capitalists in investing in young, fast-growing companies.

1. *A Condensed Summary Statement*
   Brief definition of business in clear, simple language

   - Description of product or service
   - Diagrams, illustrations, or pictures (if practicable)

   Summary of marketing approach
   - Segment of market aimed for
   - Channels through which to be sold: retail, wholesale, distributors, brokers, mail-order, or other

   Summary of financial estimates
   - Approximate annual dollar sales aimed for
   - Anticipated profit on this volume
   - Estimated starting capital required

2. *Statement of Objectives*
   Statement of desirability of product or service

   - Advantages, improvements over existing products or services, and desirability of product or service
   - Statement of long-range objectives and short-range goals of the business
   - Description of your qualifications to run the business
   - Statement of *character* of business and *image* to be projected

3. *Background of Proposed Business*
   Brief discussion of present state of the art

   - Where and how product or service is now being used (supporting articles or patent in appendix)

   Detailed explanation of your place in the state of the art
   - Projections for the state of the art, trends, and predictions
   - Competition that must be met (competition's printed material in appendix)
   - Intended strategy for meeting competition
   - Uniqueness: patentability of proposed product or special qualities of proposed service that will ensure identity and leadership in the field

4. *Technical Description of Product or Service*
   Full technical description of product or service

   - Summary of tests conducted and test data, or statement of tests to be made and purposes of tests
   - Technical description of how product or service is to be used
   - Sample brochure or dummy
   - Brief statement of follow-on (next generation) of products or services

5. *Selling Strategy and Tactics*
   Selling strategy

   - Comprehensive statement of basic selling approach: retail, door-to-door, jobbers, wholesalers, brokers, mail-order, or other
   - Proposed segment of intended market
   - Share of market expected versus calendar time from introduction of product or service

FIGURE 5–1. Outline for a Prospectus on a New Business

FIGURE 5-1. (continued)

Selling tactics
- Statement of methods to be used in meeting sales goals: direct calling, telephone, advertising, or other
- Data supporting ability to meet sales goals: actual orders, personally known prospective key accounts, potential customers, or others
- Explanation of margins of safety allowed

6. *Plan of Operation*

Description of initial organization
- Statement describing key positions and identifying personnel to fill them
- Resumés of key personnel
- Organization chart showing needed functions and relationships: administrative, engineering, production, sales, and others
- Research and development facilities required
- Kind of production to be done in-house and subcontracted
- Equipment and space required

7. *Supporting Data*
- Set of drawings of product or outline of service to be rendered
- Priced bill of materials, with prices scaled to various production quantities
- List of tooling required and estimated costs
- Layout of proposed plant, supported by manufacturing flow chart including estimated costs of manufacturing
- Packaging and shipping analysis
- List of capital equipment and costs
- Price schedule
- Market surveys
- Financial data:

  1) Projected profit and loss statement and balance sheet for first two years by months
  2) Cash flow analysis for two years
  3) Break-even chart for minimum sales goal
  4) Fixed asset acquisition schedule by month (item and dollars)

8. *Conclusions and Summary*

Statement of proposed approach for intiating new organization, in brief:
- Total capital needed and safety factor used
- Profit expected and expected times of receipt
- Ownership interest reserved for self and partners
- Total capital required
- Entrepreneur's share of initial capital investment
- Additional capital sought
- Share to be given for investment or loan of additional capital required
- Anticipated time schedule for starting the business

CONDENSED SUMMARY STATEMENT

The first section of the prospectus for the new business presents a brief summary giving the key points of the plan. This summary centers on three critical aspects of the plan: the kind of business, the marketing approach, and the financial estimates. These are the data that the prospective investor will want to know before all else. Unless this material is given in the very first page or two, the sophisticated investor will read no further. The summary statement therefore deserves careful preparation. It should be written last so that the entrepreneur can review the logic and supporting data as a final check on the accuracy, clarity, and integrity of the business plan presented in the prospectus.

Brief Definition of the Business

The first portion of the summary describes the product or service in clear, simple language. New or especially desirable features are briefly noted. The narrative is supported by diagrams, artist's illustrations, or photographs of a model or prototype.

Marketing Approach

An outline of the marketing strategy and tactics follows the description of the product or service, then a precise definition of the segment of the market aimed for is given. A statement of the marketing channel to be used follows, indicating whether the product is to be sold through retail establishments, wholesalers, distributors, brokers, or directly to the consumer. Sales tactics next described indicate whether direct mail, telephone, door-to-door selling, or some other way of reaching the customer is to be used.

Financial Estimates

The introductory section closes with a summary of financial estimates, concentrating on three items the prospective investor is particularly interested in at an early stage of the examination of the prospectus: the approximate annual gross sales in dollars, the anticipated profit on this volume of business, and the estimated starting capital required. These values come from the quantitative planning described later in this chapter. The estimates should be given for the first three years of operation as projected in the financial planning.

STATEMENT OF OBJECTIVES

The second section of the prospectus presents the desirability of the product or service. Here are spelled out the advantages and improvements over existing products or services. Answers are given to the questions: What special niche in the market is to be filled? Why should the intended customer be willing to part with hard-earned dollars to buy the product or service?

Next comes a statement of the long-range objectives of the business and the short-range subobjectives that feed into them. Major objectives flow from a carefully thought out answer to the question: What business is the entrepreneur really entering? Once the mission of the business has been established, in product or service and market terms, objectives in key areas are worked out that state the desired results to be achieved by specific dates. Typical subjects for objectives are sales, profits, marketing, research and development, and finance. Objectives may be formulated for any element of the proposed business considered important enough to require planning.[1]

The next paragraph in this section outlines the entrepreneur's qualifications to run the business. Here care must be used to be straightforward and persuasive without being brash. The entrepreneur's experience and special competencies as needed in the proposed business are clearly stated. The message should reflect confidence and the reliability of the entrepriser's character.

Not only is the character of the enterprise an important factor in the prospectus, the character of the business is also important. This section of the plan concludes with a statement of the image that the business seeks to project. Does the founder intend that the business shall deal only in high-priced, high-quality merchandise? Then every effort must be bent on building an image of quality and reliability in everything the business does or touches. Choice of letterhead, decor of the establishment, and treatment of the individual customer—these and many other aspects of the business contribute to its image. The plan states the image desired as a reflection of the character of the business and treats some of the major steps proposed to achieve it.

BACKGROUND OF THE PROPOSED BUSINESS

This section of the prospectus starts with a discussion of the present state of the art. Its purpose is to tell about the existing products or services in the general area of the proposed venture and where or how these are being used. Articles giving information about existing products or services are placed in the appendix to the prospectus. The prospective investor gets an overall perspective of the field from these data and is thus prepared to make an initial judgment of how the product or service being proposed would fit in the market.

---

[1]George A. Steiner, *Comprehensive Managerial Planning*, Oxford, Ohio: The Planning Executives Institute, 1972, pp. 13–15.

Where Does the Proposed Product or Service Fit?

The discussion then treats the projected state of the art in some detail. What are the trends in the field? What new or emerging forces in the environment indicate a growth of the market for the new product or service? How do the trends support the forecasted growth of the venture? Answers to questions such as these substantiate the planning incorporated in the prospectus. For example, if the proposed venture aims at bringing adult games onto the market, income and population by age as projected from U.S. Census data might be used to show the market potential for the near future.

Competition that must be met is outlined in the following paragraphs. Supporting evidence, for example, advertisements or brochures describing the competitive items, is placed in the appendix.

The final steps in this part of the prospectus outline the intended strategy for meeting competition. The emphasis in a competitive field is on identifying the precise segment of the market desired and showing how the product or service is different and better in some way from those offered by competition.

Differentiation implies uniqueness. What special properties of the product serve a consumer need that is not now being served? What features of the service being offered are superior to those available? If a product, can it be patented? What steps are proposed to ensure identity, consumer recognition, and leadership in the field? These are the kinds of questions the prospective investor would like to see answered in a credible way.

TECHNICAL DESCRIPTION OF PRODUCT OR SERVICE

The investor will next want to know in detail what the product or service is. A full technical description of the product or service is required at this point. The data include a summary of any tests conducted and the results. If none have been made because of the developmental status of the project, a statement is given of the tests to be made and their purposes.

The technical description is rounded out by a description of how the product or service is to be used. If the venture is to provide a new form of service for testing etched circuit boards used in electronics manufacturing, for example, the explanation might well include photographs of an actual test setup. It would show the circuit board in process of being tested on the special equipment designed for the purpose. A detailed explanation would make clear that the service focuses on developing the special adaptor needed to connect the circuit board to the test instrument. An accompanying picture might show the contrast between the older way of doing the job and the proposed method: a technician using probes and meters to check each point on the board by hand—a laborious and costly procedure—compared with the proposed fast and inexpensive automated method.

A sample brochure or a dummy of a brochure to be used for promoting the sale of the product or service accompanies the technical material.

The concluding discussion in this section gives a brief statement of the next generation, or follow-on, versions of the product or service. The sophisticated investor knows that the profitability of an innovative product or service is transitory. Evidence that the entrepreneur has thought of the need to improve the product or service with time tells the investor that the deal is with a knowledgeable person. In this way the entrepreneur builds credibility as a likely prospect for success in the proposed business.

SELLING STRATEGY AND TACTICS

The next stage in the prospectus treats the very important factor of the selling strategy to be adopted and the tactics necessary to support it. The tactics are the methods used to meet the projected sales goals.

As an example of strategy for a small company, the Abbott-Lane Company of Portland, Oregon, which introduced etched plywood as a decorative wall panel before World War II, decided to confine its selling effort to the eastern United States. This decision came from knowledge that Douglas fir plywood was commonly known in the west. The unique decorative value of the product would be novel in the east where plywood was relatively scarce at that time.

The company decided to concentrate its selling efforts on large wholesale firms of impeccable credit rating. This strategy would permit selling by carload lot, the most feasible way to handle production and distribution of this bulky product. In addition, selling to well-rated firms would permit the company to finance shipments through the bank, a well-established procedure in wholesale lumber business.

Selling tactics were simple. Sales were made by one of the two partners, a very competent salesperson, who traveled the eastern part of the country and sold by direct demonstration to key executives. (The other partner concentrated on production and management of the finances.)

The Abbott-Lane Company believed that success in introducing etchedwood would bring competition quite rapidly. The company estimated that its original monopoly would vanish within twelve to eighteen months. As competitors encroached on the etchedwood market and as profitability reached a plateau, the partners planned to introduce new products.

Whatever the strategy and tactics are, they must fit the business. The projected segment of the market and the share of the market anticipated over time are clearly stated.

The most powerful way to demonstrate the prospective company's ability to meet its sales goals is through actual orders from legitimate customers. If that is not possible, recourse may be had to listing personally known prospective key accounts or potential customers. This information should be made believable by an explanation of the margin of safety allowed.

PLAN OF OPERATION

The plan of operation opens with a description of the initial organization of the proposed company. The key positions and the personnel who will fill them are identified. Resumés of the key personnel follow. Care is taken to emphasize the special skills and experience of the individuals who bring management strength to the proposed organization. Particular attention should be paid to competencies in the management of production, marketing, and finance. These are the areas, it will be recalled, in which the prospective sophisticated investor is particularly interested.

Organization

If the proposed company is of sufficient size to require a management group beyond two or three key persons, an organization chart is included. This chart shows the needed functions and the managerial roles and relationships. It covers general management, administrative, engineering, marketing, production, and other major functions required to operate the technical and administrative processes of the organization.

R and D and Production

In a technical business the facilities for research and development are described. These include laboratory, model shop, test equipment, and other special facilities required to develop and test new products and features.

A statement is then made of the kind of production to be done inhouse and that to be subcontracted. The new business would probably do well to subcontract as much work outside as is practicable to preserve its cash. If, however, its proposed business is based upon special know-how or proprietary production equipment, it will want to do this part of the work within its own plant.

This section of the prospectus concludes with a description of the equipment to be employed in R and D and production and a statement of the floor area required for the plant.

SUPPORTING DATA

This part of the business plan provides enough information to support the sections that have gone before. Detailed data and quantitative material are presented in sufficient depth to show without question that the entrepreneur has prepared carefully for the initiation of the proposed business. Tables and reference material may well be placed in the appendix to the report. The body of this section, however, should contain the significant conclusions of the studies and projections that have been made. The prospective investor may then study the details in the appendix when convenient.

Technical Information

A set of drawings of the product or a comprehensive description of the service to be rendered starts this portion of the report. A priced bill of materials follows. The costs listed are scaled to various production quantities in keeping with the projected levels of production. The quantities assumed should fit the forecasts of sales made for at least the first two years of operation by the month, and the third year by quarters.

These data are followed by a list of the tooling required to make the product and the estimated cost of the tooling. The enterpriser should recognize that production may well be started with simple tooling. As production passes a predetermined level, it would be replaced by "hard" tooling, which would be considerably more costly. Financial estimates are adjusted accordingly and entered into the projections.

A simple layout of the proposed plant follows. It is accompanied by a manufacturing flow chart showing the stages of manufacture and the steps of assembly. If the product is fairly complicated, a straightforward way to develop the flow chart is to trace the "Christmas tree" of drawings from details through subassemblies to final assembly.

The flow chart of manufacturing prepares the way for the next item, a table of estimated costs of making the product. This table shows projected costs for several estimated quantities to be produced per unit of time and should conform with the kind of tooling to be employed, as previously determined.

A packaging and shipping analysis is included at this point. These are cost factors that must not be overlooked. Bulky, sturdy products sold by carload lots or equivalent, like the etchedwood panels previously mentioned, can be shipped by rail or truck without special wrapping or crating. On the other hand, delicate electronic equipment may have to be shipped in specially designed cartons with compliant plastic form-shaped fillers to prevent damage in transit. Air transport may be the most desirable way to ship this kind of product. When the price of the product is very high for its weight and the product is delicate, shipment by air may reduce the amount of handling and the incidence of rough treatment that could cause damage.

Careful design must be given to the packaging of consumer products. It often proves desirable to display a picture of the product on the carton so that prospective buyers can visualize what is inside. This can be helpful to the retailer also. The stacking and storage space for cartons or shipping boxes must also be considered. Shelf space in retail stores is valuable and often hard to get. Anything that helps the retailer store and display the product readily helps to promote sales.

The technical information having to do with product and production is concluded with a list of the capital equipment required and the costs of such equipment. Again the enterpriser must recognize that there are some options in the acquisition of capital equipment. Machinery may be purchased new or secondhand. It may be leased with option to buy or it may be rented. Choice at the beginning should usually be made with the aim of preserving available cash.

Market Survey

The results of the market survey and market feasibility analyses are summarized at this point. Supporting data—demographic studies, isolation of the desired market segment, product or service specifications as determined from these studies, pricing strategy, and other pertinent information—are referenced and placed in the appendix. A schedule of proposed selling prices for the product, product line, or service line concludes this portion of the presentation.

Financial Data

The final supporting data presented include the following:

- Projected profit and loss statement and balance sheets for the first two years by months; for the third year by quarters

- Cash flow analyses for two years by months; for the third year by quarters
- Break–even chart for minimum sales goal by years
- Fixed asset acquisition schedule by months, showing item and dollars

Figures 5–2 through 5–10 show a simplified set of examples illustrating such financial plans for a small retail bookstore. They have been completed for two and a quarter years of operation. The reader who has no experience with these kinds of plans may gain familiarity with them by carrying the data forward through the second and third years.

Ms. Edna Hodes, the entrepreneur who launched this bookstore, had worked for five years as a salesperson in a bookstore before deciding to venture into her own business. She had been fortunate enough to accumulate shares in blue-ribbon companies worth about $37,000 in the stock market of 1976. She also had some $15,000 in savings.

She estimated that $10,000 would be an adequate original investment in the proposed bookstore. Of this amount, Ms. Hodes decided to put into the business $7,000 cash from her savings. This would leave a balance of $8,000 for living expenses, which she believed enough until she could start drawing money from the business.

Ms. Hodes then made an arrangement with her bank to borrow funds as the business might need them during the start-up period in her bookstore operation. She put up $25,000 worth of stock as collateral against which to borrow money as the need arose.

Her financial planning for the business was based upon the assumptions shown in figure 5–3.

FIGURE 5–2. Financial Estimates for a Retail Bookstore: Background

---

1. Begin business on 1 January 1977.
2. See Figure 5–4 for initial balance sheet. Proprietor invests 70% of total $10,000 investment.
3. See Figure 5–5 for sales forecast.
4. Fixtures depreciated at 1% monthly (straight-line, 8⅓ years).
5. Cost of merchandise for resale = 65% of sales (average book, sold at $10 costs $6.50).
6. Beginning inventory set at cost of sales for next four months.

FIGURE 5–3. Financial Estimates—Assumptions

FIGURE 5-3. (continued)

7. Two-thirds of purchases are for cash. One-third of purchases paid in 30 days.
8. Three-fourths of sales are for cash. One-fourth of sales are for credit, with collections in 30 days.
9. Taxes at 30%, paid in April of following year.
10. Beginning cash balance for any month should be one-half of sales for that month. Beginning cash balance for January 1977 was $650.
11. Borrowing and repayment of debt done in increments of $200. Interest at 0.75% monthly is paid monthly. Initial loan as of 1 January 1977 was $3,000.

1 January 1977

Assets		Liabilities and Equity	
Cash	$ 650	Bank loan	$ 3,000
Inventory	5,850	Proprietor's capital	7,000
Fixtures	3,500	Total	$10,000
Total	$10,000		

FIGURE 5–4. Financial Estimates—Balance Sheet

	1977	1978	1979
Jan.	$ 1,000	$ 6,000	$7,000
Feb.	2,000	6,000	7,000
Mar.	3,000	5,000	8,000
Apr.	3,000	7,000	8,000
May	4,000	4,000	
June	5,000	5,000	
July	4,000	6,000	
Aug.	6,000	6,000	
Sept.	5,000	5,000	
Oct.	6,000	5,000	
Nov.	7,000	7,000	
Dec.	14,000	18,000	
	$60,000	$80,000	

FIGURE 5–5. Financial Estimates—Forecasted
Monthly Sales

	Jan.	Feb.	Mar.	Apr.	May	June	July	Aug.	Sept.	Oct.	Nov.	Dec.
1. Sales forecast	$1,000	$ 2,000	$ 3,000	$ 3,000	$ 4,000	$ 5,000	$ 4,000	$ 6,000	$ 5,000	$ 6,000	$ 7,000	$14,000
2. Cash sales (75%)	750	1,500	2,250	2,250	3,000	3,750	3,000	4,500	3,750	4,500	5,250	10,500
3. Plus credit sales	0	250	500	750	750	1,000	1,250	1,000	1,500	1,250	1,500	1,750
4. Total cash receipts [(2) + (3)]	750	1,750	2,750	3,000	3,750	4,750	4,250	5,500	5,250	5,750	6,750	12,250
5. Cost of goods sold (65%)	650	1,300	1,950	1,950	2,600	3,250	2,600	3,900	3,250	3,900	4,550	9,100
6. Plus ending inventory	7,800	9,750	10,400	12,350	13,000	13,650	15,600	20,800	21,450	21,450	20,150	15,600
7. Total available	8,450	11,050	12,350	14,300	15,600	16,900	18,200	24,700	24,700	25,350	24,700	24,700
8. Minus beginning inventory	5,850	7,800	9,750	10,400	12,350	13,000	13,650	15,600	20,800	21,450	21,450	20,150
9. Purchases required [(7) − (8)]	2,600	3,250	2,600	3,900	3,250	3,900	4,550	9,100	3,900	3,900	3,250	4,550
10. Cash payment (66.7%)	1,733	2,167	1,733	2,600	2,167	2,600	3,033	6,067	2,600	2,600	2,167	3,033
11. Credit payment	0	867	1,083	867	1,300	1,083	1,300	1,517	3,033	1,300	1,300	1,083
12. Total payment [(10) + (11)]	1,733	3,034	2,816	3,467	3,467	3,683	4,333	7,584	5,633	3,900	3,467	4,116
13. Salaries—proprietor	0	0	0	0	0	0	200	200	200	400	400	400
14. Salaries—other	0	0	200	200	300	300	300	300	400	400	400	600
15. Total salaries [(13) + (14)]	0	0	200	200	300	300	500	500	600	800	800	1,000

18. Supplies	50	50	50	50	50	50	50	50	50	50	50	50
19. Telephone	100	100	100	100	100	100	100	100	100	100	100	100
20. Utilities	40	40	40	40	40	40	40	40	40	40	40	40
21. Insurance	20	20	20	20	20	20	20	20	20	20	20	20
22. License fees & miscellaneous	100	0	0	0	0	0	0	0	0	0	0	0
23. Total payments [(15) to (22)]	610	510	710	710	810	810	1,010	1,010	1,110	1,310	1,310	1,510
24. Beginning cash balance	650	1,034	1,602	1,570	2,131	2,529	2,103	3,132	2,543	3,136	3,534	7,176
25. Plus cash receipts (4)	750	1,750	2,750	3,000	3,750	4,750	4,250	5,500	5,250	5,750	6,750	12,250
26. Total cash available	1,400	2,784	4,352	4,570	5,881	7,279	6,353	8,632	7,793	8,886	10,284	19,426
27. Minus total cash outlays [(12) + (23)]	2,343	3,544	3,526	4,177	4,277	4,493	5,343	8,594	6,743	5,210	4,777	5,626
28. Minus interest expense	23	38	56	62	75	83	78	95	114	131	131	144
29. Cash balance before borrowing	(966)	(798)	770	331	1,529	2,703	932	(57)	936	3,534	5,376	13,656
30. Additional borrowing	2,000	2,400	800	1,800	1,000	(600)	2,200	2,600	2,200	0	1,800	(10,600)
31. Cumulative borrowing	5,000	7,400	8,200	10,000	11,000	10,400	12,600	15,200	17,400	17,400	19,200	8,600
32. Cash balance after borrowing [(29) + (30)]	1,034	1,602	1,570	2,131	2,529	2,103	3,132	2,543	3,136	3,534	7,176	3,056

FIGURE 5–6. Financial Estimates—Cash Flow Analysis for 1977

	Jan.	Feb.	Mar.	Apr.	May	June	July	Aug.	Sept.	Oct.	Nov.	Dec.
Sales	$1,000	$2,000	$3,000	$3,000	$4,000	$5,000	$4,000	$6,000	$5,000	$6,000	$7,000	$14,000
Cost of sales	650	1,300	1,950	1,950	2,600	3,250	2,600	3,900	3,250	3,900	4,550	9,100
Gross margin	350	700	1,050	1,050	1,400	1,750	1,400	2,100	1,750	2,100	2,450	4,900
Cash payments	610	510	710	710	810	810	1,010	1,010	1,110	1,310	1,310	1,510
Interest	23	38	56	62	75	83	78	95	114	131	131	144
Depreciation	35	35	35	35	35	35	35	35	35	35	35	35
Total	668	583	801	807	920	928	1,123	1,140	1,259	1,476	1,476	1,689
Before-tax profit	(318)	117	249	243	480	822	277	960	491	624	974	3,211

FIGURE 5–7. Financial Estimates—Income Statement by Month

Sales		$60,000
Cost of sales		39,000
Gross Margin		21,000
Salaries	$5,200	
Rent	3,000	
Advertising	600	
Supplies	600	
Telephone	1,200	
Utilities	480	
Insurance	240	
License fees & miscellaneous	100	
Interest	1,030	
Depreciation	420	
Total expenses		12,870
Before-tax profit		8,130
Taxes (20%)		1,626
After-tax profit		6,504
Proprietor's capital (1 Jan. 1977)		7,000
Proprietor's capital (31 Dec. 1977)		$13,504

FIGURE 5–8. Financial Estimates—Yearly Income Statement, 1977

31 December 1977

Assets			Liabilities and Equity	
Cash		$ 3,056	Accounts Payable	$ 1,517
Accounts Receivable		3,500	Taxes payable	1,626
Inventory		15,600	Bank loan	8,600
Fixtures	$3,500		Proprietor's capital	13,504
Minus depreciation	420		Total	$25,200
Net fixed		3,080		
Total		$25,200		

Note: Totals rounded out to 3 figures.

FIGURE 5–9. Financial Estimates—Balance Sheet

This chart has been prepared on the basis of the following assumptions for the year 1978:

Sales	$80,000	(proprietor and salesperson
Salaries	14,400	each draw $600 per month)
Rent	3,000	
Advertising	1,200	
Supplies	600	
Telephone	1,200	
Utilities	480	
Insurance	240	
License fees	100	
Interest	1,200	(estimated on bank loans
Depreciation	420	projected for 1978)
Miscellaneous	160	
Total	$22,800	(costs for 1978)

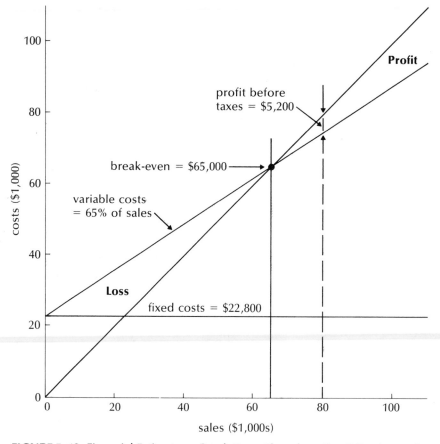

FIGURE 5–10. Financial Estimates—Break-Even Chart for a Retail Bookstore for One Year, 1978

FIGURE 5-10. (continued)

Sales in dollars are plotted along the horizontal line and costs in dollars are shown along the vertical line. Both scales are identical. The horizontal line at $22,800 gives the total of costs that may be considered essentially fixed for the year. The variable costs line, which originates at the left end of the fixed costs line, shows the costs of the books sold for the year as a function of the total sales for the year. This cost is given by the vertical distance between the fixed costs line and the variable costs line for any yearly sales volume.

A break-even line bisecting the horizontal and vertical intersection at 45 degrees permits identification of the break-even point for the year. This point is at the intersection of the 45 degree break-even line and the variable costs line. The break-even line shows the total cost of doing business for any given volume of sales for the year.

The graph shows the profit or loss for any specific volume of sales dollars. For the example of the retail bookstore given, profit may be seen to be about $5,200 for the year, before taxes.

Many useful variations of the break-even chart serve different managerial purposes. The small business owner will find them appropriate for managerial control purposes and for profit planning.[2]

CONCLUDING STATEMENT

The prospectus ends with a statement summarizing the key points of the proposed approach for starting the new business. Although the preceding discussion assumes in several places that the prospectus describes a manufacturing operation, it can be readily adapted to a retail business by substituting items pertinent to the specific enterprise. For example, in a retail bookstore, display cases, counters, and shelves would replace shears, punchpresses, and lathes; and in a wholesale company distributing roofing material, storage racks, shelving, and fork-lift trucks would replace the production machinery of the manufacturing organization.

The summary statement presents the following items in brief form:

1. The total capital needed to launch the business and the safety factor used in arriving at this total. Many entrepreneurs new to business tend to be overly optimistic about the funding that will be needed. It is wise to allow some reasonable percentage of overage to take care of contingencies and unexpected delays, which can be costly. If the entrepreneur has planned carefully and is confident of the estimates, this safety factor might range from 10 to 30 percent.
2. The profit planned and the dates when it should be available. Figures on profit will come from the profit and loss statements previously prepared.

[2]See Spencer A. Tucker, *The Break-Even System*, Englewood Cliffs, N.J.: Prentice-Hall, 1963, for a thorough treatment of the various forms and uses of break-even charts.

3. The total capital required and the percentage of this amount the entrepreneur is prepared to put up. It will be found that the sophisticated investor will insist that the enterpriser invest in the business to the limit of personal resources.
4. The additional capital sought from the investor.
5. The ownership interest the entrepreneur and partners seek for themselves.
6. The share of the business to be given to the investor for making the investment or lending the capital required.
7. The anticipated time schedule for starting the business. Here it should be recognized that the steps taken in starting the business often require more time than an optimistic approach might suggest.

SUMMARY: Key Purposes of the Prospectus

This chapter describes the steps to be taken in putting together the planning for the new business through the vehicle of a prospectus, or business plan. The reader should refer to Figure 5–1 for an outline of the content of the prospectus. The prospectus has two basic functions: it gives entrepreneurs a way to check the accuracy and completeness of their planning, and it prepares them to seek financing. The prospectus itself is the formal document required by the sophisticated investor to make a first assessment of the viability of the proposed venture. When carefully prepared, the prospectus opens the transactions that can lead to successful financing of the new business.

SUGGESTED READINGS

Baty, Gordon B. *Entrepreneurship—Playing to Win*. Reston, Va.: Reston Publishing Co., 1974, chapter 11.

Baumback, Clifford M., and Mancuso, Joseph R. *Entrepreneurship and Venture Management*. Englewood Cliffs, N.J.: Prentice-Hall, 1975, pp. 100–7.

Gross, Harry. *Financing for Small and Medium-Sized Business*. Englewood Cliffs, N.J.: Prentice-Hall, 1969.

J. K. Lasser Tax Institute. *How to Run a Small Business*, 4th edition. New York: McGraw-Hill, 1974, chapter 8.

Morrison, Robert S. *Handbook for Manufacturing Entrepreneurs*, 2d edition. Cleveland: Western Reserve Press, 1974, chapter 51.

Rautenstrauch, Walter, and Villers, Raymond. *The Economics of Industrial Management*, 2d edition. New York: Funk & Wagnalls, 1957, chapter 2.

Steinhoff, Dan. *Small Business Management: Fundamentals*. New York: McGraw-Hill, 1974, chapter 24.

Steinmetz, Lawrence L., Kline John B., and Stegall, Donald P. *Managing the Small Business*. Homewood, Ill.: Richard D. Irwin, 1968, chapter 14.

Summers, George W. *Financing and Initial Operations of New Firms*. Englewood Cliffs, N.J.: Prentice-Hall, 1962.

Timmons, Jeffry A., Smollen, Leonard E., and Dingee, Alexander L. M., Jr. *New Venture Creation*. Homewood, Ill.: Richard D. Irwin, 1977, chapter 14.

CHAPTER 6
_____

Financing New and Growing Businesses

In the office of a venture capital investor hangs a small cartoon that captures the plight of the entrepreneur. It shows the King in the Wizard of ID standing on his castle balcony, scanning a crowd of peasant subjects. They look appropriately servile and he regal. With his finger pointing high he proclaims, "Remember the Golden Rule." The cartoon shows nothing else except a small footnote at the bottom: "Whoever has the gold makes the rules." This chapter analyzes those "rules" that can simplify the entrepreneur's task of raising capital for beginning enterprises and for growing established businesses. It looks backward toward earlier chapters that discuss starting a business and forward toward Part II, which discusses managing the business, once established. Thus, this chapter bridges these two major parts of the text. Financing working capital requirements for accounts receivables, inventories, and other short-term needs are discussed in Chapter 12. This chapter deals with the following subjects:

- looking at common fund-raising difficulties
- determining the company's financial needs
- preparing the private placement memorandum
- locating sources of venture capital
- dealing with the venture capitalist.

LOOKING AT COMMON FUND-RAISING DIFFICULTIES

Every entrepreneur who has raised money knows the frustrations of this task. The process is just as frustrating for the investor, though perhaps

This chapter was prepared by Bruce G. Rossiter, Senior Vice-President, First Small Business Investment Company of California and Security Pacific Capital Corporation, Los Angeles.

not as tedious. The investor spends months investigating and screening scores of proposals before finding a suitable opportunity. Most professional venture capitalists invest in only 1 to 2 percent of the proposals submitted to them. This percentage does not include telephone or personal inquiries, which are received two or three times more often than written proposals.

A review of some of the common difficulties encountered should help the entrepreneur avoid the waste of effort many experience in seeking financial support. Five problems occur with regularity, as demonstrated by a sample of 100 typical situations submitted to First Small Business Investment Company of California (FSBIC). The problems, in the order of their frequency of occurrence, are:

- mediocre company performance or concept
- failure of the company to follow up
- lack of business experience or acumen
- unique preferences of the venture capitalist
- inadequate exposure to sources of venture capital.

Mediocre Company Performance or Concept

The greatest single reason for refusing financing to existing or starting companies is mediocre, or worse, performance or concept. In the FSBIC sample of 100 typical situations, this reason accounted for 72 percent of the refusals. Two elements underlie the typical venture capitalist's disinterest. Either the company or concept involves too high a business risk (53 percent of this sample category) or too low a profit or low return on investment (47 percent).

High Risk Investor risk is the risk of losing capital or the risk of tying up funds without realizing expected returns. There are as many factors causing risk as there are companies. Several that occurred in the sample were lack of proprietary product or competitive advantage (22 percent of the high-risk category), difficulty in monitoring the investment (for example, overseas investment), pending litigation of a significant nature, or the fact that the company was just starting. Proposals from start-ups are frequently rejected because most aspects of the new venture are unknown: unknown product acceptance; untested management, both individually and as a team; unknown production capability; and unknown expense levels.

A common argument among entrepreneurs is that venture capital should be risk capital available for start-ups. However, the average professional investor reviews hundreds of situations a year. In a tight money market, when new public offerings are scarce and money from commercial banks is restricted and expensive, competition for the venture dollar is acute. Having a wide choice, the venture capitalist will tend to invest in less risky ventures. However, some investors will finance a start-up, especially if they envision very high returns, if the use of proceeds is for assets that are easily liquidated, or if there is some other secondary source of repayment such as a personal guarantee if the venture fails.

The entrepreneur can play a significant role in minimizing the risks the venture capitalist is asked to take. Most investors will require a significant personal investment by the entrepreneur to ensure commitment to the project. Although some entrepreneurs feel their time and "opportunities foregone" should be enough of a commitment, the investor knows that as the day-to-day pressure of running a business intensifies, a high-salary job offer from an established company can become attractive. It is easier to walk away from time sunk into a project than it is from one's own dollars. If the entrepreneur does not have a significant net worth and cannot borrow to share in the initial investment, occasionally the investor may lend the money for personal investment. The entrepreneur then has the loan liability as an incentive to stick with the company if the going gets rough. This compromise is used more by individual venture capitalists than by institutional venture groups.

The selection of the business to be funded is just as important in reducing risk as are monetary contributions and personal guarantees. If the entrepreneur is starting from scratch, seeking a business in an area that has less risk makes more sense than choosing one in a high-risk field. Most venture capitalists will avoid high-risk situations, even if there is a chance for a high payoff. At some point it becomes more profitable to roll dice at Las Vegas than to invest in a high flyer.

The entrepreneur can also reduce risk significantly by reducing the risk of the unknown. The less investors know about the company the more risk they perceive. An investor may raise a number of general arguments about the risk of a particular deal, many of which can be lessened by explaining the facts. An oil production company recently asked a venture group to invest several million dollars in exploration. No historical record of past drilling successes was given. During initial screening this request was viewed as a high-risk venture; there was little chance that it would be funded. Through probing for details on past drilling programs it was learned that this company had a much greater drilling success ratio than the average oil company. Further investigation showed that a large second position could exist behind the banks that were lending on already producing property. Thus an activity that initially seemed high in risk was later viewed as one of only moderate risk. The venture group funded the project and also reduced its risk by funding in stages. As performance benchmarks were met, additional monies were released.

Low Profits and Low Return on Investment Profits as an absolute amount are important. If a company has a low margin there is little to intrigue the investor. For example, a company earning only 1 percent on $1,000,000 in sales does not warrant the time, trouble, and risk for the miniscule profit of $10,000. Companies with low sales volumes after a long period of operation (for example, several hundred thousand dollars after five years of growth), low growth potential, insufficient backlog, or unrealistic projections also suffer from low absolute dollar returns. Companies with a long break-even time horizon (over one year), historical losses with no demonstrable turnaround, negative cash flows, and requirements for large amounts of investment dollars are also likely to be turned down as giving too low a return on investment.

The investor will be looking instead for companies that can efficiently use capital and thus produce high returns. The rate of return sought by venture groups on their investment varies but will range from 20 to 25 percent for low-risk ventures, to very high returns such as 70, 80, 100 percent, or even more, for riskier ventures. Returns of these magnitudes can be expected if the company's stock price increases significantly above the investor's purchase price. They are well within reach if the company generates good returns on assets employed and increases profits, and if its stock rises to a satisfactory multiple in the market.

The entrepreneur may believe that the investor is seeking an extraordinary return on the investment. However, generally only a small number of the investments in the venture capitalists' portfolio are highly successful. The investor must make a sufficient return on successful investments to achieve an acceptable overall return on the portfolio. As an example, an unpublished study showed the returns generated by nine public Small Business Investment Companies (SBICs) as a compound rate of return from 1965 to 1970 of only 19 percent. This study included unrealized gains in the calculation of return and covered a period when the stock market was kind to over-the-counter stocks. Every year the Small Business Administration (SBA) publishes an industry survey of SBIC returns on realized gains. The returns on investment fluctuate above and below negative returns for the industry; the large institutional venture groups average returns from 10 to 12 percent at the best.

The large number of companies that fall into the low profit, low return, or turnaround category may represent sound companies in which the entrepreneur can earn a respectable salary. But an investor needs to have returns considerably above the profit history or potential of such a business. Passive investors draw no salary and thus can invest only in those businesses in which the returns are so high that they cover both rewards to the entrepreneurs for their efforts and to the investors for their capital.

Failure of the Company to Follow Up

Failure to follow up is the second major reason for companies' failing to receive capital. It accounted for 13 percent of the rejections in the sample. Typically the company made initial contact without any prepared private placement memorandum. The management seemed to be testing the waters to see if they could receive an infusion of cash—only to drop their pursuit upon learning of the major educational effort required to instill enough confidence in the investor to risk investing venture money. The entrepreneur is best advised not to approach investors in a casual fashion. That approach will produce a negative feeling toward the company's management, suggesting lack of ability to utilize venture or expansion capital effectively.

The search for funding should begin well in advance of the date it is required. It usually takes two to three months to locate a venture source, assist the investor in the analysis, and structure a deal. Many companies underestimate the time necessary to carry through a successful negotiation.

Lack of Business Experience or Acumen

A favorite truism among venture investors is that investments are made in men and women, not in companies or concepts. Some investors state: "First and foremost [investors] . . . look at the management of a soliciting company. If it does not measure up, nothing else is likely to make them want to invest."[1] While the entrepreneur in the equation entrepreneur–idea–money is vital, because of the difficulty in measuring management performance apart from profit performance, this category accounted for only 8 percent of the refusals.[2] Weak management is, of course, a primary factor in accounting for low profits and high risks, but profit performance can be reviewed, while the quality of management can only be guessed.

An investor will be concerned with the management team's individual successes before the proposed venture, experience in the business, and depth of management in key areas.

Lack of investor confidence may arise from a feeling that management's talent is promotional, not operational; that management does not have a good grasp of the key factors for success in its business; that

---

[1]"Venture Capital: What Is It/Where Is It/How to Get It," *Business Management* 26, July 1964, p. 32.

[2]*Venture Capital, A Guidebook for New Enterprises*, a U.S. Government Printing Office Publication prepared for the New England Regional Commission by The Management Institute, School of Management, Boston College, March 22, 1972, p. 6.

financial control skills are lacking; that management is not tough, not capable of rolling with the punches; that management is not honest; that management is not creative or imaginative; or that management is not realistic.

A willingness to work with the venture group in whatever ways practicable can do much to establish needed rapport. The investor group also needs to be in tune with the problems faced and overcome by management and to view management's talents with openness. Unfortunately, some entrepreneurs and investors, flushed with past success, adopt a take-it-or-leave-it stance. In practice, both sides need to establish bonds of respect. Each is asking the other to become a partner in a venture designed to produce high returns for both.

Unique Preferences of the Venture Capitalist

The difficulties previously described derive from the project or management. Not all deals fail because of defects in the business proposal. Problems unique to the venture group account for some refusals (8 percent in the FSBIC sample). A review of these refusals highlights the following factors:

1. The deal is too small. A request for $30,000 requires as much investigation as one for $500,000. Because of the limited return possible on the minor investment, it will be classified as too small for consideration.
2. The use of proceeds is questionable in the eyes of the investor; for example, a large portion of the investment capital is to be used to advertise an untested product.
3. The venture group has a general dislike for the investment area: the company may be operating in a cyclical industry, or the company may be dependent on competitive bidding.
4. Too many problems need to be overcome. Some deals have so many intermediate steps that must be completed before the investment that it is not worth the effort required to put the deal together.

Inadequate Exposure to Sources of Venture Capital

The foreword to a recent government study best sums up the problem facing the entrepreneur seeking capital: "The authors and sponsors felt there was a need to remove some of the aura of 'black art' of mysticism from the entrepreneurial process, especially the financing aspects."[3] As

---

[3]Ibid, p. v.

Stanley Rubel states, "Many venture capitalists occupy unmarked offices, have unlisted telephones, and shun publicity."[4] The average entrepreneur will approach a banker, attorney, or CPA for assistance in locating venture capital. These professionals, even if they have worked in the past with a venture source, will usually have only one or two references for the entrepreneur. However, it has been estimated that over $3 billion is available from organized venture sources, and that 99.9 percent of the venture industry will never see any specific entrepreneur's proposal. The few venture references given the entrepreneur may well be inappropriate in that these sources will very likely not have an interest in the entrepreneur's industry or company's stage of development.

Thus far, the discussion has focused on the reasons entrepreneurs fail to get venture capital. The remainder of this chapter concentrates on the basics of how to launch a successful fund-raising effort.

DETERMINING THE COMPANY'S FINANCIAL NEEDS

To raise venture capital, one needs to know how much money is needed. Yet many entrepreneurs do not know the mechanics of estimating the financial needs of a company. Financial planning falls into two broad categories: planning for liquidity and planning for profit. Planning for liquidity centers in planning the company's cash flow. One element of the cash flow projection involves projecting the company's future sales and profits. The profit projection also has independent validity as a statement of future company income. It is the cash flow projection, supported by profit projections, that is of greatest use in determining the company's financial needs. Determining the cash needs for starting a business will be considered first, then the cash needs for an existing business.

Determining Cash Needs for Starting a Business

The cash needs for a starting venture may be projected in a number of ways. Kelley, Lawyer, and Baumback review several techniques for merchandising, manufacturing, and service businesses.[5] Three approaches are outlined for each type of business. The *desired income* ap-

---

[4]Stanley M. Rubel, *Guide to Venture Capital Sources,* Chicago: Capital Publishing Corporation, 1972–73, p. 8.
[5]Pearce Kelley, Kenneth Lawyer, and Clifford Baumback, *How to Organize and Operate a Small Business,* Englewood Cliffs, N.J.: Prentice-Hall, 1973, pp. 175–84.

proach develops the amount of capital needed to produce a given amount of annual personal income. The *rental rate* approach determines the amount of sales and then the capital needed to support an assumed rental. The *cash available* approach starts with an amount of capital assumed to be available to determine the probable income resulting from its efficient use.

A standard method is to project an expected sales level, its associated expenses, and additional funds needed for capital assets.[6] Several texts illustrate methods for sales projections.[7]

Assuming sales for the year of $200,000, the analysis shown in Table 6–1 can give a quick approximation of the amount of initial investment required for a typical merchandising store.

In reviewing this simplified approach for determining the capital needs to start a business, two major flaws become apparent. No account is taken of the extra demands for cash necessitated by the buildup of sales to the required level. Also, cash needs after the first several months are not dealt with, but are assumed as satisfied by normal cash flow from operations. This assumption can be fatal. The approach used by an existing business to determine cash flow helps solve these problems.

Determining Cash Needs for an Existing Business

For an existing business, full income statement, balance sheet, and cash flow projections are helpful to both management and the investor. Management benefits from the discipline of thinking through each element of the company's growth and its profit and cash impact. The exact financial needs of the company, given various assumptions, and the various potential sources to fill these needs are pinpointed. A surprising number of companies seek amounts of venture capital that cannot be justified by projected operations. Entrepreneur and investor can come to agreement only from disciplined planning. The investor benefits, since the sources and uses of cash are specified and the effect this cash infusion will have on the business can be estimated. Finally, the investor can test the reasonableness of the assumptions used in the projections.

There are various ways to project a company's cash needs.[8] Figures 6–1 through 6–5 present one helpful method. It is a six-step procedure outlined around a hypothetical company called Any Industries, Inc. The planning is for a six-month period for illustrative purposes. However, a

---

[6]This approach is used in the retail bookstore example of Chapter 5.

[7]See, for example, J. Fred Weston and Eugene F. Brigham, *Managerial Finance*, 5th edition, Hinsdale, Ill.: The Dryden Press, 1975, chapter 4.

[8]See Perry Mason, *"Cash Flow" Analysis and The Funds Statement*, Accounting Research Study, No. 2, American Institute of Certified Public Accountants, 1961.

TABLE 6–1. INITIAL INVESTMENT FOR A TYPICAL
MERCHANDISING STORE

	Investment Needed*
Operating expenses (one month)	
General and administrative	$ 500
Rent (2,000 sq. ft. at $0.30 per sq. ft.)	600
Selling	1,500
Payroll	1,800
Total	$4,400
Beginning inventory expenses	
$BI = \frac{S^*}{T}$ (CGS), where	
BI = beginning inventory,	
S = sales, $200,000 per yr. or $16,666 per mo.,	
T = turnover,3,	
CGS = Cost of goods sold, $0.50,	
$BI = \frac{16,666}{3}$ ($0.50) = $2,777.	
Total	$2,777
Down payment on fixtures and equipment	$4,000
Reserves	
One month inventory reorder	$2,777
Operating expenses, one month	4,400
Miscellaneous (10% of operating expenses)	440
	$7,617
Total initial investment	$18,794

company should prepare at least a three-year forecast, on a monthly basis for the first two years and quarterly for the third year. Footnotes should be used for each forecast category, keying that category to a backup sheet specifying the underlying assumptions and calculations. Any Industries, Inc., is assumed to be a manufacturer in the recreational field. It has just received several orders that will cause it to double its sales within the next six months. The company is reviewing the profit and cash impact of accepting these orders, knowing that a capital ex-

*Ratios of expenses to sales or actual expenses for various types of business may be obtained from *Financial Ratios*, Robert Morris & Associates, Research Department, Philadelphia National Bank Building, Philadelphia, Penn. 19107; various studies by the Small Business Administration; and Dun & Bradstreet, Industry Studies Department, New York, which publishes an annual report, *Key Business Ratios*.

penditure of $500,000 for equipment will have to be made to allow increased production.

Step 1. Prepare income statement projections (Figure 6–1). Sales were forecast on results projected by the sales force and validated by management, and with information on current backlog. The expected doubling in sales is the occasion for the current financial needs of Any Industries, Inc., both to finance the increased receivables and to purchase fixed assets necessary to handle the expanded sales.

Cost of goods sold before depreciation was assumed to equal 78 percent of sales but would decline to 74 percent of sales from volume efficiencies in purchasing and labor efficiencies from the new fixed assets. Depreciation was treated as a separate expense so that all noncash items could be properly segregated in the cash flow. Operating expenses were projected at 13 to 16 percent of sales. The results of the expansion for the six months would be revenues of $7,192,000 and net income of $287,000.

Step 2. Prepare work sheet for cash flow and balance sheet items (Figure 6–2). This work sheet provides the detail necessary to recast a monthly balance sheet based on changes in operations, and to assist in the preparation of the cash flow. In Figure 6–4, the pro forma balance sheet, cash is the first item to be updated. Cash is not treated in step 2 work sheets, since this figure is a result of the final cash flow. Thus, the first account updated was accounts receivable. Receivables were calculated as if collected within 60 days and were updated as shown in the work sheet. The inventory update is also self-explanatory. In updating accounts payable, note that Any Industries, Inc., purchased $500,000 of fixed assets in November and December in increments of $250,000. These assets were originally financed by increases in accounts payable. However, it was assumed that payment would have to be made within 30 days, thus giving rise to a cash need. Other payables were assumed paid in 60 days. The ending balances for each account are then used in the monthly balance sheet updates and cash flow projections.

Step 3. Prepare cash flow projection (Figure 6–3). This step is the heart of the planning operation. For Any Industries, Inc., new debt or equity requirements will be determined by the cumulative cash needs from this projection. Inflows from operations and from balance sheet changes are accumulated and offset against operational and balance sheet outflows. Operational flows are taken from the income statement projections shown in Figure 6–1. Notice that noncash outflows are not used. Thus, cost of goods sold is taken from the income statement before depreciation. For balance sheet flows, recall that an increase in an asset from one period to the next represents a use of cash and thus an outflow. A decrease in an asset represents a conversion of an asset to cash and thus an inflow. Similarly, an increase in a liability represents a source of cash; a decrease, a use of cash.

Any Industries, Inc.

	(1) Sept.	(2) Oct.	(3) Nov.	(4) Dec.	(5) Jan.	(6) Feb.	(7) Totals
Net sales	$705	$1,079	$1,184	$1,304	$1,420	$1,500	$7,192
Cost of goods sold							
Material	219	338	361	398	428	445	2,189
Labor	244	375	401	443	477	498	2,438
Factory overhead	86	131	140	154	165	173	849
Subtotal	549	844	902	995	1,070	1,116	5,476
Depreciation	8	8	8	11	14	14	63
Total cost of goods sold	557	852	910	1,006	1,084	1,130	5,539
Gross margin	148	227	274	298	336	370	1,653
Operating expenses	108	150	191	197	198	202	1,046
Interest	5	5	5	5	5	5	30
Profit before income taxes	35	72	78	96	133	163	577
Income taxes at 50%	18	36	39	48	67	82	290
Net profit after taxes	17	36	39	48	66	81	287

FIGURE 6-1. Income Statement Projections (in $1,000s)

Any Industries, Inc.

Pro Forma Balance Sheet Detail (in $1,000s)	(1) Sept.	(2) Oct.	(3) Nov.	(4) Dec.	(5) Jan.	(6) Feb.
Accounts receivable detail						
Beginning receivable balance	$1,090	$1,145	$1,524	$2,003	$2,228	$2,468
Add: Sales	705	1,079	1,184	1,304	1,420	1,500
Deduct: Cash receipts	650	700	705	1,079	1,180	1,300
Ending receivable balance	1,145	1,524	2,003	2,228	2,468	2,668
Change from beginning to ending	55	379	479	225	240	200
Inventory flow/cost of goods sold						
Beginning inventory	1,112	1,453	1,515	1,658	1,763	1,869
Add:						
Material purchases	360	380	452	484	521	562
Direct labor	390	385	440	458	485	525
Factory overhead	140	141	153	158	170	185
Subtotal	2,002	2,359	2,560	2,758	2,939	3,141
Deduct:						
Material used	219	338	361	398	428	445
Direct labor used	244	375	401	443	477	498
Factory overhead used	86	131	140	154	165	173
Subtotal (cost of goods sold)	549	844	902	995	1,070	1,116
Ending inventory	1,453	1,515	1,654	1,763	1,869	2,025
Change from beginning to ending	341	62	143	105	106	156
Accounts payable detail						
Beginning payable balance	$1,492	$1,643	$1,741	$2,170	$2,386	$2,225
Add:						
Material purchases	360	380	452	484	521	562
Factory overhead*	128	128	135	139	147	160
Interest & operating expenses*	73	110	132	136	140	144
Capital equipment items	—	—	250	250	—	—
Deduct:						
Cash disbursements	410	520	540	793	969	810
Ending accounts payable balance	1,643	1,741	2,170	2,386	2,225	2,281
Change from beginning to ending	151	98	429	216	(161)	56

FIGURE 6-2. Work Sheet for Cash Flow and Balance Sheet Items

*These figures exclude payroll, since this expense is assumed to be made by cash payments in the month incurred.

Any Industries, Inc.

	Sept.	Oct.	Nov.	Dec.	Jan.	Feb.
Inflows						
Sales	$ 705	$1,079	$1,184	$1,304	$1,420	$1,500
Increase in accounts payable	151	98	429	216	—	56
Increase in debt & equity		to be determined by viewing cumulative cash (needs)				
Total inflows	856	1,177	1,613	1,520	1,420	1,556
Outflows						
Cost of goods sold (less depreciation)	$ 549	$ 844	$ 902	$ 995	$1,070	$1,116
Other expenses	113	155	196	202	203	207
Taxes	18	36	39	48	67	82
Increase in accounts receivable	55	379	479	225	240	200
Increase in inventory	341	62	143	105	106	156
Decrease in accounts payable	—	—	—	—	—	—
Increase in capital expenditures	—	—	250	250	161	—
Principal repayments on debt	—	—	—	—	—	—
Dividends	—	—	—	—	—	—
Total outflows	1,076	1,476	2,009	1,825	1,847	1,761
Net change in cash						
Inflows less outflows	($ 220)	($ 299)	($ 396)	($ 305)	($ 427)	($ 205)
Add: Beginning cash	25	(195)	(494)	(890)	(1,195)	(1,622)
Cumulative cash (needs)	(195)	(494)	(890)	(1,195)	(1,622)	(1,827)

FIGURE 6-3. Cash Flow Projections (in $1,000s)

Finally, outflows are netted against inflows to arrive at a cumulative cash balance. Thus, $1,505,000 cumulative need in February represents the company's greatest need for outside cash to finance its coming expansion. It is this amount that the company will work with in step 6 in determining sources of new funds to supply the needed cash.

Step 4. Prepare balance sheet projections (Figure 6–4). Starting with the company's current balance sheet (Figure 6–4, column 1 *Balance at Prior Month*) various adjustments are made from the work sheet. *Notes payable* and *capital stock* were assumed to remain unchanged. The balance sheet projection plays an important role in allowing management to check the reasonableness of various assumptions, as reviewed below.

Step 5. Prepare summary sheet for cash needs and uses (Figure 6–5). In order to approach an investor successfully, management must specify the uses for the cash to be invested. The method advocated here allows management to pinpoint these uses. In step 5, cash from operations is added as a source. Noncash deductions from operational results such as depreciation are added back. The sources and uses of cash are aggregated from the balance sheet by determining the change in each account, from the current balance (Figure 6–5, column 1, *balance at prior month*) to the period end balance (Figure 6–5, column 7). The net cumulative cash required is then totaled, $1,852,000. Aside from the amount needed, management can specify the uses directly. Of the total $2,991,000 uses of cash, $1,578,000 will be used to support increased accounts receivable, $913,000 for increased inventory, and $500,000 for fixed asset expenditures.

Step 6. Determine portion of total cash needs to be financed by venture capital. Any Industries, Inc., had never used accounts receivable financing. Upon consultation with a bank officer, management was informed that because of the rapid increase of new accounts, many of a marginal credit nature, the bank would finance only 45 percent of the company's accounts receivables, to a maximum of $1,100,000. The bank informed the company that it would finance $100,000 of its new fixed asset needs of $500,000 on a long-term note. This combination of $1,200,000 of new bank debt was the limit for bank-supplied funds.

Further, this new debt, when combined with the company's existing notes payable of $600,000, gave the company a debt-to-equity ratio of two to one. Although the bank was willing to lend on this ratio, it recommended an increase of the company's equity (or subordinate debt) to provide a cushion against unexpected cash needs resulting from the rapid increase in company volume. The company therefore decided to seek $650,000 in venture capital to supply the difference between bank-supplied financing and its cash needs, and further to seek these funds either as equity or subordinate long-term debt.

It would be helpful to review the advantages of the six-step procedure at this point. Through this procedure, management and the investor can

Any Industries, Inc.

	(1) Balance at Prior Month	(2) Sept.	(3) Oct.	(4) Nov.	(5) Dec.	(6) Jan.	(7) Feb.
Assets							
Cash	$ 25	($ 195)	($ 494)	($ 890)	($1,195)	($1,622)	($1,827)
Accounts receivable	1,090	1,145	1,524	2,003	2,228	2,468	2,668
Inventory	1,112	1,453	1,515	1,658	1,763	1,869	2,025
Fixed assets—net	522	514	506	748	987	973	959
Total assets	2,749	2,917	3,051	3,519	3,783	3,688	3,825
Liabilities & Net Worth							
Accounts payable	$1,492	$1,643	$1,741	$2,170	$2,386	$2,225	$2,281
Notes payable	600	600	600	600	600	600	600
New debt/equity	—	—	—	—	—	—	—
Capital stock	500	500	500	500	500	500	500
Retained earnings	157	174	210	249	297	363	444
Total liabilities & net worth	2,749	2,917	3,051	3,519	3,783	3,688	3,825

FIGURE 6–4. Pro Forma Balance Sheet (in $1,000s)

Any Industries Inc.

	Source	Use
Cash from operations	$ 287	$ —
Add back noncash deductions (depreciation)	63	—
Increase in accounts receivable	—	1,578
Increase in inventory	—	913
Increase in capital equipment	—	500
Increase in accounts payable	789	—
Add beginning cash	25	—
	$1,164	$2,991
New cash needs		$1,827

FIGURE 6–5. Summary Sheet for Cash Uses (in $1,000s)

understand what factors give rise to the cash needs, since specific uses are highlighted. Because the uses are tied to the balance sheet and income statement, different outside sources of financing can be considered in the light of the company's ability to handle various types of debt. The investor is able to check the reasonableness of the assumptions used in the forecast and can determine and question the projected growth rate in sales, assumptions about various expenses as a percentage of sales, aging of receivables and payables, working capital, and debt-to-equity ratios. As an example, the investor may question whether accounts payable can increase $789,000 as shown in Figure 6–5. If this increase is not reasonable, a greater amount than $1,852,000 may be needed. As the balance sheet (Figure 6–4) shows, accounts payable (column 1, *balance at prior month*) is 81 days of that month's annualized cost of goods sold (see Figure 6–1). At the end of the six-month period it has been reduced to 60 days. Thus, instead of the $789,000 increase being an unreasonable expansion, it represents an improved position, probably consistent with a bank's requirement for an accounts receivable loan.

PREPARING THE PRIVATE PLACEMENT MEMORANDUM

Having determined the company's investment needs, the entrepreneur should prepare a written presentation designed to do two things— interest an investor in exploring the investment opportunity and give the investor sufficient information to gain an initial understanding of the company. The private placement memorandum is the typical document used for these purposes.

A private placement solicitation for funds is one in which a security such as stock, warrants, or a convertible debenture is offered for value. The private placement is exempted from legal registration requirements if the offer is confined to sophisticated investors. Although an attorney should be consulted about individuals who may be safely approached, all venture institutions qualify legally as sophisticated investors.

The entrepreneur should consider the competing roles inherent in this presentation document. It is a selling document; it embodies the corporate business plan and thus is a document supposedly representing reality; and it is also a legal document. It is a legal document in that it is the basis for the investor's decision. Charges of fraud and security violations can arise from misleading statements or omissions in this document. The following outline should be reviewed with these several, and sometimes competing, needs in mind.

Outline for Private Placement Memorandum*

Investment Highlights

This section presents those essential facts designed to interest the investor in continuing to read. It is similar to the highlights one might give in introducing the situation over the telephone when quick *yes* or *no* decisions are made. Table 6–2, p. 170, illustrates a typical summary of investment highlights based upon a successful memorandum prepared by a manufacturer in the recreational vehicle field.

Summary of the Company

- Description of products or services and company's function (manufacturer, retailer, wholesaler, or other).
- Significant company history.
- Capsule statement of financial history and operating statistics.
- Statement of company goals.

The Offer

- Amount of money needed, timing, and use of proceeds.
- Proposed structure of the deal:
  If convertible debt, assumed interest rate, term of loan, availability of collateral, subordination assumptions, and terms of conversion (see *If equity,* following).
  If equity, number of shares, price per share given for the proceeds, and the percentage to the total shares outstanding this represents.

---

*The information given to potential investors can be presented in various formats. The outline for a prospectus for a new business given in Figure 5–1, Chapter 5, suggests one such format. The outline for a private placement memorandum given here focuses on the needs of an ongoing company for an infusion of capital to support rapid growth.

If a starting business, investment contribution from entrepreneur toward total capital needs.

- Range of potential returns to investor.
  Range of projected net income.
  Reasonable multiple range to assume in a public offering.
  Range of rates of return on the investor's capital based on valuation of company, investor's percentage of ownership, and timing of investment and returns. (See sections on Structuring the Deal and Rate of Return Method, below.)

Business

- Company organization
  Legal structure
  Organization of functional units (for example, administration, production, R and D, etc.) with key management noted.
- Company history
- Principal products or services—include sales analysis for several years, special competitive advantages and protections, and underlying factors influencing demand. Where technical in nature, describe uses for product or service.
- Marketing methods
  General description of marketing methods, including effort of company sales personnel, advertising methods, pricing, types of buyers.
  Principal distributors.
  Principal customers.
- Competition
  Structure of industry (for example, fragmented competition among many "mom and pop" stores accounting for 75 percent of the volume).
  Direct and indirect competitors (for example, direct competition, as between Hertz Rent-A-Car and Avis; indirect, as between airlines and buses).
  Nature of competitive practices within industry in pricing, quality, location, advertising, services, and other key items.
- Industry
  Sales and profit record, if available, for industry for the last three years.
  Growth prospects and projections for industry.
  Technological, marketing, or other trends that might advantageously or adversely affect subject's business.
- Production and facilities
  Production methods.
  Problem areas in the production cycle.
  Quality control and reject level experience for principal products.
  Facilities and capacities.
  Breakdown of fixed versus variable production costs.

Management

- Resumés of key managers.
- Remuneration of key managers and copies of employment contracts, if any.

- Number of employees in each functional area.
- Stock option arrangements for key managers.

Principal Stockholders

- Number of shares and percentage of ownership.

Financial Statements

- Sales/net income summary for last five years, including breakdown of cost of goods, selling, general and administrative expenses; balance sheet and income statement for last fiscal year, plus interim statements.
- Summary of sales backlog and comparison to prior year or years.
- Aging of accounts receivable and payable.
- Explain unusual fluctuations in both income statement and balance sheet accounts.

Financial Projections

(See previous discussion on Determining the Company's Financial Needs.)
- General factors concerning industry.
- Specific factors concerning company, including any litigation company is involved in and any known health problems of managers. This section is included at the end of the memorandum as sound marketing practice in making this kind of presentation.

  Unless some aspect of the presentation catches the interest of investors quickly, they may tend to screen the deal by looking for the negative aspects. After having uncovered one or more significant negative aspects, they may hurriedly complete the review. It is to the advantage of the entrepreneur to lead with strong points. If these have merit, investors, when encountering negative aspects, may be in a positive frame of mind, now interested in discovering factors that outweigh these obstacles.

Miscellaneous

- Include names of principal accountants, attorneys, bank officers; special studies about company, and other pertinent data.

A good write-up will not hide mediocre company performance or business concept, but will highlight these problems more quickly for both the entrepreneur and the investor. Treating the reality of the company in an open and detailed way builds the investor's confidence. The outline given here is a checklist, not a prescription. Entrepreneurs should use ingenuity in designing the presentation to fit their needs. Photographs, product brochures, advertising copy, or other pictorial highlights, should be included to increase reader interest.

Having reviewed and avoided the common pitfalls in raising venture capital, determined financial needs, and prepared a private placement memorandum, the entrepreneur is now ready to locate sources of capital.

LOCATING SOURCES OF VENTURE CAPITAL

Before considering the sources of money, the entrepreneur should consider capital substitutes. Money has been viewed as the most flexible form of power, but its power to cause results can be achieved in other ways. A Los Angeles based company was formed by leveraging the expertise of several teachers who were interested in developing educational products for gifted children. The products' economic potential was not their primary motive. All worked without salary to develop products; they received instead stock in the company. Offering stock to key individuals in return for assistance is a traditional way to start a company.

In some cases barter can be a powerful resource. A start-up corporation in the process of purchasing two radio stations in the northern California area reduced its equity capital needs by trading advertising air time for various offices and furnishings.

Suppliers of raw materials may sometimes agree to be paid only after the finished product is sold. The Abbott-Lane Company of Portland, Oregon, a small firm that orginated etchedwood decorative wall panels, made such an arrangement with a major plywood producer. This major wood products manufacturer believed that the uniqueness and attractiveness of Abbott-Lane's product offered a new way to market their plywood. They agreed therefore to allow Abbott-Lane to order plywood by the carload from their mill, process it into etchedwood wall panels, and pay for the material after receipt of payment from the customer.

In another example a new recreational vehicle manufacturer was paid within three to ten days by its newly established dealers (the dealer was financed by its local bank with a "flooring" line). However, the manufacturer did not pay its suppliers until 120 days after delivery, on the average. At one point, the net 110 days of supplier credit represented over $600,000 of venture financing.

Sources of Financing

An entrepreneur has access to two categories of finances: personal and the public at large. Most ventures start from personal resources. In the mid-sixties a typical conglomerate was founded from the accumulated personal savings of two former management consultants when they purchased a small Los Angeles lawn sprinkler company. A multimillion dollar sales company was developed from this original purchase.

The entrepreneur's cash may well be the most significant, if not the only source, available to many starting ventures. Other personal resources include bank borrowings against collateral, borrowings against life insurance policies, or against the equity in a house. Boutiques, antique stores, beauty salons, and a myriad of businesses are financed from the personal resources and borrowings of the entrepreneur.

Friends and relatives can also be a personal source of financing. Their willingness to lend or invest lies in their knowledge of and confidence in the individual's experience, character, and capabilities. This knowledge reduces the risks of the unknown faced by outside investors.

The public at large represents another category for finances. As used in this context, it includes private placement investors, institutional sources, and individuals willing to invest in franchising and distributorships. Franchising and distributorships are valid and creative ways to harness the financial resources of individuals who share with the entrepreneur the desire to own a business. McDonald's has thousands of franchisees who have helped finance the company's expansion by purchasing an outlet. This type of financing is best applied when the company has something of value—a trade name or a patented product—to offer the franchisee and the franchisee has the capability to run a personally operated business successfully. Many books on the subject of franchising are available, as a check of any public library will show.

Many wealthy individuals desire to invest in starting ventures. The private placement is the vehicle used to locate and attract these potential investors. The Securities and Exchange Act of 1933 exempts private placements from registration requirements, and the SEC has formulated guidelines that qualify a private placement. In order to qualify, the placement must not be publicly advertised, the information supplied must be of the same quality as would appear in a registered prospectus, the number of actual investors must not exceed 35, and the investor must be able to afford the risk of the investment.

Locating wealthy individuals who may be attracted to invest in a venture is not easy. Individuals who have an interest or expertise in the functional area of the enterprise are candidates. American Tennis Ball Company, created in 1972 to manufacture and distribute machines to vend cans of tennis balls on public tennis courts, was initially financed in part by individuals who were interested in the game of tennis.

Reputable finders can be helpful. Finders make it their business to know many potential sources of investment capital, contacts built up over time. The company formed in 1971 to purchase two radio stations in northern California was financed by the board chairman of a large transportation company. A finder was aware of the investor's interest in broadcasting and arranged the introduction. Locating a finder of good reputation and quality might seem as difficult as locating the original source of capital. However, by inquiring of commercial loan bank officers, stockbrokers, institutional venture capital sources, and other service professionals who are involved with growing companies, a number of qualified referrals can be obtained.

Institutional Sources of Venture Capital

Significant sources of available money and diversity of investment interests have recently emerged with the advent of institutional venture capital. The first institutional sources were corporations and partnerships formed in the 1940s. Until 1958 only a handful existed. With the enactment of the Small Business Investment Act of 1958, a surge of venture capital company formations occurred as Small Business Investment Companies (SBICs). Currently there are over 300 SBICs and at least that number of additional non-SBIC venture companies.

SBICs range in size from $150,000 paid-in capital to larger companies with over $40 million in assets. By law, SBICs can invest in only "small businesses" that have assets not in excess of $7.5 million, a net worth not exceeding $2.5 million, and average net income over the previous two years not exceeding $250,000, these rules subject to various exemptions. Of course, non-SBIC sources have a much wider range of self-imposed limitations.

All SBICs are readily identifiable at any Small Business Administration office. The National Association of Small Business Investment Companies, 512 Washington Building, Washington, D.C., 20005, publishes a membership directory of SBIC members including over 200 SBICs and MESBICs (Minority Enterprise SBIC), representing approximately 85 percent of the industry's resources.

Several active associations of venture capitalists have been formed in the United States. The membership lists of these groups list localized sources for venture capital.[9]

Several excellent books have been published that discuss both non-SBICs and SBICs.[10] *Venture Capital*, published by Technimetrics, Inc., 919

---

[9]Typical venture capital associations are the Western Association of Venture Capital Companies in San Francisco at 244 California Street, Suite 500, San Francisco, Calif. 94111; and the Pacific Southwest Association of SBICs, Association Secretary at 333 South Hope Street, Los Angeles, Calif. 90017.

[10]See, for example, Stanley M. Rubel, *Guide to Venture Capital Sources*, 4th edition, Chicago: Capital Publishing Corporation, 1977; James M. Johnson, *Johnson's Directory of Risk Capital for Small Business*, Kalamazoo: Business Research and Service Institute, Western Michigan University, 1976; John R. Dominguez, *Venture Capital*, Lexington: Lexington Books, 1974; Leroy W. Sinclair, ed., *Venture Capital*, New York: Technimetrics, 1971; Albert J. Kelley, Frank B. Campanella, and John M. McKiernan, *Venture Capital, A Guidebook for New Enterprises*, Chestnut Hill: The Management Institute, Boston College, 1971.

Third Avenue, New York, N.Y., 10022, lists over four hundred venture companies with a brief description of whom to contact, preferred areas for investment, approximate range of financings, special help provided to the company, and some examples of recent investments. *Venture Capital, A Guidebook for New Enterprises,* published by The Management Institute, Boston College, covers ninety-nine venture firms in the New England and New York area. It includes whom to contact, general information about the company, and individual investment approaches. Another comprehensive book is *Guide to Venture Capital Sources,* Stanley M. Rubel, published by Capital Publishing Corporation, 10 South LaSalle Street, Chicago, Ill., 60603. Over six hundred firms are listed geographically. Preferred investment limits and areas are listed as well as an extensive bibliography of articles, books, and published studies about venture capital. This book is recommended to the serious fund seeker.

Corporations as a Source of Financing

Many operating corporations make venture investments for a variety of reasons, such as gaining access to emerging technologies, assisting in corporate diversification plans, or providing the potential for a high return on investment. Corporations active as investors at various times include Hercules, Borden, Dow Chemical Company, Singer Company, ALCOA, Boise Cascade Corporation, Coca-Cola, DuPont, Ford Motor Company, General Electric Company, International Paper Company, Mobil Oil Corporation, Standard Oil Company, General Mills, and Union Carbide Corporation, to name a few.

Corporations as a source are hard to categorize, since some corporations that have gained a reputation for venturing in the past are no longer active, and many more are not visible as venture sources but will venture if an appropriate deal is shown to them. A rule of thumb may be useful in this area—the entrepreneur should approach those corporations that could logically benefit from the venture. But the entrepreneur should be cautioned that ultimate acquisition of the venture may be a goal of the corporation.

An Emerging Source of Venture Capital

A new source of quasi-venture capital may be emerging under the auspices of the SBA. Small businesses not qualifying for conventional long-term bank financing can seek an SBA guaranteed loan. This is a regular loan funded by a bank, but guaranteed by the SBA. The company has to fall within the SBA's definition of a small business. Roughly, the company would be eligible to be considered if it was in a retailing or service business that had less than $1,000,000 in sales for the last fiscal year, or, if in wholesaling or manufacturing, less than $5,000,000 or less than 250 employees (manufacturing only). The business must not be in a prohibited area such as the sale of alcoholic beverages. Based on the SBA's analysis and bank's recommendation, the SBA will guarantee up to $500,000, requiring the bank to risk at least 10 percent of the funding, for a total availability of $550,000. The bank can fund a greater amount, but its percentage guarantee would be less.

Many smaller banks aggressively seeking the smaller corporate accounts are using this program. Those actively participating can be determined by consulting a local or regional SBA office.

Investor Preferences

Locating sources of venture capital in itself is not enough, since all sources will have investment preferences and dislikes. It is important to know at what stage of company development the venture capital company will invest. The process can be put in context by examining the stages of corporate development as delineated in *Venture Capital, A Guidebook for New Enterprise*.[11]

Stage zero—Usually at Stage zero some monies (usually the principal's own) have been invested, a great deal of effort (on a part-time basis) has been expended, a prototype may have been developed. Or, on the other hand, it is possible that only the time and effort required to organize and plan for the new enterprise have been expended prior to entering Stage I.

Stage I—Is the start-up phase. It is during this period that the operation is formalized and the product or service is developed and produced. This start is made with seed capital, which can come from a number of diverse sources.

Stage II—Occurs when the company has built up a bit of a track record. It has moved through the initial growth phase and some of the conventional techniques of investment analysis can be applied to it. At this point also, the company has developed capital equipment and can begin to plan for long-term growth.

Stage III—Further expansion is warranted due to favorable indications regarding the company's potential. The quantities of funds required are much greater than those raised in the earlier stages and the early investors are seeking both realized gains and liquidity. It is at this point that the public equity offering is usually

---

[11]Albert J. Kelly, Frank B. Campanella, John M. McKiernan, *Venture Capital, A Guidebook for New Enterprises*, Chestnut Hill: The Management Institute, Boston College, 1971, pp. 30–31.

made for the dual purpose of raising additional funds for the company (primary offering) and enabling the initial investors to realize a gain by selling a portion of their shares (secondary offering).

Stage IV—The mature company has established itself and become a viable corporation.

The entrepreneur should approach venture capitalists who have a preference for the kind of business the company is in. Most of the guides to venture capital sources indicate the industry preferences of the listed venture capital companies.

In further determining a venture group's characteristics, their preferred investment amounts should be identified, as well as possible maximums and minimums.

The entrepreneur should cautiously screen venture sources with respect to their preferred limits for investment. Clearly a request for $3,000,000 would find little likelihood of success among investors whose preferred investments are in the range between $500,000 and $1,000,000. One typical SBIC is a good example. It has a house limit of investing up to $1,000,000 in any one deal. However, if a $2,000,000 request is made by a company in which it desires to invest, it will syndicate the remaining $1,000,000, at no cost, among interested institutional colleagues.

The liquidity of the venture group at the time of inquiry will influence its interest in the deal. The entrepreneur will have to determine this factor through inquiry of each venture firm.

Finally, many venture firms have developed an expertise in one or more functional areas such as high technology, retailing, or the construction industry. This understanding of an area can be invaluable. Lack of knowledge about an area tends to increase perceptions of risk. A venture capitalist familiar with the industry and its key factors will be more likely to accede to a strong contender's financial request. If the venture capitalist has investments in businesses similar to the one for which funds are being sought, it indicates interest in the industry.

Once a number of appropriate sources have been identified, the entrepreneur encounters the critical procedure of dealing with the venture capitalist.

DEALING WITH THE VENTURE CAPITALIST

Dealing with the venture capitalist involves four steps:

- making the initial contact
- analyzing the deal
- structuring the deal
- continuing relationships

Making the Initial Contact

Having located the names of likely sources of venture capital, the entrepreneur may ask: What is the best approach for introduction—initial contact by the entrepreneur or contact through an accountant, lawyer, finder, investment banker, or other person who knows "who to talk to" in any given firm? This dilemma recalls a story told by Jerry Perenchio, promoter of the Bobby Riggs–Billy Jean King "Battle of the Sexes" tennis tournament. Asked how he had contacted Bobby Riggs in the promotion, Jerry responded by saying he had contacted a mutual friend to make the introductions, promising to pay a $10,000 finder's fee. After the tournament, when computing expenses to be offset against participants' share of income, Riggs noticed the fee to the friend. Asked what it was for, Jerry said he had paid the friend for the introduction. With real shock on his face Riggs exclaimed, "Jerry, I'm listed in the phone book!" In many instances the benefit of an introduction is not worth the price. Value usually comes from locating sources of capital one would not otherwise have been aware of, or from assistance in preparing a presentation. Once the overtures have been made, an investor will consider the merits of the proposal regardless of who introduced the deal.

The entrepreneur with an ongoing business often seeks an initial meeting "at the plant" before submitting a written proposal. The entrepreneur is wise to push for such a meeting. Initial enthusiasm for the management team and a first-hand feeling for the results embodied in the financial statements may cause the investor to proceed further in the investigation. The investor will not make plant visits on every inquiry. Acceptance of an invitation to visit the plant generally depends on the investor's interest in a few key items such as product area, results to date, backlog, or other strengths of the proposal.

There are several reasons for and against approaching a number of venture capital sources at the same time. To increase the chances of funding, the entrepreneur should not initially rely on any one source. The investor sees a large number of proposals and tends to defer many deals. Knowledge of being in competition, within reasonable bounds, may increase the chances that the investor will give the proposal early consideration. Although most investors will not willingly become involved in a bidding contest over a deal, the entrepreneur can benefit from having several different offers to choose among. Finally, the existence of a lead investor many times facilitates the securing of the total amount sought. Fairness demands that the venturer be told that other sources are being considered when that is the case.

The risks of "shopping" a deal vary. Depending on the deal and the sources being consulted, the investor may wish to await the results of their analyses before proceeding. Management also runs the risk of lack of investor enthusiasm if a deal may be made by a competing venture capital source. The investor is not inclined to spend investigatory time where there is little hope for making a deal.

Once investors have reached the point of being reasonably satisfied that they will make an investment, they may require a commitment fee to help assure good faith in the negotiations. A typical arrangement would be for the investor to provide the company a letter of conditional intent to invest, subject to certain verifications and analysis, in return for a fee of 1 percent of the funds sought. If the investor later decides not to fund, the fee is returned in full. However, if the investor later makes an unconditional offer and it is refused by the entrepreneur, the fee is forfeited.

Analyzing the Deal

Most venture capital investors have a strong aversion to risk. Their screening and analytic procedure is designed to minimize two types of risks: 1) risk of the unknown that can cause loss of capital, and 2) risk of loss of time spent on unproductive projects.

Risk of the unknown is both the risk of not perceiving those key elements for success in a business and the risk of not knowing the outcome of events on issues raised. The investor can control the risk of not knowing key factors for success and related issues by learning about the people, the company, and the industry. The risk of unknown outcomes from future events can be lessened only through contingent planning by capable management.

Counterbalancing the need for extensive education is the risk that the investor may spend an inordinate amount of time investigating a deal that may not be consummated. This risk of time lost on unproductive projects impels the investor to become knowledgeable quickly through screening out much information not considered immediately valuable. The screening and analysis procedures described below are often used by the institutional investor to acquire relevant information quickly.

Conducting the Initial Screening Much of the intial screening is done on an informal basis. A telephone conversation will eliminate a large number of requests. Of those resulting in submission of a proposal, only a handful will intrigue the venture capitalist enough for the next stage of review.

Conducting the Secondary Screening When the venture capitalist has become convinced that a fairly extensive investigation is warranted, an initial meeting with the management team will occur, either at the plant or in the venture capitalist's office. Extensive details will be requested covering the topics outlined in the section on Preparing the Private

Placement Memorandum, page 155. Back-up documents will be sought to verify key elements of the proposal. Further information requested may include:

- home address and social security number of managers for the purpose of credit checks
- names and phone numbers of former employers for reference checks
- list of customers and creditors for reference checks
- research reports on the industry
- prospectuses and annual reports of competitors
- internal control reports from auditors
- IRS reports on any tax audits

In short, the secondary screening process involves gathering and verifying information so that the investor can feel comfortable about making an offer.

Conducting the Final Analysis If there is a meeting of minds on both the proposal and the structure of the deal (to be discussed in the next section), the final analysis ensues. In this analysis, the investor completes the verifications started in the secondary process, gathers final documents such as certified statements to replace ones prepared by management, and has the needed legal documents prepared. If the venture group is an institutional one requiring board approval, a final write-up would be submitted to the board for approval.

A certain amount of irrationality exists in the process. Personality conflicts between the investor and entrepreneur can cause rejection of an otherwise good venture. If the venture organization is large, the personal dislikes of one investor may cause the premature rejection of a proposal that might have fared better had another individual been approached. (Venture capital firms can avoid this outcome by several means, including distributing a summary control sheet listing the characteristics of all company proposals and the reasons for rejection, so that all staff members can check the screening process and call for a review of the specific reasons for rejection.)

Structuring the Deal

At some point the venture capitalist will have made a decision that if the company and management check out, if the problem areas uncovered can be corrected, and if no unforeseen problems arise, negotiations toward structuring the deal can begin. This process will usually start before the intensive analysis is much under way, since failure to reach agreement on basic terms will stop negotiations before management and the venture capitalist waste inordinate amounts of time.

At this point, factors such as the amount of investment, the form of investment vehicle, required controls, the amount of stock required, and pricing will be negotiated.

Most venture sources have a ceiling on the amount they will invest in any one company. If the company's request exceeds this ceiling and analysis demonstrates that a smaller amount will not suffice, the venture group must decide whether or not to syndicate the deal to other venture groups. This decision is based on the venture group's willingness to spend the time and effort to syndicate the deal (usually at no charge to the company), participate as part of a group, and assume partial responsibilities for analysis and follow-up. The company must decide whether the venture firm is strong enough to attract other partners. The company must be concerned with the extra time and resources it now needs to bring several different groups to agree to invest. In some instances a syndicate will be to the company's advantage if the presence of several well-respected venture groups helps bring in other groups. On the other hand, flexibility in negotiating price is lost, since interested venture groups will join on the basis of the lead investor's structure of the deal.

Often the venture group's analysis demonstrates that either more or less money than the amount requested is needed. Occasionally a company will request an amount from a venture source that can be satisfied by working collaboratively with less expensive sources. For instance, working with a bank-related SBIC gives the SBIC flexibility in recommending that some portion of the total request be satisfied by conventional bank debt with the SBIC providing the subordinated debt or equity base.

The form of investment preferred by many venture capitalists is the convertible debenture. A debenture is a debt instrument containing protective provisions but usually without a specific lien on any asset. Conversion features provide that some or all of the debenture may be converted into some number of shares at given conversion price. A nonconvertible debenture with attached warrants can also provide the equity needed, but suffers in that the time period for freely trading the underlying stock under Rule 144 (SEC Act 1933) does not start running until the warrant is exercised.

The advantages to the venture capitalist of using a convertible debenture are many, including the ability to build in controls, tailor the amount of equity and pricing on a flexible basis, allow for protection against dilution, give registration rights, and provide for the return of invested capital.

If the company is a start-up, a pure equity investment in common stock might be more advantageous, since no cash drain occurs for interest payments or debt amortization, and the equity base can be used for leverage to secure bank debt. However, the convertible debenture can be tailored to accomplish these goals through arrangements for a suspension of interest and payments on debt during the early critical periods, long pay-out terms, and full subordination to bank debt.

A minority shareholder has little leverage to influence management if the business starts to have significant problems. However, by structuring the investment in the form of a debenture, the investor can include those restrictions necessary to safeguard the investment. Typical restrictions might include one or more of the following:

- maintenance of a minimum net worth
- restrictions on dividend payments
- restrictions on acquisition of fixed assets
- restrictions on certain types of expenses, such as research and development
- restrictions on mergers or acquisitions
- provisions to limit salaries and benefits paid top management
- restrictions on further pledges of assets as collateral.

These restrictions are incorporated in the debenture in various forms.

Determining the amount of stock to be exchanged or converted for the financing and its price hinges on expectations of return and risk. The procedures described below may be used to determine the amount of ownership and pricing of stock to structure an attractive offer.

Method 1—Price/Earnings Multiple Method First, compare the company to similar public companies. Such comparison should be conducted on the basis of similarity of balance sheet ratios, income statement margins and levels of expense, share of market served, gross sales per employee, assets per employee, asset turnover, and other generally accepted measures of efficiency. Then determine a comparable price to earnings ratio (P/E), assuming that a 25 to 50 percent discount should be given for letter stock. Apply this adjusted multiple to current earnings per share and divide the resulting stock price into the amount of funds sought to detemine the number of shares to be issued. A comparison of this number of shares to the new total of shares outstanding (current outstanding plus this new amount to be issued to the investor) will show the percentage of the company that must be negotiated.

Method 2—Rate of Return Method Estimate the rate of return range required. Most investors seek a 25 to 80+ percent compound rate of return depending upon the riskiness of the company.

Translate the desired return into the amount of ownership required by one of two ways: use an actual rate of return range method; or use a factor of return method. The following illustrate the mechanics of determining ownership by these two methods.

Example 1—Rate of Return Range. Table 6–2 illustrates this method, as well as other principles used in pricing a deal. In this example a com-

TABLE 6–2. DEAL PRICING WORK SHEET (IN $1,000s)

	(1)	(2)	(3)	(4)	(5)	(6)	(7)	(8)	(9)	(10)
	% of Forecast	NPAT*	P/E†	Total Company Value	Investor Ownership (%)	No. of Shares to Investor	Cost of Conversion	Investor's Share of Total Value	Total Investor Return	ROI (%)
Net profit after taxes with $ one million	100	1,525	15	22,875	8	69,565	800	1,830	2,030	43
Net profit after taxes without $ one million	100	1,000	12	12,000	—	—	—	—	—	—

*Net profit after taxes.
†Price to earnings ratio.

pany requested $1,000,000 long term debt at 10 percent interest. The company was agreeable to a convertible debenture but would look to the investor for guidance in establishing the amount of equity at conversion and the conversion price to make it an attractive investment. After studying the company and its management, the investor judged that a return between 35 and 50 percent would be acceptable in relation to risks assumed. Another assumption was that the company would reach the position for a public offering within two years. The investor would charge a 10 percent interest, a rate above the then prime rate. Because interest rates were considered high at 10 percent, the investor believed that any portion of the remaining debt after cost of conversion would very likely be repaid, either from the proceeds of underwriting or from refinancing at a lower interest rate. The investor had requested that management prepare an income statement forecast for each of the next two years, both with the effect of the $1,000,000 financing and without its effect.

An investor might utilize a work sheet such as that shown in Table 6–2 to assist in structuring a conversion amount and price as follows. First, the investor must either reforecast net profit after tax (NPAT) based on assumptions he feels more comfortable with, or accept those given by management. Here NPAT the second year is of key concern, since it is this year the company is aiming for a public offering. Column 2, row 1 shows forecasted income of $1,525,000 with the use of $1,000,000 debenture capital (and possibly additional bank leverage because of the subordination of the debenture to bank debt). Next the investor used a best guess as to a multiple the company could expect, here 15 times earnings as in column 3, row 1. Multiplying total earnings times the multiple gives the company's valuation of $22,875,000, column 4, row 1. The investor had been advised that management would not accept dilution above 15 percent. Backing away from this percentage, an 8 percent interest to the investor was tried to see its effect on the investor's return on investment. It is assumed that 800,000 shares are outstanding. The investor must divide the shares outstanding (800,000) by 92 percent to find out the new total of shares of which he will receive 8 percent. Column 6, row 1 shows that the investor will receive 69,565 shares representing 8 percent of the new total shares after the dilution (800,000/0.92 = 869,565, therefore 0.08 = 69,565).

Next the cost of conversion must be determined. Not yet knowing the rate of return from owning 8 percent of the market value of the company, the investor can choose a cost of conversion somewhat at will to see the combined effect of number of shares and return of debt (corollary to cost of conversion) on his total return on investment. Here an $800,000 cost of conversion (column 7, row 1) is chosen for the 8 percent $11.50 per share).

At this point the investor can determine the rate of return. Column 8, row 1 shows a return of $1,830,000 for the 8 percent share of the total value of $22,875,000. Adding the return of $200,000 debt, the investor's total return is $2,030,000, column 9, row 1. Using present value tables or other convenient means[12] to determine the rate of return as 42.5 or approximately 43 percent. Note that interest earned at 10 percent was excluded from returns, since the investor's cost of capital and administration just about negate this return.

The 43 percent return is well within the range acceptable to the investor. However, the investor will probably apply various other tests to determine whether the share number and cost are acceptable. The investor might ask what value the company must reach for the investor to break even on an 8 percent investment. By dividing the $800,000 cost of conversion by the 8 percent interest to be received, the investor can determine that the company must reach a value of at least approximately $10,000,000 for an 8 percent interest to return $800,000. A variety of

---

[12]The formula to determine compound rate of return is

$$0 = I - \frac{R_1}{(1 + r_1)^1} + \ldots + \frac{R_n}{(1 + r_n)^n}$$

where
R = return in relevant time period,
r = ROI,
n = number of time periods, starting with 1 and progressing by units to last period,
I = initial outlay.
To use this formula, an r is estimated as probably being the true rate of return and used in the formula. If the result is not zero, r is re-estimated and the formula reworked till the result approaches zero; for example,

$$0 = \$1,000,000 - \frac{0}{(1.43)^1} + \frac{2,030,000}{(1.43)^2}$$

lesser net income or multiples than assumed in the example yielding a $22,875,000 value will produce a market value of $10,000,000, all of which may be highly attainable by the company if problems do not occur. The company's current net worth can be matched against this $10,000,000 value to gauge how close to this value the company already is, just in current net worth.

Another test might be for the investor to match the share of the company being received in relation to the contribution of cash to the new effective net worth. In this case, assume that the new effective net worth of the company is $4,000,000. This figure represents $3,000,000 of existing net worth plus the addition of the $1,000,000 "quasi" equity (money effectively like equity, since it is totally at risk and subordinate to all other debt). Here the investor is contributing 25 percent of the new capital base, but receiving only 8 percent of the company. The investor may wish to adjust this percentage to make the reward match the contribution more equitably.

The investor will be interested in noting the multiple to be paid for an 8 percent share. To determine this the investor would divide the forecasted value of the company by the new number of shares outstanding; this calculation gives the implied value per share of the company. In this example it would be $26.30 per share ($22,875,000/869,565). Then by dividing this price by the current earnings per share the resulting multiple can be compared with current market valuations. Here, assuming earnings per share of $0.80, the investor would be paying 33 times current earnings. This may be much too high a multiple and cause the investor to adjust the desired share of the company higher, or cost lower, or both.

After trying various ownership shares and costs and using these various tests, a final percentage and cost will be settled upon; the investor must now test to make sure that the company's shareholders will benefit by taking this offer. By taking the forecast supplied by the investor as to the net income level of the company in two years without the infusion of $1,000,000, a value of the company based on some multiple can be determined. Assuming a multiple of 12 (column 3, row 2 of Table 6–2), a total company value of $12,000,000 is determined (column 4, row 2). Assume that 15 percent of the company had been chosen finally as the share necessary to meet the investor's various criteria. By multiplying the $22,875,000 company value with the infusion of cash by 85 percent, the remaining amount owned by existing shareholders, the investor can see that shareholders' value is $19,443,750, or substantially above the $12,000,000 they would have if they did not take the cash. In fact the investor may use this type of analysis to show that the maximum acceptable dilution of 15 percent might be too restrictive, and that shareholders can accept more dilution and still be better off than in not making any deal.

One final variation is worth mentioning. The investor may structure a deal in which the number of shares and cost are based on the achievement of various profit levels. In this way the investor may be able to accommodate the company's desire for lesser dilution if it reaches forecasted profit levels. However, if management falls far short, by receiving a greater number of shares at a lower cost the investor is not penalized for accepting bad management forecasts. The investor provides management the incentive for achieving its own forecasts while achieving a more consistent rate of return over a broader range of earnings.

Example 2—Factor of Returns Method. This example is the same as the previous one except that management assumed that an investor would seek a return of five times the investment within three to five years:

$$\text{investment required } (\$1,000,000) \times \begin{array}{c} \text{factor of returns} \\ \text{greater than} \\ \text{investment (5)} \end{array} = \begin{array}{c} \text{total return required,} \\ (\$5,000,000) \end{array}$$

$$\frac{\text{total return required}}{\begin{array}{c}\text{projected value of}\\\text{company in third}\\\text{to fifth years}\end{array}} = \begin{array}{c}\text{\% ownership needed to}\\\text{realize return}\end{array}$$

The following table illustrates this manner of calculating the required return.

Time	Projected Market Value of Company	% Ownership Given up
3rd Year:	5,000,000 / 34,312,000	15
4th Year:	5,000,000 / 42,890,000	12
5th Year:	5,000,000 / 49,323,000	10

In example 2 the range of rate of return was between 71 and 38 percent, that is 71 percent for an original investment of one million dollars that returns five million dollars in three years or 38 percent for the same investment that returns five million dollars in five years. One should note the substantial decline in return as time passes. Table 6–3 illustrates the relationship of the factor of returns to rates of return, in effect emphasizing the relationship of timing of returns on the overall rate of return.

TABLE 6–3. TRANSLATION OF FACTOR INTO A RATE
OF RETURN (%)

Factor	Rate of Return for Year:				
	1	2	3	4	5
1	0	—	—	—	—
2	100	41	26	19	15
3	200	73	44	32	25
4	300	100	59	41	32
5	400	124	**71**	59	**38**
6	500	145	82	57	43
7	600	165	91	63	48
8	700	183	100	68	52
9	800	200	108	73	55
10	900	216	115	78	58
11	1000	232	122	82	62
12	1100	246	129	86	64
13	1200	261	135	90	67
14	1300	274	141	93	70
15	1400	287	147	97	72

Continuing Relationships

Most venture groups prefer to play a passive role in the ongoing management of the company. If all is well with the company's progress, the
venture group will monitor this performance by a monthly review of
financial statements and other key data pertaining to the specific company and industry. The investor group may advise the company on
specific problems and contribute their thinking to the policy formation of
the company. They are often well qualified, having seen numerous
other businesses resolve similar problems. The venture capitalists will
aid the business to increase its bank credit lines and other long-term
debt, and establish relationships and assist in negotiations with under-
writers to facilitate public offerings.

If performance falters, and especially if the investment falls into
jeopardy, the venture capitalist may play a more active role in helping
make key business decisions. As an example, if management is ineffective in areas of cost control, the investor may help the company find a
competent chief financial officer. If current operations are not yielding
satisfactory returns, the investor may help devise plans to curtail expansion, stop acquisitions or diversifications, or arrange divestments until
current operations are in order. In the extreme, if the company is approaching insolvency, the investor may lead the effort to turn the situation around, or consolidate operations to effect a better yield from liquidation of assets. Some venture firms charge for consulting, but most do
not, believing their just reward comes from stock appreciation.

It is important for the company to live up to the terms of agreement with the investor. Also important is the continuing effort to keep the investor informed and aware of the company's changing environment. Special care should be taken to supply all required information, observe the warranties and covenants, and avoid events that could precipitate a default in the debenture. If a breach of a provision should be imminent or actually occur, management should promptly consult with the investor to gain understanding and support. Surprisingly, many companies promptly forget these requirements after closing the deal. The ensuing breakdown in communication leads to discord between the investor and the company. In addition to the required information it is often wise to ask for an informal meeting with the investors at which the current developments of the company can be reviewed. This type of working relationship fosters mutual respect for the working style and needs of both groups and promotes accommodations on issues of mutual concern. If the company manages its relations well, the venture capitalist group can be a source of informed and seasoned judgment in helping the company grow and prosper.

SUMMARY: Key Points in Raising Capital

A review of this chapter brings to mind the wealthy executive behind his desk pontificating to the eager junior executive. Winding up his review he says: "You've asked me my secret for success. It was something my father told me long ago; 'Son, here is a million dollars, don't lose it.' " This chapter has reviewed how the investor attempts to make his "million dollars," and not lose it.

This review of common fund-raising difficulties stresses the need for the entrepreneur to represent a high caliber of management capable of producing better than average results. It is this performance translated into high returns that generates investment enthusiasm.

In determining the amount of cash needed, a preferred approach highlights the sources and uses for cash and allows for checking the forecast assumptions. A simplified approach can be used for starting a business. After determining the cash needs, the private placement memorandum is developed. This document covers many topics, but its main purpose should not be lost—to give enough information early in the memorandum to capture the interest of the investor while providing a basis for initial judgments and questions.

There are many sources of venture capital, and in some cases alternative resources to capital, such as barter or stock for services, should be considered. If venture capital is required, noninstitutional and institutional sources can be explored. Various publications and associations identify the specific venture sources. In choosing a source, it is important to match the investor's preference areas with the nature of the enterprise. The match between the amount of money sought and the investing limits of the source should also be considered.

In establishing a relationship with an investor, the entrepreneur must decide whether to use a finder or direct contact. After the contact has been made, the investor will need to analyze the prospective investment carefully, but quickly in the initial stage. A screening process is usually used to help the investor avoid spending excessive time on deals that will not be consummated.

If the request for capital passes the screening process, the venture capitalist and the entrepreneur begin negotiations for structuring the deal. These negotiations consider the amount and type of investment, the amount of stock required, pricing, and possible restrictions. Various techniques can be used in this process, but the investor's expectations of return must be considered.

After the deal has been consummated, the entrepreneur should consider the value of maintaining an ongoing relationship with the venture capitalist. Because of their experience with a number of businesses, venture capitalists can often offer effective advice in financial matters. However, institutional investors usually desire to remain passive unless the business takes a dramatic turn for the worse.

SUGGESTED READINGS

Allen, Louis L. "Venture Capital Financing—an Innovation." *Journal of Small Business Management* 7, January 1969, pp. 3–4.

Baumback, Clifford M., and Mancuso, Joseph R. *Entrepreneurship and Venture Management.* Englewood Cliffs, N.J.: Prentice-Hall, 1975, chapter 4.

Casey, William J. *How to Raise Money to Make Money.* New York: Institute for Business Planning, 1970.

Dominguez, John R. *Venture Capital.* Lexington, Mass.: Lexington Books, 1974.

Flink, Salomon J. *Equity Financing for Small Business.* New York: Simmons-Boardman, 1962.

Goulden, Joseph C. *The Money Givers.* New York: Random House, 1971, pp. 19–50.

Kelley, Albert J., Campanella, Frank B., and McKiernan, John M. *Venture Capital, A Guidebook for New Enterprises.* Chestnut Hill, Mass.: The Management Institute, Boston College, 1971.

Liles, Patrick R. *New Business Ventures and the Entrepreneur.* Homewood, Ill.: Richard D. Irwin, 1974, pp. 461–94.

Noone, Charles M., and Rubel, Stanley M. *SBICs: Pioneers in Organized Venture Capital*. Chicago: Capital Publishing Company, 1970.

"Venture Capital and Management," *Proceedings of the Second Annual Boston College Management Seminar*. May 28–29, 1970.

PART II

MANAGING A SMALL BUSINESS

INTRODUCTION

In Part II it is assumed that the entrepreneurial idea is being carried out in a small business organization. The focus is therefore on the principles and practice that undergird effective management of an ongoing small business enterprise.

The Nature of a Small Business

The obvious question that begs an answer is: What is a small business enterprise? Any attempt to answer this question with *precision* and *exactitude* is an exercise in futility. There is no standard definition that could possibly include the diversity and variety of small firms. The Small Business Administration (SBA) uses the number of employees or sales volume for defining a small enterprise. The SBA calls a manufacturing firm small if it employs 250 persons or less. This measure varies, however, from industry to industry. For example, the SBA considers a steel mill with no more than 2500 employees a small firm. For nonmanufacturing firms the SBA uses sales volume as the criterion for defining smallness. Thus a retail store with one million dollars net sales and a wholesale business with five million dollars net sales per year are considered small.

Over the years the SBA has found it necessary to change the numerical indicators for identifying small firms. It is clear that a small firm cannot be adequately defined in terms of arbitrary quantitative indicators such as the number of employees, annual sales volume, or the magnitude of its assets. Quantitative indicators are only supplementary to those more qualitative characteristics that cause the management problems of small firms to be significantly different from those of large firms. The following five sets of qualitative criteria are typical for small enterprises:

- *Scope of operations:* Small firms serve predominantly a local or regional market rather than a national or international market.
- *Scale of operations:* Small firms tend to have a very limited share of a given market; they are relatively small in a given industry.
- *Ownership:* The equity of small firms is generally owned by one person or at most very few. Small firms tend to be managed directly by their owner or owners.
- *Independence:* Small firms are independent in the sense that they are not part of a complex enterprise system such as a small division of a large enterprise. Independence also means that the firm's owner-managers have ultimate authority and effective control over the business, even though their freedom may be constrained by obligations to financial institutions.
- *Management style:* Small firms are generally managed in a personalized fashion. Managers of small firms tend to know all the employees personally; they participate in all aspects of managing the business and there is no general sharing of the decision-making process.

These five sets of attributes give rise to most of the problems and special needs that small firms have to cope with. They are also the determining factors for most of the management differences between small and large firms.

Essential Differences in Managing Small and Large Companies

The success of any business depends upon the capabilities and ingenuity of its management. The managerial responsibilities are, however, conditioned by the size and unique operating characteristics of the individual enterprise. It is for this reason that a management approach appropriate to a large firm does not necessarily work in a small firm and vice versa.

Countless executives who have changed from a large company to a small one have had to learn this lesson. For example, Thomas J. Murray reports case histories of executives who left high-level positions in large companies to become chief executive officers of small companies.[1] Many discovered too late that their previous work within fairly narrow, well-

---

[1]Thomas J. Murray, "The Big Problems of Thinking Small: Taking on the Presidency of a Small Company," *Dun's Review*, February 1976, p. 70.

defined functional responsibilities, for which they had the support of staff specialists, did not prepare them adequately for the top management job in a small enterprise. In a small company they had practically no staff support; they had to assume a wide range of responsibilities in financial, marketing, manufacturing, public relations, labor relations, and other business matters. These executives could have avoided serious mistakes had they been more sensitive to the differences between managing small and large firms. John S. Deeks summarizes some of the key differences as follows:[2]

	SMALL FIRM	LARGE FIRM
Source of authority	a) tradition (ownership) b) personal	a) expertise b) office
Basis of philosophy	a) no diffusion between ownership and control b) no conflict between personal and company objectives c) no distinction between person and role d) integration of work and social values e) not subservient to economic goals	a) control without ownership b) conflict between individual and organizational goals c) very clear distinction between the individual and the office filled d) values of the work place divorced from both individual and social values e) economic "performance" as ultimate criterion
Characteristic skills	a) adaptive b) diagnostic c) exploitation of change (opportunism) d) tactical facility e) pragmatic use of techniques as aid to problem solving f) social skills applied g) consequence-mitigating decision making	a) predictive b) prognostic c) control of change d) strategic facility e) coordination and control of specialists f) manipulative skills applied largely on an impersonal basis g) event-shaping decision making

[2]John S. Deeks, *The Small Firm Owner-Manager*, New York: Praeger, 1976, p. 227.

	SMALL FIRM	LARGE FIRM
Organization	a) informal relationships b) no divorce between planners and doers c) appointment and promotion often on the basis of birth or personal friendship d) everyone prepared to muck-in as required e) open system of communications	a) formal relationships b) divorce of planning from doing c) technical qualifications as basis of appointment and promotion d) precise definition of rights and obligations, duties, and responsibilities e) structured communications system

It is obvious that there will be exceptions to these general characterizations of small and large firms. These do, however, highlight the essential differences that cause the performance and management problems of most small firms to be significantly different from those of most large firms. The differences are not clear cut, but they are significant nonetheless.

The Analytical Approach

Although the scope and complexity of management problems and decision making may be different, the basic managerial functions and the operational activities are essentially the same in both small and large companies. In order to be effective and to accomplish the organizational objectives, small and large firms require planning, close attention to organizational considerations, systematic control, and technical competence in their business. However, in the small firm with its limited resources and financial constraints, these functions must be carried out differently than in a large firm. Furthermore, in the small firm these functions are generally the responsibility of just one person: the entrepreneur. This person's managerial skill, drive, ingenuity, resourcefulness, and dogged determination are a small firm's major source of strength. The entrepreneur plans, organizes, directs subordinates, controls their performance, and is not afraid to pitch in personally whenever an operational task requires added effort.

Generally the various managerial and operational responsibilities in small firms are not neatly segregated and assigned to different persons. An assortment of jobs and activities are either performed by just one person or are assigned to different employees at different times. These operating conditions typical of most small firms reflect the interrelatedness of the functional activities of a business enterprise much more explicitly than do the conditions in larger firms.

Yet from a pedagogical point of view we found it desirable to treat the management functions of small firms in separate chapters. The emphasis in the following chapters is on the ideas and techniques that are particularly suitable for coping with small business management problems and for improving the effectiveness of small businesses.

We are aware that there are seemingly successful small enterprises characterized by only some form of intuitive planning, a poorly structured organization, informal controls at best, or some other violation of sound management practice. But these are exceptional cases. They prove only that inadequate management does not always lead to immediate disaster. There is, however, a high probability that small companies that ignore sound management practice will sooner or later become crisis ridden and eventually fail. The material presented in Part II is intended not only to emphasize effective small business management, but also to serve as a diagnostic tool kit for identifying and overcoming problems and weaknesses in small business management.

CHAPTER 7

Planning

Purposeful decision and effective action require foresight and planning. Planning can be defined as a rational process for predetermining an appropriate course of action to achieve a specific set of objectives effectively and economically within a specified time. This definition indicates that planning is an important management tool in any organization, large or small. The organization's success depends essentially on how well its management is able to use this tool. Generally, one of the most serious operational problems for small firms is lack of effective formal planning. The seriousness of this problem is underlined by the number of small business failures every year. According to the Small Business Administration, in 1971, a typical year, there were approximately twenty thousand small business failures with an estimated loss of over three billion dollars. Dun & Bradstreet indicates that about 90 percent of these failures could be traced to a lack of planning, inexperience, or inadequate managerial competence. The remaining 10 percent are accounted for by neglect, fraud, and disaster.

BARRIERS TO PLANNING IN SMALL FIRMS

Lack of effective planning and its negative consequences are recognized as a major problem area by small business managers.[1] Three conditions must be met to improve this situation. Small business executives must:

1. develop understanding of the specific *causes* for the limited planning generally found in small firms

---

[1]Harold K. Charlesworth, "Urgently Required: A Reordering of Priorities to Save Small Business," *MSU Business Topics* 20, No. 3, 1972, p. 51.

2. be convinced that formal planning is worthwhile and a basic pre-requisite for successful operations

3. be made aware of planning methods that are suitable and appropriate for small business situations.

The low planning intensity is caused by both the typical operating characteristics of the small firm and the attitudes of its managers. Generally, the most common barriers to effective formal planning in small firms are those discussed in the following paragraphs.

Small firms are relatively simple. In small firms the most pressing problems are generally easier to identify than in large and complex businesses. This simplicity frequently misleads their managers into thinking that there is no need for formal planning. When asked why they do not develop formal plans for their organizations, managers of small businesses frequently answer: "My business is simple and I know what the problems are." As a result, formal planning is often considered as an unnecessary luxury. To the extent that any planning is done, it is informal and inconsistent. In these cases the managers follow their intuition, rules of thumb, or past experience for making their short-term as well as their long-term decisions. They neither develop nor follow a formal, systematic, and coherent plan of action.

Most small firms are the creation of one entrepreneur. The individual owner feels deeply involved in all operating problems that arise and takes personal responsibility for their solution. To the extent that the owner maps out a future course of action for the firm, there seems little need to formalize it. All plans can be kept in the head, with the added advantage of keeping them secret as well.

Most small firms have a short-range orientation. Small business management tends to focus on day-to-day survival. Small firms have only one or very few managers; they are consequently involved in all the operating problems that arise and are seemingly always fighting "brush fires." They seldom seem to have time to reflect on the long-range prospects of the organization and to formalize them into specific action programs.

Small business executives frequently lack planning skills. Since small business executives must deal with a broad range of functional responsibilities, they tend to concentrate on the most crucial current aspects of their business such as marketing or engineering problems. Thus one finds among small business managers many who are excellent salesmen or engineers, but who have little or inadequate planning skills. It is therefore not surprising that they neglect the critical planning functions in their business.

Small business lacks adequate staff support. Lack of adequate staff is probably the single most serious cause for deficiency of planning in small firms. Most small firms do not have the services of a specialized staff. In larger organizations staff specialists accumulate relevant internal and external information that reflects existing market opportunities and corporate capabilities and provides the basis for sound planning. Small firms rarely have the necessary staff specialists to do this type of intelligence work.

These various obstacles—alone or in combination—are the major reasons for the low planning intensity among small firms. Yet, overcoming these obstacles would permit the small business executive to gain the advantages offered by systematic formal planning and to grasp opportunities and forestall the threats that lie in the future.

THE ESSENCE OF SYSTEMATIC PLANNING

It has been pointed out that business planning is a rational process for selecting a future course of action aimed at achieving desired objectives profitably with minimal unsought consequences. This characterization suggests the four major dimensions of systematic business planning.

1. *Planning is a rational process.* Ideally, the planning process involves: a) the development and specification of a balanced set of organizational objectives; b) a realistic assessment of the organization's internal resources (resource analysis); an objective evaluation of the external environmental conditions that affect the organization (environmental analysis); c) an analysis of the organization's situation as compared with its direct competitors (competitive analysis). On the basis of these three sets of information—a systematic investigation of a firm's internal, external, and competitive situation—managers become aware of the firm's opportunities and risks, strengths and weaknesses. Taking into account their personal value orientations, managers can then relate the specified objectives to the observed opportunities and risks. This matching process leads to the development of strategies for achieving the organization's objectives by fully exploiting opportunities and strengths while averting or minimizing risks and weaknesses. Each systematic approach to planning has to go through such a process. The diagram in Figure 7–1 shows the interrelationships in a rational planning process. One essential aspect of systematic business planning is that it directs the future activities of the firm by determining, insofar as possible, the internal and external conditions that are likely to hold in the future, and by specifying appropriate strategies that will enable the company to reach its objectives in an optimum way. In summary, planning "is a process of deciding in advance what is to be done, when it is to be done, how it is to be done, and who is going to do it."[2]

2. *Planning is the creation of an integrated structure of plans.* Each comprehensive plan consists necessarily of various subplans with either dif-

---

[2]George A. Steiner, *Comprehensive Managerial Planning*, Oxford, Ohio: The Planning Executive Institute, 1972, p. 4.

ferent time perspectives (long-, medium-, short-range plans) or with different functional orientations (such as marketing, production, or finance). These various plans must be consistent with each other; they must be integrated. Creating an integrated structure of plans has both a time perspective and a functional-operational perspective.

As far as the time perspective is concerned, systematically structured plans integrate long-, medium-, and short-range plans. An organization's long-range or strategic plan forms the framework for the development of more detailed medium-range plans that in turn provide a basis for short-range operational planning. These three sets of plans are not subject to any fixed time spans (or time horizons). In small companies the time horizon of long-range plans tends to be considerably shorter than in large corporations. In large firms long-range strategic plans may cover five or more years, whereas in small firms a time horizon of two years may constitute a long-range plan.

The criterion for the appropriate time horizon of a company's long-range plans is the ability to predict with a high degree of certainty future developments that may affect its success. Business plans have to be based on a realistic assessment of those future developments that have an impact on present organizational decisions. For instance, a long-range plan with a time horizon of five years that does not reflect the external and internal changes that might reasonably take place during this period is worthless if not actually misleading. Therefore, the time horizon of a firm's long-range plans has to be congruent with the ability to predict relevant changes during a given period with a high degree of certainty. Generally, the efficacy of planning is not improved by extending the time horizon of the plans; for small firms it is preferable to increase the frequency with which plans are developed rather than to extend their time span. For the majority of small firms a long-range plan covering three years hence, two-year medium-range plans, and one-year operational plans would make an optimum planning structure.

Integrated planning also requires coordination among the various functional plans such as the marketing, production, finance, personnel, and investment plans. Each component plan must not only be consistent within itself, but must also be in harmony with the other plans developed for *all* the major functional or problem areas of a business: the products or services, marketing and distribution, production, administration, and finance. Several approaches to the development of coordinated functional plans are presented in greater detail later in this chapter.

3. *Planning is a philosophy.* Effective planning requires that everyone in a managerial position accept a systematic predetermination of future courses of action as a way of life. It means making a commitment to periodic identification of future opportunities and risks for the company, and it means using this knowledge for making current decisions.

A commitment to formal and systematic planning—in contrast with an intuitive and random concern with the future effects of current decisions—requires a specific organizational setup that assigns responsibilities for the various steps in the planning process. In a small firm, the one to be concerned with all aspects of planning is clearly the entrepreneur-owner. However, the entrepreneur must instill a planning consciousness in other managers in the organization so that planning becomes a cooperative endeavor. In this sense, planning is a philosophy that permeates all other managerial activities; it is also a political process in practice.

4. *Planning is a political process.* Planning involves relationships between people. Supervisors and managers try to direct their planning toward ends important to them, but their plans must necessarily fit in the network of plans that guide the work of the company. Thus they inevitably find it necessary to negotiate, compromise, and make trades with each other in order to mesh their individual plans. The process is essentially political; it involves discussion, debate, sometimes confrontation, resolution of differences, and often consensual decision making. The interplay of planning procedures can be materially eased and the planning process shortened and improved when the planners handle interpersonal relationships competently.

Planning that incorporates the four major dimensions outlined above provides a series of distinct benefits: a) it enables a company to minimize the negative consequences of uncertainty and change; b) it focuses attention on objectives and thus provides a consistent direction for strategic and tactical decisions; c) it ensures efficiency in operation; d) it facilitates control by allowing comparisons between actual achievements and the stated objectives; e) it induces flexibility and adaptability to change without dislocating the business.

APPROACHES TO PLANNING

Figure 7–1 shows the analytical steps in any systematic, comprehensive planning effort. These steps are essential in small as well as large organizations. However, the scope of planning, the depth and the sequence of analysis differ depending on a number of characteristics of the enterprise such as its size, the type of business, the nature and the magnitude of the problems the organization faces, the planning capabilities of its management, and the available staff support for planning purposes.

In general, the smaller the firm and the more limited its experience with systematic, formal planning, the simpler must be its first approach to planning. Therefore, the manager of the small firm should start with a simple, uncomplicated approach to planning and increase sophistication as the firm's planning experience and its management's planning skills

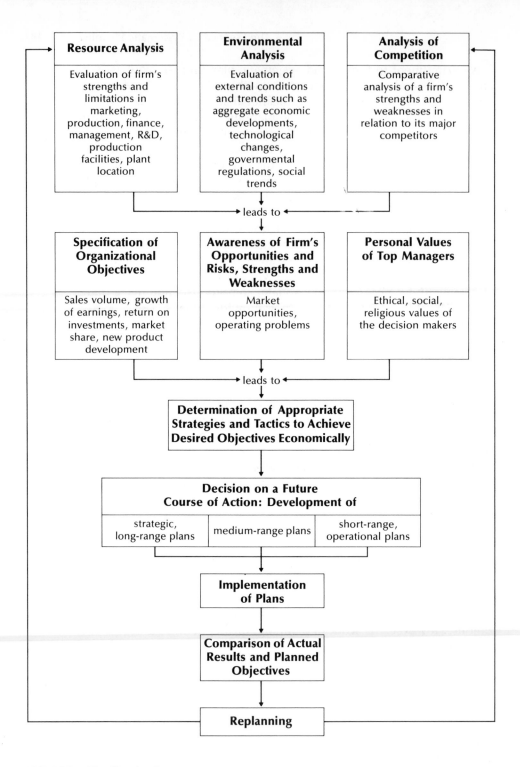

FIGURE 7–1. The Planning Process

improve. The following sections are keyed to this concept and present two effective approaches to small business planning reflecting different degrees of sophistication.

Focus on Key Problems and Strategic Factors

A first step in developing a formal, comprehensive planning system in a small firm is to analyze those forces that are of critical importance for achieving success. This process can be described as "a search for the strategic factors."[3] Every firm is subject to a variety of internal and external forces that are potential obstacles or constraints on an organization's achievement of its desired objectives. Obviously there is no standard list of these crucial factors that apply to all organizations. Every firm has its own peculiar set; in one case the most important strategic factor may be customer service, in another the ability to raise short-term capital. It is also important to recognize that each firm faces a dynamic environment and therefore the relative importance of individual strategic factors changes over time.

As an uncomplicated approach to planning, small business managers should start with identifying and evaluating those strategic factors that are hindering their firm from reaching its full potential. Once these factors are identified, the next step is to search for ways to overcome these problems. George Steiner developed a list of over seventy items that may be of critical importance to a company's success.[4] Table 7–1 represents a modification of Steiner's list of strategic factors. It can be used as a basis for identifying specific problem areas, assessing the significance and severity of the problems, and planning remedial actions.

This list of strategic factors may be used as a basis for planning in small business. It is a flexible planning tool; the list can be expanded or reduced depending on the specific characteristics of the firm. Its main benefit is that it leads small business managers to identify critical managerial and operational problem areas, it gives them a basis for establishing priorities for these crucial issues, and it makes them conscious of the changes that must be planned.

The outline advocated by Roger A. Golde (see Table 7–2) gives a somewhat different approach to planning for factors critical in business success. Focusing on critical strategic factors is an appropriate way for small firms to start developing a formal planning effort. The specific advantages of this approach are: 1) it does not require an elaborate

---

[3]Chester I. Barnard, *The Functions of the Exeuctive*, Cambridge, Mass.: Harvard University Press, 1938, p. 202.

[4]George A. Steiner, *Strategic Factors in Business Success*, New York: Financial Executives Research Foundation, 1969, pp. 4–5.

TABLE 7–1. STRATEGIC FACTORS—PLANNING GUIDE

Strategic Factors	Degree of Satisfaction with Present Level of Competence*					Remedial Actions to Improve Competence
	1	2	3	4	5	
General Management						
Clearly established objectives						
Ability to attract competent personnel for management positions						
Ability to communicate policies to employees						
Ability to provide effective leadership and to motivate employees						
Management information system						
Use of quantitative tools and techniques in decision making						
Effective organizational structure						
Effective overall control of company operations						
Ability to perceive new needs for company's products or services						
Finance						
Ability to raise short-term capital						
Ability to raise long-term capital						
Debt						
Equity						
Ability to achieve satisfactory return on investment						
Effective cost control						
Ability to reduce costs						
Ability to finance new product development						
Marketing						
Ability to gather needed information about markets						

*The scale for ranking the degree of significance of particular strategic factors for a firm's future success may be interpreted as 1—not meeting requirements at all; 2—not very satisfactory; 3—a little better but not good enough; 4—average, just about passing; 5—quite satisfactory

TABLE 7–1. (continued)

Strategic Factors	Degree of Satisfaction with Present Level of Competence*					Remedial Actions to Improve Competence
	1	2	3	4	5	

Marketing (continued)
Ability to establish a wide
    customer base
Effective sales organization
Effective distribution system
Imaginative advertising and
    sales promotion
Effective pricing
Reduced warranty costs
Improved product service
Development of new markets
    for existing products

Products
Improvement of present
    products
Improved rate of new product
    development
Improvement of product
    quality
Expansion of existing product
    line
Improvement of product line
    selection
Effective subcontracting of
    manufacturing

Engineering and Production
Location of production facilities
Plant layout
Technical efficiency of
    production facilities
Product quality and control
Possibilities for cost reduction
Ability to achieve economies of
    scale
Flexibility in using production
    facilities for different
    products
Product engineering
Automation of production
    facilities

TABLE 7–1. (continued)

Strategic Factors	Degree of Satisfaction with Present Level of Competence*					Remedial Actions to Improve Competence
	1	2	3	4	5	
Personnel						
Ability to attract qualified employees						
Effective personnel relations with employees						
Effective use of incentives to motivate employees performance						
Financial incentives						
Nonfinancial incentives						
Relations with labor unions						
Ability to level peaks and valleys of employment requirements						
Employee turnover						
Absenteeism						
Employee morale						

Source: Adapted from George A. Steiner, *Strategic Factors in Business Success*, New York: Financial Executives Research Foundation, 1969, pp. 4–5.

planning organization; 2) it does not require any extensive or exact quantification of the strategic factors under consideration; 3) it leads to a better understanding of the interdependencies of the various strategic issues; 4) it leads the planner to an explicit recognition of the urgency of the crucial problem areas that require planned change; 5) it provides a basis for the development of remedial actions; and 6) it can be used as a communication device to get information from the employees as well as to inform them about planned activities. A most important benefit from this way of planning is its effectiveness in revealing problems and changes that require deliberate, planned reactions by the small business executive.

Focus on Opportunity and Risk Analysis

The major purpose of business planning is to discover opportunities that would enhance the firm's success and to identify threats that could cause its failure. To accomplish this purpose business planning concentrates on detecting external opportunities and risks, and internal strengths and weaknesses. This approach to planning can be implemented in three phases:

TABLE 7–2. CRITICAL FACTORS PLANNING FORM

	Planned Change	
	Next Year	Year after Next
Research & development		
Products		
Product mix		
Service		
Supplies		
Suppliers		
Inventory		
Subcontracts		
Storage & handing		
Quality control		
Space		
Leasehold improvements		
Equipment		
Employees		
Fringe benefits		
Customers		
Sales outlets		
Terms of sale		
Pricing		
Transportation		
Advertising		
Promotion		
Packaging		
Market research		
Financing		
Insurance		
Investments		

Instructions: All changes are estimated in relation to the preceding year.

If a quantitative change is anticipated—as change in size or amount—use the following symbols: L = large, M = medium, and S = small. Quantitative changes are assumed to be increased unless preceded by a minus sign.

If a qualitative change is anticipated, use the following symbols: l = large, m = medium, s = small.

Note that the notions of small, medium, and large changes are obviously subjective and will vary with the person using the form.

In general, a small change denotes some sort of minimum level of change that is thought important enough to make note of. Most of the expected changes will probably fall in the medium category, indicating significant change of some magnitude. The large category will usually be reserved for unusual changes of striking impact.

The notion of qualitative changes may need some clarification. This category of change would cover such items as a change in customer mix (which might or might not result in an increased number of customers). Using a new source of supply for raw materials and changing the media allocation of the advertising budget would also be examples of qualitative changes.

Source: Adapted from Roger A. Golde, "Practical Planning for Small Business," *Harvard Business Review* 24, No. 5, 1964, p. 151.

- *Phase 1: Situation Audit:* determination of a firm's current operating situation and of the relevant environmental characteristics that affect its operations.
- *Phase 2: Plan Development:* determination of a future course of action based on the situation audit as the point of departure.
- *Phase 3: Plan Assembly:* formalization and summarization of the information produced during Phase 2 into a comprehensive set of working documents representing the organization's master plan.
- *Phase 4: Plan Reviews, Revisions, Replanning:* analysis review, revision, and replanning to correct deviations from course desired to reach objectives.

The following sections deal in greater detail with these four phases in the planning process.

Phase 1: Situation Audit For the purposes of small business planning, a situation audit should preferably concentrate on four aspects: determination and analysis of organizational objectives, analysis of current sales performance and sales trends, analysis of currently available resources, and identification of current strengths and weaknesses.

Every planning effort should be goal oriented, which requires that a *specific set of objectives* be predetermined. The objectives pursued by small firms usually reflect a growth strategy—such as growth in sales, growth in earnings, an increase in the company's market share, expansion of the product line, or improvements in productivity. In determining organizational objectives the conflict among divergent sets of objectives must be reduced and the desired objectives must be stated in an operational manner. To accomplish the latter, overall business objectives must be split into more specific subobjectives, which in turn provide a basis for further specification. This relationship among objectives is shown in Figure 7–2.

As the figure shows, a precise statement of objectives is required in any planning effort. The more clearly small business managers identify their objectives and subobjectives, the more effective their planning effort will be.

A second part of a situation audit is an *analysis of current sales and past sales trends*. Planning should be based on a clear picture of the "anatomy" of a company's sales. For this purpose the changes in the sales volume by product should be reviewed periodically, as should sales to key customers and the various customer segments. Sales for each channel of distribution and sales for each geographic region should be analyzed. A detailed examination of past sales experience along these lines automatically reveals strengths and weaknesses of the sales effort. If a firm finds, for example, that 90 percent of its sales revenue is generated by only one-third of its products, and that only 10 percent of its customers account for 75 percent of total sales, the firm's management

Long-Range Objectives	Subobjectives	Sub-Subobjectives Set in These Areas
	Increase sales to $ . . . in 5 years	Increase market share
		Analyze advertising expenditures for increased effectiveness
		Penetrate new markets
		Redesign products
		Develop new products for market
		Begin new R & D in selected area
Make a return on investment of . . . % after taxes by end of 5 years (specify for each year)	Raise gross profits to $ . . . in 5 years	Reduce overhead costs by consolidating functions
		Sell obsolete plant and equipment
		Reduce advertising outlays
	Build modern facilities and operate them at capacity over the next 5 years	Build new buildings
		Replace tools
		Improve production schedules
		Improve plant utilization rates
		Install better inventory control
		Reduce defective products
	Upgrade and maintain a skilled work force	Institute management training programs
		Add personnel
		Analyze management hiring schedules
		Replace skills lost through promotion, discharge or attrition

FIGURE 7-2. Interrelationship of Business Objectives

has a clear basis for deciding on a contraction of the product line and a shift in the sales effort.

A detailed sales analysis over time will usually reveal trends that can be used to project future sales potential and to establish the magnitude of the so-called planning gap.[5] As the diagram in Figure 7–3 shows, the planning gap is the difference between a particular sales goal and the projections of revenues from the present product line plus the expected sales generated by product improvements and new products.

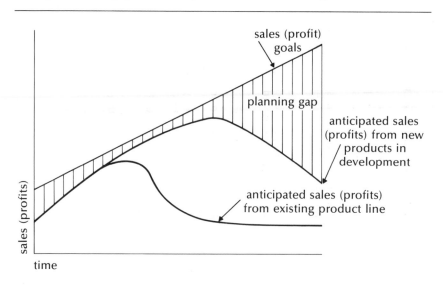

FIGURE 7–3. The Planning Gap

The sales analysis is not only a means for evaluating past performance. It also provides a way to project future sales and defines the gap that new activities will have to close if the sales goal is to be achieved.

The third part of the situation audit should be a systematic analysis of the small firm's *available resources*. These include the capabilities of the management team and the work force, the physical facilities, their location, and the firm's financial situation. The purpose of a careful resource analysis is to know clearly the quantity and quality of the resources the firm has at its disposal and to evaluate the efficiency with which the firm is using them.

In a small business an effective resource analysis can be done by selecting and regularly evaluating a set of ratios. This procedure serves two purposes: 1) it allows comparisons with other firms in the same

[5]George A. Steiner, "Making Long-Range Company Planning Pay Off," *California Management Review* 4, No. 2, 1963, pp. 28–41.

industry and therefore permits appraisal of the company's competitive performance, and 2) it provides ratios that indicate the direction and magnitude of changes that show opportunities and risks the planner should be aware of.

The most useful ratios for a situation audit are usually those derived from balance sheets and income statements. The focus should be on the firm's profitability, operating expense, gross margin, and use of financial resources. The following paragraphs list specific ratios and explain what they mean in the context of a firm's resource analysis.

Profitability ratios:

$$\frac{\text{profit}}{\text{sales}}$$

$$\frac{\text{profit}}{\text{total assets}}$$

$$\frac{\text{profit}}{\text{net worth}}$$

The profit/sales ratio shows what percentage of sales revenue is retained as net earnings and expresses essentially the cost/price effectiveness of the operation. The profit/total assets ratio shows how effectively the firm's assets are employed in generating earnings—the real test of the economic success or failure of an enterprise. The profit/net worth ratio reflects the return from operations in relation to the owner's investment.

Expense ratios:

$$\frac{\text{various expense items}}{\text{sales}}$$

Expense ratios reflect the relative magnitude of individual expense categories such as administrative costs, advertising expenditures, materials, and labor costs in proportion to the sales revenue. Changes in these ratios or a comparison of the various expense ratios with the same ratios of competing firms reveals a company's strengths and weaknesses. The company can then assess its costs and pinpoint areas that require particular attention.

Contribution ratio:

$$\frac{\text{net sales} - \text{direct (variable) costs}}{\text{net sales}}$$

The contribution ratio reflects the contribution of sales to the coverage of the firm's fixed costs and to the generation of profits. This ratio is essentially an indicator of a company's flexibility in pricing and cost control at different production levels. The determination of the contribution ratio is also important for the establishment of a firm's break-even point. This is the point at which the sales volume equals costs and therefore neither profit nor loss occur.

Break-even volume:

$$\frac{\text{fixed costs}}{\text{contribution ratio}}$$

The break-even volume gives important information for planning, since it shows how a change in the volume of output, cost, or changes in sales will affect the firm's profitability.

Turnover ratios:

$$\text{asset turnover} = \frac{\text{sales}}{\text{assets}}$$

$$\text{inventory turnover} = \frac{\text{sales}}{\text{average inventory}}$$

$$\text{accounts receivable turnover} = \frac{\text{total credit sales}}{\text{average accounts receivable}}$$

$$\text{average collection period} = \frac{365}{\text{accounts receivable turnover}}$$

$$\text{accounts payable turnover} = \frac{\text{purchases on credit}}{\text{average accounts payable}}$$

$$\text{average payment period} = \frac{365}{\text{accounts payable turnover}}$$

Turnover ratios are a way of evaluating effectiveness in the employment of the firm's financial resources. Generally, the higher the turnover, the more efficient is the use of the available capital.

Ratios reflecting the financial structure:

$$\text{current ratio} = \frac{\text{current assets}}{\text{current liabilities}}$$

$$\text{debt exposure} = \frac{\text{long-term debt}}{\text{net worth}}$$

The higher the current ratio, the greater the availability of working capital; but an excessively high current ratio may also indicate poor credit management and an underutilization of the company's current borrowing power. The debt exposure ratio reflects a company's use of its debt capacity and provides an indication of the company's ability to raise additional long-term debt.

A wide range of financial ratios can be developed.[6] However, each company must decide which ratios are most useful for its purposes. Once a set of ratios has been selected, it is important to determine them periodically and to watch for changes. To the planner they not only provide information about trends, they also reveal weaknesses in the firm's financial management. Planning effort should be directed toward overcoming these weaknesses.

Small business firms should also develop ratios other than financial. These may reflect inefficiencies or problems in the management of other resources such as its work force and its production capacity. Several such ratios are discussed below.

Production capacity utilization ratio:

$$\frac{\text{potential maximum utilization of machines}}{\text{actual utilization}}$$

A knowledge of the capacity utilization rate is a significant factor in production and investment planning. It should always be included in a situation audit of small manufacturing enterprises.

Personnel turnover ratio:

$$\frac{\text{separations (over a given period)}}{\text{average number of employees}}$$

Awareness of the personnel turnover rate is an important input in personnel planning because it indicates the rate at which a company is changing its personnel. New employees tend to be less productive than those who are familiar with the company's operations; high personnel turnover has a depressing effect on productivity. A relatively high personnel turnover may also reflect inadequacies in leadership. Other personnel-oriented ratios are the rate of absenteeism and work hours lost because of accidents or illness.

A regular check of the indicated ratios gives a simple but powerful method for appraising current strengths and weakness of an organization; this effort ensures guidance for the planning functions. Although many ratios possess no great significance in themselves, analysis of their changes or comparison with industry standards can help small business managers plan better use of their firm's competitive advantages.

Dun & Bradstreet regularly publishes sets of ratios for many industries. The individual firm will find it informative to compare its ratios with those given by Dun & Bradstreet for its industry. Table 7–3 summarizes the Dun & Bradstreet survey of ratios for a selected group of industries.

---

[6]See, for example, Richard Sanzo, *Ratio Analysis for Small Business*, Washington, D.C.: Small Business Administration, 1960.

TABLE 7-3. SELECTED KEY BUSINESS RATIOS

Line of Business	Number of Concerns Reporting	Current Assets to Current Debt (Times)	Net Profits on Net Sales (%)	Net Profits on Tangible Net Worth (%)	Net Profits on Net Working Capital (%)	Net Sales to Tangible Net Worth (Times)	Net Sales to Net Working Capital (Times)	Collection Period (Days)	Net Sales to Inventory (Times)	Fixed Assets to Tangible Net Worth (%)	Current Debt to Tangible Net Worth (%)	Total Debt to Tangible Net Worth (%)	Inventory to Net Working Capital (%)	Current Debt to Inventory (%)	Funded Debts to Net Working Capital (%)
Retailers															
Furniture stores	163	2.68	2.16	6.54	6.73	3.03	2.99	91	4.5	11.9	60.0	125.5	67.3	82.5	19.9
Gasoline service stations	84	2.08	5.86	21.71	52.21	3.59	8.11	—	10.0	37.8	43.4	66.7	85.5	115.1	42.7
Grocery stores	133	1.58	1.00	11.57	25.60	12.43	24.75	—	15.4	82.0	73.4	120.6	167.9	95.4	74.1
Hardware stores	84	3.11	1.93	7.45	10.07	3.03	3.64	—	4.1	13.6	39.8	57.7	87.5	54.6	18.1
Household appliance stores	86	19.2	1.27	8.66	9.09	5.25	6.20	28	5.0	20.0	96.3	202.0	121.3	94.5	32.5
Lumber & other bldg. mtls. dealers	86	2.80	2.93	9.78	12.87	3.99	5.11	40	5.9	28.1	42.6	94.4	82.6	77.0	42.6
Motor vehicle dealers	93	1.58	1.12	7.68	11.33	8.33	11.50	—	5.8	23.0	125.7	180.9	189.8	87.1	36.1
Retail nurseries, lawn & garden supp. stores	58	2.09	4.27	18.50	30.91	4.59	7.06	—	7.6	30.6	52.6	83.0	85.8	113.8	34.7
Shoe stores	86	3.22	1.60	4.71	5.77	3.39	4.51	—	3.8	14.6	41.8	93.7	108.9	46.0	34.5
Wholesalers															
Automotive parts & supplies	135	2.83	2.88	10.83	12.90	3.92	4.54	34	4.6	14.6	46.4	92.0	94.1	61.7	19.3
Beer, wine & alcoholic beverages	92	1.86	1.19	9.51	13.29	8.55	11.57	19	8.0	24.3	78.1	136.3	114.7	93.8	38.4
Chemicals & allied products	48	1.80	3.07	20.05	27.27	5.94	8.08	45	10.0	30.6	83.6	134.2	82.9	141.5	27.8
Drugs, drug proprietaries & sundries	87	1.84	1.00	6.56	7.14	7.12	8.05	38	6.5	25.0	100.0	165.5	116.6	91.0	32.9
Electrical appliances, TV & radio sets	98	1.75	1.18	8.24	9.00	6.55	7.44	38	5.9	8.5	122.0	167.5	126.4	100.1	23.3

TABLE 7–3. (continued)

Line of Business	Number of Concerns Reporting	Current Assets to Current Debt (Times)	Net Profits on Net Sales (%)	Net Profits on Tangible Net Worth (%)	Net Profits on Net Working Capital (%)	Net Sales to Tangible Net Worth (Times)	Net Sales to Net Working Capital (Times)	Collection Period (Days)	Net Sales to Inventory (Times)	Fixed Assets to Tangible Net Worth (%)	Current Debt to Tangible Net Worth (%)	Total Debt to Tangible Net Worth (%)	Inventory to Net Working Capital (%)	Current Debt to Inventory (%)	Funded Debts to Net Working Capital (%)
Electronic parts & equipment	57	2.31	2.45	11.69	12.37	4.93	4.96	43	4.6	14.3	77.2	177.9	102.2	82.8	27.6
Hardware	161	2.55	2.21	9.29	10.29	4.26	5.02	39	5.0	12.3	54.8	101.1	101.0	64.4	22.2
Scrap & waste materials	63	1.87	3.40	24.57	41.45	5.50	8.65	31	16.6	26.0	66.2	125.4	46.6	191.0	24.0
Tires & tubes	42	1.84	1.78	10.33	10.46	5.02	6.59	45	5.6	26.3	94.0	156.9	104.9	117.9	34.7
Manufacturers															
Agricultural chemicals	46	2.26	5.20	18.53	33.73	3.57	5.27	36	8.6	32.4	51.2	117.3	72.1	137.9	35.9
Concrete, gypsum & plaster products	85	2.22	3.56	7.71	18.83	2.46	5.76	46	9.5	64.3	40.9	81.5	61.0	132.6	68.5
Cutlery, hand tools & general hardware	80	2.50	3.79	11.84	15.68	2.76	4.09	45	4.3	39.8	45.8	73.6	94.2	70.7	38.7
Drugs	62	2.44	6.73	16.29	25.03	2.11	3.09	59	4.4	45.8	45.6	66.8	75.2	90.0	30.7
Electrical industrial apparatus	65	2.25	3.53	11.32	14.55	3.03	3.79	61	4.1	45.2	57.8	109.5	89.5	81.2	37.0
Engineering, laboratory & scientific instruments	58	2.72	3.80	9.19	11.24	2.29	2.78	69	3.7	36.6	49.9	99.3	75.8	67.7	39.8
Household appliances	41	2.40	2.44	8.14	9.12	3.17	3.98	53	4.0	41.6	64.2	89.4	99.0	76.4	32.5
Metal stampings	67	2.07	3.39	11.18	19.81	3.81	6.10	44	7.4	58.5	59.1	98.3	92.6	111.9	51.4
Motor vehicle parts & accessories	99	2.33	3.23	11.25	14.55	3.00	4.27	48	4.5	52.6	49.9	100.5	94.4	80.7	56.7
Paperboard containers & boxes	70	2.71	4.18	13.41	24.42	3.25	5.57	31	7.8	52.2	33.4	77.2	77.3	78.0	60.4
Special industry machinery	98	2.49	3.53	9.95	11.93	2.81	3.51	60	4.3	32.6	51.7	92.4	89.8	88.6	23.4

Note: The ratios on pages 200 and 201 are calculated periodically by Dun & Bradstreet on the basis of financial statements from a sample of companies. The figures represent the *median* (the figure that falls just in the middle of a series) and can thus be considered typical ratios for all the companies surveyed in a particular line of business.

Definitions of Terms

Collection Period—The number of days that the total of trade accounts and notes receivable (including assigned accounts and discounted notes, if any), less reserves for bad debts, represents when compared with the annual net credit sales. Formula: divide the annual net credit sales by 365 days to obtain the average credit sales per day. Then divide the total of accounts and notes receivable (plus any discounted notes receivable) by the average credit sales per day to obtain the average collection period.

Current Assets—Total of cash, accounts and notes receivable for the sales of merchandise in regular trade quarters, less any reserves for bad debts, advances on merchandise, inventory less any reserves, listed securities when not in excess of market, state and municipal bonds not in excess of market, and United States government securities.

Current Debt—Total of all liabilities due within one year from statement date including current payments on serial notes, mortgages, debentures, or other funded debts. This item also includes current reserves, such as gross reserves for federal income and excess profit taxes, reserves for contingencies set up for specific purposes but does not include reserves for depreciation.

Fixed Assets—The sum of the cost value of land and the depreciated book values of buildings, leasehold improvements, fixtures, furniture, machinery, tools and equipment.

Funded Debt—Mortgages, bonds, debentures, gold notes, serial notes, or other obligations with maturity of more than one year from the statement date.

Inventory—The sum of raw material, material in process and finished merchandise. It does not include supplies.

Net Profits—Profit after full depreciation on buildings, machinery, equipment, furniture, and other assets of a fixed nature; after reserves for federal income and excess profit taxes; after reduction in the value of inventory to cost or market, whichever is lower; after charge-offs for bad debts; after miscellaneous reserves and adjustments; but before dividends or withdrawals.

Net Sales—The dollar volume of business transacted for 365 days net after deductions for returns, allowances and discounts from gross sales.

Net Sales to Inventory—The quotient obtained by dividing the annual net sales by the statement inventory. This quotient does not represent the actual physical turnover, which would be determined by reducing the annual net sales to the cost of goods sold and then dividing the resulting figure by the statement inventory.

Net Working Capital—The excess of the current assets over the current debt.

Tangible Net Worth—The sum of all outstanding preferred or preference stocks (if any) and outstanding common stocks, surplus and undivided profits, less any intangible items in the assets, such as goodwill, trademarks, patents, copyrights, leaseholds, mailing list, treasury stock, organizational expenses, and underwriting discounts and expenses.

Turnover of Net Working Capital—The quotient obtained by dividing annual net sales by net working capital.

Turnover of Tangible Net Worth—The quotient obtained by dividing annual net sales by tangible net worth.

Source: *Dun's Review*, October 1975, p. 82–87 and December 1975, p. 86–91, reprinted by permission.

The fourth basic ingredient of a situation audit as part of the first step in the planning process is to get broad participation by managerial and operational personnel in *identifying strengths and weaknesses*. This approach employs the experience of the firm's members in identifying problems and opportunities that require attention *in planning*. Wide participation may be encouraged through use of a standardized form similar to the one shown in Figure 7–4.

Issue No. _____

Planning Issue

Identification as:
Weakness ☐   Strength ☐
Threat ☐   Opportunity ☐

Statement of the Issue:

Observation based on:

Recommended Action:

FIGURE 7–4. Form for Identifying a Firm's Strengths and Weaknesses

This approach stimulates planning consciousness among managers and others in the organization. Identifying problems and determining a future course of action is seen not only as the responsibility of one person or a small select group of managers, but also as a collective activity that obliges individuals to point out opportunities and problem areas from their personal perspectives.

After the current situation has been analyzed in this systematic and comprehensive manner, the organization is ready for the development phase, the next logical step in the planning process.

Phase 2: Plan Development The results of the situation audit provide reference points for setting planning priorities. Every firm is faced with a unique situation; it is therefore difficult to make uniform recommendations on methods of plan development. In general, those involved should start by reaching agreement on the relative importance of the threats or opportunities that were diagnosed during the situation audit phase. Once a ranking of the issues has been achieved, the planners must identify the choices that seem feasible for exploiting the potential opportunities and for remedying the existing or anticipated problems. A particular course of action then chosen becomes an action program for dealing with a specific issue. Related actions can be grouped along functional lines such as production, product development, marketing and distribution, administration, and finance.

Action programs for each functional area can be developed on this basis. Finally, the financial consequences of each program must be synthesized in a financial plan. Figure 7–5 shows the basic blocks in the development of a financial plan.

Phase 3: Formalization of Plans The final phase in this approach to small business planning is the assembly of the various working documents into a set of written formal plans. Documentation of planning makes it easier to communicate the plans to those who will be carrying them out. It also provides an effective basis for control, and eventually a deviation analysis between what has been planned and what has been achieved.

Phase 4: Plan Reviews, Revisions and Replanning Formalized plans should never be considered as unchangeable. In fact, every plan must be reviewed and revised regularly to avoid obsolescence caused by impact of unforeseen events. To keep updated and effective, planning must become a continuous process in which planning cycles overlap.

Summary Table 7–4 summarizes the elements of a systematic and somewhat more sophisticated approach to small business planning than that presented earlier in this chapter and illustrated in Tables 7–1 and 7–2.

THE ORGANIZATION OF PLANNING

The explanation of various approaches to small business planning makes it obvious that every planning effort must be organized. Effective

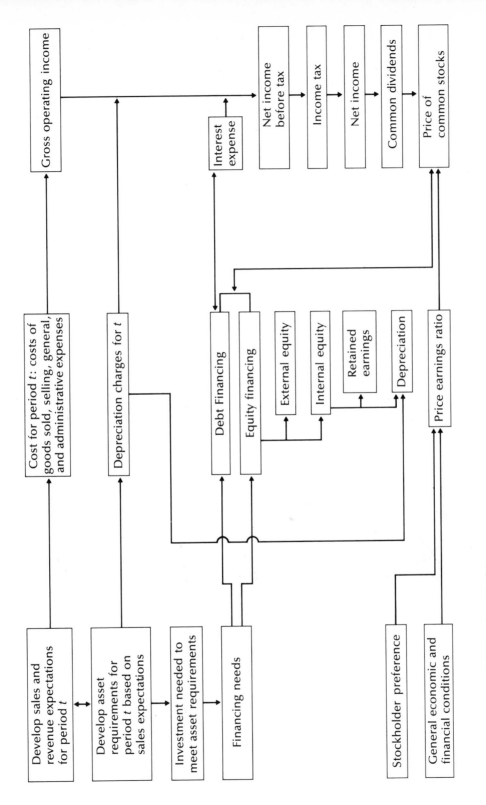

FIGURE 7-5. Financial Planning Model

TABLE 7–4. SYSTEMATIC PLANNING APPROACH

Phase 1 Situation Audit	Phase 2 Plan Development	Phase 3 Formalization of Plans	Phase 4 Plan Reviews, Revisions, Replanning
Review and restatement of company's goals and basic strategies:	Establishment of of planning priorities	Documentation of the planning decisions in a set of formal plans covering various time horizons and functional areas	Periodic reviews of accomplish-ment of plans, plan revisions or replanning as necessary
growth objectives, profitability, sales volume, market share	Determination of possible alternatives to exploit diagnosed opportunities and to avert threats		
Analysis of past sales trends:			
development of sales per customer group, regional development of sales, development of profit margin	Selection of a particular course of action for each planning issue		
Analysis of external opportunities and risks, internal strengths and weaknesses.	Grouping of planning issues into sets of action programs for different functional areas		
Analysis of available resources and their utilization:	Scheduling of action programs: the timing of future actions		
product performance, production capacity utilization, manpower situation, financial resources			

planning, even in small firms, requires a structure that assigns specific responsibilities for the various steps and tasks in the process. Ideally, all people in managerial roles should be planning conscious and must be aware of the contribution they are expected to make to the planning effort. Thus their actions, the information they are expected to provide, and the timing of both should be specifically stated. The timing is particularly important; organizing the planning effort requires both assigning specific responsibilities and setting up time schedules. These schedules enforce regularity in planning and prescribe the sequence and allotted time for each major step in the process.

SUMMARY: Guidelines to Planning in Small Firms

Planning in small businesses is often overlooked entirely or carried out in a haphazard manner. The following guidelines can help the management of a small business develop effective planning.

Getting a formalized planning system started

1. Understanding the barriers to small business planning is the first step toward overcoming them.
2. Formalized planning in small firms should preferably start with a relatively simple approach that can be progressively expanded as the firm's planning experience increases. Initially, a planning-oriented checklist covering the strategic factors for business success is an appropriate way to introduce formalized planning in a small firm.
3. A strong commitment to formal planning should be made by chief executives of small firms. To a large extent, the actual planning is their responsibility. But in addition, chief executives should instill a high degree of planning consciousness among subordinates. Whenever possible their experience should be used in identifying internal weaknesses and problem areas, and external opportunities and threats.
4. Small business managers should not expect that formal, systematic planning will lead to immediately noticeable benefits. However, formal planning does provide significant advantages when it is a regular endeavor and when it is used as a basis for control.
5. A successful planning approach cannot be moved from one company to another without change. Each company has to design a planning approach that reflects its own specific operating characteristics.

6. In general, formal, comprehensive planning cannot be introduced into a small firm without a careful reappraisal of current managerial practices and decision-making processes.
7. In organizing the planning process, attention must be paid to the existing organization structure.
8. Planning should be considered a learning process and the approach to planning changed as a company's planning experience and sophistication increases.

The Planning Process

9. Effective planning requires a clear identification of realistic objectives and subobjectives as a basis for developing specific plans.
10. Planning is a rational process and should be approached systematically. First, effective planning requires a clear awareness of the current strengths and weaknesses of a company, an awareness of the available resources and their utilization. Second, planning requires forecasts of future changes that will affect the firm. Forecasts plus an awareness of the available resources provide a basis for determining a future course of action.
11. It is not necessary to give all planning areas equal weight. For example, some companies may have to pay close attention to marketing planning, whereas other companies may find financial planning the most crucial planning area.
12. The planning horizon of a company should relate to the degree of certainty with which future changes can be anticipated. It is of little use to develop five-year plans if a company cannot predict with a high degree of certainty the changes over this period that will affect its operations.
13. Planning should be a continuous process in which planning cycles overlap.
14. Planning is a managerial process than can be used to improve managerial capabilities throughout the company.
15. Plans should be used as a control tool. Planned and actual results should be compared regularly and major deviations accounted for and corrected.

SUGGESTED READINGS

Ackoff, Russell L. *A Concept of Corporate Planning*. New York: Wiley Interscience, 1970.

Anthony, Robert N. *Planning and Control Systems: A Framework for Analysis*. Boston: Harvard University Press, 1965.

Branch, Melville C. *The Corporate Planning Process*. New York: American Management Association, 1962.

Golde, Roger A. "Practical Planning for Small Business." *Harvard Business Review*, September–October 1964.

Haas, Raymond M.; Hartman, Richard I.; James, John H.; and Milroy, Robert R. *Long-Range Planning for Small Business*. Bloomington, Ind.: Bureau of Business Research, Graduate School of Business, Indiana University, 1964.

Nickerson, Clarence B. *Accounting Handbook for Non-Accountants*. Boston: Cahners Books International, 1975, pp. 181–90.

Pickle, Hal B., and Abrahamson, Royce L. *Small Business Management*. New York: Wiley/Hamilton, 1976.

Schabacker, Joseph C. *Cash Planning in Small Manufacturing Companies*. Washington, D.C.: Small Business Administration, 1960.

Steiner, George A. *Top Management Planning*. New York: MacMillan, 1969.

Warren, Kirby E. *Long-Range Planning: The Executive Viewpoint*. Englewood Cliffs: Prentice-Hall, 1966.

CHAPTER 8

Organization

We assume at this point that the business has grown to require more personnel than one or two managers can handle—perhaps 30 or 40 employees or more. To ensure a sound basis for cooperation in achieving common objectives, some form of logically designed organizational structure becomes indispensable. Efficiency is fundamental to the success of any enterprise; the small firm can least afford the inefficiencies caused by a poor organization.

Although it is often hard to establish what a poor or a good organization is, the presence or absence of specific conditions can offer clues, as the simple test in Figure 8–1 suggests. For each yes answer, 10 points are given. A total score of 80 points or more suggests that a business is well organized. A score of 40 points or less indicates a poor organization with significant deficiencies. A score falling between 50 and 70 suggests the need for improvements. The value of the rating scheme is that it pinpoints the essential issues in properly organizing a business enterprise. This chapter discusses these issues and gives guidelines for developing and maintaining an effective small business organization.

THE MEANING OF ORGANIZATION

The term *organization* has a variety of meanings when used in different contexts. Frequently the term means an entity in itself; for example, the Small Business Administration is often called an organization. In this view an organization is a group of people who, as members of a formalized structure, are expected to cooperate in the achievement of a common organizational purpose. The term is also used to characterize the process of developing and maintaining a system of working relationships among the people of an enterprise and of dividing the work that has to be done. In this view an organization is a "formalized intentional

Rating Your Firm's Organization

Yes   No

1. The term *organization* has real meaning in your firm.
2. Basic company objectives and policies are clearly stated in writing.
3. Duties and responsibilities are spelled out in detail.
4. Standard operating procedures have been established.
5. Everyone in the organization is accountable to just one superior.
6. Organizational relationships are formally charted.
7. Actual organizational relationships are recognized and reflected in the organization chart.
8. The top management operates within the organization framework.
9. The organization structure is reviewed periodically.

FIGURE 8–1. Test for Effectiveness of Organization

Source: Adapted from Erich M. Haner, "Rating Your Firm's Organization," in *Management Aids for Small Manufacturers,* edited by Robert A. Sitzberg, Annual No. 6, Washington, D.C.: Small Business Administration, 1960, p. 23.

structure of roles or positions,"[1] that is, the formal organization as reflected in an organization chart.

However, the *formal organization* may not accurately show the actual interpersonal relationships and interactions among a group of people pursuring common objectives. Often some employees, not necessarily in management positions, may have significant influence on other employees. They command a leadership role that enables them to alter the formal organizational relationships. These interpersonal relationships, which fall outside the formally prescribed organizational patterns, are generally called the *informal organization.* Every organization normally has informal groups. Each has its own goals, values, and group norms that regulate the behavior of its members. Informal groups satisfy certain social and psychological needs at the work place; they provide their members with status, recognition, and a feeling of belonging.

The formal and the informal organization exist side by side. Ideally, they should be reasonably congruent. Significant discrepancies between them tend to lead to conflicts and consequently to a loss in organizational effectiveness. An important task for any manager, therefore, is to review regularly the formal organizational structure, to develop an awareness of the existing informal relationships, and to bring them in line with each other. In some cases this realignment may require a

[1]Harold Koontz and Cyril O'Donnell, *Principles of Management: An Analysis of Managerial Functions,* 5th edition, New York: McGraw-Hill, 1972, p. 241.

change in the formal organization structure; in other cases it may require a subtle effort to change the informal relationships. The small business manager must, however, realize that changing the formal organization structure is almost always easier than breaking up a disruptive informal organization.

CRITICAL ORGANIZATION ISSUES

It is generally recognized that to be effective the structure and internal functioning of an organization must be compatible with the demands of the organization's tasks, the technologies that are used, and the relevant conditions of the external environment.[2] Since practically every enterprise has its unique operating characteristics and environmental conditions, the validity of universal principles of organization might be questioned. Yet there is evidence that effective organizations show certain common traits. The small business executive should use these guidelines in organizing any endeavor.

The Human Use of Human Beings A good organization integrates the requirements of the work with the desires and capabilities of its people. Modern organization literature tends to focus on this issue and stresses a philosophical disparity that Douglas McGregor referred to as Theory X versus Theory Y.[3] Theory X outlines the traditional work-centered approach to organization design; it views the organization as structured around the tasks to be performed. Theory Y, on the other hand, defines a people-centered set of values; it stresses the intrinsic needs of employees and the human relations aspects of management. In reality, organizational effectiveness is the result of a balanced approach that takes into account the requirements of work *and* the desires of employees for harmonious, satisfactory interpersonal relationships on the job.

Proper Division of Work The total range of activities that need to be accomplished should be divided into meaningful tasks that can be performed by individuals. Each set of tasks should fit the capabilities, skills, and motivations of the people who are assigned to do them. Thus, any

---

[2]Much of the more recent organization literature focuses on this issue; see Joan Woodward, *Industrial Organization: Theory and Practice*, London: Oxford University Press, 1965; Paul R. Lawrence and Jay W. Lorsch, *Organization and Environment: Managing Differentiation and Integration*, Boston: Harvard University Graduate School of Administration, Division of Research, 1967; Fremont E. Kast and James E. Rosenzweig, *Contingency Views of Organization and Management*, Chicago: Science Research Associates, 1973.

[3]Douglas McGregor, *The Human Side of Enterprise*, New York: McGraw-Hill, 1960, parts I and II.

organizing effort must focus on establishing compatibility between specific tasks or activities to be performed by an individual and that person's capacity for carrying them out efficiently. In addition, proper division of work also implies differentiating activities so that clear boundaries of responsibility may be drawn between them.

Appropriate Departmentalization of Activities Similar tasks should be grouped into the same organizational units or departments. The most commonly used criteria for this grouping are:

1. function, such as marketing, engineering, finance, accounting, or personnel
2. product or product lines, such as electrical equipment, instruments, or electronic components
3. groups of customers, such as industrial customers, private households, or retail stores
4. region, such as sales territories, domestic operations, or foreign operations
5. process, such as distillation, bottling, or labeling

An important consideration in establishing organizational units is the need for interaction between various groups of employees. This need may arise because people are using similar skills, working toward solutions of essentially the same problems, or using the same sets of information. The greater the task-oriented need for interaction among a group of people the more compelling it is to group them into the same organizational unit.

Unity of Command Organizational conflict tends to be reduced if each employee reports to and is accountable to a single superior. Orders and direction should come only from this superior. When the employee has more than one superior, accountability is divided and there is a danger of receiving conflicting instructions—a situation that usually reduces efficiency and lowers morale.

Balance of Authority and Responsibility Authority is the right to act or to direct the actions of others in order to achieve specific results. The authority that is delegated to someone should be congruent with that person's responsibility for specified actions and results. This means an employee's responsibility for achieving certain results should not be greater than his authority to effect those results, nor should it be less.

Clear Specification of Authority and Responsibility for Every Position To achieve an effectively functioning organization every position should have a clearly defined statement of responsibilities and authority to discharge these responsibilities. Statements of this kind are generally referred to as *job descriptions*. Job descriptions specify the required tasks, the reporting relationships, and the necessary interactions between that position and other positions in the organization. Job descriptions should provide position holders with a clear understanding of what is expected of them and a description of the resources at their disposal. Job descriptions may range from a mere listing of the required duties to lengthy statements that not only specify the responsibilities but also include specific policies governing the activities on the job, the expected standards of performance, and a specification of the resources that can be used at discretion. Although job descriptions must be viewed as effective organizational tools, they do not automatically guarantee performance. An important task of every manager is to ensure reasonable compliance between what a job description specifies and what the incumbent actually does.

Proper Degree of Delegation There is an appropriate place in the organization for every task that must be performed. Management should not burden itself with tasks that can be performed effectively at a lower level in the organizational hierarchy. To obtain the greatest benefit from a sound organizational structure it is imperative to delegate authority and responsibility for particular results as far down in the organization as possible.

Proper Span of Control Supervisors must control the performance of their subordinates. The number of subordinates a supervisor can manage effectively depends upon the diversity of tasks performed by the subordinates and their competence. The span of control (also referred to as span of management) states the number of subordinates directly accountable to and effectively managed by a supervisor.

The span of control has a direct bearing upon the number of levels in an organization, which in turn affects the length of that organization's lines of communication. Figure 8–2 illustrates this point for an organization that requires 21 positions to achieve its goals. In the Type A organization (a), with three organizational levels, every supervisor controls four subordinates. In contrast, the Type B organization (b) has only two hierarchical levels and all 21 employees are directly accountable to one executive. The span of control—4 versus 20—therefore has a direct effect on the shape of the organization, the length of its communication lines, and its internal working relationships. A significant amount of research has been done to determine whether a tall or a flat organization structure is preferable.[4] The findings do not provide clear evidence of the

---

[4]See, for example, J. C. Worthy, "Organization Structure and Employee Morale," *American Sociological Review*, 15, April 1950, pp. 169–79; W. W. Suojanen, "The span of Control—Fact or Fable," *Advanced Management*, November 1955, pp. 5–13; R. Carzo and J. N. Yanouzas, "Effects of Flat and Tall Organization Structures," *Administrative Science Quarterly*, 14, No. 2, 1969, pp. 178–91; H. R. Jones, Jr., "A Study of Organization Performance for Experimental Structures of Two, Three and Four Levels," *Academy of Management Journal*, 12, No. 3, 1969, pp. 351–65; Joseph A. Litterer, *The Analysis of Organizations*, New York: John Wiley & Sons, 1973, pp. 559–69.

(a)

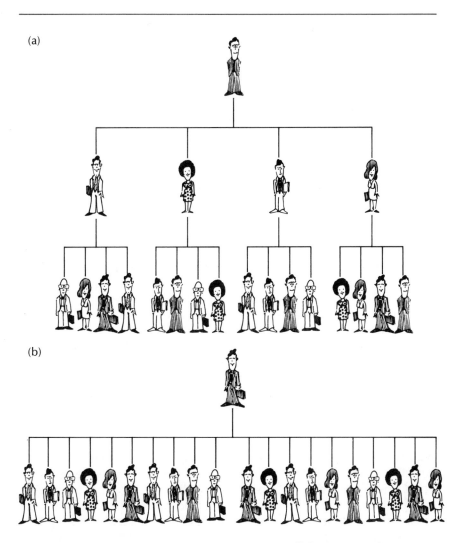

(b)

FIGURE 8–2. Organization Structures: a. Type A—Tall, b. Type B—Flat structure

superiority of one type or the other; each has certain advantages as well as disadvantages. The only clear recommendation that can be made is that in practice management should seek a balance and select a span of control that takes into account 1) the characteristics of the task to be performed, 2) the ability of a given superior to supervise a given number of subordinates effectively, 3) the capabilities of the employees, and 4) the required degree of coordination.

Small companies tend to have a somewhat broader span of control than large companies. A major reason for this is that small companies cannot afford the costs of additional organizational layers that go with reduced spans of control. Furthermore, there is a tendency among the chief executives of small firms to avoid clear delegation of authority to subordinate managers. They seem to prefer an organization in which a relatively large number of employees report directly to them. This situation creates an inherent danger and is frequently the major cause of executive inefficiency in small firms. A broad span of control combined with insufficient delegation creates a very heavy work load for many small business executives, which in turn is the cause of poor decisions, lack of planning, and weak control of subordinates, which may reduce work efficiency. Fixing a proper span of management is a crucial organizational issue requiring continuous attention.

Organizational Flexibility An organization should not be conceived of as a static structure but rather as a dynamic structure that *can* adjust rapidly to changing external or internal conditions. An inflexible, rigid firm often fails to meet the challenges of change in its economic, technical, social, or competitive environment. In contrast, flexible organizations are capable of adapting to change in environmental conditions; they tend to be successful because they see and seize opportunities. For this reason the management of a small firm should review its organization structure regularly to assess its effectiveness under current conditions and to ensure its ability to adapt rapidly to anticipated change.

The preceding discussion outlines the variables involved in the creation and maintenance of an effectively functioning organization. There are no off-the-shelf solutions to any of these issues; the small business manager should be conscious of them and treat them in the light of the specific operating conditions of the company. It would be wrong for any small business manager to assume that organizational matters are unimportant and easy to resolve, or that these matters take care of themselves; small firms cannot afford such negligence. In small businesses organizational deficiencies can be more readily identified than in large firms. Small firms are well advised to review these readily seen critical organizational issues periodically as a means for improving their effectiveness and their competitive advantages.

CREATING AN EFFECTIVE ORGANIZATION

The process of organizing a new enterprise or of reorganizing an already existing one involves three steps:

- determining the specific activities necessary to achieve organizational objectives efficiently (*activity analysis*)
- grouping these activities into a logical framework or structure (*departmentalization and developing the organization structure*)

- assigning specific positions and activities to individual employees (*job assignments, manning the organization*).

These steps are basic to organizing. They are the same in developing an organizational structure for a total enterprise or for specific parts of it.

Activity Analysis

The development and maintenance of an efficiently functioning organization rests on a clear conception of the desired objectives and of the specific activities necessary to achieve them. A thorough analysis of the required activities—including basic business functions such as production, marketing, procurement, and finance—is an indispensable part of any organizing effort. This analysis should provide answers to such questions as:

- What major functions are involved in achieving the organizational objectives?
- What subfunctions are required in each major function?
- What volume of work is generated by each major function and its subfunctions?
- How many positions are necessary to perform the activities?

It is obvious that each business requires its own set of activities. The importance of each varies with the kind of business, its size, and scope of operations. Table 8–1 gives a guide for a simplified activity analysis of a manufacturing or service organization.

A carefully performed activity analysis, besides showing the range of tasks to be performed, breaks down complex tasks into specialized units that can be assigned to individual employees so that their capabilities are fully utilized. It also indicates the skills and experience necessary to perform each job effectively. Last, but not least, an activity analysis gives a foundation for the proper grouping of positions and the development of a coherent organizational structure.

Departmentalization and Development of the Organization Structure

It has already been pointed out that to form the basic organizational units a number of criteria can be used: functions, products, processes, customers, or geographic regions. In a small company the functional approach is most commonly used. Once the departmental units have been established, they are integrated into a formal organization structure, which can then be shown on an organization chart. An organization chart shows graphically the major positions of the enterprise, their hierarchical order, and the formal reporting relationships among them.

Three basic forms may be used in designing an organization structure—a *line structure,* a *line and staff structure,* or a *matrix structure.*

TABLE 8–1. ANALYSIS OF ORGANIZATIONAL ACTIVITIES

Manufacturing		Service Organization (Including Retailing)	
Major Functions	Subfunctions	Major Functions	Subfunctions

Production	Engineering
	  Product design
	  Mechanical engineering
	  Electrical engineering
	  Packaging
	Production planning and control
	Tooling
	Fabrication
	Assembly
	Quality control
		Merchandising	Buying
			Sales
			Budgeting

Marketing	Market research Marketing planning Pricing Sales administration Distribution Advertising, sales promotion Customer service	Publicity	Advertising Display Sales promotion

Finance	Financial management
	  Financial planning
	  Cash management
	  Credit
	  Disbursements
	  Budgeting
	Accounting
	  Financial accounting
	  Cost accounting
	Tax management
		General administration	Customer service
			Store protection
			Inventory management and control
			Receiving
			Marking
			Delivery

Purchasing	Materials procurement Inventory management Receiving Inspection of purchased materials	Finance	Cash management Credit and collections Accounting

Personnel	Manpower planning
	Employment
	  Hiring
	  Layoffs
	Personnel training and development
	Compensation
	Employee benefits administration
	Employee and union relations
		Personnel	Employment
			Personnel training
			Compensation
			Employee services

the typical organization form for a small company is a *line structure* as shown in Figure 8–3. In this form of structure a straight line of command exists from the highest position in the organization to the lowest. Each line manager has a clearly defined area of responsibility and is accountable to only one superior. Within the limits of their authority all members of the organization have the right to make decisions, assign tasks to subordinates, and expect satisfactory performance from them. The primary advantage of a line organization is its simplicity. The work-related interactions among the members of the organization, as well as their responsibilities and accountabilities, are clearly delineated. An additional advantage is the ease with which a line organization can be changed or new positions fitted into the existing structure.

As a firm grows, its managers may no longer be able to deal with all the specialized technical details that their jobs demand. In this situation a *line and staff organization* may become advisable. Here staff positions, filled by experts in specialized fields, are created to advise the line managers and the operating personnel. Staff positions provide either a specific service to line positions or offer advice on particular problems. Final authority for making decisions and issuing orders rests with the line positions. However, staff members may be granted functional authority in their area of expertise, so they often acquire considerable authority to make decisions. Figure 8–4 shows a line and staff organization.

A line and staff organization allows the use of the expertise of staff specialists without increasing the number of decision making centers in the organization. However, the existence of two types of authority, line authority with the right to command, and staff authority with the right to advise—the latter often powerfully authoritative because of its expertise—can create problems of status, misunderstanding, and interpersonal conflict. Line managers frequently regard advice from staff members as an infringement of their authority. The resulting tensions show in such statements as "the staff do not appreciate the technical problems" or "staff people always try to take credit when things go well and are unwilling to accept responsibility for failure."

A line and staff organization is recommended for small firms that are growing rapidly in size and are operating in a dynamic, volatile environment. For most other small businesses a strict line organization or the use of functional task groups is preferable to a line and staff organization.[5]

A third choice for designing an organization structure is a matrix

---

[5]It has been argued that the line and staff concept for structuring an organization is obsolete and that "functional teamwork" is a more effective alternative. See Gerald G. Fisch, "Line—Staff is Obsolete," *Harvard Business Review,* 39, September–October 1961, pp. 67–79.

organization (sometimes referred to as grid organization or project organization).[6] A matrix organization combines functional and project responsibilities. As Figure 8–5 indicates, a company may assign responsibility for a specific project to a project manager who uses the existing, relatively stable, functional organization for carrying out the project. The managers in charge of projects depend on the cooperation and the resources of the functional departments for the technical efforts required to complete their projects. The project managers are responsible for the successful completion of their projects; the departmental managers are responsible for the technical activities required and the quality of the work. As Figure 8–5 implies, all project managers have the same access to line departments as that shown for the manager of project B. A major disadvantage of a matrix organization is that it can easily lead to authority conflicts between project managers and departmental managers.[7]

The main advantage of a matrix form of organization is that it focuses management's attention on the completion of specific projects. Small firms can effectively use a matrix organization under certain operating conditions, for example:

- if individual projects are clearly divisible and if several projects are being carried out simultaneously
- if each project is unique
- if each project is technically complex, requiring a high degree of coordination among different technical specialties.

Although there are considerable differences among line, line and staff, and matrix forms of organization, the basic structural considerations are essentially the same. To be effective each of the three forms requires clear delineation of responsibilities for every position, logical grouping of interrelated positions into departmental units,and proper hierarchical arrangements of the various departmental units, reflecting their importance to the achievement of business objectives. Although a pure line organization tends to be the most appropriate form for the majority of small firms, small firms facing rapid growth, offering a technically complex product, or operating in a rapidly changing external environment should consider the use of a line and staff structure. There are few small firms that meet the preconditions for an effective use of a matrix form of organization.

---

[6]For a detailed description and analysis of matrix organizations see George Steiner and William G. Ryan, *Industrial Project Management*, New York: Macmillan, 1968; Andre J. Grimes, *Matrix Organization*, Madison, Wisconsin: Bureau of Business Research and Service, University of Wisconsin, 1969; C. J. Middleton, "How to Set Up a Project Organization," *Harvard Business Review*, 45, No. 2, 1967, pp. 73–82.

[7]See Richard A. Goodman, "Ambiguous Authority Definition in Project Management," *Academy of Management Journal*, 10, No. 4, 1967, pp. 395–407; David I. Cleland, "The Deliberate Conflict," *Business Horizons*, 11, No. 1, 1968, pp. 78–80.

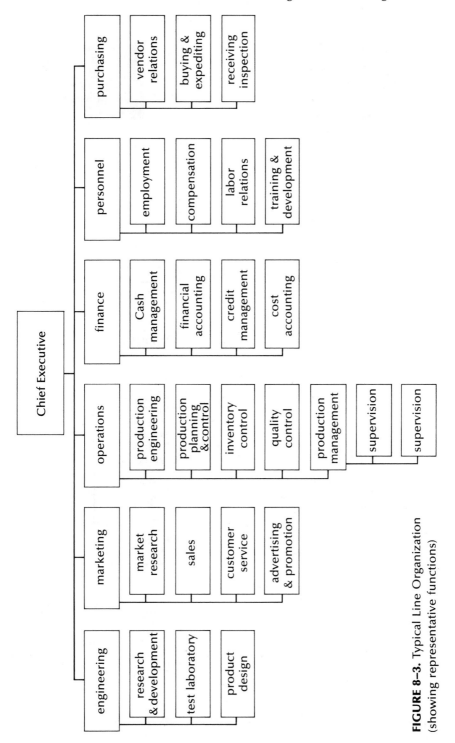

FIGURE 8–3. Typical Line Organization (showing representative functions)

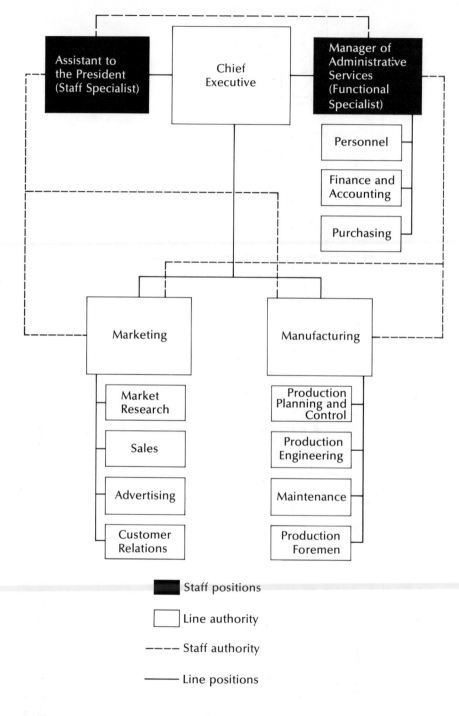

FIGURE 8–4. Line and Staff Organization

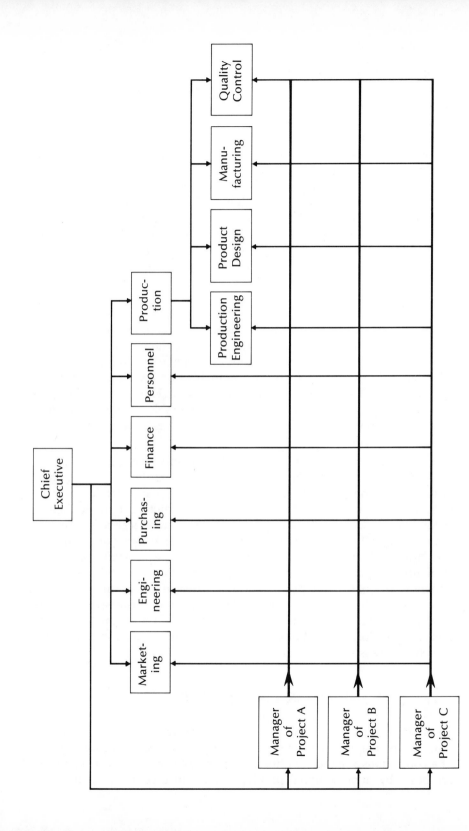

FIGURE 8-5. Matrix Organization

Staffing the Organization

The third step in the process of organizing is to find the right person for each position in the organization. In order to match the requirements for the position with a person having adequate knowledge and skills, a job description and a job specification based on an activity analysis should be developed for each position.

A job description defines the functions, responsibilities, work relationships, authority, and accountability of the person in a particular position. A job specification states the personal qualities, capabilities, and skills that are deemed essential for satisfactorily executing the functions specified in the job description. Job descriptions are an effective organizing tool in a small business. They show whether functional responsibilities are fully covered; they play a useful role in the recruitment, development, and evaluation of employees; and they help the person placed in a job understand its requirements. Job specifications should indicate the desired educational background, experience, skills, aptitudes, and other important qualifications of the person to be placed in a given position. Since the attributes that enable a person to perform a job effectively are not often sharply definable, job specifications tend to be more difficult to develop than job descriptions. However, job descriptions and job specifications do provide a workable basis for matching persons and positions, and thus help in successfully manning the organizational structure.

In summary, the process of establishing an effective organization requires a continuous effort involving three essential steps. 1) A systematic analysis of the activities necessary to achieve the organization's objectives must be made. 2) An organizational structure that delineates individual positions and places them in some hierarchical order must be designed. For this purpose three basic organization forms are available; the choice of one of these forms—line, line and staff, or matrix structure—depends on the internal operating characteristics and interdependencies of the organization and on external environmental conditions. 3) The organization must be staffed, which means finding the ideal person for each position, the culmination of the organizing effort; accurate position descriptions and job specifications are basic prerequisites for successfully completing this task.

PITFALLS TO AVOID IN ORGANIZING

Thus far the discussion has focused on creating an effective organization. The management of small firms often fails to realize the importance of a continuous organizing effort. Many small firms, as a consequence, are beset by organizational problems that cause conflict, inefficiency, and waste. This part of the analysis focuses on some common organizing pitfalls and ways of avoiding them.

Overcentralization and Insufficient Delegation

The terms centralization and decentralization refer to the degree of delegation of authority and decision making in an organization. Both terms express relative concepts; no organization can be completely centralized nor can it be completely decentralized. Complete centralization would mean that all decision-making authority would be held by one person, and complete decentralization would imply no central authority and no coordinated activities. An organization could not exist under either of these extremes; rather centralization and decentralization are matters of degree. The greater the delegation of authority for making decisions to lower levels in the organization, the more it is decentralized; the greater the retention of power and authority by the top management of an enterprise, the more it is centralized.

The balance between centralization and decentralization reflects basic management philosophy. Although there is no clear empirical evidence that a decentralized organization is superior to a highly centralized one, there are some specific advantages to decentralization. A decentralized organization tends to provide more opportunities for personal growth, self-actualization, and satisfaction in work among its employees. Their jobs tend to become more challenging, which in turn can be a factor in stimulating creativity, ingenuity, and efficient performance. And yet in many small firms there is an unduly high degree of centralization. Decision-making authority is retained by top management. Many small business executives are unwilling or unable to delegate managerial responsibility. As a consequence they tend to be overburdened with routine operating decisions, thus robbing themselves of time for long-range planning and other important strategic functions.

Small business executives should realize that they could make a far more significant contribution to their firms' success if they would focus more on strategic planning, control, and the exercise of leadership rather than day-to-day routine decisions and tasks that could be dealt with by subordinates. Koontz and O'Donnell recommend the following guidelines for moving toward a greater degree of decentralization and for overcoming aversion to delegating:[8]

- Define assignments and delegate authority in the light of results expected.
- Select the person on the basis of the job to be done.

---

[8]Harold Koontz and Cyril O'Donnell, *Principles of Management: An Analysis of Managerial Functions,* 5th edition, New York: McGraw-Hill, 1972, pp. 352–53.

- Maintain open lines of communication.
- Establish proper controls.
- Reward effective delegation and successful assumption of authority.

Failure to Clarify Job Responsibilities and Organizational Relationships

A prerequisite for an effectively functioning organization is clear delineation of the responsibilities of each position and clarification of the interrelationships among the various positions. The means for accomplishing these purposes are accurate job descriptions and organization charts. Yet in many small firms there is neither an explicit specification of the responsibilities of each position nor an organization chart giving organizational relationships, lines of authority, and channels of communication. A lack of clarity in these matters invites a lack of understanding by the employees about what is expected of them. Such a lack causes some responsibilities not to be covered at all and others to be assumed by more than one person. Failure to clarify job responsibilities is a common pitfall in small firms and can lead to intra-organizational frictions, buck-passing, and exasperating and costly inefficiencies. To avoid these problems small companies should pay special attention to written specifications of job responsibilities and organizational relationships. These documents should:

- Specify the tasks for which every employee is responsible.
- Where there are multiple tasks, set task priorities.
- Specify the amounts and types of expenditures that each manager can control without approval.
- Specify the managers' responsibilities and their relationships with others on the job.

Imbalance between Responsibilities and Authority

One criterion of good organization is that employees' responsibilities be commensurate with the authority granted them. A mismatch often occurs in small firms. Managers may hold their subordinates responsible for results they cannot possibly achieve simply because they have not been granted sufficient authority over the use of the company's resources. On the other hand, the subordinates in small companies have frequently been granted sufficient authority, but management fails to exact responsible and efficient performance from them. Both conditions are detrimental to organizational effectiveness. Small business executives should try to maintain a balance between the employees' responsibilities and the means put at their disposal for carrying out their responsibilities. One way to achieve this balance is through a management by objectives (MBO) program[9] or any other periodic performance review system. Management by objectives is a technique as well as a continuing process. It stresses a review of each employee's job-related performance objectives between the employee and his immediate superior. Supervisors and their subordinates meet on a regular basis (perhaps every three or six months) to evaluate the actual achievements against the established objectives and agree on new objectives for the next period. In this review it is advisable to check whether an employee's authority and responsibility are commensurate—and adequate for achieving the objectives agreed upon.

Organizational Inflexibility

Most business firms operate in a dynamic environment that affects their organizational arrangements. Internal developments such as the introduction of a new product line, personnel turnover, or a reorientation of production and marketing strategies tend to have an immediate impact on organizational relationships. External developments such as fluctuations in economic conditions, changes in consumer taste, or technical innovations by competitors may have an even more dramatic impact. To be successful a company must have the ability to adapt rapidly to the changing conditions that affect it. That requires organizational flexibility—an ingredient often missing in small companies. There are several reasons for lack of organizational flexibility in small companies. First, the resources of time, money and specialization tend to be in short supply. Second, in small firms the consequences of change are likely to be great, the cost of failure drastic, and the inherent resistance to change strong. Third, the management turnover in many small companies is relatively low and, as a result, the organizational relationships among the management group may become "petrified." Fourth, owner-managers of small companies are frequently hesitant about taking steps toward reorganization because it would require them to change their management style. All these factors combine to create inertia and organizational rigidity, which prevent many small firms from promptly adapting to changing environmental conditions. The managers of small firms can, however, use two approaches to facilitate organizational flexibility:

- Periodically review the organization structure.
- Use the normal personnel turnover to make changes in the organization structure rather than merely to replace employees.

---

[9]See, for example, Stephen J. Carroll, Jr., and Henry L. Tosi, Jr., *Management by Objectives: Applications and Research*, New York: Macmillan, 1973.

Insufficient Attention to Informal Organizational Relationships

Side by side with the formal organization there exists the more nebulous informal organization. The informal organization arises from a free association of employees. They form social groups whose members tend to share common values, sentiments, and group activities.[10] Informal group relationships provide opportunities for satisfying individual needs that are not met within the structure of the formal organization. The informal organization can have a positive, negative, or neutral impact on the effectiveness of the formal organization.

On the positive side, the informal organization can provide opportunities for satisfying social needs of the employees. These include recognition, status, friendship, congeniality, and gregariousness or a sense of belonging, which when fulfilled may lead to great satisfaction with the formal organization and to high morale. In addition, the informal organization can facilitate the flow of information and may provide a safe release of emotional tensions caused by pressure of work.

On the negative side, the informal organization can have a disruptive effect on the achievement of the formal organization's objectives. Sabotaging the "rate buster," pressure for work restriction, extended work breaks, idle chatter around the coffee machine, gossiping, and horseplay are well known examples of counterproductive activities to which the informal organization can give rise.

The management of a small firm should try to determine the specific effects of the informal organization. When the effects are negative, it may become necessary to identify the informal group leaders and to counsel them to an improved attitude. At the same time, management should try to detect and eliminate the underlying causes of counterproductive informal group behavior. If this does not succeed, it may well become necessary to discharge unreasonably antagonistic informal leaders or to make it difficult for the members of a disruptive clique to interact during working hours.

Whether the informal organization has a negative, positive, or neutral effect on the achievement of a firm's objectives, it should never be ignored. If an effective work organization is to be established, management should be aware of the informal relationships and should continuously work to produce synergistic interaction between the formal and informal organizations for the benefit of the company. To accomplish this objective the management of a small firm should:

---

[10]On the nature of the informal organization see George C. Homans, *The Human Group*, New York: Harcourt Brace & Company, 1950; Daniel Katz and Robert L. Kahn, *The Social Psychology of Organizations*, New York: John Wiley & Sons, 1966; T. N. Whitehead, "The Inevitability of the Informal Organization and its Possible Value," in *Readings in Management*, edited by Ernest Dale, 3rd edition, New York: McGraw-Hill, 1975, pp. 208–10.

- Seek to understand the basic reason for the existence of a given informal group.
- Seek to understand why specific attitudes and behavior patterns occur.
- Identify the informal leaders.
- Work through the informal leaders for the achievement of desired organizational objectives.
- Ask for the informal leaders' advice and participation in decisions directly affecting the informal organization.
- Attempt to establish close congruence between the formal and informal organizations.

COPING WITH ORGANIZATIONAL GROWTH AND CHANGE

Like living organisms, business organizations are subject to a life cycle. They have a period of youth, a period of maturity, and a period of decline. Some organizations go through their life cycle in a very short time; others last for decades, or even centuries. To be successful every organization must grow in some way—not necessarily in size, but perhaps in technical competence or managerial expertise. Furthermore, to be successful an organization must undergo and adapt to change. Growth and change impinge upon an organization's structure and its interpersonal relationships. To ensure the survival of a small firm, its management must anticipate and take proper action in response to the impact of growth and change.

Stages of Organizational Growth

The term *organizational growth* is used broadly and refers to the concept that organizations are complex social structures with identifiable stages of development. Each stage of development tends to be associated with one or more crucial organizational issues. When an enterprise copes successfully with these issues, some form of growth occurs. That does not mean it has to grow in size. In fact, the tendency among many small businesspersons to see increasing sales volume as a solution to all problems is a fallacy. Shrinking the number of products or product lines and reducing the number of employees is often a better route to a higher return on investment.[11]

Organizational growth may be measured not only by an increase in size such as a larger number of employees, a higher sales volume, or an

---

[11]See Herbert N. Woodward, "Management Strategies for Small Companies," *Harvard Business Review,* January–February 1976, p. 114.

Growth Stages	Likely Sales (——) and Profit (----) Trends	Dominant Organizational Issues
Launching the venture		Assess opportunities and risks realistically Determine feasible organizational objectives Achieve unity of purpose Delineate responsibilities and specify lines of authority
Take-off		Move toward decentralization of decision making Emphasize organizational flexibility that facilitates rapid growth Adjust to growth Recognize limiting conditions
Drive to maturity		Decentralize further and delegate authority to lower organizational levels Develop organizational stability Build pride and reputation
Maturity		Avoid excessive organizational rigidity Avoid organizational sprawl: too many organizational levels, empire building, unnecessary expansion of administrative services
Decline		Regain organizational flexibility Recognize the need for change Identify relevant external and internal changes Search for new product and market opportunities Attract new leadership with progressive ideas
Revitalization and renewal		Concentrate organizational energies on new opportunities Reduce resistance to change Adopt new, aggressive strategies Develop team spirit Build faith in the future success of the enterprise

FIGURE 8–6. Stages of Growth and Dominant Organizational Issues

increased market share, but also by qualitative improvements such as a greater technical competence or movement toward the successful accomplishment of the company's objectives. Organizational growth therefore results from a process of development in which increase in size may be only a by-product.[12] This process of development tends to take place in stages of varying lengths of time. Figure 8–6 outlines the important stages in the growth of business organizations. It also maps the likely sales and profit trends during each stage and the dominant organizational issues that must be dealt with. If a firm's management fails to deal with these organizational issues, the enterprise is likely to become crisis ridden and may not survive.

Although the stages of growth, as characterized by the framework shown in Figure 8–6, give a somewhat arbitrary and limited way of looking at the progression of a business enterprise, there is an inner logic to the sequence of the indicated developments.

Launching a new business venture is always an entrepreneurial act. It combines human and material resources into a coordinated, goal-oriented endeavor aimed at capitalizing on perceived opportunities. At this stage of the firm's development an important organizational issue is determining a feasible set of objectives based on a realistic assessment of opportunities and risks. These objectives must be clearly communicated to all the members of the organization in order to achieve unity of purpose. What follows then is a clear delineation of responsibilities, which is another crucial issue during the firm's initial struggle for survival.

If a company finds a market niche for itself and overcomes the typical start-up difficulties of inadequate capitalization, inexperienced leadership, and lack of planning, it may find a high degree of market acceptance and relatively rapid growth. This can be called the take-off stage.[13] During this phase the company achieves a decisive breakthrough in its struggle to gain a solid, albeit limited, customer base.

During the take-off stage a firm tends to experience considerable turbulence stemming from the need to expand productive capacity, increase employment, and add administrative services. This expansion generally requires additional organizational and managerial levels. As a consequence, a move toward greater decentralization becomes a critical organizational issue. The chief executive of a small firm, who is very likely to be the one who started the business, must now be able to delegate a greater share of the decision-making authority to lower man-

---

[12]For a more detailed discussion of this interpretation of the term *organizational growth* see Edith T. Penrose, *The Theory of the Growth of the Firm,* New York: John Wiley & Sons, 1959, pp. 1–8.

[13]The terms *take-off* and *drive to maturity* have been used by W. W. Rostow to characterize phases in the economic development of countries. They are used here in an analogous manner to describe phases in the growth of a business enterprise. See W. W. Rostow, *The Stages of Economic Growth,* London: Cambridge University Press, 1960.

agement levels. Otherwise occupation with daily routine matters may thwart managerial effectiveness. The take-off stage also requires change in leadership style from an autocratic approach to a more participative approach.

Equally important to resolving the delegation problem is achieving organizational flexibility so that the firm's expansion is not stifled by a rigid organization structure.

Financial success during the take-off period may cause management to disregard the firm's limitations and weaknesses. This kind of blindness may be overcome by developing sensitivity for those conditions that might imperil further growth of the firm.

The third growth stage, referred to as drive to maturity, may be viewed as a phase of consolidation. It is keyed to overcome the turbulence of the take-off stage by emphasizing organization stability. In addition, the firm's "ego" now becomes an issue; effort is directed to developing the employees' pride in their organization and to gaining the respect of customers, suppliers, competitors, and the public at large. Also during this stage the company should move further toward decentralization and the development of a management team.

An enterprise approaching maturity can experience both positive and negative influences: positive from achievement of a secure position in the marketplace, and negative from relative stagnation because of a complacent attitude. Two developments that management should take care to prevent often occur during this stage: excessive organizational rigidity and organizational sprawl. These conditions can be seen in an unproductive increase in layers of management, an undue expansion of administrative services, and empire building. Through mismanagement of this kind a firm may easily slip into decline.

The decline of a firm is always caused by some form of mismanagement, although external developments may increase its difficulties. The management of a mature company often believes itself immune from the necessity for innovation and change. Without innovation and change conventional practices and tradition take over. The result is rigidity, coupled with reduced drive, ingenuity, and efficiency on the part of the employees. In such a case a firm tends to grow in an unproductive manner—one that may be called organizational sprawl.

Once in decline, key executives and managers must face the situation boldly and diagnose the underlying factors realistically. In the last analysis, some form of neglect or inappropriate managerial decisions are always the true cause of the decline. Corrective actions rest on management's addressing four major issues:

- It must recognize the need for change.
- It must identify relevant external and internal developments that require some form of adaptation.

- It must conduct a concerted search to identify new product and market opportunities.
- It must try to regain organizational flexibility.

The latter may require changes in organization structure as well as changes in established organizational procedures. For example, the required changes may necessitate reorganizing to eliminate too rigid departmental lines; reassigning responsibilities to younger, less tradition-bound employees; or abandoning cumbersome, outdated procedures. All these measures may be used to achieve a greater degree of organizational flexibility for meeting the requirements of changing conditions.

The management of a firm that is in a phase of decline is often unable or unwilling to recognize the need for change. John Gardner observed that "ailing organizations frequently develop a functional blindness to their own defects. They are not suffering because they cannot solve their problems, but because they cannot see their problems."[14] If the decline of a firm is to be reversed, its management must recognize the need for change. Outside consultants can be helpful in this regard; they may be able to pinpoint sources of trouble and they may help management to discover its blind spots. Furthermore, they may stimulate a concerted effort to identify new product and market opportunities. Figure 2–1, p. 31, shows the range of alternatives in this search.

The firm, as mentioned in Chapter 2, can focus on existing markets and an existing product line in the attempt to achieve better market penetration. This strategy is particularly appropriate for small firms with unused production capacity; a deeper market penetration may then be achieved with a modest amount of additional working capital. Emphasis on the development of new products for an existing market would constitute product diversification; the development of new markets for an existing product line would lead to market diversification.

These are possible alternatives. If a company is in a stage of decline, however, the search for new opportunities through product and market diversification may strain the financial resources of the firm, and also may be beyond its managerial capabilities. Change of leadership often becomes a critical organizational issue in this phase of a firm's development. If the company succeeds in attracting new leadership with drive and progressive ideas, it may then enter a stage of renewal or revitalization.

Revitalization brings out a new set of organizational issues requiring close attention. Most importantly, the company should concentrate its resources in realizing new opportunities. That in itself will necessitate change in strategic emphasis and in organization structure. Since change always implies some degree of uncertainty, it tends to arouse

---

[14]John W. Gardner, "How to Prevent Organizational Dry Rot," *Harpers Magazine*, October 1965, p. 20.

resistance among the members of the organization. If management neglects to deal effectively with overt or covert resistance to necessary change, revitalization cannot occur. Reducing resistance to change rests on management's ability to inspire faith in the future of the organization and to develop a team spirit among its members.

This analysis outlines organizational growth as an evolutionary process that proceeds in a series of phases. Each phase in the life cycle of a firm brings to the fore a unique set of critical organizational issues that management must deal with promptly and effectively if the firm is to survive and prosper.

The Limits to Growth

Every enterprise is confronted by a range of conditions or factors that prevent it from realizing its full potential for growth. These factors are not constant; their relative importance may change over time. Management should search for these limiting factors and try to eliminate or at least reduce their negative consequences. There are externally imposed limits to growth over which the management of a firm has little or no control. There are also internal limitations that can be affected by management. Among external factors limiting organizational growth and development are change in the economic, political, or regulatory conditions; change in consumer preferences; and change in technology. These external conditions can be viewed as the variables proscribing the range of economic opportunities for a firm. However, there are many examples that show that in spite of the limiting conditions in the external environment of a firm, its management may be able to reorient the firm's activities, thus enabling it to continue to grow.

When seen in this light, the limiting factors to the growth of a firm are ultimately the limitations of its management. One of the most important—and most difficult—organizational requirements is to ensure that the role played by the chief executive officer (or the top two or three members of the management team) of a small firm evolves with growth. Figure 8–7 indicates the changing demands on top management as the organization grows.

During the early life of an organization the managers of new small firms who are also the owners and initiators of the ventures spend most of their time personally carrying out major functional responsibilities such as selling to key customers, raising funds, developing new products, and hiring and training employees. As the firm grows, the demands on the chief executive or the top management team change. They spend more and more time coordinating the activities of subordinates, developing strategic plans, and handling public relations. However, many small business executives fail to make this transition; they retain their entrepreneurial orientation. They prefer to make operating deci-

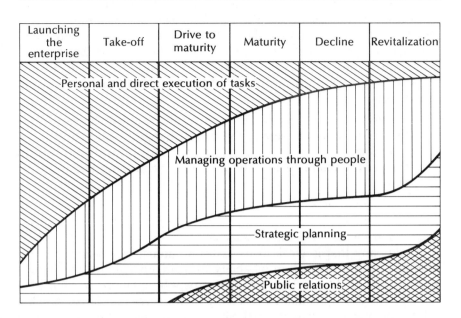

Launching the enterprise	Take-off	Drive to maturity	Maturity	Decline	Revitalization

Personal and direct execution of tasks

Managing operations through people

Strategic planning

Public relations

FIGURE 8–7. The Changing Role of Top Management

sions and carry out major activities themselves rather than delegate increasing responsibilities to lower levels in the organization. This inability to break away from the old routine and to acquire new skills tends to be a severe restriction limiting the growth of the firm. It is not easy to find a small business manager who can guide a firm successfully through the various stages of growth. Those who succeed do so through formal retraining, counseling with experienced outsiders, and determinedly adjusting their management style to the changing requirements of the growing firm. To keep the organization viable it is important to recognize the point at which an enterprise tends to outgrow the capabilities of its current management. If its top management is replaced, the firm may continue to grow—otherwise, having reached its limits of growth, it will stagnate.

Organizational Change and Resistance to Change

Every business enterprise is affected by environmental changes such as fluctuating economic conditions, market movements, technological inventions, and emerging societal demands. In order to be effective and to prosper an enterprise must not only adapt to these changes but must also initiate changes that will give it new competitive advantages. All these changes, induced by dynamic external and internal environments, tend to create uncertainties, or even chaos, against which the members of an organization attempt to defend themselves. For this reason, every organization is also subject to strong forces that aim to preserve the status quo, constancy, predictability, and stability. The management of a firm therefore must cope simultaneously with three conflicting pressures:

1. the need to adapt to relevant external and internal change
2. the need to be innovative, to initiate change to gain competitive advantage
3. the need to maintain stability, to preserve constancy and predictability

The ideal organization shows high ability to be adaptive, to be innovative, and to provide a relatively stable internal work environment. Figure 8–8 shows these three dimensions.

A company that is weak in its ability to adjust to relevant external change and is also weak in its ability to maintain stability and initiate change (block 8, Figure 8–8), is a likely prospect for failure. In contrast, a company that can maintain a relatively high degree of internal stability while creating an organizational climate conducive to innovation and adjustment to external change (block 1) meets the basic requirements for success and growth. All other combinations shown in the diagram imply varying degrees of threat to the survival of the firm, although any one deficiency may not be sufficient to cause the firm to fail. To assure a high probability of success the management of a company should periodically appraise its level of adaptability, stability, and innovation. High values for these three criteria produce a combination that may be considered the touchstone of effective leadership.

It has been pointed out that a major obstacle to a firm's ability to grow is resistance to change. Small companies tend to be particularly prone to this phenomenon. An analysis in the *Behavioral Sciences Newsletter*[15] gives the following reasons why resistance to change in smaller companies tends to be greater than in larger ones. First, in small companies the resources of time, money, and specialization tend to be in short supply and make it hard to effect change. Second, the consequences of change are likely to be great, the stakes high, the cost of failure more drastic, and therefore resistance to change tougher. Third, small companies frequently don't have the "critical mass" needed for change. Even if some people in a small firm advocate change, conflicts about the desirability of change and the ways to accomplish it are likely to become explosive when enclosed in a small space. Fourth, because there is more face-to-face contact in smaller companies than in larger ones, personal-

---

[15]*Behavioral Sciences Newsletter*, September 24, 1972.

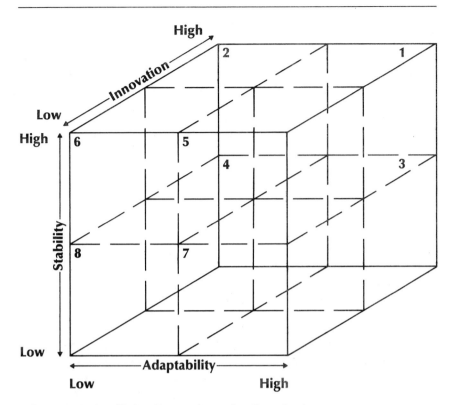

FIGURE 8–8. Conflicting Demands on the Organization

ity factors, as opposed to objective criteria, are likely to play a bigger role in the evaluation of proposals for change. All these issues combine to make the typical small firm resistant to change.

The attitude of the top executive of the small firm is the most critical issue in dealing with this resistance. The chief executive must become convinced that change and adaptation to change are basic to the long-run prosperity of his enterprise. Overcoming resistance to change among the employees of a small company should start from the premise that it is to a large extent an organizing issue. Research and practical evidence show that the greater the understanding of the need for change by those who are affected, the more readily the change will be accepted and the required adjustments made.[16] In addition, people are more

---

[16]See Alfred J. Marrow, David G. Bowers, and Stanley E. Seashore, *Management by Participation—Creating a Climate for Personal and Organizational Development*, New York: Harper & Row, 1967; L. Coch and J. R. P. French, "Overcoming Resistance to Change," *Human Relations*, 1, 1948, pp. 512–32.

favorable toward change when they see it as a means for accomplishing not only organizational but also personal objectives such as promotion, pay increases, easier working conditions, and an improved self-image. For these reasons, a managerial strategy for reducing resistance to change requires developing an awareness throughout the organization of the need for change and an understanding of its likely effects. To reduce anxiety about necessary change, those affected by it should be asked to participate in and contribute their ideas to the planning, introduction, and implementation of the change. They should also be made aware of the specific advantages that a change may have for them personally.

SUMMARY: Central Issues in Organizing the Small Firm

Finding effective solutions to problems of organizing is as important for the small company as it is for the large enterprise. Organizational deficiencies tend to be easier to diagnose in the small firm, but they also pose a more imminent threat to survival. Organizing should be viewed as a continuous process of developing the system of relationships among functions, personnel, and physical factors so that all work will be directed toward achieving organizational objectives. To be successful in this effort requires close attention to critical organizational issues such as the necessity for functional differentiation; the importance of a clear specification of responsibility, authority, and accountability for every position; and the urgent need for organizational flexibility. These issues provide objectives for the organizing process, which involves three essential steps: a comprehensive, systematic analysis of the required activities; the design of an organization structure appropriate to the process of the business; and the selection of persons to fill each position of the organization structure.

In organizing, the small business owner-executive faces a large number of potential pitfalls, which can cause inefficiencies and waste if they are not avoided. Small firms frequently become entrapped by overcentralization, inadequate specification of job responsibilities, imbalance between responsibility and authority, organizational inflexibility, and lack of concern for the informal organizational relationships. If a small firm is to flourish, its management must develop sensitivity in detecting the onset of these conditions and responsiveness in taking corrective action.

The ability to cope with growth and change is of vital importance for any small company. It must recognize that both growth and change require organizational adaptation. At each stage of growth in the life of a small enterprise a unique set of organizational issues becomes dominant. These issues must be resolved effectively or the survival of the business may be at stake. Organizational change represents both opportunity and threat. The management of any firm faces the task of reconciling three conflicting pressures: the need for adapting to external change, the need for initiating change to improve the firm's competitive position, and the need for maintaining stability in the internal work environment. Effective organizational response to these three pressures depends on the firm's ability to cope with resistance to change among the members of the organization. Reducing resistance to change depends largely on an approach to organizing that emphasizes widespread employee participation in planning and instituting the required change.

SUGGESTED READINGS

Bennis, Warren G. *Changing Organizations.* New York: McGraw-Hill, 1966.

Dale, Ernest. *Planning and Developing the Company Organization Structure.* New York: American Management Association, 1972.

Gibson, James L.; Ivancevich, John M.; and Donnelly, James H., Jr. *Organizations, Behavior, Structure, Processes.* Dallas, Tex.: Business Publications, 1976, chapter 10.

Hall, Richard H. *Organizations: Structure and Process.* Englewood Cliffs, N.J.: Prentice-Hall, 1972.

Hampton, David R. *Contemporary Management.* New York: McGraw-Hill, 1977, chapter 9.

Kuriloff, Arthur H. *Organizational Development for Survival.* New York: American Management Association, 1972.

Litterer, Joseph A. *The Analysis of Organization,* 2d edition. New York: John Wiley & Sons, 1973.

Thompson, James D. *Organization in Action.* New York: McGraw-Hill, 1967.

Trewatha, Robert L., and Newport, M. Gene. *Management—Functions and Behavior.* Dallas, Tex.: Business Publications, 1976, part IV.

CHAPTER 9

Personnel Management

The small firm, and particularly the new small firm, is notoriously deficient in its practice of personnel management. Too often this aspect of its management is haphazard. Hiring is done by random selection among the first applicants who apply at the door as the need for help arises. There is no basic policy and no planning.

Entrepreneurs are usually so busy selling and getting the product out the door that they give little or no thought to the consequences of an unplanned approach to hiring, let alone to the total management of the human resources upon which the future of their firm depends.

Some companies miss the opportunity to increase their effectiveness by operating their personnel functions loosely and informally. Organizational competence can come only from the purposeful activity of competent people—and in a competitive world it is the competent firm that survives.

NEED FOR SOUND PERSONNEL POLICY

Small business owners usually have little background in management theory and practice. They operate by handling individual problems as they arise, and they see no connection between the decision they make in a specific instance and the establishment of a policy that will govern the outcome of similar situations in the future. They view policies as something that executives in large companies are concerned with but as not pertinent to the way small business owners conduct their affairs.[1]

Failure to formulate clearly defined policies causes many problems for the small and growing business. This statement holds true in personnel

---

[1]Roland C. Christensen, *Management Succession in Small and Growing Enterprises*, Boston: Graduate School of Business Administration, Harvard University, 1953, chapter 11.

management as well as in other areas. With the hiring of the first employee, the entrepreneur sets standards that can help or hurt future efforts. Too often entrepreneurs believe that they cannot afford high-quality help. They hire the first person they can find regardless of background, education, and potential for growth—perhaps a brother-in-law or cousin. Repeating this procedure they set a pattern and one day wake up to discover themselves surrounded by semicompetent people who cannot meet the challenges of their growing company.

Objectivity and courage may be required to resist the easy path of hiring relatives and close friends who may not meet high standards. However, the small business executive who sets a sound hiring policy from the beginning, even though the cost may be somewhat more than desired, avoids the problems of nepotism and civil warfare often seen in companies employing relatives and friends.

Budding enterprisers would do well to set standards for the kind of personnel around whom to build their company. They should look for competence and potential growth—and for people with whom they feel compatible. These standards should reflect their personal values and form the basis for a policy that attracts high-quality personnel. In this way they can avoid the distressing experience of ridding the company of deadwood when it has grown beyond the limited capacities of its early employees. The problem of finding competent replacements becomes acute at such a point in the company's history. A much healthier way is to start with people of high potential who can grow with the organization.

STEPS IN RECRUITMENT

The small firm is not equipped to use sophisticated techniques in recruitment and selection. Since it does not have qualified staff specialists to handle employment matters, it should use simple techniques. Simplicity, however, does not imply ineffectiveness. The key managers in a small company can do a good job in hiring by following well-tested, straightforward procedures.

Hiring is a three-step process of 1) identifying the position to be filled, its responsibilities, and the skills and background required to meet them, 2) attracting those people who have the qualifications for the position, and 3) hiring the most promising candidate. Step 1 is discussed fully in Chapter 8; steps 2 and 3 are discussed in the following sections.

Attracting Qualified Applicants

The small company does not have the advantages in money, recruiting staff, or attractive fringe benefits of the large company. It must use every resource at its command in the search for qualified applicants for a position. Among the resources available to the small company are the following:

1. *Newspaper advertisements.* The advertisement should outline the requirements of the position specifically to attract individuals with appropriate qualifications. The small firm should concentrate on the advantages it offers: uniqueness of its product or service, opportunity for growth, camaraderie of working in an intimate group, wide scope for individual contribution, and such other features as may be pertinent to that firm.

2. *Business friends and acquaintances.* Company heads usually know many of their counterparts. By making the specific need known to other company heads, the owner of a small firm may find a likely prospect for the open position.

3. *Suppliers and customers.* Key managers among suppliers and customers offer another source of possible prospects.

4. *Trade associations.* There are over five thousand trade associations in the United States, covering almost every business that can be named. Many have employment services that can be used in the search for candidates to fill an open position.

5. *Technical publications.* There are technical publications in almost every field. An advertisement in a selected publication may be fruitful in turning up candidates with specific technical qualifications and background.

6. *Universities and technical institutes.* Universities and technical institutes maintain employment services for new graduates and alumni. Qualified young graduates and mature candidates with experience may be located through these services.

7. *Personal file.* A useful tactic for heads of smaller companies is to keep a personal file of likely prospects for employment. They should build records by noting the name, background, and impressions of individuals they meet in the course of business or social affairs.

8. *Friends and relations.* Soliciting friends and relations for the names of likely candidates has some attendant danger but can be a useful source of information. If the prospect is hired and doesn't work out, there is the risk of losing a happy relationship with friend or relation. This route should clearly be among the last to be used.

9. *Employment agencies.* Employment agencies vary from free government agencies to private firms that charge for their services. A management search firm, carefully selected for integrity and record of success, can do a good job of locating qualified candidates. An agency of this kind might well be chosen to fill a high-level position, with the knowledge that the service would be costly,

perhaps several thousand dollars, and would probably require several months. The small new firm cannot usually absorb the cost of this approach, but might be able to use it later in its growth.

10. *Self-help clubs.* Organizations such as Forty Plus aid mature unemployed executives to find employment. Among the members are those who have lost their positions not for lack of competence, but for reasons beyond their control: mergers, displacement for reasons of sudden change in the economy, or even bankruptcy of the company they have been with. Persons over forty have not necessarily lost their drive or competencies; indeed, many at that age are just beginning to reach their full power and have a quarter of a century of full productivity ahead of them. These clubs are a possible source for filling a vacant management position.

Small business owners, recognizing the problems of competing with large companies, should use every resource available to attract competent people. By knowing thoroughly the requirements of the position to be filled, they are prepared to mount a search for competent candidates. When the search has produced candidates, they can then select and hire the most promising person for the position.

Selecting and Hiring the Right Person

The small business is at a disadvantage in its ability to offer generous fringe benefits. It must therefore attract personnel through the advantages it does have, as has been mentioned: benefits of small size, individuality, close-knit teamwork, and the opportunity for rapid personal growth with the growth of the company. If it cannot meet competition in fringe benefits, it must at least pay comparable salaries.

This means that entrepreneurs must learn about salary levels in their particular business and in their immediate geographic area. They must be familiar with usage and custom in fringe benefits as well, so they can cope with deficiencies in their own programs by suggesting alternative advantages of working for their small firms. They should be aware of the customary hours of work in their area, working conditions, incentives, insurance programs, medical coverage offered employees, deferred compensation programs, and other fringe benefits that may be given by firms with which they must compete for personnel, particularly management personnel. So armed they are ready to fight the battle of selecting and hiring the right person for the position.

The entrepreneur should look for two kinds of competence in candidates during the selection and hiring procedure: technical competence and interpersonal competence. Technical competence means understanding the requirements of the position and having the skills and experience necessary to achieve them in satisfactory fashion. In the small company, particularly in its early stages, candidates will very likely be required to bring more than one set of competencies to the firm. They will have to wear several hats. In addition, they will have to get their hands dirty. Any prospect showing unwillingness to engage actively with the work should be rejected. The small company cannot afford gentility at that stage in its history.

Interpersonal competence refers to collaboration within the firm. Organizations, even the smallest, require cooperation among members. Without teamwork based on interpersonal competence the organization cannot be effective. Effectiveness implies the ability to identify major problems impeding achievement and to solve them so that they stay solved by using the available resources in knowledge and skill. Problems should also be solved in a cooperative fashion so that the problem-solving process itself is not damaged and tomorrow's problems can be solved as competently as today's.[2]

Procedure in Interviewing The small business executive should be aware of the importance of objectivity when interviewing the candidate for a position. Research in the interviewing process shows that interviewers tend to form a favorable or an unfavorable impression of the applicant very early in the meeting. They then search for confirmation. Having found it, they press for proof substantiating their first impression.[3] This tendency should be avoided.

Sound procedure suggests a balanced approach. When the candidate makes a favorable impression, the interviewer should search deliberately for unfavorable evidence—and, in the opposite case, should try to evaluate carefully unfavorable impressions. The small businessperson is more likely to reach a sounder conclusion by following these guidelines and withholding judgment until after the interview.

A widely accepted screening procedure includes three steps. If the company has an individual responsible for personnel matters, that person should take care of the first step, preliminary screening. The second step should be the responsibility of the first-line supervisor for whom the applicant would work directly. The third step should be performed by the enterpriser personally, to make sure that there is a reasonable chance for success of the new hire in fitting into the company. If the company is very small and lacks personnel management, these three steps may be performed by the owner alone. In the latter case, the screening might be compressed into two steps, or possibly even one. The recommended procedures for these three steps are described below.

---

[2]Chris Argyris, *Interpersonal Competence and Organization Effectiveness*, Homewood, Ill.: Dorsey Press, 1962, chapter 2.
[3]Edward C. Webster, *Decision Making in the Employment Interview*, Montreal: Industrial Relations Centre, McGill University, 1964, pp. 112–14.

Step 1. Preliminary screening. This step is aimed at gathering information on the candidate's background and potential. It seeks answers to some basic questions: What has the candidate done in previous jobs, and what does he or she know from education and experience? What skills have been acquired? Does the candidate seem to have the capacity to grow? What are the candidate's motives, drives, interests, and aspirations? From the responses to questions such as these the interviewer can form a judgment about the applicant's potential. An application form filled out by the applicant before the interview is a useful tool for guiding the interview. The information customarily asked for on such a form is given in Figure 9–1.

Personal

Name: Social security number:

Address: Phone number:

Date of birth:*

Educational

High school and location: Dates:

College or university:

Degrees obtained: Year:

Other educational training, including trade, business or military:

References

Name three persons, preferably former supervisors or teachers familiar with your qualifications, whom we have your permission to contact:

Name   Address and phone no.   Position

1.

2.

3.

Personal Comments

Use this space for comments about your special abilities, special work you have done, or special work you would like to do.

FIGURE 9–1. Typical Application Form

---

*The employment Act of 1967 prohibits discrimination on the basis of age with respect to individuals who are at least 40 but less than 65 years of age.

FIGURE 9–1. (continued)

Work Experience

List all periods of employment since school. Start with the most recent employment.

Dates

Company: _____   _____

Address: _____   _____

Company: _____   _____

Address: _____   _____

Company: _____   _____

Address: _____   _____

(If more space is required for work experience, please attach additional sheet.)

I authorize _____ Company to obtain information about my employment and educational records from former employers, school officials, and persons named above as references, and I release all concerned from any liability in connection with the release of such information.

_____
Applicant's signature   Date

Step 2. Second interview: Assessing technical competence. The purpose of the second interview is to assess the candidate's technical competence. Here the individual's capacity to meet the requirements of the position is explored: Is the applicant's background in the business adequate to enable him or her to take hold in a reasonably short time? Does the applicant know the technology required in the position? Does the applicant know enough about management principles and practice to qualify for a management position? This interview is intended to probe more deeply into the specifics of the candidate's qualifications to handle the position. During the interview, the candidate should be asked about particular instances of success or failure in previous employment.

A telephone call to the candidate's previous immediate boss is the preferred way to check this information. People will generally say things in a telephone conversation (or in person) that they wouldn't say in a letter. The former employer can verify the data the candidate has given and serve as a check on the truthfulness of personal information. A typical telephone reference guide list is given in Figure 9–2.

_____(Applicant)_____ is being considered for a
position as _____ and has given us permission
to contact you, _____(reference, title)_____, for a confidential
reference. We would appreciate your answering the following questions:

What was the applicant's technical assignment (company, relationship, time supervised, etc.)?

How did the applicant perform?

Does the applicant get along well with people?

Do you have any reservations about recommending the applicant for hire in our proposed work assignment?

Would you rehire the applicant if the opportunity arose?

Additional comments: (potential, goals, interests, etc.)

Interviewer	Date

FIGURE 9–2. Telephone Reference

Step 3. Third Interview: Final judgment. The third interview is intended to verify the findings and impressions of the first two and, particularly, to solidify judgment about the candidate's interpersonal competence: Would this person tend to display a consultative or an authoritarian manner in managing subordinates? Would the candidate face up to the boss when the boss's approach left something to be desired? How would the candidate respond if questioned about a decision? Would the experience of subordinates be used in a cooperative way to solve problems facing the group? Does the person's behavior indicate rigidity or a reasonable but not wishy-washy flexibility? These questions, and similar ones that may suggest themselves, provide the basis for judging whether the individual could successfully direct problem-solving efforts so that problems would stay solved without impairing the problem-solving process—the ultimate test of interpersonal competence.

These interviews furnish successively finer screens in the selection process. The candidate passing through them would be offered the position. The entrepreneur should recognize, however, that even the most elaborate interviewing and testing procedures cannot ensure that the candidate selected will be successful on the job. There are too many variables in practice to certify the outcome of any selection procedure. The implication is that the entrepreneur, having been very careful in selecting the individual, has tilted the odds toward a favorable outcome. The boss must take a chance. The new person should come to work on a trial basis for a specified period. If the person does not work out well, a clean severance is the best answer. This understanding should be clear at the time of hiring.

The three-step procedure outlined above offers the entrepreneur-owner the chance to make reasonably sure that the candidate is the kind of person upon which to build the organization. When hiring the first employee, the entrepreneur sets standards for the future of the company and begins to form its culture. Executive actions should be based on consciously appraised values and consistent striving to incorporate these values in the organization.

Use and Misuse of Testing It was assumed in the foregoing discussion that the owner-enterpriser was screening the candidate personally. The small business executive may wish to seek outside help on occasion. A psychologist may be employed to check out the candidate's personality. Here the attempt would be to find out whether the applicant *can do* and *will do* the job.[4]

In theory, it is possible to list the aptitudes needed to perform a specific kind of work. For example, an engineering designer must be able to visualize in three dimensions, a statistician requires high accounting ability to analyze and organize data rapidly and accurately, and a writer of fiction relies heavily on creative imagination. Aptitude testing performed by a qualified consultant can be helpful in making decisions about hiring. The results, however, should be used with caution. The information is best treated as another set of data in forming an opinion about the candidate.

The basis of aptitude testing is statistical, resulting from a large number of tests of many individuals. If one assumes an acceptable correlation between selected aptitudes and success in performance on the job, there still remains considerable question about the particular individual's response to the tests. Human beings are complex organisms, capable of enormous adaptability—and the *can do* may be more than made up for by the exercise of *will do*.

Assessing *will do* may be attempted through personality testing. Many kinds of tests are used for this purpose. Some are intended to disclose particular traits such as anxiety under stress, initiative, or self-confidence. Others are aimed at giving a general picture of the personality. Assessment depends upon clinical methods, generally relying on

---

[4]George S. Odiorne, *Personnel Administration by Objectives*, Homewood, Ill.: Richard D. Irwin, 1971, pp. 263–66.

projective techniques. The subject may be asked to tell stories about particular pictures or to describe some standard ink blots. The psychologist then interprets these responses for themes indicative of the subject's dominant needs, such as attitudes, major internal conflicts, and tolerance of frustration. The report the clinician prepares for the entrepreneur is descriptive, representing the professional's individual point of view. It is likely to be full of general statements, somewhat qualified, and guardedly written.

The data in the report should not be considered conclusive. In the final analysis, it is up to the entrepreneur to decide. Testing should be used with the understanding that it can be helpful when treated with caution.[5]

The entrepreneur should recognize that there are federal and state laws that place constraints upon the use of testing for hiring or promotion. Testing procedures must be nondiscriminatory and must be clearly tied to the requirements of the specific job for which candidates are being assessed. The small business executive would be well advised to consult counsel if there is any doubt about the legal propriety of the intended testing.

PITFALLS OF TRADITIONAL PERFORMANCE APPRAISAL

Performance appraisal as practiced historically has been a manifestation of the traditional organization's implicit purpose of detecting and correcting error. As McGregor has indicated, it has usually been an administrative technique to control the behavior of subordinates through reward and punishment. It has also been used to control the behavior of superiors by forcing them to address problems of inferior performance and to communicate with subordinates their judgments of the subordinates' performance.[6] Performance appraisal practiced in this way indicates a directive managerial strategy issuing from the assumptions of Theory X.

The traditional performance appraisal starts with consideration of the position description, which tells what the position holder is supposed to do. It is used for administrative purposes in the organization, for informative purposes in telling incumbents how they're doing, and for motivational purposes in stimulating them toward improved performance. Each of these elements contains pitfalls that subvert the beneficial intentions of the appraisal procedure.

---

[5]Harold J. Leavitt, *Managerial Psychology*, 3d edition, Chicago: University of Chicago Press, 1972, chapter 7.

[6]Douglas McGregor, *The Human Side of Enterprise*, New York: McGraw-Hill, 1960, chapter 6.

Inadequacies of Position Descriptions

People are unique. They do things in different ways. The same job is therefore performed differently by different people. One salesman, for example, may rely on superior technical competence to sell a job, another on charismatic personality. One person may write a report by first preparing a meticulous outline on paper, another may outline the report mentally.

Conditions within and outside the organization change, changing the nature of the work to be done. As people gain competence, they approach the task in a different manner. The technology of the company changes as new methods become available. For these and similar reasons the position description that may have been reasonably applicable at one time no longer applies. It is almost impossible to keep the position description congruent with the actual requirements of the work.

Managers, understanding the inadequacy of position descriptions, generally scan them to see if there is some semblance of agreement between what the descriptions say and their knowledge of the requirements. If there is rough agreement, the position descriptions are casually tossed into the file and ignored from then on.

Superiors and subordinates have been found to have widely different views of the subordinate's job.[7] The position description appears to be an ineffective tool of communication. Those who suppose that writing it down is the sure way to clarify the requirements of a position are sadly in error.

Although the position description does have some usefulness in charting the organization and in hiring and salary administration, its value as a basis for understanding performance requirements of the position is limited.

Inadequacies of the Appraisal Process

The performance appraisal process is customarily used for administrative purposes, including the adjustment of salary; promotion, demotion, or transfer; and termination. Here too the traditional procedure has run into trouble.

Because there are no absolute standards for judging many of the characteristics often stipulated in the traditional appraisal form—which is keyed to traits such as initiative, quality of work, cooperativeness, and adaptability—managers judge by personal standards. These vary widely, since what one manager may consider excellent another may

---

[7]Rensis Likert, *New Patterns of Management*, New York: McGraw-Hill, 1961, pp. 52–53.

think only passable. Bias and prejudice, all too human failings, affect even the fairest managers. Evaluations are not comparable as a result, and the reliability of the performance appraisal is shadowed by serious doubt.

Traditional appraisal methods frequently try to make judgments much finer than the necessarily rough data will justify. To specify the point at which an individual should be rated on a scale of twenty for *adaptability* or for *attitude toward coworkers* certainly seems too much to ask of human judgment. And yet this requirement comes from an actual form used in practice and is not atypical of the traditional approach.

The purposes of the performance appraisal are thwarted in yet another way. Managers very quickly learn to manipulate the process for their own purposes. If they want to give a raise or improve a person's chances for promotion, they simply adjust their responses to the forms in the appropriate direction. Manipulation can, of course, be used for negative purposes as well.

It would seem that the appraisal procedure involves far more than its design intends. It is a complex function of the subordinate's characteristics and performance and the psychological profile of the manager. The procedure is further complicated by the quality of the relationship between the two.

In summary, these common deficiencies of the traditional appraisal practice raise questions about its reliability. Traditional appraisals tend to show wide differences in ratings of the same personnel by different managers, and they do not necessarily measure accurately the qualities being rated.

Failure to Communicate

It is a truism that people want to know where they stand. Most managers seem to translate this adage to mean "people want constructive criticism." When managers practice constructive criticism it somehow turns into censure—or so it seems to subordinates. They find it hard to hear and accept criticism, as do most of us. We become defensive. We reject what we do not want to hear. The more serious the criticism, the more likely we are to shut it out. Defensiveness is after all a mechanism that arises when the self feels threatened. The four most frequently threatening experiences are anxiety, conflict, frustration, and failure.[8] The subordinate may feel any or all of these under the stress of criticism that is perceived as censure.

Traditional interviews, which are supposed to be informative in telling subordinates where they stand, too often develop into censure in which

---

[8]Chris Argyris, *Personality and Organization*, New York: Harper & Row, 1957, pp. 36–39.

subordinates are told what they have done wrong and what their deficiencies are. Under these circumstances, it is highly questionable whether subordinates want to know where they stand. They tune out. If the situation becomes truly frightening, however, they may start fighting back. Interviews then turn into lose-lose arguments in which neither party can win. Many managers have had this experience even though they may have entered an interview with the best of intentions and in the kindliest spirit. The manager soon discovers that appraisal interviews are fraught with danger. The result is that the interview becomes anything but a vehicle for communication; its informative purpose is subverted. The manager learns to avoid possible conflict in the future, and performance appraisal depreciates to a perfunctory ritual.

Failure to Motivate The traditional appraisal procedure is poorly calculated to provide the motivational impact intended. It is based on the concept that people change by being told. The motivation to change must originate within the person. Since behavior is goal directed, individuals must see the change as beneficial in some way, as an objective of value, before they are stimulated toward self-initiated efforts to change.

The traditional performance appraisal is customarily conducted semiannually or annually. This timing violates the *law of effect*, and thus the appraisal fails to reinforce desired behavior. The law of effect states that people tend to repeat behavior they expect will be rewarded and avoid behavior they expect will not be rewarded or will lead to punishment.[9] But reward or punishment must be perceived as connected with a specific behavior if it is to affect the individual's behavior. When there is too long a time lag between the act and its consequence, this connection is lost; the person does not become motivated to change. The annual or semiannual performance appraisal fails in this regard. The lag between performance and result is usually too long.

AVOIDING THE PITFALLS OF TRADITIONAL PERFORMANCE APPRAISAL

The new small firm is unlikely to use position descriptions. But as it grows the need for a more-or-less formal array of position descriptions will arise for administrative purposes, if for no other reason. Position descriptions should then be prepared with a full understanding of their inadequacies.

As conditions within the company change, the requirements of work are likely to change. Managers soon learn that position descriptions do not tell with reasonable accuracy what the job requirements are. They do

[9]Lyman W. Porter and Edward E. Lawler, III, *Managerial Attitudes and Performance*, Homewood, Ill.: Richard D. Irwin, 1968, p. 8.

not, therefore, take the position descriptions literally. Some attempt should be made to update the position descriptions on a regular schedule to keep them somewhat in line with actuality. This procedure will help in administering wages and salaries.

The system of managing by results, which is described in Chapter 14, incorporates methods and techniques for avoiding the other pitfalls of the traditional performance appraisal—its inadequacies in appraising, communicating, and motivating.

COMPENSATION POLICIES AND PRACTICES

The small firm usually cannot afford to hire a specialist in wage and salary administration. The entrepreneur will more than likely perform this function during the early period of the company's history. As the firm grows, the duties of wage and salary administration are customarily transferred to one of the managers, perhaps a financial officer. With further growth, a staff specialist may be added to perform wage and salary administration. It is extremely important that the responsible individual, whether boss or staff specialist, keep abreast of developments in this field so that the firm can maintain a competitive position.

Wage and salary administration presents perhaps the most complex and difficult problem in management. A handy outline for examining the elements of this problem is that suggested by David W. Belcher. It covers the following categories:

1. wage and salary levels
2. wage and salary structures
3. individual wage determination
4. method of payment
5. indirect compensation or fringe benefits
6. exempt employees
7. management control[10]

The small firm should adopt the simplest means to administer its compensation practices. For the sake of efficiency, several of these categories can be dealt with in combination, as for example, wage and salary levels and salary structures.

Wage and Salary Levels and Structures

The small firm can develop guides for setting wage and salary levels by answering the following four questions:

---

[10]David W. Belcher, *Wage and Salary Administration,* 2d edition, Englewood Cliffs, N.J.: Prentice-Hall, 1962, chapter 2.

1. Are our wages and salaries competitive for the industry and for the geographic area in which we operate?
2. Do we meet the minimum wage laws and other legal requirements governing compensation?
3. Do we meet the standards implied by the values of the owner-executive and management staff?
4. Are we concerned with meeting or exceeding union wage policies?

Many sources of information are available on prevailing compensation. Among these are national trade associations, which generally maintain data on wages and salaries in their specific industries; local business associations; city, county, and federal agencies, which publish these data regularly; and several national and local associations of personnel and compensation specialists. Specific sources of data can be identified by referring to the local library, business school libraries, and local government offices at the city, county, state, or federal level. A telephone call to a personnel manager in a large local company can be immediately productive, since these managers must maintain up-to-date information. They are usually willing to give the small businessperson names and telephone numbers of agencies that can provide information. Some effort in seeking help can produce a wealth of information from which practicable wage and salary levels and structures may be established.

By setting wage and salary levels in keeping with these data, the small firm assures its ability to hire and retain a productive work force. It can hire at rates that represent sound averages for its various jobs and positions.

Wage Determination and Method of Payment

Setting wage and salary structures provides a way of judging what compensation should be paid for each job or position with respect to others. The more responsible and difficult jobs command more pay than those at lower levels. The structure also shows the range of compensation available to each position. This gives the basis for administering individual wages and salaries within each range. The procedure establishes policy for individual wage determination. It also provides motivation by showing the members of the company how their compensation can be increased by moving up the position ladder.

Establishing the payment method requires determining which jobs are to be paid on hourly rates and which are to be salaried on a weekly or monthly schedule. In addition, incentive and bonus programs must be settled with respect to position levels.

Indirect Compensation

The small company faces a special problem in setting policy on indirect compensation, often called fringe benefits. The list of fringe benefits in American business practice is long and varied. In many companies the financial equivalent of the benefits ranges from about 15 to 25 percent of direct compensation in wages and often exceeds 30 percent for high-level managers. The term *indirect compensation* seems more appropriate than fringe benefits in view of the increasing importance and cost attached to this form of pay. Because of the high cost of indirect compensation, the small firm, and particularly the new small firm, must be cautious in administering this part of the compensation program.

It will have to pay fringe items required by law. Federal and state laws govern hours of work and overtime pay for hourly rated, nonexempt employees. Exempt personnel include managers, professionals, and outside salespersons. Base compensation for exempt personnel is called salary; for nonexempt personnel, wages. A distinguishing difference between the two is the time interval of payment. Hourly workers are customarily paid each week, salaried personnel every other week or twice a month.

Other indirect compensation that must be paid includes workers' compensation and disability insurance, required by state law. These are generally considered to be payroll taxes. The federal Social Security Act provides for one more benefit that must be paid. It is another contribution to indirect compensation.

Beyond compulsory indirect compensation to meet state and federal laws, the small business must provide some forms of indirect compensation to meet competition. As it grows and prospers, the entrepreneur-owner may wish to add elements of indirect compensation for both personal and business reasons.

From a personal standpoint, the entrepreneur may wish to reward loyal and hard-working members of the firm who have helped build it and make it successful. From a business standpoint, such compensation will be necessary to attract qualified workers and managers and to retain superior performers at all levels. Special rewards for high performance can also be used as motivational devices.

Indirect compensation takes many forms and the list grows longer each year. Belcher suggests the following five categories, which cover a great number of items in current compensation practice:

1. extra payments for time worked, such as holiday premiums or overtime premiums, or extra vacation time
2. nonproduction awards and bonuses, such as attendance or quality bonuses

3. payments for time not worked, such as jury duty, voting, or military service allowance
4. payments for employee security, such as accident and hospitalization insurance or life insurance
5. payments for employee services, such as educational assistance or suggestion awards[11]

These items of indirect compensation are typical, but are only indicative of the wide range of such benefits. The entrepreneur should keep abreast of developments in fringe benefits for the sake of maintaining a competitive position.

Benefits for managers present special problems. Here the enterpriser-owner wants to hire, motivate, retain, and reward outstanding performers in this most critical element of business. Bonuses, stock options, profit sharing, deferred compensation programs, and, at less significant levels, use of company autos, membership in clubs, and reserved parking space represent a wide range of special compensation items for this purpose. Three critical factors influence the executive benefit program:

1. the financial ability of the company to offer such benefits to its managers
2. the desirability of the particular benefits to the individual manager
3. the way benefits are administered

The small company should use its limited resources carefully in selecting those executive benefits that are most productive in meeting the objectives for which they are employed. Typically these include the goals of remaining competitive, of being able to attract managers of superior caliber, of rewarding superior performance, and of influencing managers toward higher levels of achievement.

Adoption of the so-called cafeteria style of compensation for managers would appear to be most helpful in being competitive and attracting qualified management personnel. The purpose of cafeteria compensation is to permit executives to select that combination of salary and benefits they consider most useful in filling their needs. Young married managers with small children, for example, usually have immediate need for cash. Older managers whose children have grown and left home generally require less cash and are more interested in setting aside funds for retirement. The underlying principle in cafeteria compensation is that managers who can satisfy their personal needs by combining base salary with an appropriate selection of benefits will be attracted to and remain with the company.

The motivational effect of benefits tends to produce the most effective

---

[11]David W. Belcher, *Compensation Administration*, Englewood Cliffs, N.J.: Prentice-Hall, 1974, pp. 364–65.

results when administered so that reward is seen by the manager as being attached to performance.[12] Company policy should clearly define the relationship between superior performance and reward, and the reward should be given as soon after superior achievement as practicable so that the connection between achievement and reward is firmly established. When consistently applied, managerial expectancies of reward for superior performance are fulfilled and help to undergird an achieving climate in the organization. This form of administering benefits for managers is completely consistent with the methods of managing by objectives and results, as will be seen in Chapter 14.

Terminating Personnel

Even the best managed businesses find it necessary to terminate personnel. The small businessperson should be aware of several important considerations when faced with this distasteful task. These include proper timing, satisfying the requirement for replacement, warning the unsatisfactory performer, terminating the employee, deciding on severance pay, and conducting the terminal interview.[13]

The proper approach to releasing an employee will vary according to circumstances. Sometimes management wishes to release the employee. At other times the employee wishes to quit.

It is manifestly unfair to discharge employees without prior warning except in unusual situations. Employees who cannot meet the requirements of a job should be given the opportunity to improve. They should be told that they have a reasonable time, one month or two, perhaps more depending upon the nature of the job, to bring their performance up to standard. They should be coached if possible, or given special training if they are deemed capable of making the required improvement. If the desired improvement is not evident in the specified time, they should be given notice. One or two weeks is customary in most cases. They should then be terminated. In the meantime, management should solve the problem of replacement.

If employees indicate a desire to leave, it is usually the wisest course to let them go immediately. Persons who want to leave no longer have their hearts in their jobs. To retain them may precipitate some unwanted consequences. They may spread disaffection among other employees. They may, if managers, recruit others whom they see as competent to leave with them. It is far better for the company to give them reasonable severance pay and ask them to go at once.

There are some delicate questions that may have to be answered be-

---

[12]Porter and Lawler, *Managerial Attitudes*, pp. 176–80.

[13]William Wayne, *How to Succeed in Business When the Chips Are Down*, New York: McGraw-Hill, 1972, chapter 12.

fore terminating a key employee in some situations. Does the employee alone have special knowledge that should be imparted before departure? Is the employee involved in an important negotiation with a good customer that should be settled before severance? Can someone else take over the job? If not, would it cost the company more to have the employee leave before a replacement is found than it would to put an uninformed person in the position? Is it desirable to try to change the employee's mind? Answers to questions such as these help to decide the time of termination.

In any event, it should ordinarily be the responsibility of the person who did the hiring to do the firing. Termination interviews should be conducted with care. This procedure allows the company to receive important feedback on its practices and can often pinpoint opportunities for improvement. At the same time the company can deal openly with questions employees may raise. Employees may want to know exactly why they are being terminated if the company is letting them go. They should be told honestly so that they can avoid similar difficulties on their next job. The discussion should not be permitted to degenerate into a debate over the issues. When management has taken the time and trouble to discuss performance deficiencies in prior warning meetings there should be no need for debate. Decisive termination interviews are healthier for the company and the employees.

Occasionally a special case arises stemming from long-term absence of a key employee because of illness. Issues of morality and equity are involved. It is difficult for the small company to decide policy in this situation because of its usually limited resources. The owner will have to decide how generous the company can afford to be. Answers to the following questions can serve as guides: How long has the employee been with the company? How long is the absence likely to last? How adequate is the available hospitalization insurance coverage? Does the insurance program provide funds for maintenance of the employee's family? If so, how adequate is the payment in meeting their needs? Is it feasible to cover the difference between the returns from insurance and maintenance requirements? Would a loan be a possible solution? What is a reasonable length of time for the company to provide support? Perhaps three or four months would be generous; a longer period might be questionable. The owner will be forced to compromise on occasion between satisfying the dictates of good judgment and those of conscience.

DEALING WITH UNIONS

Successful small business enterprisers usually believe that the best union is no union. They have hauled themselves up by their bootstraps through their own initiative and very likely resent sharing management prerogatives with outsiders. It disturbs them that their people should look to a union instead of to them for satisfaction of demands, for they see themselves as fair-minded persons, willing to listen and compromise.

The law of the land, however, says that the owner and the union must sit down and bargain collectively in good faith. Entrepreneurs would be wise to sublimate their feelings by devoting their energy to planning for and managing relationships with the union in a way calculated to be most beneficial to their businesses in both the short and the long haul.

The Typical Situation in Small Companies

Small companies facing unionization have probably achieved a modicum of success. They must have grown to somewhere between 20 and 200 employees to be attractive to a union, which generally prefers big game where the payoff is greater in dues and prestige.[14]

The business is likely doing well, but is undercapitalized. It therefore suffers cash flow problems from time to time and depends on customers paying their bills promptly and reordering. New customers are added slowly as this process goes on, primarily through the efforts of the owners in building confidence and trust with the new customers.

The businesses have small management groups, but the owners are involved in everything that goes on, and particularly in developing sales and customer relations. These companies have no industrial relations specialists. No one in these firms really understands federal law and the way it affects relations with the union. The entrepreneurs and their managers are amateurs. They may at first not recognize their incompetence to deal with union representatives, who are professionals with broad experience and determination.

These companies cannot stand a long labor dispute. They do not have the financial resources to meet ongoing obligations during a lengthy strike, and management realizes that the companies must produce continuously to maintain the lifeblood of cash flow. Union representatives also know these facts. They know their psychological advantage, which comes from their recognition that owners have limited knowledge in union relations, do not know the law, have no plans for the upcoming negotiations, and hope to get it over with quickly for as small a settlement as possible.

What owners don't realize is that the union, too, has problems. Union representatives are caught, more often than not, in a political bind. They

---

[14]Donald J. Grabowski, "Labor Relations and the Small Employer," in *Managing the Dynamic Small Firm: Readings,* edited by Lawrence A. Klatt, Belmont, Calif.: Wadsworth, 1971, pp. 249–53.

know what they can realistically hope to achieve in the negotiations. The local bargaining committees, which represent the employees of the firms, may not. The representatives must "sell" their ideas to these committees. Even if they are successful, the committees may not be able to get the employees to go along. Their expectations may be unrealistic, perhaps much higher than the hard facts can possibly warrant.

Frequently the union representatives find themselves in the midst of a fight for leadership. This puts another political pressure on them. The whole picture then becomes muddled. The negotiating problem is exacerbated, and the owners, were they aware of the ramifications of the situation, could negotiate more adroitly with the union representatives and give away less to reach settlement.

Small businesspersons faced with unionization should recognize their amateur status in a role that demands professional competence. They would be well advised to seek the most competent counsel to represent them. They should employ a labor lawyer who has the requisite experience and skill to represent their interests in the negotiations. In the long run, the expense of counsel is usually a pittance compared to the savings counsel can gain for the company.

Avoiding Unionization

The owner-enterpriser who understands the forces that drive personnel toward unions could lessen their strength by proper managerial action. Employees want unions for such reasons as improved wages, inability to seek redress for wrong, job security, freedom from fear of capricious action by the employer, and desire for recognition.

Unfortunately, the majority of small businesspersons are the victims of their own ignorance in dealing with this problem. They do not know, except in the vaguest way, what the prevailing wage scale is in their industry. If they were aware of the importance of this information, they would make it a point to keep wages competitive. This action would, of course, eliminate this cause of unionization.

Entrepreneurs, being rugged individuals, incline toward a directive approach in dealing with personnel. Such persons are often critical of the shortcomings of others and may perceive effective activity differently than do the people who work for them. They are often made to feel insecure in their jobs by the precipitate response of the boss to something they may have done in all good faith. They see the boss's forthright criticism as capricious and unwarranted. Their sense of safety is threatened, and their response may be to seek a union as a shield against a threatening management. Through the union they see the chance to be treated more humanely and to have a means for redress of wrong. They believe their grievances will be heard and attended to.

If the firm faces an effort to unionize, the small businessperson should be prepared to work with counsel in planning to meet the challenge. Questions that should be answered include the following:

- What is a competitive wage scale for the industry in the local area?
- What maximum benefits can the company afford?
- What minimum will the company have to pay, as determined by what competitors are paying, in wages and benefits?
- What management prerogatives, such as policies about hiring, firing, overtime scheduling, and administration of benefits, must be retained by management at any cost?
- What are the terms in competitors' union contracts?

Careful planning, keyed to the answers or suggestions triggered by these and similar questions, would provide the basis for a contract at the least cost, that would retain the greatest number of management's rights. The ultimate objective is a contract that is seen as equitable by both parties. It should produce a win-win solution.

SUMMARY: Key Points in Personnel Management of the Small Firm

The entrepreneur historically has been remiss in personnel management and planning. When the need for sound personnel policy is accepted, recruitment and selection of qualified personnel are carefully planned.

The behavior of the entrepreneur is the most important influence affecting the development of personnel. The boss with a warm, supportive manner encourages the development of a climate of achievement. Such a person clearly values learning, personal growth, and the acquisition of mastery and competence throughout the organization.

In the administration of compensation, the enterpriser should make sure that wage and salary levels are competitive and that the indirect compensation the firm provided is as generous as it can manage. Personnel should be treated fairly with the aim of minimizing problems of equity, misconception, and internal strife.

The small businessperson, aware of the pitfalls of the traditional performance appraisal, should rely on open and informal meetings with employees to give motivational impact and to improve performance. The owner-enterpriser can meet on a one-to-one basis and with small groups to learn what is going on and to inform people about conditions in the business.

The entrepreneur managing in a style congruent with the assumptions of McGregor's Theory Y, operating in a group-participative mode, and communicating openly and truthfully with personnel at all levels would more than likely not be pressured for unionization. However, if faced wth a drive for unionization, the enterpriser-owner should hire expert counsel immediately.

SUGGESTED READINGS

Danco, Leon C. "What's Wrong with Closely-Held and Family-Owned Companies." *CE News* (Construction Equipment), August 1967, pp. 15–19.

————. "Why Nepotism Should Be Saved." *Industry Week*, May 18, 1970, p. 40.

Eisenberg, Joseph. *Turnaround Management*. New York: McGraw-Hill, 1972.

Fear, Richard A. *The Evaluation Interview*, 2d edition. New York: McGraw-Hill, 1973.

Lasser, J. K. *How to Run a Small Business*, 4th edition. New York: McGraw-Hill, 1974, chapter 16.

Pickle, Hal B., and Abrahamson, Royce L. *Small Business Management*. New York: John Wiley & Sons, 1976, chapter 12.

Steinhoff, Dan. *Small Business Management Fundamentals*. New York: McGraw-Hill, 1974, chapter 20.

CHAPTER 10
_____

Management Succession

_____

Small firms that grow in sales and profits sooner or later require more managerial efforts than the founders can provide. A sure way to lessen the problems of growth is to plan carefully for acquiring competent management personnel.

IMPORTANCE OF PLANNING FOR MANAGEMENT SUCCESSION

Management needs are a function of both the present and the future organization. Predicting future needs is the key to hiring and developing qualified personnel at all levels and particularly in management. Planning for developing an effective organization is based on knowing the work to be done and the resources and techniques available to do it. One logical way to start is with an audit of current personnel.

In small firms it is relatively easy for enterpriser-owners to assess the qualifications and the potential of the members. They know everyone in the firm personally and have gained insight into individual strengths and weaknesses through daily contact. When these data are compared with present and future needs, they can judge with considerable accuracy the possibilities for moving people into management positions as the need arises. This process can be quite informal in the small firm, although entrepreneurs would be well advised to maintain a written log of the strengths and weaknesses of key personnel (see Figure 10–1). In this way they can keep a running inventory of their firms' human resources and can draw upon it to fill management positions.

The work to be done and the technical requirements that must be met with the growth of the firm determine the future of the organizational

---

Personnel Log

Date: July 2, 19—

Name: Earl Farley

Age: 36

Education: BSME, MBA

Present position: Technical sales

Candidate for position of: Marketing manager

Estimated time when ready: 6 months to 1 year

Strengths: Fair to good salesman, excellent planner, keen analytical approach to problems, gets on quite well with others. Other salespeople like him.

Weaknesses: As a salesman, tends to be overly cautious in grasping opportunities that could be profitable. Engineering training seems to make for too structured approach; not loose and easy enough to be superior salesman.

Notes: Would make a first-rate marketing manager. This placement could convert present weakness to strength, using analytical ability and structured approach in market analysis and feasibility studies. MBA should provide good background for the position. Suggest that Farley take a refresher course in marketing through university extension immediately.

FIGURE 10–1. Sample Form of Log on Strengths and Weaknesses of Key Personnel

structure. The organizational structure in turn will define the management positions to be filled. These requirements stem from the business plans laid down to guide the growth of the firm, as has been indicated in Chapter 7.

In general, the procedures for making a personnel audit and inventory should be kept simple in the small firm. A small concern cannot afford the luxury of staff to mount and maintain such a program. The assessment of strengths and weaknesses must necessarily be done by the chief executive and key managers. It is important that they keep some kind of written record of their judgments, for these will undoubtedly be the forerunners of a more formal and elaborate system of record keeping as the firm grows. The evolution from simple choice based on recorded notes to a sophisticated formal inventory and selection system[1] will be

---

[1] A system for managing managerial resources as the firm grows larger is outlined in Chapter 14.

smooth and easy when a sound elementary system underpins later efforts.

RECRUITMENT AND SELECTION

When the small business has developed a management inventory, it can select qualified candidates for positions that must be filled from the outside. A sound hiring policy will provide the strategy for assessing prospective personnel.

Any organization, whether a manufacturing or service business, has jobs to be done at different levels. Positions of all kinds require a mixture of routine and innovative performance. At lower levels, jobs tend to be narrow in scope and complexity because they are limited by the technical process of the organization. At higher levels, jobs expand in scope and become more complex. The need for innovation increases with status in the management hierarchy. Since the proportion of creative to routine content of positions depends upon their level and the technical process of the organization, strategy for assessing candidates should be keyed to these factors.

Creative or innovative activity implies risk taking. When successful, such activity can produce a high payoff for the firm. The organization engaged in a fast-moving technological field might well assume the risk of placing a creative person in a key management position, knowing that one major success would more than compensate for several unsuccessful efforts. On the other hand, in a stable business such as an insurance service, there would be less need for highly creative personnel. It should be recognized, however, that even the most conservative business needs some creative talent in its organization.

At lower levels, the firm might seek to minimize failure in filling positions by choosing those with adequate competence to meet the requirements, but without innovative flair. Here the strategy aims at avoidance of failure, with a low-risk modest payoff. The small firm looking toward the future would do well, however, even in filling lower level positions, to seek people who have aspirations and potential for personal growth.

As a final point, strategy for selection should recognize that the work in any position has both prescribed and discretionary content.[2] The more discretionary the content, the more sound judgment would be required for effective performance and the greater the need for innovative solutions to management problems. The smaller the freedom of choice in the position and the greater the prescribed content, the less would be the need for exercise of judgment and creativity.

---

[2]Wilfred Brown, *Exploration in Management*, New York: John Wiley & Sons, 1960, p. 21.

PROBLEMS OF SUCCESSION

The problem of management succession is common in small business. Bankers and trust officers who deal with the owners of small enterprises report that 70 to 90 percent of the owners of small companies fail to plan for their replacements or for management succession in general.[3] This situation seems universal whether the business is retail, wholesale, service, or manufacturing. Neglect of planning for management succession in the small firm seems to stem from the characteristics of single ownership. The entrepreneur is so busy filling many roles—in finance, selling, production, and other pressing management functions—that the need for a succession program is overlooked. In some cases the thought of having to give up power because of retirement, ill health, or death is so repugnant as to be repressed. The owner-boss consequently takes no action.[4]

Running an independent show, the entrepreneur seldom calls on outside help and is not accustomed to seeking counsel from accountant, lawyer, or directors if the company is a corporation. Indeed, the directors tend to be figureheads, family members, or friends who are not intimately aware of the affairs of the company. They are generally not knowledgeable enough to be concerned with critical problems such as succession, or to be able to offer sound advice. An active board of experienced people with diverse business or professional backgrounds can provide sound counsel. They would force the owner to face up to the question, "Who will run this company if something happens to you?" The forward-looking entrepreneur invites counsel by setting up a powerful board of directors and by seeking help from competent outside sources. Such owners follow the advice given, including planning for their own succession and building a management staff.

Another kind of problem that the enterpriser-owner should be aware of as the company grows is the long-term implications of promotion of the personnel who started with the company or were hired early in its history. If the management group are in the owner's age bracket, the company may one day face the problem of the key managers retiring at about the same time. The owner should protect the company against a management void of this kind and ensure continuity of management by bringing in younger people as need arises.

The Position to Be Filled

Positions open up through promotion or loss of the incumbent, or because of needs created by growth of the firm. The requirements of an

---

[3]Roland C. Christensen, *Management Succession in Small and Growing Enterprises*, Boston: Graduate School of Business Administration, Harvard University, 1953, p. 107.
[4]H. N. Broom and Justin G. Longenecker, *Small Business Management*, 3d edition, Cincinnati: South-Western, 1971, pp. 73–75.

open position and the qualifications needed to fill it are definable. A new position created by growth can be described by the requirements stated in the company's long-range business plan and its attendant management succession program. The need to fill a vacancy opens the opportunity to examine the position critically. Questions that should be answered include:

1. Is there really a need for the position? Or can its content be distributed among other positions without loss of effectiveness?
2. What performance will the new manager be expected to be responsible for?
3. What skills, educational background, and experience are required to ensure the performance expected?
4. Who are the managers and people the new manager will be working with most closely? What kind of leadership style seems indicated for best results in the position?
5. What are the possibilities for advancement attached to the position? Will the position expand in scope with expected growth of the company? Or is there a clearly perceivable career ladder for the new person?

Answers to these questions and others of a similar nature will permit a brief description of the position to be prepared and provide a guide for assessing the qualities of the candidate. Selection of the right individual is admittedly a chancy business and pains should be taken to increase the odds for success.

TRAINING AND DEVELOPMENT OF MANAGERS

The continuity of the organization depends upon the continuity of effective management. This fact often poses a novel problem to entrepreneurs, who are not prone to think of a supporting managerial staff or their own successors. It is a hard fact of organizational life that performance depends upon specific competencies. These are not, by and large, genetically coded. Human beings must acquire them, and the only way to acquire competence is through education and training.

The small firm has limited resources to apply to this problem, but many practical things can be done to develop a management team and to ensure the managerial continuity of the firm. The owner-manager should understand first of all what it is that training and development are intended to change. Change in this context implies movement from a present state to one of improved ability of some kind. Change should be beneficial for both the individual and the organization. The target is increased personal *and* organizational competence.

Growth should take place through beneficial change in five broad areas: 1) knowledge, 2) attitude, 3) abilities, 4) job performance, and 5) operational results.

1. *Knowledge* refers to the individual's store of information, facts, and data that can be drawn upon for innovative purposes, problem solving, or decision making. The greater the supply of knowledge, the better equipped the manager is to do a sound job.
2. *Attitude* reflects the unique way in which the person constructs a vision of the world. If attitude is to change, the person must view the world differently. This fact suggests the importance of creating a psychologically healthy environment that stimulates personal and organizational growth.
3. *Abilities* include the proficiencies required to achieve performance. The complement of skills possessed by individuals defines their competence; more highly developed skills mean higher levels of competence.
4. *Job performance* measures how well the individual meets the requirements of the position. Superior performance results from the application of competence to the tasks of the position.
5. *Operational results* are the outcome of efforts of personnel at all organizational levels. Operational results indicate how well the organization has been able to achieve its objectives and goals.

The significant factor in the attainment of organizational effectiveness and growth lies in the training and development of human beings. The critical personnel upon whom the growth of the small firm depends are the managers who direct and control its destiny. Change through training and development is therefore usually intended to accomplish one or more of the following ends:

- improve the performance of managers in the present job
- prepare managers for future requirements of the job
- prepare managers for promotion to higher level jobs

Limitations on Training and Development

Research reported by C. Roland Christensen underlines major limitations experienced by the small firm in its training and development efforts.[5] The small size of its management group imposes a number of job responsibilities on each of its managers. They must shift from one area of responsibility to another at the demand of the situation. The time available to them for training is both limited and broken into short periods.

---

[5]Christensen, *Management Succession*, p. 120 and chapters 2 and 3.

The firm is frequently dominated by one individual who may be reluctant to share or delegate tasks that can provide learning experience. The company is often unable or unwilling to devote any of its limited funds to support training and development. Frequently its methods of operating concentrate on keeping the company alive in the face of strong competitive pressures. Training effort is viewed as diversionary under these circumstances.

The family-owned firm has the additional problem of preserving leadership within the family. When the family insists on having its members run the firm, there is little inducement to bring in qualified managers or to train present personnel to assume positions of responsibility.

Although these factors inhibit the introduction of training and development, the forward-looking entrepreneur takes advantage of the opportunities available for developing key personnel.

Conditions Facilitating Training and Development

Opportunities for developing managers in the small firm arise during the course of business. Decisions must be made about what tactics can be used to overcome a competitive threat, whether or not to buy a large quantity of material at a special price, or whether to delay entering the market with the newly developed product. Situations such as these present real problems that can be used for developmental purposes. The trainee may be given responsibility for making the necessary decision. Because the situation poses an actual problem of the business, the trainee will be put under some stress in solving it—stress that can reinforce learning provided it is not overly intense. The owner-manager should give both the opportunity for learning and unobtrusive support as needed during the learning.[6]

Several conditions facilitate training and development efforts in the small company. Among the more important are:

1. An active board of directors that insists on a management succession program and follows up to ensure that it is carried out.
2. Steady growth of the company, which stimulates the training and development of managers to fill the needs that are foreseen in the management structure.
3. The entrepreneur-manager who recognizes the need for management development and gives time and energy to it, assuming the role of trainer personally.
4. The entrepreneur-manager who allows younger executives freedom to run their own show and accepts the risk of this practice,

---

[6]Robert L. Trewatha and M. Gene Newport, *Management-Functions and Behavior*, Dallas, Tex.: Business Publications, 1976, p. 152.

understanding that truly delegating responsibility is the only way younger managers can develop management capability and the perspective needed to assume higher positions successfully.

5. The company that has access to executive training programs appropriate to small business management and sends its candidates for succession to them. The programs should be offered in a series of short sessions to avoid prolonged absence of participants from their jobs. Furthermore, the content of the programs should be specifically focused on the management problems of small business, which in many ways are considerably different from those of big business.

Christensen reports that in small firms observed to be successful in developing managers, the top managers show several pertinent characteristics.[7] They are able to sense teaching opportunities in the course of operations. They recognize that they must behave differently from the way they did in running an individual show when the business was young. They loosen the reins to permit subordinates to gain experience and skill. They realize that developing successors takes time and effort. And finally, they show willingness to accept the problems that arise when inexperienced people handle management situations that they themselves manage competently.

Techniques for Developing Managers

Some specific techniques for developing managers particularly fit the small company. These include developing an heir apparent; developing an executive group; splitting off a discrete operation, which the trainee-manager can run individually; using day-by-day training and formal educational services.

In the heir apparent technique, the entrepreneur identifies a younger person to be trained for the top job. This method allows sharp focus on the training effort, as every possible opportunity to learn about the company and its operations can be used to speed the growth of this individual.

Everyone in the company knows that the young person is being groomed as successor to the chief executive. The heir is rotated through various positions in the company and is given gradually increasing responsibility. Permitted to sit in on company meetings and encouraged to participate in the discussion and decision making, the young executive acquires experience. The boss coaches, trains, and shares experience with the heir.

This technique can work well. When there are no qualified persons to

---

[7]Christensen, *Management Succession*, chapter 7.

follow in the shoes of the owner-manager, bringing in a younger person as the heir apparent can be eminently successful. However, this technique often has its own peculiar problems.

In a company that has a small group of older managers, the heir must demonstrate a very high level of interpersonal competence to gain acceptance and cooperation. The heir may have been selected by the boss because of showing a kindred spirt—entrepreneurs both. The entrepreneurial personality of the younger person may present an obstacle in working with the older managers. Confident, used to winning, optimistic, and impatient with those who react with less certainty to obstacles, the young executive is likely to be insensitive to the needs and reactions of others. Unchastened in life's battles, the heir may alienate the older managers by forthright actions and responses, thus diminishing desirable collaboration with them. This kind of behavior defeats the developmental purpose in the long run.[8]

Unless harmonious relations with the older management group develop, they are likely to sabotage the heir's efforts. The young executive is almost sure to fail when repeatedly blocked by managers who know the company procedures so well as to be able to manipulate them in a careful, covert manner. These efforts would frustrate the heir and thwart the boss's developmental program.

This technique can be dysfunctional in another way. When the heir is identified, the other executives may lose their ambition. Some may leave; others may become passive, lose their desire to achieve, and take refuge in routine performance.

Developing a small executive group as a whole presents a way of overcoming the difficulties of the heir apparent approach and may provide a superior answer in the long run. Here the top executive tries to bring the whole management group along together. This procedure aims to increase organizational effectiveness while developing individuals. The managers are stimulated to gain personal competence and to develop collaborative purposeful activity by the process. The chief executive lets them in on company data, seeks their suggestions, and helps them coordinate their problem-solving activities. Since there is no designated successor, the managers see possibilities for themselves. Developing the whole group as a pool from which the next chief executive will be selected stimulates the managers toward growth. They become active team members rather than passive observers of the development of a single heir.

When the top executive has singled out managers who show promise, those managers' development can be speeded by giving them a separate element of the company to manage when the opportunity arises. The

---

[8]Saul W. Gellerman, *Motivation and Productivity*, New York: American Management Association, 1963, pp. 140–41.

operation should be self-contained so that its performance can be readily measured. This procedure forces the managers to stand on their own feet. They should, of course, be given counsel when a difficult situation arises. Here the board of directors can provide help and the chief executive should play a supportive, coaching role. The reality of running a complete operation and being held accountable for its performance bulwarks the previous training. It is the test by fire of managerial competence.

Conditions That Stimulate Learning and Growth

In the long run, individuals must develop themselves. Whether they choose to do so or not depends to a great extent on the environment in which they work. Certain environmental conditions stimulate self-development. Among the more important influences are the behavior of the boss, the informal group in which the individual has membership, the characteristics of the formal organization, and the economic and technological characteristics of the industry and the firm.

Behavior of the Boss The behavior of the chief executive is the most important influence affecting management development. The boss is the key figure in the organization and the model that subordinates emulate. When the boss's behavior shows that development is important, supporting managers are stimulated to develop themselves. Every meeting between boss and subordinate presents a teaching-learning situation— the subordinate experiences learning of some kind. As Douglas McGregor put it:

> When the boss gives an order, asks for a job to be done, reprimands, praises, conducts an appraisal interview, deals with a mistake, holds a staff meeting, works with his subordinates in solving a problem, gives a salary increase, discusses a possible promotion, or takes any other action with subordinates, he is teaching them something. The attitudes, the habits, the expectations of the subordinate will be either reinforced or modified to some degree as a result of every encounter with the boss.[9]

That is why day-to-day training is so important. It is immediate, pertinent to the job to be done, and highly significant to subordinates, who see reward or punishment as a consequence of their response to the training. The entrepreneur, to support development of subordinate managers, should show a leadership style that values learning and personal growth.

---

[9]Douglas McGregor, *The Human Side of Enterprise*, New York: McGraw-Hill, 1960, p. 200.

Behavior of the Informal Group The informal group to which the individual belongs expresses organizational culture through its behavioral norms. The group can provide support for or resistance to change. When the top executive values development, the group reflects this value. It will support developmental effort.

A manager in such a group will be stimulated to educational effort by the support of the group. When development is seen as an important goal, cooperative relationships tend to develop within the group. Support for change in the quest for competence thus proves beneficial for the individual and for the building of teamwork.[10]

Influence of the Formal Organization The formal organization influences the management development effort in significant ways. The organization structure, policies, procedures, controls, objectives, and practices define the boundaries of legitimacy within which trainees can improve their behavior.

Training and development has as its objective beneficial change in behavior, which is fundamental to the acquisition of competence and personal growth. In organizations where autocratic influences have exerted pressure over a long time, the cultural norms and the formal organization may inhibit personal or organizational growth. For example, in a small company that keeps its top management within the family there is little hope for the development of others. Where controls are rigid, freedom of individual action is likely to be severely restricted. In such circumstances there can be little opportunity for growth, for growth means trying, making mistakes, and learning by correcting them. The learning climate requires a certain amount of openness and lack of constraints so that people may explore new ideas and new ways of doing things without fear.

The structure of the organization materially influences the implementation of a management development program. In a closely knit, centralized structure with sharply drawn lines of authority, controls tend to be tight. The individual manager's opportunities to experience higher levels of responsibility and to explore newer and better ways of doing things are limited. The small company has the advantage of simple structure. When coupled with relatively lenient controls, the situation is conducive to successful management development. The management development program can be further supported by clearly stated objectives in which the managers have had some say. These objectives should cover both goals of the business and those pertinent to the management development and succession program.

Economic and Technological Influences The economic climate in which

---

[10]Arthur H. Kuriloff, *Reality in Management*, New York: McGraw-Hill, 1966, p. 45.

the firm operates and the technology of the industry affect the development effort. A rapidly growing company in an expanding technological field obviously offers more opportunity for managerial growth than a static company in a stable or contracting field. The rapidly expanding company is forced by its growth, if nothing else, to tend to its needs for management. On the other hand, the stagnating company can improve its condition only by strengthening its entrepreneurial management functions, especially through innovation and improved marketing. This need may mean bringing in outside talent, stimulating talent within the firm, or both. Beneficial responses to economic and technological forces require changes in norms and climate to support the growth of managerial and organizational competence.

SUMMARY: Ensuring Succession in Management

The small business owner can plan for management succession by looking ahead to the needs of the growing firm for competent managers. The key to success in this effort lies in identifying the positions that will need to be filled and the people capable of filling them. A simple record of strengths and weaknesses of potential managers within the firm will show possibilities for promoting from within. It will also point up training and development needs for these persons. This record will, of course, also identify positions for which recruitment from the outside may be necessary.

The small business owner who is aware of the importance of careful planning for management succession will overcome the often seen reluctance to delegate authority to others. Overcoming this psychological block will ease the way to finding and placing the right person in the right management position at the right time.

With this awareness, the boss will also be prepared to put into effect a program of developing managers within the firm. This effort would be underpinned by supportive executive behavior in encouraging a climate of learning and achievement.

SUGGESTED READINGS

Desatnick, Robert L. *A Concise Guide to Management Development.* New York: American Management Association, 1970.

Myers, M. Scott. "Conditions for Manager Motivation." *Harvard Business Review* 44, January–February, 1966, pp. 58–71.

Reeves, Elton T. *Management Development for the Line Manager*. New York: American Management Association, 1969.

Wainer, H. A., and Rubin, I. M. "Motivation of Research and Development Entrepreneurs: Determinants of Company Success." *Journal of Applied Psychology* 53, 1969, pp. 178–84.

CHAPTER 11

Marketing Management

Small business owners should see marketing as a critically important, challenging function of their business. They should view it as the culmination of an organized effort to achieve the overall objectives of their firm. However, some consider marketing merely as the art of selling, merchandising, and promotion for the purpose of separating unwary customers from their money.

More farsighted businesspersons realize that the achievement of their firm's objectives in the long run is inevitably linked to attracting and holding customers by satisfying their needs better than competing firms. Marshall Field, an expert merchandiser, is supposed to have summarized this idea in a simple statement: "Give the lady what she wants!" Theodore Levitt gave an equally succinct recommendation:

> A business enterprise should view itself as a customer-creating and customer-satisfying organism. Management must think of itself not as producing products but as providing customer-creating value satisfaction. It must push this idea into every nook and cranny of the organization. It must do this continuously and with the kind of flair that excites and stimulates the people in it. Otherwise the company will be merely a series of pigeonholed parts, with no consolidating sense of purpose or direction.[1]

Marketing should not be viewed as a conglomeration of activities. It should be seen as a managerial attitude that sees customer needs and their satisfaction as the guiding concern of business.

---

[1]Theodore Levitt, "Marketing Myopia," *Harvard Business Review* 38, No. 2, 1960. p. 56.

THE MARKETING CONCEPT

The literature refers to the marketing concept as centering on *identifying* and *anticipating* customer needs and *satisfying* these needs with products or services. A whole cluster of additional activities such as packaging, arranging delivery, and adequate servicing are also included. Marketing management includes all activities that have to do with the implementation of this concept. It is the process of integrating and coordinating the following:

- identifying and measuring the need of customers for some type of product or service that the company is equipped to provide
- translating this perceived need into product or service development
- developing and activating a plan that makes the product or service available
- informing prospective customers about the availability of the product or service and stimulating their demand at a price that generates a satisfactory profit for the firm.

Difficulties in Implementing the Marketing Concept

Many research studies have shown that implementing these activities is more difficult than it might seem. For example, few businesspersons would quarrel with the advice that they should know the characteristics of their customers. Yet a typical study of a sizable group of electrical appliance dealers showed that many had "little knowledge about their customers' characteristics. In fact a number of them found it extremely difficult to describe their customers in terms of the most common demographic characteristics."[2] Concerning customer needs, a study among executives and customers of department stores found that the management of these stores believed telephone sales merely replaced floor sales and that customers did not value delivery service for small packages. A survey of the customers revealed that both beliefs were misconceptions; the researcher concluded that these two services could well play a larger role in building sales.[3] Another study among managers and customers of retail stores about the best- and least-liked features of each store concluded that most retailers do not even know the key strengths and weaknesses of their own store. They therefore miss a

---

[2]John K. Ryans, Jr., "An Analysis of Appliance Retailer Perceptions of Retail Strategy and Decision Processes," in *Proceedings of the Conference of the American Marketing Association*, September 1965, p. 669.
[3]Stewart U. Rich, *Shopping Behavior of Department Store Customers*, Boston: Division of Research, Graduate School of Business Administration, Harvard University, 1963, p. 227.

major opportunity to develop a uniquely effective merchandising strategy.[4] These examples illustrate that although many small business owners think of themselves as marketing experts, their actual marketing efforts and practices leave much to be desired. This situation suggests that many small businesspersons do not perceive the complexity of marketing decisions. The rest of this chapter highlights fundamental marketing issues and describes essential steps in the process of identifying, anticipating, and satisfying customer needs.

IDENTIFYING CUSTOMER NEEDS

Since meeting customer needs is the primary requisite for business success, the first step in the marketing effort of a small firm should be to identify the needs of the customers it intends to serve. A major cause of small business failure is that this essential step is *not* taken. Many newly created entrepreneurial firms focus their energies on the technical perfection of a new venture idea without finding out if it really satisfies customer needs. New products are often developed and launched at considerable expense by enthusiastic entrepreneurs, only to find that the market potential of what they plan to sell is very limited or nonexistent. The following are a few examples of products launched by small firms without much prior analysis of actual customer needs: a bicycle speedometer with digital readout, pocket-sized sports games, and laundry machines using ultrasonic sound waves instead of a mechanical agitator. In each case the companies developing these novel products assumed that a market existed for them. They did not check to see if there was an actual demand. As a result, the companies failed.

Entrepreneurs are likely to become victims of their own enthusiasm; they assume that their enthusiasm is shared by others and that a "better product" will generate its own demand. In the majority of cases this is simply not so. The Ski Kit Case in Part III of this book illustrates this point. The initiators of the ski luggage venture inferred that the rapid expansion of the skiing population and the increasing frequency of damages to skis in transport to and from skiing resorts would naturally mean a rise in demand for some type of protective luggage for skis and related ski gear. These entrepreneurs failed to recognize that their potential customers had a very different attitude toward the benefits of using ski luggage because of its price. The entrepreneurs could have found that out had they done more systematic market research.

An interesting empirical study involving pairs of businesses in identical markets concluded that among a long list of factors identified as

---

[4]H. Lawrence Isaacson, *Store Choice: A Case Study of Consumer Decision Making,* New York: Retail Research Institute, National Retail Merchants Association, 1966, p. 78.

having a high correlation with business success, the two most important were understanding user needs and paying attention to marketing.[5] Although large and small firms are about equally negligent in this regard, most small companies lack the resources and the financial strength to absorb losses caused by these failings. As part of their marketing effort small firms must therefore strive for awareness of the specific needs of the customers they want to serve. The small firm should preferably make no assumptions about what potential customers might want, but should continuously probe the practicality of harmonizing the needs of potential customers with the firm's own capabilities of meeting them.

Firms should not only identify customer needs before developing new products; they should also make certain that the needs of customers for their existing products have not changed. In the turbulent world of the twentieth century, the needs and desires of customers change frequently and abruptly. For example, the sudden surge in demand for bicycles and waterbeds in the early 1970s led to the opening of many small retail outlets for these products, yet the actual demand was already declining. Many owners of these newly opened small stores were surprised to find their sales far below the level they had expected. The ensuing losses could have been averted had they done even a cursory demand analysis instead of merely following a quickly changing fad.

Entrepreneurs and small business owners should take heed from examples such as these. They cannot afford the mistakes larger companies can often weather; they should proceed only on the basis of a thorough knowledge of customer needs and an awareness of forces that cause changes in buying habits.

Sources of Information about Markets and Customers

To identify customer needs and market trends a small firm should use a variety of information sources. These can be classified broadly in two categories: primary and secondary sources of market intelligence. Primary sources are those that the company develops itself for its own specific data requirements. Secondary sources are published reports by industry associations, government agencies, university research bureaus, and others. These sources are not directly geared to the data requirements of an individual firm.

Primary Sources of Information From a marketing perspective the three major sources of primary information are:

- information derived from an analysis of the firm's own records such as invoices, inventory audits, and reports from salesmen

---

[5]Andrew Robertson, "The Marketing Factor in Successful Industrial Innovation," *Industrial Marketing Management* 2, No. 4, 1973, pp. 369–74.

- mail surveys, telephone interviews, or personal interviews of actual or prospective customers
- information derived from direct observations of customers and competitors.

A frequently neglected source of customer and market information is the small firm's own internal records. Invoices or sales slips can be used to get customers' addresses, which in turn reveal a firm's geographic market area, the concentration of customers in a given area, some of their social characteristics, and their purchasing patterns. Analysis of invoices gives information about changes in the demand pattern for existing products. This information may be useful in predicting the acceptance of related products ready for introduction. Sales records may not accurately describe the total market, but they provide important clues about a firm's market standing. Similarly, a small firm may require its salespersons to submit market reports, which when properly analyzed can help to pinpoint new business opportunities or provide a better picture of the firm's competitive weaknesses, as the following statement indicates:

> Once we pulled together a complete picture of a competitor's distribution from reports by our salesmen even up to and including its warehousing in the most strategic locations, it put us in a better position to plan and implement our own distribution needs. We have a planned program of sending questionnaires to our salesmen requesting information for a competitive analysis and we get a great deal of valuable information from them. We get research into how our competitors are marketing their products, how many salesmen they have, and how their products compare as to service, function and quality.[6]

Small firms can also use surveys to gather worthwhile marketing information with little expense. Most commonly used are mail surveys, although telephone surveys or personal interviews tend to generate better and more reliable results.[7] In using the various survey techniques small business owners should carefully plan the information gathering process and the questions to be asked. In a survey made to ascertain the market prospects of a new product, those surveyed must first be well informed about the product. Otherwise the results of the survey could be quite misleading, as the following example shows. A Los Angeles

---

[6]Philip Gustafson, "Let Salesmen Help You Plan," *Nation's Business*, July 1961, p. 62.
[7]For a thorough discussion of these issues see Mildred B. Parten, *Surveys, Polls and Samples*, New York: Harper & Row, 1950; Gerald Zaltman and Philip C. Burger, *Marketing Research*, Hinsdale, Ill.: Dryden, 1975. There are many literature references on this subject in Leslie Kanick and Conrad Berenson, "Mail Surveys and Response Rates: A Literature Review," *Journal of Marketing Research* 12, No. 4, 1975, p. 440–55.

company developed a new type of filter to be used in car air conditioning systems. Interviews conducted in parking lots of shopping centers showed that owners of cars with air conditioning systems, those who had allergy problems, and those who were very concerned about air pollution reacted favorably; they indicated that they were likely to buy this filter once it was available. The company decided that this response was good enough to proceed immediately with the introduction of this new filter. When actual sales did not meet expectations, another survey was carried out. It was discovered that during the initial survey those queried were not told that the filter needed to be changed periodically. This was the major reason for the product's lack of market success.

Secondary Sources of Information The range of publications that serve as secondary sources of information from which small businesses can draw potentially useful marketing information is overwhelming.[8] The federal government, particularly through the Department of Commerce and the Small Business Administration, collects and disseminates market data on practically every type of business. Industry-specific market data are published by trade or professional associations. Similarly, most large banks, newspapers, and broadcasting and television stations periodically produce studies on market opportunities or market characteristics for their geographic area. Typical are studies on the bridal market, the youth market, the black market, and the Spanish-speaking market. Secondary information sources such as these are ordinarily available at no cost in public or university libraries. Although differences may exist between the precisely desired data and those actually available in published sources, the conclusions to be drawn from the published data may not differ enough to warrant the cost of a specific, company-related study.

The foregoing description of primary and secondary sources of market information suggests that small business owners can be well informed about the needs and wants of their customers and their firm's market opportunities.

Pinpointing the Real Customers

So far in this chapter it has been implicitly assumed that the customer is a single individual who makes the purchase decision. This is a gross oversimplification, for there may be many actors playing a variety of different roles in the purchase decision process. If the firm understands

---

[8]A useful and free bibliography of readily available secondary sources of information is the Small Business Administration's *Basic Library Reference Source for Business Use,* Washington, D.C.: U.S. Government Printing Office, 1966. This publication is available at all field offices of the Small Business Administration.

the characteristics of the decision process in its market, it will be able to serve the needs of that market better.

People play a number of roles in the decision process:

User: the person who consumes the product or service
Buyer: the person who actually makes the purchase
Decider: the person who decides what should be purchased
Influencer: the person who has some influence on the purchase process
Informer: the person who controls the flow of information to the decision-making group

In the typical household the wife or husband may play several of these roles. However, the more complex and costly the decision, the more likely that additional family members will play a part in the process. In the decision to buy a television set, for example, all family members are users. The buyer may be just the husband, although both husband and wife may be joint decision makers. The children may exert influence on the decision makers. Any member may act as informer and provide or withhold information from the decision making group.

An early understanding of the role structure of the decision process is particularly important to small firms serving the needs of larger companies. Purchasing agents, engineers, production managers, mechanics, marketing managers, and others may play crucial roles in the decision to buy a product or service. Far too often the focus of marketing effort is solely on the purchasing agent. For many items the purchasing agent may function as both purchaser and decider, but the more complex the product or service, the more likely it is that the agent's influence is reduced. Quite often the agent may act only in the role of purchaser, and other organizational members take the key roles.

The successful small company identifies the decision process and the roles different members of the customer organization play. It is then able to generate influence at the pressure points. Although it is often difficult for the representatives of small firms to get past the purchasing agent, who acts as informer, it is imperative that they reach the influencers and deciders. The owner-manager of the small company dependent upon the large company for sales should make sure that there is one individual, at least, in the firm who is able to identify, reach, and influence the proper people in the customer company.

MARKET SEGMENTATION

It has already been stressed that any marketing effort should be customer oriented, which means it should be centered around the needs and desires of the firm's actual and potential customers. If this were the only criterion for action, a firm might be expected to produce a wide variety of products or services, each tailored to the needs or preferences of customers. Although some small firms actually use this approach, it usually leads to high unit costs, since benefits of standardization and economies of scale in production cannot be realized. Conversely, if a firm focuses its effort solely on achieving relatively low costs to achieve standardization and mass production, it may not be able to satisfy the needs of some of its customers. An example of this dilemma is the small firm that was formed to customize Cadillacs by installing sun roofs and adding other features that General Motors Corporation did not provide. Soon afterwards, in the same area, another company was formed to customize a wide range of cars from Volkswagens to Cadillacs. This company offered customizing packages geared to the desires of various groups of customers who wanted certain features associated with sports or racing cars, or those who were more interested in specific convenience or increased technical performance. Judging from the usual financial performance criteria, the latter firm was considerably more successful with its strategy of satisfying the wants of different groups of car owners than the company that offered to customize Cadillacs only. What the second company did was to use a more successful strategy of *market segmentation* than the first.

Market segmentation involves grouping customers into segments, each segment having similar needs, characteristics, or requirements. This technique helps a firm to relate its products or services to the requirements of unique target groups. It aims at making a particularly strong appeal to some identifiable subpart of a total market. Carefully conceived market segmentation is a marketing strategy that small firms can often use with more success than larger enterprises. The small firm's efforts in this regard can be characterized as "fine-tuning" to customer wants; the larger firm is forced to pay greater attention to standardization, mass production, and the adoption of fairly large market segments. Market segmentation can create for small firms protected niches in which larger firms may not be able to compete because of insufficient market volume.

Before a market segmentation strategy can be successfully pursued, the market segments must satisfy three criteria. First, the needs of customers must be both identifiable and measurable. A strategy of market segmentation cannot be followed unless the needs to be satisfied can be clearly identified. Second, the firm must be able to develop products or services that will meet the requirements of customers in the chosen market segments. Third, the segments must be sufficiently large to be worthwhile for the company to cultivate. Sufficient volume must be availble to strike a balance between the needs of a particular target group and the benefits of standardization or mass production.

Identifying Market Segments

When a firm decides to segment its market, how should it determine which market segments to serve? First, it should identify its own particular capabilities to see what market segments and what sets of needs it is best able to satisfy. A firm may be able to serve many market segments, but it will generally be able to serve some better than others. For instance, a small manufacturer of wood surface preparations for do-it-yourself customers may be able to satisfy the needs of those who shop in small paint and hardware stores and those who shop at chain and discount stores. However, even though it may have the capabilities to serve the paint and hardware store customers well, it may not have the financial, promotional, or distributive capabilities to operate successfully in the chain and discount store market segment. As another example, the owners of a photographic business may decide to concentrate their activities in their immediate geographical market area. They might wish to expand their business to serve the needs of customers in a city hundreds of miles away, but if they do not have the processing facilities or the management expertise to operate at that distance, they would be foolish to try.

Second, the firm should identify the characteristics and the extent of competition in the various market segments it could serve. If a number of market segments appear to have equally attractive market potential and the firm is able to serve those segments, all other conditions being equal, the most attractive segment would be the one with the weakest competition. The choice is seldom that simple, however, for the firm's ability to serve different segments varies, the size of segments varies, and the competitive activity may vary considerably.

As a general rule, the larger the market segment, the fiercer the competition is likely to be. For small enterprises with limited resources, a strategy of identifying and serving market segments too small for large firms to be concerned with, yet substantial enough for the small firm, is often the most judicious procedure. Small companies are well advised to search for small market niches that provide protection from vigorous competition, particularly by larger firms. Since some competition can rarely be avoided, small business management must strive to identify market segments in which it has a competitive advantage. No strategy is likely to be more disastrous for a small firm than a direct, head-on competitive battle, particularly with a large competitor. Even highly innovative small firms can seldom withstand a direct competitive struggle with a giant in the industry. For example, in the electronic calculator business, the small pioneer, Bowmar Instrument Corporation, was unable to survive a head-on battle with Texas Instruments. In contrast, Checker Motors Corporation, a tiny company among the automobile manufacturers, has remained successful by concentrating primarily on the production of taxicabs. Small firms are thus well advised to search continuously for market segments that provide them, at least for a time, with a competitive niche. If larger competitors are crowding into this same niche, the small firm should use its greater flexibility to position itself in a new niche.

Segmentation Criteria

One of the most creative challenges in marketing is the identification of appropriate segmentation criteria. The number of possible dimensions by which to segment a market is extremely large, although they tend to fall into two categories:

- criteria that focus on consumer characteristics, such as the geographic region where they live, their sex, age or income brackets, personality traits, or life styles
- criteria that focus on consumption patterns, such as frequency of usage, brand loyalty, or the importance that consumers attach to certain product attributes

A most common segmentation criterion is geography. The company identifies a particular geographic area and aims to serve customers only in that area. All small retailers implicitly practice geographic segmentation. The location of their store defines the customer group they serve. Demographic segmentation is practiced by firms that define their markets on the basis of personal characteristics of customers: their income, age, educational achievements, or sex. A further group of segmentation criteria focusing on consumer characteristics includes the psychographic or life-style variables. Dimensions employed include compulsiveness, conservatism, or other behavioral modes of consumers.[9]

Segmentation criteria that focus on consumption patterns, such as segmentation of markets on the basis of heavy and light users, also have a high intuitive appeal. Similarly, market segmentations on the basis of cultural, ethnic, or social class groupings are frequently used because they can represent very different consumption patterns.

The possible segmentation criteria are legion. It is, however, important to keep in mind that there is no magic formula that will profitably segment a market in all cases and under all circumstances.[10] Market segmentation decisions should come from an analysis of the validity of

[9]See Joseph Pernica, "The Second Generation of Market Segmentation Studies: An Audit of Buying Motivations," in *Life Style and Psychographics*, edited by William D. Wells, Chicago: American Marketing Association, 1974, pp. 279–313.

[10]See Joel P. Baumwoll, "Segmentation Research: The Baker Versus the Cookie Maker," in *Combined Proceedings*, edited by Ronald C. Curhan, Chicago: American Marketing Association, 1975, pp. 3–26.

the several criteria used, coupled with an analysis of those variables that shape the firm's marketing strategy.

MAJOR MARKETING DECISION VARIABLES

Once the company has identified potential customers and targeted marketing segments, it should develop a coordinated marketing strategy that can contribute to the achievement of the firm's objectives. In developing a marketing strategy, the management of a small firm ought to concentrate on those marketing decision variables over which it has some degree of control and those that it must manipulate in response to environmental conditions beyond its direct control. The development of a firm's marketing strategy therefore centers on decisions that align or relate marketing variables that the firm can control (referred to as *marketing controllables*) with those marketing-relevant environmental conditions that it cannot control (referred to as *marketing uncontrollables*). Table 11–1 shows the most important variables in both categories. The composite of the controllable marketing decision variables used by a firm to achieve its marketing objectives is generally referred to as its *marketing mix*. It is obvious that a firm's marketing success depends on how well its management manipulates the marketing mix. If decisions about the firm's marketing mix fit the environmental dimensions of the market segments to be cultivated, the firm is more likely to be successful. The basic marketing decision situation is shown in Figure 11–1.

It is important to recognize that decisions about the marketing mix package (products, prices, promotional efforts, channels of distribution, and so forth) must be coordinated and integrated. An emphasis on only one of the variables in the marketing mix is usually not sufficient to guarantee marketing success. For example, Wilkinson Sword was at one time a relatively small manufacturer of high-quality, high-priced home garden tools and of competitively priced yet superior razor blades. Both product lines were sold through the same retail outlets, hardware stores. When the company tried to expand its sales, it started to sell razor blades in the United States using the same distribution outlets as in Britain: hardware stores. Although Wilkinson Sword razor blades were considered better than competitive blades and were priced at a level American customers were willing to pay, the venture was initially quite unsuccessful because of the firm's poorly integrated marketing mix program in the United States. Customers in the United States were not accustomed to buying razor blades in hardware stores.

Although the following parts of this chapter focus on the major marketing decision variables separately, the reader is reminded that an effective marketing strategy requires the integration of all of the variables that form a firm's marketing mix. The marketing management of a small

TABLE 11–1. MAJOR MARKETING DECISION VARIABLES

Marketing-Relevant Variables Largely under the Control of the Firm—Marketing Controllables	Marketing-Relevant Variables beyond the Direct Control of the Firm—Marketing Uncontrollables
Target market segments on which the firm's marketing effort is concentrated: location or geographic area target customers timing	*Resource availability* availability of required materials cost and quality of required materials
Product(s) or service(s) offered type of product or service range of products or services design features quality standards	*Competition* direct competition indirect competition *Economic conditions* total market size economic trends income situation
Price price level price variability (discounts) price maintenance	*Socio-cultural conditions* societal values affecting consumer behavior life style fashion consciousness consumer preferences
Advertising and promotions advertising level advertising media advertising image sales promotions	
Distribution distribution channels type of distributors number of sales outlets warehousing facilities inventory levels	*Political and legal conditions* political risk situation legal regulations power of regulatory agencies *Technological situation* state of technology rate of technological change
Servicing extent of servicing service facilities	

firm must be sensitive to the interrelationships of all the marketing-relevant variables under its control, and it must manipulate them in a coordinated fashion to achieve its marketing objectives.

Decisions about Product or Service

Decisions about a firm's product or service offering are among the most crucial its management has to make. The firm can be viewed as a portfolio of products or services, and choices of these products and

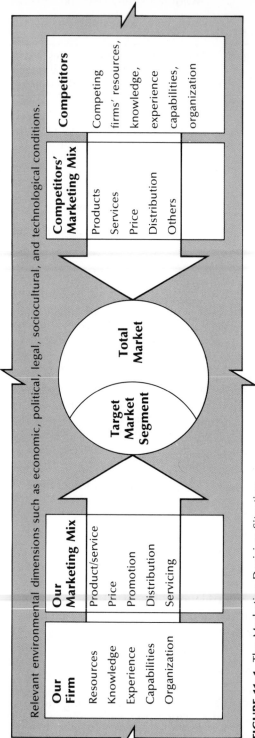

Relevant environmental dimensions such as economic, political, legal, sociocultural, and technological conditions.

Our Firm

Resources
Knowledge
Experience
Capabilities
Organization

Our Marketing Mix

Product/service
Price
Promotion
Distribution
Servicing

Target Market Segment

Total Market

Competitors' Marketing Mix

Products
Services
Price
Distribution
Others

Competitors

Competing firms' resources, knowledge, experience capabilities, organization

FIGURE 11–1. The Marketing Decision Situation

services determine the basic character of the business, its customers, and competitors. These decisions have become even more critical as the basis of competition has shifted. In the first half of this century a firm's operating objectives were often efficiency in production and distribution, and a major factor in competition was price. Today, competition tends to focus on *what* is offered and not necessarily on how cheap it is. Customers are no longer content to be told they can have any color car they want as long as it is black.[11] Firms desiring market success must come up with a product or service offering that derives from recognized consumer needs or provides some betterment for the customers. Another reason why product decisions have become so important is that the length of time over which a product can be expected to be profitable has shortened drastically. Frequent technological innovations and the proliferation of new products and new production processes have shortened the length of the product life cycles. At the same time the costs of new product development have increased and the time from conceptualization to commercialization has lengthened. Even if a new product development promises to be a marketing success, a small firm often does not have the financial or managerial resources to exploit this market by itself. For example, a small company developed an ingenious technology for treating water in heating and cooling systems in such a way that undesirable deposits and corrosive action in metal pipes were virtually eliminated. Although the market potential for this new water treatment system was very favorable, the company's financial strength to market it was too weak; its owners therefore decided to merge with a large, diversified firm.

The Scope of Product Decisions Product decisions are a critically important part in the development of a firm's marketing strategy. Close attention must therefore be paid to the question of whether a firm's existing products and its efforts to improve them are in harmony with the overall objectives it wants to achieve. The company must periodically monitor the range of characteristics that seem to be important in its existing products. The major categories for analyzing product characteristics are:

- performance and functional features—for example, the product's ability to perform, its durability, reliability, and precision
- use characteristics—for example, the ease in handling and serviceability
- sense qualities and aesthetic properties—for example, styling, design, color, and ornamentation

---

[11]This statement is attributed to Henry Ford. For several years the Ford Motor Company sold only black cars. More recently, Head Ski Company, the pioneer in metal skis, offered only black metal skis until it was forced by a declining market share and financial losses to branch out into colored and fiberglass skis.

- gratifications and extrinsic values—for example, the uniqueness of the product or its use as a status symbol

An analysis along these lines gives the company valuable insights for developing an appropriate marketing strategy for the product it is selling.

Similarly, a firm's management should develop awareness of the stage the existing product is at in its life cycle. The sales and profit trends for a product (or a product group) are affected by the various stages in the product's life cycle. Most products go through a life cycle that can be broken down into various stages: product development, introduction, early growth, late growth, maturity, and decline. Figure 11–2 illustrates the effect these stages typically have on sales and profits. For some products the life cycle may be very short; for others it may last decades.

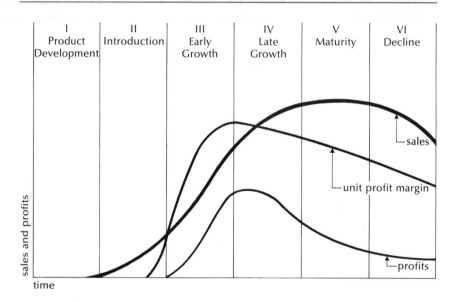

I Product Development	II Introduction	III Early Growth	IV Late Growth	V Maturity	VI Decline

FIGURE 11–2. Effect of the Product Life Cycle on Sales and Profits

Although these stages are somewhat arbitrary, an understanding of these changes in a product's market position can be a very useful aid in planning product strategies. The situation of a small company fabricating window shades and screens offers an example. The company originally produced roller-type window shades using white cloth material, then shades of plastic materials, after that horizontal and vertical louver drapes, and most recently window screens and louver drapes with a variety of colorful designs printed on them. The president of this company made the following statement:

Our objective is to enjoy a normal rate of growth and a satisfactory return. The sale of any product we are manufacturing will reach a peak sooner or later—mostly much sooner than we would like. Our strategy is to predict that peak in terms of time and other factors, such as developments by our competitors, and to have additional products ready for marketing as close to those peaks as possible.

Another example of the successive introduction of new products in response to changes in the life-cycle patterns of existing products is the deodorant business. Successive innovations produced cream, stick, roll-on, and finally aerosol deodorants. When aerosols were introduced, creams and sticks were entering the decline stage, and the roll-on type deodorants had reached maturity. With the rapid acceptance of aerosol deodorants, the decline of creams and sticks quickened and roll-on types also reached the decline stage. Aerosol deodorants opened a new market segment, the male segment, since other types of deodorants had been sold largely to women.

These examples indicate the importance of identifying life-cycle stages correctly and of maintaining a balanced product mix with the various products at different stages. It is obviously desirable for a firm to produce an assortment of products that are at different stages in their life cycle. At any given time the company can then concentrate on the improvement or the development of one new product segment rather than having to cope with upgrading several of its products at the same time in order to achieve desired sales and profit levels.[12] Thus, an awareness and understanding of the product life-cycle concept is critical in reaching proper product decisions, particularly those requiring product modifications, product elimination, or the development of entirely new products.

Proper attitudes toward the development of new products or the improvement of existing ones are usually found among managers of small manufacturing concerns. Many small business managers have, however, an entirely irrational attitude toward the elimination of weak products. Entrepreneurially oriented small business managers often have a psychological investment in a product. They keep producing it beyond any economic justification. This psychological investment prevents them from recognizing that weak products exert cost pressures that reduce the firm's profitability. Weak products tie up scarce resources, cause misgivings among customers, and make excessive demands on the time and energy of management and sales personnel. Although the marketability of weak products can be enhanced by add-

---

[12]For a more detailed discussion of the product life-cycle portfolio mix see Seymor Tilles, "Strategies for Allocating Funds," *Harvard Business Review* 44, January–February 1966, pp. 72–80; Donald K. Clifford, Jr., "Leverage in the Product Life Cycle," *Dun's Review*, May 1965, pp. 62–70.

ing new features or by finding new uses, it is better to drop weak products from the manufacturing program sooner rather than later. For this reason, small companies should frequently review the products they market. Those products characterized by falling sales and profit margins or a shrinking market share should be considered as candidates for elimination. It is, of course, possible that a firm may want to continue marketing weak products because it wants to offer a complete line or because it wants to use them as loss leaders to attract customers. However, in the absence of these considerations, a decision to drop a marginal product should be taken without delay and without concern for the psychological investment in it.[13]

The Product Mix Small firms producing only a single product are quite rare; most small manufacturing companies fall into the multiproduct category. Service-oriented small firms, too, customarily offer multiple services. Therefore it is appropriate to consider the product mix issue in the context of marketing decision making.

The term *product mix* refers to the number of different products a company offers. Product mix decisions are a typical optimizing problem. On the one hand, a broad product spectrum tends to enable a company to keep all its bases covered and to serve various segments of a market. In addition, a broad product spectrum can give a company relatively steady sales and profits if it sells products with different seasonal demand peaks, or if competitive developments cause a sudden decline in demand for some of the company's products. On the other hand, the larger the number of items in a firm's product mix, the greater the resource requirements. For example, a broad product spectrum often causes increased investments in production facilities and higher inventory levels. The marketing task tends to become more complex, since different distribution channels and a multiplicity of promotional schemes may have to be used. In contrast, a company concentrating on a product mix with only a few items may benefit from increased production efficiency; it may also have to contend with the disadvantages of having all its eggs in one market basket.

In making product mix decisions, management will be forced to weigh the advantages and disadvantages of a broad versus a narrow product mix. It will also have to take into account its available resources, existing and future market opportunities, and the product mix strategy of competitors. Small companies faced with a choice between a broad or a narrow product spectrum should as a rule choose that which requires

---

[13]For a more detailed discussion on the elimination of weak products, see R. S. Alexander, "The Death and Burial of 'Sick' Products," *Journal of Marketing* 23, April 1964, pp. 1–7; Philip Kotler, "Phasing Out Weak Products," *Harvard Business Review* 43, March–April 1965, pp. 107–18.

the fewest number of items to reach the desired objectives. The optimal product mix is reached when neither an enlargement nor a reduction of the product spectrum would enhance the company's chances for achieving its objectives. To spot this point is often very difficult; it is generally easier to recognize symptoms of suboptimality. According to Philip Kotler, any one of the following symptoms can be used as an indicator that a firm's current product mix is less than optimal:[14]

- disproportionately high percentage of total profits from a few products. For example, the frequently encountered 70:30 situation is a case in point (70 percent of the company's sales, or profits, are generated by only 30 percent of the products it markets).
- insufficient product breadth to exploit sales force contacts efficiently.
- excess productive capacity on a chronic or seasonal basis.
- steadily declining sales or profits.

Since small companies stand to gain significantly from the maintenance of an optimal product mix, they should invest some resources in regularly checking for these symptoms with a view to changing the product line when necessary.

Developing New Products Most companies, including small ones, view the development of new products or the improvement of existing ones as a key to their marketing success and survival. As the high failure rate among new products indicates, a marketing strategy emphasizing the frequent introduction of new or improved products can be very risky. Yet successful innovations can offer high rewards in profitability, market standing, and prestige. Small business managers must recognize that the frequent introduction of new products as part of their firm's marketing strategy can be a boon as well as a bane. The process of generating new product ideas and actually implementing them should be performed in a *systematic* manner. None of the essential steps should be skipped or abbreviated. Although each new product has its own development process, the major steps are almost always the same: proper search for new product ideas, screening ideas, establishing technical and market feasibility, reviewing internal resources and capabilities, product development, product testing, test marketing, and successful commercialization. At each of these steps there should be go/no-go decision criteria built into the process. Figure 11–3 shows the major steps in the new product development process. This process and related methodologies are described at length in Chapters 2 and 3 of this book from the viewpoint of launching a new business venture. The process is

---

[14]Philip Kotler, *Marketing Management,* 2nd ed., Englewood Cliffs, N.J.: Prentice-Hall, 1972, p. 444.

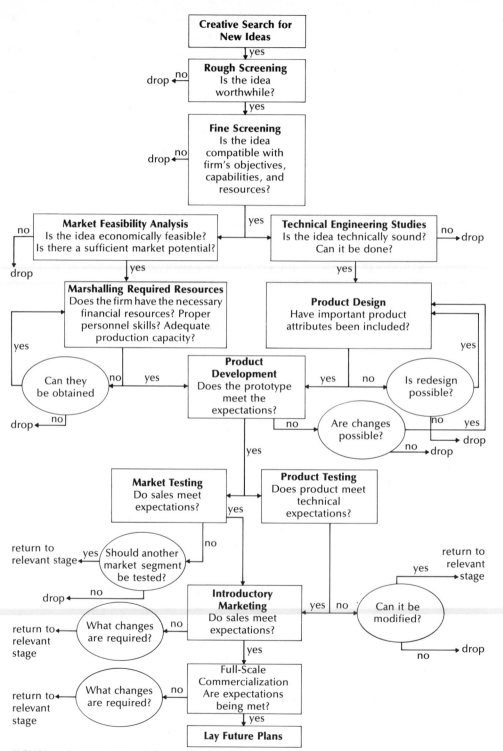

FIGURE 11-3. Major Steps in the New Product Development Process

essentially the same for the generation and introduction of new product ideas in an ongoing small business. There is therefore no need for a detailed description of it in this chapter except to stress the following point: The development of a new product or the improvement of an existing one is usually very expensive and full of pitfalls. Most small firms don't have the resources to survive major new product blunders; the development of a new product must be approached with prudence. This prudence is generally reflected in adoption of sound analytical decision criteria. Each intended new product should be subjected to careful analysis of the firm's resources and capabilities, the existing market opportunities, and the important product attributes in view of consumer needs and wants.

Pricing Decisions

Pricing is one of the most obvious marketing decision issues every businessperson must settle, although it may not be the most important one.[15] But customers and competitors alike tend to be sensitive to a firm's price decision; they are also likely to notice price changes much quicker than changes in product characteristics, advertising efforts, distribution methods, or any other element in a firm's marketing mix.

The complexity of price decisions is well known. A large segment of microeconomic theory focuses on the pricing process under various market and demand situations. Every introductory course in economics shows that monopolistic, oligopolistic, and competitive market conditions lead to very different pricing behaviors. Similarly, price changes under inelastic demand have a different effect than those under elastic demand.[16] These price theory considerations must be complemented by some operational guidelines for management decision making.

Approaches to Price Setting Firms enjoy varying degrees of latitude in setting prices depending on market and demand conditions. This latitude allows the decision maker to stress certain considerations more than others, although all of them may affect price decisions. The most

---

[15]Studies on the importance of pricing as an element in a firm's marketing strategy have shown that other issues are frequently considered to be more important. For example, one survey found that about half of the responding business executives did not rate pricing as among the five most important decision issues in their firm's marketing strategy. See John G. Udell, "How Important is Pricing in Competitive Strategy?" *Journal of Marketing* 28, January 1964, pp. 44–48.

[16]For extensive exposition of price theory see, for example, Milton Friedman, *Price Theory*, Chicago: Aldine Publishing Company, 1976, chapter 2; Jack Hirshleifer, *Price Theory and Applications*, Englewood Cliffs, N.J.: Prentice-Hall, 1976, chapter 5; Donald S. Watson and Mary A. Holman, *Price Theory*, 4th ed., Boston: Houghton Mifflin Company, 1977, chapters 2, 3, 13.

common variables in setting price are costs, the demand situation, and competitive conditions.

Cost-oriented pricing is a widely used approach among small firms. It involves compiling known (or projected) costs and adding a mark up, or cost-plus, for the profit target. The pricing issue in this case is to find out what the direct costs are and to add a given percentage to cover the fixed costs and the desired net profit margin. For example, if retailers purchase an item for $10, they will typically add on 35 percent and set the selling price at $13.50. If the item is actually sold for this amount, the gross profit margin of $3.50 might make a contribution of $2.96 to the coverage of operating expenses, leaving $0.54 as net profit before taxes. The obvious drawback of this simple cost-plus pricing approach is that it ignores the demand side of the market. In addition, small companies often have no clear picture of what their actual operating costs are. They tend to use a customary mark up of, for example, 35 percent to the price they pay to their supplier for an item they sell. There is no guarantee that this fixed mark up will actually yield a profit.

Instead of straight cost-plus pricing, some companies use an approach that yields a desired rate of return on investment above the fixed and variable costs. Figure 11–4 shows how this method is used. In this case a firm must carefully review the demand and cost situation, as the equations derived from the usual break-even analysis show (see Figure 11–4). The specified condition is that the firm should achieve a desired profit target. This means that the firm's revenue (unit price times quantities sold) must cover the firm's fixed costs, the variable costs, and the profit target. Equation (2) in Figure 11–4 indicates the number of units that a firm must sell to reach the predetermined profit target with a given price and cost. Equation (3) suggests the price that must be charged if the profit target is to be achieved, given a projected number of units sold and a related cost. The drawback to this approach is that it focuses too rigidly on a predetermined profit target without paying sufficient attention to the price elasticity of demand.

In general, the cost-oriented approach to pricing is fraught with pitfalls. Small firms often lack a sufficiently detailed cost accounting system. Even if they have one, the allocation of a share of fixed costs to the unit price of individual items tends to be most arbitrary. In addition there is, as has been pointed out, an insufficient concern for the demand side. The question then remains: What is the role of costs in price setting? The answer is that the only role costs should play in pricing is that of setting a benchmark or pinpointing a floor price. If the company has to sell below this level, it must absorb losses, and eventually its survival will be at stake. That costs should not play the primary role in pricing decisions has been very well stated by Henry Ford:

> Our policy is to reduce the price, extend the operations, and improve the article. You will notice that the reduction of price

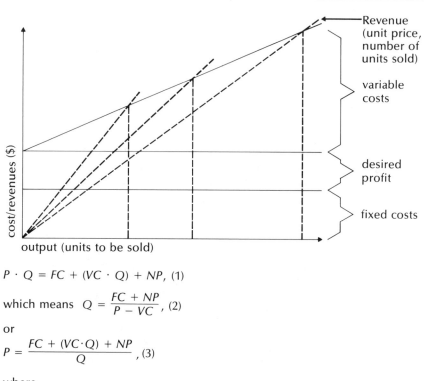

$P \cdot Q = FC + (VC \cdot Q) + NP$, (1)

which means $Q = \dfrac{FC + NP}{P - VC}$, (2)

or

$P = \dfrac{FC + (VC \cdot Q) + NP}{Q}$, (3)

where

  P = unit price
  Q = number of units to be sold
  FC = fixed cash
  VC = variable unit costs
  NP = desired net profit (or desired sale of return on investment times investment)

FIGURE 11–4. Cost-Plus Pricing for a Specific Profit Target

comes first. We have never considered any cost as fixed. Therefore we first reduce the price to the point where we believe more sales will result. Then we go ahead and try to make the prices. We do not bother about the costs. The new price forces the costs down. The more usual way is to take the costs and then determine the price, and although that method may be scientific in the narrow sense, it is not scientific in the broad sense because what earthly use is it to know the cost if it tells you that you cannot manufacture at a price at which the article can be sold? But more to the point is the fact that, although one may calculate what a cost is, and of course all our costs are carefully calculated, no one knows what a cost ought to be. One of the ways of discovering . . . is to name a price so low as to force everybody in the place to the highest point of efficiency. The low price makes everybody dig for profits. We make more discoveries concerning manufacturing and selling under this forced method than by any method of leisurely investigation.[17]

Competition-oriented pricing implies that a major determinant for a firm's price decision is neither cost nor demand but the price charged by the competition for equivalent products or services. This is not to say that a firm subscribing to this approach necessarily has the same price as its competitors. It may actually charge a somewhat higher or lower price, depending on perceived differences in quality, service, or product availability. However, when the competition changes its price, the firm using a competition-oriented pricing approach will generally follow suit with a similar rate of price change.

Strictly competition-oriented pricing makes sense only in a highly competitive industry where firms offer a rather homogeneous product. In this case the prices demanded by competing firms will necessarily be very close and no firm can afford to deviate much from the going rate. In all other situations competition-oriented pricing has undesirable consequences. First, this approach removes price as an active weapon in a firm's marketing armory. Second, this approach can lead to price changes without apparent logic and in the case of fierce competition to ruinous pricing for all competitors. Third, this approach neglects unduly the cost and demand condition of the individual firm.

Customer- or demand-oriented pricing allows the demand and the consumers' response to a given price to become the focus of attention. The price is set on the basis of what the market will bear, which makes the best sense of all. The demand sets a ceiling for the price that can be asked and the firm must find out whether its cost structure and operating conditions will allow it to reach a satisfactory profit under these conditions.

The conclusion is that in setting a price the management of a firm should start with a demand analysis and an evaluation of the competitive situation. Sensitivity to these two conditions will provide an indication of what the upper price limit is likely to be. The lower price limit, viewed from a long-range, and not just a short-term perspective, has to be determined through a cost analysis. All three sets of conditions—demand, competition, and cost—play key roles in pricing decisions. Any approach leaning toward only one of these conditions is misleading.

---

[17]Henry Ford, *My Life and Work*. New York: Doubleday, Page & Company, 1923, pp. 146–47, as quoted by Theodore Levitt, "Marketing Myopia," *Harvard Business Review* 38, July–August 1960, pp. 51–52.

Other Pricing Considerations Beyond the three basic considerations—demand, competition, and cost—pricing decisions must take into account additional factors. First, pricing decisions for established and well-known products will differ from those for new and unknown products. In fact, these decisions may vary at each stage of a product's life cycle. Second, whether the price is to be set for a single product or a group of interrelated products must be considered. Third, the issue of pricing calls for an awareness of a wide range of legal regulatory requirements.

Since demand should play a dominant role in pricing decisions, it follows that the product life cycle, which is simply a reflection of the changing demand during the product's life, has important implications for pricing strategy. During the early life-cycle stages (see Figure 11–2) a firm often has the greatest flexibility in setting a price; it has a choice of pursuing either a *market penetration strategy* or a *market skimming strategy*.[18] Penetration strategy implies pricing close to direct cost. That means covering essentially only the variable costs in order to increase the quantities sold as quickly as possible. The aims here are to obtain economies of scale and to deter the entry of competitors. In contrast, the skimming strategy stresses an initially high price, thus "skimming the cream" of any market segment that is relatively insensitive to high prices. This approach tends to produce early profits and a quick recovery of product development costs, but it also encourages competitive entry. A company should weigh the benefits and drawbacks of an initially high versus a low price in bringing out a new product.

The later stages of a product's life cycle, maturity and decline (see Figure 11–2), are often associated with increased competition and eventual overcapacity among the competing firms. This condition limits a firm's pricing discretion. The recommended price strategy in this case is to lower the price close to the cost level. The relatively low price may not yield much profit but it may attract new customers. The company might then be able to produce close to capacity until a new or improved product is ready to replace the old one.

Pricing of interrelated products is also an important issue in the development of marketing strategy. If a company sells a number of competing products, the price of each product should bear a sensible relationship to the others. For example, a company may produce a deluxe, a special, and a standard model of a product geared to a corresponding high-, middle-, and low-income market segment. If the price of the standard model is relatively high and the price of the special model is

---

[18]This distinction has been introduced by Joel Dean and is now widely accepted as having important ramifications in marketing strategy considerations. See Joel Dean, "Pricing Policies for New Products," *Harvard Business Review* 28, November–December 1950, pp. 45–53.

close to it, some of the potential customers in the low-income market segment may not be able to afford the standard model, and some may choose to buy the special. This situation will lower the sales of the standard model. If the price of the standard is low compared with the special and the deluxe, and if the price difference between the three models is high, there is little chance that customers will eventually trade up to the more expensive models. The prices of related products must be set so that customers consider prices fair in view of the products' value and the possibility of trading up (or down) the product line corresponds with the marketing objectives the company wants to achieve.

Finally, pricing is one of the areas in marketing in which companies have to be careful of government regulation. The pricing practices of firms engaging in interstate commerce are closely regulated by federal laws that impose numerous restrictions on practices such as price discrimination (different prices for purchasers of commodities of like grade and quality), price fixing (collusion among competitors), granting of price discounts or allowances unless they are granted to all customers, and various restraints of trade. The cautious manager should be aware that price policies, more than any other marketing variable, attract the attention of federal investigators.

Distribution and Channel Decisions

The term *distribution channel* refers to the organizational setup through which a firm brings its products or services to the ultimate users. The selection of distribution channels ordinarily involves a long-term commitment to a given mode of distribution. Changes in distribution system are difficult to effect and they tend to be disruptive of the business. For this reason small business executives must plan their firm's distribution strategy very carefully. They must be knowledgeable about the availability of proper channels and the way a chosen channel may affect the firm's marketing efforts. They must be perceptive about any changes that affect the channel structure.

The Range of Distribution Alternatives As Figure 11–5 shows, a manufacturing organization can usually choose from among a fairly broad range of distribution alternatives. A firm may decide to sell its output directly to the ultimate consumer, which is referred to as direct selling. Some small firms are quite successful in using this approach, following the lead of companies such as Fuller (brushes, toiletries), Avon (cosmetics), Dart (plastic containers), or the encyclopedia publishing companies whose salespeople sell directly to consumers by making house calls. Selling by mail order is also a direct selling strategy. Other forms of distribution use a variety of intermediary organizations to bridge the gap between the producer and the ultimate user. Because of their specialization, experience, and close contact with the customers, these inter-

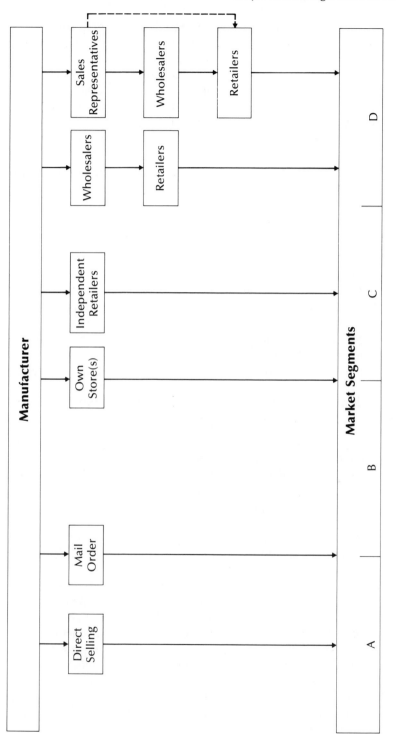

FIGURE 11-5. Alternative Distribution Channels

mediary organizations, wholesalers and retailers, can help the producing companies to achieve a larger sales volume than they could through their own efforts. However there is no one "best" distribution set up for all organizations producing similar products or serving the same end users. Each firm's distribution system must be developed within the framework of its marketing capabilities and resources. In addition, each must take into account the characteristics of its output, the strength and weakness of available intermediaries, and the nature of competition.

If a firm serves different market segments, it may find it worthwhile to use multiple channels of distribution. For example, a small producer of handicraft ceramic items may sell directly through a retail store, fill mail orders, and market some wares through wholesalers and independent retailers.

Before making channel decisions a small business executive should find answers to six important questions:

1. Is it more advantageous to sell directly to the ultimate user or to use intermediaries such as wholesalers and retailers?
2. Is there any advantage in using both direct and indirect distribution?
3. If direct selling seems preferable, what must be done to put this strategy into practice?
4. If indirect distribution seems preferable, what type of resellers are most appropriate?
5. What is the optimum number of resellers for each market segment?
6. What are the specific demands of the resellers that will ensure their cooperation in the marketing effort?

Answers to these questions vary from company to company; there are no general answers that hold for different companies. The following comments on the various distribution alternatives suggest decision criteria for choosing among the major channel possibilities.

Direct Selling. The advantage of direct selling is that the seller remains in control of all aspects of the marketing effort and market development activities. The seller is not dependent on the cooperation of intermediaries. However, direct selling tends to be rather expensive. It is unlikely that a small manufacturer of consumer products has the financial resources, the marketing capabilities, or a broad enough product line to sell directly to the end user and still achieve a satisfactory profit volume. Direct selling should be chosen by a small manufacturer if some of the following conditions prevail: 1) there are large purchases by relatively few customers, 2) customers are concentrated geographically, 3) the demand is reasonably stable throughout the year, 4) the customer knows how to use the product and there are no installation or servicing requirements by the manufacturer, 5) the seller can afford to employ a relatively large, trained sales force, and 6) the sales volume is large enough for an efficient use of the sales force. In most other situations small manufacturing firms may have to rely upon retailers, wholesalers, or both as the efficient way to reach the ultimate user.

Retailer Decisions. Most firms have a variety of possible types of retail outlets through which they can merchandise their products. For example, a small company that produces paint for do-it-yourself customers could sell its products through independent hardware stores, chain hardware stores, paint stores, department stores, supermarkets, drugstores, and discount stores. The firm must decide what type of outlet is most appropriate for the particular market segment it wishes to reach, then attempt to secure that distribution. The needs of people in the market for paint differ widely; different groups of people will tend to buy their paint in different types of stores. The manufacturer must decide which sets of needs he wishes to fill and distribute his products accordingly.

The importance of choosing the right retail outlet is illustrated by the following example. An enterprising student interested in astrology discovered that many of his fellow students were curious about their horoscopes. He developed monthly horoscopes for the twelve zodiac signs, then asked himself how he should market this service. He approached a few monthly magazines, inquiring whether they would publish a monthly horoscope column. None of the magazines was interested. He then developed an approach that gave him a first success as an entrepreneur. The monthly horoscopes for the twelve zodiac signs were printed on three-by-five inch simulated parchment. These were individually rolled and inserted into slots in a cleverly designed counter top display. Placed beside the cash register in bars and restaurants, the horoscopes attracted the attention of customers as they paid their bills. Many couples, particularly those out on a date, were induced to spend an extra fifty cents for their horoscopes. At the beginning of each month the entrepreneur filled the display with a new set of horoscopes and got paid for those that were sold the previous month. His decision to use bars and restaurants as retail outlets proved to be highly successful.

The appropriateness of the store or retail outlet for reaching the defined market is, however, only half of the story. The supplier also has to persuade the retailer to put the product on the shelves or on display. In some types of outlets that may be extremely difficult. The demand for space in supermarkets, for example, is so intense that products that cannot promise a high immediate volume of sales will not be given shelf space. To the supermarket management the promise of high sales is often related to the anticipated level of advertising that the supplier will undertake. Satisfactory levels are generally out of reach for small firms, therefore so is their access to distribution through supermarkets.

The firm must not only decide which type of outlet to distribute through, it must also decide on the intensity of distribution. There are three basic possibilities: *exclusive, intensive,* and *selective.*

In exclusive distribution the producer grants exclusive rights to a retailer in a given geographic area. In granting a degree of monopoly, the manufacturer expects the retailer to direct extra effort to promoting the product. This strategy is often used in marketing consumer durable products such as carpets and furniture.

With intensive distribution the product is sold in every conceivable retail outlet. This policy is particularly appropriate for products that are used and purchased frequently. Soft drinks, cigarettes, candy, and razor blades are prime examples of these kinds of products.

Selective distribution falls between exclusivity and intensity. This policy does not provide any retailer with a monopoly, but it does reduce the likelihood that there will be untoward price competition from other retailers. For example, watch manufacturers may decide to sell their product to jewelers and high-class department stores but avoid selling them to drugstores and discount stores. By avoiding the latter outlets the manufacturers enhance the probability that prices will hold firm and that they will receive the benefits of strong support from the retailers they have chosen.

The retailer outlet decision is an important one for the firm. The type of outlet chosen determines the group of customers that will be exposed to the product. The number of outlets determines the number of customers likely to be exposed and the intensity of promotional support that the retailer is likely to give. In addition, the type of outlet modifies the image of the product. If Accutron watches, for example, were distributed through discount stores, customers would hold a lower impression of these watches than if they were found only in jewelry and high-class department stores.

Wholesaler Decisions. After the retailer decision is made, the company must then decide whether to sell its goods directly to the retailer or whether to sell through a wholesaler. By selling directly to retailers, the firm can have strict control over the distribution of its goods. The firm both knows and can control the retailers that sell its goods. It is in a good position to influence the amount of merchandising effort the retailer provides. The price the firm realizes can be higher than if it had to pay a margin to the wholesaler.

These benefits do not come without considerable cost. The direct sales effort required is much greater in serving retailers than in serving a significantly smaller number of wholesalers. The firm dealing through wholesalers gains the advantage of bulk shipping not available in direct selling to retailers. In addition, the firm selling to wholesalers needs a smaller total inventory at a given sales level, and it is relieved of credit collection problems at the retail level.

The decision of whether to sell directly to retailers or through wholesalers carries both advantages and disadvantages. In general, the greater the volume of business done by each retailer, the more likely it is that direct distribution is worthwhile. For the small company it is not likely that direct distribution will be very profitable, and therefore many small firms supplying the consumer market make use of wholesalers. However, if a company employs a geographic segmentation strategy and seeks to serve concentrations of customers, direct distribution to retailers can be profitable. The firm may decide to distribute directly in major cities and employ wholesalers in rural areas if such a segmentation strategy is used.

If the company decides to sell through wholesalers, great care should be taken to select the right wholesalers. The firm should employ wholesalers serving retail outlets most appropriate for its products. These outlets should be prepared to put selling effort behind the firm's products.

Far too often small firms do not select wholesalers well. They may have built good relations with a wholesaler doing an excellent job in selling their products. They may then decide to introduce a quite different product line. The original wholesaler, doing a good job for the firm's existing product line may be quite inappropriate for the new product line. Companies often find it difficult to make the decision to give the new line to a different, qualified wholesaler instead of to the one with whom they have an existing relationship. Such was the case with Wilkinson Sword, as has been mentioned, whose original products were cutting tools and garden implements sold through hardware stores. When the company started to market razor blades, they were sold through hardware stores also—a strange outlet for razor blades.

Management must also keep in mind that distribution systems are in a dynamic state of change. A distribution channel that was appropriate at one time may not be appropriate later. The proliferation of retailers during the last two decades, the increasing specialization among lines wholesalers carry, and changes in the functions they perform are indicative of the dynamic changes in the distribution system.

The small firm, depending on these intermediaries in its marketing effort, should periodically reevaluate whether the use of a specific distribution channel is still appropriate in the light of changing conditions.

Industrial Distribution Decisions The preceding discussion has focused exclusively on consumer goods, but the selection of an appropriate distribution system is equally important for industrial goods. The major distinction between industrial and consumer goods is that industrial goods undergo some change in form between the time they leave the producer and the time they are finally consumed.[19] Since manufacturing processes intervene between the sale of the product by a particular firm and final consumption, the possibilities for complications in the distribution system are greatly increased. In addition, the likelihood of a firm's being able to excercise control at the retail level is very small. Only a few of the really large companies are able to do it, the synthetic fiber manufacturers being a good example. Small companies that sell industrial goods cannot hope to control retail distribution unless the circumstances are exceptional.

But just as the manufacturer of a finished product can choose to sell directly, through a retailer, or through a wholesaler, so the firm producing an industrial item can sell directly to the manufacturing customer or through a wholesaler. In general, the same issues that are relevant to the finished goods producer apply in the industrial sector. Selling directly ensures control of distribution and the firm realizes a higher price, whereas distribution through wholesalers requires less selling effort, reduces inventory and credit costs, and gives the advantages of bulk shipment.

Control becomes more important when the finished product is associated with the producing firm in the mind of the final consumer. For example, a small manufacturer of monofilament polypropylene used in the production of fishing nets may have gained a good reputation among tuna fishers who have used nets made of this twine. However, trawler operators are not direct customers, since they buy nets from a net maker, who in turn buys twine from a spinner, who in turn buys monofilament polypropylene from the manufacturer. The polypropylene producer is concerned with maintaining an impeccable reputation and therefore wants to make certain that only competent spinners and manufacturers of high-quality nets use the yarn. The company may tend, therefore, not to sell through wholesalers but rather to deal directly with spinners, and further, to try to influence spinners to direct sales to specific net manufacturers. Management will, of course, have to trade off the advantages of this control against the cost of achieving it.

Advertising and Promotional Decisions

Most entrepreneurs and also many small businesspersons seem to accept as true an assertion attributed to Ralph Waldo Emerson: "If a man write a better book, preach a better sermon, or make a better mousetrap

---

[19]Capital goods such as machinery and equipment used in the manufacturing process are excluded from this discussion.

than his neighbor, though he build his house in the woods, the world will make a beaten path to his door."

This claim suggests that there is always a market ready and waiting for ingenious products or services and that only those not able to offer "a better mouse trap" are required to advertise and to promote their wares. This is obviously a fallacy to which many entrepreneurs subscribe; they convince themselves quite easily that what they offer is better than that offered by their competitors. Viewed objectively, this is usually not the case; but even if it were true, small businesses are advised to adopt an attitude that nothing should be expected to sell itself. The management of small firms must realize that successful marketing requires careful attention to promotional efforts to achieve the firm's objectives. There are three major decision areas in promotion:

- advertising
- personal selling
- sales promotion

These three decision areas constitute the so-called promotional mix, which includes the ways by which a firm communicates with its potential customers and informs them about what it has to offer. The basic aim of any promotional effort is to make potential customers aware of an offering and to present the offering accurately in a way to stimulate its sale.

In the promotional mix there is a clear conceptual difference between personal selling on the one hand and advertising and sales promotion on the other. The firm can gain immediately feedback on its promotional attempts in personal selling. That does not hold in advertising and sales promotion in which the communication is one-way, without any direct feedback on how the intended message was received. Personal selling is a promotional device of much greater flexibility than advertising and sales promotion. For this reason personal selling is often more effective; it is also more expensive.

Although some companies may invest resources in all three promotional areas, others may find it appropriate to select from among these alternatives. As a general rule, the greater the number of persons in the customer group with which the company wishes to communicate, the greater will be the reliance on advertising and sales promotion. Conversely, the smaller the number of persons within the customer group, the more likely it is that the firm can use personal selling effectively.

Advertising Decisions The essential purpose of advertising is to support the achievement of the firm's basic marketing aim—to move prospective customers to purchase the goods or services offered. In order to affect the choice of potential consumers the small business executive must understand what triggers the desired consumer behavior. That is a complicated issue on which there is a significant amount of research.[20] Advertising should be viewed essentially as communication with prospective customers. To be effective in this regard, a firm's advertising should meet a series of requirements:

1. The target group of the market segment at which the firm's offer is aimed must actually be exposed to the information that the firm tries to get across. That means a good deal of attention must be given to the media through which potential customers can be reached.
2. Since all who make purchasing decisions are continually bombarded with advertising messages, the firm must try to give its advertising effort a creative twist in order merely to attract the attention of prospective customers.
3. The advertising message must be readily understood and accepted as valid by the target group.
4. The message should aim at a need and arouse a desire to acquire the product or service that is offered.
5. Both need and desire should be strong enough to stimulate prospective customers to buy what is offered.
6. Ideally, the expectations customers had when they bought the product or service should be satisfied so that they will come back and buy again.

These six requirements clearly show that the adoption of an advertising program requires many decisions. All these decisions, which are mutually dependent, are centered around the objective of communicating with a target segment in the most efficient possible way. Decisions of how much to spend, in which media to spend it, when to spent it, what messages to use in the media, are all decisions that interact and should jointly result in the most effective advertising program.

How Much? Perhaps the most difficult decision is the budgeting or *how much* decision. The company should set its spending at a level such that the marginal return on advertising is equal to the marginal cost. That is extremely difficult to do in practice. Although measurement of the cost of advertising is comparatively straightforward, it is much more difficult to measure the return from advertising. Further, since advertising in one year can result in sales in a subsequent year, the calculation of return becomes quite complex.

Even though it is difficult to estimate the return, management should

---

[20]See the references in William J. McGuire, "Some Internal Psychological Factors Influencing Consumer Choice," *The Journal of Consumer Research* 2, No. 4, 1976, pp. 302–19.

view resources committed to advertising as an investment that will reap a return—if the advertising is being done properly. Far too often firms employ arbitrary criteria for setting advertising expenditures, such as a fixed percentage of last year's sales, or the amount left over after other expenses have been paid. The potential sales in this year's marketing requirement, however, may have little relationship to last year's sales or the funds left after paying all expenses.

Although the budgeting decision is difficult, management should recognize that the use of arbitrary decision rules is no substitute for attempting to understand the relationship between advertising expenditures and future sales. Continual study of this relationship must inevitably improve the return in sales per dollar spent on advertising.

Where? The *where to advertise* decision is also complex. A variety of communication channels are available—television, radio, cinema, newspapers, magazines, direct mail, and poster display—and there are a variety of media within each. Advertising on television during a soap opera is obviously quite different from advertising during a college basketball game; and advertising in a campus newspaper with a limited coverage but rather homogeneous readership, such as the *Daily Bruin*, is different from advertising in *The New Yorker*, a weekly magazine of international circulation with a sophisticated yet heterogeneous readership.

A number of aids can be used to simplify the decision making process. First, since the target market segment has been previously defined, no medium should be considered that does not reach a significant number of people in the segment. Second, certain channels are more suitable for specific products than others. For instance, television advertising was entirely appropriate for communicating the instant photography benefits of the Polaroid camera. On the other hand, complex products for which a detailed message is required may be better advertised in print. Third, the cost of using a particular medium may be prohibitive. Although television advertising might be an appropriate medium for a given small firm, it may be too expensive.

Despite these aids to decision making, many questions may still remain to be answered: Should the advertising be concentrated in one medium or spread among different media or channels? Should the advertising budget be concentrated in one or relatively few periods of a year? Or should it be spread out more or less continuously throughout the year? These are often hard decisions and most small companies will not have the expertise to make sensible judgments. For this reason even small firms might find it worthwhile to work with an advertising agency qualified to make sound decisions in these matters. There are many small advertising agencies that will do an effective job even with a relatively small budget. For example, the *31 Flavors* ice-cream chain was at one time a very small, two-man operation of its founders, Baskin and Robbins. When they had only two outlets these two entrepreneurs engaged a small, Los Angeles-based advertising agency that developed for them, at a cost of but a few hundred dollars, the ideas and advertising characteristics that *31 Flavors* is still using successfully as a large chain operation.

What? Either the firm itself or its agency will have to develop the message to be used in the advertisements. The message and image the company wishes to communicate depend upon the group of customers it wants to reach and on the particular customer needs it expects to fill. The message should be interesting enough to attract the attention of potential customers; it should be easily understood; it should point to a need and stimulate a conviction that the offered product or service can meet the perceived need better than any alternative or substitute.

Who? Management must have a clear concept of the recipients of the message in making advertising decisions. Final consumers are obviously a key group to be communicated with, but other groups should also be considered. If sales are made through wholesalers, advertising may be directed at retailers to influence them to request the firm's products from the wholesaler. In addition, other groups may be influential in the decision process. Recently a small financing institution identified commercial bank lending officers as desirable targets for their advertisements. Small firms requiring accounts receivable financing tend to go to their commercial banks when in need. The loan officer unable to accommodate them would usually refer them to other financial institutions. The small financing firm therefore developed an advertising campaign aimed at persuading bank loan officers to refer potential clients to them.

Despite the apparent difficulty of resolving advertising problems, small business managers should not despair. A clear identification of which specific groups it wants to communicate with and what it wants to say will do much to ease the problem of decision making.

Personal Selling and Sales Force Decisions Personal selling, a conversation with one or more prospective customers for the purpose of making a sale, plays a key role in the marketing effort of most small businesses. Personal selling requires the selection, training, and organization of an effective sales force. The related decisions are of a complexity equal to that of advertising decisions. The major distinction between sales force decisions and advertising decisions is that sales force costs are much more fixed than advertising costs. In making the advertising decision for the year the firm can set a desired pattern, for example start at a high level of investment, then drop to zero for three months, and finally reinstate advertising at a medium level for the remainder of the year.

Management can seldom treat sales personnel in such a manner; changes in the size of the sales force tend to be more gradual. There are of course sound business reasons for this. The budgeting decision for a sales force therefore involves a long-term financial commitment.

How Much? The accepted framework in setting the sales force budget, although sometimes difficult to adopt in practice, is again one of equating marginal returns with marginal costs. The company should determine which customers it wants to have salesmen call upon, and the optimal number of sales calls for each customer. From knowledge of the length of time a sales call takes and the geographic location of its customers, the company can determine the optimal size of the sales force. This analysis should be updated from time to time, for requirements and locations change over time; there may be a significant shift in the optimal distribution of sales calls. The results may well indicate the need for a larger or smaller sales force, or rerouting of sales calls.

How to Pay? A subset of the budgetary decision is the issue of compensation of sales personnel. Three types of compensation are customary: 1) straight salary regardless of the results a salesperson achieves over the short run, 2) commission, as a fixed percentage of the achieved sales for each pay period, 3) a relatively low fixed salary plus a bonus based on performance.

Compensation packages vary from 100 percent salary or 100 percent commission to arrangements involving combinations of two or even all three types of payment. The more concerned the firm is with the short-term behavior of its sales personnel, the greater will be the percentage of compensation paid on a commission basis. Since all compensation is a function of short-term performance in a 100 percent commission arrangement, the salesperson is likely to be more motivated to achieve a high sales volume.[21]

The company may wish its sales force to engage in long-term sales development efforts and to fulfill additional functions such as gathering market information or report writing. If so, it is more likely to obtain the desired behavior if compensation of the sales force comes in two forms: a percentage on the basis of short-term sales volume and a larger percentage in a fixed salary.

Bonuses are usually employed when the sales effort tends to be long-term and the firm wishes to relate the reward for this effort to perform-

---

[21]The extreme example of this compensation system is the manufacturer's representative. Typically paid 100 percent on commission, manufacturers' representatives are independent businessmen who frequently carry the product lines of several manufacturers.

ance. Bonuses are usually granted as reward for exceptional achievement, normally when sales exceed a predetermined volume.

How to Organize? One of the more critical sales force decisions is organizational: Should the sales force be specialized, and if so, on what basis? This decision becomes more acute as the firm's product mix becomes more heterogeneous. For firms with simple product mixes and a homogeneous customer group, sales forces are normally specialized on a geographic basis. Each salesperson is held responsible for the customers (including the potential customers) in a geographically defined sales territory. The more complex the firm's product mix and the more homogeneous the customer group, the more likely that other forms of specialization would be appropriate.

If the product mix is complex, sales may be specialized on the basis of products. Each salesperson would be responsible for a well-defined group of products. If customer uses of the products are very different, the sales effort may be specialized according to the different customer types. Alternatively, company size may be a dimension of specialization. Some salespersons may be more effective in working with large organizations, which have complex decision processes, and others with small companies. Finally, some individuals may be better able to work at maintaining a sales relationship with existing customers; others may be skilled in bringing new customers to the firm.

Carefully selected specialization increases the efficiency of the sales effort. Salespersons comprehend the needs and problems of specific customer groupings far better than if they have to deal with widely differing situations from day to day. The main disadvantage of specialization is the decrease in total time that can be spent with customers because of the need to cover a large geographic area. Negative consequences may also result from having more than one sales representative from a firm visit a customer. Finally, the greater the specialization, the lower the degree of flexibility in transferring sales personnel from one part of the organization to another.

The decisions involved in the recruitment, selection, and training of an effective sales force are essentially personnel management decisions. The development of an effective sales force involves many trade-offs. For example, by spending more time and money on the recruitment and the selection of salespersons, a company may possibly reduce training costs and turnover among the sales force. By carefully thinking through the decisions that have to be made, the company can arrive at a selling strategy most appropriate to its needs.

Sales Promotion Marketing efforts often involve appropriate sales promotion of product or service. Sales promotion activities include a host of promotional devices that are intended to stimulate sales and improve marketing effectiveness. Most people are familiar with the games used by gasoline companies or the giveaway drinking glasses and food samples in supermarkets. Sales promotions include giveaways, displays, participation in shows and exhibits, demonstrations, and a broad range of other nonrecurrent selling efforts. Small firms should generally shy away from gimmicky sales promotions. These can involve considerable expense without making a noticeable contribution to the achievement of the firm's marketing aims. As in any other business effort, sales promotions require careful analysis and planning. The company that wishes to engage in such activities should learn from the experience of others and use the services of qualified people to develop appropriate schemes for its business.

Other Marketing Decision Variables

The preceding sections discussed the major marketing-relevant variables that the management of a firm can affect (marketing controllables) such as the product or service offering, the selection of target markets, the price, the distribution setup, and promotional efforts. In addition to these issues there are other marketing controllables that can be equally important. For example, *packaging* may be considered only from the perspective of providing protection for the product during shipping or from the perspective of economy. Yet packaging can also be used as a major marketing tool. That requires carefully considered decisions about the emotional appeal or promotional impact of the package, the information it provides about the product and its use, the visibility of the package in a mass display, stocking and stacking requirements, and protection against shoplifting. All these are packaging decision issues that may have important impact on the firm's marketing success. The handling of problems arising after purchase such as servicing or customer complaints are also decision issues in the development of a firm's marketing strategy.[22]

A detailed discussion of these decisions is beyond the scope of this chapter. However, the following recommendation can be made: Small business managers should always consider whether any decision would affect the firm's marketing effort. If so, managers will come up with the right decision more often than not, if they consider their firm as the purveyor of customer utility and if their efforts are directed toward satisfying customer needs and interests.

---

[22]See C. L. Kendall, and F. A. Ross, "Warranty and Complaint Policies: An Opportunity for Marketing Management," *Journal of Marketing* 39, No. 2, 1975, pp. 36–43.

MARKETING DYNAMICS

Marketing, like any other business function, is constantly affected by a wide range of changes in both the firm's external and internal environments. Consumer attitudes and preferences change quite rapidly; new products become fashionable and reduce the consumers' disposable income for goods and services they used to buy; competitors come up with innovative products or imaginative advertising campaigns; and many other marketing-relevant changes tend to occur in rapid succession. Most of these changes are predominantly economic, and businesspersons are quite used to dealing with them. During recent years a number of social shifts have occurred. These have a significant impact on marketing practices and require special attention from the business community.

1. The consumer movement or *consumerism* is a force to be reckoned with. In the mid-1960s vocal consumer organizations and consumer advocates arose. These groups aim to protect individuals from business or government practices that could be detrimental to their interests or rights as consumers. They vigorously oppose certain practices such as planned obsolescence of products, the proliferation of "useless" products, wasteful packaging, and the related waste of resources. They also expose malfuntioning, unsafe, unhealthy products; shoddy product quality; poor servicing; deceptive advertising claims; and gimmicky sales promotions. Furthermore, they take direct action to press for improvements.
2. There is now a heightened awareness that available resources are limited and should not be used in a wasteful manner. As a consequence, conservation of resources and recycling of used materials has become an important social issue worldwide.
3. A broad spectrum of the population has a strong opposition to a further decline in environmental quality. Since both production and consumption can contribute to environmental pollution, it is widely felt that there are merits in curbing demand rather than in stimulating it. Kotler and Levy, for example, characterize this idea as *creative demarketing*.[23]

These are some of the trends that have a profound impact on marketing practices. Small firms are neither immune to these developments nor can they afford to ignore them. It is impossible to prescribe how small firms should respond to these developments and challenges; they can, however, adopt some general principles and guidelines:

- Marketing practices must reflect a concern for societal values and

---

[23]Philip Kotler and Sidney J. Levy, "Demarketing, Yes, Demarketing," *Harvard Business Review* 49, November–December 1971, pp. 74–80.

considerations. Consumer needs and human welfare and not merely economic gain must be emphasized.

- The firm's marketing effort should center more on the intrinsic values of what is being sold, rather than on extrinsic ones. For example, product quality, durability, economy of consumption, and freedom from harmful effect are product features that should be stressed, rather than mere style, prestige, novelty, or even worse, planned obsolescence.
- Marketing should be more concerned with *why* a product or service should be sold, rather than *how* it can be sold.
- The promotional efforts of the firm should be objective and explicit and free from any form of deception.
- The firm should try to minimize the detrimental impact of its operations on environmental quality. From a marketing perspective, the firm should advise the consumers on the proper disposal of used products or packaging material and consider the possibility of recycling used materials.

In essence, firms should be sensitive to the welfare of their customers and of the physical environment in which they operate. It would be a mistake to argue that small firms can do little harm in this regard and that whatever they are doing has a very limited impact as compared to the actions of the large firms. On the contrary, the management of small companies should adopt a positive approach toward these issues and should develop sensitivity toward all marketing-relevant changes as a means for strengthening their firms' competitive advantages.

SUMMARY: The Essence of Marketing Management

In this chapter the major marketing decision variables under management control have been discussed at some length. Having defined the market segments that it wishes to serve, the firm can then manipulate marketing-relevant decision issues such as the product, price, distribution, and promotion in the light of existing external market conditions over which it has no direct control. The resulting marketing strategy ought to be aimed at satisfying customer needs in specific market segments and achieving profit by filling those needs.

The setting of objectives and subobjectives, and the development of an effective marketing strategy, however, are just the first two phases in the development of a total marketing program. The third key phase is measurement and analysis. Having set objectives and applied a strategy to meet these objectives, the firm must identify whether or not the strategy was successful. If the objectives were not achieved as desired, other decisions might have been made that would have been more effective. Management must get feedback on the crucial variables so that marketing strategy may be improved in the next planning period. Feedback data should focus on the results of the marketing program. The firm should measure its achievements in profit, market share, consumer awareness, extent of distribution penetration, or whatever objectives or subobjectives were set at the beginning of the planning period. When the firm has determined the deviations of actual achievements from forecast, and the reasons behind those deviations, it will be better able to reestablish objectives and subobjectives, and to plan its marketing strategy for the following period.

SUGGESTED READINGS

Britt, Stewart H., and Boyd, Harper W., Jr. *Marketing Management and Administrative Action*, New York: McGraw-Hill, 1973.

Engel, James F.; Fiorillo, Henry F.; and Cayley, Murray A., eds. *Market Segmentation: Concepts and Applications*. New York: Holt, Rinehart & Winston, 1972.

Engel, James F.; Wales, Hugh G.; and Warshaw, Martin R. *Promotional Strategy*, 3d edition. Homewood, Ill.: Richard D. Irwin, 1975.

Enis, Ben M., and Cox, Keith K. *Marketing Classics: A Selection of Influential Articles*. Boston: Allyn & Bacon, 1969.

Govoni, Norman A.P. *Contemporary Marketing Research: Perspectives and Applications*. Morristown, N.J.: General Learning Corporation, 1972.

Howard, John C. *Marketing Management: Operating, Strategic, and Administrative*, 3d edition. Homewood, Ill.: Richard D. Irwin, 1973.

Kelley, Eugene J., and Lazer, William. *Managerial Marketing: Policies, Strategies, and Decisions*. Homewood, Ill.: Richard D. Irwin, 1973.

Kotler, Philip. *Marketing Management: Analysis, Planning and Control*, 3d edition. Englewood Cliffs, N.J.: Prentice-Hall, 1976.

Levitt, Theodore. *Marketing for Business Growth*. New York: McGraw-Hill, 1973.

Luck, David J.; Wales, Hugh G.; and Taylor, Donald A. *Marketing Research*, 4th edition. Englewood Cliffs, N.J.: Prentice-Hall, 1974.

McCarthy, E. Jerome. *Basic Marketing: A Managerial Approach*, 5th edition. Homewood, Ill.: Richard D. Irwin, 1975.

Palda, Kristian S. *Pricing Decisions and Marketing Policy*. Englewood Cliffs, N.J.: Prentice-Hall, 1971.

Rachman, David J. *Marketing Strategy and Structure*. Englewood Cliffs, N.J.: Prentice-Hall, 1974.

Shapiro, Stanley J., and Chebat, Jean-Charles, comp. *Marketing Management: Readings in Operational Effectiveness*. New York: Harper & Row, 1974.

Stanton, William J. *Fundamentals of Marketing*, 4th edition. New York: McGraw-Hill, 1975.

Webster, Frederick E., Jr. *Marketing for Managers.* New York: Harper & Row, 1974.

Wotruba, Thomas R. *Sales Management: Planning, Accomplishment, and Evaluation.* New York: Holt, Rinehart & Winston, 1971.

Zaltman, Gerald, and Burger, Philip C. *Marketing Research: Fundamentals and Dynamics.* Hinsdale, Ill.: Dryden, 1975.

CHAPTER 12

Production and
Operations Management

The entrepreneur bent on producing a product should carefully decide on policies in several critical areas. These include setting basic guidelines for ownership of assets, buying, leasing, or building a plant; buying or leasing equipment; managing inventory; making or buying parts or components; designing the product line; and controlling production and costs. By establishing sound policies in matters such as these, the small manufacturer can practice good husbandry through proper decisions—and good husbandry will conserve time and money in producing and getting out the product.

POLICIES IN PRODUCTION AND OPERATIONS MANAGEMENT

Small entrepreneurs starting in manufacturing usually have limited funds. Their first decisions should be made with a view to using those funds judiciously. They should often make a choice that may be a bit more expensive for the moment in order to preserve liquid cash. For example, rather than buy a large quantity of raw materials at an attractive discount, they would choose to buy a modest quantity at a higher price, avoiding the trap of loss of cash flow for the sake of the immediate bargain.

Similarly, the beginning manufacturer would probably be compelled to lease a building rather than buy or build. When the company has achieved growth and a measure of profitability it may be desirable to buy or build. It then becomes important to project future requirements to ensure the adequacy of the manufacturing facility. Whether leasing, buying, or building, criteria for assuring the suitability of the plant should be considered. These are given later in this chapter.

The small manufacturer should exercise prudence in the acquisition of equipment and machinery with which to start manufacturing. It often makes more sense to lease or buy on terms rather than to invest heavily in outright purchase. The objective here again is to preserve available cash.

Other areas that can absorb cash and that should be critically examined are inventories of raw materials and work in process. Naturally, small inventories tie up less money. The small businessperson will have to use sound judgment here to keep enough inventory on hand to meet the needs of sales without freezing too much cash in inventory and work in process.

Improper make-or-buy decisions can be costly in use of funds. The beginning enterprise should farm out as much production of parts and components as good judgment dictates. Only when special expertise possessed by the entrepreneur is required, or special machinery unique to the manufacturing facility is needed, should the small new firm take on the manufacturing chore. It is wiser in general to have as much as possible made on the outside and to confine internal operations to assembly. As the firm grows and becomes profitable, it may choose to add manufacturing of parts and components to its operations. But that should never be done without due analysis of the benefits in profitability, ability to get quality or production that cannot be obtained outside, or other valid reason.

If the product line requires a number of related items, the manufacturer would do well to design the product with standardized parts and subassemblies that can be combined in various ways to make the different model numbers. This approach can also be used to provide a variety of features.[1]

Caution should be observed to control design changes. When a design is frozen for production, no changes should be permitted unless mandatory for performance. Changes for improvement of the product should be gathered, tested, and introduced at a stipulated model number in the future. Several improvements can then be incorporated at one time. This procedure ensures control of product quality, replacement parts, maintenance instructions, and costs.

These are some of the more important aspects of sound policy for the newly formed manufacturing operation. As the business grows and prospers, long-range plans should be made to include the broadening of policies, or to adjust them, to expand the scope of operations in ways appropriate to building on the strengths and avoiding the weaknesses of

---

[1]Peter F. Drucker, *The Practice of Management*, New York: Harper & Row, 1954, pp. 99–102.

the business. The balance of this chapter is given to examining manufacturing issues in a small firm that has gotten over its starting pains and is reasonably well established.

SMALL PLANT DESIGN

The small manufacturer should be aware of three cardinal sets of criteria in leasing, constructing, or buying a plant. These criteria concern location, community features, and plant layout. In leasing or buying, it may not be possible to fulfill all the desired requirements in detail. However, many will be found to be mandatory and others only desirable. The owner will have to meet the mandatory requirements and should try to fill the desirable ones insofar as possible. When building a new plant, the entrepreneur has the opportunity to meet them all.

Location

The location of the plant determines the ease of access to the firm's market and raw materials. The particular freight and transportation facilities required will depend upon the characteristics of both market and product. A high cost per unit weight product, such as electronic instruments, with a widespread national market, may well use air transport for receiving many of its small, lightweight, often expensive components. On the other hand, bulky and heavy products, such as clay tile, would require both raw materials and finished product to be shipped by rail or truck.

The plant site should be picked with careful attention to zoning restrictions. The ecological impact of manufacturing processes plays an important part in zoning ordinances. Many communities restrict manufacturing to light industry that emits no noxious smoke, fumes, noise, or waste products. Heavy industrial operations are relegated to outlying areas specially designated for the purpose. The site should be selected with both present and future requirements in mind. If it is possible that the characteristics of the manufacturing operation will change over time, the location should be selected to permit such changes without disrupting the business.

Not the least among the requirements for site location is the availability of labor. The labor supply should be checked to see if the necessary skilled personnel are to be had. The requirements of the work may be such that it is possible to train unskilled people to do what is needed. If so, provisions should be made to train new personnel upon hiring.

The site location should provide needed power, gas, and water. The specifications for electric power should be worked out ahead of time and the availability of electricity in the right quantity, voltage, and phase assured. Provision should be made for increase in demand for power as the firm grows. The same is true for gas and water. If the manufacturing process uses large quantities of water, an adequate supply must be arranged. Often the disposal of large quantities of wastewater presents a serious problem. Many municipalities limit the amount of wastewater that can be emptied into the sewer system. This problem can be solved on occasion by pumping effluent water into a return well of sufficient size and percolation effect to return it into the ground. Drilling a large return well can be expensive. Needs of these kinds should be anticipated in the planning for the new plant. They can present difficult and costly problems if they arise after the plant is under construction.

Another aspect of site location that should be noted in the original search is the tax burden that would be assumed. Some communities offer inducements in the form of tax relief for a specified period to encourage new industry to locate there. Anticipated tax benefits should not override the more important considerations given above. Taxes on property and real estate usually represent but a small percentage of the overall tax bill for the manufacturing operation. They would typically be between 2 and 5 percent of the estimated true value of the real estate and property. Nevertheless, the tax assessment policy and rates should be checked as another variable in deciding where to locate a new plant.

The size of the plot for the new plant should be given careful consideration. Space should be allocated not only to accommodate the buildings proper, but also to provide for growth, sufficient parking for cars, access by trucks and freight cars, and open space for landscaping.

Design Features

A design that lends itself readily to expansion allows for future growth at minimum cost. Modern construction methods incorporate this flexibility. Among the methods available are modular construction, shell structures, geodesic domes, and independent steel frame and independent long-span concrete frame construction.

Planning for the new plant should be influenced by the needs for good citizenship. This means that provisions should be made to subdue noise and to eliminate pollution. It is far easier to incorporate the necessary abatement processes in a new plant design than to add them to an existing plant—and usually less costly. Very often these costs of installation more than pay for themselves. A furnace combustion process that is carefully designed and run to minimize undesirable effluents usually means an efficient burning process that reduces the cost of fuel.

The buildings and grounds should meet aesthetic requirements. Grounds should be landscaped and well maintained. A pleasant place for the members of the company to work in also means a good neighbor in the community. The investment in appearance is well worth the return in good relations with the community.

OVERALL PLANT LAYOUT

The manufacturing plant provides the vehicle by which the inputs of human effort, money, and material are joined to make a product, which is a major output. The objective of the operation in economic terms is to achieve a high contributed value—the difference between the total income received through the sale of the poduct and the total amount paid out for raw materials and the services of outside suppliers. Contributed value measures the cost of all the efforts of the business and the total income received for these efforts.[2] Anything that detracts from the smooth flow of process from raw material to finished product lowers the contributed value. Therefore great care should be exercised in designing the layout of the plant to ensure the efficiency of the process. This includes, of course, the provision of safe and comfortable working conditions.

Layout

The layout usually takes the form of a drawing that shows the arrangement of facilities and machinery within the plant. The layout may also be a scale model that shows the arrangement physically in miniature. A good layout allows material to be moved easily over the shortest distance while permitting the manufacturing process to be carried out smoothly.

Moving raw material and work in process is wasteful. Minimum handling promotes efficiency. Any arrangement that cuts out a stage of handling or reduces the distance that the material must be hauled is beneficial. The layout can show how to streamline the operation to reduce unnecessary handling costs.

Efficient handling is supported by effective storage arrangements for raw materials and work in process. Adequate shelving, bins, and pallets ease storing and carrying. These facilities should be designed to accommodate quantities of materials required to maintain normal production, with some overage capacity. Materials should be moved in a straight line from stage to stage whenever possible to avoid backtracking and clutter. Good housekeeping practices help to streamline movement of material and work in process and to ensure safety in the plant.

---

[2]Ibid. p. 72.

Flexibility in Design

Managing the business to adapt to change will inevitably mean change in product design or adding new products to the line. The basic plant should incorporate design features permitting easy adjustment to new production requirements. Provisions for adaptability include unsluttered floor space without posts or columns, high enough roof space and sturdy enough structure to accommodate overhead materials handling equipment or tall equipment and machinery, under-floor ducts or overhead conduits for high voltage lines that may be needed in the future, movable mounts to ensure ease of relocation for production machinery, and floors of sufficient strength to take high concentrated loads. Forethought in these matters may incur some additional expense in construction but will more than pay off in reduced costs of remodeling required by growth and change.

Ease of Maintenance

Forethought in the selection of construction materials can lower the costs of maintaining the factory. There are no building materials that are free from maintenance, but some are more suitable than others for specific purposes. Natural concrete walls may not need paint, but may need to be cleaned occasionally to remove soot and dirt. Stainless steel panels or tile for the walls of washrooms are easier to keep clean than other materials. In any event, the cost over the long term should be considered in the selection of building materials. The payoff may be well worth a somewhat higher initial cost.

Considerable care should be given to the regular upkeep of production machinery and equipment. Selecting the machine for the job is the first step in ensuring steady performance. It is usually wiser to buy more capacity than first estimates indicate. A machine that can handle more than the specific task with ease has capacity for larger jobs and will ordinarily require less maintenance than one of smaller capacity. The extra capacity will generally cost a little more but will usually pay off many times over in the long run.

Plant Design and Employee Morale

The design of the new plant should make it a desirable place to work. Despite the fact that working conditions do not increase motivation, as reported by Herzberg and his associates, uncomfortable or dangerous conditions reduce motivation.[3] Today's owner will want to provide con-

---

[3]Frederick Herzberg, *Work and the Nature of Man,* Cleveland: World Publishing Company, 1966, chapter 6.

veniences and aesthetic features as well as safety in the new plant. Adequate parking lots, air conditioning, a clean employee lunch room, colorful and cheerful decor, and well-kept grounds are some of the features that can serve to make the plant an attractive place in which to work. A good-looking plant on carefully groomed grounds makes itself known as a good neighbor in the community and maintains its investment value. Furthermore, it need be no more expensive than an ugly installation. An aesthetically pleasing result reflects the thought and taste put into the design by owner and architect.

INTENSIVE OR EXTENSIVE USE OF FACILITIES

The small plant can turn out considerably more volume by operating three shifts per day rather than one. A three-shift operation is intensive use of the manufacturing facility; single-shift operation is extensive use.[4] The owner-manager of the small plant may find it desirable to operate two or three shifts per day to get maximum productivity from the available equipment.

It would seem that overhead costs per unit of production might be less with three-shift operation. This would be true for many items of expense, such as taxes, insurance, building depreciation, interest on investment, and obsolescence of machinery. Less expensive rates for electric power are sometimes available during off-shift night operation. However, countervailing costs usually offset the gains. Labor costs for second- and third-shift operations are generally higher. Saturday and Sunday work commands higher labor rates than normal. Labor on other than the standard first-shift tends to be somewhat less productive, increasing the unit cost of production. Maintenance of machinery and equipment is easier to perform on a one-shift, five-day operation. Repairs and adjustment can be made without interfering with production. All in all, it is generally more desirable to have a larger plant that can produce to normal needs on a standard workday and workweek.

Many plants use part of their facilities intensively and part extensively. Very expensive machines are purchased in limited number and worked two or three shifts a day. Other equipment is worked only during the normal first shift.

Trends in Working Hours

The small business owner should note the trend toward the four-day workweek. The four-day workweek originated in relatively small man-

---

[4]Franklin G. Moore, *Production Management,* 6th edition, Homewood, Ill.: Richard D. Irwin, 1973, chapter 6.

ufacturing firms in the late sixties. Since then it has captured the imagination of top management in many different endeavors. Organizations now using this approach include retail trade, hospitals, police forces, banks, trucking, wholesalers, and a variety of services. But small manufacturing concerns seem to be in the forefront of the movement.

In practice, the customary five-day week is reduced to four. The general plan is to maintain the number of working hours at forty per week. However, there are many variations of this practice. Some companies reduce the hours somewhat. Typical variations include workweeks of 34 hours and 40 minutes, 35 hours, 37 hours, and 39 hours. Hourly rates are normally reduced a bit, minimizing the effect of higher rates for overtime so that the worker's take-home pay stays the same as it was before the change.

Scheduling the workforce for the four-day workweek poses problems that vary with the nature of the business. Some companies place the total workforce on four days, including male and female workers. Others exclude employees who must serve customers, such as salespersons and shipping clerks. Each organization must plan the move to the four-day workweek in the light of its unique requirements for doing business.[5]

Preparation for the Four-Day Workweek

Surprisingly few disadvantages to the company and its employees have turned up with the four-day workweek. After initial adjustments to scheduling work and educating customers to the new hours, the problems that arise seem relatively minor. The small business owner should consider adopting the four-day workweek to gain its advantages for the business.

In a study of 139 firms having more than one year of experience with the four-day workweek, Richard I. Hartman and K. Mark Weaver found three major advantages management experiences with the short work schedule. These findings are as follows:

1. Successful implementation of a four-day workweek significantly increased productivity.
2. Successful implementation of a four-day workweek significantly improved job satisfaction of the workforce.
3. Reduced absenteeism was one of the benefits of the four-day conversion.

The first two items showed a statistical significance value of 0.001 and

---

[5]Riva Poor, ed., *4 Days, 40 Hours*, Cambridge, Mass.: Bursk and Poor, 1970.

the third a significance value of 0.10, indicating less certainty than the first two but still of appreciable importance.[6]

Successful introduction of the short week depends upon painstaking preparation. Planning should be based on a detailed study of the entire operation of the company. The ultimate aim should be a design of a four-day workweek that provides maximum benefits to the company, its workers, and its managers.

Background Study The background study should include a careful analysis of the flow of company process, the transactions that define the relationships between departments, the relationship with the community served by the company, and such factors as manufacturing costs, productivity, and profitability in its many ramifications.

Human factors must be considered. These involve the physical effort required in the various kinds of work and an analysis of the makeup of the workforce: male-female ratios and numbers, average age, family constituency, and other variables that may influence the choices to be made. Even such items as employee car pools should be considered.

Work Scheduling Great care should be given to the scheduling of work and personnel. The switchover from the old to the new schedule will often prove complex. Proper planning will prevent crises in operations, particularly in production where the problems of changeover to the short week can be critical.

The following factors should be studied in preparation for scheduling the changeover:

- the flow of work, which will depend upon the kind of manufacturing being done: continuous process, small batch fabrication, or job shop
- shipping requirements, which reflect the needs of both manufacturer and customer
- sales requirements, which determine the time salespersons should be on the job
- start-up and shutdown sequencing as required by the manufacturing process and maintenance of production machinery
- sequencing of switchover, which is critical in its impact on personnel scheduling

The data produced by these studies usually permit the development of several combinations of timing from which management may select that which seems best. The most desirable schedule would fulfill the criterion of giving maximum benefit to the company, its workers, and its managers when viewed as a whole package.

---

[6]Richard I. Hartman and K. Mark Weaver. "Four Factors Influencing Conversion to a Four-Day Work Week," *Human Resource Management*, Graduate School of Business Administration, University of Michigan, Vol. 16, No. 1, Spring 1977, pp. 24–27.

As in introducing any critical change, it is important that accurate records be kept before and after the changeover. These would give comparative data upon which to judge the effectiveness of the shorter work schedule. If the experience of many firms that have made the change holds true, the new schedule should show improvement in the criteria that have been discussed.

In summary, management should follow two key guidelines in switching to the short workweek: 1) The plan it develops for the changeover should fit the unique characteristics of its organization, and 2) any program it evolves from the plan should produce a win-win situation. The outcome must be good for the company, and for its workforce and managers.

Learning Curve

Both managers and workers approaching a strange new production task tend to be slow and somewhat less than efficient in their procedures. Learning comes with experience, with trial and correction of less effective ways of performing the elements of the task. As skill is acquired, productivity goes up and costs come down. Typical curves of productivity and cost per unit of production are shown in Figure 12–1.

The reduction in time and cost to accomplish a production run that comes with learning reflects a variety of factors: better planning by management; increased skills by workers; improved tooling, jigs, and fixtures; specially developed production machinery; and reduced scrap.

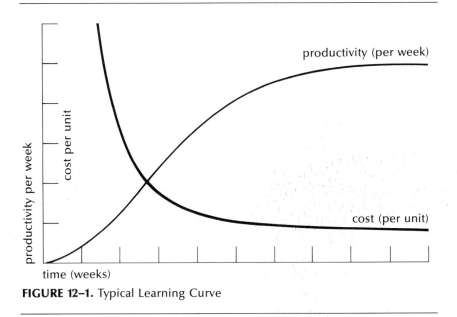

FIGURE 12–1. Typical Learning Curve

Management in the small manufacturing firm can predict unit cost on the basis of accumulated records when a production batch of an item is to be rerun. A rule of thumb gleaned from the aircraft and electronics industries says that every time the production quantity doubles, the direct labor goes down to 80 percent of its former level.[7]

MANAGING SEASONAL CHANGE

Some manufacturing businesses are intensely seasonal. Toy manufacturing requires the production of large quantities of goods during the summer months. Quantity requirements taper off after retailers are stocked with merchandise for the Christmas season. Other businesses follow their own patterns of seasonal ups and downs. The small plant must manage very carefully to meet the cyclical demands imposed by a seasonal business. It is not feasible, nor is it desirable, to hire and fire in keeping with the current demand for production. The organization cannot build an effective workforce unless it offers steady employment. Actions may be taken to meet the problem of seasonal demand. Among these are the following:

- The company can do a certain amount of building to inventory. Its ability to stockpile will depend upon its financial strength and credit rating. Care must be taken not to tie up too much cash in this way.
- Special marketing efforts can often stimulate off-season sales. These include developing a new market for the existing product line, developing export sales, or offering special discounts for off-season sales.
- Increasing and decreasing the number of hours of shop work can sometimes be used as a method of leveling out costs. This procedure requires skillful handling to ensure maintenance of the workforce. It might be possible to employ retired or semiretired personnel, who prefer not to work full time, during periods of peak production.
- Another approach is to keep a steady small workforce and to farm out work during heavy production periods. When slack periods are encountered the work would then be brought back into the plant.

These courses of action may be drawn upon singly or in combination to help meet the problems of peaks and valleys of production.

RESEARCH AND DEVELOPMENT

The small firm with its limited resources must necessarily use the simplest approaches in its research and development efforts. It can ac-

---

[7]Moore, *Production Management.*

complish major achievements through applying ingenuity, and it can add to its own resources those of outside vendors and other small firms qualified in specific specialties. Any metropolitan region abounds with small companies that offer services of various kinds: electro-plating, balancing of rotating machine elements, precision grinding, chemical milling, tool and die fabrication—services that the small firm's research and development department can draw on to supplement its own efforts.

The small firm with a unique product will find it important to build a research and development facility particularly capable of treating the problems in its own specialty. A firm concentrating on manufacturing very small high-precision electric motors, for example, would want to combine model shop and research and development laboratory. It would install power supplies and switchboard capable of providing both AC and DC current at a variety of voltages and phases. It would very likely be equipped with a small punch press and a dynamic balancing machine for balancing armatures and rotors. A small paint manufacturer would provide itself with a complete chemical laboratory and bench-sized ball mills, miniature test ovens, and other special equipment for developing formulas for new finishes.

The laboratory-model shop should never be allowed to be used in production. It should be considered a tool, as much as a computer or a set of Jo blocks. The function of the R and D operation is to reinforce the forward-looking, proactive attitude of the company. Tempting as it may be on occasion to use R and D facilities for production processing, this practice should be discouraged, for it takes management's focus away from the main purpose of the function: to ensure the availability of new products when needed to take up slack caused by obsolescence or competitive products. Model shop short-sightedness can be just as disastrous inside the plant as marketing short-sightedness outside the plant. Management should not trade the future for the sake of a bit more profit today.

Research and development effort in the small plant should be keyed to the marketing function. Ideas generated within the plant should be tested for commercial worth from the outside in, which means subjecting them to the acid test of acceptance in the marketplace. Opportunities for new product development should be related to the resources available within the small organization. A small plant might well take on the development of a new laboratory test oven, but would be foolish indeed to try to develop a new blast furnace for making steel.

Whatever the nature of the R and D function, the projects undertaken should be managed as carefully as the finances of the company. The three elements of personnel, money, and time are the variables with which the project leader must work to achieve R and D objectives. R and D performance is measured by three criteria: an excellent job accomplished to specifications, finished on time, and completed within budget.

The project leader should plan the job through any simple and convenient planning technique that fits the development purpose: Gantt charting, PERT, CPM, or equivalent.[8]

Designing for Production

The smaller manufacturer often overlooks the importance of designing products for producibility. Products should be designed to minimize scrap and to reduce machining as much as possible. That requires careful study of alternative ways of producing the product, of making appropriate production equipment available, and of minimizing costs.

The selection of methods stems from the original design, which must be dictated by the quality of the product desired for the intended segment of the market. Even in apparently simple products a multitude of choices must be made. Some could be readily managed by the small manufacturer, and some are clearly too complex and too costly.

So seemingly trivial a problem as joining two sheets of metal together cannot be taken lightly. Choices abound: spot welding, riveting, seam welding, seam bending, fastening with special adhesives—all require different kinds of tooling and fabrication equipment. Costs of equipment vary depending on the process. The basic design should take into account the end use of the product, the quantities required, and the most satisfactory way to produce the joint soundly and economically.

In another example, a skillet may be made from different materials and in different ways. Materials may include cast iron, sheet steel, copper, aluminum, or ceramics. Fabrication from cast iron is ordinarily done by sand casting, which requires patterns and molds. Sheet steel fabrication involves stamping and requires proper dies. Copper and aluminum skillets may be stamped or spun; handles are fabricated separately and attached by riveting or possibly welding. Aluminum skillets may be cast through the use of sand molds or permanent steel molds. Ceramic skillets require special materials, special know-how, and proprietary processes involving costly production equipment. Some manufacturing methods leave a rough texture on the surfaces of the skillet, needing secondary grinding and polishing operations. Of the many ways to make a skillet some are suitable for the small manufacturer and some are not.

Ensuring the producibility of products commands careful attention.

---

[8]See Arthur H. Kuriloff, *Reality in Management,* New York: McGraw-Hill, 1966, pp. 183–95 for an example of the use of simplified Gantt planning and scheduling in R and D.

The small company should explore every possibility in designing the product to make it easy to fabricate economically and soundly with the resources the company has at hand.

PURCHASING ISSUES

The owner-chief executive of a small manufacturing firm should view purchasing as an overall job that links together the major functions needed to make the product and serve the customers' needs. Purchasing is not merely a matter of buying. Purchasing must contribute to and be involved in joint planning with the marketing, sales, distribution, production, and engineering functions. These functions are interdependent and all must be supplied with the right materials and components at the right time to meet delivery schedules.

Planning for purchasing can be done only by knowing the status of present and expected sales. From these data, materials and components and services to be used in production can be scheduled with due regard to lead times, quantities, costs, and availability of various items from specific vendors. Those responsible for purchasing must keep abreast of vendors. They should be aware of changes in quality, price, delivery, and availability of goods and services. Alertness often pays off in special deals on price and delivery. Establishing close relationships with vendors can be enormously helpful in buying in a tight market. Beyond that, good working relationships with vendors can allow the small businessperson to stretch credit in a time of stress. This practice is one that should not be overdone, but on occasion it may stand the manufacturer in good stead.

Purchasing should work closely with receiving inspection. In the small firm, it is sometimes desirable to attach an inspection function to the purchasing operation. Purchasing provides the feedback link through which vendors are told of the quality of the goods they deliver. In this way purchasing can enforce the delivery of materials and components that meet specifications.

Costs of Ordering and Inventory

Ordering materials and components and managing inventory involve costs that should be identified and carefully controlled. The major costs of ordering include placing orders, receiving and checking material, and handling and stocking inventory. Each step of the process should be studied. The simplest possible paperwork should be adopted for ordering and record keeping. One purchasing form with four or five copies for ordering, receiving and inspection, confirming receipt of materials, record keeping, and payment will usually suffice.

Careful control of inventory is mandatory to avoid unnecessary tying up of money. The costs involved include investing in, handling, stocking, and insuring inventory. Variables to be taken into consideration are the kinds and variety of products, the seasonal nature of sales, the methods of assembly and operations used, and the shelf life of such materials as chemicals and paints. Consideration of these variables underlines the need for cooperative planning among marketing, sales, production, and engineering departments. The objective in purchasing should be to keep sufficient materials on hand to meet expected deliveries without building inventory excessively.

Identifying maximum and minimum quantities of the various materials and components needed to meet anticipated production requirements improves management of inventory. The profitability of the manufacturing operation, indeed of the business, depends to a great extent on the immediate usefulness of the inventory. Care must be taken to ensure that materials do not become obsolete. That can be accomplished only by continual surveillance of the status of inventory.

One helpful device is to keep an up-to-date graph of the total inventory. In the small firm that is best achieved by regular physical count and evaluation of current inventory on a four-week basis. Four weeks rather than a monthly count is suggested in a small manufacturing operation wherever practicable. It will be found that there is a reasonably regular periodicity to the ebb and flow of total inventory value. Irregularities may be seen by a glance at the graph and may be investigated immediately. Unwanted variance can then be corrected by appropriate measures.

The four-week period provides an equal measure of time throughout the year. Accounting for value of inventory by the month gives periods with unequal numbers of manufacturing days, which makes it difficult to compare the financial status of the business from one period to another. The only variance the four-week count produces is one short period in a year's operation.

In the small manufacturing organization it is useful for the chief executive and the purchasing manager to work out a minimum and maximum amount for the total dollar value of inventory that should be maintained to meet the current level of production. This budgeting procedure ensures effective allocation of purchasing funds as a part of the total cash flow of the business. High and low values may be adjusted as the business grows. Involvement of purchasing personnel in setting this guideline assures their understanding of their contribution to company profitability and gains their commitment to intelligent monitoring of the purchasing function.

PRODUCTION ISSUES

Successful management of production requires control of costs by eliminating waste and operating at a high level of efficiency. Production scheduling emerges from the needs of the customer—it is the customer who sets production goals.

Planning for production must therefore start with the sales forecast. Production needs may be judged and production schedules set by tabulating orders actually on hand, orders that may reasonably be expected within the next one-, two-, and three-month periods, and orders that seem fairly likely to come through in these periods. Expectancy percentages may be set for these anticipated orders: 90 percent for those orders that look certain and 50 percent for those that seem fairly likely. By comparing anticipated deliveries and sales with shipping dates, scheduling may be worked out for production quantities. Here, as in many managerial realms, judgment must be applied to smooth the data. Purchasing and production may then be performed with some assurance that the overall plant operation will be reasonably steady.

The planning meeting involving marketing, sales, production, and engineering personnel provides the logical vehicle for arriving at the basic data for production scheduling. These meetings should be held regularly, perhaps weekly in a new business. As the planning procedure improves through the development of teamwork among the representatives of the several functions, the interval between meetings can be lengthened. A four-week period ordinarily serves in a company that is well established. The basic planning, iterated and reiterated, fuses the interests of all parties and supports increasingly efficient operations.

Scheduling Production

The key factors in scheduling production are the production volume and the rate of production required. These are influenced by such essential ingredients as required delivery dates; seasonal variations in the business; availability of raw materials, components, and outside services; and lead times. It will be seen that the customer's need for delivery is only one element that affects production scheduling. The others depend on the cooperation of vendors in delivering materials and services when agreed upon. Lead times become critical in meeting production schedules.

The small business must walk a tight line between developing reliable suppliers and keeping a trim inventory of raw stock. Two courses of action can help to ensure a balance between the outflow to customers and the inflow of goods or services from vendors: the nurturing of a warm relationship with suppliers and careful attention to the planning process described. The trick is to build a favored relationship with suppliers while practicing sound husbandry in managing the flow of materials in the manufacturing process.

Control of Product Cost

A high level of productivity coupled with efficiency helps to build a high contributed value, which is a measure of the effectiveness of the organization in converting raw material into value. In many companies, particularly in the small firm, labor represents a large part of the cost of the product. Managerial effort devoted to building productivity adds materially to contributed value—and to profit for the company.

But increasing productivity implies keeping regular records. These records give the feedback that tells how well the managerial effort is doing. They furnish data for the planning and control of operations so vital to the financial health of the company.

Management in the small company should know the cost of each part and component. It should have up-to-date information on the cost of each operation in the fabrication process. Records should be kept current by periodic review. The most critical common variable that threads through all operations is time. Anything that can be done to shorten the time required to perform an operation, if the capital investment required can be recovered expeditiously, will pay off in higher contributed value. And anything that can be done to reduce scrap and waste will have the same effect.

The costs associated with manufacturing may be divided roughly into fixed and variable categories. Fixed costs include items of expense such as rent, insurance, indirect labor, telephone, and miscellaneous small supplies. These costs may be thought of as spread uniformly throughout the year. Variable costs, however, change with the volume of production. These include the cost of materials and direct labor, in the main. If the manufacturing process depends upon use of electricity or gas in large volume, costs for these supplies would change with the volume of production and should be taken into account as a variable.

Variable costs, in general, are the most important to control, since they contribute significantly to the cost of the manufacturing operation.

Control of Scrap and Waste

Three variables determine the amount of scrap and waste: 1) complexity of the product, 2) suitability and condition of the production equipment, and 3) the skill and experience of the production personnel.

Complexity of the Product Increasing the complexity of products increases the amount of scrap and waste. Obviously, to hold a tolerance of

0.0001 inch on the diameter of a two-inch shaft is many times more difficult than to hold it to 0.001, which in itself is a very close tolerance. The level of craftsmanship required to get the tighter tolerance would be much higher, and one would expect the amount of scrap to increase considerably.

Rougher kind of work requires less skill and should be accomplished with less scrap. For example, to make planter boxes of redwood does not demand fine craftsmanship. Tolerances are of the order of a quarter of an inch. One would expect very little scrap in the assembly, which is performed by nailing sides to a bottom plate. The approach to minimizing waste here, as in that of most products, is to design in such a way as to use the raw material to best advantage and to keep tolerances as wide as possible without impairing the usefulness or appearance of the product.

Suitability and Condition of Production Equipment It is of paramount importance that production equipment be suitable and adequately sized for the job and that equipment be maintained at peak performance. The small businessperson should determine the capability of a piece of production equipment before buying it. It is wiser, in general, to purchase some excess capacity than to buy a less expensive machine, only to discover later that its performance is marginal. For example, it is possible to cut three-quarter inch fir plywood on a table saw of one-quarter horsepower. The job becomes much faster and easier, however, at three-quarters horsepower. The larger motor costs more, of course, but it is much more adequate for the job. Investment in the larger machine would pay off quickly in time saved alone.

Maintenance is another critical factor in preserving the capability of equipment to perform efficiently. Keeping machines clean and well lubricated, and replacing worn parts before they impair performance are the essence of good husbandry. Proper maintenance can be the key to profit. One West Coast concern specializing in screw machine job shop work has been able to maintain an excellent record of profit over the years by running its machines at double the speed of the manufacturer's recommendations. It can do this only by continual inspection of the machines, proper lubrication, and replacement of parts that show wear before the wear becomes excessive.

Skill and Experience of Workers The skill and experience of craftsmen and workers is the third great factor in limiting scrappage and waste. Precision work obviously requires a high level of mastery. Complex tasks require higher levels of skill, and perhaps intelligence, than less difficult tasks. In any event, performance depends upon skill at a level appropriate to the task. But people do not acquire skill without training. The modern perspective in management suggests that a major part of the management job is to train—to ensure that members of the firm receive the necessary training and education to acquire mastery and skill.

In the small firm, the process of training and education carried on at all levels from bench worker to vice-president is one of the best ways to ensure upgrading of competence throughout the organization. Not only does scrap and waste diminish, but efficiency of the various operations in the company also improves.

Salvage of Scrap and Waste Materials The value in scrap and waste materials should not be overlooked. The screw machine company mentioned previously centrifuged all metal turnings to recover cutting lubricant. Brass, copper, and aluminum turnings were segregated and stored in a covered shed at the back of the plant. When the scrap price of a particular material rose to a figure the president considered acceptable, that material was sold for recycling. This practice added to the profitability of the screw machine operation. It is recommended practice if the company has the space and can afford to store the scrap for long periods, several months in some cases.

Other kinds of businesses offer other opportunities for recovering value from scrap. Companies engaged in etched circuitry production in electronics can reclaim the silver salts washed off in the process. Fabricators of sheet metal usually have odd-shaped pieces that are cut off in their fabrication processes. These can sometimes be used for special purposes or sold to other manufacturers. The guiding principle once more is the practice of good husbandry in the manufacturing operation.

Value Analysis

The small manufacturer can well employ value analysis to improve profitability of its manufacturing operation. Value analysis may be defined as an orderly method for accomplishing maximum performance at minimum cost. The basic techniques of value analysis are applicable to every aspect of company operations. However, they are particularly useful in improving contributed value in material selection, fabrication methods, and manufacturing processes.

Two basic steps must be taken in applying value analysis:

- Discovery through uninhibited creativity of promising alternatives for reducing the complexity of design and production or purchased cost of each item, part, component, or assembly of the product.
- Decision based on intensive study and evaluation of the alternatives. The alternative chosen should give the optimum combination of high utility and low cost while retaining the desired features.

The application of value analysis depends upon the ability of management to mount an effective approach based upon comprehensive sources of information. The reference material required includes cost records, data sheets, catalogs, and test reports. The analysis also requires design and production experience as represented by a wide background in various types of manufacturing, fabrication, shop practice, materials handling, and design. Above all, value analysis demands a climate supportive of innovativeness and creativity. This kind of climate would be demonstrated by the ability to freewheel in generating ideas, to develop fresh ways of combining old ideas, to stimulate ideas in others, and to conceive alternative ways of accomplishing desired results.

An example of value analysis properly applied involved the replacement of a special finish on a sheet metal environmental temperature test chamber by a standard, much less expensive baking enamel. The function of the test chamber was to provide a very stable, controllable temperature within its insulated interior. Electromechanical and electronic equipment could be soaked in this stable environment for test purposes. The original design called for a special vinyl baking enamel on the outside skin. This material gave a textured, rough, but good-looking finish. The rough texture was intended to provide more radiating surface than a smooth enamelled sheet metal surface. This feature would allow the internal temperature to stabilize very quickly when compared with a smooth skin. Unfortunately the vinyl material was very expensive and had a short shelf life. It had to be ordered in small quantities as required, posing an awkward purchasing problem.

Management decided to conduct a value analysis of the problem. The objective was three-fold: to reduce the cost of the material, to eliminate the troublesome purchasing problem, and to maintain or improve performance of the test chamber. Investigation showed that it was possible to purchase aluminum sheets called *seconds* from which to fabricate the outside skins of the chambers. These seconds had slight surface defects, scratches or pits, that developed in manufacture or handling. They were considerably less expensive than the first quality material that had been used previously. It was found that the second sheets could be embossed with a small pattern at minimal cost. The pattern increased the radiating surface without impairing the strength of the material—indeed, stiffened it somewhat.

It was now possible to substitute a standard baking enamel for the vinyl finishing material at one-third the cost and with no shelf life problems. Tests conducted with chambers made of second sheets and finished the new way showed performance superior to the previous design at a substantial decrease in cost.

Tests for Values The following questions are applicable to assess the worth of a proposed value analysis. They may be applied in whole or in part to materials, parts, components, processes, or assemblies:

- Does it contribute value?
- Is its cost proportionate to its usefulness?
- Does it need all the features it possesses?
- Is there anything better for the intended use?
- Can a usable part be made by a lower-cost method?
- Can a standard product replace one specially fabricated?
- Is the piece made on proper tooling, considering quantities used?
- Is a reasonable cost reflected by its labor content, material, and overhead?
- Will another dependable supplier provide it for less?
- Is anyone buying it for less?

Answers to these questions will suggest the desirability of pursuing a value analysis in depth for the particular item under consideration.

Quality Control or Quality Assurance?

Quality starts with a sound concept, a sound design, and a thoroughly tested, well-proved product. Even with these ideal conditions, small manufacturers have a special problem in ensuring the quality of products. They cannot usually afford a special quality control function as can a large manufacturer with adequate means to support the necessary staff. This lack suggests an alternative very much in keeping with the modern management concept of training as a part of job enrichment.

Too often the quality control function in the traditional organization takes on a policing aspect. It is quite clear that policing can do nothing but find faults that must be corrected. Policing does not build quality into the product. What builds in quality is superior workmanship. Superior workmanship, in turn, comes from the skill and mastery of the worker.

Skill and mastery of the task result from education and training— know-how that can be acquired in large part on most jobs under the coaching guidance of the boss. When that is done successfully, quality is assured because each step of the manufacturing process is performed with excellent craftsmanship. Thus quality is built into the product.

When the firm can afford a separate quality assurance staff, it should focus its efforts on teaching and training rather than surveillance. An excellent procedure that works well in practice is to name the function *quality assurance* and give it the authority to inspect finished goods selected at random from stores. If defects in workmanship are found, the quality assurance representative helps the individual who did the job gain skill through coaching and teaching.

Group Assembly versus Assembly Line

We have inherited some notions about how manufacturng should best be done from the early days of the industrial revolution. So-called scientific management developed the concept that the most efficient way to assemble a relatively complex product was by the progressive assembly method. Here the work moves from station to station. At each station a worker does some small bit of assembly: inserts some screws, spins up nuts on bolts, solders an electrical connection, or the like. The main task is broken into small, easily learned chores, which can be performed by relatively unskilled people. The training required is minimal.

A demanding management problem in progressive assembly is planning the logistics of the assembly line. The necessary parts, fittings, subassemblies, and supplies must be at the right station at the right time to keep the line moving. With a complex product such as an air compressor, electric motor, or a television set, the logistics of supply assume major proportions.

Some products lend themselves admirably to a group method of assembly. Here the objective is to take advantage of what we have learned about human capability in recent years. The job itself becomes the focus for infusing beneficial motivational factors into the working environment. People take on an enriched job of doing a whole complex task. They are supported by training and coaching designed to help them acquire the mastery necessary to do the job.

When competent people are permitted to team together to do a whole complex job and are allowed to proceed in their own fashion, they usually perform very well. Performance and quality improve and many management problems issuing from the robot-like quality of work on the assembly line diminish.[9] The small firm making a product that can be handled this way does well to take advantage of the group-centered approach to assembly.

This method trades the complex logistic system of the assembly line for a simple system of delivering kits of parts to be assembled by the group. As soon as one product has been assembled, a kit for the next is delivered from stock. People are required to think, to plan, and to arrange the work in an orderly sequence. It is possible for the small manufacturer to achieve productivity levels above and beyond that of the assembly line in this way—through the human use of human beings.

This is not to say that all products can be or should be assembled by

---

[9]See for example, Robert N. Ford, *Motivation through the Work Itself*, New York: American Management Association, 1969, chapter 9; and Arthur H. Kuriloff, *Reality in Management*, chapter 3.

group methods. Obviously some products can be better built by automated processes. The general guideline should be to give routine operations that can be readily performed by machines to machines, and to give more complex problems that require intelligence to human beings.

The Need to Know

The boss should also realize that people need to know what is happening whether they can use the information or not.[10] The top executive of the small manufacturing concern should take advantage of the motivating effect of letting employees know the status of affairs within the company. There may be a few things that should be kept secret, but the status of orders and deliveries is not one of them. When people are not told honestly what is going on, rumor and distorted tales tend to rush in to fill the vacuum of ignorance.

Clear, accurate information removes the dysfunctional impact of rumor on morale, removes fear of the unknown or ill-defined situation, and stimulates people to productive activity. For example, the small manufacturer soon discovers that it is the effort of the last one or two days of the four-week period that produces the profit. When the members who are responsible for getting out the product understand that it is the effort of the last one or two days of the period that produces the profit on which the longevity of the company—and their well-being—depends, they are stimulated to improve the productivity that results in profit. In this way both the individual and the company gain.[11]

SUMMARY: Key Points for Small Manufacturing Firms

The small businessperson setting up in manufacturing should establish basic policies to guide the firm successfully through the difficulties that beset the start-up period. The decisions in the early stages of the business should be made with due regard to minimizing cash outflow.

If a new manufacturing plant is built, sound judgment should be used in selecting a location. The features of the community where the plant will be should be carefully scrutinized. The layout of the proposed plant should meet present needs and should incorporate flexibility for accommodating future growth.

---

[10]Abraham H. Maslow, *Toward a Psychology of Being,* New York: D. Van Nostrand, 1962, chapter 5.

[11]For some suggestions on how to convey information to manufacturing personnel, see chapter 4, "The Need to Know," in Arthur H. Kuriloff, *Reality in Management.*

In setting employment policy, the small manufacturer may do well to consider the possibilities of the four-day workweek. Advantages to employees, managers, and customers should be weighed against possible disadvantages. Careful planning and scheduling should precede the adoption of the short workweek. On balance, most firms that have moved in this direction report favorable outcomes with few disadvantages.

The small firm producing a product should recognize the transitory nature of market leadership for its products. It must keep a continuous research and development effort going to produce improved features and new products to replace existing products as they fade in the marketplace. Research and development effort should be keyed to the special strengths of the company, and the small company should build its capability to do research and development in its own field. By increasing its special competencies it bulwarks its unique expertise. In addition, products should be designed to be readily and economically produced.

Purchasing should be viewed as a function that links with marketing, sales, production, and engineering. It should not be viewed as an isolated entity that simply buys what is needed. When purchasing effort is linked with the efforts of other functions, a smoother, less wasteful, more economical overall manufacturing and business operation is achieved. Careful planning, scheduling, and budgeting allow control of product cost while meeting the needs of the customer.

A number of techniques can be used to improve the production process. In general, manufacturing effectiveness increases as workers gain skill and mastery of the task. Management that provides such training takes a great stride in increasing the efficiency of the manufacturing operation.

Another technique, value analysis, offers the small manufacturer a way to decrease cost without impairing the utility of the product—and often actually increases its usefulness. This technique may be applied to materials, parts, assemblies, and processes.

Quality assurance, as opposed to quality control, can also improve the production process. Quality in the product may be achieved in the small firm by training personnel to do the job right, step by step. Competence and mastery ensure building in quality. When those are evident, the inspection function may be replaced by a quality assurance function keyed to teaching and coaching rather than to policing to discover error.

In many manufacturing operations, group assembly methods offer the chance for a more productive approach than that of the assembly line. The group assembly method simplifies the logistics of supply while placing the responsibility for relatively complex work on the members of the group. This approach takes advantage of the findings of behavioral research by enriching the job, offering challenge to the group members, and stimulating them toward achievement.

Finally, management should realize that when the members of the manufacturing organization know the truth about what is going on in the company they are relieved of uncertainty and often of fear. Knowledge of the situation tends to motivate employees and stimulates improved productivity. Truth serves the needs of both the individual and the company.

SUGGESTED READINGS

Ammer, Dean S. *Manufacturing Management and Control.* New York: Appleton-Century-Crofts, 1968.

Buffa, Elwood S. *Modern Production Management,* 5th edition. New York: John Wiley & Sons, 1977.

———. *Production Inventory Systems.* Homewood, Ill.: Richard D. Irwin, 1968.

"Building Types Study: Industrial Building." *Architectural Record,* July 1964.

Cooper, Arnold C. "R & D is More Efficient in Small Companies." *Harvard Business Review* 43, May–June 1964, pp. 75–83.

———. "Small Companies Can Pioneer New Products." *Harvard Business Review* 44, September–October 1966, pp. 162–79.

Dearden, John. "Profit-Planning Accounting for Small Firms." *Harvard Business Review,* March–April 1963.

Feigenbaum, A. V. *Total Quality Control.* New York: McGraw-Hill, 1961.

Fitzgerald, C. T. *Organizing for New Product Evolution in Small, Technically-Based Manufacturing Companies.* Cambridge, Mass.: MIT Press, 1966.

Gross, Harry. *Make or Buy.* Englewood Cliffs, N.J.: Prentice-Hall, 1966.

Henke, Russell W. *Effective Research and Development for the Smaller Company.* Houston: Gulf, 1963.

An Introduction to Material Handling. Pittsburgh: The Material Handling Institute, Gateway Center, 1966.

Juran, J. M., ed. *Quality Control Handbook.* 3d edition, New York: McGraw-Hill, 1974.

McBride, H. J., and Skinner, G. S. "Small Firm Research Activity." Business Research Bulletin, Ohio State University, August 1970.

Morrison, Robert S. *Handbook for Manufacturing Entrepreneurs,* 2d edition. Cleveland: Western Reserve Press, 1974.

PERT Guide for Management Use. Washington, D.C.: National Aeronautic and Space Administration, June 1963.

Reiter, S. "A System for Managing Job-Shop Production." *Journal of Business* 39, July 1966, pp. 371–93.

Suggested Readings 343

Sayer, J. S., Kelley, J. E., Jr., and Walker, M. R. "Critical Path Scheduling." *Factory*, July 1960.

Wheeler, Kenneth E. "Small Business Eyes the Four-Day Work-Week." *Harvard Business Review*, May–June 1970.

CHAPTER 13

Management Control

A common shortcoming among small business firms is lack of systematic, formal control of operations. Many small business managers believe that organized control is unnecessary because of the small size of the enterprise. Frequently they believe that they are well in control of operations although in fact they suffer unwittingly from deficiencies that could be remedied by closer attention to the control function. In order to manage a small firm effectively, its executives must not only be planning conscious, they must also be control conscious. Planning and control are closely interrelated. It is impossible to have an effective control system without plans and predetermined standards that provide a basis for evaluating and controlling actual performance. It is similarly impossible to have an effective planning system without efficient controls to pinpoint discrepancies between planned performance and actual results.

Whether a business enterprise is large or small, a key to its success is an effective control system. The fact that operations of a small firm may be easier to control than those of a large enterprise should not be used as the rationale for deemphasizing controls in a small firm. On the contrary, a well-organized control system can enhance the small firm's competitive advantage over the large enterprise.

THE CONTROL PROCESS

The managerial control process has four essential steps:

1. specification of performance standards consistent with planning objectives
2. design of an information feedback system to give prompt, adequate, and accurate information or data about operational activities

3. systematic and continual comparison of actual achievements with predetermined standards in order to ascertain the variances and to determine their significance
4. taking corrective action when necessary to eliminate (or to minimize) the negative consequences of the variances between the planned and the actual results[1]

These four steps are interrelated and of equal significance. Together they constitute what can be called the control process. The process must be systematic and organized and must include establishing an information system. The specific steps outlined above will be discussed in greater detail in the following sections.

Specification of Objectives and Performance Standards

Objectives and performance standards provide a basis for assessing actual achievements. To ensure effective control, appropriate performance standards must be specified for various achievement areas, which may differ from one firm to the other. In general, the more important achievement areas are:

product quality
production cost
productivity
new product development
market share and sales
distribution costs
profitability

Since there are many potential control areas, a balance must be struck between the control of all possible areas and the costs of control. A small firm is well advised to concentrate its effort in key areas most critical to the success of its business. Each firm will have to decide what its most important control areas are.

Management must establish specific performance standards for each control area selected. These set the levels of achievement under the prevailing operating conditions.

The following criteria can be helpful in developing performance standards:

• *Historical standards*—levels of performance that have been achieved in the past.

---

[1]Robert J. Mockler, *The Management Control Process*, New York: Appleton-Century-Crofts, 1972, p. 2.

- *Comparative standards*—levels of achievement of similar firms in the same industry. For example, the key financial ratios for specific industries, as published periodically by Standard and Poors, can be used by a small business manager as performance standards against which to measure the company's achievements.
- *Ideal standards*—standards reflecting a level of performance that might be achieved under optimum operating conditions. Even if such ideal standards are difficult to attain, they may be used as a motivating force for raising individual performance and for making full use of the existing organizational capabilities.

Although it is important to determine *specific* performance standards, certain variations may be considered normal. It may be advisable in some cases to establish a range of acceptable variation from the specified standards.

In summary, the determination of appropriate standards is fundamental to any control process. These standards should be specified for all critical control areas. They should be timely and should provide an early warning, telling when corrective managerial intervention may become necessary.

Design of an Information Feedback System

It has been frequently observed that information is the lifeline of a business enterprise. That is especially true from the point of view of managerial control. Timely and accurate information about the firm's operations and relevant environmental conditions is the essential prerequisite for intelligent decision making and effective control. The design of an information system for a small firm should start with an examination of the basic information needs of the company. These generally fall into three categories:

- *Environmental information,* which includes information about macroeconomic data and their effect on prices, costs, demand patterns and information about technological developments, sociological changes, and relevant legal and regulatory issues.
- *Competitive information,* which includes information on the past performance of direct competitors (such as their profitability, market share, product line) as well as their present activities and, if possible, their future plans.
- *Information on internal, operational activities,* which includes essential information or data that indicate the company's operational strengths and weaknesses, such as financial and cost accounting data, delivery performance, personnel resources, and marketing effectiveness.

Every company needs information in these three basic categories for

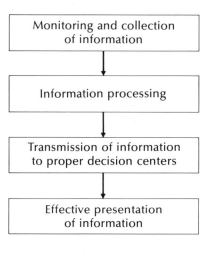

FIGURE 13–1. Flow of Information

its control effort. The amount of data required for intelligent decision making varies from company to company; the information system must be tailored to the specific needs of the firm. In developing such a system, attention must be paid to the four aspects shown in Figure 13–1. These are the essential building blocks of an information system. The system should monitor all relevant developments in the internal and external environment of the company; systematically collect information about these developments; process all important information; quickly transmit the information to the proper decision centers; and present the information in a clear form that can be readily used.[2] Once an information system has been established, it must be reviewed regularly to ensure that it continues to satisfy the control requirements of the firm.

Systematic Comparison of Actual Performance with the Predetermined Standards

Checking on performance is one of the basic steps in the control process. Actual performance must be compared with the standards set and the results reported to the responsible decision makers. If the actual results

---

[2]There is a substantial literature on this subject. See, for example, Robert G. Murdick and Joel Ross, *Information Systems for Modern Management,* Englewood Cliffs, N.J.: Prentice-Hall, 1971; Robert I. Benjamin, *Control of the Information System Development Cycle,* New York: John Wiley & Sons, 1971; Sherman C. Blumenthal, *Management Information Systems,* Englewood Cliffs, N.J.: Prentice-Hall, 1969.

fall within the limits of the preestablished standards, it may be assumed that the system is functioning properly. However, management must be constantly alert to detect internal and external developments that may require reevaluation of the established performance standards.

There are control areas in every organization—particularly in non-routine tasks—for which no clear quantitative standards can be set. Consequently, actual performance may be difficult to assess. In these situations a manager must rely on personal observations, discussions with subordinates, and qualitative judgments for achieving control of activities.

One important question is how frequently performance should be assessed. Timing of corrective measures depends largely on the cost and importance of improving substandard performance. Ideally, an effective control system should detect declining performance before it becomes serious. Forward-looking control is much more effective than after-the-fact control; therefore the frequency of assessment should be decided on the basis of cost and importance of the activity.

Because of the generally broad spectrum of problems in a small business, the manager should make a commitment to the *exception principle*.[3] This principle, applied to control, suggests that a manager should concentrate on the exceptions—on those areas where actual performance deviates significantly from the established standards.

Corrective Action

The final phase in the control process is to take corrective action whenever a serious discrepancy between actual performance and the predetermined standard has been identified. The first step in taking corrective action should be to investigate the cause of the variance from the standard. This analysis tends to identify the corrective measure that should be prescribed. For example, if poor performance can be traced to inadequacies of an individual to perform the task, that person can be given more guidance or training or can be replaced by someone better qualified. If unforeseen external developments are found to be the major cause of a variation, a revision of the standards might be in order.

Effective control requires that appropriate remedial measures be taken without delay; control is exercised by acting. Small business managers frequently tend to delay acting when inadequate performance has been revealed. They seem to hope that the situation will correct itself. This approach usually tends to compound the difficulties. Effective control results from continuously monitoring the key performance areas, analyzing the causes of significant variations between planned results

---

[3]Frederick W. Taylor, *Shop Management*, New York: Harper & Brothers, 1919, pp. 126–27.

and actual achievements, and taking corrective actions without delay.

Sometimes plans are subject to a high degree of uncertainty because of rapid change in the external environment. Sound practice includes the development of contingency plans to ensure managerial control in a turbulent environment.

Criteria for an Effective Control Process

In addition to fulfilling the four basic steps described above, the control process should be organized in such a way that the following important characteristics are realized:

1. *Cost/Benefit.* The benefits derived from a systematic control effort should be greater than its costs.
2. *Flexibility.* The control system should allow ready adjustments to changes in the internal and external environment of the organization.
3. *Clarity.* Relevant parts of the control system and the standards to be achieved should be well understood by everyone affected by them.
4. *Consistency.* Controls and performance standards should be consistent with organizational policies and objectives.
5. *Comprehensiveness.* An effective control system should give systematic, comprehensive guidance in all significant performance areas.
6. *Continuous feedback.* Control data and information should be expeditiously transmitted to appropriate decision centers where they can be analyzed and evaluated so that adverse developments can be acted upon quickly.
7. *Corrective action without delay.* The reasons for significant variations from standards should be identified and remedial measures taken without delay.

Adequate controls and a well-organized control process along these lines are essential elements in managing a small enterprise successfully. Yet a manager who relies too heavily on controls is often perceived as threatening and is likely to create a company climate that is the opposite of that desired. Strict controls may make employees resentful and antagonistic. Their dissatisfactions with the way control is exercised may cause them to be less productive, unreliable, cynical, or even dishonest, and the boss may find more and more management time being wasted on nonproductive control efforts. A small business manager soon learns that there is an ill-defined line separating a control effort that can improve organization efficiency from one that detracts from it. A most important criterion for effective control is therefore sensitivity, awareness of the possibility for both productive and dysfunctional effects of any control effort.

Dysfunctional effects of control tend to be minimized when managers follow the criteria given above in setting up a control process. In addition, managers should develop confidence in the ability of subordinates to do an adequate job, should seek their understanding of the necessity for controls, and should promote their participation in the planning of change.[4]

The analysis in this chapter has thus far dealt with the basic characteristics of an effective control system. The following sections deal specifically with key control areas. Although the control requirements differ from company to company, the following five areas deserve close attention in any small business enterprise:

- financial controls
- cost control and budgeting
- control of operations (production control)
- quality control
- inventory control

FINANCIAL CONTROLS

The business enterprise employs its resources in the attempt to generate a surplus. Its effectiveness in this regard can best be judged by periodically analyzing its financial statements. These disclose the firm's general financial condition, its liquidity, its profitability, and its effectiveness in the use of financial resources.

Control through Analysis of Financial Statements

No small business manager should neglect or do without periodic comparative analyses of balance sheets and income statements, since these are the fundamental means of financial control. It is advisable to express individual components of the balance sheet as percentages of total assets and the components of the income statement as percentages of total sales (see Tables 13–1 and 13–2). This procedure gives the manager a better idea of the relative size of the various components of the company's financial situation than a report of aggregate amounts only. In addition, a comparison of the various components of financial statements for different periods reveals intervening changes and identifies shifts in the company's financial condition. An analysis of the flow of funds (see Table 13–3) during a particular period is another financial control measure. Tables 13–1 through 13–3 exemplify the basic forms of financial control.

---

[4]Rensis Likert, The Human Organization. New York: McGraw-Hill, 1967, pp. 156–88.

TABLE 13–1. COMPARATIVE BALANCE SHEET (in $1,000s)

	Amount		Percentage of Total Assets		Amount of Increase/ Decrease*	Percentage of Increase/ Decrease*
	Month . . . (p_1)	Month . . . (p_2)	Month . . . (p_1)	Month . . . (p_2)		
ASSETS						
Current assets						
Cash	2.5	2.8	0.5	0.6	0.3	12.0
Short-term investments	4.0	—	0.9	—	(4.0)	(100.0)
Accounts receivable	90.8	104.0	20.2	21.7	13.2	14.5
Inventories	101.2	110.5	22.5	23.0	9.3	9.2
Prepaid expenses	0.8	—	0.2	—	(0.8)	(100.0)
Total current assets	199.3	217.3	44.4	43.3	18.0	9.0
Fixed assets						
Land	85.0	85.0	18.9	17.7	—	—
Buildings, machinery and equipment net of depreciation	165.0	177.5	36.7	37.0	12.5	7.6
Total assets	449.3	479.8	100.0	100.0	30.5	6.8
LIABILITIES						
Current liabilities						
Accounts payable	82.6	90.4	18.4	18.8	7.8	9.4
Notes payable	28.8	33.0	6.4	6.9	4.2	14.6
Accrued taxes	5.6	7.3	1.2	1.5	1.7	30.4
Total current liabilities	117.0	130.7	26.0	27.2	13.7	11.7
Long-term debt	55.0	70.0	12.3	14.6	15.0	27.3
Reserve for contingencies	10.0	10.0	2.2	2.1	—	—
Owner's equity	100.0	100.0	22.3	20.8	—	—
Retained earnings	167.3	169.1	37.2	35.3	1.8	1.1
Total liabilities and net worth	449.3	479.8	100.0	100.0	30.5	6.8

*Parentheses denote decrease.

TABLE 13–2. COMPARATIVE INCOME STATEMENT (in $1,000s)

	Amount		Percentage of Total Assets		Amount of Increase/ Decrease*	Percentage of Increase/ Decrease*
	Month . . . (p_1)	Month . . . (p_2)	Month . . . (p_1)	Month . . . (p_2)		
1) Gross sales	88.5	93.0	102.9	104.3	4.5	5.0
2) Sales returns and allowances	2.5	3.9	2.9	4.4	1.4	56.0
3) Net sales (1 − 2)	86.0	89.1	100.0	100.0	3.1	3.6
4) Cost of goods sold (5 + 6 + 7):						
5) Materials used	58.7	63.4	68.2	71.1	4.7	8.0
6) Direct labor	35.0	38.0	40.7	42.6	3.0	8.6
7) Other manufacturing expense	15.5	16.6	18.0	18.6	1.1	7.0
8) Gross profit (3 − 4)	8.2	8.8	9.5	9.9	0.6	7.3
9) Selling expenses	27.3	25.7	31.8	28.9	(1.6)	(5.9)
10) Administrative expenses	12.0	13.2	14.0	14.8	1.2	10.0
11) Operating profit (8 − 9 − 10)	6.3	6.5	7.3	7.3	0.2	3.2
Other income and expenses	9.0	6.0	10.5	6.8	(3.0)	(33.3)
12) Interest on debt	2.5	3.0	2.9	3.4	0.5	20.0
13) Interest income	0.3	—	0.3	—	(0.3)	(100.0)
14) Earnings before tax (11 − 12 + 13)	6.8	3.0	7.9	3.4	(3.8)	(55.9)
15) Income taxes	2.7	1.2	3.1	1.4	(1.5)	(55.6)
16) Net Income (14 − 15)	4.1	1.8	4.8	2.0	(2.3)	(56.1)

*Parentheses denote decrease.

TABLE 13–3. STATEMENT OF SOURCES AND USES OF
FUNDS (in $1,000s)*

Sources of Funds	
Net income (increase in retained earnings)	$ 1.8
Decrease in short-term investments	4.0
Decrease in prepaid expenses	0.8
Increase in accounts payable	7.8
Increase in notes payable	4.2
Increase in accrued taxes	1.7
Increase in long-term debt	15.0
Total sources of funds	$35.3
Uses of Funds	
Increase in cash	0.3
Increase in accounts receivable	13.2
Increase in inventory	9.3
Increase in fixed assets	
(buildings, machinery, equipment)	12.5
Total uses	$35.3

*Figures given for the changes from month . . . (p_1)
to month . . . (p_2).

These tables—consisting of comparative income statements, balance sheets, and a flow of funds statement—provide a wide range of information that demonstrates the concept of financial control. The presentation of the elements of income statement and balance sheet in percentages reflects better than the absolute figures the relationships among the various items. The comparison of financial statements of different periods provides insight about changes and trends. For example, the income statement reflects a significant decrease in earnings from about 5 percent of net sales to only 2 percent while net sales increased by almost 4 percent during the same period. An analysis shows that the company encountered strong market resistance: selling expenditures rose by 10 percent, the company had to extend its credit (as can be seen by the 15 percent increase in its accounts receivable), and sales returns and allowances jumped by 56 percent. The company's profitability was further reduced by a 9 percent increase in material costs, which accounted for over 40 percent of total sales. These observations point up the control measures that the manager must take to improve the financial condition of the company: less emphasis on an increase in the volume of sales, reduction of sales returns and allowances, closer control of selling expenses, faster collection of accounts receivable, effort to reduce material costs, and a reduction of inventory levels.

As the above example indicates, a systematic and periodic analysis of the financial statements is a control device that pinpoints problems requiring corrective action and can provide a better basis for management decisions in all functional areas.

Control through Analysis of Financial Ratios

The measurement and control of a company's performance is further enhanced by the use of financial ratios that indicate trends and patterns of change. Four sets of ratios are particularly relevant for control purposes in small business:

1. *Profitability ratios* show net profits to equity (return on equity), or total assets (return on assets), or sales (return on sales).
2. *Liquidity ratios* indicate a firm's ability to meet its payment obligations by relating financial resources such as cash, marketable securities, and accounts receivable to current liabilities.
3. *Turnover ratios* show a firm's effectiveness in using its resources. For example:

$$\text{inventory turnover} = \frac{\text{sales}}{\text{inventory}},$$

$$\text{asset turnover} = \frac{\text{sales}}{\text{assets}},$$

$$\text{receivables turnover} = \frac{\text{sales}}{\text{receivables}}.$$

4. *Financial structure ratios* provide insight into the basic financial strategy of a firm. For example:

$$\text{current ratio} = \frac{\text{current assets}}{\text{current liabilities}},$$

$$\text{leverage} = \frac{\text{total debt}}{\text{equity}}.$$

Financial ratio analysis gives a manager checkpoints for judging the effective use of the company's resources. Further insights may be gained by comparing the company's ratios with the same ratios of other companies operating under similar conditions. For example, the ratios periodically published by Dun & Bradstreet in *Dun's Review* may be used as performance standards against which the company's achievement may be compared.[5] How well the company is doing within the industry can be judged in this way. A wide range of ratios can be calculated. Firgure 13–2 gives key ratios that are best interpreted when viewing the business as a system of interconnected conditions.

---

[5]See, for example, "Key Business Ratios," *Dun's Review,* generally the September, October, and December issues of each year.

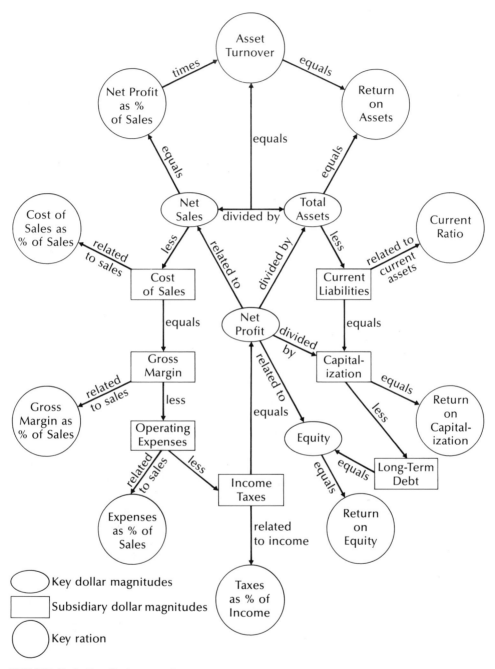

FIGURE 13–2. Key Ratios as a System

Source: Erich A. Helfert, *Techniques of Financial Analysis,* Homewood, Ill.: Richard D. Irwin, 1972, p. 71.

Financial analysis is a powerful control technique because it identifies strengths and weaknesses in key managerial decision areas. Each company must, however, decide on the specific financial analyses most critical to its control requirements.

COST CONTROL AND BUDGETING

Small firms frequently suffer financial crises because of lack of cost consciousness and cost control; these must necessarily become prime concerns in managing a small enterprise. The effectiveness of any cost control system depends largely on the company's efficiency in collecting and analyzing cost information. For this purpose the company can choose between two cost accounting systems: *actual cost system* and *standard cost system*. The first deals only with costs that have actually been incurred by the company; the second relies on predetermined cost standards that reflect cost levels under optimum operating conditions. As a rule, a standard cost system does not make an actual cost system superfluous but should be considered as supplementary, enabling management to make comparisons between actual and standard costs. In addition, the company has the choice of collecting cost data on the basis of specific job orders (*job costing*) or for a specified period of time (*process costing*).

The choice between job costing and process costing depends largely on the operational characteristics of the company. Under job costing, costs are identified and collected for each job or batch of work as it is performed, regardless of the accounting period in which the work is done. This approach is particularly appropriate when a company produces a variety of different products and there is little repetitive work. Under process costing, all costs are collected for a specified period of time, such as one month, then spread over the number of units of products that were manufactured during that period. This method is advantageous when only one product or relatively undifferentiated products are produced. Since process costing usually requires less record keeping than job costing, it is less costly to administer. Each of the two approaches emphasizes, however, the clear identification of specific cost elements.

The range of alternatives for collecting cost information is shown in Table 13–4. The matrix can be used as appropriate to the circumstances for analyzing cost data and for cost control purposes.

Cost Elements

The most important aspect in cost control is reliable information about the specific cost elements that the company has incurred. In general it is

TABLE 13–4. COST SYSTEMS AND INFORMATION COLLECTION METHODS

Methods for Collecting Cost Information	Cost Systems	
	Actual Cost	Standard Cost
Job costing		
Process costing		

advisable to distinguish among six major cost elements:

1. *Direct material:* cost of materials that enter directly into the manufactured product and that can be identified with specific jobs or processes.
2. *Indirect material:* cost for materials used in the operation of the business that cannot be identified with specific jobs or processes, for example, shop supplies or lubricants for machines.
3. *Direct labor:* labor costs that are directly attributable to specific jobs or processes.
4. *Indirect labor:* labor costs that cannot be identified with specific jobs or processes; for example, wages paid to janitors and truck drivers.
5. *Manufacturing expenses:* all expenses other than material and labor costs associated with the manufacture of the company's output; for example, expenditures for light, power, heat, insurance, maintenance, and depreciation.
6. *Selling, general, and administrative expenses:* indirect costs incurred in the marketing of the company's outputs and the administration of the organization; for example, salaries and expenses of salesmen, avertising costs, warehousing costs, legal expenses, financing costs, and executive salaries.

The essence of an effective cost control system is timely and reliable information on cost elements. Important cost items must be clearly identified. Since the cost structure tends to be different from one company to another, each company must develop its own system for grouping cost data. The six major cost elements outlined above provide, however, a general and useful framework for collecting and analyzing these data. In addition, it is advisable to establish cost standards for various performance levels against which actually incurred costs can be compared periodically. An analysis of the variance between actual and standard costs is a control procedure that can pinpoint the items to which management must pay close attention in the effort to reduce costs.

Cost standards are usually developed in one of four ways: 1) on the basis of an average of past actual costs; 2) on the basis of lowest costs that have previously been attained; 3) as a reflection of projected costs at a normal level of operations; and 4) as the result of operations at the company's maximum level of effectiveness. Whatever approach is used in establishing cost standards, the most significant benefit stems from the development of a basis on which to assess actual costs. Analysis of the variance between actual costs and cost standards is the first and most important step in any cost control system.

Control of Specific Cost Elements

Cost control in a small company should focus primarily on the most important cost items. For example, if material costs account for 65 percent of the total cost, then close attention to material cost control would obviously be warranted. For controlling specific cost elements, the following guidelines deserve consideration.

Material Costs A prerequisite for controlling material costs is establishing proper quantitative (in addition to qualitative) material requirements. An excessive material inventory causes unnecessary storage costs and possible losses because of spoilage or obsolescence. In addition, the cost of financing a too-large material supply may be a considerable financial burden. For this reason, it is advisable to set upper and lower limits for materials on hand to avoid impeding the company's operations or building excessive material inventories.

Appropriate quality standards for the materials that the company uses also play a significant role in controlling material costs. The company may be able to achieve substantial savings by reducing excessive quality requirements in some materials. Standards that emphasize minimization of scrap loss also offer a way to control and reduce material costs.

Labor Costs Since most small firms use labor-intensive operations, the control of labor costs becomes a vital element in improving operating efficiency. As in any control attempt, the first step toward effective control of labor costs is a rational determination of the actual labor requirements and the establishment of standards of performance for all job categories. At the operating level standards of labor performance are generally established by time and motion studies; at the clerical and managerial levels criteria for determining standards of performance focus more on qualitative characteristics such as administrative or leadership skills. To control labor costs the company must guard against an excessive buildup of its labor force. It must be realistic in the assessment of the personal qualifications required in each job.

Manufacturing costs The problems encountered in controlling manufacturing costs tend to be more complicated than those involved in controlling material and labor costs. The major reasons for this are that 1) the responsibility for controlling manufacturing costs is usually delegated to several people in the organization, and 2) manufacturing costs tend to be composed of a variety of cost items, such as costs for tools, jigs, fixtures, and power, for which it is difficult to assign control responsibility. This complexity makes it necessary to analyze each of the major manufacturing cost items separately to determine whether there is a practical basis for establishing a standard for each.

Selling, General, and Administrative Costs This category contains a wide range of different cost items. Their control poses the same difficulties as the control of manufacturing costs. Effective control of these costs requires, again, a clear identification of the individual cost items and the determination of standards against which actual costs can be compared. There is usually a wide range of opportunities for reducing selling, general, and administrative costs. For example, it is imperative that the small firm assess regularly the effectiveness of its sales force, its advertising effort, and its distribution strategy. Control over expenditures such as office equipment and its maintenance, office supplies, and postal and telephone expenses may in addition yield significant savings.

A systematic effort to control specific costs should be integrated in a comprehensive, well-organized *cost reduction program* that ought to be viewed as a continuous, long-range effort. A crash program to reduce just one particular category of costs without much concern for other cost items may have a temporary benefit, but in the long run may do more harm than good. It is the responsibility of the management of a small firm to pay close attention to costs and to impress upon all members of the organization the need for cost consciousness.

Cost Centers

Specific cost centers can be set up to establish responsibility for specific costs and their control. Cost centers can be defined as areas of responsibility (such as a department) for which it is desirable to accumulate cost data separately from the rest of the organization. In general, production (cost) centers are distinguished from service (cost) centers. A production center is one that is directly involved in the manufacture of the product, such as a bank of machines. A service center is one that provides a service to other cost centers of the organization, such as the maintenance department or the general offices. The advantages of using cost centers are that 1) cost data tend to become more specific and actionable, 2) the responsibility for controlling costs becomes linked with clearly identified organizational units, and 3) cost centers facilitate the development of accurate cost standards.

The Role of Budgeting

Budgets, which are critical tools for managerial control, are statements of anticipated results expressed in monetary terms. For small firms three types of budgets are particularly useful:

- operating budgets
- cash budgets
- capital budgets

An operating budget follows the same format as an income statement, starting with the sales budget and corresponding cost budgets for materials, labor, manufacturing overhead, selling, and administrative expenses. The sales budget summarizes the expected sales revenues per product line or per division. The various cost budgets, which represent the expected costs, are related to the expected revenues. The sales (revenue) budget minus the corresponding cost (expenditure) budget leads to the profit budget.

Cash budgets are simply a reflection of the anticipated cash flow and represent expected cash receipts and disbursements for each of the planning periods. Cash budgets are managerial control devices for assuring the company's ability to meet its bills. Carefully developed cash budgets show management to what extent it will have to find additional money when liquidity is strained or to what extent it has excess cash available.

Capital budgets focus on expected long-range expenditures for specific investments such as construction of buildings, new machinery, or equipment.

Budgets are essential control devices in that they enable a company to check on variations between planned and actual achievements. To the extent that these variations are systematically analyzed, management gains insights into the causes of the variations and can take positive corrective actions.

Although the importance of comprehensive and systematic cost control in the small enterprise can hardly be overstated, its management must nevertheless guard against a cost control system that is unduly expensive or cumbersome. Cost control must not be viewed as an end in itself; it is only a means to assure that the company chooses effective courses to achieve its objectives.

PRODUCTION CONTROL

The aim in controlling the operations of a business enterprise is to assure that all the required activities are on schedule and that preestablished quality and cost standards are met. An effective production control system should reflect the company's operating conditions and production characteristics. For example, in a *job shop system* that groups machines according to the operations they perform, production control is necessarily different than it is under a *production line system,* which places machines in the sequence in which work is being done. The kind of activity a company performs also affects its production. A company that produces one-of-a-kind products made to customers' specifications would employ a job shop organization for which an *order control system* is most appropriate. In this system the focus is on the progress of each order through the successive operations in its fabrication and assembly. In contrast, a production line organization, as might be found in an assembly plant, would use a *flow control system.* Here the control centers on the rate or flow of production from one work station to the next. An intermediate form, between a flow control and an order control system, is called a *block control system.* The block control system tends to be most suitable in situations where the production process is regulated by batches or lots. Here the control focuses on the progress of blocks of shop orders through the production cycle. Under each of these different production systems the actual control activities concentrate on four basic functions:

- *Routing*—determining where a required operation or job is to be done.
- *Scheduling*—determining when the operation or job is to be done.
- *Dispatching*—issuing production orders at the right time.
- *Expediting*—determining whether or not the required work is progressing as planned.

Figure 13–3 shows the various elements of a typical production control system and identifies the control activities that need to be performed. Within this general framework, emphasis may be placed on elements of control selected according to need. The approach taken will depend on the production method, alternatives for organizing the production process, and differences in technological requirements. There are, however, a number of guidelines that have general validity in controlling production:

1. The complexity of production control increases progressively with increasing variety of components or of products being manufactured. An increase in product variety tends to decrease production efficiency. For these reasons a careful analysis should be made to determine whether the company might benefit from buying a larger proportion of the required components from outside suppliers, rather than relying upon in-house production.
2. Work measurement and time studies are indispensable prerequisites to an effective production control system. The existing produc-

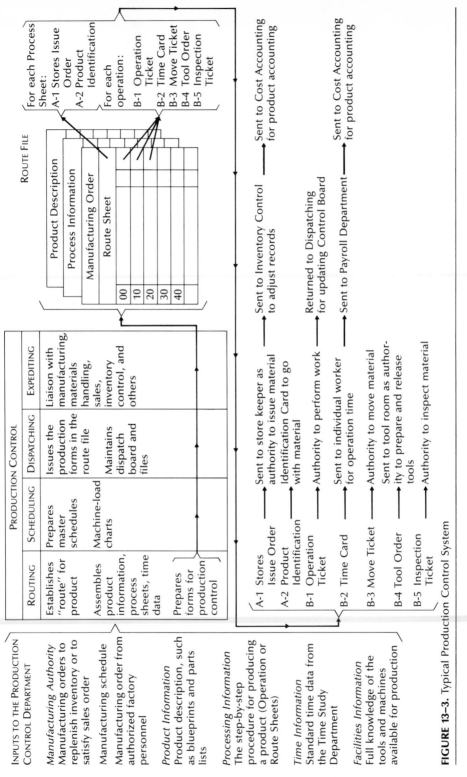

FIGURE 13-3. Typical Production Control System

Source: James H. Greene, *Operations Planning and Control,* Homewood, Ill.: Richard D. Irwin, 1967, p. 19.

tion capacity and available machine loads must also be accurately known.

3. Control over the use of materials, particularly when they constitute a large percentage of the total cost of the manufactured product, should be emphasized in production control.
4. The personnel performing specific operations should have accurate, clear drawings or specifications of what they are expected to do. Blueprints and other production documents should be routed back to the dispatch point as a part of the production control procedure.
5. The determination of optimal production lot sizes is important not only in lowering production costs but also in production control.

The essence of production control is to predetermine as precisely as possible the standards of control against which actual performance can be evaluated. The aim is to achieve effectively the basic objective of any production control system—to produce on schedule, according to planned quantity and quality standards, and at acceptable cost.

QUALITY CONTROL

Quality control is often considered a part of production control. For the small company a superior quality product or service is a major factor in improving its competitive position. Conversely, poor quality or repeated delays in delivery are significant contributing causes in the failure of small business. For these reasons quality control merits separate and special consideration.

The term *quality* generally means "fitness for the intended purpose." It therefore is a relative concept. The aim in a business context is to provide the customers with a product at a level of quality that assures customer satisfaction while minimizing cost. To pursue a quality standard higher than customers reasonably expect, so-called unnecessary gold plating, adds cost for the company but gives no economic advantage. The interrelationship between quality levels and associated costs that may exist for a given product or its components is shown in Figure 13–4.

As the quality of a product (or its components) is raised, the costs tend to increase progressively. However, the value consumers attribute to increasing quality tends to be degressive. Any product tends to have a most economical quality level. To determine this level, one starts by assessing what the customers consider to be an acceptable quality in relation to the product's price. The next step is to develop a consistent strategy for product quality control and to use a quality control system for implementing the strategy chosen. The function of quality control is thus 1) to determine optimal quality standards, and 2) to monitor pro-

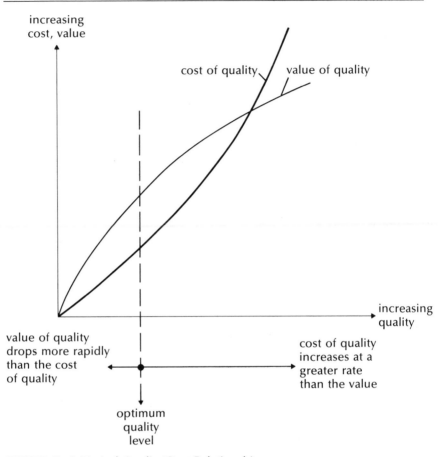

increasing
cost, value

cost of quality   value of quality

increasing
quality

value of quality
drops more rapidly
than the cost
of quality

cost of quality
increases at a
greater rate
than the value

optimum
quality
level

FIGURE 13–4. Typical Quality/Cost Relationships

duction so that goods of the specified quality are produced. The latter function entails inspecting and measuring what is happening in the production process. If substandard work is found, the information is fed back into the production system at appropriate points where corrective action can be taken.

The Quality Control Process

Every company has its own peculiar quality control problems. The actual quality control process must therefore be designed to reflect these peculiarities either in the specified quality standards, in permissible tolerances from these standards, or in the way quality inspection is carried out. Quality control generally consists of a series of planned measurements designed to verify compliance with all specified quality standards. It must be recognized that quality control cannot be limited to the final product but must include the materials and components that go into the product and the adequacy of its design. This suggests that quality control must be considered as an integral activity in the flow of operational events.

Defective work that does not meet established quality standards can be detected only through an appropriate inspection program. Management must therefore determine specific control points for quality inspection. The frequency of inspection depends on the inspection cost and the costs that the company might have to absorb for not detecting a defect in quality. For example, suppose that a simple production process has an average defective rate of 3 percent (3 out of 100 do not meet specified quality standards). The cost resulting from an undetected defect (expenditure for return shipment, cost of repair or replacement, loss in goodwill) amounts to $15, while the average inspection cost for each unit produced amounts to 60 cents. In this case an inspection of the total output would not be economical, since inspecting 100 units would cost $60 and the expected costs from the undetected defects if no inspection were made would amount to only $45 (3 times $15). Under the assumptions stated in this example, the break-even point for inspecting the total output would be a defective rate of 4 percent of the output. In this situation the inspection costs would equal the costs resulting from undetected defective output, but quality inspection on a sampling basis would still pay off simply to make sure that the average rate of defective products does not rise above 4 percent.

Decisions should be made not only about the frequency of inspections, but also about the specific characteristics of the product that should be checked. It is essential to identify and inspect those features that are most crucial to the performance of the product.

Another important aspect of the quality control process is to specify the documentation necessary to show that the required controls have actually been carried out. In its simplest form quality documentation consists of a stamped inspection mark indicating acceptable quality, or the attachment of a rejection or rework tag to defective parts. In its most complex form, quality documentation may record the quantitative results of all inspections and measurements, which are subsequently analyzed; from this analysis, the company may detect areas posing specific problems with quality. Quality documentation in a small company should be used in such a way as to give motivational impetus to the inspectors to carry out their responsibility with integrity.

Quality Control Techniques

The specific techniques for setting standards for quality should be selected after the quality control problem has been identified and analyzed. The available techniques for controlling quality fall into three categories: mechanistic, statistical, and motivational techniques.

Mechanistic quality control techniques use automatic sensing and feedback devices to register whether the tested parts conform with established quality limits.

Statistical quality control techniques, involving sampling and probability concepts, minimize the number of inspections. That reduces inspection costs while maintaining an acceptable quality level. For example, in a batch of 1,000 identical components, if there must be 100 percent certainty that each piece falls within established quality tolerances, then there is no choice but to inspect every piece of the batch. On the other hand, if 98 percent certainty is acceptable, a statistically valid sampling scheme can be devised; inspection can then be carried out at a fraction of the cost of inspecting every piece. The premise for using statistical techniques in quality control is that 100 percent inspection is economically wasteful and that inspection of a selected sample can save inspection cost but still attain an acceptable quality level. To achieve this economy all sampling schemes must be based on probability statistics.[6]

Motivational quality control techniques are based on the premise that quality defects are caused by human errors resulting either from a lack of knowledge or a lack of attention. The latter is an attitudinal problem that can be corrected only by the employee. What is required is a conscious effort to perform the task correctly the first time. To create motivational incentives the *zero defect system* may be used. Zero defect programs, which were developed by aerospace companies in the early 1960s, are designed to motivate each employee to eliminate all quality defects in their assigned tasks. These programs use posters, slogans, letters to the employees, and financial rewards for outstanding performance as motivational incentives. Small companies with a small cohesive work force can make effective use of such programs. It should be recognized that motivational programs intended to stimulate high quality performance can be effective supplementary means, but are not substitutes for either mechanistic or statistical quality control in achieving high quality products. Figure 13–5 summarizes the elements of a quality control system. The figure specifies the areas subject to quality control and the way the quality control process should be organized.

The power of quality control to contribute significantly to the operating efficiency of a small enterprise is often overlooked. Because of problems with quality, many small firms are faced with substantial warranty costs—and their negative effects on the company's image. The management of small firms should recognize that emphasis on superior qual-

---

[6]For a detailed analysis of sampling inspection and statistical quality control techniques see, Robert B. Fetter, *The Quality Control System*, Homewood, Ill.: Richard D. Irwin, 1967, pp. 8–98.

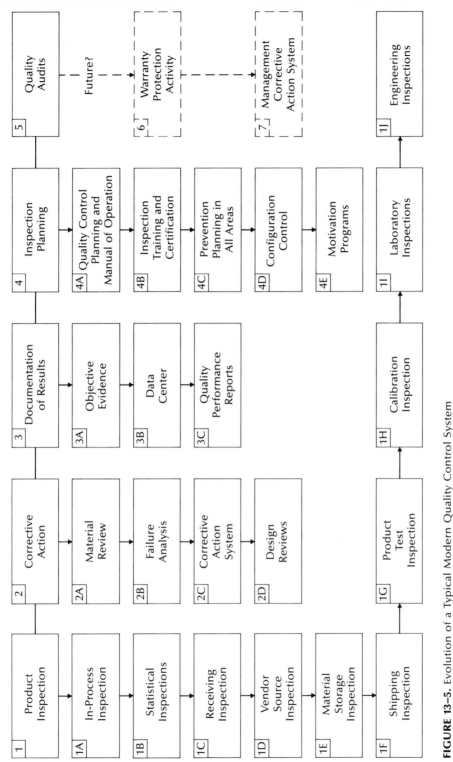

FIGURE 13–5. Evolution of a Typical Modern Quality Control System

Source: John T. Hagan, *A Management Role for Quality Control*, New York: American Management Association, July, 1968 p.46

ity is an effective strategy for improving their firm's competitive advantage. A well-functioning quality control system is the foundation for gaining the advantages of such a strategy.

INVENTORY CONTROL

Many small firms do not succeed as expected simply because of poor management of inventory. A company that permits a substantial portion of its working capital to be tied up in an inventory that is disproportionate to its volume of sales, or one that carries in inventory an assortment of poorly chosen, obsolescent items, will probably face liquidity problems—problems that may eventually lead to bankruptcy. The widespread lack of inventory controls among small- and medium-sized firms has been documented by an empirical investigation. This study revealed that about 20 percent of the annual investment in inventory by small- and medium-sized companies is actually unnecessary.[7] Poor inventory management drains the financial resources of these companies. Yet relatively simple inventory control schemes can lead to significant savings in cost of inventory.

Types of Inventory Items The term *inventory* refers to the movable parts of a business that are expected to enter the flow of production or trade. For control purposes it is important to differentiate among the various types of goods that compose the total inventory. The classification given below is the most common for inventory items:

- *Raw materials*—all items or goods that are not yet worked up but that will not be sold before some processing has taken place.
- *Materials in process*—items on which some work has been done in preparation for assembly.
- *Finished products*—items that have been completed and are ready for sale or shipment.
- *Component parts*—items that go into the assembly of finished products such as hardware, electric relays, and electronic units.
- *Maintenance, repair, and operating supplies*—items that are required in the production or the administrative process but that do not become directly a part of the finished product, such as tools, cooling fluids, spare parts for machines and equipment, paper, pencils, and forms.

Each inventory category poses unique control problems. The general aims of inventory control are, however, the same for all categories.

---

[7]Wilbert Steffy, William Buer, and Lawrence Schultz, *Inventory Controls for the Small and Medium Sized Firm.* Ann Arbor: Institute for Science and Technology, University of Michigan, 1970, p. 1.

Proper inventory control should enable the company 1) to maintain a sufficient stock of all required items so that productive operations can proceed without interruption, 2) to satisfy customers' orders as quickly as possible, and 3) to minimize carrying costs and capital tied up in inventory.

Approaches to Inventory Control

Several basic questions should be answered in setting up an inventory control system intended to accomplish these three objectives:

- What quantities of required items are really needed at any point?
- In view of anticipated price changes what quantities of stock should actually be carried?
- What are the economic order quantities so that an optimum balance between ordering costs and carrying costs may be achieved? (In general, the larger the order, the larger carrying costs tend to be and the larger the amount of capital tied up in inventory).
- How up-to-date must inventory records be?

Answers to these questions provide the basis for designing an inventory control system. A small company is often faced with an additional question: Should all inventory items or only selected items be subject to systematic, periodic control? There is no uniform answer to this question. For some companies with a homogeneous inventory the answer should probably be yes. For most small firms the proper answer would indicate that control measures should focus on critical high-value items. For example, in a company in which three-fourths of all inventory items represent only 10 percent of the investment in inventory, the control effort should concentrate on the one-fourth of the items that account for 90 percent of the inventory investment. Of course, special attention should be paid to those parts that are really critical in maintaining a continuous flow of production, even though their cost may be small.

To determine which inventory items are critical a four-step approach is recommended: 1) prepare a list of all inventory items that must be carried and specify the average unit price and the approximate annual volume for each item; 2) calculate the annual dollar usage for each inventory item by multiplying annual usage by the average unit price; 3) rank the inventory items in descending order according to the annual dollar usage; and 4) establish three groups of inventory items. Category *A* should contain all items that account for the greatest dollar usage; for example, the top 10 percent of the items that may account for 75 percent of the dollar usage. Category *B* should contain items of secondary importance; for example, the middle 25 percent of the inventory items that may account for 20 percent of the dollar usage. Category *C* should contain all other items that may be very numerous but are also relatively

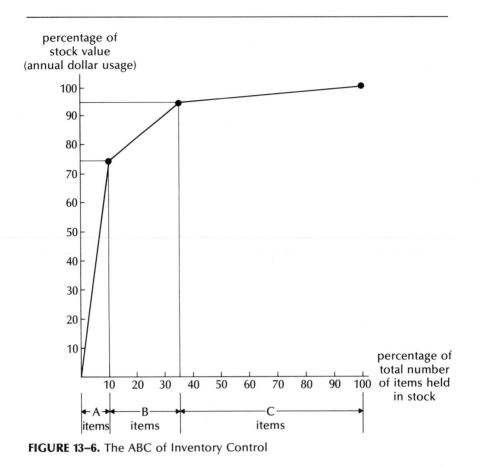

FIGURE 13–6. The ABC of Inventory Control

inexpensive. For example, 65 percent of the inventory items that may account for only 5 percent of the dollar usage. Figure 13–6 depicts this example. This approach is sometimes referred to as the *ABC* method of inventory control. It enables management to concentrate the inventory control effort primarily on the most expensive (*A*) items. For the rest of the items a relatively large reserve can be carried inexpensively. The *ABC* method helps to put first things first and get the most control for the least amount of controlling.

A somewhat different approach from the *ABC* method is to focus on the *turnover* of individual inventory items by relating the approximate annual usage volume (or usage value) of each required inventory item to the existing quantity of this item actually on hand. As this ratio decreases, there is usually good cause to suspect either overstocking or possible obsolescence of the item. Although each inventory item should be treated as a special case, particular attention should be paid to those items that show a slow turnover. Both approaches described—focus on high-volume, high-value items, and emphasis on the turnover of each item—are complementary to each other. They are easy to implement in small firms and can yield high benefits by reducing inventory carrying costs.

Inventory Control Systems

Inventories are used for satisfying present and future demands. For this reason effective inventory controls must not only focus on the current demand for specific items but must also take into account the potential future demand. The company's forecast of the future demand for particular inventory items can be used to answer the three essential inventory control questions in order to optimize inventory costs:

1. What are the proper inventory quantities of the required items?
2. When should inventory items be ordered (what are the order points)?
3. How much should be ordered of each required item (what are the economic order quantities)?

The answer to the first question, that of the most economical inventory level for each required item, depends on the expected usage rate, which can be estimated from past usage on the basis of the company's marketing plans.

The second question, when to order, can be answered by determining the expected demand during the time it takes for the item to be produced or received from outside suppliers. This period is frequently referred to as *lead time*. Since the lead time can fluctuate, it is advisable to keep some reserve stock on hand to avoid running out of a critical item.[8] The greater the fluctuation and the higher the potential cost of a stock-out, the higher should be the reserve stock that the company carries. (The inventory carrying cost will also be higher.) Management must therefore balance the inventory cost of a given reserve level against the savings in avoiding a stock-out and its adverse consequences on the flow of production.

The economic order point, the date at which a replenishment order must be placed to avoid a stock-out, can be determined by the following formula:

$$\text{economic order point} = \text{lead time (in days)} \times \text{usage rate (in units per day).}$$

Figure 13–7 shows the relationship between the economic order point, usage rate, lead time, and reserve stock in an idealized manner. It shows

---

[8]Suggestions for managing reserve stocks are given in Chapter 12.

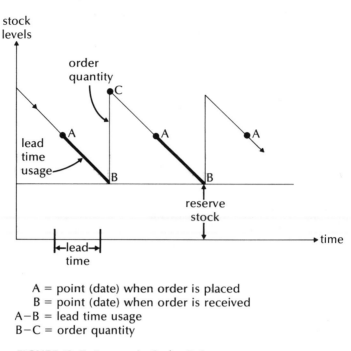

A = point (date) when order is placed
B = point (date) when order is received
A−B = lead time usage
B−C = order quantity

FIGURE 13–7. Economic Order Point

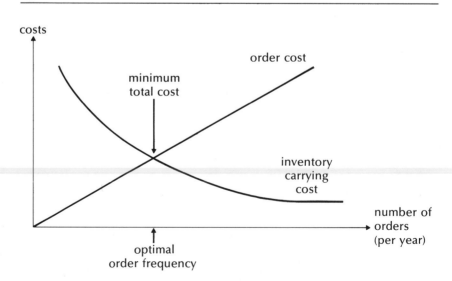

FIGURE 13–8. Relationship between Order Costs and Inventory Carrying Costs

when an order should be placed, given a certain usage, lead time, and desired reserve stock.

The third question, how much to order, determines the economic order quantity. It can be answered by getting information on two sets of costs: 1) inventory carrying costs, and 2) order costs. These two sets of costs tend to move in opposite directions: increasing the order quantity (and thus reducing the order frequency) reduces order costs and also tends to lead to a lower price per unit because of quantity discounts. At the same time, an increase in order quantities increases the amount of capital tied up in inventory and increases inventory carrying cost. Therefore it is important to determine—at least for high-volume, high-value inventory items—the size of an order that minimizes the total expenditure for ordering and carrying these items in an idealized manner. Figure 13–8 shows that the optimal order quantity can be found by dividing the optimal number of orders per year (optimal order frequency) into the total usage of an item per year. For calculating the optimal order quantity of an item in a somewhat more refined way the following formula can also be used:[9]

$$Q = \frac{2 \times D \times A}{C \times I},$$

where
Q = economic order quantity,
D = average demand for the item during period (usage),
A = preparation cost per order,
C = cost per unit of the ordered item,
I = percentage inventory carrying cost per unit.

The same basic approach can be used for determining the economic order quantity of in-house production of the required item, generally referred to as the *economic lot size*. The formula for calculating the economic production quantity is:

$$Q_P \quad \frac{2 \times D \times A_p}{C \times I},$$

where
Q_p = economic order quantity,
D = average demand during period (usage),
A_p = setup and internal order processing cost,
C = total cost per unit of the produced item,
I = percentage inventory carrying cost per unit.

[9]For a detailed discussion of the statistical rationale of this formula see R. Stansbury Stockton, *Basic Inventory Systems: Concepts and Analysis,* Boston: Allyn & Bacon, 1965; also J. W. Prichard and R. H. Eagle, *Modern Inventory Management.* New York: John Wiley & Sons, 1965.

These formulas should be considered only as guidelines for establishing the actual order qantities, since they do not reflect factors that sometimes become influential in determining the size of an order. For example, anticipated strikes, anticipated price increases, or the use of special, temporary price discounts are all factors that may affect decision on the order quantity, yet these factors are not included in the above formulas. These formulas, nevertheless, give guidelines that can help a small firm to reduce costs.

Emphasizing economic order points and economic order quantities to determine optimal inventory levels is one aspect of an effective inventory control system. There are other issues that should be considered in a systematic effort to control inventory. The following procedures are recommended:

1. Periodically all inventory items should be physically verified; for example, a monthly physical inventory pinpoints slow-moving items that take up space, helps to use older stock first, and may reveal pilferage.
2. Storage facilities should be appraised. A small company should know the cost of maintaining its own warehouse as compared to the cost of using public warehousing for its inventories.
3. Inventory costs can be cut not only by reducing the quantities of each item kept on hand, but also by reducing the number of different items kept in stock. An inventory control system in a small company should try to reduce stock carried by standardizing on inventory items. Standardization means that fewer items need to be stored, ordered, tested, and kept track of. Proper inventory management also implies eliminating unnecessary inventory items.
4. The specified levels of reserve stock should be re-examined periodically to find out whether a reduction in some items might be feasible under changed conditions.
5. Since the availability of accurate and timely inventory information is the fundamental prerequisite for any worthwhile inventory control effort, the management of a small firm must pay particular attention to establishing and maintaining inventory records appropriate to the needs of the company.

A Concluding Note

The preceding analyses stress the significance of five control areas: financial, cost, production, quality, and inventory control. For each of these areas a variety of approaches or techniques can be used to make controls truly effective. For an individual firm, other areas may also require control. Examples of these are sales effort, marketing services, research and development, and the human organization. Five general guidelines deserve re-emphasis at this point.

1. The management of a small firm should always be control conscious, since an effective control is basic in managing an enterprise successfully.
2. The control effort should be tailored to the specific requirements and operating characteristics of the firm.
3. Control should be viewed as a continuous effort encompassing all crucial areas of an enterprise.
4. Individual areas should not be controlled in isolation; on the contrary, the various control efforts should be coordinated.
5. The company's control system itself should be controlled; it must be regularly reviewed and reappraised to determine its effectiveness in regulating current operations.

SPECIAL CONTROL TOOLS AND TECHNIQUES

Control depends upon the use of suitable tools and techniques for collecting, organizing, transmitting, and displaying control data to the responsible decision makers in the company. In smalll business, complicated control techniques such as industrial dynamics,[10] linear programming,[11] model building, and simulation[12] are not generally feasible either because of their complexity or, more importantly, because they require a computerized data processing system that most small firms do not have at their disposal. Although these control techniques are difficult to apply in a small firm, there are control tools that can be effectively used; these include graphic control charts and network analysis.

Graphic Control Charts

Graphic control charts communicate control data that facilitate corrective decision making and motivate performance. An effective control chart is the well-known Gantt chart, which consists of horizontal bars representing planned and actual accomplishments plotted against time. This chart shows at a glance whether a task or group of tasks is on schedule, ahead

---

[10]Jay W. Forrester, *Industrial Dynamics,* Cambridge, Mass.: MIT Press, 1961.
[11]Billy E. Goetz, *Quantitative Methods: A Survey and Guide for Managers,* New York: McGraw-Hill, 1965.
[12]Joel M. Kibbee, "Management Control Simulation," in *Management Control Systems,* edited by Donald G. Malcolm and Alan J. Rowe, New York: John Wiley & Sons, 1960, pp. 300–20; Thomas R. Prince, *Information Systems for Management Planning and Control,* Homewood, Ill.: Richard D. Irwin, 1970.

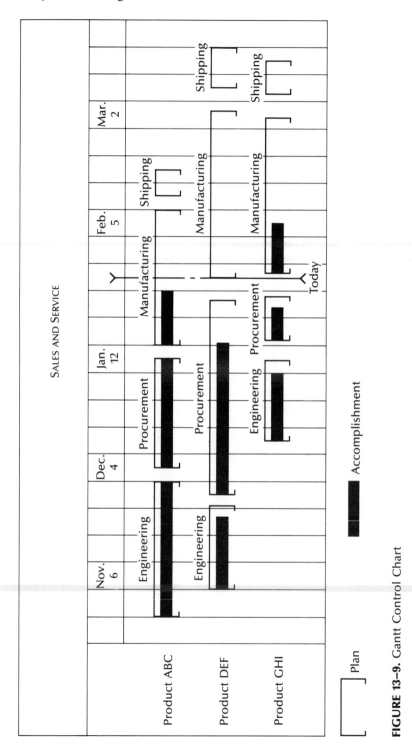

FIGURE 13–9. Gantt Control Chart

Source: Earl P. Strong and Robert D. Smith, *Management Control Models*, New York: Holt, Rinehart and Winston, 1968, p. 85.

of, or behind schedule. Figure 13–9 illustrates the basic principle of the Gantt chart.

This chart can show the progress of any conceivable project or planned performance over time. Kept up-to-date, it shows any discrepancy between planned and actual achievement at any given date. With this knowledge, management can act speedily to make additional resources available to a project that has fallen behind schedule. The Gantt chart can also show the degree of conformity between budgeted and actual costs. Cost overruns can be seen at a glance and corrective action taken.

Other examples of graphic control charts are break-even charts, line charts displaying actual sales against projections, and organization charts. Examples of these and other charts are found throughout this book.

Pictorial and graphic representations are effective control tools that are easy to use in the small business. It should be emphasized that these charts are useful only to the extent that they are accurate and timely. Particular attention must be paid to updating the charts regularly.

PERT and CPM

PERT (program evaluation and review technique) and CPM (critical path method) are planning and control techniques using network logic. These techniques were developed in the late 1950s. They have proved their worth over the years and have come into wide use. In essence, both techniques attempt to formulate a group of project functions into a coherent, integrated, manageable system. These techniques help to speed completion of a project by showing management how to reduce time, cost, and confusion.

PERT and CPM are designed to highlight potential problem areas that could disrupt achievement of program goals. They give management tools for controlling and accelerating progress of a project toward its objective.

PERT and CPM are vehicles for planning as well as control. Since planning always involves problems of uncertainty, PERT uses a statistical concept that makes it possible to assign probability factors to targets of time and cost.

PERT and CPM require a four-stage approach.

Stage 1. A project's structure is first analyzed as to the specific activities and events that have to be achieved to reach a predetermined goal. Then a network is constructed graphically representing the sequence and interrelationships of the required activities. A simplified analysis of structure, or network, showing the execution of an order is illustrated in Figure 13-10.

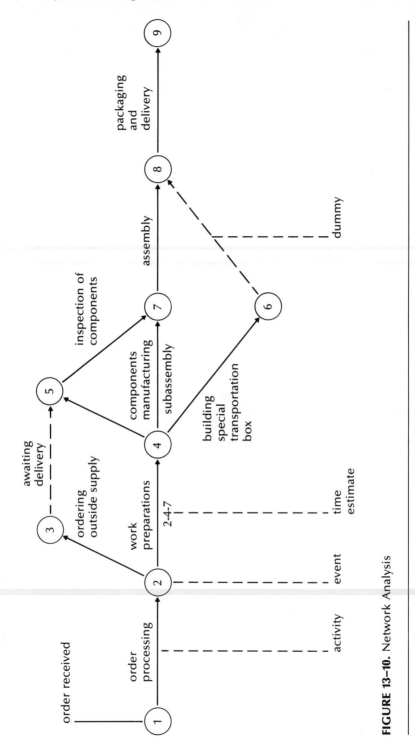

FIGURE 13–10. Network Analysis

Source: Hans Schollhammer, "PERT—Practicalities and Promise of the Network Planning and Control Method," *European Business Review,* No. 6, 1965, p. 5.

Stage 2. Next an estimate is made of the time that will probably be required to accomplish each activity. It is often easy to make a reasonably accurate forecast of the time it takes to do a job, but on many occasions the time deviates considerably from the average expected value. To make this uncertainty explicit, PERT uses a three-value system; it uses time estimates for favorable, unfavorable, and most likely conditions for each activity. The time assigned for most favorable conditions is called *optimistic time (a);* for least favorable conditions, *pessimistic time (b);* and for usual conditions, the *most likely time (c).* The most likely time represents the most accurate forecast based on normal circumstances. The three time estimates are used in the following simple statistical formula to get the average or *expected time (t_e):*

$$t_e = \frac{a + 4c + b}{6}.$$

The most likely time is given four times the weight of the estimated optimistic and pessimistic times.

After calculating the expected duration for each individual activity the earliest expected time (T_E) for each event in the network is found. The T_E value of a given event can be calculated by summing all average activity times (t_e) of all activities leading to this event. If several activities lead to the same event then the longest duration (T_L) is considered the earliest expected time for this event. The slack time (T_D) is the difference between the earliest event time T_E and the longest time T_L. The network in Figure 13–11 shows seven specific activities with a total of six events, event six being the completion of the project. The estimated duration for each activity and the calculated expected time for each are indicated.

This example shows that the earliest expected completion of this project would be 20 days. The network also shows that for activities 2 - 4 and 3 - 5 there is slack time, as Figure 13–12 illustrates.

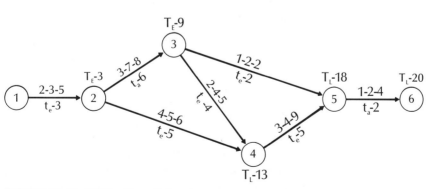

FIGURE 13–11. PERT—Time Estimates

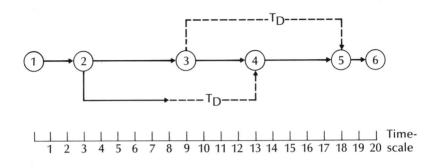

FIGURE 13–12. Slack Time in an Activity Network

Source: Hans Schollhammer, "PERT—Practicalities and Promise of the Network Planning and Control Method," *European Business Review,* No. 6, 1965, p. 7.

Stage 3. Determining the critical path in an activity network requires identifying the critical activities that form a chain running through the network. The critical path represents the string of activities for which there is no slack time. Knowing the critical path permits controlling progress of a project strictly on the critical activities rather than on all activities involved in the project.

Stage 4. Time-cost relationships can be found by analysis of the activities and events of a project. This analysis provides a basis for planning and controlling the costs of the project. Costs for each activity are estimated in a fashion similar to that for finding the time of each activity; the expected cost per activity guides management cost control. A carefully developed PERT/time–PERT/cost system makes an ideal tool for controlling the operations of a firm. The system is simple enough to be used effectively by organizations of any size—even small firms. It focuses attention on critical areas and enables management to employ forward-looking controls.

SUMMARY: Key Factors in Management Control

Developing and maintaining comprehensive, systematic controls in the small business is a most important and demanding task. An effective control system requires the development of control standards, an analysis of the deviations between standards and actual performance, and prompt action to correct significant variances. But more important than understanding the control process is management's attitude toward this function. The management of the small firm must be control conscious and should instill this attitude in all members of the organization.

In addition to developing control consciousness, management must organize the control effort. Controls should be flexible, but they should encompass all important operational areas of the enterprise. Of particular importance are control in the areas of finance, costs, production, quality assurance, and inventories. For each of these areas a variety of approaches and techniques can be used. The firm must, however, develop a control system that is tailored to its specific operating characteristics. In general, adequate controls should:

- report deviations promptly
- be forward-looking
- point up exceptions and critical points
- be objective
- be flexible
- be economical
- be understandable
- lead to corrective action[13]

Controls should be viewed as a continuous, integrated effort. This effort itself should be regularly reviewed to determine whether its elements are in tune with changes in the external and internal environment of the company.

SUGGESTED READINGS

Anthony, Robert N. *Planning and Control Systems—A Framework for Analysis.* Boston: Graduate School of Business Administration, Harvard University, 1965.

Anthony, Robert N., Dearden, John, and Vancil, Richard F. *Management Control Systems: Cases and Readings.* Homewood, Ill.: Richard D. Irwin, 1965.

Basso, Lee L. *Cost Handbook for Small Manufacturers.* St. Louis: L. B. Associates, 1964.

Bonini, Charles P., Jaedicke, Robert K., and Wagner, Harvey M. *Management Controls: New Directions in Basic Research.* New York: McGraw-Hill, 1964.

---

[13]Harold Koontz and Cyril O'Donnell, *Principles of Management: An Analysis of Managerial Functions,* New York: McGraw-Hill, 1972, pp. 587–90.

Deming, Robert H. *Characteristics of an Effective Management Control System in an Industrial Organization.* Cambridge: Harvard University, 1968.

Hobbs, John A. *Control over Inventory and Production.* New York: McGraw-Hill, 1973.

Hopeman, Richard J. *Production Concepts and Controls.* Columbus, Ohio: Charles E. Merrill, 1965.

Jerome, William Travers, III. *Executive Control—The Catalyst.* New York: John Wiley & Sons, 1961.

Malcolm, Donald G., and Rowe, Alan J. *Management Control Systems.* New York: John Wiley & Sons, 1960.

Mockler, Robert J. *The Management Control Process.* New York: Appleton-Century-Crofts, 1972.

————. *Readings in Management Control.* New York: Appleton-Century-Crofts, 1970.

Stokes, Paul M. *A Total Systems Approach to Management Control.* New York: American Management Association, 1968.

Strong, Earl P., and Smith, Robert D. *Management Control Models.* New York: Holt, Rinehart & Winston, 1968.

Tipper, Harry. *Controlling Overhead.* New York: American Management Association, 1966.

Vancil, R. M., Dearden, J., and Anthony, R. D. *Management Control Systems.* Homewood, Ill.: Richard D. Irwin, 1965.

CHAPTER 14

Organizational Development

The entrepreneur has a great opportunity to build an effective organization from the moment of starting a business. Organizational effectiveness develops as technical and interpersonal competencies increase. The enterpriser has at command the relatively new methodology of organizational development to effect improvement in both.

Elaborate preparation is not needed to acquire skill in organizational development. The ideas and techniques in its methodology, which stem by and large from the behavioral sciences, are neither startling nor strange. The enterpriser will find them quite in keeping with modern managerial thinking and practice. The mode of management supported by organizational development is consistent with the assumptions of McGregor's Theory Y and the principles of Likert's System 4 management style.

System 4 managerial style assumes that management adopts the following fundamental principles:

1. development of a warm, supportive relationship with all personnel
2. consistent use of a participative, group-centered method of decision making and planning
3. establishment of high performance goals for the organization.[1]

The enterpriser who employs these principles with conviction opens the way for developing a highly competent organization.

THE FIRM AS A SOCIOTECHNICAL SYSTEM

With the hiring of the first employee the enterpriser has begun to build a social system. As more people are added, complexity increases in both

---

[1] Rensis Likert, *The Human Organization*, New York: McGraw-Hill, 1967, p. 47.

structure and interrelationships within the organization. The norms of behavior formed at the very beginning gradually become enculturated. If these norms are shaped by the principles of System 4 management, the organization is well started toward gaining competence and effectiveness. The culture that evolves in the firm will support achievement and the organizational climate will support psychological health.[2] A sound foundation for the growth and longevity of the firm develops in this way.

The small firm shows the characteristics of a purposeful organization as it becomes more than a one-person operation. It may now be conceived of as an open sociotechnical system. This system in turn is composed of three internal systems: the administrative, the technical, and the social.

Characteristics of the Open Sociotechnical System

The term sociotechnical combines the ideas that the firm is an organization of people in various groupings working together to achieve a central purpose and that such achievement comes from the application of technical competence of one kind or another.

An open system is defined as one that maintains itself by exchange of material, or in broader terms energy and information, with its environment. At any moment it may be considered in a state of relative stability, but it has the capacity to grow to a higher state through the dynamic interaction of its internal elements or subsystems. The path of growth may not necessarily be steady. Growth may follow any of an infinite number of paths, including false start and overshoot, before steadying at a relatively higher state. Growth occurs as order between internal elements increases and interdependency relationships become more productive.[3]

The open sociotechnical system of the firm is essentially an organic system much like the human body. It endures and can grow through exchange of energy and information with its environment. It may be in an unstable state at a given time, but it can move toward a steady state by using its internal resources. Such movement shows the phenomena of growth and development.

The steady state may be disturbed by a change in the external environment. This change would then trigger organizational behavior toward regaining the steady state. In practice this process implies that the

---

[2]Chris-Argyris, *Intervention Theory and Method*, Reading, Mass.: Addison-Wesley, 1970, chapter 2.

[3]Ludwig von Bertalanffy, *General System Theory*, New York: George Braziller, 1968, chapter 6.

firm should strive for adaptive, flexible behavior—behavior that permits it to recover quickly and effectively from upsetting forces. If, for example, a competitor comes out with a new product offering significant improvement over a major product the firm has on the market, management should be prepared to release an advanced version of its item. Flexibility of this kind can come only from forward planning and alertness to the needs and wants of the customer.

Characteristics of the Closed System

The open sociotechnical system of the firm may be usefully thought of in a management framework as being composed of three major subsystems—the administrative, the technical, and the social.[4] Managers working within a major subsystem often consider the subsystem as closed, although it is clearly open to the influences of the internal environment of the firm and the external environment in which the firm is embedded. By thinking in closed-system terms, variables may be isolated as internal and rational; the environment is held constant. Decision making and planning become more manageable. However, when thinking of the firm as a whole, managers go beyond the closed-system concept and take into account the impact of selected environmental forces of both the internal environment around their domain, and the external environment surrounding the firm, yet keep their problems within manageable limits.[5]

Owners of small firms should take advantage of the closed-system concept in planning and decision making, understanding that they must always take into account the impact of external forces. The closed system, self-contained and isolated from its environment (except for the input of information) permits the top managers to see clearly the variables with which they must deal and to take the steps needed for improving performance.

The closed system may be roughly likened to a sealed container enclosing a vacuum. If water is admitted through a valve, the container will fill up. It is now in a steady state, isolated from its environment. This end state represents a static or null condition. Similarly, managers who have thought through the solution of a major problem or come to an important decision in the firm by isolating the variables through the closed-system approach, have reached a null condition. The planned activities that follow take place in an open system of reality.

---

[4]Newton Margulies and Anthony P. Raia, *Organizational Development: Values, Process and Technology,* New York: McGraw-Hill, 1971, p. 2

[5]Barry M. Richman and Richard N. Farmer, *Management and Organizations,* New York: Random House, 1975, pp. 282-83.

Administrative System The administrative system is that part of the firm that regulates internal affairs. Its activities revolve around such matters as the development and issuance of policies and procedures, budgets, payments and collections, financial statements, payroll and withholding accounts, taxes, and various other aspects of accounting and financial planning, personnel administration, public relations, and similar functions. Many administrative tasks are generally considered staff functions.

Technical System The technical system includes the personnel, processes, and productive equipment that in combination accomplish the mission of the organization. Typical activities in this system include research, innovation of new products or processes, market feasibility studies, production, quality assurance, purchasing, and inventory control.

Social System The social system is composed of people acting individually, in pairs, groups of various sizes, departments, and divisions. The quality of the relationships between people, the level of their ability to work together cooperatively, determines the level of interpersonal competence in its broadest sense. It will be recalled that interpersonal competence can be seen in an organization when people show the ability to identify relevant problems, to solve them so they stay solved, and to do so without impairing the problem-solving process.[6] Organizational development focuses on the social system of the organization.

Regulation of the Total Sociotechnical System

The administrative, technical, and social systems are interlinked and mutually dependent. A change in one almost always effects change in the others. Therefore management must regulate the performance and growth of the whole firm to ensure that it adapts successfully to both internal change and change imposed by its environment. The enterpriser-owner of the small firm can gain such control through the use of two closed-loop systems that cut across the whole organization. These are management by objectives and management of managerial resources.

The closed system is essentially a *regulatory* system: both the open and closed systems of the organizational pattern described above have one feature of regulatory systems in common: they use information as the basis for planning, for detecting deviation from desired performance,

---

[6]Chris Argyris, *Organization and Innovation,* Homewood, Ill.: Richard D. Irwin and The Dorsey Press, 1965, p. 4.

and for adjusting performance to reach a desired goal. As that goal is reached, the closed system reaches a null condition, one that is at least temporarily stable. Attention and energy devoted to this achievement may now be directed toward other goals intended to increase organizational effectiveness and competence.

ORGANIZATIONAL DEVELOPMENT

The small business owner, having successfully carved out a segment of the market, recognizes the need to adjust to its constant changes. The owner comes to see that adapting to the changing environment is a way of life. It is adaptive, proactive management, not reactive management, that enables the business to survive and grow in an inconstant world. Adaptive management depends upon building organizational competence and effectiveness. These qualities are the objectives of organizational development.

Organizational competence measures the firm's ability to achieve its objectives, to maintain its internal environment, and to adapt to and control certain elements of external environment over the long term. *Organizational effectiveness* reflects the firm's ability to manage these variables in any given situation, a short-term measurement.[7] Organizational competence and effectiveness increase as technical and interpersonal competence increase. The methodology of organizational development does not ignore the need to update and improve technical competence. Its main focus, however, is on developing interpersonal competence throughout the organization.

Organizational Development Defined

Organizational development may be defined as a managerial methodology employed to increase the competence and effectiveness of the organization. The methodology uses findings from the behavioral sciences and allied fields of knowledge to effectuate desirable change for the organization and its individual members. Although organizational development addresses primarily the human side of management—values, attitudes, norms, relationships, management style, and organizational climate—it does not neglect the more structured aspects of management—planning, organizing, staffing, directing, and controlling.

The methodology of organizational development centers in educational processes. Since the subject matter involves the relationships between human beings *and* logical processes of management, the educa-

---

[7]Argyris, *Intervention Theory*, p. 36.

tional approaches include experiential and cognitive methods—that is, learning through trying and undergoing experience and learning intellectually.

The methods and techniques of organizational development are designed to change what members of the firm do to adjust behavior in ways that are beneficial for both the individual and the organization. Organizational development is concerned with the ethical qualities of both means and ends. With persistent and continuing effort, its methods and techniques are used to develop a climate of achievement in a psychologically healthy organization.

This process of change is essentially a cultural change affecting the whole organization. In the new small firm, the enterpriser can spearhead the development of an achieving culture by employing the methodology of organizational development. The boss's behavior and attitudes set the pattern for the firm's personnel. There is no existing culture to convert. The boss may therefore induce a rapid cultural evolution aimed at the qualities that support competence and effectiveness.

MOTIVATION IN THE SMALL FIRM

Enterpriser-owners of small firms want to be supported by highly motivated people, as do managers everywhere. They should therefore acquire some understanding of human behavior in order to build motivational forces in the environment. A simple model of human behavior useful for this purpose may be described as follows.

All human behavior is directed toward the satisfaction of needs. Behavior originates in a *cause* of some kind, which determines a need. The cause triggers a *stimulus,* which then develops within the person a need, a want, a tension, or a motivation toward behavior that will satisfy the need. The behavior is therefore goal directed. As the goal is achieved, the need is satisfied, and the stimulus is wiped out. The cycle is completed and another cycle of behavior, aimed at satisfying some other need, is initiated. This process goes on continuously, following the cycle shown in Figure 14–1.

A simple example will explain the cycle. A person whose stomach is empty experiences the pangs of hunger: Cause equals empty stomach; stimulus equals feeling hungry. The person now experiences the need for food. The discomfort or tension then *motivates,* impels activity aimed at filling the stomach, which is the goal. The motivation shows itself in behavior, searching for food. When food has been found and eaten, the person has reached the goal. The cause of the behavior has now been removed and the stimulus reduced to zero. The person then *becomes motivated* toward some other goal-directed behavior.

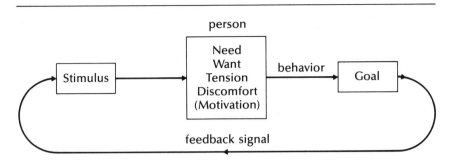

FIGURE 14–1. Basic Cycle of Human Behavior (after Leavitt)

Three basic concepts are involved in this model of human behavior:

1. Human behavior is caused. It is not random, although often times the cause is difficult to identify. The cause of behavior lies outside the person, in a psychological sense. This implies that heredity and environment affect behavior, since individuals may be motivated toward different goals by the same external influences, or the same goals by different external influences. The individual's response reflects heredity, conditioning, education, and the behavioral norms of the culture in which the person was brought up.
2. Human behavior is goal-directed. It is not random. People behave in ways intended to satisfy their needs.
3. People are motivated toward goal-seeking behavior in response to an internally experienced need, which may be stated as a tension, discomfort, or want. These terms are roughly equivalent to *motive*.[8]

The important point here for our purpose is that motivation occurs within the person. What is outside affects what is inside; the manager must work outside to set up conditions conducive to motivation. Thus the manager must create the kind of environmental forces that will stimulate the members of the firm toward beneficial goal-directed behavior, for the organization and for themselves.

Human Needs and Management Values

A set of concepts useful in understanding the way motivational forces operate in the business environment is the *hierarchy of human needs*

---

[8]Harold J. Leavitt, *Managerial Psychology*, 3d edition, Chicago: University of Chicago Press, 1972, chapter 1.

proposed by Abraham H. Maslow.[9] He stated that the human being is a wanting animal whose behavior is directed, consciously or not, at satisfying needs of various kinds. These needs may be classified in sets, which form a hierarchy. The most basic set of needs is the *physiological,* followed by the *safety, social, esteem,* and *self-actualization* needs in order, from the most to the least tangible. These sets of needs may be described briefly as follows:

1. Physiological needs include the fundamental requirements of the physical organism for existence: food, water, air, exercise, rest, sex, and sleep are typical.
2. Safety needs refer to the powerful desire to be free from fear and deprivation—to prefer the known over the unknown, the clearly defined over the unformed, and the familiar over the unfamiliar.
3. Social needs define the human being's wants for belongingness and love. They reflect the fundamental requirements of society for healthy interdependency and cooperative relationships.
4. Esteem needs are composed of two basic subsets: the need for competence and the need for recognition. The first stems from the desire of the individual for self-confidence and self-respect, which come from mastery demonstrated through skill or special achievement. The second comes from appreciation or recognition of such competence by others.
5. Self-actualization needs encompass the human being's desire for self-fulfillment, for the urge to bring to actuality latent talents or abilities.

Figure 14–2 illustrates Maslow's hierarchy of needs.

The more basic needs have greater potency to motivate behavior than the less basic. As the human being behaves in one way or another to satisfy existing needs, the more potent need takes precedence. However, when the needs in a set are reasonably well satisfied, a need in a less potent set becomes a stimulus that motivates behavior toward its fulfillment.

Another characteristic of the hierarchy is that needs coexist; the average normal person is partially satisfied and partially unsatisfied in meeting the needs at the five levels at the same time. In the culture of the United States, Maslow suggests some arbitrary figures for the sake of illustration: the average citizen may be satisfied 85 percent in physiological needs, 70 percent in safety needs, 50 percent in social needs, 40 percent in esteem needs, and 10 percent in self-actualization needs at a given time. So, for example, as the physiological, safety, and social needs become reasonably well satisfied, the esteem needs gradually

---

[9]A. H. Maslow, *Motivation and Personality*, New York: Harper & Row, 1954, chapter 5.

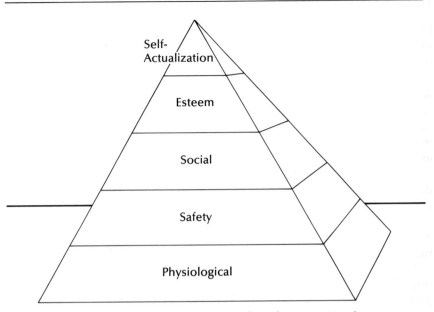

FIGURE 14–2. Model of Maslow's Hierarchy of Human Needs

emerge as a motivating force, impelling the individual toward the achievement of competence. And as the esteem needs become fulfilled to a greater extent, the need for self-actualization gradually emerges as a motivating force. The individual might then devote energy toward developing some latent talent, perhaps in acquiring some special skill in the business.

Maslow presented the foregoing hierarchy of human needs as a theoretical construct. Empirical studies aimed at testing his theory conclude that some modification is in order.[10] Once the physiological and safety needs are reasonably well fulfilled, the less tangible higher order needs for social, esteem, and self-actualization fulfillment may not necessarily emerge in the sequence Maslow suggested. Self-actualization needs, for example, may arise before esteem needs. The individual's state at any given time would determine which higher level need is emergent. Although Maslow's concept of a hierarchy of human needs may have to be modified, managers should be aware of the importance of the higher order needs in stimulating individual motivation. The trend in today's management is in this direction.

---

[10]Wahba, M. A. and L. G. Bridwell, "Maslow Reconsidered: A Review of Research on the Need Hierarchy Theory." *Proceedings of the Academy of Management,* 1973, pp. 514–20.

From Theory X to Theory Y

Douglas McGregor described two sets of values underlying contrasting managerial philosophies, and therefore differing styles of management; one he called Theory X, the other Theory Y.[11]

Theory X outlines assumptions about human behavior that are pervasive in the literature of management and are often heard in conversations between managers even today. These assumptions are traditional values inherited from the industrial revolution and may be summarized in the following way. Personnel who work for a business organization are considered hands, all very much alike and essentially interchangeable. They are somewhat lazy and unwilling to learn. They must be directed, controlled, and threatened with punishment if the productivity required by the organization is to be attained. And to cap it all, these hands are seen as somewhat dishonest; they can't be trusted. Management style, therefore, is geared to ensuring that the company receives full worth for the money it spends for labor.

The resulting organization, as a consequence, follows what is sometimes called the accounting model of organization; it is set up to detect and correct error. As McGregor indicated, the widely accepted principles of management current in the literature until fairly recently could only have been derived from assumptions such as those of Theory X.

The values of Theory Y are quite different and are consonant with ideas such as those expressed by Maslow in his hierarchy of human needs. They are also in keeping with emerging cultural and legislative changes that call for respecting the dignity of the individual and eliminating discriminatory practices of all kinds. Theory Y values underline the worth of the individual and the individual's potential for growth, psychologically and intellectually.

Theory Y may be summarized as follows. People who work for a business organization are unique; they have their own complement of aptitudes and talents. Learning is as natural as breathing, given the climate that supports it. Human beings are inherently energetic and will devote prodigious amounts of energy to the achievement of goals they consider important. In addition, they will seek and accept increasing responsibility under the proper conditions. The capping statement, quite the contrary of that of Theory X, is that most people are fundamentally honest; they can be trusted.

From the concepts of Theory Y, a different management style emerges. Here the climate of the organization would be open and supportive. A large part of the management job would be that of coaching, training, and educating members of the firm to help them increase their

---

[11]Douglas McGregor, *The Human Side of Enterprise,* New York: McGraw-Hill, 1960, chapters 3, 4.

competence and gain mastery in their work. People would be encouraged and helped to grow. The firm would gain effectiveness and grow with the growth of individuals. That these concepts are not wild-eyed, blue sky ravings of rocking chair idealists is clearly shown in recent trends in business, industry, and other kinds of organizations.[12]

Motivation and Management Style

Frederick Herzberg and his associates have found that certain factors in work cause dissatisfaction; others give satisfaction.[13] The major dissatisfiers, in order of their intensity as measured by their impact on change of attitude, were identified as company policy and its administration, technical incompetence of the boss, salary, interpersonal relations with the boss, and working conditions. These factors tend to reduce motivation.

The major satisfiers were found to be achievement, recognition for achievement, joy in the work, increase in responsibility, advancement, and personal growth in mastery and competence. The satisfiers motivate people toward achieving behavior.

It will be seen that dissatisfiers have to do with the conditions surrounding the work, whereas satisfiers are directly concerned with the work itself. Herzberg points out that the two cannot be equated. A pound of satisfaction does not equal a pound of dissatisfaction.

Dissatisfiers are concerned with the psychological environment of work, the *surround* that influences human behavioral responses. People are disaffected by having company policy about which they have had nothing to say imposed on them, or by working under an incompetent boss. On the other hand, achieving a difficult task in good style and having that achievement recognized by the boss makes the person feel good. These factors, which relate more to the work itself, motivate toward further achievement.

In the overall picture, as Herzberg points out, the dissatisfiers have to do with one part of the duality of human nature, the animal aspect that urges people to avoid pain and seek safety. The other part of the human being's dual nature, the persistent need for personal growth, for mastery and competence, is served by the satisfiers. It is through the work itself that mastery and competence are developed and demonstrated.

It should now be clear that the work of Maslow, McGregor, and Herzberg tie together. Motivation toward further achievement is stimulated by achievement—and achievement results from mastery and competence in work. The acquisition of mastery and competence is best

---

[12]See, for example, Peter F. Drucker, "Hysteria Over the Work Ethic," *Psychology Today*, November 1973, pp. 87–92.
[13]Frederick Herzberg, *Work and the Nature of Man*, Cleveland: World Publishing Co., 1966, chapter 6.

supported in the organization that encourages and helps people to grow. Such an organization displays an open and supportive managerial climate consonant with the values of Theory Y. Support for this statement comes from years of research in many different kinds of organizations performed by the Institute of Social Research of the University of Michigan, under the guidance of Rensis Likert.[14]

Organizational Effectiveness and Managerial Style

Likert sees the interaction between boss and subordinates as the critical factor in building a supporting relationship. The boss's behavior should be such as to be helpful and ego building for subordinates. It is the subordinate's perception of an interaction that determines whether the experience has enhanced a sense of personal worth and importance. Understanding this, the boss would try to view the situation through the subordinate's eyes, taking into account the individual's background, values, and expectations. The boss would then be ready to be supportive by confirming the essentiality of a subordinate's contribution to the operation of the firm, and thereby to increase that person's feeling of personal worth.

The group method of decision making and supervision, when properly managed, can produce both superior decisions and self-discipline in the conduct of affairs. With practice, the group learns to improve its communications and to avoid wasting time on trivia. Decisions are based upon data contributed by those individuals most experienced and knowledgeable in the subject being considered. In addition to drawing on the wisdom of the group, the participative process of decision making tends to induce the members to *own* their decisions. They are moved to support the actions that come from the decisions. The result is a self-disciplined approach requiring managerial direction but very little overt managerial control.

Participative group management tends also to support the setting of high performance goals. The group often chooses goals that are higher than those the manager might establish. The manager's purpose should be to guide the goal-setting effort toward targets that are achievable, requiring some stretch of the group's capability, but not so high as to be beyond reach. This procedure encourages the use of the members' capacities and promotes the acquisition of increasingly higher levels of competence. When successfully met, the challenge of achievement stimulates personal growth of the members.

Participative group management of this kind, called System 4 management by Likert, fulfills the requirements for motivation indicated by

---

[14]Likert, *Human Organization*, chapter 4.

Maslow's concepts and Herzberg's studies. Its rewards for the individual stem from personal achievement, which is in turn ministered to by a supportive managerial climate.

As a concluding note, a supportive style of management implies constant attention to reduction of the dissatisfiers that surround work. To practice good management in the small firm, the entrepreneur would constantly seek to improve the conditions in which work is done *and* to help people gain mastery and competence.

STRUCTURED METHODS IN ORGANIZATIONAL DEVELOPMENT

The structured methods in organizational development encompass the more traditionally identified functions of management: planning, organizing, staffing, directing, and controlling. These functions fall within the scope of the two major regulatory systems of the organization: management by objectives and self-control (MBO) and management of managerial resources (MMR). Both will be discussed briefly here to show how they fit into the concept of organizational development.

Management by Objectives and Self-Control

The process of management by objectives and self-control, described originally by Drucker,[15] was elaborated by McGregor, who called it management by integration and self-control.[16] Since then the process has come to be known as management by objectives, commonly abbreviated to MBO.

MBO is a systematic way of managing derived from observation of the procedures that effective managers use in working with their subordinates; its basic process is keyed to the values of Theory Y. MBO applies to the total group of managers in the firm, from president to first-line supervisor. It therefore includes the basic planning for the whole organization and provides the vehicle for integrating the planning at all levels.

A tested vocabulary for the elements of the planning in MBO uses the following definitions:

Objective. An objective is the highest level plan in a three-level tier of planning. It is the statement of an overall position or condition that is to be reached. Objectives are stated for the firm, division, department, and

---

[15]Peter F. Drucker, *The Practice of Management,* New York: Harper & Row, 1954, chapter 11.
[16]McGregor, *Human Side of Enterprise,* chapter 5.

individual management position. They are inherently long range, usually requiring from one to five years to attain.

Subobjective. A subobjective is an end result, narrower in scope and usually shorter in time span than the objective to which it applies. Several subobjectives must usually be achieved to accomplish an objective.

Action Plan. A step, task, project, program, or activity requiring action by one or more members of the firm. Several action plans will usually have to be completed to achieve the subobjective at which they are aimed.

Action plans imply activity of some kind inside and outside the firm. The success of the firm in achieving its objectives—and therefore its performance—ultimately depends on the appropriateness of its action plans and the effectiveness with which they are carried out. Objectives, subobjectives, and action plans have several characteristics in common:

1. Each should be clearly defined in simple language; each should start with an active verb as a reminder that activity is required to make the plan work.
2. Each should be limited to one idea to avoid confusion.
3. A target by calendar date should be set for each.
4. A method of measuring the accomplishment of each should be established, together with an appropriate frequency of measuring performance along the way.
5. The achievement of objectives should require extending the capabilities of the organization to some extent; similarly, the achievement of subobjectives and action plans should challenge individuals, requiring stretching personal capacities to a reasonable extent.
6. Objectives, subobjectives, and action plans should be limited in number. When the number of plans in each category exceeds a half-dozen or so, the planning is probably getting too complicated for its intended purpose, which is to provide guides for what should be done. Planning should not give step-by-step instructions.
7. Objectives, subobjectives, and action plans should be attainable; they should not be so difficult as to exceed the capacities of persons or the organization.

Planning is best started at the top. The enterpriser-owner should set the objectives for the company. It is the chief executive's responsibility to develop the overall objectives for the company, using all the help available from subordinate managers and the board of directors if there is one.

Once the key objectives for the company are set, the entrepreneur then works with managers at the next level to define subobjectives under each objective. These managers are expected to make major contributions to the formulation of company subobjectives, for they assume responsibility for achieving them. The second-level managers now work out action plans for achieving company subobjectives with their subordinate managers who, in turn, are expected to make contributions to the plans and assume responsibility for their accomplishment.

It will be seen that the scale value changes at each level. Company subobjectives once set by agreement between the top boss and managers at the next level become objectives for them. In turn, second-level subobjectives and action plans may become objectives and subobjectives for third-level managers. Figure 14–3 shows this hierarchical arrangement clearly.

In addition to the basic set of company plans, individual managers in the firm are expected to add their personal objectives for the special requirements of their jobs. These may cover routine, innovative, emergency, or personal growth objectives.[17]

The most important element in the system of MBO is the individual managers. It is they who do the basic planning for their own activities and consult with and secure the consent of their bosses for these activities. Above all, it is the individuals who accept personal responsibility for the achievement of the results desired of them—and agree to be judged by the results they achieve. How the individual managers use the planning process in MBO and how their activities are governed by its basic concepts are shown in Figure 14–4.

The small business owner who uses MBO from the beginning can readily set an effective planning style by indoctrinating the first managers employed in the system. As new management positions are created with the growth of the firm, the new managers will find it relatively easy to adopt MBO, which will be the accustomed way of managing—the norm of the firm.

MBO, when skillfully employed, works to free the individual manager for innovative effort. MBO is concerned with setting high but attainable standards of performance, that is, with results—and not with the idiosyncracies of the individual style or method. Through the managerial methodology of MBO, the enterpriser-owner can control the destiny of the firm—can ensure an integrated system of planning and achievement in which the firm's managers are free to act in accordance with their individual desires, proclivities, and talents within a framework of legitimacy defined by the planning process.

Performance Appraisal in MBO

In management by objectives and self-control (MBO), managers accomplish their objectives in their own fashion without minute directions

---

[17]George S. Odiorne, *Management by Objectives*, New York: Pitman, 1965, chapters 7, 8, 9.

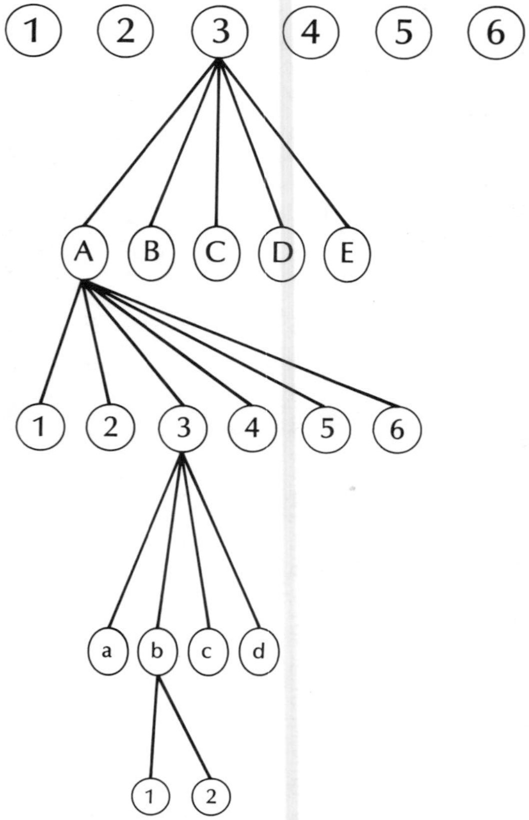

COMPANY OBJECTIVES—PRESIDENT'S OBJECTIVES
1. Increase sales from $6 million to $7 million by January 1 next year.
2. Complete development of new product program by March next year.
3. Install management succession program by December 20.
4. Develop total management compensation package by January 15 next year.
5. Install management by objectives in manufacturing department by November next year.
6. Complete preliminary plans for new plant by September 25.

COMPANY SUBOBJECTIVES—MANAGEMENT OBJECTIVES
A. Develop base management salary program by July 1.
B. Develop profit participation program by September 30.
C. Develop stock option plan by November 30.
D. Develop deferred compensation plan by March 1 next year.
E. Upgrade executive insurance program by December 10.

MANAGEMENT SUBOBJECTIVES—PERSONNEL ADMINISTRATION OBJECTIVES
1. Gather position questionnaires on existing and projected management positions by June 15.
2. Prepare position descriptions for key jobs from questionnaires by August 15.
3. Evaluate and rank key positions with management team by October 15.
4. Review evaluations with president by October 20.
5. Develop salary trend line, salary midpoints, and ranges by November 15.
6. Review and secure final approval of program by December 1.

PERSONNEL ADMINISTRATION SUBOBJECTIVES
a. Identify key management positions by August 30.
b. Identify management ranking team by September 7.
c. Evaluate and rank key management positions by October 1.
d. Review and submit rankings for president's approval by October 15.

PERSONNEL ADMINISTRATION ACTION PLANS
1. Select position ranking team by September 5.
2. Hold position ranking team meeting by September 7.

FIGURE 14–3. Relationship of objectives, subobjectives, and action plans

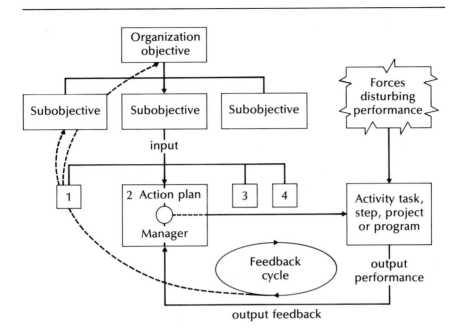

- Subobjective or end result desired, stated in measurable terms, becomes an input for the individual manager.
- Manager develops action plans for achieving subobjective, leading to activity and output performance.
- Changing conditions or personal factors produce disturbing forces that cause variance from desired performance.
- Manager measures output performance against input data from desired subobjective and adjusts or revises plans—including subobjective, or even objective, when appropriate—leading to corrective changes in activities.
- The planning process depends on a continuing series of feedback cycles in which the manager measures performance against subobjectives, revises plans, and thereby develops more effective activity.

FIGURE 14–4. The Planning Process in Management by Objectives
Source: Used with permission of the Society of Manufacturing Engineers.

from the boss. They consider the boss a resource person who may be consulted for advice or counsel as necessary.

The appraisal of performance in MBO includes self-evaluation of progress by subordinate managers themselves. When the manager and the boss agree on the results to be achieved during a stipulated period, say six months or a year depending on the nature of the subobjective, the subordinate has in essence agreed to a contract of work. Figure 14–5 illustrates a typical memo of agreement prepared by a subordinate man-

To: Jim Kemper (President)

From: John Haskell (Marketing Manager)

Dear Jim:

Here's confirmation of our discussion about my plans for marketing in 1978:

> **Objective 1:** Increase market penetration on product A in New York and Boston areas from 12 percent in 1977 to 15 percent by January 1, 1979.
>
>> **Subobjective A:** Add two salespersons, one in New York City and one in Boston, by March 1, 1978. This will add $38,000 to our salary budget for 1978, as we agreed.
>>
>> **Subobjective B:** Increase scope of mail advertising by adding 1,000 potential customers to our mailing list by April 20, 1978. This will require increasing the sales promotion budget from $12,000 in 1977 to $17,000 in 1978, as we agreed.
>>
>> (Note: I plan to measure achievement of this objective by checking our sales of product A each month during the year.)
>
> **Objective 2:** Determine the future of product B by June 30, 1978.
>
>> **Subobjective A:** Identify causes of rapid obsolescence of product B during the last eighteen months.
>>
>> **Action Plan 1:** Analyze impact of competing products brought on the market by the Garth and Moody companies during the past two years by March 15, 1978.
>>
>> **Action Plan 2:** Determine our customers' responses to these competing products by April 20, 1978.
>>
>> (Note: I intend to make a tour of our customers in the Boston and New York areas myself, to gather the data needed for the above action plans.)
>
> **Objective 3:** Conduct a market feasibility study of product C now under development by November 15, 1978.
>
>> **Subobjective A:** Determine acceptability of product C to our customers by September 15, 1978.
>>
>> **Action Plan A-1:** Carry out two focus group meetings of present customers on product C in New York and two in Boston by May 25, 1978.
>>
>> **Action Plan A-2:** Test the market by making a selling tour personally with both our New York and Boston salespersons by July 10, 1978.
>>
>> **Action Plan A-3:** Develop strategy and tactics for an intensive marketing campaign on product C in 1979, upon the basis of the data gathered in action plans 2 and 3, by October 1, 1978.
>>
>> **Action Plan A-4:** Train our sales staff in promoting and selling product C by December 15, 1978.
>>
>> (Note: I'll measure effectiveness of the foregoing actions by watching sales of product C weekly for the first quarter of 1979 and by continual feedback from our salespersons during that time. We can incorporate any needed changes in price or selling strategy as indicated by the information from the field. I'll keep you up to date on our progress in this campaign.)

FIGURE 14–5. Informal Confirmation of Managerial Planning

ager for the boss. The subordinate expects to be appraised by the results achieved. This method of performance appraisal is considered an integral procedure in MBO.

Performance appraisal by results affords a management process in keeping with the values of Theory Y and capable of motivating human beings toward achievement and personal growth. Its strategy and procedures automatically fulfill the organization's *administrative, information,* and *motivation* needs when the appraisal process is carried out competently. It is particularly suited to the small company, as its relatively informal procedures and minimal paperwork admirably fit the small firm's management climate.

Meeting Administrative Needs The administrative needs of the firm in managing personnel include salary adjustment, promotion, transfer, demotion, termination, and often the adjudication of fringe benefits and bonuses.

Salary administration becomes a relatively straightforward procedure when performance is measured objectively by the results the individual has achieved. The superior manager no longer has to play God in judging attributes or traits that even the most skillful psychiatrist balks at assessing. Both superior and subordinate manager are aware of the subordinate's performance through the feedback process inherent in the planning system. Subordinates don't have to be told how they are doing. They know. If a raise is due, both individual and boss know. If a person has failed significantly to meet most of the objectives agreed upon, both know—and the lack of a raise comes as no shock.

One caution is to be observed here. If managers have been unable to achieve an objective because of environmental conditions beyond their control, they should not be penalized. A sudden change in the economy through a jump in interest rates, an unexpected change in fashion, or an unanticipated technological breakthrough by a competitor can sometimes abort the best conceived plan. The program of appraisal by results should include a policy for dealing equitably with situations like these.

Promotion, transfer, and demotion are decisions more readily made with the background of data from performance appraisal by results.

Meeting Information Needs Performance appraisal by results opens channels of communication between boss and subordinate by the inherent design of the process. The dialog between the two, which starts the subordinate's planning for the achievement of specific objectives, sets the stage for a continuing, reciprocal relationship. The boss learns a great deal about the subordinate—personal strengths, weaknesses, and idiosyncracies. The subordinate learns the boss's characteristics, and, if the boss performs the managerial role of coach and counselor with some skill, the subordinate sees in this behavior a model of warm support.

The mutual planning procedure is a vital factor in the coaching, counseling relationship that the superior uses to help the subordinate gain increased competence. As the relationship develops, the boss can coach the subordinate in improving skills and in acquiring special know-how related to the job. If the subordinate runs against personal obstacles that block progress, the boss can help by adopting a counseling role.

Performance appraisal by results for these reasons builds a supportive climate of management by developing open communications between boss and subordinate. As an informative device, it is extremely effective because it is based on frequent contact and feedback; the boss knows when help is required and can furnish it immediately. The personal transactions between the two allow the boss to identify the special strengths of the subordinate. They can then work out plans that build on these strengths—the surest way to accelerate achievement of both personal and organizational objectives.

Meeting Motivational Needs We have noted that the environmental forces to which a person is subject stimulate motivation toward behavior of one kind or another. What the chief executive of a small firm wants (as do managers everywhere) is beneficial behavior—that is, behavior that achieves organizational objectives. We have also seen that it is imperative to meet social norms of respect for the worth and the dignity of the individual. Beneficial behavior therefore implies building a psychologically healthy climate, which supports both personal growth *and* increase in organizational effectiveness.

We have also noted that the opportunity for achievement, for doing a difficult job well, provides motivational impact. Achievement of a difficult job implies competence—and the achievement itself is a demonstration of mastery. Competence, which comes with mastery, is an indicator of self-actualization—the individual has been motivated to acquire knowledge, skills, and know-how.

The process of setting objectives by mutual agreement between boss and subordinate lays the foundation for establishing environmental forces that stimulate individuals to motivate themselves.

The organization is bound together by the interactions of people, individually and in groups. These are interdependent relationships in which people work together toward the common purposes of the organization. The binding element cementing the organization is the set of organizational objectives that guide its activities. The organization becomes a social institution as people share tasks and interact.

Members behave in keeping with the values and norms that evolve with the development of the unique organizational culture. They identify with the organization beyond the requirements of the tasks to be performed. Underlying individual and organizational behavior are motives—and the objectives of the organization and the individual reflect the values toward which behavior and activity are directed. In other words, values that motivate behavior are embedded in objectives. When an individual sets objectives for certain activities, and those objectives help to satisfy needs for achievement, self-actualization and personal growth, a self-motivating drive toward the attainment of those objectives is generated. Performance thus flows from self-motivation. Performance appraisal by results meets the motivational needs of the firm through the process of planning and setting objectives for achievement.

Management of Managerial Resources

Management of managerial resources (MMR) provides the second major control system for regulating the growth of the firm. It cuts across the whole organization, as does MBO, which it parallels in general concept. MMR concentrates on the human resources of the firm. It functions to ensure the availability of competent managers to meet the needs of growth and replacement.

A simple approach suitable to the management of human resources in the small firm has been given in Chapter 9. As the small firm grows, it will find that this effort will require more formal administration. A comprehensive strategy for developing a system of MMR includes considerations of personnel planning, staffing and development, factors that influence organizational performance, appraisal and analysis of results, personnel inventory, and feedback loops for adjusting the performance of the system.[18] The basic scheme is diagrammed in Figure 14–6.

As will be seen from the diagram, each major factor is influenced by a number of different elements. These have been covered throughout this book; therefore they will be merely outlined here to show their interrelationship.

Personnel Planning Planning to fill future needs for personnel starts with consideration of economic forecasts, labor market forecasts, and business plans.

Economic forecasts reflect environmental forces over which the entrepreneur has no control. There are many sources of information that may be used to gain some understanding of what is likely to happen in the near future: Graduate schools of business do a creditable job of forecasting the economic climate for state and country. Many forecasts are updated quarterly. Major banks do a similar job of forecasting economic conditions. Some of these are notably on target.

Labor market forecasts can also be made on the basis of data that are available through governmental and private sources. Among these are

---

[18]Arthur H. Kuriloff, *Organizational Development for Survival*, New York: American Management Association, 1972, chapters 11, 12, 13.

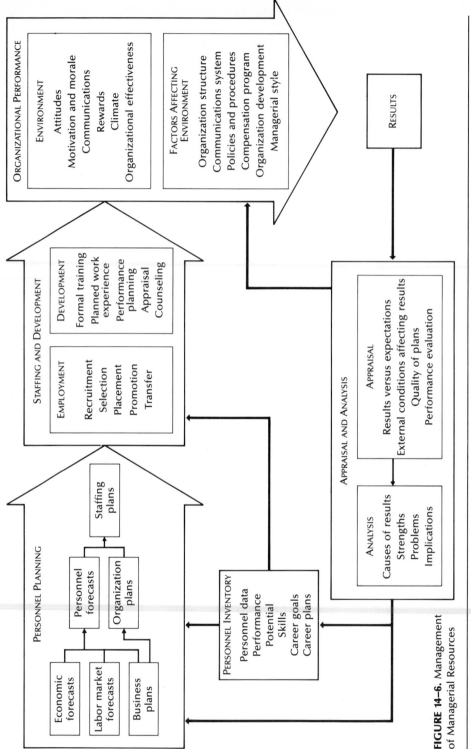

FIGURE 14–6. Management of Managerial Resources

Source: Used with permission of Cresap, McCormick and Paget, Inc.

merchants and manufacturers associations; chambers of commerce; the U.S. Department of Commerce, which has offices strategically located throughout the country; and metropolitan newspapers, which often have highly competent researchers who compile and update pertinent data for their communities.

Business Plans The business plans that the entrepreneur develops provide a guide to the future of the firm. These plans result from the effort to ensure growth and longevity and, in general, center on newer and better things to do or newer and better ways of doing older things. To develop these plans, the enterpriser-owner has engaged in transactions with the environment in which the company is embedded. A potentially profitable new product or service has been identified, or a new way to segment the market profitably has been conceived. The business plans may now call for such activities as expanding existing facilities, adding a new department, or mounting a new promotional campaign.

From business plans, organizational planning can be established. The structure of the new organization can be projected, and the management positions that will need to be filled can be defined. Personnel forecasts may be made from an integration of economic forecasts, labor market forecasts, and business plans.

Staffing plans are next projected from a combination of organization plans and personnel forecasts. Data from the firm's personnel inventory are used to identify likely candidates for the new positions and positions that will have to be filled from the outside. These data are also used in the next major stage of MMR, staffing and development, as shown in Figure 14–6.

Staffing and Development Staffing and development involve considerations of employment and specialized training. Employment deals with matters of recruitment, selection of personnel deemed qualified for promotion, placement of qualified individuals in new positions as they open, promotion from within existing ranks, and transfer from one segment of the firm to another. Development aims at increasing the competence of personnel through the methods of formal training, planned work experience, performance planning designed specifically to meet individual needs, appraisal of performance, and counseling as required.

Staffing and development are intended to put the right people in the right place at the right time and to ensure that those people have acquired sufficient competence to gain mastery over the job. The integration of individual efforts produces some level of organizational performance. But organizational performance can be supported or eroded by the managerial environment within the firm.

Organizational Performance The environment in the firm stems from a number of interrelated elements, which in turn are intertwined with several factors that shape and modify them.

The environment may be characterized by the attitudes shown by the members of the firm, which influence morale and motivation; the quality of the communications and timeliness of rewards for superior performance; the quality of openness and trust among people and groups; and the level of organizational effectiveness—that is, how well the firm overcomes obstacles and solves problems on an ongoing basis.

The factors that affect the environment include organizational structure, which can aid or impede cooperative effort; the communications system, which should provide open channels for the flow of data, down, sideways, and up; policies and procedures, which can be particularly effective when developed with the help of the members of the firm; the compensation program; and the style of management that pervades the firm.

The operational outcome of performance is results. The quality of the results indicates the level of organizational competence—that is, how well the company is able to meet its objectives and thereby fulfill its central purpose. The enterpriser discovers ways for improving performance through appraisal and analysis of results.

Appraisal and Analysis Feedback on performance of the firm and individual managers provides data for improving the competence of both. Undesirable variations from plan can be pinpointed and corrected. Opportunities for improvement in personal performance can be identified and made the basis for developmental effort.

Appraisal includes an assessment of results against the expectations expressed in planning, an examination of the forces in the environment that may have affected results, study of the quality of the plans to see where improvement might be made, and evaluation of performance against the standards agreed upon when the plans were set. The next step in the cycle of MMR is the analysis of data generated to this point.

The purpose of the analysis is to formulate improved strategy upon which to base the next round of planning in the MMR cycle. Analysis concentrates on isolating and understanding the causes of the results achieved, finding the special strengths of firm and people, stating the problems and weaknesses uncovered, and , finally, detailing the implications of the data brought to light by the analysis, which provides inputs for planning strategy. In addition, the analytic procedure produces information about the capabilities of individual managers. These data are entered into the personnel inventory. Feedback from the appraisal and analysis process furnishes data for modifying factors or elements that influence organizational performance and for the basic personnel planning that underlies staffing plans.

Personnel Inventory The final step in the MMR cycle, personnel inventory, outlines information that should be collected about individual managers, as follows: usual personnel information, such as age, prior employment and education; a record of performance in each of the positions held during tenure with the company; an estimate of potential for assuming higher level positions; a catalog of special skills; and a statement of personal career goals and plans.

The system of MMR will be seen as having planning and feedback procedures similar to those of MBO. A small firm that has become accustomed to planning in the MBO mode would find MMR easy to adopt. The record keeping requires nothing more complicated than three-ring binders with loose-leaf pages for companies up to three or four hundred personnel. Beyond that size, record keeping could be done with a punched card sorting system, a straightforward transition from the three-ring binder.

Enterpriser-owners who install and maintain the system of MMR improve their chances for seeing their company grow and endure. They will have ensured the development of a group of competent managers to meet the needs of company growth and renewal.

BEHAVIORAL METHODS IN ORGANIZATIONAL DEVELOPMENT

The objective of organizational development is to help the firm achieve a high level of organizational competence, that is, to increase its ability to fulfill it central purpose and to endure. Organizational competence is a function of technical competence and interpersonal competence. The methodology of organizational development aims primarily at building interpersonal competence. Its scope, however, includes helping the members of the firm identify needs and means for enlarging their technical knowledge and skills.

The development of interpersonal competence, as has been noted, is significantly influenced by the style of management in the firm. Autocratic management tends to thwart the emergence of norms of behavior that support the building of interpersonal competence; participative-group management, which Likert calls System 4, encourages and supports it.[19]

Three norms of behavior associated with the development of interpersonal competence are 1) *individuality*, 2) *concern*, and 3) *trust*. These are described essentially as follows:

1. *Individuality:* behavior by members of the firm that encourages the individual to express ideas or feelings openly. The norm influences

---

[19]Likert, *Human Organization*, chapter 2.

members to protect and develop the uniqueness of the individual.
2. *Concern:* behavior that induces members to be solicitous about the ideas and feelings of others. The norm encourages members to protect and develop the uniqueness of others, both in ideas and feelings.
3. *Trust:* behavior that induces members to take risks and to experiment with ideas and feelings.

(The opposing norms, which are destructive of interpersonal competence, are conformity, antagonism, and mistrust.)[20]

Organizational development operates to build teamwork, which depends upon interaction and cooperation among people. The methods and techniques of organizational development address the building of norms of individuality, concern, and trust, and these in the largest measure are seen in the activity and behavior of the group.

Working With Groups

Entrepreneurs in small firms should school themselves to observe the behavior of their people when they work in groups. By observing carefully and responding intelligently to the behavior observed, the boss can stimulate the development of the norms of individuality, concern, and trust. These, in turn, support the emergence of an achieving climate and organizational competence.

Content and Process

When the boss observes what the group is talking about, the focus is on *content*. When the boss concentrates on how the members are communicating, the focus is on *process*. The key point to remember is that it is the process that determines how well the group is functioning. The process tells about such things as hidden fights for leadership, dissatisfaction with conditions surrounding work, or bad feelings between members. The process can, of course, indicate smoothly functioning teamwork—as it will when the behavioral norms produce beneficial results. By observing process, the boss can decide when to take action to remove a barrier to teamwork.

Communication

The boss should observe the pattern of communication in the group. Answers to the following questions can give valuable insight into the way the group functions:

---

[20]Argyris, *Intervention Theory,* pp. 289, 290.

1. Who does most of the talking?
2. Whom do people address when they talk? A specific person? The group? No one?
3. Who interrupts whom?
4. Who needles, blocks, or thwarts others?
5. What signals of emotion are there? Anger? Emphasis? Tone of voice?[21]

The direct observations and inferences that the boss can make from different behaviors can provide data that help to adjust the functioning of the group toward more effective problem solving and decision making—that is, toward more capable handling of the content with which they are involved.

Answers to the questions posed above may seem to produce trivial data. That would be true if the process stopped at this point. However, to obtain operational effect, the boss must share these data with the group so that they can together explore what is going on beneath the surface. The discussion that follows may unearth difficulties in the relationships between people, power plays, or informal relationships that tend to disrupt formal operations. When the boss brings situations such as these out for consideration by the group, a cathartic and healing process begins. Techniques in the methodology of organizational development for handling matters of these kinds are outlined later in this chapter.

Consensus in Decision Making

An important procedure in building teamwork is to encourage the group to reach decisions by consensus. A consensual decision means that the members have contributed to the discussion, debated the key points, considered different points of view, and have generally converged in their individual thinking to the point where all can agree to the merit of the proposed solution. It does not necessarily mean that each person is wholeheartedly convinced that the solution is the best possible, but that each sees sufficient advantage in the approach to concur in it and to support its application.

The boss can suggest the following guides to the group for achieving consensus:

1. Persons should avoid defending their own position beyond a reasonable point simply because it is their position.

---

[21]An informative discussion of the communication process and how to analyze it will be found in Edgar H. Schein, *Process Consultation: Its Role in Organization Development,* Reading, Mass.: Addison-Wesley, 1969, chapter 3.

2. Each person should try to maintain logical objectivity in responding to what is said and not be swayed by who is saying it.
3. The group should not vote on propositions, average approaches, or "horse trade" simply for the sake of reaching a group decision.
4. Members should be admonished not to change their minds just to avoid conflict and reach agreement.
5. Members should support only those proposals with which they agree sufficiently to be able to devote their wholehearted efforts to the action proposed.
6. The group should be instructed to view differences of opinion as a healthy starting point for their resolution. When persons support differences of this kind with their best thinking and information, the group has the chance to compare one against the other and to arrive at what is usually the approach most likely to succeed. In addition, open discussion of differing viewpoints often draws the opponents closer together. A synergistic solution is likely to occur—one better than any of the differing viewpoints. Individuals and group both benefit from discussions of this kind. Resolution of differences in this fashion will be found helpful rather than dysfunctional in reaching a sound and practicable solution.

Purpose of Individual Behavior

It is often useful for the boss, or manager, to understand the purpose of individual behavior as seen in the group. The member who says something is primarily trying to 1) help get the task of the group accomplished, 2) improve or patch up a relationship among members, or 3) express some personal feeling or goal aside from the group task. The following outline identifies the more common behaviors observable in groups, as suggested by the NTL Institute of Applied Behavioral Science:

Behavior Oriented toward the Group's Task Much behavior within groups focuses on the group's task. Examples of this kind of behavior are:

1. *Initiating:* proposing tasks or goals defining a problem, suggesting a procedure or an idea for solving a problem.
2. *Seeking information or opinions:* requesting facts and seeking relevant information about a concern of the group, asking for expressions of feeling, requesting a statement or estimate, soliciting expressions of value, seeking suggestions and ideas.
3. *Giving information or opinion:* offering facts, providing relevant information about group concern, stating a belief about a matter being considered, giving suggestions or ideas.

4. *Clarifying and elaborating:* interpreting ideas or suggestions, clearing up confusions, defining terms, indicating alternatives and issues before the group.
5. *Summarizing:* pulling together related ideas, restating suggestions after the group has discussed them, offering a decision for the group to accept or reject.
6. *Consensus testing:* asking to see if the group is nearing a decision, sending up a trial balloon to test a possible conclusion.

Behavior Oriented toward the Group's Process The behaviors often observed in the individual's attempts to keep the temper and problem-solving climate of the group at an effective level include the following:

1. *Harmonizing:* attempting to reconcile disagreements, reducing tension, getting people to explore differences.
2. *Gate keeping:* helping to keep communication channels open, facilitating the participation of others, suggesting procedures that permit sharing thoughts.
3. *Encouraging:* being friendly, warm, and responsive to others; indicating by facial expression or remark the acceptance of others' contributions.
4. *Compromising:* offering a compromise when one's idea or status is involved in conflict, admitting error, modifying one's statement in the interest of cohesion or reaching group consensus.
5. *Standard setting and testing:* testing whether the group is satisfied with its procedures, suggesting procedures, pointing out behavioral norms that should be critically examined for their impact on group processes.

Emotional Issues The foregoing issues deal with the group's attempt to work. There are other forces, usually concealed, that tend to be disruptive of group cohesiveness and process—the underground emotional issues that cannot be neglected if the group is to perform at a high level. As the group develops effectiveness, the boss must create conditions that will permit these emotional factors to be dealt with and channeled in the direction of group effort.

The basic emotional issues may be stated as the following problems:

1. *The problem of identity:* Who am I in this group? Where do I fit in? What kind of behavior is acceptable here?
2. *The problem of goals and needs:* What do I want from this group? Can the group's goals be made consistent with my goals? What have I to offer to the group?
3. *The problem of power, control, and influence:* Who will control what we do? How much power or influence do I have?
4. *The problem of intimacy:* How close will we get to each other? How

personal? How much can we trust each other and how can we achieve a greater level of trust?

The behaviors that emerge in response to these problems may be outlined as follows:

1. *Dependency-counterdependency:* leaning on anyone in the group who represents authority; resisting anyone who represents authority.
2. *Fighting and controlling:* asserting personal dominance; attempting to get one's own way regardless of others.
3. *Withdrawing:* removing oneself from the group psychologically in the attempt to remove sources of uncomfortable feelings.
4. *Pairing up:* forming an emotional subgroup by joining forces with one or two others for mutual support.

Although there are other kinds of behavior to be observed in a group, these represent the more usual patterns that can serve as bases for understanding what is going on, and thereby what actions may be taken to improve teamwork for the sake of the business. The enterpriser-owner and the managers can provide the necessary supportive management by increasing their skill in observing and responding appropriately to correct dysfunction and improve effectiveness of the group process.[22]

PROBLEM-SOLVING PROCEDURE

The methodology of organizational development has evolved a generally accepted procedure for solving problems and making decisions. This procedure is based on the concept that in a wide variety of situations superior solutions or decisions are more possible through collaborative effort among group members than if made by the boss alone.[23]

The problem-solving procedure starts with identification of a relevant problem. A relevant problem is one that is impeding achievement in the group or organization; it is significant and has an effect on the situation or issues involved in it. The entrepreneur-owner may see a problem or difficult situation or it may be identified by an individual, perhaps in a group meeting. As the process of organizational development takes hold, it becomes more and more likely that group meetings will bring out relevant problems that need to be solved.

Once the problem (or need for decision) has been singled out, it must be clearly understood so that it can be sharply stated. Too often symptoms are mistaken for problems. And too often we are prone to

[22]The foregoing paragraphs on the behavior of the individual in the group have been adapted from the *Reading Book of the NTL Institute for Applied Behavioral Science*, associated with the National Education Association, Washington, D.C., 1969, pp. 21–23.
[23]Richman and Farmer, *Management and Organizations*, pp. 315–17.

propose solutions before the problem has been clearly defined. We human beings seem to have more answers than we have problems to fit. Once the problem has been carefully outlined and clearly understood, it will usually be found that appropriate answers will suggest themselves. The boss, then will find it sound practice to refrain consciously from trying to find answers, and to restrain others from doing so, until the problem has been accurately defined.

The following steps are recommended for ensuring that premature answers are not proposed and that the problem-solving procedure will be handled effectively. (Specific techniques for use in each step will be suggested later.)

Step 1. Data gathering. The first step in the problem-solving process is that of gathering pertinent data. This may seem obvious, but the implications are highly significant, for it is here that the enterpriser-owner can start the dual role that organizational development can play in the firm.

First, the boss can help the organization learn to understand its own processes and how these affect its performance. By feeding back to the members and sharing perceptions, feelings, and information about the technical aspects of the work, groundwork is laid for self-assessment that removes misconceptions and clears the way for cooperative problem-solving effort.

Second, the enterpriser-owner can stimulate the collaborative process upon which effective problem solving and decision making depends by ensuring that people are involved and share in the data-gathering and feedback process.

The kind of data to be collected will depend upon the problem being studied. Problems may range from the strictly technical to those of the most sensitive relationships between people. The former may cover such diverse subjects as overcoming an unforeseen difficulty in a product development project to deciding on the best way to finance a major expansion of the business. The latter may include situations from improving the quality of information communicated to the boss to resolving a major conflict between two managers. Whatever the problem or situation, a variety of useful techniques for collecting pertinent data are available. The important point in gathering data is to seek it from any who may have information to contribute to the understanding of the situation; it is particularly important to involve those who are intimately concerned with the problem.

Step 2. Diagnosis. The diagnosis of the problem is the second step in the problem-solving process. Here the boss should see that the data are fed back to the members, monitoring the process of outlining the problem clearly and accurately. When the problem has been sharply defined to the satisfaction of the group, the third step may be taken, that of developing a solution.

Step 3. Problem-solving strategy and tactics. In this step, the group works to develop a strategy for solving the problem. Alternative strategies may be proposed and considered. That thought most likely to succeed should be selected by consensus. The group then takes on the task of developing tactics for solving the problem in the form of action plans. Responsibilities are assigned, time for accomplishment agreed upon, and a date set for a meeting to report on progress.

It will be seen that the planning process of MBO neatly fits the management needs of problem solving. The boss plays the role of resource person and coach as required by the situation.

Step 4. Activating the planning. The fourth step requires that the action plans be put into effect. The assignments made in the action-planning meeting are carried out by the members. At the scheduled time the group reconvenes to report on progress in a feedback meeting.

Step 5. Feedback meeting. This meeting is designed to elicit feedback on performance. The group has the opportunity to assess achievement of the plans intended to solve the problem. If there are variances from desired results, the group uses its resources to adjust the plans and change the activities to bring performance to the target level. This evaluation and assessment procedure is repeated as required to achieve the results desired. The boss manages the operation as unobtrusively as possible, but manages it to ensure the outcome and to reinforce the learning that the process can develop for the group members.

DATA-GATHERING TECHNIQUES

Many techniques are available for collecting data. They cover a spectrum from intensely personal to impersonal or anonymous.[24] At the impersonal end is the survey questionnaire. This technique is often used to gather data quickly from a relatively large number of people. Surveys are used to determine such things as attitudes of personnel toward the company, members' perceptions of management style, and satisfiers and dissatisfiers in the work. At the other end of the scale is the intensely personal interview on a one-to-one basis. If the boss is conducting the interview with a manager, the content is likely to include expressions of feeling as well as statements of fact. The interview tends to be much more flexible and much richer in its potential for conveying important data. The boss will need to be skillful enough to observe behavior and draw proper inferences from what is seen and experienced. Fortunately this kind of awareness and responsiveness can be heightened through practice.

---

[24]Margulies and Raia, *Organizational Development: Values, Process, and Technology,* pp. 129-214.

Other measures for gathering data fall between the objective questionnaire and the personal interview. These take various forms from highly structured to quite unstructured. Small businesspersons would seldom have use for the more formal data gathering means. Their relationship with their people is generally close and informal. The personally conducted meeting affords the most logical vehicle for the boss to obtain important information upon which to build organizational competence. Personally conducted meetings can take different forms. Some of the more useful for the enterpriser-owner of the small business are described here.

Interviewing

The most direct way of obtaining data on "what goes on around here," which is the first step in making beneficial change, is the personally conducted interview. This one-to-one interview gives the boss a straightforward means for finding out how people feel and what they think about important issues in the company. Many aspects of organizational functioning may be explored: How the person feels about proposed company policy; difficulties an individual has with a new manufacturing process; problems an employee is experiencing in relationships with peers. In general, personal interviews, when conducted with reasonable skill, can be productive in bringing out opinions and sentiments about almost any subject the owner-executive thinks needs attention.

When conducting the interview, the boss should maintain an objective, nonevaluative attitude, remembering that people see the world differently, that each person constructs a vision of reality through unique perceptions. The boss's objective is to gather as much data as possible about the relevant problem. By being nondirective and nonevaluative the boss increases the possibility of receiving more, and more valid, data.

Several general questions can help interviewees express their opinions. Some examples are the following:

- How are things going in your group?
- Is there any way you see that we could speed things up around here?
- Are there changes you'd like to see that would make the company go better?
- What kinds of steps might we take to improve the quality of our product?
- Do you and your people think you know as much as you'd like about what goes on in the company?

When the boss has gathered data from a sufficient number of representative individuals so that the information required to understand the problem has been acquired, it can be fed back to the group in the problem-solving process described earlier in this chapter.

Sensing

Sensing offers the enterpriser-owner an organized way of identifying relevant problems and discovering needs, concerns, strengths, weaknesses, and other issues that may be important in the management of the company. This method is particularly useful when the company has reached a size such that the boss no longer has intimate contact with personnel.

A sensing meeting is conducted as an open, unstructured group meeting. Members are selected to represent various segments of the organization. They would include personnel from all levels. The size of the group is limited to a small number, usually not more than twelve. With permission from the group, the boss may tape record the proceedings so the discussions can be reviewed carefully to make sure that no important point has been missed. The boss may also wish to review the meeting with key managers. Each attendee must understand the purpose of the meeting; each is informed that the meeting is intended to give management information that will help improve the company's operations. No direct actions that would impinge on the participants will be taken, therefore each attendee should feel able to speak freely. The meeting is to be nonstructured and discussion open and informal. Attendees may ask that the tape recorder be turned off if they do not wish to have their statements recorded.

The boss listens actively most of the time, trying to absorb the data without diverting the conversation, occasionally asking a question, but only for the purpose of clarification. The boss's thoughts and intentions may be interjected if such a contribution would clear up a confusion or point out a direction in which the company should move.

In sensing, the group acts as a sounding board that can provide important data on the state of well-being of the company. Symptoms of organizational dysfunction can be detected. These serve to direct management's attention to problems that may need resolution. Grumbles and metagrumbles, in Maslow's terms, allow the boss and management to identify the kind and seriousness of the issues that the symptoms represent.[25] Understanding that human beings will always complain about something, management would see low-level complaints—those

---

[25]Abraham H. Maslow, *Eupsychian Management*, Homewood, Ill.: Richard D. Irwin and The Dorsey Press, 1965, pp. 236–46.

that deal with basic concerns such as lack of ability to earn enough to meet living expenses, lack of adequate safety devices on the job, or dictatorial managerial procedures—as danger signals showing the poorest kind of management and managerial climate.

High grumbles reflect a much more hygienic climate. These complaints emerge from such happenings as lack of acknowledgment of superior achievement, inequities in pay, and reward being accorded the wrong person. Metagrumbles such as complaints about inefficiency, not getting the last 5 percent of possible performance from a machine the company builds, and not being given comprehensive information about a company situation peripheral to the immediate job—statements issuing from perceptions of imperfection in the surround of the job—concern higher level human needs.

Grumbles indicate the psychological health of the company and the motivational level of the person making the complaint. The owner-enterpriser should view these grumbles as signals identifying areas for improvement in management practices.

In the United States today, one would hardly expect to hear too many low-level grumbles in industry or business. These complaints suggest a cruel or harsh situation, in which the individual can earn scarcely enough to meet the bare necessities of life.

High grumbles might indicate problems about pay practices that are seen as inequitable, lack of respect from a superior, not being heard when making a suggestion, or other complaints centering in the esteem or self-concept needs of the individual.

Metagrumbles indicate a reasonably high level of civilization within the company. They reflect desire for improvement where conditions are already good or excellent. Such complaints seem to flow from the human practice of accepting personal or situational improvement as a normal state once the novelty has worn off and finding some new, albeit minor, flaw to complain about. The important point for the small businessperson to remember is that grumbles are significant feedback data. They add richness to the information being gathered. And they often furnish important clues for clarifying understanding of a problem in the organization.

Feedback to the Group

The organizational development problem-solving process stresses the desirability of feeding back the data to the group from which it was gathered. This feedback is an integral part of the participative-group method of management. It is consistent with the needs of the members of the company to participate, to grow, and to contribute toward the development of organizational effectiveness and competence.

MEETINGS AIMED AT CHANGE

The participative-group method of management necessarily uses meetings of various kinds for its purposes. Several kinds of meetings are designed to bring about desirable change. These include meetings for diagnosing situations where change is desired, planning for change, and instituting change operationally.

Meetings for Diagnosis

The enterpriser-owner usually tends to be so deeply involved in the affairs of the company as to be unaware of serious deficiencies that should be corrected. A wise action to take is to conduct periodic diagnostic team meetings. These meetings focus on the assessment of the effectiveness and competence of the company. They are aimed at uncovering the need for change to make improvement.

The boss picks representatives from the several levels and functions in the company. The purpose is to assure representation on a broad base. The team gathers to consider the health of the organization and to identify specific objectives for beneficial change. When these specific changes have been agreed upon, the team decides on ways of gathering data pertinent to their implementation.

They may decide to use a questionnaire, to engage in personal interviewing, or to use sensing. The team then meets to consider the information produced. The objectives are reviewed and adjusted in accordance with the results of this study of the data. The team develops strategies and tactics for introducing and following up on the changes agreed upon. These include meetings for diagnosing situations where change is desired, planning for change, and instituting change.

Goal-Setting Meetings

Small business owners can take advantage of the resources of their people in addressing organizational problems through goal-setting meetings. The problems dealt with in this manner are generally more immediately pressing than those dealt with in diagnostic meetings. There are many variations of goal-setting meetings, but that outlined here is representative.[26]

The goal-setting meeting usually requires one day of concentrated effort by a relatively large representative group of company members. The objective is to set goals for beneficial change. There are two phases to the meeting: collecting information and setting goals. The boss starts

---

[26]Richard Beckhard, *Organization Development: Strategies and Models*, Reading, Mass.: Addison-Wesley, 1969, pp. 38–40.

by describing the procedure to be followed but does not participate in the proceedings personally, merely guiding and monitoring the process.

Collecting Information The participants are divided into subgroups of five or six. It is often good practice to arrange the subgroups so that subordinates are not together with their immediate superior. The subgroups are instructed to take an hour to collect a list of changes that they believe would be helpful to the company. They may address any aspect of organization they wish: policies and procedures, management style, group relationships, process flow, or any other matter they consider important. A recorder in each group lists the items on a sheet of newsprint. All lists are placed on the wall with masking tape. Each group in turn presents its list to the total assemblage. The boss permits no debate at this time. However, questions for clarification may be asked and answered.

The boss then sorts the items on the several lists into general categories with assistance from the subgroup members. Copies of all lists are prepared, including the list of categories. These are distributed to each participant.

Goal Setting New subgroups are now formed, but managers meet with those regularly reporting to them. Each subgroup then comes to consensus on the following three items:

1. Identification of two or three of the items they think most important; agreement on what action to take and when to start on each.
2. Decision on the priorities that should be set on these items.
3. Plan for communicating the results to the remainder of the firm.

Follow-up The total group then assembles to hear and review the results of the discussions in the subgroups. The boss decides on the priorities for all items presented. The schedule is set for a follow-up meeting, usually four to six weeks later. At the follow-up meeting each group reports on its progress in accomplishing its action plans. The boss's view of the progress made is also reported. Action steps for improving progress or correcting deviation from desired achievement are planned in each group. The next follow-up meeting is scheduled.[27]

Organization Mirror

The organization mirror is a special kind of meeting in which one element or group in the firm can see how it is perceived by other groups.

---

[27]A generalized excellent outline of this procedure will be found in Jack K. Fordyce and Raymond Weil, *Managing with People,* Reading, Mass.: Addison-Wesley, 1971, pp. 93–97.

Members of the firm must have reached a fair level of sophistication in dealing with interpersonal relationships before this kind of meeting can be successful. The impetus for the meeting should come from the group that sees itself as being disregarded or in contention with another group. The enterpriser-owner should be careful to monitor the planning for and conduct of the meeting to ensure that its purpose of improving relations between groups is carried out and that divisive incidents do not worsen an existing situation. The boss has several tasks: preparing the way for the meeting by interviewing key people from the two groups that will be involved; gaining understanding of the general nature of the problem, the key issues that divide the groups; and preparing the members for the meeting.

The boss feeds back the important data gathered in the interviews, having the information summarized on newsprint. Subgroups of six people, three from each group, are then asked to assess the data. They are to identify the half-dozen or so major changes that they see necessary to improve collaboration between the groups. Each group records its list on newsprint.

The lists are placed on the wall where all can see. The total group combines the lists and reduces the findings to one master list, which now shows beneficial changes as perceived and desired by the whole group.

The subgroups then develop goals and action plans for the accomplishment of each change. Personal responsibilities for each activity are assigned, target dates for each achievement agreed upon, and dates for reporting on progress set.

The boss concludes the meeting by reviewing the purposes and achievements of the day and announcing the date of the feedback session. The results of the meeting can be discussed with several people from each group later to discover what their personal reactions are. These data may give the boss information useful in preparing for the feedback meeting.

The organization mirror is a powerful tool for cementing relations between groups that must work together, overcoming deteriorating relationships between groups, correcting misuse of staff group functions, and, in general, improving the quality of transactions across organizational interfaces.

Conflict Resolution

The technique described here is useful for resolving conflict between two people or between two groups. Although many variations are possible, this procedure gives a well–tested and effective approach.

The enterpriser-owner of the small firm, observing civil war between two individuals or two groups, discusses the situation privately with each. The purpose is to get commitment to an attempt to resolve the difficulty; each should therefore be sufficiently receptive to the procedure to permit its healing function to operate.

Each party (or group) is then asked to prepare three lists on newsprint: 1) a list of qualities and behaviors that each values in the other, 2) a list of intensely disliked behaviors that the other exhibits ("bug" list), and 3) a list predicting what the other's lists will contain (empathy list).

Each party in turn presents the lists (a representative presents the lists for a group). The boss stipulates that each is to listen carefully to the other. The only talking permissible is to ask and answer questions to clarify points being made. The objective at this time is for each to gain a clear understanding of what the other is saying.

The parties then discuss and agree upon changes they wish to make in their relationship. The boss facilitates the negotiations if necessary, records actions the parties have agreed upon, and notes unresolved issues that may have to be dealt with later. The parties may then work on action plans to resolve these issues or agree to hold them in abeyance for later resolution. In the last step, the parties set a time for a follow-up meeting to check progress and adjust plans as the circumstances dictate.

The "bug" list procedure here described has proven a simple and effective way for clearing the air between persons or groups in conflict. It should be used only under conditions where the conflict is severe and damaging to the organization. It is not intended for routine problems that can be overcome by the more common coaching and counseling methods good managers generally use.

Team Building

Any of the meetings described in the foregoing pages can have a team-building outcome, but some meetings may be designed specifically to build teamwork. For example, when two newly formed groups must work together it may be desirable to explore the possibilities of the new relationship before actual working operations begin. A meeting for this purpose may take two or three days.

A significant point in the conduct of such meetings is that the groups consider both the feelings and ideas that crop up. Hidden animosities brought out in the open should be faced and talked through. Role relationships should be clarified; candid examination of dysfunctional behavior should be encouraged. But concern for behavioral aspects of group functioning should not interfere with the overall concept of improving the effectiveness of working operations. It is wise, therefore, to focus the purpose of team-building meetings on a substantive issue, such as planning for the joint venture or project or setting major objectives for a period ahead.

A team-building meeting should be based on information gathered well ahead of the meeting date by any suitable means: questionnaires, sensing, or personal or group interviews. The usual procedures are employed for feeding back the data to the total group, having them set the agenda for the meeting, work up goals and action plans, assign responsibilities, and plan for a follow-up meeting. The boss who has gained some skill in these procedures can steer the activities unobtrusively to achieve sound results.

SUMMARY: Organizational Development in the Small Firm

The enterpriser-owner of the small business can develop healthy forces for growth in the company by managing with the methods of organizational development. When used intelligently, these methods support improvement in both technical and interpersonal competence—key capabilities in building an achieving firm.

The company may be considered an open sociotechnical system. Three major subsystems make up the total organization: the administrative, the technical, and the social. Organizational development aims its efforts mostly at the social system. It also works to smooth out any difficulties with the structured aspects of the organization, which involve planning, organizing, staffing, directing, and controlling.

The administrative, technical, and social systems are embedded in a special environment within the open sociotechnical system of the firm. Two regulatory closed systems give the owner means for controlling the growth of the small firm. These are management by objectives (MBO) and the management of managerial resources (MMR). Both are based on the concept that individual growth and teamwork underpin organizational effectiveness and competence.

Organizational development, designed to help the company find newer and better things to do and better ways of doing older things, employs a variety of methods and techniques. These range from ways to identify relevant problems to ways of solving them through individual and group methods.

The entrepreneur managing by the methods of organizational development can gain great power to plan and control the destiny of the organization for the common good of the members and the firm.

SUGGESTED READINGS

French, Wendell L., and Bell, Cecil H., Jr. *Organization Development: Behavioral Science Interventions for Organization Improvement,* Englewood Cliffs, N. J.: Prentice-Hall, 1973.

Gibson, James L.; Ivancevich, John M.; and Donnelly, James H., Jr. *Organizations: Behavior, Structure, Processes,* Dallas, Tex.: Business Publications: 1976, chapters 15, 16.

Golembiewski, R. T. *Men, Management and Morality,* New York: McGraw-Hill, 1965.

Lippitt, G. L. *Organization Renewal,* New York: Appleton-Century-Crofts, 1969.

Margulies, Newton, and Wallace, John. *Organizational Change,* Glenview, Ill.: Scott, Foresman & Co., 1973.

Maslow, Abraham, *Eupsychian Management,* Homewood, Ill.: Richard D. Irwin, 1964.

Rush, Harold M. F. *Organization Development: A Reconnaissance, Research Report.* New York: The Conference Board, No. 605, 1973.

Vaill, Peter B. *The Practice of Organization Development.* Madison, Wis.: American Society for Training and Development, 1971.

Wexley, Kenneth N., and Yukl, Gary A. *Organizational Behavior and Personnel Psychology.* Homewood, Ill.: Richard D. Irwin, 1977, chapter 15.

Afterword: The Future of Small Business

There can be little doubt that there is increasing interest in owning one's own small business. That men and women of all ages are intrigued by this idea is shown by the steadily increasing enrollment in courses and seminars aimed at teaching people how to start and how to manage a small business.

Increased interest in small business courses in colleges and graduate schools seems to have its roots in the student turmoil of the sixties. In the seventies students have seen the image of the large corporation dulled by ethical scandals and by socially irresponsible activities. Young people have been stimulated to re-examine their values—and many have chosen to carve out their own destiny in their own fashion.

Women show an increasing interest in starting and running their own business and for the first time have the opportunity to do so. Reports from continuing education programs for adults from universities across the country state that the attendance by women has risen from 10 percent to 40 percent in the five-year period from 1972 to 1977. And the typical audience in seminars on small business is no longer dominated by men in their early and mid-thirties. Participants are men and women of all ages, of all colors, and from a great variety of backgrounds.

FACTORS INFLUENCING THE GROWTH OF SMALL BUSINESS

Any attempt to predict a sound future for small business in the United States must start with the assumption that there will be reasonable stability in the economy. Inherent in this assumption is the belief that federal policy will be such as to support steadiness in the economy.

The federal government, through the activities of the Small Business

Administration, and several state governments now aid small business by making funds available and by numerous assistance programs.

Several major forces in the environment will surely affect the growth of small business in the United States. These are briefly outlined below.

Growing Population

The total market for goods and services grows with increase in population. Although increase in population in the United States has slowed since the decades immediately following World War II, the country is still experiencing a growth rate of about 1.5 percent per year. There are increasing numbers of young and old, and a stationary segment of the population in the prime working years between 35 and 55. The need for goods and services is therefore increasing as the population grows.

Increase in Educational Level

A significant increase in the level of education has occurred. More young people have more years of schooling since World War II than ever before. For example, the proportion of twenty to twenty-four year olds enrolled in schools increased from 13 to 17 percent between 1960 and 1964.[1] This trend has continued to the present. Therefore, in comparison with past years, many more people are better equipped for entrepreneurship and management.

Desire for Personalized Service

Large company operations have become remarkably depersonalized with the advent of automation and computerization. This arms-length relationship with the customer has created an opportunity for the small business that can offer intensely personal service. By building a warm relationship with customers small business owners can capture a segment of the market represented by customers who value the personal touch. These people will often go miles out of their way to deal with a retail store or other business whose personnel know them and their wants and treat them considerately.

Impact of Technology

One of the great forces that augurs well for the future of small business comes from the impact of technological change. Technological change is

---

[1]Edward D. Hollander, *The Future of Small Business*, New York: Frederick A. Praeger, 1967, chapter 10.

everywhere. Every scientific advance sooner or later spins off opportunity for small business. Kenneth Boulding has suggested that American industry may be likened to a huge pyramid, supported at the bottom by enormous round boulders, representing the largest corporations.[2] Succeeding layers are formed by boulders of decreasing size, to the top, representing smaller and smaller companies as the peak is approached. In the interstices between boulders are smaller rocks, pebbles, and even grains of sand; these may be thought of as smaller companies, down to the one-person operation represented by the single grain of sand.

Mammoth corporations are surrounded by a host of medium- and smaller-sized companies—down to the one-person outfit—that prosper and survive. The mammoths create markets for the midgets and very often the relationship is reciprocal. Small companies frequently create new products or services that are acquired by the large company and produced commercially.

As technology advances, companies of all sizes are involved in new opportunities. Small business can take advantage of opportunities that arise within the fields of their special competencies. A quick glance at areas that offer these opportunities for exploration indicates the enormous scope available to small business in the immediate future.

Areas of Opportunity

Many broad areas present an enormous variety of opportunities for creativity and innovation in small business.[3] A few examples are given in the list that follows.

- *Health and medicine.* Possibilities here range from the development of a nuclear-powered artificial heart to a hoverbed for supporting a patient suffering from burns on a cushion of air.
- *Power and energy.* Here ideas vary from the use of superflywheels for powering electric automobiles to the development of simple solar-powered cooking devices. In a series of articles in *The New Yorker*, Barry Commoner explores the usual sources of energy and points out the deficiencies associated with them.[4] He concludes that the most likely—and most desirable—source of energy in the immediate future is solar, with its universal availability and lack of pollution.

---

[2]Kenneth Boulding, "The Jungle of Hugeness," *The Saturday Review*, March 1, 1958.
[3]Stephen Rosen, *Future Facts*, New York: Simon and Schuster, 1976. In this fascinating book, Dr. Rosen, a research scientist, explores products, services, processes, and ideas that appear imminently practicable or are likely to be developed in the not-too-far future. Some of the ideas presented here are drawn from this source.
[4]Barry Commoner, "Energy I, II, III," *The New Yorker*, February 2, February 7, February 16, 1976.

- *Foods and crops.* The possibilities in this field cover a broad spectrum from developing nonhazardous food additives to storing foods for long periods under both cold temperature and pressure. Other ideas are, for example, for disposable, internally heated, double-walled cups capable of warming soup instantly—or an internally chilled cup that will cool the contents. Both are possible through chemical or physical reactions, and both seem economically feasible.
- *Business and work.* Improving productivity offers untold opportunity for the small business that concentrates in some portion of this field. The problems of productivity cut across all kinds of industry, organizations, and operations. Problems range from joining two pieces of metal together to improving the speed and effectiveness of response of government agencies to the needs of the public.
- *Play and pastime.* The trend of the times is toward experiential activities. Playing tennis and golf, skiing, backpacking, scuba diving, surfing, hang gliding, and bicycling are the order of the day. Play and pastime offer a great variety of possibilities for new products and services. Products might range from a tiny underwater personal propulsion device to an inflatable backpacking tent. Opportunities for innovation in products that people can use for active enjoyment of leisure are seemingly unlimited.
- *Environment.* Here, too, are unlimited opportunities for the creative entrepreneur. Ideas for future products range from converting waste products to use—for example, developing improved ways of collecting methane generated by decaying garbage—to ways of purifying water through practical ozone devices.

ENTREPRENEURIAL APPROACH TO SMALL BUSINESS

The importance of the unique, useful, and consumer-attracting product was stressed in the beginning of this book. But unique products or services come only from innovation. Many authorities have expressed the importance of innovation in business. Peter Drucker has put it well in the following words:

> But innovation is more than a new method. It is a new view of the universe, as one of risk rather than one of chance or of certainty. It is a new view of man's role in the universe; he creates order by taking risks. And this means that innovation, rather than being an assertion of human power, is an acceptance of human responsibility.[5]

Prospective entrepreneurs can, in the light of the prospects briefly

---

[5]Peter F. Drucker, *Landmarks of Tomorrow*, New York: Harper & Row, 1959, p. 19.

outlined here, face the future with the conviction that there is a place for them in it. What they will have to do first to succeed is to adopt an entrepreneurial approach to management. They will scan the environment for its risks and opportunities and will find needs that can be converted into wants. They will make rational choices among risks and opportunities. And they will convert the opportunities into desirable products or services. In short, they will accept their human responsibility, and they will launch and run successful businesses through the practice of sound management.

PART III

CASES IN ENTREPRENEURSHIP AND SMALL BUSINESS MANAGEMENT

The cases in Part III focus on an array of difficulties encountered when starting a new enterprise and on a variety of problems with which managers of small firms may have to cope. Each case describes a complex set of issues that require careful analysis. All cases are drawn from real life and although in several cases names and locations have been changed, the disguise has not altered the essential issues.

The cases are intended to stimulate thinking and discussion of fundamental problems common to starting and running a business.

SKI-KIT, INC. (A), (B), (C)

SKI-KIT, INC. (A)

SKI-KIT, Inc., a California corporation, was founded in August of 1974 to market SKI-KIT luggage. Prior to its incorporation, SKI-KIT, Inc. had been a "dba" and a partnership during the market research and product development stages.

SKI-KIT luggage was invented by Mr. Fred McAlister who, not only as a skier but also as a concerned airline pilot, recognized the need for total in-transit ski equipment protection and convenience. He perceived that the luggage (Exhibit A) should be made of lightweight molded plastic or aluminum, use the skis as a reinforcing frame, be large enough to pack skis, boots, clothing and accessories, and be versatile enough to pack other sporting goods when not used for ski equipment. Three years previously Mr. McAlister had applied for a patent, built several prototypes and, on a limited basis, personally conducted some market research. He then realized SKI-KIT luggage would have to be produced either in high volume or in a very limited, garage-type operation. In April of 1973, Mr. McAlister contracted with DYNO Enterprises, a market and product development consulting firm, to determine the market potential and the best approach to pursue.

BUSINESS FEASIBILITY STUDY

DYNO Enterprises was essentially a two-man firm consisting of Mr. Joe Ciarica, President, and Mr. Bob Wilhelm, associate consultant and MBA candidate in the University of Southern California Business Development and Entrepreneurship Program.

Over the next 5 months they proposed to investigate all aspects of the product, the ski industry, and the ski market. A business feasibility study would then be developed to analyze the market, and the technical and financial potential of SKI-KIT luggage. This would determine the need for the product, its ability to satisfy the need, and the sales volume at which it would be profitable. If the results proved acceptable, a business plan would be implemented.

Prepared by Robert F. Williams under the direction of Hans Schollhammer and Arthur H. Kuriloff.

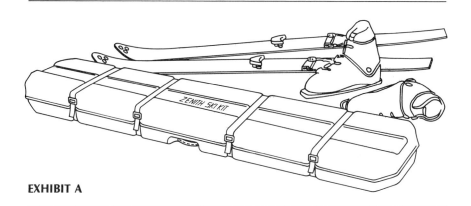

EXHIBIT A

DYNO Enterprises decided that a questionnaire to 3,000 United States Ski Association members would provide the necessary information on skiers' interest in the concept. An additional 500 people including ski industry executives, retailers, ski officials, distributors, competitors, travel agents, ski resort managers, ski magazine personnel, and other skiers would be contacted.

Experiencing a return of 23% of the questionnaires, the partners tabulated the following results:

Skiers acceptance of SKI-KIT
1. 79% of the skiers who responded were in favor of SKI-KIT and its one-piece durability.

Skiers dissatisfaction with current protective coverings
2. 80% of the skiers desired improved luggage equipment.
3. Nearly 85% of the skiers indicated dissatisfaction with the ski protection techniques employed by commercial carriers.

Ski equipment damage
4. Ski damage was experienced by 40% of those surveyed. Automobile and airplane travel cause most of the beyond-repair damage to skis.
5. Bus and train travel cause almost as much damage as the airlines but not as severe as the beyond-repair category.

Present protective covering
6. Of those skiers suffering ski damage, 70% owned some kind of protective covering; the majority of these were vinyl bags.

Another important result indicated how much a skier was willing to pay for SKI-KIT luggage. The percentage breakdown was as follows:

$ Price Range	Percentage
50–65	58
66–81	20
82–97	8
98–113	2
greater than 114	1
no reply	11
	100

Realizing that SKI-KIT was a new concept, and initially limited low volume production would require a higher selling price than desired in the long run, Ciarica and Wilhelm were satisfied with the 11% acceptance in the $82 and up categories. Their marketing strategy was now coming into focus. They believed that the serious, affluent skier would buy it at the initially high selling price. Then, by exposure, word-of-mouth, and a lower price through high volume production, SKI-KIT would be purchased by the occasional recreational skier who represented the mass market.

Desirable Features

Analysis of the questionnaires showed that the respondents thought durability the most important SKI-KIT feature, followed by transit protection, equipment safety, lightweight, hard-covered, convenience (one-piece), protective lock, slimline design, ability to satisfy airline requirements, and compact storage (off season).

SKI INDUSTRY

After investigation of the industry using information from Ski Industries America (SIA, the Ski Industry's trade association), *Ski* magazine and *Skiing* magazine, DYNO compiled the following information:

The retail trade sales volume in skis was expected to grow from $405 million during the 1972–73 ski season to $1,070 million during the 1979–80 ski season.[1] This represented an average annual growth rate of approximately 13%.

A 1972–73 *Ski* magazine survey showed that well over half the skiers surveyed had purchased new ski equipment: 61% bought skis, 59% bought boots, 78% bought ski clothing, and 71% bought other new equipment. This "other new equipment" (which would be SKI-KIT's classification) comprised 46% bindings, 38% poles, 18% car ski racks and 37% goggles.

Of those skiers responding to the SKI-KIT questionnaire, 58% valued their equipment at $500–$1,000; 20% at $1,000–$1,500; 7% at $1,500–$2,000; 4% at greater than $2,500. There was no correlation between the value of the skiers' equipment and their interest in buying SKI-KIT luggage.

According to an executive of SIA, the total amount spent on ski equipment (equipment, travel, lodging, etc.) for the 1972–73 ski season was $1.74 billion and would increase an average of 13.3% through the 1979–80 ski season to $4.65 billion.

Checking channels of distribution, DYNO discovered approximately 180–200 ski equipment distributors. Less than 10% had sales in the multi-million dollar category, approximately 75% were in the $600,000–$1.5 million category, and the balance had sales of $500,000 or less. The major national and regional distributors operate on a 33–35% gross margin; a national sales force with administrative facilities but not buying and stocking merchandise operates on a 20–25% gross margin; and independent representatives on a regional basis operate on a 6–15% gross margin depending on the product. Retail shops expect a 35–50% gross margin depending on the merchandise.

---

[1]Mr. Doc Des Roches, Executive Vice President, Ski Industries of America.

Ciarica and Wilhelm found from a *Ski* magazine survey that skiers purchase their equipment at the following retail outlets:

Retail Outlet	Percent
Ski shop	70
Sporting goods store	26
Department store	7
Discount store	2
Mail order	1
Other	4
	110*

Of the almost 6,000 retailers selling ski equipment, approximately 80% are specialty ski shops.

On the basis of this industry information, DYNO concluded that with industry and retail sales growing at an average annual rate of 13% and with a high percentage of skiers making yearly purchases, the potential of SKI-KIT looked bright. The data pointed to the desirability of focusing sales on the specialty ski shop. This would require a sales force capable of contacting specialty ski shops successfully.

Ski Market

According to a 1970 *Ski* magazine survey, the demographic data for a typical skier are the following: skiers' average income was $21,113; skiers' average age was 29.5 years. Approximately 3 times as many men as women ski. 50% of the men were single and 50% were heads of household. The occupational status breakdown showed skiers were: 33% professionals; 12% proprietors and managers; 18% clericals and sales personnel; 12% craftspeople and supervisors; and 25% in a variety of work.

Not only is the ski market an affluent one but it is also very close knit. According to *Skiing* magazine,

The serious skier is the hub around which the entire skiing market revolves. The serious skier sets the trends which others follow. Their influence is felt not only in the sale of skiing clothing and equipment. . . . Word-of-mouth influence is the crucial factor for the successful movement of goods in the ski market. Skiers participate in the sport in a very concentrated area. From the time they leave their home to the actual skiing and staying in a ski location, they are in constant communication and association with each other.
Sell the serious skier and you win the best customer there is for everything skiers use. More importantly, you gain the skiing markets best "salesman" . . . using and recommending the products he knows and believes in, as others emulate his example and follow advice.

*Exceeds 100% because of multiple answers.

According to an SIA executive, growth of the ski population may be shown and projected as follows:

Year	Hard-Core, Serious Skier[1]	Percentage Increase	Occasional Skier[2]	Percentage Increase
1970–71	3,273,700 +	9.75	2,119,200 +	9.75
1971–72	3,633,900 +	9.90	2,352,300 +	9.50
1972–73	4,033,600 +	10.20	2,611,000 +	9.80
1973–74	4,477,300 +	10.00	2,898,200 +	12.25
1974–75	4,969,800 +	9.75	3,217,000 +	7.50
1975–76	5,515,500 +	9.50	3,570,900 +	9.50
1976–77	6,123,200 +	9.75	3,963,700 +	9.80
1977–78	6,796,700 +	9.80	4,399,700 +	10.00
1978–79	7,544,400 +	9.80	4,883,700 +	9.75
1979–80	8,374,300 +	10.00	5,420,900 +	9.50

On the basis of information from a 1970–71 survey of 1,000 skiers by *Skiing* magazine, DYNO discovered that on a relative scale, 15% of the skiers traveled to Europe, 55% to other states outside their home state, and 30% traveled to Canada. DYNO further determined that 15% travel by airline, 4% by train, 16% by bus, and 67% by automobile.

Interestingly, ski trip duration varied as between DYNO's questionnaire results and *Ski* magazine's survey of 1971–72. DYNO's percentage breakdown was:

Duration	Percent
1 day	16
2 days	35
3–5 days	30
6–7 days	10
greater than 7 days	12
	103*

Ski magazine's survey showed far greater emphasis on one- and two-week vacations. In any event, skiers would be carrying a considerable amount of equipment and luggage awkwardly, and SKI-KIT luggage would quite easily eliminate the need of all other baggage.

Several other important marketing aspects DYNO considered were the retail and consumer buying cycles and the accounts receivable policy. *The Sporting Goods Dealer* magazine indicated that the majority of sales to retailers were in March, April, and December. March and April were important because of the

---

[1]Those who ski 12 or more days per year.
[2]Those who ski fewer than 12 days per year, but visit ski areas and purchase clothing and equipment.
Note: The two groups are considered independent markets by the industry; estimates as of September 17, 1970.
*Exceeds 100% because of multiple answers.

trade shows and December because of Christmas and the peak of the ski season. The consumer buying cycle followed the ski season with December being the most important month followed by November, October, January, and February. SKI-KIT luggage would therefore expect its strongest sales commencing in October and increasing through December, then tapering off in January to practically nothing during the summer months.

From various ski manufacturers and distributors, it was found that accounts receivable were dated December 10th. However, the majority of revenue did not come in until January, February, and March. This meant that a manufacturer or distributor wrote orders at the March and April shows, produced an inventory against these orders, and shipped the merchandise in late August through September. The manufacturer thus had to carry the receivables from date of shipment for several months—sometimes to March. This was not viewed favorably by DYNO but there appeared to be little alternative other than to sell to financially sound retailers, keep close watch on accounts receivable, and offer favorable cash discounts to entice early payment.

One of the most important aspects of DYNO's feasibility study was the analysis of the competition. DYNO divided the competition into two categories: indirect and direct. The indirect competition consisted of airline cardboard cartons or plastic bags, and vinyl or canvas bags. Since the airlines discontinued using cardboard boxes because of the expense, and the plastic bags offered no protection at all, as DYNO's questionnaire had indicated, competition from the airlines appeared to be no problem.

The sales of vinyl and canvas bags over the past couple of years had increased tremendously, pointing out the trend to cover and protect ski equipment. The industry retail sales for these bags were approximately $4 million in 1972 with the average retail price for a ski bag at $12 to $15, boot bag at $10 to $12, and a carry-all bag at $10 to $20. Therefore, the total price for all bags was approximately $32 to $47 not including a car rack, which was also needed. These bags, according to the DYNO questionnaire, offered little protection and no convenience.

A thorough search within the industry for direct competition showed that there had been seven previous attempts at hard-shelled luggage. They consisted of two imported models, several homemade models, and the attempt of a major U.S. ski manufacturer. None of these units were now on the market. The viewpoint of the ski executives interviewed was that a need might exist, but the market potential was too small for them to pursue. Most individuals who had made their own units still believed in the concept. Previous attempts had many things in common but not the advantages of SKI-KIT luggage. The most important deficiencies compared with SKI-KIT included:

1. Carried skis and poles only
2. No patented feature
3. No research directed towards consumer demand
4. No market plan
5. Poorly designed

Ciarica and Wilhelm concluded that the primary advertising and promotion thrust should be geared to the skier, who would in turn create a consumer demand at the retailer level.

TECHNICAL PRODUCTION AND PRODUCT DESIGN FEASIBILITY

On the basis of information gathered, DYNO believed that SKI-KIT would be purchased by the serious and affluent skiers for the first couple of years. At low volume production, the cost versus performance difference between aluminum and plastic appeared insignificant. Aluminum was considered to be more prestigious. (According to DYNO's questionnaire, the three most important SKI-KIT features—durability, transit safety, and equipment safety—also pointed to aluminum.) Therefore, DYNO concluded that SKI-KIT should be produced out of aluminum for the first two years. In the second year a plastic SKI-KIT should be introduced to the mass ski market. This would allow time to investigate the many different kinds of plastic processes.

With this in mind, DYNO surveyed 24 plastic and metal fabricators in Southern California. This effort revealed 15 different candidate materials and processes for SKI-KIT construction. These processes had a variety of cost/performance trade-offs (Exhibit B).

SKI-KIT could be tooled for production in aluminum in the range of $3,000 (extrusion) to $30,000 (cold forming); in plastic for as little as $2,000 to $30,000 (FRP, foam molding, extrusion) to $15,000 to $25,000 (thermoforming, air molding, rotational molding, or structural foam molding); or as high as $50,000 to $95,000 (injection molding). The per unit cost varied from $10 to $15 (injection molding) to $40 to $45 (thermoforming).

It was clear to the DYNO partners that the selection of optimum manufacturing technique depended on market strategy. Therefore, the most practicable approach would be to select initially the manufacturing process that offered the most flexibility and the least start-up costs with no attendant sacrifices in quality. Choice of initial process appeared to be open as several product design firms stated the patent would be easy to adapt to metal or plastic.

Taking all this into account, DYNO formulated a business plan—a step-by-step process on how to launch what appeared to be a potentially successful venture.

BUSINESS PLAN

Marketing Strategy

DYNO believed that the marketing strategy should be heavily weighted towards the skier, but major sales effort to retail outlets by a sales force should be launched at the same time.

During the feasibility study DYNO had sent letters to the major airlines. It had received positive responses from most of the airlines, expressing an interest in the DYNO questionnaire and SKI-KIT luggage. DYNO believed that a leasing program could be developed in which SKI-KITs would be leased or sold to the airlines, which would provide SKI-KITs for their passenger skiers. The distribution points would be at ski shops or travel agencies.

Other areas of strategy would be in promotion. The first phase would be extensive use of free promotion through the major ski and related publications. Over 100 U.S. ski writers would be contacted. The releases would consist of the typical product release and also editorials analyzing the results of the SKI-KIT questionnaire. This free publicity would indirectly stimulate demand.

DYNO believed the most direct way to expose SKI-KIT was to give presentations at ski clubs. In Southern California alone there were over 11,000 members in 67 United States Ski Association clubs. A representative from each club could solicit orders and submit them to retailers. This concept would be developed in all nine regions across the United States.

National trade shows in Las Vegas and Boston, and regional shows would be attended and orders taken. Primary emphasis would be placed on those regional shows where maximum results could be realized. There were a number of other shows geared toward professional skiers and ski patrolmen, which would also be attended.

A limited number of SKI-KIT packs would be made available as gifts and donations. They would be given to the most influential people in the industry and used as prizes at the consumer ski shows.

Paid advertising would be limited to the several major ski consumer and trade publications. Cooperative advertising with original equipment manufacturers and major retail shops, and other important purchasers would be used extensively to get maximum exposure at least cost, and to gain recognition by association with known products and retailers in the industry.

DYNO next laid out a time schedule of major events to be accomplished each quarter for the following year-and-a-half.

4th Quarter 1973—October–December
1. Conclude business arrangement for necessary financing and manufacturing
2. Contact airlines for leasing program
3. Schedule presentations to ski clubs
4. Send out new product releases
5. Produce brochure
6. Design metal SKI-KIT
7. Apply for foreign patents

1st Quarter 1974
1. Finalize details for airline leasing program
2. Conclude arrangements with a distributor
3. Prepare for and attend SIA trade show in Las Vegas
4. Fabricate metal prototypes
5. Commence tooling for full production of metal SKI-KIT
6. Contact suppliers for material requirements
7. Initiate limited production scheduling

2nd Quarter 1974
1. Implement mechanics of commercial carrier arrangement
2. Attend regional ski shows
3. Make presentations to ski clubs in key cities
4. Commence designing plastic SKI-KIT
5. Initiate full production for metal SKI-KIT
6. Conclude all foreign licensing programs
7. Schedule cooperative advertising programs

3rd Quarter 1974
1. Finalize plastic design
2. Execute foreign licensing program
3. Fabricate metal SKI-KIT according to sales schedule
4. Implement cooperative advertising programs

EXHIBIT B—SKI-KIT, Inc. (A) Comparative Manufacturing Economics

Process	Material	Estimated per Unit Costs (total assembly)	Estimated Tooling Costs	Estimated Production Facility Costs	Advantages	Disadvantages
Thermoforming	ABS	$30–$40	$5,000/mold	$100,000–$150,000	Durable, lightweight; flexible operation	Expensive per unit costs; poor full production expenses
	HDPE	$25–$30	$20,000 total	$100,000–$150,000	Good initial production	Less expensive than ABS but high for PE
Profile extrusion	Vinyl	$25–$30	$2,000–$5,000	$0.5–$1 million	Good structural design	Weight increase; labor intensifies with considerable part assembly
	ABS or HDPE	$30–$35	$2,000–$5,000	$0.5–$1 million	Low start-up costs	
	Aluminum	$30–$40	$1,000–$3,000	$1 million	Good flexibility to operations	
Injection molding	ABS	$13–$20	$60,000–$100,000	$0.6–$1 million	Highest quality plastic process & material; low unit cost	High tooling costs; high volume
	PE or PP	$10–$15			High quality; inexpensive; durable; lightweight	High tooling costs; high minimum volume
Blow molding	PE or PP ABS	$15–$20 $18–$25	$15,000–$25,000	$0.5–$1 million	Air mold modification of blow mold provides good volume economies and excellent	Conventional blow molding has major technical difficulties with quality; surface detail fair

Process	Material					
Rotational molding	PE or PP ABS	$17–$24	$8,000–$15,000	$0.5–$1 million	Inexpensive per unit and tooling costs; good flexibility in process for limited production quantity	Serious weight penalty of up to 7% weight increase; wall thickness required greater for quality; fair surface detail
Structural plastic foam molding	Open-cost ABS	$13–$20	$3,000–$5,000 Total $12,000–$20,000	$20,000–$50,000	Cheap start-up costs; fair quality surface expected	Questionable structural integrity; extensive tests required; weight penalty expected
VCC	N2 Pressure PE	$14–$18	$10,000–$15,000 (Total)	VCC license + $0.5–$1 million	Poor quality surface; low volume economics; durable container	Up to 70% weight penalty; surface finished required
Fiber reinforced plastic	Fiberglas + polyester or epoxy	$17–$30	$3,000–$6,000 Total $15,000–$25,000	$20,000–$40,000	Lightweight; flexible operations; low start-up costs	Labor intensifies; high costs for good surfaces
Cold forming	6063 aluminum	$25–$45	$20,000–$35,000	$0.5–$1 million	Readily coatable surface for better inventory flexibility; durable, high prestige unit	High percentage costs; mass market acceptance for metal limited

4th Quarter 1974
1. Make presentations to ski clubs
2. Publicize plastic SKI-KIT to all news media
3. Prepare full plastic production
4. Continue cooperative advertising programs

1st Quarter 1975
1. Organize a cooperative program between ski clubs and ski shops
2. Prepare for and attend trade shows with new plastic product design
3. Complete tooling and material arrangements for full production of plastic SKI-KIT

2nd Quarter 1975
1. Update previous SKI-KIT operations for future implementation

Financial Projections

DYNO utilized their questionnaire results and the SIA ski population projections to calculate SKI-KIT sales projections. The formula used was the following:

23% return on questionnaire × 79% who stated they were in favor of the
SKI–KIT concept × number of hard-core serious skiers and
occasional skiers will give the potential SKI-KIT market.

This total was then multiplied by a reasonable market share percentage for varying degrees of success (see table footnotes 3, 4, and 5).

CALCULATIONS FOR SALES PROJECTIONS

Year	Hard-Core Serious and Occasional Skiers[1]	Potential SKI-KIT Market[2]	SKI-KIT Units		
			Most Pessimistic[3]	Most Probable[4]	Most Optimistic[5]
1973–74	4,500,000	818,000	3,000	4,000	6,000
1974–75	5,000,000	908,000	9,000	21,500	26,500
1975–76	5,500,000	999,000	15,000	50,000	93,000
1976–77	10,100,000	1,835,000	36,000	68,000	110,000
1977–78	11,200,000	2,035,000	40,000	78,000	120,000
1978–79	12,400,000	2,253,000	50,000	90,000	145,000
1979–80	13,800,000	2,507,000	40,000	90,000	150,000
1983–84	18,400,000	3,343,000	40,000	90,000	150,000

[1]The number of hard-core serious skiers is indicated as the total for the years 1973 through 1976 ski season (first 3 years). The remaining years include both serious and occasional skier population.
[2]See calculation formula.
[3]Depending on the year, the most pessimistic estimates are based on a market share of 0.4% to 2.2% of total SKI-KIT potential and less than 0.5% of the total ski population.
[4]Depending on the year, the most probable estimates are based on a market share of 0.5% to 5% of total SKI-KIT potential and less than 0.5% of total ski population.
[5]Depending on the year, the most optimistic estimates are based on a market share of 8.7% to 9.3% of total SKI-KIT potential and less than 2.0% of total ski population.

Dyno believed that the most probable business analysis (Exhibit C) would be the most likely to occur.

DYNO's basic thought about the metal/plastic ratio was that the commercial carriers would probably be more inclined to use the plastic version for its overall durability while the skiing public would lean toward the metal fabrication. Leasing arrangements with the airlines and ski retail shops were figured at $5 per usage for both metal and plastic units. The usable life of each leased unit was considered to be one year.

Year	Lease Price	Number Leased	Usage per Unit per Year	Leased Units (metal)	Leased Units (plastic)
1974	$5	1,200	10	1,000	200
1975	5	6,500	15	2,500	4,000
1976	5	10,000	20	4,000	6,000
1977	5	14,000	24	6,000	8,000
1978	5	18,000	30	8,000	10,000
1979 & on	5	20,000	30	8,000	12,000

DYNO used the following cash analysis to determine the overall profitability of a leasing arrangement in which the SKI-KIT luggage principal would be the lessor. However, they decided that the leasing program should be financed by an independent agency at a 20% rate, which would include all administrative duties associated with the leasing operations.

	1974	1975	1976	1977	1978	1979 & on
Total leased units	1,200	6,500	10,000	14,000	18,000	20,000
Cost of goods sold	$64,000	$265,000	$ 280,000	$ 370,000	$ 480,000	$ 520,000
Leasing costs	15,000	100,000	200,000	350,000	500,000	600,000
Total costs	79,000	365,000	480,000	720,000	980,000	1,120,000
Total revenues	60,000	487,500	1,000,000	1,680,000	2,500,000	3,000,000

The cost of goods sold schedule below outlined the direct manufacturing costs. The initial costs of $45 in plastic and $55 in metal should reduce to $18 in plastic and $35 in metal in larger volume runs.

	1974		1975		1976	
	Unit Cost	Total Cost	Unit Cost	Total Cost	Unit Cost	Total Cost
Metal	$55	$192,500	$50	$450,000	$40	$800,000
Plastic	45	22,500	35	437,500	20	600,000
Total costs		215,000		887,500		1,400,000

	1977		1978		1979 & on	
	Unit Cost	Total Cost	Unit Cost	Total Cost	Unit Cost	Total Cost
Metal	$35	$1,050,000	$35	$1,155,000	$35	$1,330,000
Plastic	20	760,000	20	900,000	18	936,000
Total costs		1,810,000		2,055,000		2,266,000

DYNO figured the marketing costs (commissions) to independent representatives would be 10% for the first 2 years and 7% thereafter. The retail outlet
gross margin would be on the basis of a 35% markup. However, to be on the
conservative side, an additional 20% commission expense was allowed for, to
be split among the distributor/sales representatives and/or retail outlets.

The most probable case showed mass SKI-KIT acceptance by the third year
(1976). DYNO's rationale was that the plastic units would be more popular,
particularly for the leasing arrangements. Also, the lowest possible sales price
of $80 in plastic and $140 in metal would be achieved in that year.

The Pro Forma Cash Flow and Business Planning Schedule (Exhibits C and D
respectively) showed that between $400,000 and $500,000 would be required
over a 2½ year period to finance SKI-KIT adequately. The overall breakeven
point would occur at about the third year of operation. The overall long-term
profitability (greater than 5 years) showed a pretax profit/sales ratio of
10%–25%.

DYNO concluded the most probable case represented a realistic analysis of
the SKI-KIT operation. The three-year mass market acceptance was considered
conservative in view of the impulsive buying characteristic of the ski market.
Also, the 5% maximum SKI-KIT market penetration and the overall 0.5% or less
total ski market penetration were considered well within realistic probabilities.

DYNO then used the information from a ski magazine survey to determine
where the highest concentration of serious skiers was. This identified the
primary revenue-producing regions in which to concentrate their sales effort.

Area	Percentage
Alaska and Southern states	1
Northern states	1
Rocky Mountain states	3
Pacific Northwest	4
Central	10
Intermountain	12
Far West	22
Eastern	48
	100

With the 200-page Business Plan complete, DYNO was ready to make presentations to raise capital or to find a manufacturer to provide working capital
and to produce SKI-KIT. DYNO projected that at least $250,000 would be
needed for initial start-up cost and working capital during the first ski season.

This would carry the project to the second quarter of 1974, at which time a "go/no go" decision would be made on the basis of actual sales and market acceptance. If the decision were a "go," then an additional $150,000 to $250,000 would be required.

FINDING CAPITAL/MANUFACTURER

In the fall of 1973, DYNO ran an advertisement in the "Business Opportunities" section of the *Wall Street Journal*, which read:

> Recently completed nationwide market test by outside firm demonstrated over 79% market need and acceptance for new plastic and/or metal ski luggage product. Designed to contain all necessary ski equipment in one piece, lightweight luggage eliminating multiple luggage pieces and assured durable protection and convenience. U.S. patent issuing within month; now filing foreign patents. Seeking business arrangements regarding commercialization or patent sale. Complete thorough business development feasibility study available to principals only.

DYNO received twelve inquiries from this advertisement, mostly from business brokers. One inquiry was from a major leisure-time company. However, none proved fruitful. At the same time, DYNO was giving presentations to Southern California corporations with the capabilities of financing and producing SKI-KIT luggage. Finally, in October, a licensing agreement with Zenith Manufacturing Co., Inc.—a well-known Southern California specialized aluminum container producer for military, industrial, and consumer products—seemed certain. Zenith's only concern was how SKI-KITs they manufactured would be distributed.

DYNO presented three alternatives, each one showing a different means of distribution, profit, and market participation. The choices were: use a national distributor, use a regional distributor, or develop an independent sales force. A national distributor was the safest but least profitable because Zenith would be acting almost as a contract manufacturer, receiving a manufacturing profit only. On the other hand, using independent representatives was the most profitable but riskiest because it meant producing SKI-KITs without any assurance of selling the inventory. Developing an independent sales force appeared too difficult and time consuming to be worth the effort. Zenith elected to go with an intermediate plan: use regional distributors and participate in both manufacturing and marketing profits. DYNO was retained to coordinate the marketing operation.

Zenith acquired exclusive manufacturing and marketing rights under a licensing agreement. They agreed to pay a 5% royalty to Mr. McAlister, the inventor, throughout the life of the contract.

Zenith also agreed to pay the product design expense, to produce promotion brochures, and to determine if SKI-KIT could be tooled and manufactured in production quantities at a total manufactured cost of $40. If this could be done, twelve prototypes would be produced in time for the March SIA trade show, tooling would be fabricated, and production begun. DYNO would be responsible for coordinating all aspects of product development, setting up national distribution, and making sure SKI-KIT was in the trade show.

The minimum performance agreement stated that Zenith was required to sell

EXHIBIT (C). SKI-KIT, Inc. Pro-Forma Cash Flow—Most Probable Forecast

	1974	1975	1976	1977	1978	Annual Entries 1979–84
CASH-IN[1][2]						
Metal	$ 248,000	$ 585,000	$1,411,000	$2,117,000	$2,205,000	$2,646,000
Plastic	15,000	434,000	1,210,000	1,512,000	1,764,000	2,016,000
Leasing	60,000	488,000	1,000,000	1,680,000	2,500,000	3,000,000
Total Cash-In	323,000	1,507,000	3,621,000	5,309,000	6,469,000	7,662,000
CASH-OUT						
Cost of Sales	215,000	888,000	1,400,000	1,810,000	2,055,000	2,266,000
Gross Operating Cash	108,000	619,000	2,221,000	3,499,000	4,414,000	5,396,000
Indirect expense						
Marketing						
Leasing	15,000	100,000	200,000	350,000	500,000	600,000
Promotion	20,000	35,000	80,000	100,000	125,000	125,000
Warehousing, shipping, delivery @ 3% of total cash-in	10,000	45,000	109,000	159,000	194,000	230,000
Commissions @ 20% total cash-in	65,000	301,000	724,000	1,062,000	1,294,000	1,532,000
Technical						
Product development[3]	10,000	4,000				
Overhead						
Legal	3,000	1,000	1,000	1,000	1,000	1,000
G & A @ 5% total cash-in	16,000	75,000	181,000	265,000	323,000	383,000
Management (DYNO)	18,000	25,000	40,000	50,000	50,000	50,000
Sub-Total Indirect	157,000	586,000	1,335,000	1,987,000	2,487,000	2,921,000
10% Contingency	16,000	59,000	134,000	199,000	249,000	292,000
Total Indirect	173,000	645,000	1,469,000	2,186,000	2,736,000	3,213,000
NET CASH (OUT)	(65,000)	(26,000)	752,000	1,313,000	1,678,000	2,183,000

EXHIBIT C (continued)

CAPITAL INVESTMENT (tooling and start-up)	75,000	100,000	140,000	75,000	75,000	75,000
NET NET CASH (OUT) (expensing all tooling)	(140,000)	(126,000)	612,000	1,238,000	1,603,000	2,108,000
¹Sales Schedule (units/year)						
Metal	3,500	9,000	20,000	30,000	33,000	38,000
Plastic	500	12,500	30,000	38,000	45,000	52,000
Total	4,000	21,500	50,000	68,000	78,000	90,000
²Wholesale Price Schedule ($/unit)						
Metal	99.00	90.00	88.20	88.20	88.20	88.20
Plastic	51.00	51.00	50.40	50.40	50.40	50.40

³Product development costs do not include $40,000 tooling expenditures during 1973.

Retail List Price ($/unit)						
Metal	165	150	140	140	140	140
Plastic	85	85	80	80	80	80

	1973 1st Quarter			2nd Quarter			3rd Quarter			1974 4th Quarter			5th Quarter			6th Quarter			7th Quarter	
	April	May	June	July	Aug.	Sept.	Oct.	Nov.	Dec.	Jan.	Feb.	March	April	May	June	July	Aug.	Sept.	Oct.	Nov.
MARKETING																				
Feasibility Study	Commence ──────▶ Completed																			
Business Program																				
Airlines				Preliminary ──────────▶			Discussions	──Finalize Arrangement												
Bus & Train							Preliminary Discussion		◀──Finalize											
Distributor							Preliminary		Final Arrangements											
Retail			Feas. Survey			Set up Joint Mkt. Efforts with Ski Clubs														Preparat
Advertising & Promotion																				
Publication Promotions							New Product Release													New
Shows										Ski Shows Preparation & Attendance										
Clubs							Ski Club Presentation Preparation & Presentation													
Advertising													Cooperative Schedule			Implement				
Brochure				Photog-raphy	Bro-chure	Show & Presentation Material							Prepare Flyers & Mailers							
TECHNICAL																				
Feasibility Study	Commence ──────▶ Completed																			
Product Design							Design Dev. (Metal)	Final (Metal)			Feasi-bility (Plastic)	Design & Process Development (Plastic)		Final						
Prototype Development							Handmade Samples (20)									Handmade Samples (10)				
MANUFACTURING																				
Feasibility Study	Commence ──────▶ Completed																			
Prototypes							First Metal Samples (20)									First Plastic Samples				
Limited Production																				
Tooling										Tooling──Limited Metal Production						Limited Production Plastic Toolin				
Material							Order Materials									Order Materials				
Fabrication							Fabricate									Fabricate				
Full Produciton																				
Tooling												Tooling	Full Metal Production						Tooling	
Material											Materials								M
Fabrication																				
LEGAL		1,000			2,000						1,000		1,000			1,000				
Patent	Domestic				Foreign															
General				Domestic						Domestic			Domestic & Foreign							
Business Licenses																				
GENERAL & ADMINISTRATIVE	1,000				2,500		1,500	750	750	1,200	1,200	1,200	1,200	1,200	1,200	1,200	1,200	1,200	1,700	1,700
MANAGEMENT (DYNO)	3,000			1,500	1,500		1,500	1,500	1,500	1,500	1,500	1,500	1,500	1,500	1,500	1,500	1,500	1,500	2,000	2,000
TOTAL EXPENSES	5,000			7,500			7,500			2,700	2,700	3,700	2,700	2,700	3,700	2,700	2,700	3,700	3,700	3,700
CAPITAL EXPENDITURES { TOOLING							40,000													
{ MANUFACTURING							80,000													

EXHIBIT D. Ski-Kit, Inc. Business Planning Schedule

5 Quarter		9th Quarter			10th-11th Qtr.	1976	1977	1978
Feb.	March	April	May	June	July–Dec.	12th-15th Qtr.	16th-19th Qtr.	20th-23rd Qtr.

Efforts (Plastic)—Clubs

...se

Ski Shows

Advertisements

Show Exhibits

Ski Club Presentation

Advertising Materials

Further Development

Full Plastic and Metal Production

	1,000					1,000		1,000
	Domestic					Domestic		Domestic
	Foreign					Foreign		Foreign

...50	6,250	6,250	6,250	6,250	6,250	37,500	180,000	265,000	323,000
...00	2,000	2,000	2,000	2,000	2,000	7,000	40,000	50,000	50,000
...50	8,250	9,250	8,250	8,250	8,250	44,500	221,000	315,000	374,000

a minimum 1,000 SKI-KITs during the first 18 months of the agreement ending May 31, 1975, and 3,000 SKI-KITs per year each year thereafter. Zenith would also be required to pay Mr. McAlister, in the form of a rebate, $30,000 for his prior expense. If Zenith failed to meet such minimums, Mr. McAlister had the right to convert the exclusive licensing agreement to a non-exclusive agreement allowing him to seek other licensees; in return, he would be required to repay Zenith $25,000 out of SKI-KIT net sales at a 5% rate. There were no minimum royalty payments.

Lastly, Zenith decided to fabricate the first SKI-KITs out of plastic rather than metal. They reasoned that, in the short run, subcontracting the thermoforming operation and fabricating in-house would be less expensive than forming aluminum. Besides, they questioned the technical feasibility of manufacturing in metal.

EXTERNAL ENVIRONMENT

At almost the same time of the signing of the licensing agreement, the Arab oil embargo surfaced and conditions grew steadily worse as 1973 drew to a close. Gasoline and plastic prices shot dramatically upward and a general reduction in plastic supplies on the West Coast compounded the difficulties of the situation. As one executive for the Society of the Plastics Industry, Inc., stated, "I firmly believe that Southern California stands ready to have its entire manufacturing industry grind to a halt within the next few months unless something is done to reverse the trend in the resin shortage for the plastics industry." Fortunately, ABS high-impact, low temperature plastic was selected for SKI-KIT luggage fabrication. This material was available but was one of the most expensive plastics on the market. It had increased 50% in price in only three months.

By the end of 1973, the shortages were at their worst and a recession looked imminent. In addition, the ski industry was going through its third successive year of poor snow conditions in the Eastern and Mid-Western United States, forcing retailers into bankruptcy and creating the highest level of accounts receivable the ski industry had ever experienced. In early 1974 Zenith's management was becoming concerned, but they were assured by DYNO that serious skiers will find a way to ski regardless of the economic conditions. Besides, there was plenty of snow in the Western United States. Skiers could travel by commercial carrier, which suited SKI-KIT's purpose perfectly.

Following the Business Plan, DYNO did a feasibility study to determine the trends in the size of ski equipment in order to fix the SKI-KIT luggage dimensions. After speaking with major ski and boot distributors and measuring existing equipment, DYNO and Zenith concluded that luggage 84 in. (214 cm.) × 15 × 6¾ in. would capture at least 95% of the market.

With these results, Zenith contracted with a well-known design firm to do the product design, determine the cost of materials, and fabricate a production prototype. The firm designed into the SKI-KIT a car rack, interior bracing pods (to incorporate the patent), shoulder strap, and luggage handle. Zenith wanted a prestigious looking plastic case, so aluminum extrusions, latches, and hinges were added to the unit. These additions increased the labor and material costs as well as the weight. The finished product weighed 18 pounds.

The production prototype cost $49.50 to make, almost $10 over the agreed upon $40, but Zenith decided to continue with the project. With G & A and

R & D expenses for the year, the wholesale price would increase considerably, as shown in the following cost breakdown:

COST BREAKDOWN

	Anticipated Units Produced		
	1,000	2,000	3,000
Material	$ 36.00	$36.00	$36.00
Labor and overhead: 1.5 hours @ $9.00 per hour	13.50	13.50	13.50
Subtotal	49.50	49.50	49.50
G & A @ 10%	4.95	4.95	4.95
Subtotal	54.45	54.45	54.45
R & D			
Sales—DYNO $10,000 (contract to coordinate marketing program)			
Promotion 5,000 (brochures, travel, etc.)			
Design firm 10,000			
Prototype 4,000			
29,000	29.00	14.50	9.65
Production tooling $10,000			
(amortized over 5,000 units)	2.00	2.00	2.00
TOTAL	85.45	70.95	66.10
Zenith's profit @ 15%	12.81	10.64	9.91
	98.26	81.59	76.01
McAlister's royalty @ 5%	4.91	4.08	3.80
TOTAL (distributor price)	$103.17	$85.67	$79.81

On the basis of an annual production of 3,000 units the retail price would be $200, giving the wholesaler a 40% gross margin at the wholesale price of $120. The distributor price would be $80, at a gross margin of 33⅓% on the wholesale price.

DYNO was disappointed that Zenith intended to amortize the tooling and R & D costs over so few units. They also believed that labor and overhead costs were too high. By making a nominal adjustment in quantity of units and cutting labor and overhead costs somewhat, DYNO believed the retail price could be reduced to about $115, still too high but considerably closer to the questionnaire results. Zenith was unwilling to reduce the distributor price below $80, the 3,000 unit production level. Zenith's management stated that if the product could not sell at a profitable price, then SKI-KIT was not a viable product.

MARKET DEVELOPMENT

A trademark determination and distributor search was made during the cost studies. Out of 90 names compiled, SKI-KIT was voted by Zenith management to be best. Zenith's name would precede SKI-KIT to assure it from being too generic.

From November to February continuous efforts were made to conclude arrangements with a distributor. Over 50 distributors and independent represen- tatives were contacted; all declined because the inquiries were too late in the season, because they did not believe in the concept, or because it was too expensive. In early February, an Eastern distributor consented to show Zenith SKI-KIT in the Chicago National Sporting Goods show in mid-February. After evaluating the retail interest they would decide whether they and their Western associate would distribute it.

Few retailers of skis were at the National Sporting Goods show, but most of the major mass merchandisers attended. All mass merchandisers expressed interest in SKI-KIT luggage but stated it was far too expensive. Throughout the entire show, this was always the major complaint. To a lesser extent, weight and bulkiness were also mentioned. Since the SIA show was only three weeks away, it was too late to make any changes. DYNO also was not very impressed with the Eastern distributor and would try to find another one prior to the ski show.

In the following two weeks all efforts to interest a distributor failed. At the last possible day DYNO reached an informal agreement with Sako Industry Sports, Inc., one of the largest ski distributors in the United States. They agreed to show SKI-KIT in the ski show, evaluate the results, and decide whether to distribute it. They warned, however, that because of lack of time prior to the show, their salesmen would not have proper knowledge and few positive results were expected until September when their salesmen visited the ski retailers. Sako also questioned the need for SKI-KIT and said the price was definitely too high.

At the Ski Industries America show, SKI-KIT luggage stirred a lot of interest among the retailers but few orders were written. They said the price was far too high. They were not sure who among their regular clientele would buy it, and they would prefer to talk to a Sako salesman when he visited their shop in September, or wait until a customer asked for a SKI-KIT. At the show, there was also considerable interest from European, Japanese, and Canadian dis- tributors. However, because of high shipping costs, SKI-KIT would have to be licensed to be manufactured in foreign countries.

The DYNO partners then redesigned SKI-KIT, eliminating all latches, hinges, and extrusions thereby utilizing the patented concept to its fullest. A drawing was made and displayed at the SIA Boston ski show, where the new SKI-KIT was priced at $137.50 retail, $82.50 wholesale, and $60.00 distributor price. It re- ceived more favorable acceptance but very few orders. Back in Los Angeles, a prototype was made using straps and buckles rather than the previous hardware. This not only reduced the manufactured cost but also reduced the weight to 15 pounds. Bob Wilhelm went to the San Francisco regional ski show with the prototype, received very little sales support from Sako, returned to Los Angeles convinced SKI-KIT would sell at the lower price, but that it would be necessary to find a new distributor.

Meanwhile, Zenith was growing disappointed, not seeing the expected sales results they were assured would be forthcoming. DYNO agreed that it was the price that was still too high, and Zenith remarked they were led to believe skiers were affluent and the price should not be a critical factor. If the price was the major factor, then the product was not viable. Zenith's management stated despite the lack of sales force and the high price, they would probably produce

500 units in an attempt to recover some of their R & D costs, but they would allocate very little money for promotion and advertising.

FOUNDING OF SKI–KIT, INC. (B)

Confronted with the possibility of not recovering the capital already invested and of never seeing SKI-KIT luggage on the market, Mr. McAlister and DYNO evaluated the following alternatives:

1. Continue the licensing agreement with Zenith and hope that the first 500 units would be easily sold and more produced
2. Mr. McAlister would look for a new licensee/subcontractor, even though he would be required to pay Zenith $25,000 at 5% of net sales
3. Acquire the licensing rights from Zenith and raise enough capital for Mr. McAlister to start his own manufacturing facilities
4. Sell the manufacturing, technical, marketing information, and patent rights
5. Scrap the entire project and use it as a tax write-off.

McAlister and DYNO reasoned that the fifth alternative would always be available. Because the patent would become more valuable the more developed the product, the fourth alternative was also a last resort. The third alternative would require at least $100,000 immediately, which would be extremely difficult to raise in the existing economic situation. The first and second alternatives therefore seemed the most feasible.

McAlister contacted several of his friends and received an $11,000 loan commitment; he got oral commitments from other friends for approximately $90,000 more at a future date. McAlister and Zenith then discussed a new business arrangement. Zenith was willing to let McAlister have only the marketing rights; Zenith would retain the manufacturing rights.

The following amendment to the licensing agreement was made:

1. For McAlister's initial $25,000 investment, Zenith would provide a $2 trade discount on the first 12,500 SKI-KITs purchased by McAlister.
2. Zenith would not participate in any leasing revenues.
3. Zenith would agree to sell a minimum of 500 SKI-KITs the first year, ending May 31, 1975, and 1,000 SKI-KITs each succeeding year, ending May 31. In any year McAlister was not the distributor, he agreed to give Zenith an additional year to sell the minimum quantity.
4. McAlister would still receive the 5% royalty on all SKI-KIT sales.

A distributor agreement was also signed by McAlister and Zenith. This agreement read as follows:

1. McAlister agrees to spend, in addition to purchasing the SKI-KIT luggage, $15,000 annually for advertising and promotional materials or services.
2. McAlister agrees to purchase from Zenith a minimum of 500 SKI-KITs by May 31, 1975, and 1,000 SKI-KITs in each succeeding year ending May 31. If these minimums are not met, Zenith has the right to terminate the distributor agreement.

3. Zenith agrees to produce a minimum of 500 SKI-KITs and sell them to McAlister at $58 each. Zenith's price to McAlister for SKI-KITs in subsequent years shall include a 15% pretax profit. Included in Zenith's cost will be the recovery of $35,000 in development costs; this will represent $5 a unit on the first 7,000 units.
4. After the initial 500 units, if McAlister places a firm order with Zenith, McAlister will determine design and quantities to be manufactured.

CORPORATE STRUCTURE AND OPERATIONS

With these agreements signed, Zenith began gearing up for production and McAlister began organizing SKI-KIT, Inc. He retained Mr. Bob Wilhelm to organize and manage the company. Two of McAlister's friends who provided loans became corporate officers; legal counsel was retained for proper incorporation; and an accounting firm was hired to establish an accounting system.

McAlister's lawyer stated the best plan was to incorporate as a small business corporation capitalized at 500,000 shares with a par value of $1 per share. Stock would be issued on a private placement basis to McAlister's friends. A total of 326,806 shares would be distributed accordingly:

Stockholder	Corporate Office	% of Equity	Shares of Stock	$ Value of Stock	Reason
Fred McAlister	President, Chairman of the Board	51	166,161	166,161	prior advances prior services patent value
Bob Wilhelm	Executive Vice Pres., Director	7	22,807	22,807	prior services
Bill DuVaugh	Vice Pres. Advertising Promotion Director	5	16,290	16,290	prior advances
Bob Nemon	Treasurer	5	16,290	16,290	prior advances prior services
Charlotte Castle		1	3,258	3,258	prior advances prior services
Joe Ciarica			1,000	1,000	prior services
Jim Sabot	Secretary				
McAlister's friends		31	100,000	100,000	investors

SKI-KIT, Inc., now became the legal entity to market SKI-KIT luggage.

Mr. Wilhelm would be the only individual to receive money for his services and Ms. Castle would act as the secretary until SKI-KIT, Inc., had sufficient funds to hire one.

SKI-KIT, Inc., revised the pro forma financial projections to show that in the first full year of operation they would gross $337,000 (3,600 SKI-KITs by direct sales, wholesale, foreign licensing, export and commercial carrier) and incur a $6,000 loss. The second year revenues would rise to $937,000 (10,000 SKI-KITs) and pre-tax profits of $103,000. The third year of operation would have sales of $2,342,000 (25,000 SKI-KITs) and pre-tax profits of $475,000. On the basis of these projections, SKI-KIT, Inc., would need slightly more than $100,000 in working capital during the first year of operation. A loan would be needed to finance SKI-KIT, Inc., during the slow period from April to July.

All business operations would be conducted from an office SKI-KIT, Inc., rented. However, Zenith would warehouse the SKI-KITs and drop ship orders according to SKI-KIT, Inc.'s instructions. Zenith would then bill SKI-KIT, Inc., 60 days from the end of the month in which the SKI-KIT luggage was shipped.

Consumers buying directly from SKI-KIT, Inc., would be required to pay in advance of shipment by check, money order, or major credit card. Because of SKI-KIT, Inc.'s modest capital support, adverse economic conditions and poor credit rating of many ski retailers, orders by retailers would require 50% down payment and the balance according to normal ski industry terms.

MARKETING

SKI-KIT management rationalized that the ski market was faddish and fashion conscious with respect to color; SKI-KIT luggage should also follow this market characteristic. Instead of offering SKI-KIT in white only, they added yellow, orange, blue, and green. This would cost SKI-KIT, Inc., several dollars more per unit but they would pass the cost on to the consumer. The car mounting straps and shoulder strap would be optional features priced separately to keep the price of the SKI-KIT luggage as low as possible.

Because the major retail shows were over and it was too close to the ski season to hire and train a national sales force, SKI-KIT, Inc., would have to devote the majority of its efforts to direct consumer marketing. This would not only generate needed sales at the highest profit margin but would also provide maximum national exposure at least cost. It would also create a consumer demand at the retail level.

An advertising agency was retained for three months to develop a national advertising campaign. This would include full-page advertising in a major consumer ski magazine, advertising in retail trade magazines, local advertising, product brochures, and contacts with other ski companies for cooperative advertising.

The final arrangements between SKI-KIT, Inc., and three airlines and a car rental company proved to be somewhat disappointing because these commercial carriers did not purchase any SKI-KITs nor did they want to participate in a leasing program the first year of SKI-KIT's operation. Their decisions stemmed from SKI-KIT's being a new product and consumer acceptance not yet proven. They believed the total ski equipment damage incurred during transit was not significant enough to warrant an investment in SKI-KITs; their budgets had already been approved and it was too late to make any major changes.

These commercial carriers did include SKI-KIT luggage in their promotion programs to analyze consumer interest. If there were sufficient interest, they would then create a more elaborate program during SKI-KIT's second year of operation. The first year promotional programs included the commercial carriers' endorsements by displaying SKI-KIT luggage at 23 consumer ski shows across the United States. One airline gave SKI-KITs away as a grand prize for a consumer game they sponsored. This same airline also promoted it in their in-flight magazine and used SKI-KIT luggage as an employee sales incentive. A second airline had their ski team carry it to all ski races they participated in to promote the airlines' new colors and logo. A third commercial carrier, an international airline, offered SKI-KIT as an optional purchase to skiers traveling on their ski charters to Europe. They also demonstrated SKI-KIT luggage while promoting their ski vacations to all ski clubs in the Southern California area.

Other promotion programs included:

1. Endorsements by three major professional and amateur ski associations providing international exposure and credibility to the skier population
2. Giving SKI-KITs to ten movie stars, for product identity.
3. Demonstration of a SKI-KIT on television
4. Endorsement of SKI-KIT by an international travel tour organization.

One hundred new product releases were sent out to the major national magazines and largest newspapers in the United States. These releases were eventually printed in all the major ski publications and several major international general interest publications.

October is the beginning of the ski season. Consumer ski shows begin then and go on through late November. SKI-KIT, Inc., presented SKI-KIT luggage in San Francisco, Los Angeles, Chicago, and New York, and the commercial carriers displayed it in other consumer shows.

At the first show in San Francisco, SKI-KIT management was shocked to discover another ski manufacturer with similar ski luggage. It was the same color and had almost the same dimensions and general appearance. However, its quality was far inferior to SKI-KIT's. A skier could not pack his boots in it and there was no car mounting feature. This luggage was priced under $100 at retail. SKI-KIT management learned that Zenith's plastic supplier had told this competitor about SKI-KIT four months prior to the ski show.

SKI-KIT at first wanted to take legal action against the competitor. However, on second thought SKI-KIT management decided that their competitor did not pose a threat during the first year because they had an inferior product, no sales force, and no advertising or promotional effort. In the future SKI-KIT would be so advanced in marketing and product development that they would not have to worry. Also, if the competitor were selling its product in the future, it would actually improve SKI-KIT's position because competition would help to create a consumer demand, increase the overall market share for ski luggage, and provide the consumer the opportunity to see SKI-KIT's superior quality.

Skiers at all the consumer shows indicated that SKI-KIT luggage was a highly desirable product and they would very much like to own one—but could not afford it. This convinced SKI-KIT management that they had a good product, but that they would have to find a way to reduce the price.

Sales and Financing

The original loans were spent rapidly on start-up for organizational and advertising costs. More capital would be needed for SKI-KIT to survive until their stock permit was issued, and income from sales of the product was generated. McAlister and several of his friends together lent SKI-KIT an additional $12,900.

In October, the full-page advertisement was printed and several promotional programs were initiated. Sales were a disappointing $1,000. By November, a sales force for California had been established to sell to retail ski shops. The advertisement, product releases, and retail SKI-KIT displays were widely seen by skiers. SKI-KIT sales displays increased sales to $9,000; the majority of these sales were directly to the consumer. SKI-KIT experienced a flurry of orders in late November and through December; skiers called by telephone from across the United States and Canada, causing sales to jump to $15,199.

Unfortunately, skiers wanted their SKI-KITs immediately or before Christmas. Many of these orders were impossible to deliver in that short time. Normal shipping to the East Coast was 4 to 6 weeks but the truck company SKI-KIT was using developed a backlog because a competing truck company went on strike. SKI-KIT management was forced to spend a considerable amount of time on customer relations.

FUTURE OF SKI-KIT, INC. (C)

SKI-KIT management was pleased with the December sales but they knew sales would taper off substantially in the following months because of the seasonal characteristic of the sport.

The financial statements for the first quarter of operation (Exhibit A) showed SKI-KIT, INC., to be in a precarious position. SKI-KIT, INC., management knew they had to do the following:

1. Maintain the previously high level of sales for the next two quarters. This was necessary not only for needed revenue, but also to sell the balance of the 500 units required to retain the exclusive distributorship.
2. Continue efforts to get the stock permit issued.
3. Reduce the retail price to under $100.
4. Establish national distribution and warehousing.
5. Broaden the product mix to include other ski items and counter-seasonal products.

EXHIBIT A—SKI-KIT, Inc. (C) Statement of Income and Retained Earnings (Deficit) from October 1, 1974, to December 31, 1974 (Unaudited)

Sales, Net	$ 25,199
Cost of Sales	14,940
Gross Profit	10,259
Operating Expenses	
Advertising	33,878
Consulting fees	5,305
Show expense	1,903
Freight and delivery	599
Amortization of organization costs	249
Depreciation	12
Sales promotion and entertainment	255

Professional fees	250
Miscellaneous	219
Office	696
Telephone	1,547
Travel	651
Rent	1,310
Commissions	175
Equipment rental	32
Bank charges	58
Dues and subscriptions	10
	47,149
Income (loss) before Taxes on Income	(36,890)
Taxes on Income (Note 1)	200
Net Loss	(37,090)
Retained Earnings—October 1, 1974	—
Retained Earnings (deficit)—December 31, 1974	$(37,090)

Balance Sheet as of December 1, 1974 (Unaudited)

Assets

Current		
Cash		$ 9,515
Accounts receivable		5,102
Advances to officers		221
Total Current Assets		14,838
Property and Equipment, at Cost		
Net of accumulated depreciation of $12		1,374
Other		
Unamortized organization costs	$4,722	
Deposits	262	4,984
		$ 21,196

Liabilities and Stockholder's Equity

Current Liabilities	
Accounts payable and accrued expenses	$ 33,574
Loans payable	4,500
Taxes other than income	412

Note 1: Summary of Significant Accounting Policies
Inventories: Inventories are stated at the lower of cost (first-in, first-out method) or market.
Depreciation: Depreciation and amortization are computed using the straight-line method for both book and tax purposes.
Fiscal Year End: The company has adopted June 30 as its accounting year end.
Income Taxes: Investment tax credit is treated as a reduction of tax expense in the year the related asset is placed in service (flow-through method.) Income for financial reporting and tax purposes will be substantially the same.

Total Current Liabilities	38,486
Advances from Incorporators	19,800
Commitments and Contingencies (Note 2)	
Stockholders' Equity	
Common stock, authorized 500,000 shares; par value	
$1 each, issued and outstanding, none	—
Retained earnings (deficit)	(37,090)
	$ 21,196

Statement of Changes in Financial Position October 1, 1974 (Unaudited) to December 31, 1974

Source of Funds	
Advances from incorporators	$ 19,800
Application of Funds	
From operations	
Net loss	37,090
Non-cash charges against income,	
depreciation and amortization	261
	36,829
Purchase of equipment	1,386
Organization costs	4,971
Deposits	262
	43,448
(Decrease) in Working Capital	$(23,648)
Increase (Decrease) in Components of Working Capital	
Cash	$ 9,515
Accounts receivable	5,102
Advances to officers	221
Accounts payable and accrued expenses	(33,574)
Loans payable	(4,500)
Taxes other than on income	(412)
(Decrease) in Working Capital	$(23,648)

Sales for the next three months totaled only $5,000, which meant that 30% of the inventory still remained. Complications with the stock permit further delayed its issuance. Other means of acquiring capital were pursued, but venture capital companies, which at one time had invested in leisure companies, were

Note 2:
The company is contemplating suit against one of its creditors because of various deficiencies in their performance. There is approximately $6,000 in dispute.
Payment to a national organization to promote SKI-KIT luggage has been terminated because they have not complied with the agreement. To date, SKI-KIT, Inc., has paid $1,000 and the unpaid portion of $9,000 was not included in the accounts at December 31, 1974.

no longer investing in anything. Several banks indicated that they were no longer granting SBA loans because of the uncertain economic situation.

Private investors showed interest but took too long to make a decision. And SKI-KIT principals, having already lent $50,400, were not willing to lend any more or secure a loan with their personal assets.

Not until after the major ski retail show in March was SKI-KIT, Inc., able to establish a firm relationship with a national ski equipment distributor with warehousing. At about the same time, SKI-KIT management succeeded in obtaining new manufacturing costs from another manufacturer. This allowed the retail price to be reduced to $99.

SKI-KIT, Inc., also succeeded in acquiring the rights to represent several other ski products and a full line of tennis gear and clothes. The only goal not achieved was raising the capital to keep the company going.

The principals now came to believe that their only alternative was to sell the company. The national sales force was queried to determine how many SKI-KITs they could sell during the next ski season. An analysis of the sales for the first year showed that 70% were direct sales to the skier and 30% were sales made through retail shops. From this information financial pro formas were made, showing the following:

	1975–76	1976–77	1977–78
Units	7,000	12,000	20,000
Sales	$364,500	$556,000	$814,000
Pretax profits	$ 25,760	$ 91,000	$139,000

The sell-out proposal SKI-KIT, Inc., offered was a small upfront cash or equivalent stock payment partially to compensate for SKI-KIT principals' loans. In addition, the buyer would assume all SKI-KIT, Inc., liabilities and pay a 5% royalty on net sales for the life of the agreement.

After a three-month search, SKI-KIT, Inc., began negotiating with a leisure-time company. This company gave their own buy-out proposal stating they would give no upfront cash or stock, assume no liabilities, and would pay only a 5% royalty. SKI-KIT, Inc., was again confronted with a most precarious situation, which would require a decision very soon.

Geochron Laboratories, Inc.— Getting a Company Started

Geochron Laboratories, Inc., was incorporated in June, 1960, for the purpose of offering a commercial service to persons and firms interested in determining the ages of rocks and minerals. The company's four founders were Robert Lemer, Marc Altman, and Richard Freedman, all members of the class of 1960 at the Harvard Business School, and Harold Krueger, a graduate geologist employed by MIT until June, 1960, as research assistant in the department of geology and geophysics.

CONCEPTION AND FORMATION OF GEOCHRON, INC.

The company had grown out of preliminary discussions among the four men which culminated in a report written by Mr. Freedman, also a graduate geologist, for a second-year course in new businesses at the Harvard Business School. The report had examined the feasibility of commercially exploiting a rock-dating technique known as potassium-argon isotope analysis. This technique was based on the well-established fact that a particular radioactive type of potassium, K^{40}, decays, with a half-life of approximately 1.3 billion years, into Ar^{40}, an isotope of the inert gas argon. By measuring the ratios of the amounts of the two isotopes, where the initial amount of K^{40} was known and the radiogenic (decay product) argon had been sealed in, it was possible to estimate with comparatively great precision the age of the rock in which the isotopes were contained. Estimates could be made of ages in the range of 1 million to 4.5 billion years.

The technique used by Geochron was not the only means of rock-dating available to the geologist, but other known methods appeared to have greater limitations. Dating through fossil analysis was less precise, and had the further disadvantage that fossils were not always found where they might be most helpful. Other isotopic analyses in existence made use of the decay series involving uranium lead, rubidium strontium, and thorium lead; but these required the presence of rarely occurring elements, whereas potassium was one

---

This case was copyrighted in 1962 by the President and Fellows of Harvard College and is reproduced by permission.

of the more commonly occurring elements. Carbon dating had been a great help to scientists, but its use was limited by the fact that it measured only ages less than some 70,000 years. The gap between 70,000 and one million years, the approximate period of the Ice Ages, was not capable of accurate estimation by K–Ar or other existing methods. The founders of Geochron felt confident, given this state of dating technology, that K–Ar dating provided three significant advantages which would make it an especially salable service: (1) it was precise by existing standards, (2) it had wide geographic applicability, and (3) it spanned a large period of geologic history.

When Geochron was formed, Mr. Lemer became president; Mr. Krueger, vice-president and technical director; Mr. Freedman, vice-president and geologist; and Mr. Altman, treasurer. They felt that their service would be of primary interest to geologists employed in academic establishments, oil or mining firms, or government service. Little present competition was thought to exist. While there were laboratories performing K–Ar dating, there were perhaps less than 20 in the Western Hemisphere, and these were principally government and university installations. Several of the largest oil companies had the facilities, but they were not interested in selling the service. The great majority of oil companies were not set up to perform the analyses. Only one potential commercial competitor, Isotopes, Inc., existed, but it was not considered to be a serious threat.

Concerning potential competition, Mr. Lemer was aware that neither the process nor the apparatus was patentable. He also knew that the separation equipment, flame spectrophotometer, mass spectrometer, and other necessary laboratory hardware could be acquired for less than $70,000. Technically trained people were not so easily found, although several schools (MIT among them) had been training scientists in geochronology since 1955. In any case, an exclusive option on the services of Mr. Krueger had been obtained by the company. He had acquired considerable experience in geochronology at the University of Minnesota and at MIT, training under several of the leading geochronologists in the country.

MARKET FEASIBILITY SURVEY

In the spring of 1960, before forming the company, the principals made their first effort to measure the market for commercial K–Ar dating. Already aware that there were essentially no laboratories available for routine commercial service, they decided on a mail survey of geologists as the fastest and least expensive means of assessing market potential. A questionnaire was constructed and mailed with a covering letter (Exhibit 1) to 500 geologists early in March, 1960. In selecting their sample, the founders drew largely from people who had been members of the Geological Society of America for at least five years. The principals realized that the true universe of geologists was far larger than the 5,000-member GSA, with perhaps 35,000 in the U.S.A. alone and over 100,000 in the world. At the time, however, Mr. Lemer, who assumed responsibility for preliminary market analysis, was a student at the Harvard Business School, and his survey was severly limited by time and financial restraints.

Of the 210 respondents to the questionnaire, 41 percent indicated that they would utilize the proposed service at the quoted price of $300 to $600. This range had been chosen after a cursory estimate of operating costs indicated that, with an operation of 200 to 300 determinations per year, prices within this span would yield a profit. (The break-even point at an average price of $350 per determination would be less than 200 units annually, figuring monthly costs to be about $5,000. Above 200 units, marginal profit would rise sharply, since most of the costs were thought to be fixed.)

LETTER AND ACCOMPANYING MAIL QUESTIONNAIRE

24 Blackstone Street
CAMBRIDGE 39, MASSACHUSETTS

February 29, 1960

DR. JOHN SMITH
Mammoth Oil Company
TULSA, OKLAHOMA

DEAR DR. SMITH:

In recognition of the growing importance of age determinations in geological research, we plan to establish a commercial geochronological laboratory. The laboratory staff is presently associated with one of the major research centers in the country, and has been active in the field of geochronology for a number of years.

Commencing in the fall of 1960, we shall be equipped for potassium-argon age determinations. Accuracy ranges from plus or minus 1 percent for Precambrian rocks, to plus or minus 2½ percent for Early Tertiary specimens. We expect that this information should be useful to university researchers, governmental surveys, mining companies, and oil companies.

As potassium-argon age determinations have been heretofore unavailable to most geologists, it is difficult for us to determine the laboratory size needed to provide adequate service. For this reason, it would be very helpful if you would fill out and return the enclosed questionnaire, even if you have no use for the facilities.

It is nearly impossible for us to compile a complete list of geologists with interest in age determinations. Therefore, our survey would be much more complete if you would pass on the extra questionnaire to an interested colleague.

Procurement of this information is the best way we can think of to determine and fill your requirements. Thank you for your cooperation.

Yours very truly,

(Signed)
ROBERT J. LEMER

Enclosure

EXHIBIT 1. Geochron Laboratories, Inc.

EXHIBIT 1 (continued)

POTASSIUM-ARGON SURVEY*

This questionnaire is designed only to help us to determine your requirements. This is not a commitment on your part; we just want your best guesses.
If you prefer to write us a note or letter rather than filling out this form, that
would be equally helpful. You need not give your name unless you wish to.

1. Name ——————————————————————————————————
   Address ————————————————————————————————
   ——————————————————————————————————————

   Specialty ————————————————————————————————
(Petrology, Sedimentation, etc.)

2. The exact cost per determination will depend very largely on the scale of
operations that proves possible. We expect, however, that the charge will
probably exceed $300, but will certainly be less than $600. Do you think you
would utilize this service for potassium-argon age determinations?

   Yes ————————— No ————————— Probably —————————
   As a rough estimate, how many determinations do you think you might
require per year? ————————————————————————————

3. Are there any other age-determination methods you would like to have
available? Other uses of isotope analyses? Would you like us to provide a
consulting service as well as the raw data?

4. Any additional comments, criticisms, or questions would be appreciated.
Please use the reverse side if required.

The respondents who indicated that they would utilize the age determination service estimated an average annual requirement of 2.5 determinations, or
a total of 225 per year from the 87 who responded affirmatively. If questionnaires mailed to 500 geologists indicated an expected volume of 225 per year,
how many requests for determination might be forthcoming from the entire
universe of geologists? It was thought that the first year might produce 750,
with succeeding annual increments of 750 not unreasonable to expect, though
clearly a wide range of possible demand levels existed.

With these encouraging thoughts in mind, it was decided that Geochron
would purchase equipment, at a cost of approximately $35,000, which would
afford a sample-analyzing capacity of about 400 per year. The price schedule
would be $350 for raw (unseparated) rock and $300 for purified samples. On
June 8, 1960, the firm was incorporated with one million common shares (no

---

*Prepared by Geochron Laboratories, Inc.

par) authorized, and arrangements for the acquisition of laboratory equipment were initiated. Shortly after incorporation, most of the original list of 500 geologists was approached again, this time through the mailing of Technical Bulletin No. 1 and a covering letter. The bulletin described the laboratory as it would be in the fall, introduced its principal staff members, and provided information of a technical nature about the analyses that would be performed. Also, Mr. Freedman made plans to visit academic geologists and technical employees of oil and mining companies in an attempt to develop familiarity with Geochron's services throughout the geological profession. He expected as well to attend professional and trade conventions where he would discuss age determinations and provide literature on the company.

FINANCING

Shortly after incorporation, the four principals as a group loaned the corporation approximately $1,000 to cover out-of-pocket expenses. They had expected that substantial financial backing would be forthcoming by the fall of 1960 from one of several private investors who had evinced strong interest in Geochron. As the summer wore on, however, it became apparent that no backing could be expected from these sources, so the principals accelerated their solicitations (which had begun on a modest scale in January) of Boston investment houses and SBIC's. Receiving little encouragement and no definite offers, they began to pound pavements in New York City, first utilizing personal contacts and later working on references and cold-call prospects. September came and went, and still no funds. Mr. Lemer realized that most of Geochron's anticipated business would occur in the fall, after geologists had returned from their summer explorations, and without capital to purchase equipment Geochron would have to turn away business.

One day late in September, a Canadian friend of Mr. Freedman's got in touch with him in Cambridge. The friend had received one of the 300 publicity folders (Exhibit 2) which the company had distributed to a wide range of personal contacts in the United States and Canada. He suggested that the Geochron management contact one of the smaller brokerage firms, Globus, Inc., of New York. When Mr. Freedman hesitated, mentioning the immediacy of the company's cash needs, the Canadian source remarked that Morton Globus could often make a decision to commit funds to a company in as little as three hours' time.

An appointment with Mr. Globus was arranged, and within three hours he had agreed in principle to underwrite a public issue of Geochron common stock in the amount of $150,000. Since preparations for the public offering would undoubtedly require several months' time, both the officers and Morton Globus agreed to seek out sources of temporary funds. These creditors could then be repaid out of proceeds from the public issue. One private investor advanced the company $5,000 cash in return for a promissory note due July 31, 1961, or convertible into 8,000 shares of common stock at the time of public issue.

Also, Globus, Inc., and some of its officers and associates took a $30,000 convertible promissory note on the same terms. At the time of issue of the two notes, mid-October, 1960, the company sold to the private investor 2,000 common stock purchase warrants, and to the holders of the $30,000 note

60,000 warrants. These warrants were purchased at 2½ cents apiece, and each warrant entitled its holder to buy one share of Geochron common stock at $1.00 until October, 1965. With these proceeds, the company was able by the end of October to make progress payments of $15,000 on laboratory equipment under construction, and to defray its general expenses.

On February 16, 1961, Globus, Inc., and Ross, Lyon & Co., Inc., offered to the public, under a long-form registration, 150,000 shares of Geochron common stock at $1.00 per share. Proceeds to the company were $105,000. The issue was oversubscribed. At the same time, the four founders as a group received 70,000 shares at 1 cent per share, in return for $700 of the $1,000 they had originally loaned to the company. The other $300 was repaid to them in cash. Just prior to the public issue, the four founders had authorized themselves options to purchase 17,500 shares apiece at $1.10 per share over the five subsequent years. Thus, if all options and warrants were exercised, the number of common shares outstanding after the public issue would be:

Founders	70,000	18.0%
Founders, option plan	70,000	18.0
Globus, Inc., et al.	30,000	7.7
Globus, Inc., et al., warrants	60,000	15.4
The public	150,000	38.4
Private investor	8,000	2.0
Private investor, warrants	2,000	0.5
Totals	390,000	100.0%

EXHIBIT 2. Geochron Laboratories, Inc. Publicity Folder

POTASSIUM-ARGON AGE DETERMINATIONS

Here, in a few pages, we have tried to outline some of the most important aspects of geological age determinations by the potassium-argon method. Geochron is happy to make this service generally available for the first time.

Naturally, in a brief booklet, we cannot anticipate the specific problems our readers may have. Our technical staff welcomes the opportunity of corresponding with members of the geological profession concerning particular problems or applications of interest to them.

Please contact either:
H. W. KRUEGER, *Technical Director*
R. O. FREEDMAN, *Geologist*

GEOCHRON LABORATORIES, INC.
24 Blackstone Street, Cambridge 39, Mass., U.S.A.

WHAT ARE POTASSIUM-ARGON AGES?

The potassium-argon method of age determination is based on the radioactive decay of K^{40} to Ar^{40}. K^{40} has a half-life of approximately 1.3 billion years,

EXHIBIT 2 (continued)

enabling a wide range of geologically useful ages to be measured by potassium-argon analysis. Ages from less than 1 million to over 4,500 million years have been measured by this technique. As a result of recent advances, incorporated in our facilities, even younger materials may be dated, although with reduced precision. Thus, virtually the entire geological time-scale is encompassed.

The analysis of a sample for potassium and radiogenic argon determines the parent-to-daughter ratio. This, plus the known decay constants for K^{40}, allows the calculation of the time elapsed since formation of the potassium-bearing sample.

Recently, technological advances have made possible the extremely precise measurements necessary in this work. For example, our mass spectrometer enables us to measure argon content with a precison of a few parts per billion.

APPLICATIONS

Uses of age data in regional studies or mapping programs, structural studies in complex areas, and localized petrological studies are fairly self-evident.

Less widely known, but no less important, are applications to petroleum geology, mining geology, mineral exploration, and economic geology.

Tuffs, bentonites, and volcanic ash-falls in general provide excellent material for the petroleum and stratigraphic geologist, when in sedimentary sequences. They are ideal from the standpoint of representing a single instant in time. Even where recognized as important key-beds, most such units remain to be dated. Many other strata may be dated directly, by means of their glauconite content.

Under certain structural conditions, the dating of crystalline rocks (e.g., dikes, sills, basement complexes) may help solve difficult stratigraphic problems. Dating of detrital sedimentary grains may help determine the source(s) from which they were derived.

Applications to economic and mining geology range from delineating metallogenetic epochs on a possibly continent-wide scale to solving age relationships in the vein systems of a single mine. In between, geochronology provides a key to recognizing metallogenetic provinces. It thus becomes possible to direct mine development or mineral exploration programs with more efficiency (and less money) than otherwise would be the case.

MATERIALS SUITABLE FOR ANALYSIS

Any potassium-bearing mineral is potentially suitable for K-Ar age determinations. In actual practice, certain materials have proven superior to others. The list below discusses those of particular interest and widest applicability.

Neither grain size nor percentage of potassium-bearing mineral normally affects the reliability of an age determination. For example, a volcanic ash with ½% very fine-grained biotite is just as suitable as a pegmatite with 25% very coarse grained sheets of biotite. An exception is the case of a few extremely fine-grained rocks where mineral separation may pose a problem.

Micas: Biotite, Muscovite, Phlogopite, and Lepidolite. These minerals retain all

EXHIBIT 2 (continued)

of their radiogenic argon, and have become the standard for K-Ar age determinations. Naturally, where the mica is of metamorphic origin, the age determined reflects the date of latest recrystallization of the rock rather than that of original emplacement or deposition.

Glauconite: The most widespread and reliable of sedimentary minerals suitable for age determinations. Glauconites have proven useful throughout the age range 1 million to 1600 million years.

Amphiboles: Hornblende and soda amphiboles have recently been proven suitable for age determinations in a large number of cases, notwithstanding their low potassium content. Much of the interest in amphiboles stems from their apparent ability to withstand considerable thermal metamorphism without argon loss.

Pyroxenes: Although presently unproven, pyroxenes have arroused considerable interest from the standpoint of suffering small argon loss under thermal metamorphism. This lab is interested in cooperating with researchers in investigating the pyroxene group further.

Feldspars: The feldspars as a group are not good minerals for age determinations, with the important exception of sanidine.

Others: A great many other potassium minerals are suitable under particular conditions or have potential as age indicators. These include leucite, sylvite, and other with essential potassium, plus a host of minerals with minor potassium content.

In addition, certain unseparated materials may be dated directly; slates, phyllites, and young fine-grained volcanics have proven especially useful.

If in doubt as to the suitability of a sample, please correspond with our Technical Director. Better still, submit the sample for free examination.

SAMPLE REQUIREMENTS

Prepared Mineral Separate:

Send 10 or more grams of clean mineral, if possible. The *minimum* size ranges from 2 grams for an ancient, potassium-rich sample to 10 grams for a young, potassium-poor sample. If prepared samples of mineral separates are sent, they should meet high standards of purity.

Unprepared (Whole Rock) Samples:

An unseparated rock sample (hand specimen, core, chips) should generally be large enough to yield the quantities of mineral separate noted above. Usually, to obtain 10 grams of pure mineral, we find that we need a sample containing about 30 grams of the mineral. A hand specimen or equivalent quantity generally suffices; however, if you have 5 or 10 lbs., send it along.

We do not return unused material unless asked to do so; however, it is kept on file, available to the sender on request.

SHIPPING

Air freight, railway express or parcel post (securely packed!) is recommended. Where time is of little importance, rail or ocean freight is satisfactory. Samples

EXHIBIT 2 (continued)

from abroad should be clearly labeled, "Scientific Specimens—No Commercial Value."

LABORATORY FACILITIES

Sample preparation facilities include complete comminution equipment, magnetic separators, heavy liquid equipment, and petrographic equipment for control of separations.

The argon extraction systems are patterned after the best features of those at the University of Minnesota and at M.I.T. The systems are all directly connected to the mass spectrometer, athough otherwise completely independent. A 'continuous' spike system, similar to that in use at M.I.T., serves each system.

Mass spectrometric analyses are made on an instrument patterned after that designed by J. H. Reynolds of the University of California. This is the most sophisticated instrumentation available for the purpose, and, indeed, ranks among the most sensitive of measuring devices known to man. Its capability to analyze extremely minute quantities of argon enables us to determine the age of very young or potassium deficient specimens.

Rigorous quality control is exercised throughout the operation. The Ar^{38} spike is repeatedly calibrated by two independent methods; mass spectrometric analyses are fractionation and discrimination corrected. Regularly scheduled standard samples, and random replicate analyses of routine samples ensure constant precision levels. Potassium analyses, determined by means of a flame spectrophotometer, are regularly repeated gravimetrically. The overall analytical error of the age determination is thus held to less than 2%.

We welcome the opportunity
of answering any questions you may have

CHARGES

(All Prices in U.S. Dollars)

Age Determinations

Complete Potassium-Argon age determination,
   on unprepared sample $350
Complete K-Ar age determination on prepared sample
   (pure mineral separate) $300

Separate Services Available

Mineral Separation & Purification (an overage is charged
   when technician's work exceeds 15 hours) .... $ 60
Potassium Analysis .... $ 40
Argon extraction, mass spectrometric analysis, and reduction
   of data to Ar^{40} content, or age $275
Analysis of received pure argon sample for Ar^{36}, Ar^{38}, and Ar^{40} $125

Fees Arranged: For counsulting service, and analysis of other alkali metals.

EXHIBIT 2 (continued)

Delivery: Generally, we return results within 30 days of receipt of specimen. In cases of extreme urgency, a priority service can be arranged.

GEOCHRON LABORATORIES, INC.
24 BLACKSTONE STREET, CAMBRIDGE 39, MASS.
Telephone TRowbridge 6-3691

LATER DEVELOPMENTS

Shortly after the successful public issue, the four founders sat down to take stock of their progress. A source of extreme disappointment had been the sales volume; during the eight months from July, 1960, through February, 1961, only eight requests for age determinations had been received, and all were still being processed. The management believed that the low level of orders stemmed primarily from the forced absence of advertising due to lack of capital. Since the issuance of Technical Bulletin No. 1, shortly after incorporation, no mailings had been sent to potential customers; consequently, the anticipated inflow of fall orders had failed to materialize. Also, no personal visits to conventions or to the geologists of potentially large customers had been made by Mr. Freedman, again because of financial limitations. Since the principals found themselves, in March of 1961, with equipment affording an annual capacity of about 400 determinations, for which they had paid $35,000, they felt compelled to spare no reasonable expense necessary to generate a substantial level of orders.

Accordingly they began advertising in various technical journals and trade publications. A large-scale direct-mail effort was begun, including a covering letter, a pamphlet describing the laboratory, and the offer of a complete bibliography of geochronology on return of a reply card. This mailing was sent to 5,000 geologists, of whom 10 percent were foreign. In April, 1,000 pamphlets and 2,000 wallet-size plastic geological time scales were distributed at a petroleum geologists' convention. In May, a second direct-mail promotion was sent to the same 5,000 geologists who had received the first mailing. This time, a letter, an information sheet on the subject of sample requirements for K–Ar age determinations, and a small cloth bag for use in collecting samples were enclosed. Also, Mr. Freedman made several sales calls on large firms in the eastern sections of the United States and Canada.

By the fall of 1961 it became obvious, in the words of Mr. Lemer, that, ". . . development of demand for our age determination services, as indicated by rock samples received, has been slower than expected. It seems likely that demand for a service as advanced and complex as ours will take longer to develop than was originally anticipated." Only 41 requests for determinations had been received from February, the time of the public offering, through November, 1961. Consequently, the six-month report to stockholders, arriving in December, announced the resignation of Messrs. Lemer and Freedman. Though Mr. Altman retained the title of treasurer, he accepted fulltime employment elsewhere. The company had shown an operating loss of $33,000 on no sales in its first year, and a loss of $31,000 on sales of $7,300 for the first six months of its second year.

THE CURRENT SITUATION

In the second half of its second year of operation, the company began to show signs of improvement. Requests for determinations averaged eight per month during the six months ending May 31, 1962, and the company showed a loss of only about $3,000 during that period. Though there was a two-year deficit of some $67,000, the working capital position was far from desperate. There were net current assets of about $75,000, of which $70,000 was cash, as of May, 1962. Since Lemer and Freedman had relinquished their options to all except 2,500 shares apiece under the company option plan, potential dilution had been reduced by 30,000 shares to 360,000 shares. As of May, 278,100 shares were outstanding and the remaining 81,900 were reserved for potential conversion of warrants and options. The stock was quoted over the counter at about 25 cents per share in October, 1962. It had traded at a price as high as $7.00 per share shortly after the public offering date. Recent balance sheets for the company appear as Exhibits 3 through 6.

Balance Sheet, October 31, 1960

Assets:		
Cash	$19,470.20	
Progress payments for laboratory equipment under construction	15,000.00	
Leasehold improvements	666.66	
Organization expenses	801.65	
Administrative and general expenses	2,478.77	
Telephone deposit	60.00	
Total Assets		$38,477.28
Liabilities:		
6% unsecured convertible notes	$35,000.00	
Unsecured loans from officers	654.59	
Accrued officers' salaries	240.00	
Accrued interest	87.50	
Accounts payable	245.19	
Total Liabilities		$36,227.28
Capital:		
70,000 Common shares issued and outstanding	$ 700.00	
Additional paid-in capital	1,550.00	
Total Capital		$ 2,250.00
Total Liabilities and Capital		$38,477.28

EXHIBIT 3. Geochron Laboratories, Inc.

EXHIBIT 4. Geochron Laboratories, Inc.

Balance Sheet, May 31, 1961

Assets

Current Assets:

Cash	$ 21,715	
Marketable securities, at cost (which approximates market value)	64,931	
Advances to employees	947	
Prepaid expenses	847	
Total Current Assets		$ 88,440

Property and Equipment, at Cost:

Laboratory equipment	$ 34,753	
Furniture and fixtures	1,067	
Leasehold improvements	2,013	
	$ 37,923	
Less: Accumulated depreciation and amortization	4,277	33,696
Organization expense, less amortization of $262		2,877
Total Assets		$125,013

Liabilities

Current Liabilities:

Accounts payable	$ 2,055	
Accrued taxes	917	
Total Current Liabilities		$ 2,972

Stockholders' Investment:

Common stock, 1 cent par value; 1,000,000 shares authorized, 267,100 shares issued and outstanding	$ 2,671	
Additional amounts paid in on common stock	152,475	
Retained earnings (deficit)	(33,105)	122,041
Total Liabilities		$125,013

EXHIBIT 5. Geochron Laboratories, Inc.

Balance Sheet, November 30, 1961

Assets

Current Assets:

Cash	$ 20,477.77	
Marketable securities at cost, approximate resale value	49,706.00	
Accounts receivable	2,303.70	
Accrued interest	256.54	
Deposits	161.80	
Prepayments	491.54	
Total Current Assets		$ 73,397.35

EXHIBIT 5. (continued)

Property and Equipment, at Cost:		
Laboratory equipment	$ 33,943.44	
Furniture and fixtures	1,376.80	
Leasehold improvements	2,102.79	
	$ 37,423.03	
Less: Accumulated depreciation and amortization	10,604.47	26,818.56
Organization expense, less amortization of $575.43		2,563.42
Total Assets		$102,799.33

Liabilities

Current Liabilities:		
Accounts payable	$ 238.14	
Accrued taxes	874.38	
Total Current Liabilities		$ 1,112.52
Stockholders' Investment		
Common stock, 1 cent par value; 1,000,000 shares authorized, 278,100 issued and outstanding	$ 2,781.00	
Additional amounts paid in on common stock	163,365.44	
Retained earnings (deficit)	(64,479.63)	101,666.81
Total Liabilities		$102,779.33

EXHIBIT 6. Geochron Laboratories, Inc.

Balance Sheet, May 31, 1962

Assets

Current Assets:		
Cash	$ 9,797	
Deposits in savings banks, including accrued interest of $567	60,767	
Accounts receivable	6,014	
Prepaid expenses	987	$ 77,565
Property and Equipment, at Cost:		
Laboratory equipment	$ 34,452	
Furniture and fixtures	1,630	
Leasehold improvements	2,103	
	$ 38,105	
Less Accumulated depreciation and amortization	16,815	21,370
Organization expense, less amortization of $889		2,250
Total Assets		$101,185

EXHIBIT 6. (continued)

Liabilities		
Current Liabilities:		
Accounts payable	$ 734	
Accrued liabilities	2,029	
Total Current Liabilities		$ 2,763
Stockholders' Investment:		
Common stock, 1 cent par value; 1,000,000 shares authorized, 278,100 shares outstanding	$ 2,781	
Additional amounts paid in on common stock	163,365	
Retained earnings (deficit)	(67,724)	98,422
Total Liabilities		$101,185

In the summer of 1962, Mr. Krueger, the only founder remaining with the company on a full-time basis, hired a technician to help him in performing K –Ar analyses, raising to three the number of employees. Requests for determinations were still sporadic; the company had received 29 such requests in June, 8 in July, and 1 in August. Mr. Krueger emphasized that the company was operating profitably at that time, with cash expenses averaging less than $2,500 per month. His long-term objective was to gradually build up the company's reputation, primarily through word of mouth from satisfied customers, to the point where it could generate a reasonable return for the common stockholders. He recognized that a carefully managed program of corporate acquisitions might also improve the firm's profit picture.

Datamax Corporation

In late July 1969, Mr. Samuel T. Harmon, president of Datamax Corporation, sat in his office in Ann Arbor, Michigan, and talked at length about the events and circumstances which had led to the formation of one of the few black-owned electronics firms in the nation. He spoke at ease about his background, his work experience, his first attempt at entrepreneurship, the work which eventually led to the creation of Datamax, and the present and future prospects for his own career development and the developmental strategies for the company.

This case describes the background and career development of Mr. Harmon and the organization and current status of the Datamax Corporation.

Datamax Corporation, located at 3941 Research Park Drive in Ann Arbor, was incorporated in Michigan on November 1, 1967, and is engaged in the development, manufacture, and marketing of data communications devices. The initial efforts of the company have been concentrated upon the development of data communications devices in order to exploit the inventions of its president, Mr. Harmon.

The first contracts for the company's products were negotiated in late 1968 with two large American corporations for whom the company built prototype models of the data communications device. In November 1968, the company had limited sales, only a few prototype orders, and a monthly cash outflow of $40,000 to $50,000 (see Exhibit 1).

It is anticipated that Datamax's total sales for the twelve-month period ending March 31, 1970, will be approximately $1.5 million with total bookings in the approximate amount of $2 million. Sales in the second twelve-month period are projected in the amount of $4.0 million. Sales are expected to increase by at least multiples of two for the succeeding 36-month period. By the time sales levels of $2.8 million are attained, it is expected that Datamax's unique proprietary position, combined with the high expertise of its technical staff, will enable Datamax to achieve net profit margins of 30% of sales before federal income taxes.

This case was prepared by Clifford E. Darden under the direction of Professor Paul R. Lawrence. The case was copyrighted in 1970 by the President and Fellows of Harvard College and is reproduced by permission.

The Product

The principal products being developed by the company now employ applications of a proprietary device invented by Mr. Harmon. The basic principle of the device is to utilize redundant codes so as to increase the data through-put utilizing the facilities of the A.T.&T. dial telephone network, while at the same time increasing the reliability of the data so transmitted.

The Datamax system accomplishes the faster and more reliable through-put utilizing the dial network by encoding data signals at the transmitting terminal and decoding the encoded signal at the receiving terminal, using digital and decoding processes. As a result of the encoding and decoding processes, transmission errors due to line disturbances are detected and corrected at the receiving terminal.

In addition to the encoders and decoders the Datamax system also employs a modulator and demodulator (it is called "modem" by the company) designed by Datamax. The various components of the Datamax system can be designed to interface with the various types of communications terminal equipment now being offered.

Another unique feature of the Datamax system is that it can be coupled acoustically to telephone transmission lines.

In order to satisfy the particular needs of different types of customers, the company has developed three basic models of Datamax error-correcting communications system, each having its own error-correcting power to fit the error and speed requirements for the particular type of communications (see Exhibit 2).

Prospects for the Company

The data communications field in which Datamax Corporation is involved is a rapidly growing one. In 1968, $50 million worth of devices for data communication were sold. Some market analysts predict that the figure for 1972 will be about $400 million. Mr. Harmon confidently predicts that Datamax will grow along with the market. He said:

> We're in a rapidly growing field, we have a superior product, and it's accepted. This suddenly forces the company to decide what kind of company it wants to be. We can become a $10 or $15 million company in terms of annual sales; or we can become a $100 million company. The latter is very, very possible. I think we have most of the resources required to get to that point.

SAMUEL T. HARMON

Personal Background

One would not normally expect a high school dropout to become one of the key contributors in signal processing technology for advanced communications, surveillance, and navigation in the United States. Inventory of the only successful electro-optical computer on which a patent has been granted, the 39-year-old Mr. Harmon has a technical background which includes management and technical direction of programs related to ballistic missile defense systems and satellite surveillance systems involving radars and multisensors. His theoretical and research experience includes plasma physics studies, plasma-microwave interaction phenomena, ballistics re-entry microwave phenomena, and high-powered cross-field microwave oscillator and amplifier techniques.

Mr. Harmon was born in Detroit in 1929, the oldest of nine children of an automotive plant laborer. Out of the nine children in his family, none graduated from high school. Mr. Harmon left school at the age of 15, "raised" his age and entered the U.S. Navy. His beginning in electronics started in the Navy when he was admitted to the Navy's electronics technician school in 1946. After completing this one-year program Mr. Harmon served for the next several years as a technician in the Pacific Fleet and as a part-time instructor at a Naval electronics school in California. After serving 8 years, he had every intention of making a career out of the Navy. He was planning on a 30-year career and had assumed that he would, after a while, get a chance to "buck for" a commission in the Navy. But, changes in Naval requirements for commissioned officers caused Mr. Harmon to alter his plans.

Harmon left the Navy in mid-1953, intending to obtain the Bachelor's degree as quickly as possible and to return to the Navy and resume his 30-year Naval career plans. He felt that, as a black man in the Navy, he was doing exactly the job which he was qualified to do without any racial restrictions. And he did not see many opportunities for reaching the same level of responsibility outside of the Navy.

Upon leaving the Navy, Harmon decided to "probe around just gently" to see whether or not he could find a job in Michigan, making use of the kind of training he had in the Navy. He applied for a technician's job at the University of Michigan and was hired immediately. At the same time, he began taking night courses at Wayne State University in Detroit. Although he did not have a high school diploma, he gained admission to Wayne State by taking an entrance examination on which he did "quite well."

Thus, Harmon embarked on a schedule of part-time technical work in the Radiation Laboratory at the University of Michigan and part-time studies at both Wayne State and Michigan Universities. Explaining that he was "a man in a hurry," Harmon obtained a Bachelor of Science degree in the summer of 1955—just 2½ years after leaving the Navy—and worked as a junior engineer at the University of Michigan for one year after obtaining the B.S. degree. By that time he no longer intended to return to the Navy; instead, he established a different set of goals for himself. With a degree in physics, and a job which he enjoyed, he decided that he would continue to do technical work outside of the Navy. He fully intended to follow a technical-scientific career and to avoid managerial positions in the technical or scientific field.

In order to insure that he would not encounter any disruptions in his career goals, Harmon proceeded to bolster his background in the technical areas in which he was mainly interested by earning a Master's degree in engineering. Receiving the Master's degree in 1956, he had done all of the research and the preliminary draft work on his Ph.D. dissertation by 1958. But he never got the Ph.D. degree because he had become far more interested in the jobs on which he was working.

Business Experience

Beginning in 1957, Harmon went to work as an engineer for a radar company—Strand Engineering Company—in Ann Arbor. He joined this company because he had a good background in radar technology and because "it looked like a growing company in which I thought I'd be in a better position than I would be if I went to work for one of the larger companies involved in the same type of technical work."

From Strand Company Harmon went to work as a research scientist for Keeve Siegel, who was then a professor of electrical engineering at the University of Michigan. Noting that "Siegel had since started two companies, one of which (Conductron Corporation) went from $0 to $40 million in sales in five years," Harmon asserted that "I mention this because he must have had some influence on my own thinking about the business world." (Siegel, Harmon pointed out, is now "a year and a half into a conglomerate which does about $50 million in sales a year.")

Harmon attributes a large part of his professional development as a specialist in radar technology to the two years of work with Professor Siegel. Some of the tasks which he was given involved going into the ballistic missiles impact areas in the Pacific Ocean and conducting instrumentation of the various ballistic missile phenomena. As a result of his focusing on a narrow scientific aspect of the ballistic missile program, he developed viewpoints and perspectives which were fairly unique to himself. Siegel, who was at that time a member of the Air Force Scientific Advisory Board, asked Harmon to attend high-level Pentagon briefings as technical back-up man. As a result of this work, he was invited to join a special advisory board to the Secretary of Defense for ballistic missile defense problems. Harmon noted that "this marked the first time in my career as an engineer where the methods of presenting the data were equally as important as the data itself." It was during this time that he learned how to be a persuasive salesman for his own particular point of view.

After two years of work with Professor Siegel and the Air Force Scientific Advisory Board, Harmon was hired by Bendix Corporation, which was one of the large corporations that had become interested in the scientific and technical aspects of the ballistic missiles program. He worked for Bendix Corporation for three years, going from a group leader to a section leader and, finally, to a department manager. Much of his job responsibility involved obtaining projects for the company and acting as a project leader for the projects which the company was already working on.

Harmon ended up with practically all of the responsibility for new business in the ballistic missile area in Bendix's Ann Arbor Division—"a fairly responsible job." But this type of management job marked a deviation from the career path that he had set out for himself, and the problems of working in a larger corporation began to bother him.

The "entrepreneurial bug" began to bite. The constant sales effort had led to a personality development which made Harmon feel fairly confident that he could maintain his expertise in technical areas. He felt that "if one knows what needs to be done and can do it and knows how to sell it, then one has two of the major requirements for tapping the wealth of this free enterprise society."

Upon leaving Bendix, he began consulting in the technical and scientific areas in which he had obtained extensive work experience. However, this consulting endeavor lasted for only a few weeks because, during that time, one of his corporate clients approached him with a proposal which triggered the beginning of his entry into business, climaxing in the creation of Datamax. The client wanted Harmon to set up and run a "Route 128" type company around Ann Arbor. Harmon rejected the offer, deciding instead that he would pursue a line of action which would lead to the creation of a corporation of which he would be the principal owner.

Although he had no money, no machines, and no contacts in particular which would enable him to create his own company, Harmon knew that there were a few much needed technological innovations, the market for which was virtually guaranteed. This was at the time that Secretary of Defense Robert McNamara had canceled the B-70 program due to a lack of a certain kind of radar which the industry could not seem to develop. There was one special signal processing requirement that this radar had, and Harmon went to work on developing some technical approaches to solving this problem. He thought that if he could develop the approaches, he could obtain funding from government agencies and he could use the funding to organize a company to carry out the development of these technical approaches to this radar problem.

In a time span of 8 months, Harmon not only conceived an approach to the signal processing problem, but discovered that the development of the hardware solution to the problem—"which looked quite feasible on paper"—would cost about a half million dollars. Emphasizing that he had, at the time, "absolutely no sophistication in knowing how to go about raising a half million dollars," Harmon decided to seek an alternative to the formation of his own independent, fully controlled company.

The first thing that occurred to him was that this signal processing system would be a key item in a larger radar system. The market potential for that larger radar system was estimated to be about $700 million. Feeling quite certain that "some large radar company ought to be interested in this gadget (the signal processing system)," Harmon carefully investigated several large radar companies and finally selected one with which to organize a joint venture for the development of the idea.

Harmon emphasized that he chose an area where the existence of the market was a proven fact. Stating that "the existence of the market for a given technical gadget is usually well known," he said that he had convinced himself, through the years of work, of his technical creativity—a creativity which had always led to special solutions to tough problems that had eluded others. He decided to concentrate on those areas in which the market was known because he felt that his role would be considerably easier.

Harmon's three years as president of Sensor Dynamics, Inc., of Ann Arbor (the company which was organized as a joint venture with the large radar company to exploit the electro-optical correlator invention of Mr. Harmon's for use in radar signal processing to work on radar signal problems) were not as untroubled as Harmon might have wished. Although the large radar company did not take the majority position in Sensor Dynamics, the development funds were supplied in such a way that the large radar company had board members and veto power, in effect, over virtually all of the company's operations.

Sensor Dynamics was built up to about three-quarters of a million a year in sales and about $35,000 a year in profits. The company had a very highly sophisticated technical staff, but had to rely on the larger company for marketing its products. Eventually, the larger company began pressing for the rights to manufacture the device, also, and apparently did not want Sensor Dynamics to grow to a size at which it could exist in the industry without the financial and marketing assistance of the larger company.

The company had "people problems," also. After it had been going for about a year, Harmon realized that there were three people in the company who thought they were the number two man. In his zeal to recruit the talented persons necessary to get the company going, Harmon had given each of the three persons plenty of reason to feel that each of them was the number two man. He had not consciously promised things which he could not deliver; but, in his haste to get the operations going, he was not as specific as he might have been.

Then, there were problems with the advisors and the technical managers who had no business experience. There was a wide variety of people in the company who had business experience and who were, at times, overbearing in their attitudes and behavior toward the technically oriented personnel. Harmon was, for a while, convinced that what they were saying was right and, in retrospect, thinks that perhaps he placed too much trust in their advice. The result was that he paid too much attention to the technology and not enough attention to the nontechnical aspects of the company. As president of the company, he had to make decisions on nontechnical problems; and he found that he just did not have the background or experience upon which to make weighty business decisions.

Additionally, there were other conflicts revolving around corporate goals and strategy. It soon became apparent to Harmon that persons in the larger radar company had different sets of goals for Sensor Dynamics than he had. On the board of directors of Sensor Dynamics were a few people who were interested in a quick cash pay-out. The company had received an offer of a million and a half dollars for the patent from another radar company. Some persons on the board wanted to sell, but Harmon was more interested in building a stable, long-term organization. Some other members of the board were more interested in keeping the company small and perpetually dependent upon the partner corporation. Finally, a third faction on the board wanted to use the patent for its own private exploitation. Since the patent was the major asset of the company, none of the three groups could achieve its objectives without acquiring rights to the patent. Harmon said that he thought there was "plenty of justification for the position of each group"; however, these divergent positions on corporate strategy did not make for harmony within the company or aggressiveness within the market place.

Finally, Harmon dissolved the company and put the patent into a trust, opening it to all users on a royalty-paying basis. The company, upon liquidation, had a cash value which was "significantly higher" than the paid-in capital, so all of the shareholders got back in the liquidation their original investment plus 12% per year. Harmon noted that this return represented "maybe twice what they would have gotten at bank rates if they had simply put their money in a savings account." The shareholders continued to receive a portion of the royalty payments which subsequent patent users paid. Although the company did a little better than breaking even, Harmon considers it "a financial failure" because the company had much greater potential than was actually realized from its operation.

DATAMAX CORPORATION

The Creation of Datamax

With the dissolution of the joint venture, Harmon decided that he didn't want to give business a "second chance" immediately. But, as a result of this experience and "having been bitten by the 'bug' a second time," Harmon spent the next year just thinking about how he would go about it if he ever had a second chance. During this year he also worked as a consultant to both government and private agencies, always reserving "just a little free time for myself for my own inventions." He continued to ask himself, "What is one of the more significant non-military problems in the electronics industry that I have the background to tackle?"

In arriving at an answer to this question, Harmon reviewed both his technical background and the nature of one of the unsolved problems in the data communication field. Signal processing—the process of extracting information from electrical waveforms where these waveforms may have been distorted by noise, etc.—was his area of expertise. Signal processing was one that was relevant to communications through the telephone network, also. However, the telephone network is only about 5% efficient for conveying machine-type signals, having been designed primarily for the transmission of electrical characteristics of voice signals. The capacity, in terms of telephone system time, is roughly equally divided between people and machines. Therefore, Harmon reasoned, any way of increasing the efficiency of the telephone system for conveying machine-type signals would have a favorable impact of considerable magnitude on a company's telephone bill, assuming that the increased efficiency could be had at a reasonable cost.

Harmon acknowledged that other researchers had been working on this problem for some time and that the key technical problem required to handle it was fairly well known. In other words, there existed a well-recognized general problem, at the base of which lay one missing technological link. The few people who knew Harmon well told him: "It's important; it's tough; and we think you've got the right background. If anybody can contribute to the solution, Sam, you're the person."

In preparation for the task which he was about to tackle, Harmon took about four months to get some mathematical background on the particular area, another month or two to familiarize himself thoroughly with what past workers had done in the problem area, and then set out to see if he could create a device which would lead to an increase in the utility of the network for machine communications.

Harmon was successful in devising a theoretical solution which he felt "a few knowledgeable people would immediately recognize as the solution to that key problem." However, he was not especially anxious to organize another company, feeling that an easier way of gaining an existence would be through selling the patent rights to the device in return for a "good healthy income" from royalties or some stock ownership in a growing company.

As he explored the ways of exploiting his technological breakthrough, Harmon was very careful to remember and to apply the "lessons" he had learned from his first business venture. One of the lessons that he had learned was "to recognize your negotiating strengths and to play the game of negotiating for the best you can get." He had also learned that "a person can negotiate most effectively only if a couple or more people are interested in buying what you have." The offer from the first company was "perhaps just enough for the annual interest from it, if conservatively invested, to have generated enough money to maintain my current standard of living."

Harmon decided for a variety of reasons to try to get more from his idea, and he decided that the way to do this was to get other companies interested. To achieve the objective of getting other companies interested, he proceeded to develop further his idea. From his basement, he built a system that would demonstrate that the principles he required were sound. Going further, he constructed a logical implementation of the product based on the system. He retained two computer design engineers to design the entire system.

At this point, he wanted to get a rough estimate of specific market for the product as an additional step in broadening still further the base of potential customers for the device. Lawrence L. Dobrin, who was then the commercial marketing manager for another electronics company, made a market study which showed that "thousands" of the devices could be sold at a price which Harmon and his associates thought was reasonable. At the conclusion of his study, "he simply offered to join the firm."

After having done all of these things, Harmon and his associates began to ask themselves, "Why not go into business and exploit this device ourselves?" They began to question seriously whether they should go out and try to sell it to someone else. Harmon explained that something inside of him said, "Don't rush." He felt that he had rushed the first time (Sensor Dynamics), but this time he decided that incorporation in itself was not a goal.

What they did was to start working through the technology in the market, pre-selling the device using their own personal resources. Both Dobrin and David E. Klinger, who had done some of the development work on the device, quit their jobs at this time and for several months operated without any income at all. The three of them—Harmon, Dobrin, and Klinger—started doing all of the things that had to be done to organize Datamax.

They finally got to the point where they recognized that they were ready to get the device to the market place. Only one big problem remained: finances. They had received numerous offers for financial assistance from other corporations, but Harmon had evolved this one principle—that a corporation investing in another automatically has a different set of goals than does a purely speculative investor. He felt that corporations just don't invest their money in others to get a return on their investment. They expect to receive a fringe benefit from being involved in the technology that the smaller company is developing. So, Harmon and his associates decided not to let other companies participate in the financing.

The three men felt that with a quarter of a million dollars in paid-in capital they could get to the point of marketing the first device. This would be "cutting it very slim," but such money would be very high risk money and, hence, would come only at a very dear price. The three most crucial considerations were: 1) that the company obtain $250,000; 2) that Harmon maintain majority ownership; and 3) that the company avoid getting involved with another corporation.

They talked with several different types of financiers. The first type were wealthy and successful individuals operating together in small groups of two or three. Although these persons were not at all reluctant to put up the money, they wanted majority control (something like 60%) of the company in return. The second type were the investment bankers, who were more astute than the first group, and who recognized immediately that Harmon and his associates would really need about $700,000 to handle the development, establish a marketing organization, and a manufacturing organization. Harmon's goal for the first quarter of a million dollars was simply to get operations to the point at which the second round of financing would be easier to obtain under more favorable terms. But the investment bankers felt that the company would need more money and offered more, but in return for a larger piece of the company.

At this point, Harmon decided to try a different route in obtaining the needed initial capitalization. He had lived in and around southeastern Michigan for several years, and many people had watched his progress in organizing and operating Sensor Dynamics. While the company had not been an unqualified success as a business, Harmon was not treated as a failure. So, he approached professional men who were generally affluent enough to be able to sustain a loss of $15,000–$20,000 without damage to their financial status. More importantly, this third type of financier was not known as an investor group and did not have the constant barrage of investment deals offered to them. Consequently, the professional persons whom Harmon approached "were a little more interested" than the other two types had been, and he was able to make an agreement with them.

With this initial capitalization, the company hired a technical staff, further developed the electronic system, and worked hard to get one system installed with "a large, prestigious '*Fortune* 500' company" before the money ran out. These achievements, it was felt, would make it easier for the company to obtain the second round of financing. At about the time that Harmon and his associates were contemplating where and how to obtain another level of financing, a major change in the environment necessitated their altering their strategic plans and, with it, their plans for a new financial structure. Harmon gave some background on the environmental changes which led to new marketing and financing strategies:

> We were all set to go into production on this limited basis with this device that was going to fit between the business machine and the terminal that Bell himself provided. Then A.T.&T. changed their policies and said that private manufacturers could manufacture the terminals themselves. This made us realize that our gadget, when put inside a terminal we could manufacture, would give our terminal competitive advantages well above and beyond any other existing one. We decided, therefore, to escalate and become a terminal manufacturer.
>
> This, then, raised the business prospects from a company that might grow to five to seven million to one that could potentially hit thirty million in sales a year, considering the market as it was. We had to decide how to handle this changed environment. We chose to go after the bigger one, and this was based on a number of considerations: the possibility of doing so, first of all; but, secondly, a three or four million dollar company is, in my opinion, just a damned uncomfortable one. A million dollar company is one that I could have seen as being quite easy and handy to have. It's based on, usually, a set of customers having loyalties to one or two people in the company; and these customers will see to it that the company rides the economic ups and downs. The three to seven million dollar company cannot rely on that personal contact for getting orders to keep the company in business. This size of company would have all the

problems of a major corporation but really not the resources of one. It has to have a diversity of customers so that it can trade off the ups and downs.

Harmon explained that his initial idea in organizing the company was to build it up to an attractive size—seven or eight million dollar annual sales— and then sell it to another corporation in exchange for securities of the buyer. But "with the possibility of getting beyond the fifteen or twenty million dollars a year sales horizon," he and his associates changed their strategy. They felt that a corporation of this size (fifteen to twenty million dollar sales) would be "the kind of company which is big enough to cope with corporate problems and has enough resources to cope with." But they realized also that if they were going to get to that size as rapidly as they desired they would have to go for public monies. Harmon explained how this was accomplished and the effects on his control position.

With the conscious strategy of raising another million dollars to expand the product line, to start production, and to develop a backlog of one or two million dollars in sales, Harmon and his associates approached a large prestigious investment banker, and within a week negotiated a total of $1.1 million of new capital for the company. He was no longer able to maintain personal control after this second round of financing, but he still had enough stock so that even in a future public offering, he could sell a significant fraction of his stock and still retain working control of the public company.[1] In order to be certain that he maintained a little more independence and freedom than he had had in the first company, Harmon sold part of his stock ownership at the time of this refinancing "just to get a nest egg aside" so that he would not have to worry about his own personal financial situation. This action also allowed him to treat himself as an employee of the corporation, without having to worry about possible conflicts between what is good for him and what is good for the company.

Marketing Strategy

After the financing matter was settled, the principals turned their attention to the problems of production and marketing. While the financial arrangements were still being specified, the principals proceeded to develop two products; one for the digital computer communications and the other for facsimile communications.

The company had initially planned to offer these products to other equipment manufacturers on an OEM basis. This strategy had been devised to allow the company to delay temporarily the problem of establishing its own sales and service organization. But, as the principals got into negotiations with the OEM

---

[1]Mr. Harmon holds 41,000 shares of Class A common stock and 5,100 shares of Class B stock. The company's present authorized capital consists of 72,000 shares of Class A common stock and 10,500 shares of Class B common stock. The rights and privileges of the Class A and Class B common stock are identical except that to the extent that options are exercised under the company's qualified stock option program, shares of the Class B common stock may be redeemed by the company at a price of $20 per share.

market, they soon learned that the price which the OEM companies offered was not based on the economies which their customers would receive from the device; instead, the price was based on the OEM companies' own manufacturing costs and other policies which had no relationship to the attractiveness of the system to the end-users. It soon became apparent to the principals that the basic advantage of their device—i.e., lowering the end-users' telephone bills—would be negated if they chose to sell to the OEM market.

The company changed its over-all strategy in early 1969, and decided to sell to end-users. It was felt that this strategy would allow Datamax to establish the price and the demand with the end-user and then work back up to the OEM companies. (The OEM companies were willing to offer only 20–30% of what the end-users would pay for the product.) This end-user marketing strategy was designed as a means of allowing Datamax to exploit its proprietary patent or monopoly position of the technology, without having the company's growth and profit margins determined by the OEM market. In selecting this strategy, the principals decided to forego the greater dollar volume which could have been generated by the OEM market, since the profit margin in the OEM market would have been much smaller.

Because the company did not yet have a sales and service organization, they had to choose relatively sophisticated end-users who were capable of maintaining the equipment with their own maintenance engineers and technicians. The airline companies, for example, were willing to purchase the device (without any special price consideration) because these companies had their own maintenance organizations. The economic motivation, in terms of the lower communications costs, was sufficient inducement for the airline companies.

While this marketing strategy was working well for 1969, Harmon noted that it had caused some problems which could have been avoided for another year or two had the company retained its initial marketing strategy. The company developed a tremendous backlog of orders as a result of the first trade show in May 1969. In one case, the company received a $1.25 million order for the device. The purchaser would have taken all of the systems as immediately as Datamax could deliver them, but Datamax decided not to use all of its productive capacity to satisfy any one customer. Instead, Datamax spread this large order over a couple of years.

American Telephone & Telegraph (A.T.&T.) had captured about 80% of the market in the field in which Datamax was competing because of some restrictive regulations which prohibited independent manufacturers from tying equipment to the telephone lines under certain conditions. At the beginning of 1969, the Federal Communications Commission struck down those restrictive regulations, thereby eliminating A.T.&T.'s virtual monopoly position in the modem field. For Datamax, this action meant that a sales and service organization would have to be established in order to take full advantage of its superior product and of the lack of restrictive regulations on the use of the telephone networks.

Harmon explained that Datamax could scatter a few of its salesmen across the country and selectively choose the kind of customer who had some degree of electronics sophistication. But competitors, in order to counter Datamax's advanced technology, were already saying in their advertising, "Remember, Mr. Customer, you're buying more than just technology; you're buying service and reliability. And you'd better look to the older, more established companies for that."

Thus, Datamax was working on plans to establish a nationwide sales and service organization which would require an additional $2 million of capital. Noting that the building of this organization "would not be an easy task," Harmon expressed confidence that Datamax could "build one that is at least as good as any other which is servicing the kind of equipment that we have here." Plans called for the division of the country into about seven regions, each of which would be under a regional sales manager who would hire the salesmen and servicemen needed for his region. The regional sales managers would be under the direction of a national sales manager who would be headquartered in Ann Arbor. Recruiting the right type of salesmen at all levels in the proposed sales organization was expected to be difficult because of the relatively few people who have experience in selling or maintaining the kind of equipment that Datamax was selling. It was expected that training would be primarily operational, on-the-job training, at least for the key executives. Harmon felt that although this was a slower way of building the sales and service organization, it would be a more efficient and safer way and would allow headquarters to control the quality of the organization as it developed.

The data communications equipment industry is concentrated in only a few areas of the country, and Harmon felt that it will be another several years before it becomes extremely widespread. Thus, Datamax would be well-entrenched in those areas of the country where there will be much equipment sold. This includes the entire East coast (from Boston to Miami), southern California, some parts of northern California, the Midwest (mainly in and around Chicago), and perhaps the Seattle area.

Harmon explained that the company was actively negotiating with investment bankers for an additional $2 million in capital, at least three-quarters of which will be earmarked for creating the sales and service organization. The remainder will be used to build more inventory which will allow the company to gear up its manufacturing operations more rapidly than the managers thought would be necessary or possible in May 1969.

Manufacturing Strategy

Datamax's present plant (16,000 square feet of space), located in an industrial park in Ann Arbor, is expected to suffice until sales reach the level of $5 to $7 million a year, making maximum use of subcontractors. The company has an option on land adjacent to this property where they expect to build 20,000 square feet of additional capacity within two to four years.

The manufacturing operations are those normal to electronic assembly and involve soldering and wiring components. The only substantial capital expenditure required is for testing equipment for inspection of both the incoming components and the completed final assembly. In order to accommodate sales of $3 million, the company estimates a direct labor force of approximately 35 will be required.

The company is currently modifying the building to accommodate an assembly line operation. They have not delivered any manufactured equipment. They have delivered a few handmade pre-production prototypes "just to test our customer acceptances after they have had them for a while." The assembly line will not be running until December 1969, at which time Datamax will begin delivering mass-produced equipment.

In the meanwhile, the backlog of orders is building up, and it's already past a million dollars in sales for the current year. Because the company is presently production-limited, the strategy has been that of getting a few of the systems into the hands of many different companies, as opposed to supplying the total needs of just a few larger buyers. Datamax is trying to place the systems into the hands of buyers who need fifty or so systems and who can perform their own evaluations. By the time Datamax is able to deliver in large quantities, potential large buyers will have overcome all the hesitations which they might have. However, the company will not be able to deliver as many systems as is needed to eliminate the backlog for this year. Harmon noted, however, that most customers are still willing to wait until Datamax can manufacture the systems, even though these customers would like delivery earlier than Datamax can promise.

In terms of the assembly line operations, Datamax has anticipated two kinds of problems, both of which have been handled. First, the assembly operation is relatively simple. The assembly characteristics of the products are those of the standard kinds of electronics equipment. There are plenty of companies, Harmon said, which specialize in manufacturing electronic sub-assemblies for manufacturers. Datamax has divided its system into eleven sub-assemblies and is having these parts manufactured by subcontractors. These sub-assemblies will be shipped to Datamax where they will be assembled into the final product. The company has tested several unskilled people to see how much training is required in order to develop the manual skills required to produce at peak efficiency. Three to four days is the time it takes to train an unskilled person to assemble the components.

The second important part of the manufacturing and assembly operations is the quality control and testing. The device is extremely obscure in its testing characteristics. It is basically a device for correcting errors that occur during transmission of data. The device is designed so that it can correct some of its own internal wiring or component errors. Rather than breaking down catastrophically when a piece goes out, its performance degrades gradually. What this means then is that the test procedures have to be extremely sophisticated. The company does not yet have a complete and sufficient set of test procedures, but they have hired the test engineering section, which is working with the development and manufacturing departments to devise reliable test procedures.

The goal is to develop the necessary set of test procedures by October 1969, so that the company will be confident that the equipment it ships will perform as it should. Harmon said that "there is no better way of stigmatizing our product than to have it not perform in the field." He noted that quality control and testing are more important in Datamax's product than they are for others, because the device goes in the buyer's communications channel. When the device breaks down, the buyer's communications stop. Understandably, the buyer would be very upset.

The only additional problems in manufacturing are those that come as a result of the fact that a significant part of the company's manufacturing cost goes into the purchase of parts and components. Harmon noted that it is necessary for Datamax to have "a pretty sophisticated purchasing department and a good inventory system." These have already been established.

The production of the modems can go from a hundred units a month to "a few thousand units" a month in the time span of three months. This will be possible because the subcontractors which the company has chosen have much larger capacities than the company will initially use.

Harmon reiterated his concern that the major limitation on production volume will be in the testing and quality control phases. He said that the company will automate these phases of manufacturing as soon as the test engineers have a complete understanding of what needs to be tested and have the manual procedures worked out.

Organizational Structure

Harmon is the chief executive, chief operating officer, and president of the company.[2] Reporting to him are four vice presidents, each of whom directs one of the four "divisions" of the company (see Exhibit 3).

The marketing division is headed by Lawrence Dobrin, and currently has a staff of three people. Dobrin, who came to Datamax Corporation from Conductron Corporation, where he had extensive experience in both government and commercial marketing, has done all of the selling to date. In explaining why Dobrin had done all of the selling, Harmon said:

> This was necessary because the hardware is not ready. What he has been selling is mainly the potential, the people, and the fact that the organization and the equipment are coming.
>
> Now that we are going into manufacturing, however, the sales function can be handled by considerably lower level persons than Larry. These salespersons will have a piece of equipment that can be sold on its own merits. So he (Larry) is beginning now to assemble a group of local salesmen, regional managers, and a sales manager. He already has some manufacturers' representatives lined up and working with him. He is using them to keep warm certain contacts that he himself has already made. But he is still closing all of the sales that have been made to date.

Harmon also pointed out that Dobrin will temporarily direct the planning and implementation of the service organization. He said:

> He'll be doing the organizational work in getting it going. I have some misgivings about having sales and service organized under the same head, but I've not yet resolved for myself the optimum way the service function should be integrated into Datamax as a whole.

The advanced development division is led by Lindsey Waldorf. The function of this division is "simply to take any new product ideas that the company is interested in exploring, to examine the theoretical aspects of those ideas to insure that they are sound, and (if the idea passes that test) to build one

---

[2]The board of Directors consists of Messrs. Samuel T. Harmon, Lawrence L. Dobrin, Howard K. Schwartz, David E. Klinger, Richard M. Mehrtens, Allen M. Krauss, George S. Odiorne, Daniel R. Fusfeld, and a gentleman representing the company's investment bankers. The first five persons are also officers of the company.

prototype or an engineering model." This engineering model is then used to prove that not only is the idea sound, but that it can be implemented. This model can then be displayed to potential customers to test for customer reaction in a sales environment. Harmon noted that generally, the marketing division works closely with advanced development in determining what types of hardware are needed in order to test the salability of the equipment.

David E. Klinger heads the manufacturing division, and has had 20 years of experience as the number one or number two technical man in a variety of small computer-related organizations. Klinger has built a sound reputation as an adept organizer and administrator, being able to "manage a lot of chaos at any one time." He has an advanced degree in engineering and has an excellent grasp of both the theoretical and practical aspects of the company's modems.

The finance division is under Mr. Howard Schwartz, a part-time administrator who is a practicing attorney in a large business law firm in Detroit. Mr. Schwartz is assisted by a full-time controller. "This fits part of my philosophy," said Mr. Harmon, "that the fund-raising activity—that is, the acquisition of operating funds under the most favorable terms possible—is quite a distinct function, requiring separate skills than those of the controller's function."

Harmon indicated that this basic organization "will exist for at least a couple of years more." He added, however, that one potential change could occur. He stated:

We will probably install an executive vice president—or maybe another president or chief operating officer. In other words, we need a man between me and the rest of the line organization. Whether he's called an executive vice president or chief operating officer has not yet been decided. A lot will depend on the individual.

Harmon indicated that he felt that the company's chief problem now is "basically an organizational development one." Emphasizing that the company's current management group and staff had done "a masterful job of creating a set of resources"—e.g., the technical product itself, the ability to manufacture it, etc.—he said that there would be a need very soon to bring in a person who would be adept at managing the resources which would be placed at his disposal.

Harmon said that some of the activities in which the company is involved would not be warranted for a $10-million-a-year company. For example, the quality of the people in the company is too high for a $10 million operation. Harmon and his associates assert that Datamax has the potential to reach the $100-million-a-year level. But, the company needs to bring in a chief operating officer who will be able to cope with the "administrative chaos" which will come with a company of that size.

Although Harmon has been exposed and has operated, by necessity, in a decision-making fashion in all of the aspects of the company's operations, he enjoys most "just probing out the need for new devices, finding a technological solution to them and engaging in the sales activities to demonstrate that they are salable." Harmon tends to demand the freedom to spend his time on the problems which he likes. The company is still small enough so that the most important problems which currently exist are the ones on which he likes to work. These are the problems in product development, market development, negotiations with financiers, etc. He indicated that financiers continue to invest in the company partly because of his technical knowledge of the product and because of his personality. But, two years from now, Harmon says, the ability of the company to raise the capital it needs will be directly related to the profit and loss statements. The company will be judged on the basis of how well it has performed and not on the basis of an assessment of the potential of any one individual in the company.

As more people become associated with the company—customers, employees, government regulatory agencies, etc.—problems will arise which Harmon thinks he will have little interest in solving personally and which he may have little ability to handle. Yet, these will be problems which will have to be handled carefully and adroitly; otherwise, the company will run the risk of "being washed out through some administrative pitfall." The recruiting of a chief operating officer is expected to minimize this possibility. Organizationally, Harmon said that the company will eventually be organized into what could conceptually be called two separate companies. The heads of advanced development and marketing and Harmon will have as their major responsibility and prerogative the investigation and selection of new products. The part of the total company will be concerned with the salability of new products also; and in order to demonstrate that selected new product developments have an economic value, this group will have the responsibility for generating a couple of million dollars in sales before transferring the product to the operations part of the total company.

The operations officer will then bring in the manufacturing operations, the sales and service organization, and the control and finance group—all of whom will be responsible for exploiting the profit possibilities represented by the new product.

Harmon says that this process "of creating new businesses within the business" will be a continuous one. The fairly autonomous product development part of the total company may ultimately involve as many as forty people. An annual budget will be allocated for this group, and the group will be held responsible for the use of that budget in terms of developing marketable new products. An executive committee composed of Messrs. Harmon, Dobrin, and Schwartz, plus the new chief operating officer, will direct activities of the total corporation. (See Exhibit 4.)

Officers and Staff

Forty-seven persons now work for the company in administrative, engineering, or secretarial jobs. There are 15 engineers and 22 technical support persons—which includes technicals, draftsmen, and purchasing personnel. The engineers and technical support personnel are under the direction of either Mr. Klinger or Mr. Waldorf. Ten persons are in administrative or secretarial positions. Of the 47 current employees, five are black: Mr. Harmon, three engineers, and one secretary-receptionist.

Harmon noted that the staff for the projected sales volume was "rather small," but that most of the work would be on the assembly line side anyhow. In describing his staff, he said:

> It goes without saying that a technological venture must have a very highly capable technical staff. It has to have this just to attract the

attention of the outside world. And if it's going to be successful, it's got to have a good marketing organization and a good financial structure. One of the personal advantages that I've had in organizing in Ann Arbor—and I doubt that I could have done this in any other city—is that, as a result of working here for 15 years, I have got to know most of the technical community. I think the things that they would say if you asked them, "Hey, how about Harmon?" is that "He has always had an idea that's a little ahead of the state of the art and the people who are involved in developing his ideas get a lot of personal glory as a result of doing so. The ideas are fun to work on and the staff gets a lot of visibility as a result of working on them and sometimes the ideas are even profitable." I'm a good technical leader. This had made the recruitment of the very best technical people in the area easy for me.

The company's employment list is expected to more than double to 100 persons by the end of 1969. Many of the new employees will be test engineers and salespersons.

Prospects for the Future
Harmon spoke with optimism about Datamax's future and discussed some of the plans for the development of the organization. He said that at the end of 1970, Datamax would have an organization with an accumulative several million dollars in sales behind it, a network of regional offices across the country, a product offering important superior technical features, large prestigious customers, and at least a two- or three-year jump on competitors. He said that the company would still be a relatively closely held corporation at that time.

Once the sales and service organizations are firmly established, the company will begin broadening its product line. Harmon said that the modem is just one piece of equipment in a chain of equipment that is necessary for business communications. For example, a person using a magnetic tape system to transmit data through the telephone network needs a modem. It is very conceivable that Datamax could develop or buy components of a magnetic tape system, combine these components with its own modem, and then offer a single product to the customer. There are other examples of this kind of a combination of existing products which can be combined into one. If the customer has only one function—to communicate—Harmon says it should not be necessary for the customer to buy three or four distinct products in order to serve that one function.

Datamax's product strategy for the future will be to use its vantage point (its superior product) to create new and better products from combinations of "state of the art" equipment which the company has not invented. The advanced development group is already beginning to implement this strategy.

Within another year or so, Harmon predicts that the company "can begin seriously thinking about reaching the $100 million sales level over the following five to seven years." The company has entered into negotiations with a Japanese manufacturer for the joint marketing of an even more technologically advanced business communications system. The Japanese manufacturer has a mechanical package which, when combined with Datamax's electronic package, produces a communications system which "has features that are at least three years ahead of the state of the art anywhere in the world." Current plans are for Datamax to ship its electronic package to the Japanese manufacturer and for the Japanese manufacturer to ship its mechanical package to Datamax. The combined system will then be assembled both in the United States and in Japan, and the system will be marketed in both the Orient and the United States. The major problem in consummating this agreement is Datamax's lack of a sales and service organization. Negotiations with third-party companies who have established sales and service organizations have begun, also.

Even though Datamax's modem is far superior to any other similar product on the market, Harmon was aware of the fact that some competitors were captives of large utility companies and would have very large resources to draw upon in competing with Datamax in the marketplace. He said:

And I constantly put myself into the position of the other management and ask myself what I would do to fight off this threat. The obvious answer is to attempt to acquire Datamax—and they attempted that. The other answer would be to begin exploiting my strengths and pointing out Datamax's weaknesses. And the only weakness they can point to, at this stage, is our lack of a sales and service organization. The airlines don't mind our lack of a sales and service organization, but we cannot become a giant corporation by selling only to the airlines. The major problem encountered to date with this end-user sales strategy is simply demonstrating to the potential customer that we can service the equipment.

Other problems exist in just starting the manufacturing operations. In spite of all the careful attention which has been devoted to the development of the production operations, the company will be a month or two longer getting into production than was expected. Yet, Harmon indicated that the company could deliver $5 million worth of the equipment immediately if the assembly line was in operation. Currently, the company is on a "crash program," examining and re-examining all of its plans to shorten the time between now and when the systems start coming off the assembly line at a reasonable rate.

Because the state of the art in data processing equipment changes rapidly, there is an incipient financial problem associated with marketing the modem. Many customers prefer to lease rather than buy the equipment. Whereas the company selected its present customers because these customers were anxious to buy the device, Harmon says that as the base of potential customers broadens Datamax will have to be prepared to increase its financial structure so that it can support leasing arrangements. As pressures to lease the equipment increase, the company will have to consider raising additional capital through either high-cost private investors or a public stock offering.

Harmon mentioned that one high-level policy problem that top management faces every six months is the problem of public vs. private financing. Although Datamax is the kind of company now that can always go to the public market, management has chosen, in the past, to get needed capital through private placements. The company has to relinquish a somewhat higher percentage of the company when the private placement route is taken, but Harmon said that there are some significant disadvantages for a dynamic, flexible company in going public. One such disadvantage is that a considerable amount of information about the company has to be divulged, and competitors can benefit from such information. Another disadvantage is that a public company loses some of the flexibility that a closely held company such as Datamax needs in order to maximize its competitive advantages. Harmon, in commenting further on the company's financial strategy, said:

> So, we always, every step of the way, end up agonizing over which of these two choices to make. Both are available to us. We have consistently followed the private placement route. We're going to go through private placement again soon. It's never an easy decision to make. I think in the long run that withholding the public offering is going to be best for me personally, for the company, and for the stockholders in general.

The management of Datamax realizes that there is some danger of having its product copied by other corporations, especially the OEM companies. The patents on the two devices have not yet been issued. The management feels that once the patents are issued, they will be able to keep others from using the technology which they have developed. When asked what the company is doing in the meantime (while the patents are pending), Mr. Harmon replied:

> Well, put yourself in the position of a large manufacturer and say, "Here's an important piece of technology in a big field. What's to keep us from stealing it? We'll put away 5% in a contingency fund to fight the patent suits, if necessary." One of the reasons we feel under a little pressure to enter into agreements with other manufacturers is that as a part of this type of agreement will be a noncompetitive clause or a clause which stipulates that so long as they are using this kind of equipment and our prices are competitive, they will buy from us. Or we might stipulate that if, for any reason, we cannot supply their needs because of the price or quantity, then they will pay us a royalty on the units which we will license them to manufacture. These restrictions in such agreements often will provide more protection than the patent laws will.

Mr. Harmon indicated that the development of new products would be launched in October 1969. He said:

> I'm spending a large part of my personal day now making decisions about those products. But we'll actually unleash the development group in the latter part of this year, and give them specific development goals. Sometime next year, we'll be in a position to begin to engineer them for manufacture. It'll probably be the end of 1970 before we introduce the first of the new line of products.

In concluding his discussion about the future prospects for the company, Mr. Harmon said:

> I think there are three stages of growth for this company: 1) through the particular proprietary product that we develop; 2) through other products where this technology is a key; and 3) through other companies, if we remain an independent company.
>
> These things that we've been discussing all fall under the category of growth through our own internal capabilities. There are other ways of fostering growth, of course. We feel that if we are just partially successful

in meeting our sales and technical objectives, then Datamax Corporation will surely become a public one—with not only glamour, but a good profit picture which will give our stock some value for use in growth through some acquisitions. This is not a subject which I'm sophisticated about, but I would assume that the operations manager that we're looking for would have an appreciation for that kind of thing.

BLACK ENTREPRENEURSHIP AND THE BLACK COMMUNITY

In response to the casewriter's question about Harmon's views on the role of the black businessman in the solution of the problems of the black community, Harmon said that "the company's contribution to the social well-being of the community is very important, but in the long term it has to be very secondary." Harmon explained that he doubted that the entrepreneur could successfully combine social goals that are not directly related to the business with economic goals. He counsels would-be black businessmen "to very, very carefully sharpen up their goals and to behave accordingly." He said:

> I've never been involved in a service industry, just in manufacturing. And one thing that's clear to me abut this industry is that to be successful at it, it's rather difficult to mix in a direct fashion any broad social goals with the business and financial goals. Yes, my own personal experiences have shown me that a black businessman will automatically have a lot of visibility in this community, and, as a result of this visibility, will get many opportunities to participate in community affairs. And in a fashion that he can use to advance, as a matter of fact, the goals of the black community. I make the observation, though, that the more successful he is, the more opportunity he gets—and the more of these opportunities he follows through on—the less successful he's going to be on his job. It just seems to me wholly incompatible for entrepreneurs in small growing manufacturing companies to have concerns or to use their time or emotional energy in any way other than full, 100% commitment to the goals of the organization.
>
> The financial backers of this company (probably might) have very lofty social ideals, but they invested in it for one purpose only: because they want to have a healthy return from their investment. And when a person spends less than full time in the company or dissipates his energy outside of it, they (the investors) become concerned. The same is true of the employees of the company. They've hitched their wagon to a star. And if the entrepreneur—myself, in this case—doesn't spend maximum time and energy on the enterprise, they'll be getting disgruntled, also. The short of this is that I, myself, haven't found it possible to be anything other than just the entrepreneur of a would-be manufacturing company. Maybe the situation is different for service-oriented enterprises. I just have had no experience, so I can't be sure. However, I can see many examples of cases where community participation leads to a very direct, straight-forward benefit for certain enterprises. But one thing must be clear: if a person does so (becomes involved in the community participation concept), then he ought to have a pretty clear understanding of how it benefits the company because in the long run, you'll be evaluated first by the success of the enterprise.

Harmon explained that there is no relation between Datamax's products and the black community at this point. None of the company's products are used by individuals; hence, the only viable avenue for contact with the black community is through the company's relationship with its black employees. Many of the persons who will be hired to work on the assembly line are expected to be black.

Harmon was once very active in civil rights and community organizations and was the first black person to hold a county-wide elective office in his section of Michigan. But, he says that the time pressures of running a business have necessitated his minimizing the amount of time which he spends on activities for community organizations. He continues to be instrumental, however, in helping black leaders establish contact with white businessmen who want to contribute to the solution of community problems. He further commented:

> All in all, I think their reaction would be that "Sam is more concerned with business than he is with the community. He doesn't do very much, but if you can identify a thing that he is uniquely capable of contributing to, he'll do it. However, if there's anyone else who can, he just won't do it." That's just the way things stand now. I am not making any judgment as to whether it is right or wrong. I hope that as time goes on we'll have a somewhat different situation. But right now that's the way it is.

Harmon systematically invites the high schools and junior high schools to send groups of black youngsters to his company, where he takes them on tours of the facilities and encourages them to pay more attention to education and to take more technical and science subjects. He has encouraged some students to take subjects such as electronics and drafting in high school and will be hiring them for the summer. When they complete their education, Harmon said that there will be jobs open to them with Datamax. He indicated that he works hard to maintain some contact with the youngsters, the students in business colleges and law schools, and the business leaders.

As a result of his being a fairly successful black businessman, Harmon said that he gets many opportunities to become involved in one program or another in the black community. But, he explained that the more he attempts to exercise these chances to become involved, the less successful he is in his business. He continued:

> They (the community activists) see a black guy who looks successful or who is doing something and they say, "Because he *is* what he is, let's give him this opportunity to participate in the community." And the more opportunity he gets to participate, the less chance he gets to do what he needs to do to remain successful.

Being black does not in any way adversely affect Harmon's relationships with the white business community. He said that it usually takes a white businessman about five minutes to overcome the surprise of meeting and talking with a very talented black engineer-inventor. After the first five minutes, the white businessman may be amazed but his amazement is usually a function of Harmon's affability and proven competence.

In responding to a question about his future personal plans, Harmon said:

Up to now, we've been saying that if the gadget works, we're going to make money. But there comes a point when we say, "It works." At that point I'll be more concerned with continuing to create other businesses within the business, so to speak. I'm just not well suited for the position of an executive, but I am very well suited for other technical functions. So I'm going to follow the technical path as soon as the development of the company allows. This will free me up from the day-to-day operating activities of the company. By the time that happens, I will have achieved a couple of echelons of wealth which will be significant. We now have a group of fairly happy investment bankers. And if this day I'm talking about comes around, we'll have even a larger group of still happier ones. I personally will be in a good position to do a lot of things which I'd like to take a crack at. I have already talked to some of these investment bankers about organizing a black-oriented venture capital fund, a very high risk one. And I have an idea of how it can be done in such a way—I've got the plan and I guess I'm not going to try to detail it. But that's the goal, and I'll more and more shift my time and concern in that direction.

I think I will have had—if things continue the way that they are, and this is a big "if" and I realize that—a degree of success and a reputation which can be used like a magic wand at times. I've seen it happen in the community. Whether it's logical or not, it happens, and I'll use it for another end. I will be able to raise substantial amounts of money from people who, at that time, will have made substantial earnings from Datamax. I have the idea for this venture capital concern which will be black-managed, if not black-funded, for the purpose of providing capital for any reasonable venture. I know that defining "reasonable" is going to be damn tough, but it has got to be designed so as to include as large a number of black entrepreneurs or would-be businessmen as possible.

Basically, what I'm saying is I'm trying to find a way of getting back to some of those social goals. The goals are changing. By the time these degrees of success occur, I'm just not going to be physically, temperamentally, or even chronologically suited for the kind of social problems that the college campus kids are into today. I intend to use the business (the venture capital fund) for these purposes. Somehow, it's going to combine venture capital and entrepreneurs.

EXHIBIT 1. Datamax Corporation

Balance Sheet as of December 31, 1968
(Subject to comments in accompanying letter)

ASSETS
Current Assets

Cash	$ 81,977.21
Accounts receivable, other	1,771.00
Unbilled portion of contracts in progress	13,870.00
U.S. Treasury Bills, at cost	887,100.75
Accrued interest receivable	3,685.50
Prepaid expenses (Note H)	21,435.36
Total current assets	$1,009,859.82

EXHIBIT 1 (continued)

Property and equipment, at cost less accumulated depreciation (Note A)	20,086.60
Cash surrender value of life insurance (Note F)	970.74
Organization costs, net of amortization (Note A)	11,370.85
Research and development expenses (Notes A and B)	158,031.84
Patent application rights (Note E)	410,041.00
Marketing and feasibility studies, net of amortization (Notes A and G)	32,966.65
Prepaid rent (Note H)	89,743.60
Total assets	$1,733,071.10

LIABILITIES AND CAPITAL
Current Liabilities

Accounts payable, trade		$ 24,864.39
Employees withheld and accrued taxes		3,772.31
Accrued expenses		29,079.17
Total Current Liabilities		$ 57,715.87
Notes payable (Notes F and H)		52,292.30
Total Liabilities		$ 110,008.17

Contingency (Note C)

Common stock, par value $10 (Note D)

Class A:		
Authorized 250,000 shares		
Issued and outstanding 106,295 shares	$1,062,950.00	
Class B:		
Authorized 10,500 shares		
Issued and outstanding 10,475 shares	104,750.00	
	$1,167,700.00	
Other capital	644,500.00	
	$1,812,200.00	

Deficit:		
January 1, 1968	$ 11,526.01	
Loss, as annexed	177,611.06	
	$ 189,137.07	
Total capital		$1,623,062.93
Total liabilities and capital		$1,733,071.10

The accompanying notes are part of these financial statements.

EXHIBIT 1 (continued)

Statement of Operating Loss
for the year ended December 31, 1968
(Subject to comments in the accompanying letter)

Sales (Note C)	$ 36,370.00
Operating expenses (Notes B and G)	359,268.55
Loss from operations	$322,898.55
Less, research and development expenses deferred (Note B)	138,305.24
	$184,593.31
Other income	6,982.25
Loss	$177,611.06

The accompanying notes are part of these financial statements.

Statement of Sources and Applications of Funds
for the year ended December 31, 1968
(Subject to comments in accompanying letter)

Working capital, January 1, 1968		$ 123,324.78
Sources		
Proceeds from issuance of common stock	$1,191,300.00	
Proceeds from notes payable:		
Life insurance	1,587.12	
Lessor	50,000.00	
Total sources		$1,242,887.12
Total funds available		$1,366,211.90
Applications		
Loss from operations	177,611.06	
Add: research and development expenses deferred (Note B)	138,305.24	
	$ 315,916.30	
Deduct:		
Depreciation and amortization	$4,636.04	
Amortization:		
Organizing costs	2,277.00	
Marketing and feasibility studies	8,600.02	$ 15,513.06
		$ 300,403.24
Additions to non-current assets:		
Property and equipment	20,500.37	
Organization costs	3,150.00	
Prepaid rent	89,743.60	
Cash surrender value of life insurance	970.74	
Total applications		$ 414,767.95
Working capital, December 31, 1968		$ 951,443.95

The accompanying notes are part of these financial statements.

EXHIBIT 1 (continued)

Notes to Financial Statements
for the year ended December 31, 1968
(Subject to comments in accompanying letter)

Note A: The company uses straight line method for computing depreciation on property and equipment and amortization of organization costs and marketing and feasibility studies. The costs, accumulated depreciation or amortization, and lives used are as follows:

Depreciation or Amortization

Property and equipment:				
Laboratory equipment	$20,208.11	$ 4,600.22	$4,013.73	3
Office furniture and fixtures	5,048.89	570.18	504.81	5–10
Leasehold improvements	235.00	235.00	117.50	1
Total	$25,492.00	$ 5,405.40	$4,636.04	
Organization costs	$14,009.85	$ 2,639.00	$2,277.00	5
Marketing and feasibility studies	$43,000.00	$10,033.35	$8,600.02	5

Note B: The company has deferred research and development expenses of a non-capital nature in the amount of $158,031.84. The expenses deferred represent those expenses which are to be charged against income systematically over a two-year period based on a percentage of cost of sales when manufacturing operations commence. It is anticipated that manufacturing operations will commence approximately April 1, 1969.

Note C: The company is contingently liable, in the event of certain circumstances, to repay all amounts received under a contract with a customer. Funds received under the contract to date are $22,500.

Note D: The authorized Class A common stock was increased by action of the stockholders on January 4, 1968, from 57,000 shares to 72,000 shares and on November 6, 1968, from 72,000 shares to 250,000 shares having a par value of $10. The stock transactions since incorporation are as follows:

EXHIBIT 1 (continued)

	Number of Shares	Amount
Class A common stock issued and subscribed:		
Balance, November 1, 1967	—	—
Stock subscriptions unpaid at December 31, 1967	1,470	$ 14,700
Stock issued for services	5,100	51,000
Stock issued for cash	7,900	79,000
Stock issued for patent rights	41,000	410,000
Balance, December 31, 1967	55,470	$ 554,700
Stock issued for cash	51,575	1,160,250
Stock subscriptions cancelled	(750)	(7,500)
Totals	50,825	$1,152,750
Balance, December 31, 1968	106,295	$1,707,540
Class B common stock:		
Balance, November 1, 1967	—	—
Stock subscriptions unpaid at December 31, 1967	750	7,500
Stock issued for cash	7,900	79,000
Balance, December 31, 1967	8,650	$ 86,500
Stock issued for cash	2,575	25,750
Stock subscriptions cancelled	(750)	(7,500)
Totals	1,825	$ 18,250
Balance, December 31, 1968	10,475	$ 104,750

Proceeds from the issuance of common stock have been credited to common stock issued and outstanding at par value of $10 and the proceeds in excess of par value have been credited to other capital.

The company has issued 2,000 shares of Class A common stock at $15 per share to a management employee subject to certain restrictions and conditions with respect to sale or disposition of the stock prior to June 26, 1971.

The stockholders of the company adopted the 1967 Qualified Stock Option Plan and have placed in reserve a total of 15,000 shares of common stock for the plan.

To date, options totalling $40,250 have been granted to employees under this plan as follows:

Exercise Date	Shares Granted	Option Price Range
1969	4,500	$10 to $15
1970	5,249	$10 to $15
1971	5,251	$10 to $15
Total	15,000	

EXHIBIT 1 (continued)

In November 1968 the Board of Directors adopted the 1968 Qualified Stock Option Plan and designated 10,000 shares of common stock to be reserved for the plan.

To date, options totaling $35,250.00 have been granted to employees under this plan as follows:

Exercise Date	Shares Granted	Option Price
1969	150	$23.50
1970	474	$23.50
1971	526	$23.50
1972	350	$23.50
Total	1,500	

The 1968 Qualified Stock Option Plan and options granted under the Plan are subject to approval by the stockholders at the next annual meeting.

All options expire five years from date of grant.

The company may at any time up to and including January 15, 1973, redeem the whole or any part of the Series B common stock by a lot, or pro rata, by payment in cash, the sum of $20 per share.

On January 16, 1969, the company agreed to issue 250 shares of Class A common stock to an attorney in consideration for services rendered to the company.

Note E: Certain of the incorporators have assigned exclusive rights on two patent applications on file with the U.S. Patent Office to the company in exchange for 41,000 shares of its Class A common stock, having a par value of $410,000.

Note F: The company owns life insurance policies on the President of the company having a face value of $600,000. Notes payable in the amount of $2,292.30 represent unpaid premiums due the insurer which will be paid out of the cash values or cash proceeds in the event of the insured's death at some future date. Cash surrender value life insurance is pledged as security for the notes payable. In accordance with the terms of the employment contract between the President of the company and the company, the company has agreed to pay to designated persons, upon the death of the President of the company while in the employ of the company, the sum of $100,000 in 60 equal monthly installments.

Note G: The company has capitalized the cost of preparation of marketing and feasibility studies. This cost was paid by the issuance of 4,100 shares of its Class A common stock having a total par value of $41,000 and $2,000 in cash. The amortization policy is discussed in Note A.

Note H: On December 31, 1968, the company purchased an assignment of the lease from the previous lessor on the facilities the company presently occupies for $100,000. The sum was paid by issuance of notes payable for $50,000 and $50,000 in cash. The notes are interest bearing at 7% per annum on the unpaid balance and principal payments are required in four equal annual installments of $12,500 beginning January 2, 1970.

The cost incurred has been capitalized and will be amortized over the term of the lease which expires October 1, 1978.

EXHIBIT 1 (continued)

Statement of Operating Expenses
for the year ended December 31, 1968

Experimental materials and supplies	$ 31,305.31
Salaries and wages	172,760.15
Taxes:	
Payroll taxes	6,245.47
Property and franchise taxes	17,230.13
Travel	28,772.22
Depreciation	4,636.04
Equipment rental	1,210.68
Office supplies	3,312.63
Telephone	6,220.19
Rent	9,475.00
Legal	35,498.98
Audit	8,857.64
Amortization:	
Marketing and feasibility studies	8,600.02
Organizational costs	2,277.00
Freight and express	607.09
Interest	82.87
Advertising	396.00
Subscriptions and dues	892.54
Insurance	10,310.05
Reproduction	1,169.81
Miscellaneous	3,104.03
Bell modems and line rental	3,266.92
Patents	3,037.78
Total operating expenses	$359,268.55

EXHIBIT 2. Datamax Corporation

Background on the Products

The principal remote communications system in the United States is the telephone network. This system was designed for voice communications where the receiving mechanism is the human ear-brain system. This human receiving system is capable of automatically compensating for most errors in transmission caused by line disturbances. An increasing portion of the message content being carried by the telephone network (estimated between 25% and 40% and growing rapidly) is data which is received by electronic and electro-mechanical devices, such as facsimile transmission equipment, punch paper tape terminals, magnetic tape recorders, computers, cathode ray tube units or related buffer units. These devices do not have the error-correcting capability of the ear-brain system. The company's initial product is an error-correcting device which is fundamentally a small, special purpose computer performing for data communication the function of the brain in the human ear-brain system for verbal communication.

EXHIBIT 2. (continued)

The maximum capacity of an average voice frequency band width (0–3,000 cycles per second) telephone line has been theoretically calculated to be 48,000 bits of information per second (hereafter bps). Because of the amount of "noise" on the telephone lines developed in the switching centers and other ambient electro-magnetic influences, the current rate of transmission of data over the telephone switching dial network for most applications is 1,200 bps (normal error rate is 1 bit per 100,000). Higher transmission rates develop unacceptable error rates. The principal method now in use to accomplish high data transmission rates is transmission over wideband or microwave circuits by those who can justify the very high rental charges for such circuits. The newspaper wire services and television network transmission are examples of such conditions.

It has long been recognized in the data communications industry that machine signals can be encoded in order to permit incrased efficiency of transmission. In 1966, Mr. Harmon (President of Datamax) studied the problem to ascertain if a low cost solution could be found. This work resulted in the filing of the patent applications in January and May of 1967.

The substance of the Harmon inventions is embodied in a device designed to increase the speed-error efficiency of data transmission over the telephone dial switching network. A schematic diagram of the position of the device (encoder-decoder) in a data transmission system is:

DATA SOURCE   ENCODER   MODULATOR   Telephone network

Telephone network   DEMODULATOR   DECODER   DATA RECEIVER

The first element in the transmitting end of the system is the data source which may be, for example, a magnetic tape unit, a punch paper tape unit, a facsimile machine, a cathode ray tube or a computer. The second link in the system is the company's encoder for processing the input signal. The third link in the transmitting end is the modulator which converts the output of the encoder to a form suitable for transmission over the dial telephone network. On the receiving end of the data communications link the process is reversed. The signal is first received by the demodulator, then is processed by the Datamax decoder for detection and correction of errors occasioned by the characteristics of the telephone line and finally is fed into the receiving terminal.

The company varies the design of its error correcting device in order to fit different user requirements of speed of transmission versus error rate, ranging from transmissions at 1,200 bps (errors: 1 in 1,000,000,000 bits) to transmissions at 9,600 bps (errors: 1 in 1,000 bits). The norm for the dial network is 1 error in 100,000 bits for transmission at 1,200 bps; without increasing this error rate, the company's device will permit transmission at a rate of at least 6,000 bps.

High Speed Moderate Error Rate Communications

Certain types of business machine systems which employ data communications can readily utilize high speed transmission of data, but can also tolerate moderately high rates of error because the output of such systems is visual or graphic copy. This area may be generally described as graphic communications. For application to this field of communications, which is exemplified by facsimile transmission equipment or cathode ray tube display, the Datamax system permits transmission of data through the dial network telephone lines

EXHIBIT 2 (continued)

at a rate of approximately 8,000 bits per second with an error rate of 1 error in 1,000 bits. This permits the transmission of a standard size (8½ x 11 inches) page of copy by means of facsimile in an elapsed time of 2 minutes and 30 seconds, as opposed to the present state of the art time of 6 to 8 minutes per standard page.

High Speed Low Error Rate Communications

Certain types of data communications require both high speed and low error rates. Examples of such systems would be communication between magnetic tape units transmitting computer program data, and communications between computers directly on line. The performance specifications of the configuration of the Datamax system for this application, using the dial network, is 6,000 bits per second with error rates of 1 in 1,000,000 bits. The present state of the art in this area of data communications is transmission speeds of 2,000 bits per second with error rates of 1 in every 100,000 bits. Thus the Datamax system both increases the speed of the transmission by a factor of 3 and decreases the error rate by a factor of 10.

Low Speed Low Error Rate Communications

In certain areas of data communications the user finds low rates of data transmission perfectly acceptable, but is unable to tolerate any errors in such transmission. Examples of this type of data communications would be communication directly between computer memories. The performance characteristics of the Datamax system for this application are approximately 1,200 bits per second, with error rates not exceeding 1 in 1,000,000,000 bits. There are no other existing techniques for reducing error rates to this level.

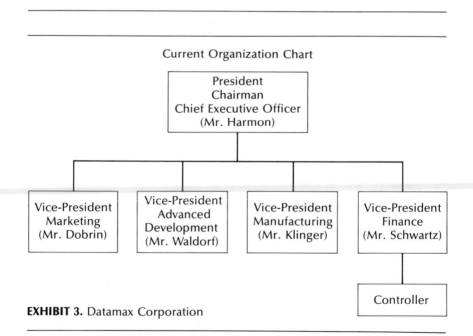

Current Organization Chart

President
Chairman
Chief Executive Officer
(Mr. Harmon)

| Vice-President Marketing (Mr. Dobrin) | Vice-President Advanced Development (Mr. Waldorf) | Vice-President Manufacturing (Mr. Klinger) | Vice-President Finance (Mr. Schwartz) |

Controller

EXHIBIT 3. Datamax Corporation

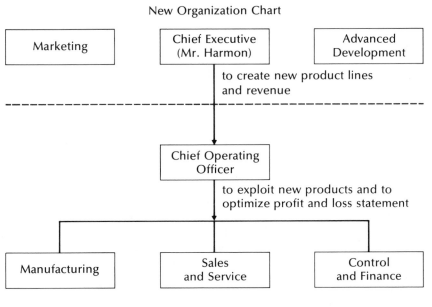

New Organization Chart

EXHIBIT 4. Datamax Corporation

Computer Services, Incorporated

COMPANY BACKGROUND

Computer Services, Inc., a St. Louis based firm, was organized in April, 1970, by a group of eight young black entrepreneurs. Its business objective was to offer a wide range of computer oriented services to the industrial and professional communities of the St. Louis metropolitan area. Among these services were the following:

1. *Programming Support.* The staff of Computer Services, Inc., was available for handling peak programming work loads and specialized jobs. The staff was proficient in COBOL, FORTRAN and other programming languages, and had experience with a wide variety of data processing equipment.
2. *Systems Design.* The staff of Computer Services, Inc., offered systems design and implementation services. Systems design was tailored to the user's specific needs, and "systems control standards" were employed to monitor design performance against design estimates.
3. *Documentation.* Under its system control standards, the company developed a generalized systems, programming, and operational documentation procedure which again could be tailored to a specific user's needs.
4. *Small Business Support.* Computer Services, Inc., combined computer technology with accepted accounting principles to provide the business and professional communities with general ledger, payroll, tax, and accounts receivable management. Comprehensive services offered by the company included preparation of original books of entry, balance sheets, income statements, payrolls, tax returns, paychecks, customer reports and various management reports and analyses.
5. *Mathematical Modelling.* With a strong background in mathematics, the staff offered expertise in mathematical modelling—including statistical analyses, simulation, mathematical programming, cost analysis and inventory control.

This case was prepared by Professor Robert E. Markland for the University of Missouri, St. Louis. Reproduced by permission.

6. *Education.* Computer Services, Inc., conducted seminars on computer applications and instruction in such programming languages as COBOL and FORTRAN. Basic education courses which were prerequisites to an understanding of these programming languages were also taught.

The eight founders and principals of the company held responsible positions within various businesses and corporations in the St. Louis area. However, they also felt a need for engaging in entrepreneurial activities, and thus most of their spare time was spent in activities associated with the company. The company maintained rented offices in the central part of the city, and utilized an answering service and a part time secretary. The office facility was used as a meeting place and for working on the various projects in which the company was engaged.

BACKGROUND OF OWNERS

The founders and owners of Computer Services, Inc., who also were its basic staff, had wide and diverse academic and professional backgrounds in data processing and related fields. The president, Mark Bradley, had a B.S. and an M.S. degree in mathematics, and was working on a doctorate in computer science and operations research. The vice-president, Robert McMurry, had over 14 years of experience in programming and systems analysis. The treasurer, Albert Clark, had a B.A. in mathematics and an M.S. in computer science and had broad experience in computer programming, systems analysis, and operations research. The treasurer, Frank Parks, had a B.S. in business administration and was a tax consultant and accountant. Other members of the corporation had experience as computer operators, programmers, systems analysts, geodesists, mathematicians, and systems engineers. In total, the staff of Computer Services, Inc., offered experience and technical expertise in nearly all phases of computing and data processing. Virtually all of the work that Computer Services, Inc., did was on a part time basis, that is, at night or on the weekend. However, several members of the firm were considering working for the company on a full time basis, if an adequate backlog of profitable projects could be obtained.

COMPANY PROBLEMS

In the early summer of 1970, the officers of Computer Services, Inc., were engaged in a thorough review of the fledgling company's problems. Among the most prominent problems they isolated were:

1. Lack of financing for the company
2. Lack of organizational structure and definition of responsibilities
3. Lack of direction as to which areas to seek as marketing objectives

Of these three prominent problem areas, the latter was considered as being most critical, as various members of the company had divergent ideas as to what types of services the company should attempt to market, and in which areas the company should concentrate its efforts.

At the same time the discussions concerning marketing objectives were transpiring, the company became acquainted with Dr. Robert Martin, a business professor at a local university. Dr. Martin had received a summer research grant from his school to investigate the potential utilization of computers within minority-owned, urban businesses. After several discussions, the members of Computer Services, Inc., and Dr. Martin agreed to pool their talents in an attempt to survey a number of small minority-owned, urban businesses to determine their potential computer and computer related needs. It was felt that the joint effort would be beneficial to both groups, and that each group could afford assistance that the other group would otherwise be unable to obtain.

THE SURVEY

The survey was conducted during the summer of 1970. During this period of time, detailed personal interviews were conducted within fifty small businesses (annual sales less than $1 million) in the St. Louis urban area. The businesses that were interviewed were typical of those commonly found in an urban area. Forty-three (86%) of the businesses interviewed were black owned, with the remaining seven (14%) of the businesses interviewed being white owned. The black-owned businesses were selected for interviewing by a stratified random sampling process, using strata determined from the 1970 *Directory of Black-Owned Businesses—City of St. Louis and St. Louis County.* The white-owned businesses were selected by simple random sampling, but were constrained to the same strata established for the black-owned businesses.

Survey Questionnaire

The research questionnaire employed in the study concentrated on four major areas of interest. First, questions concerning the type of business, ownership, capitalization, size, earnings, and profitability were asked.

Second, a set of questions concerning the general problems of the business were considered. Herein, the objectives were two-fold: a) there was a genuine need to determine the general problems of the business being examined, in order to relate these problems to possible solutions involving computers; b) by beginning the interviewing process with a set of questions concerning the general problems of the business, a degree of rapport between interviewer and interviewee was established. This was particularly important because of the technical nature of the questions which were asked in the latter part of the interview.

The third part of the interview was oriented towards determining the "computer awareness" of the interviewee. In this respect, the questions dealing with the subject of computer awareness were oriented towards the management information needs of the businesses. This was done because the interviewees could relate easily to their management information needs, but in general could not relate to sophisticated computer terminology and hardware.

The fourth and final part of the interviewing process was directed towards the computer needs of the businesses. Again, the emphasis was on computer related needs, i.e., management information systems and data processing systems. Little or no attention was given to computer hardware; obviously, the size and capitalization of the businesses being considered generally precluded direct purchase and/or lease of such computer equipment. Both general computer needs and specific needs were addressed within this section of the interview.

A copy of the questionnaire used in the interviewing process is shown below as Exhibit 1.

EXHIBIT 1. Computer Services, Incorporated

Automatic Data Processing (ADP)/Management Information Systems (MIS) Requirements—Survey of Small Businessmen and Professionals

I. Business Profile
A. Business name & location:_____
B. Type of business: _____
C. Single owner _____ Partnership _____
   Corporation _____ Other (please specify) _____
D. If partnership or corporation the number of partners or stockholders is:
   _____

E. Estimated gross yearly income:
   $ 5,000 to $10,000 _____ $30,001 to $50,000 _____
   $10,001 to $15,000 _____ $50,001 to $100,000 _____
   $15,001 to $20,000 _____   Over $100,000 _____
   $20,001 to $30,000 _____
F. Estimated yearly profits:
   $ 1,000 to $ 5,000 _____ $20,001 to $40,000 _____
   $ 5,001 to $10,000 _____   Over $40,000 _____
   $10,001 to $20,000 _____
G. Business objectives:
   Expand business in present location _____
   Expand business to other locations _____
   Expand into other types of business _____
   Other (please specify) _____
H. Method of obtaining capital to start business:
   Personal savings _____ Selling stock_____
   Business loan (specify from whom)_____
   Other (please specify) _____

II. Major Business Problems
A. What are your major business problems?
   Unreliable help _____ Unskilled help_____
   Operating capital_____ Debt collection _____
   Obtaining loans_____ Obtaining business information __
   Maintaining adequate records____ Other (please specify) _____
B. What have you done about these problems?
   _____

III. Computer Awareness
A. Do you presently use any business reports prepared by a computer?
   Yes _____ No _____
B. Do you feel that computerized reports could be helpful to your business? Yes _____ No _____

IV. Data Processing/MIS Needs—General
A. What are the major information needs of your business at present?
   _____
B. How frequently do you require various kinds of business information?
   _____

EXHIBIT 1 (continued)

C. Is your current volume of data too great for manual handling?
Yes _____   No _____

D. Could your current information needs be satisfied by better organization of existing data? Yes _____   No _____

E. Could you accumulate the data for input to a data processing system if you were given some assistance? Yes _____   No _____

F. What new information would you like to have for controlling your business?_____
_____

G. What kind of personnel do you have for working with computerized systems? _____

H. What savings might be generated through computerization of your present business systems? _____
_____

J. Would you be interested in attending a data processing/computer seminar related to your business needs? Yes _____   No _____

V. Data Processing/MIS Needs—Specific

A. Accounts payable	M. Marketing analysis
B. Accounts receivable	N. Payroll
C. Cost accounting	O. Personnel
D. Engineering	P. Production control
E. Equipment costs (capital investment)	Q. Projection/forecasting
F. Financial statements	R. Purchasing
G. General accounting	S. Sales analysis
H. General ledger	T. Scheduling (PERT/CPM)
I. Inventory control	U. Scientific applications
J. Invoicing	V. Statistical analysis
K. Mailing lists	W. Summary of sales
L. Management information systems	X. Tax reports
	Y. Work in progress reports
	Z. Miscellaneous

RESULTS OF THE SURVEY

The survey was completed in late summer of 1970. Data collected in the survey were then tabulated, edited, and summarized. The major research results are presented below.

Major Business Problems

Survey results summarizing the business profile of the firms in the sample are presented below in Table 1. Survey results concerning the major problem areas encountered within the small businesses are seen below in Table 2. As noted, the most commonly experienced business problems were:

1. Maintaining adequate records
2. Unreliable help
3. Other
4. Inadequate business information

The first two problems mentioned in Table 2 are self-explanatory. The "Other" problem area included a wide range of responses. Commonly mentioned problems were:

1. Inventories—drug stores, restaurants, furniture stores
2. Getting adequate fire & theft insurance—all businesses
3. "Rowdy clientele"—taverns and liquor stores
4. Obtaining and maintaining equipment—cleaning establishments and restaurants

A large number of interviewees (29) reported that one of their major problems was "maintaining adequate records"—primarily for tax purposes. Additionally, a sizable number of firms (12) experienced difficulty in obtaining business information.

The interviewees were also questioned as to their attempts at solving their various problems. The responses were extremely varied, and defied a concise categorization. The most common solution to the "maintenance of adequate records" dilemma was to employ a commercial bookkeeping service. This generally resulted in some type of a manual system which was partially maintained by the owner or manager of the business.

TABLE 1. COMPUTER SERVICE, INCORPORATED— PROFILE OF FIRMS STUDIED

	No. of Firms		No. of Firms
*Type (Primary Product or Service)**		Restaurant	2
Appliance Sales & Service	1	Service Stations	3
Attorneys	1	Shoe Repairs	1
Automobile—Repairs & Parts	3	Taverns	5
Automobile—Wholesale &		Taxicab Company	1
Retail Sales	1	Upholstering Company	1
Barber Shops	2	*Total*	50
Beauty Shops	2		
Cleaners	2	*Size*	
Construction Companies	3	Number of Employees:	
Dentists	2	One	3
Drug Stores	2	Two	11
Financial—Bank & Finance		Three–Five	24
Company	2	Six–Fifteen	9
Furniture Stores	1	Sixteen or More	3
Grocery Stores	2	*Total*	50
Income Tax Service	1		
Janitorial Service	1	*Annual Sales*	
Liquor Stores	2	$5,000– 10,000	10
Manufacturing	2	10,001– 15,000	8
Physicians	2	15,001– 20,000	6
Radio & TV Repairs	1	20,001– 30,000	4
Real Estate	1	30,001– 50,000	6
Recording Company	1	50,001–100,000	6
Recreation—Pool Hall &		Over $100,000	10
Bowling Alley	2	*Total*	50

*Based on random sampling

TABLE 1 (continued)

	No. of Firms		No. of Firms
Profitability (After Tax)		*Original Capitalization***	
$1,000– 5,000	13	Personal Savings	37
5,001–10,000	16	Business Loan	16
10,001–20,000	14	Selling Stock	6
20,001–40,000	4	Total	50
Over $40,001	3		
Total	50	*Business Objectives*	
		Expand—present location	28
Form of Business Organization		Expand—other business or	
Proprietorships	30	location	14
Partnerships	11	Other (specify)	8
Corporations	9	Total	50
Total	50		

**In a number of instances the original capitalization resulted from two or more sources.

TABLE 2. COMPUTER SERVICES, INCORPORATED—
MAJOR BUSINESS PROBLEMS

Problem Areas	Number of Responses*
1. Unreliable help	24
2. Unskilled help	11
3. Operating capital	6
4. Debt collection	11
5. Obtaining loans	4
6. Thefts	9
7. Obtaining new business	4
8. Obtaining business information	12
9. Maintaining adequate records	29
10. Other (specify)	18

*Respondents were allowed to state more than one problem area.

Computer Awareness

In attempting to evaluate computer awareness, two relatively simple questions were asked. These two questions and a summary of results are shown below.

1. Do you presently use any business reports prepared by a computer?
   Yes __8__   No __42__

2. Do you feel that computerized reports could be helpful to your business?
   Yes __32__   No __18__

As could be expected, very few of the businesses interviewed were presently utilizing computer prepared reports. Those responding "yes" were basically in three categories:

1. Financial (Banking and Savings & Loan)
2. jolProfessional (Doctors, Dentists, and Lawyers)
3. Drug & Grocery Stores

However, it is important to discern that computerized reports were viewed favorably by a majority of those firms interviewed (64%—Yes). Indeed, virtually all of those businesses interviewed had some awareness of the computer's potential in processing data which could be useful to the operation of their respective bussinesses.

Computerized Management Information Needs—General

Questions concerning the general management information system needs of the businesses in the survey considered nine areas. These questions were basically "open ended," and thus resulted in a variety of responses. The questions employed in this part of the study and a summary of the responses they elicited are shown below in Table 3.

TABLE 3. COMPUTER SERVICES, INCORPORATED—
GENERAL MANAGEMENT INFORMATION SYSTEM NEEDS

Question	Response
1. What are the major information needs of your business at present?	Financial and tax information
2. How frequently do you require various kinds of business information?	Weekly and monthly
3. Is your current volume of data too great for manual handling?	Yes—37% No—63%
4. Could your current information needs be satisfied by better organization of existing data?	Yes—62% No—28%
5. Could you accumulate the data for input to a data processing system if you were given some assistance?	Yes—53% No—47%
6. What new information would you like to have for controlling your business?	Sales data, mailing lists
7. What kind of personnel do you have for working with computerized systems?	Secretary, clerks, office girls
8. What savings might be generated through computerization of your present business systems?	Less bad debts, less tax delinquencies
9. Would you be interested in attending a data processing computer seminar related to your business needs?	Yes—65% No—35%

It should be stressed that the respondents indicated to the interviewers that the above areas were of interest to them without any particular "selling" of computerized systems. In spite of the generally favorable attitude expressed towards computers and computerized systems, many of the respondents expressed some skepticism concerning their usage and feasibility. Typical comments were as follows:

- Computer systems cost too much.
- Computer systems take too much time to implement.
- As a small businessman, I don't understand the computer.
- I'm too small to afford, let alone use, computers in my business.
- My employees will be afraid that their jobs are going to be replaced by the computer.
- I don't have "start up" funds for a computer system.
- A lot of computer systems don't work very well.

Computerized Management Information Needs—Specific

The final portion of the interview considered specific computerized management information system needs. Herein, the interviewees were asked to indicate specific interest areas from an extensive list of possibilities. The results are shown below in Table 4.

TABLE 4. COMPUTER SERVICES, INCORPORATED—
SPECIFIC MANAGEMENT INFORMATION SYSTEM NEEDS

Areas of Interest	Number of Responses*
1. Accounts payable	17
2. Accounts receivable	26
3. Cost accounting	14
4. Engineering	2
5. Equipment costs (capital investment)	3
6. Financial statements	25
7. General accounting	21
8. General ledger	17
9. Inventory control	22
10. Invoicing	22
11. Mailing lists	9
12. Management information system	13
13. Marketing analysis	4
14. Payroll	12
15. Personnel	11
16. Production control	10
17. Projection/forecasting	1
18. Purchasing	4
19. Sales analysis	3
20. Scheduling (PERT/CPM)	1
21. Scientific applications	1
22. Statistical analysis	1
23. Summary of sales	11
24. Tax reports	32
25. Work in progress reports	4
26. Miscellaneous	9

*Totals do not equal 50 because respondents were allowed to respond in more than one category.

As shown in Table 4, primary information needs were in financially related areas. Virtually all types of accounting information were desired by a majority of those the firm interviewed. This information was needed both for tax purposes and for internal control, with the former being more prominently mentioned as a critical factor. Additionally, interest was expressed in obtaining inventory control data, sales and marketing information, and in having payroll and personnel matters automated.

THE PROBLEM SITUATION

In the fall of 1970, the members of Computer Services, Inc., were again reviewing their problems. They felt that their joint survey had been of value, but were uncertain as to interpreting its results. Specifically, they were unsure as to which of their six major marketing areas they should concentrate in. Furthermore, they were in a quandary as to the level of effort required to develop one or more areas of opportunity. Some members favored concentration on one area, while others favored a broad development effort in several areas. This question was also tied to that of having full time employees, either externally hired, or internally on the part of one or more of the principals. Another concern was whether or not to concentrate on development within the black community solely. A final issue of concern was whether or not the company should attempt to move into application areas involving larger businesses.

Mercury Instant Printing

THE FRANCHISEE

Mercury Instant Printing is a franchised instant printing shop located in Newark, New Jersey. The business was opened in October, 1972, after capitalization with a $40,000, seven-year loan from the Small Business Administration. Of that sum, $35,000 went for the franchise fee and the remaining $5,000 for rent and operating supplies.

Mercury Instant Printing has the capability to quickly reproduce virtually any type of printed material in up to four colors, with enlargement or reduction of the original copy if desired. The operation uses two basic machines. The first is the Itek 12·18 Platemaster, which photographs the subject material and produces a paper plate for the printing press (same principle as the Polaroid Land camera). The second is the A. B. Dick 360 CD Offset Printing Press, which takes either a stencil or the paper plate and transfers the subject image onto paper. Other printing related services offered by Mercury include design and layout work to customer specification, photocopying, typing, collating, and hole punching. Business cards, rubber stamps, announcements and poster size photo enlargements are also available; however, this work is farmed out.

THE FRANCHISOR

The franchisor is Mercury Corporation, located in New Haven, Connecticut. In addition to its $35,000 franchise fee, the company receives 5 percent of the monthly gross sales from each franchisee. However, it also agrees to buy back any franchise during its first six months of operation for $40,000. The company reports that fewer than 10 percent of its franchises have been bought back, and that none has gone out of business.

Franchisees have the option either to lease their equipment from the Mercury Corporation or buy it outright. In either case, repair costs are borne by the franchisee. The company also offers printing supplies (paper, ink,

This case was prepared by Patrick L. Graham, David S. Rapoport, and Ronald G. Sharples under the direction of Hans Schollhammer and Arthur H. Kuriloff.

Platemaster film) to its franchisees at bulk prices generally lower than those obtainable through other channels.

In support of its franchisees, Mercury Corporation provides a two-week training course covering the technical and managerial aspects of running an instant printing store, a bi-monthly newsletter called "Instant Press," and randomly mails operational improvement suggestions to all its outlets. The company also maintains a group of field representatives who provide technical and managerial assistance to individual franchisees and are also available to help them solicit new customer accounts.

Franchisor Views Versus Franchisee Realities

Several telephone calls and a visit to Mercury Corporation headquarters allowed us to identify the company viewpoint about the proper way to operate one of their franchises. However, our investigation of the practices employed by our subject franchise and several other outlets in the Newark area disclosed some obvious differences of opinion as to the applicability of certain company suggested operating procedures. These areas are discussed briefly as relevant background information before we specifically address our subject franchisee's current situation.

Operating Philosophy Mercury Corporation views its franchisees as offering a business service—not merely running a print shop. The corporation therefore devotes a large portion of its energy to standardizing operating procedures and evaluating the performance of each franchisee in terms of his or her adherence to its various recommended practices. Franchisees are taught company approved managerial techniques during the training course and compile an operating manual consisting of various company handout sheets and supplemented by their individual classroom notes.

In the field we discovered that some franchisees had found their original operating guidelines to be of limited usefulness. Although they helped a franchisee to get started (supplemented by daily assistance from the field representative for the first two weeks of operation), a variety of local situational factors soon appear to take over and strongly influence the type of marketing approach that a particular store will adopt. The result is that some franchisees eventually mold their operations into businesses of narrower scope than the corporation considers most profitable. Our observations lead us to conclude that the co-existence of unsystematic market development by franchisees (generally a reflection of both their personal managerial qualities and the peculiarities of their marketing areas) and the rather inflexible performance evaluation criteria of the franchisor (reflecting both a desire to maximize its royalties and maintain adherence to company devised operating procedures) is a cause of significant misunderstanding and irritation between franchisor and franchisee.

Role of the Franchise Owner Mercury Corporation grants franchises only to individuals planning to operate with a minimum of three people. The corporation sees the owner's primary role as that of account solicitor, with a full-time pressman operating the store's equipment and a third individual to attend the counter and make pickups and deliveries. We observed this arrangement to be practical in many cases; however, it is not mandatory once the business is established.

The inclination and suitability of owners to act as salesmen are obviously subject to some variance. Also, certain owners attempt to dispense with the cost of a pressman and take on both the printing and selling chores. We quickly realized that the proper role of the franchise owner, like the definition of the franchise's scope, is subject to non-uniform interpretation and is a source of contention between the franchisor and franchisee.

Projectaform's Effectiveness as a Sales Aid Mercury Corporation places great emphasis on the use of a sales aid known as Projectaform. This device, put forward as a printing/inventory control system, is a loose-leaf binder that a franchisee can compile for each regular customer. A sample of every form, letterhead, envelope or document that a customer has ordered or intends to order is coded and placed in the binder. The sample also shows the inventory level, price and re-order time for each item. A duplicate Projectaform is maintained by the franchisee, allowing a customer to telephone an order and know its cost in advance. The company believes that the initiation of a Projectaform binder virtually locks in a customer.

We have found, however, the Projectaform can be of only marginal usefulness in certain circumstances, and its value as a sales clinching aid was disputed by several franchisees that we interviewed. For instance, if a store's major accounts are businesses needing price sheets, newsletters, or materials whose content is subject to frequent or periodic changes, Projectaform is useless since the new copy must be supplied for each job. Projectaform also seems to be of limited value in many initial solicitation situations since most customers are more interested in the quality, cost, and scope of work that a franchisee can provide than the ease with which they can re-order once an account has been established. The franchisees that we interviewed agreed that in-person solicitation is a store's best sales approach, and this effort places premiums on a specific knowledge of the owner's equipment capabilities. A personable manner is more important than offering the future convenience of telephone re-orders or even free delivery.

OWNER'S BACKGROUND

The subject franchisee, Mr. Alex White, brought a long and varied background of work experience to his venture. After graduating from high school, Mr. White worked in a print shop for a year. He then attended Rutgers University for two years, until his Marine Corps Reserve unit was activated for service in Korea. In the combat zone he served for two years as a tank crewman, rising to the rank of sergeant. After his discharge, Mr. White held jobs as an electrical installer for Grumman Aircraft (five years) and milkman for Luxor Farms (three years). He next owned a carpet cleaning business, but dissolved it after one year and for the next five years worked as a postal clerk. For the last ten years prior to acquiring his Mercury franchise, Mr. White worked as a painting contractor.

In January, 1973, Mr. White's wife began working in the store. At first her efforts were devoted to waiting on customers and making pickups and deliveries. However, the Whites soon became dissatisfied with the performance of their accounting service, which was slow in furnishing monthly statements and had on one occasion supplied erroneous data that had led to a large sales tax overpayment. In July, Mrs. White assumed all bookkeeping duties in addition to her other responsibilities. She had previously worked in her husband's carpet cleaning business and during her own work career had accumulated ten years' experience as a bookkeeper and secretary. The Whites have four children, ages ten to eighteen.

METHODOLOGY

The problem areas discussed in the following pages were identified and evaluated after compiling information from several sources. In addition to obtaining Mr. White's own estimate of his situation, we visited other Mercury outlets in the greater Newark area to determine if certain difficulties were common to many franchisees, and, if so, what corrective actions were being tried. The viewpoint of Mercury Corporation on the proper way to operate one of its franchises was obtained via telephone calls and a visit to its headquarters.

Marketing

Three areas for improvement in marketing are evident:

Market Segment and Customer Profile Prior to granting a franchise, Mercury Corporation surveys the proposed area to make sure that it contains a minimum of 1,000 on-going businesses. The corporation believes that 75–80 percent of the printing needs of any business can be accomplished by one of their franchisees.

Mr. White's immediate marketing area falls largely in postal zone 72; however, Mercury Corporation places no restrictions as to where any franchisee may seek customers. Physical distance appears to be the most significant prohibitive constraint in soliciting business outside a store's immediate area, since the time and cost of travel between customer and printer are factors that both parties would presumably want to minimize. Zone 72 appears to contain enough potential customers to sustain several small printing establishments, although Mr. White's solicitations on the fringes of adjacent zones have proven worthwhile.

Approximately 85–90 percent of Mr. White's customers are repeat business (a figure quoted by several other franchisees that we contacted). These run the gamut from doctors and lawyers to the New Jersey Egg Producers Association and include a substantial number of small proprietorships. However, due to the small size of many of the businesses in Mr. White's area, the average monthly bill for an account is only about $50.00.

Unsatisfactory Sales Volume Mr. White stated that his primary objective was to discover ways to increase his store's sales. Although there appear to be some seasonal influences upon sales, monthly gross revenues have been rather erratic and generally lower than both Mr. White and the Mercury Corporation feel are attainable at this time (see Appendix A). We found Mr. White's technical proficiency and his product's quality to be very good. Instead, we believe that his departure from the three-person operating concept is the most significant factor in the business's inability to generate a higher sales volume.

Mr. White's original pressman proved to be undependable, and during the summer of 1973, the Whites decided to discharge him and operate the business by themselves. With Mr. White spending most of his time in the store, new account solicitation (which had initially been quite successful) quickly declined. Ironically, Mr. White now feels that his financial position is such that it cannot support the pressman necessary to allow his return to customer solicitation. We concluded that, although two-person operation for the last nine months may have been workable, it has been extremely strenuous, and has led directly to the present dilemma.

Non-productive Advertising Despite the inherent advantage of being able to produce his own copy cheaply, Mr. White has had only limited success with his past promotional efforts. Several factors appear to have caused this situation. First, Mr. White did not carefully investigate both the types and number of potential customers in his immediate area of access. This made it difficult to know what kinds of advertising approaches would be most effective. Second, no systematic advertising plan has ever been implemented; there has been no determination of a budget and ways to measure the effect of a particular campaign. Third, the store's erratic sales performance and the hectic pace of the two-person operation have been a constant drain upon the White's financial and physical resources. Thus far, promotional efforts have been limited to direct mailings and the purchase of advertising space in several telephone directories.

Mr. White's advertising situation is not unique among the Mercury outlets that we surveyed. However, since the communications among most of the stores are quite good, it was logical for some type of cooperative promotional effort eventually to be discussed. Very recently, seventeen Mercury stores, including Mr. White's, formed an association. The first project it has undertaken is a thirteen-week radio advertising campaign. We believe that this pooling of resources is a step in the right direction and has advantages that could be exploited in other areas (for example, group buying of printing supplies in bulk so as to take advantage of large quantity discounts). However, we would caution against undertaking any type of advertising scheme that is not preceded by a careful profiling of the target audience and complemented by some means for measuring results.

Optimizing Equipment and Man-Hour Usage
Currently, Mr. White divides his time among the printing operation, making pickups and deliveries, and customer solicitation. This often results in his having to work after regular hours to complete jobs or catch up on other work around the store. This practice makes it difficult for him to step back occasionally and do some careful planning for the future. It can also become a serious physical strain and a source of irritation within Mr. White's family.

Press Efficiency The several claims on Mr. White's time cause the shop's press to be used at something less than maximum efficiency (we estimate from observation that there is up to 50 percent idle press time per day). At the store's present level of sales (see Appendix A), Mr. White has been able to use the press sub-optimally and still meet all his job deadlines. However, we believe that the continuation of this situation will seriously inhibit future sales growth. Apparently it has already become a misleading factor in Mr. White's thinking about expansion.

Mr. White believes that when he reaches a $6,500 per month sales plateau he should buy a second press (cost, approximately $3,000, rebuilt) and hire a full-time pressman (salary approximately $700 per month). We think that the $6,500 figure is too low and is based upon the relatively inefficient use of the existing press. If Mr. White had a full-time or at least part-time pressman now, we estimate that the present press could handle up to $8,000 per month in sales. Furthermore, the additional time this would give Mr. White for customer solicitation should make sales growth much more rapid and consistent.

Production Scheduling Implicit in the above estimate is the assumption of efficient production scheduling. Although current jobs are certainly not run haphazardly, neither is there any formalized procedure for accepting and scheduling work. We believe that the use of a production scheduling chart (even without hiring a pressman) would greatly increase the efficient use of press time and delay the need for a second press. Similarly, a large wall map of Mr. White's marketing area could help him in two ways. First, it could be used to aid in planning solicitation efforts. Second, it could be used to determine the most efficient routes for making pickups and deliveries, thereby reducing travel time and gasoline consumption.

Refining the Management Process

The management of operations could be improved in the following ways:

Improving Bookkeeping Procedures Mr. White's discontinuation of his subscription to the computerized bookkeeping service that he had initially employed did not completely eliminate his problems in financial information gathering and maintenance. For the second half of 1973, record keeping, like account solicitation, suffered unavoidable neglect resulting from two-person operation of the store. Working under the stress of both her business and family responsibilities, Mrs. White is only now completing the financial records of the past nine months. Nevertheless, our examination of current bookkeeping procedures has suggested a few areas of further improvement in the interests of greater accuracy and control over the store's operation.

Currently, receipts are filed only in alphabetical order, according to customer name. This policy makes it difficult to determine monthly sales quickly. In addition, gross revenues are determined by a cash accounting system, rather than by the usual accrual method. For example, if a sale is made in January, but the customer does not pay until March, the transaction is recorded as a sale in March, not January. These practices could generate incorrect information leading to erroneous conclusions in at least three areas. First, they make the determination of peak sales period extremely difficult. This is an important consideration if Mr. White is trying to measure the results of advertising or make supply purchasing decisions on the basis of sales data. Second, determination of the Mercury Corporation's monthly fee (5 percent of gross sales) could often be based on incorrect sales figures. Third, if monthly sales totals are used as the principal criterion, the decision to expand the store's operating capability (for example, buy another printing press) would almost certainly be miscalculated.

Another shortcoming is the absence of a journal in which to post daily transaction entries. Under the present system, receipts (vouchers) and check stubs are totalled at the end of the month to determine expenses. This practice makes it difficult to monitor out-of-pocket cash expenses that, in Mr. White's business, are not insignificant.

Systematizing Bad Debt Collection A persistent problem for Mr. White has been the collection of delinquent accounts, which currently total about $575. Although bad debts do not comprise a large percentage of receivables, their collection would obviously permit Mr. White to develop other aspects of his business, especially sales promotion. At this time the only method used in attempting to collect delinquent accounts is repeated telephone calls to the parties concerned. The only results have been a variety of excuses. Although Mr. White does not feel that this problem is serious right now, we see a strong possibility of its becoming worse in the future. This is because of the accounting system weaknesses previously mentioned, which make it difficult to monitor accurately the date of sales, and hence the delinquent status of an account.

APPENDIX A. Summary of Available Financial Data

	1973 (all figures rounded to nearest dollar)		
	Total Sales	Gross Profit	Net Income
Jan.	$1,907	$1,349	$ (308)
Feb.	3,177	2,724	1,390
Mar.	2,832	1,566	(184)
Apr.	3,869	3,567	1,520
May	3,074	2,996	1,781
June	3,481	2,617	1,197
July	3,960	Unavailable*	(14)
Aug.	4,925	Unavailable	200
Sept.	5,858	Unavailable	1,807
Oct.	5,723	Unavailable	949
Nov.	4,211	Unavailable	288
Dec.	4,373	Unavailable	283
	1974		
Jan.	$4,916	Unavailable*	Unavailable*
Feb.	5,662	Unavailable	Unavailable

*Because of difficulties explained in the report, complete financial data were not available for our evaluation during the consulting project.

Allied Plastics, Inc.

In late January 1972, Mr. Nathan Leff, vice president of Allied Plastics, located in Atlanta, Georgia, was examining the company's balance sheet with an eye toward establishing a more stable liabilities schedule. In addition, he was considering the raising of additional funds to finance expansion of the firm's plastic operations.

DESCRIPTION OF FIRM'S PRODUCTS AND CUSTOMERS

Allied Plastics was founded in 1962 by Nathan and Jenny I. Leff, who were husband and wife. The firm was a small designer and fabricator of standard and custom plastic products. Their products included such diverse fabricated items as windshields for golf carts and plastic cubes, nameplates for individual employees, directional signs for office buildings, industrial machinery and equipment, plastic furniture, indoor and outdoor nonilluminated signs of various sizes and descriptions. The company's customers included builders, industrial designers, architects, plus various industrial users of fabricated plastic items. Allied Plastics worked with all the standard materials of the industry, such as acrylics, styrene, vinyls, polyethylenes, acetates, and both rigid and flexible engraving stock.

THE COMPANY'S BEGINNING AND EARLY YEARS

The initial capitalization consisted of three hundred shares of capital stock issued at $1 par, to Jenny I. Leff, who was designated president. Nathan Leff served as vice president and was the chief operating officer of the firm.

Mr. Leff, who was now in his mid-fifties, had previous business experience in the construction industry, but following a heart attack in 1961 his doctor had strongly advised that he not return to that line of work. At the time Mrs. Leff was doing engraving work for Delta Plastics, a small Atlanta firm. Both Mr. and Mrs. Leff believed that the plastics industry was in its infancy in regard to signs with plastic bases with either engraved or applied letters. After advisement

This case is prepared by Harry R. Kunianski, copyright © 1972 by the author. Reproduced by permission.

with Mrs. Leff's brother, Dr. Donald Stein, a local physician, they decided to enter the plastic sign business. Dr., Stein agreed to endorse a $5,000 note maturing in 12 months with Allied's bank, the Atlanta National, Polly Street Branch. These funds were necessary for working capital and the purchase of needed equipment.

The firm rented a vacant store owned by the father of Mrs. Leff. The location was ideal as it was near the downtown business district, which easily afforded the Leff's the opportunity to contact possible sources of business such as engineers, architects, builders, and contractors. Sales involved two types of signs, engraving on phenolic plastic and glue-applied letters on acrylic plastic. Mr. Leff contacted prospective customers and brought the orders back to the store. Mrs. Leff, with the help of a part-time employee, would complete the engraving orders while Mr. Leff would do the applied sign work. Mrs. Leff handled the bookkeeping function and a CPA prepared yearly statements and tax returns.

Sales for the first month were $350 and for the first year in excess of $19,000. The firm suffered a negligible loss during the initial year of operations. In 1963 net profit before officers' salaries was $9,650 with officer salaries being $8,000.

The firm continued with the same product lines until mid 1965. At this time both Mr. and Mrs. Leff noted the profit potential in the fabrication of plastics. Plastic was fabricated or shaped by heating the material with a stripheater to the desired temperature and then bending or shaping to the form needed. As an example, this technique enabled the firm to sell chartholders to the medical profession. In addition, Allied was able to secure the account of a large motel chain for which it made drapery arms out of acrylic scrap. The company added another engraving machine, and sales for the fiscal year ending February 28, 1966, were over $46,000.

During 1965 Allied received debt funds through the endorsement of a note by Dr. Stein, and repaid it within 12 months. Short-term funds were borrowed from the Polly Street Branch of the Atlanta National Bank. Mr. Leff had banked at this location for a number of years and had a warm personal relationship with the branch manager, Mr. Harvey Higgins. Mr. Higgins was quite amenable to continue short-term borrowings as the company needed them. He realized that some of the firm's needs were of a permanent nature. However, he did not believe this was the appropriate time to explore term debt. For his part Mr. Leff had given some thought to term debt, as he believed this might facilitate the planning process. He believed that an inordinate amount of his time was spent on financial activities such as telephoning to inquire about outstanding receivables and worrying about whether deposits would cover outstanding payables. During some months it had been necessary to refrain from paying bills because there were not enough funds from collections to cover maturing payables. Mr. Leff thought a term loan might relieve him of some of these financial pressures, thus paving the way for him to spend more time outside the firm; namely calling on prospective customers. He believed increased time on the sales function would enable the firm to grow at a faster rate, since personal selling played an important part in stimulating sales, especially those of the applied letter variety. However, Mr. Leff thought a term loan to be somewhat risky because it committed the firm to repay debt for a period over one year. He was not at all sure that Allied was that firmly established in the Atlanta market to warrant such a commitment. Applied letter sign sales were almost totally non-recurring. Engraving sales were dominated by two or three large customers. If either sign sales declined or one of his large engraving customers switched its account, he feared that the firm might have difficulty in meeting the installments on term debt. Mr. Leff, therefore, decided at this time to forego any attempt to negotiate term-debt arrangements.

By fiscal 1967 the firm's sales had risen to $54,000 with net profits before officer salaries of $12,200. By 1967 fabrication of plastic materials was responsible for about 60% of the company's output, while engraving accounted for around 25% and applied letters 15%. In addition, fabrication was growing at a faster pace than either of the other two product lines.

THE FIRM'S COMPETITION

Allied was especially active in producing goods for architects and builders. These items not only provided profits in themselves, but enabled this type of customer to observe the quality of Allied's workmanship. Accordingly, the firm derived additional business, such as from hospitals and hotels, by doing excellent work for these clients. The company, as it had from its inception, continued to stress quality work and strict adherence to the scheduled date of delivery. Mr. Leff strongly believed that any compromise with these goals would seriously impair the competitive position of the firm. Basically, the firm was in competition with two or three well-established Atlanta firms as far as engraving was concerned and price was likely to play a major role. The applied sign competition was composed of numerous small firms scattered throughout the metropolitan area. Price played a lesser role in securing sales as most customers were more concerned with appearance and durability. Allied continually pointed out that plastic signs would last a lifetime, whereas painted signs lasted between two to five years. Profit margins on applied signs were higher than either engraving or fabrication.

Competition for fabrication sales was intense; mainly from large national and regional firms situated in the Atlanta area. Accordingly, lower profit margins were the rule, especially on large-volume orders. However, Mr. Leff believed the securing of this type order was necessary, because it provided coverage of the firm's fixed cost. In addition these orders tended to be repeaters and therefore provided the firm with a stable sales base.

THE GROWTH YEARS 1967–1970

A large jump in sales, in excess of 30%, was recorded between 1967 and 1968. Contributing materially to this growth was the building boom occurring in the City of Atlanta (see Exhibit 7). The boom reflected the development of Atlanta during the 1960's as the leading city in the Southeast. In response to the sales increase the firm added another full-time production employee. Allied added a store adjacent to the present site, and remodeled it to meet its specifications. This expansion was financed by short-term loans and profits. In 1968 Dr. Stein made a $7,500 loan with no maturity date and no interest rate. This enabled the firm to pay off some long-standing accounts payable and to withstand an operating loss that occurred in fiscal 1969. The loss was primarily due to a decrease in sales and an inability of the firm to curtail expanding operating expenses.

In 1969 the firm widened its product line by securing the distributorship of Harrison Plastics of Bradenton, Florida, producers of plastic-injected molded letters of various sizes and shapes, and the Delcy Corporation of Santa Barbara, California, manufacturers of directory boards and their interchangeable letters. Previously, Allied had purchased all of its letters at a 40% discount from Garrison Plastics in Atlanta, which was the only local distributor of plastic letters. The company used these letters in its own sign-making activities and also sold them to the general public. Mr. Leff foresaw profit potential in two ways from the new distributorship. He believed that he could materially increase letters sales to the public because the Harrison distributorship provided him with a more varied and larger inventory of letters and Harrison gave the firm a 60% discount on all letters purchased. In order to secure this distributorship Harrison required that Allied maintain a minimum inventory of $6,000 and to remit to Harrison promptly on terms of net 30 days. In order to finance this increase in assets the firm borrowed from its bank $8,000 on a 12-month note with a $5,000 balloon payment at the end. Approximately one-half of the note had been paid back by February 1970.

In January of 1970 Mr. Leff received pro forma income statements and balance sheets prepared by George H. Schafer, a nephew of Mr. Leff, and a professor of finance at a local university. Among other things these financial statements projected a gross sale in excess of $200,000 for this year ending February 28, 1973. In addition, Mr. Leff noted that he and Mrs. Leff were already spending many weeknights at the office. Mr. Leff noted the increasing difficulty in trying to sell and also supervise production in the sign and fabrication sections. Mrs. Leff found it cumbersome to oversee engraving, bill customers, and do the necessary accounting work. Especially crucial was the prompt billing of customers for work performed. This activity had to be done daily or billings would lag and therefore collections would be delayed. In view of the firm's tight cash position, this lag would only make the present cash situation more pressing. Also, Dr. Stein in conversations with him had stressed the importance of growth if the firm was to continue to prosper. Dr. Stein believed that organizations either grew or declined and that it was impossible for a firm to maintain the status quo.

All of these factors re-enforced the idea that Mr. Leff had been pondering for the past few months; namely that Allied Plastics was passing or had already outgrown the "Mom and Pop" phase of its existence. Mr. Leff believed it imperative that a general manager be hired and given the complete responsibility for production, as well as supervising bids for the fabricating jobs. In all likelihood this person would probably wish to upgrade the quality of labor in the fabricating and sign sections. Hiring and keeping skilled labor was an increasing problem and as the customers' demands grew for more complex products, the necessity for workers who possessed the prerequisite skills for manufacturing quality work became more and more important to Allied Plastics. Mr. Leff grappled with the problem of finding the right man and how to finance the required salary. He believed it would require between $10,000 and $15,000 to attract a person of sufficient ability to get the job done. He also considered some form of profit sharing or stock-purchase plan for the individual he would hire.

FINANCIAL CONSIDERATIONS AND BANK RELATIONSHIPS

By June of 1970 the company's financial condition had deteriorated to such an extent that it was having considerable difficulties meeting its current maturities. Growth in sales was occurring, but this seemed only to aggravate the liquidity problem. The managerial difficulties were compounded by the growth situation. Mr. and Mrs. Leff decided that both of these problems must be met at once. Accordingly, he began searching in earnest for a top-flight production manager. He became aware of a change in management at a large diversified Atlanta-based plastics firm, and the subsequent availability of one of its experienced managers, Mr. Lyman Miller. Mr. Miller possessed over twenty years' experience in both the production and management functions of plastic fabrication. Additionally, Mr. Miller was well acquainted with numerous purchasing agents and buyers in some of the large users of fabricated products in Atlanta and other large cities. He believed he could bring a portion of this business to Allied Plastics. Mr. Miller was hired and began work as general manager in September of 1970 at an annual salary of $12,000, plus 2 per cent of net profit before owners' salaries.

At this time Mr. Leff was also determined to tackle his financial problems, especially his schedule of maturing debts. Mr. Leff had preliminary discussions with Mr. Schafer and Dr. Stein, and it was agreed that it was necessary to secure some form of term financing. Accordingly, Mr. Schafer prepared pro forma income statement and balance sheets (see Exhibit 3 and 4) to present to Mr. Lawrence Glacken, manager of the Polly Street Branch of the Atlanta National Bank. Glacken had replaced Mr. Higgins as branch manager at the first of the year. Although relations between Mr. Leff and Mr. Glacken had been acceptable, the warm personal relationship that had existed between Mr. Leff and Mr. Higgins had not developed. Nevertheless, if at all possible, Mr. Leff wished to continue doing business at Atlanta National because of past satisfactory associations, and due to the fact the branch was located in close proximity to the firm.

Mr. Leff and Mr. Schafer approached Mr. Glacken with a proposal for a term loan of from 3 to 5 years' duration and in the amount of $15,000. Mr. Glacken seemed amenable to such a loan as he felt the prospects of the firm warranted a long-term commitment by the bank. Mr. Glacken required that all parties provide personal financial statements, Dr. Stein co-sign the note, and Mr. and Mrs. Leff sign the note personally as well as officers of the corporation, and that Mr. Leff secure a life insurance policy for the value of the loan and assign this policy to the bank. The only requirement that disturbed Mr. Leff was the latter one. He could not comprehend why he should obtain such a policy, since both he and Dr. Stein were signing the note, and their personal assets would be sufficient in case of default of the note. In addition, and more important than the cost of the policy, which would range between $330 and $600 yearly, Mr. Leff felt it showed a lack of confidence by the bank in Allied's future prospects. He asked Mr. Glacken if the bank would remove the life insurance proviso. Mr. Glacken informed him that he would give the bank's decision within a week to ten days. In the meantime, Dr. Stein suggested that Mr. Leff inquire as to the possibility of securing the loan from another Atlanta bank. He suggested that Mr. Harold Bogan, branch manager of the Metropolitan

National Bank, might be interested in making a loan on more favorable terms. Dr. Stein was a friend of Mr. Bogan and banked at Metropolitan. A conference was arranged and Mr. Bogan informed Mr. Leff that he would lend $15,000 at a 6 percent add-on-rate, to be paid back over 60 monthly installments. Personal endorsements of Mr. and Mrs. Leff and Dr. Stein were required, but no life insurance policy would be demanded. Before accepting the Metropolitan National loan, Mr. Leff informed Mr. Glacken of the terms of the loan. Mr. Glacken stated that he had discussed the loan with the bank's loan committee and they concurred in his judgment that a life insurance policy should be required. Accordingly, the firm accepted the Metropolitan National loan and switched its account to that bank.

RECENT MANAGERIAL AND FINANCIAL CONSIDERATIONS

The term loan alleviated the severe liquidity squeeze for the moment but the underlying conditions of undercapitalization and sales growth soon placed the firm in a liquidity bind again. By the fall of 1971 Mr. Leff needed to borrow again. The bank secured the borrowings ($14,000) with firm purchase orders on fabricated products from Allied's well-established customers. At this time Mr. Bogan suggested the firm look for equity financing as he felt the firm was severely undercapitalized. Mr. Bogan also suggested that the firm could benefit from managerial consultants who would assess the organizational strengths and weaknesses of the firm and report on the accounting and reporting procedures of the company. Mr. Leff was receptive to this idea as for some time certain internal managerial problems had continued to plague him. He especially desired to secure more accurate and comprehensive information about the relative profitability of the firm's various product lines. At present, no cost accounting system was in operation and the financial reporting system and balance sheets provided only periodic and annual income statements. He wanted this cost information for two basic reasons: One was to insure that each product line was making the proper contribution to the overall profitability of the firm. Secondly, he felt that this type information would help Mr. Miller and himself in the pricing decisions made by the firm. Mr. Leff believed strongly that improved pricing would greatly enhance the profitability of the firm. For example, in pricing fabrication jobs he knew the firm could accept less profit than on sign jobs, but he was not at all sure of how much he could cut fabricating job profit contribution and still have it beneficial to the firm. Fabrication and engraved sign orders were much more competitive than applied signs, and he wanted to insure that the pricing policies of the firm were neither preventing Allied from getting profitable work or pricing the job so low as to make it unprofitable. In the actual pricing decision on fabrication jobs, Mr. Miller tended to be lower than Mr. Leff and this sometimes led to inconsistently submitted bids.

By January of 1972 Mr. Leff had decided to employ a managerial consultant. This consulting team would install a cost accouting system and provide a part-time accountant who would prepare the necessary financial reports and Allied's income tax return. Mr. Leff estimated that the cost would be between $4,000 and $4,500 the first year and between $3,000 and $3,500 thereafter. In addition Mr. Leff was investigating the purchase of a vacuum forming machine which cost in the neighborhood of $8,000. Vacuum forming is a method of sheet forming in which the plastic sheet is clamped in a stationary frame, heated and drawn down by a vacuum into a mold.[1] Mr. Leff knew the purchase of this piece of equipment would enable the firm to produce such items as plastic cups, dinnerware, plastic toys, lamps and skylights. He believed it would be essential to employ a full-time salesman in order to exploit the output from the vacuum forming machine. He thought he could hire a competent person for $10,000 plus commission. Although competition was intense in this area, Mr. Leff believed the addition of vacuum forming would allow Allied to double its volume within two years. He thought the profit margin from vacuum forming was similar to that of fabrication.

Considering all these major changes, Mr. Leff thought it imperative to develop a capital structure that would enable the firm to support without undue risk a growing asset structure, and at the same time pay the firm's maturing debts within the 30 days terms furnished by his creditors.

---

[1]Source: *Modern Plastic Encyclopedia,* 1970–1971, Vol. 47, McGraw-Hill Publishing Company.

EXHIBIT 1. Allied Plastic, Inc.

Balance Sheets, February 28, 1967—February 28, 1971, and August 31, 1971

	2/28/67	2/29/68	2/28/69	2/28/70	2/28/71	8/31/71
Assets						
Cash	$ 1,006	$ 372	$ 399	$ 1,513	$(3,854)	$ 4,688
Accounts Receivable	4,328	9,462	5,690	13,836	20,077	26,237
Inventory	4,107	5,202	7,564	11,074	19,031	26,884
Prepaid Interest	1,334	698	416	251	425	340
Total Current Assets	$10,775	$15,734	$14,069	$26,674	$35,679	$58,149
Fixed Assets	10,091	10,880	12,219	13,822	19,326	20,994
Less Accumulated Depreciation	(2,715)	(4,811)	(7,015)	(5,551)	(8,452)	(7,153)
Advances to Stockholders	6,202	9,697	11,749	11,830	10,832[b]	11,694
Other Assets	525	525	525	932	1,389	1,217
Total Assets	$24,878	$32,025	$31,547	$47,707	$58,774	$84,901
Liabilities and Net Worth						
Accounts Payable	$ 4,263	$ 8,269	$ 5,729	$ 5,787	$14,741	$24,665
Accrued Taxes	604	801	643	1,694	1,518	2,039
Bank Loans Payable	9,868	5,884	5,431	9,123	12,515	25,855
Total Current Liabilities	$14,735	$14,954	$11,803	$16,604	$28,774	$52,559
Term Loans	0	0	0	0	13,500	12,000
Other Loans	0	0	7,500[a]	7,500	7,500	7,500
Total Liabilities	$14,735	$14,954	$19,303	$24,104	$49,774	$72,059
Common Stock, $1 par, 1,000 shares authorized and 300 shares outstanding	300	300	300	300	300	300
Retained Earnings	9,843	16,771	11,944	23,303	8,700[b]	12,542
Total Liabilities and Net Worth	$24,878	$32,025	$31,547	$47,707	$58,774	$84,901

[a] Loan to be converted in some future time to 20% of outstanding shares.
[b] Retained Earnings charged with $4,508 and advances to stockholders credited with $4,508.

EXHIBIT 2. Allied Plastics, Inc.

Periodic Income Statements, Period from March 1, 1966—August 31, 1971

	3/1/66–2/28/67	3/1/67–2/29/68	3/1/68–2/28/69	3/1/69–2/28/70	3/1/70–2/28/71	3/1/71–8/31/71
Gross Sales	$54,774	$73,649	$64,307	$105,397	$135,006	$111,956
Less Sales Discounts	701	881	1,083	1,149	1,430	1,168
Net Sales	$54,073	$72,768	$63,224	$104,248	$133,576	$110,788
Beginning Inventory	3,613	4,107	5,202	7,564	11,074	19,031
Purchase of Raw Materials	14,011	23,998	16,820	29,568	48,833	51,263
Tools, Hardware, and Subcontracts	1,506	1,930	2,478	3,204	5,335	2,939
Less Ending Inventory	(4,107)	(5,202)	(7,564)	(11,074)	(19,031)	(26,884)
Cost of Goods Sold[a]	$15,023	$24,833	$16,936	$29,262	$46,211	$46,349
Gross Profit	$39,050	$47,935	$46,288	$74,986	$87,365	$64,439
Operating Expenses						
Salaries[b]	$19,667	$24,354	$33,281	$39,990	$64,777	$40,219
Rent	2,400	2,400	2,600	3,600	5,800	3,200
Utilities	2,569	2,684	2,753	4,043	5,099	2,917
Sales Promotion and Advertising	1,305	1,089	1,119	1,100	1,284	510
Licenses and Property Taxes	1,689	2,160	2,001	2,609	4,003	3,539
Insurance	378	404	1,144	2,064	2,571	2,466
Depreciation	1,677	2,096	2,204	2,268	2,901	1,501
Other	4,211	4,969	5,118	6,916	9,520	5,100
Total Operating Expenses	$33,896	$40,156	$50,220	$62,590	$95,955	$59,452
Net Operating Income or (Loss)	$ 5,154	$ 7,779	$ (3,932)	$ 12,396	$ (8,590)	$ 4,987
Interest Expense	887	851	895	1,037	1,505	1,145
Net Income or (Loss)[c]	$ 4,267	$ 6,928	$ (4,827)	$ 11,359	$ (10,095)	$ 3,842
Owners Withdrawals	$ 8,000	$10,000	$12,000	$ 15,000	$ 15,000	$ 8,000

[a]Cost of Goods Sold does not include either direct labor or overhead.
[b]Salaries include all labor costs whether incurred in production or operations and owners' withdrawls.
[c]No Federal or State Income Taxes as owners choose to be taxed as individuals under Sub Chapter S of the Internal Revenue Code. Under this section of the Code all profits or losses flow directly to the individual stockholders.

EXHIBIT 3. Allied Plastics Inc.

Pro Forma Balance Sheets
Fiscal Years 1971, 1972, 1973

	Feb. 28, 1971	Feb. 29, 1972	Feb. 28, 1973	Key to Pro Forma Preparation
Assets				
a) Cash	$ 2,500	$ 3,500	$ 4,500	a) Assumed minimum balance
b) Accounts Receivable	16,469	20,585	25,732	b) Turnover 8 times or 45 days
c) Inventory	12,164	15,206	19,007	c) Turnover 3 times or 120 days
d) Fixed Assets	13,270	18,270	23,270	d) Assumed net of depreciation $5,000 increase per year
e) Other Assets	1,500	1,500	1,500	e) Assumed figure
Total Assets	$45,903	$59,061	$74,009	
Liabilities				
f) Accounts Payable	$ 6,082	$ 7,603	$ 9,503	f) 60 days Cost of Goods Sold
g) Accrued Taxes	2,000	2,500	3,125	g) 4% of salaries
h) Bank Notes Payable	11,353	13,333	14,148	h) Plugged figure
	$19,435	$23,436	$26,776	
Net Worth				
i) Common Stock	7,800	7,800	7,800	i) Loan payable of $7,500 converted to equity
j) Retained Earnings	18,668	27,825	39,433	j) 2/28/70 Retained Earnings $23,303 − $11,830 advance to stockholders written off equals $8,563
Total Net Worth	$26,468	$35,625	$47,233	
Total Liabilities and Net Worth	$45,903	$59,061	$74,009	

EXHIBIT 4. Allied Plastics, Inc.

Pro Forma Income Statements[a]
March 1, 1970—February 28, 1973

	Mar. 1, 1970–Feb. 28, 1971[b]	Mar. 1, 1971–Feb. 29, 1972	Mar. 1, 1972–Feb. 28, 1973	
a) Gross Sales	$131,745	$164,681	$205,852	a) 25% increase in sales and sales discounts each year
a) Less Sales Discounts	1,436	1,795	2,244	
Net Sales	$130,309	$162,886	$203,608	
b) Cost of Goods Sold	36,493	45,617	57,021	b) 27.7% of sales as per year ending 2/28/70
c) Operating Expenses	78,125	97,656	122,071	c) 59.3% ratio as per year ending 2/28/70; includes withdrawals by principals
Net Operating Profit	$15,691	$19,613	$24,516	
d) Less Interest Expense	1,300	1,300	1,300	d) 10% × $13,000 average balance on term loan
Net Profit Before Taxes	$14,391	$18,313	$23,216	
d) Federal Income Tax at 50%[c]	7,196	9,156	11,608	
Net Profits	$7,195	$9,157	$11,608	
e) Dividends	$0	$0	$0	e) No dividends planned during this period

[a]Prepared in September 1970.
[b]Includes actual data from March 1, 1970—August 31, 1970.
[c]Imputed, as owners are presently taxed as individuals.

EXHIBIT 5. Allied Plastics, Inc.

Revised Pro Forma Income Statements[a]
March 1, 1972—February 28, 1973

	A	B	C
Gross Sales	$279,980	$279,980	$279,980
Less Sales Discounts	2,920	2,920	2,920
Net Sales	$277,060	$277,060	$277,060
Cost of Goods Sold	110,824	115,811	96,971
General, Selling, and Administrative Expenses	138,530	148,504	124,677
Net Operating Profit	$ 27,706	$ 12,745	$ 55,412
Less Interest Expense	2,290	2,290	2,290
Net Profit Before Taxes	$ 25,416	$ 10,455	$ 53,122
Federal Income Taxes at 50%	12,708	5,227	26,561
Net Profit After Taxes	$ 12,708	$ 5,228	$ 26,561
Dividends	0	0	0

Assumptions for Pro Forma Statements
A—25% increase over annualized 8/31/71 sales and sales discounts, operating profit 10% of net sales, cost of goods 40%, and operating expenses 50% of net sales repsectively, interest expense double figure on 8/31 statement.
B—25% increase over annualized 8/31/71 sales and sales discounts, cost of goods sold and operating expenses same percent of net sales as 8/31/71 income statement, interest expense double figure on 8/31 statement.
C—25% increase over annualized 8/31/71 sales and sales discounts, cost of goods and operating expenses 35% and 45% respectively representing optimal levels of efficiency, interest expense double figure on 8/31 statement.

[a]Prepared January 1972 and does not include sales and expenses from possible acquisition of vacuum forming equipment.

EXHIBIT 6. Allied Plastics, Inc.

Monthly Sales

	1970	1971
Jan.	$ 10,277	$ 13,350
Feb.	10,366	16,508
Mar.	10,189	15,578
Apr.	10,174	18,613
May	7,283	15,571
June	10,218	20,152
July	9,487	20,195
Aug.	10,400	21,346
Sept.	9,700	14,045
Oct.	12,840	17,800
Nov.	13,526	18,000
Dec.	13,305	12,420
	$127,765	$203,578

EXHIBIT 7. Allied Plastics, Inc.

Total Private Non-Residential Construction, Metropolitan Atlanta Area
(in millions)

Year	Amount
1964	$140
1965	133
1966	172
1967	200
1968	169
1969	184
1970	238
1971	149
(Jan.–Aug.)	

Source: *Construction Review,* United States Department of Commerce, December 1970 and April 1971.

EXHIBIT 8. Allied Plastics, Inc.

Percentage Breakdown of Financial Information for Fifty-Three Manufacturers
of Miscellaneous Plastic Products
(Statements on or about June 30, 1970, and December 31, 1970)

	Sales Under $250,000	Sales $250,000 to Less Than $1,000,000
Assets		
Cash	6.9%	5.4%
Marketable Securities	0.5	0.4
Receivables, Net	30.5	25.6
Inventory	21.1	22.7
All Other Current	2.2	1.6
Fixed Assets, Net	33.3	37.4
All other Non-Current	5.5	6.9
Total	100.0%	100.0%
Liabilities		
Due to Bank, Short Term	7.0%	6.7%
Due to Trade	24.0	17.6
Income Taxes	2.8	2.2
Current Maturities, Long-Term Debt	5.5	4.7
All other Current	10.4	9.1
Total Current Debt	49.7	40.3
Non-Current Unsubordinated Debt	12.7	15.0
Total Unsubordinated Debt	62.4	55.3
Subordinated Debt	4.8	3.1
Tangible Net Worth	32.8	41.6
Total	100.0%	100.0%

EXHIBIT 8 (continued)

	Sales Under $250,000	Sales $250,000 to Less Than $1,000,000
Income Data		
Net Sales	100.0%	100.0%
Cost of Sales	71.9	77.2
Gross Profit	28.1	22.8
All other Expenses Net	25.3	20.4
Profit Before Taxes	2.8%	2.4%

Source: *Annual Statements 1971*, Robert Morris Associates, p. 53.

535

Recreation Capital Corporation

In January 1973 Recreation Capital Corporation, manufacturer of compact motor homes converted from the Volkswagen van, offered at private placement 60,000 shares of its common stock at $5 per share. The corporation intended to use the proceeds of this offering to expand their California plant production capacity, open a new production facility in northern New Jersey, and provide the necessary working capital to permit an increase in inventories and accounts receivable for the expanding business.

Recreation Capital Corporation was formed by a small group of private investors in April 1972 to acquire all the outstanding capital stock of Adventure Campers, Inc. The purchase price was $660,000, of which $190,000 was paid in cash and the balance was represented by Recreation Capital Corporation's three-year note payable in three annual installments of $50,000, $125,000, and $295,000 due August 1973, 1974, and 1975 respectively, and secured by the Capital Stock of Adventure Campers, Inc. Recreation was capitalized at $200,000, of which $190,000 went for the down payment; the rest was spent on organizational expense.

Recreation had 200,000 shares outstanding and, in addition, the employees held options to purchase 22,000 shares of Recreation's common stock at prices ranging from $1 to $3. Recreation's balance sheet as of January 31, 1973, is given in Exhibit 1.

ADVENTURE CAMPERS, INC.

Founded in Los Angeles in 1965 and incorporated in California in 1969, Adventure Campers, Inc., had become the leading U.S. manufacturer of compact motor homes converted from the Volkswagen van. As it had been closely involved in providing a comprehensive line of Volkswagen conversions, an excellent relationship had been established with VOA, the American subsidiary of Volkswagenwerk of Germany, and with many of its distributors and dealers.

The ideas of Edward J. Anderson, founder, executive vice president and a director of the company, were largely responsible for the success of the company's line of compact motor homes, the "Adventurers." Starting with the California market, sales grew sharply; the number of units converted were 584, 852, and 1434 in the fiscal years 1970, 1971, and 1972 respectively. Exhibits 2, 3, and 4 show the financial statements for Adventure Campers for the years 1972 and 1973.

In April 1972, when the present owners took over, Adventure sold directly through 200 VW dealers in California. In March 1973 the company entered into a contract with World-Wide, the New York Volkswagen distributor, to supply Adventurers from the new plant to be located in New Jersey. An initial order to supply 225 units to World-Wide through July 1973 from California was also negotiated. At about the same time Adventure obtained additional orders of 50 units for delivery in April and 100 units for delivery through May 1973 from Midvo, Inc., the VW distributor for Ohio and Kentucky. There were talks of the company also establishing production facilities in Ohio to serve the continuing requirements of Midvo. A summary of historical results of operations and projections, made on the basis of the above orders, is shown in Exhibit 5.

Recreation Capital Corporation saw substantial growth opportunity in other regions. They opened negotiations with VOA, which owned 5 of the 14 U.S. Volkswagen distributorships. Recreation anticipated increased orders on completion of these negotiations.

In 1972 Adventure developed a prototype motor home conversion of a Mercedes Benz Airport Bus. The prototype was exhibited at the Dodger Stadium Recreational Vehicle Show in October 1972 and was very well received. This resulted in a close working relationship with Mercedes Benz for further development of this product and the initiation of a joint marketing effort.

THE ADVENTURER MODEL LINE

The Adventure line consisted primarily of four models with 12 different versions. The features offered included a foldaway, fully made-up double bed; a 110-volt plug-in electrical system; a 12-volt electrical system; a 13-gallon pressurized water system with purifier and optional hot water container; a two-burner propane stove; an AC-DC electric refrigerator; a front sleeping hammock; and a special top giving 6 feet of standing room and 30 cubic feet of storage space. Cabinets were finished in teak veneer, table tops in vinyl, and floor coverings in linoleum. The motor home had 16 different major component parts and systems and about 300 subassemblies. The company expected to concentrate on two of these fully-equipped models during 1973; these would probably account for 80 percent of the units sold.

Some of the distinctive advantages the VW motor home offered were its compactness, which qualified it for a first or second family car, its economy of operation, ease of handling, durability, and its availability across the United States. All these tended to make the van well-accepted.

COMPETITION

After devaluation of the dollar in 1973, a fully equipped standard model Adventurer retailed at approximately $5,770. This price included $3,600 for the van, $1,655 for the conversion, and a dealer markup of $515. Prices to the New York distributor provided for a sharing of this markup between the dealer and the distributor.

Compared to the fully equipped Adventurer, a similar Chevrolet, Dodge, or Ford conversion cost as much as $4,000 more.

For a number of years the VW conversion market had been dominated by the

German-built Westphalia. Westphalia sales in the U.S. declined substantially with increasing competition from U.S. suppliers, particularly the Adventurer, and from converted domestic vans such as Ford, Dodge, and Chevrolet. A fully equipped Westphalia model retailed for about $4,840, and had no stove or refrigerator and in terms of features, style, and comfort seemed less appealing than most U.S. versions. The Adventure company had been advised that Westphalia had no affiliation with Volkswagenwerk other than as a customer. Unit sales of Westphalia in the U.S. for 1971 were 16,153 while sales for 1972 were about 11,750. In California sales for the similar periods were 4,282 and 3,150 respectively.

Competition from other VW conversions within the United States consisted of the Safari, Contempo, and Sun Dial models available in California; the Sportsmobile in Florida and the Midwest; and the Riviera in the Northwest. The Adventurer held about 70 percent of the U.S. converted VW market in California in 1972. There seemed to be no significant domestic competition in the South or Midwest.

PRODUCTION

In February 1973, manufacturing and installation are performed in a 14,500-square-foot facility located in Sylmar, California, occupied under a lease expiring in December 1974, for a rental of $1,460 per month. Northern California is served by a 10,000-square-foot production facility located in San Leandro, California. This plant is occupied under a lease expiring in October 1975, which requires $1,040 a month rent.

Management believes that a number of economies of scale would be obtained through a substantial increase in volume, as expected from the sales agreement with the VW regional distributors. Similarly, if the agreement with VOA materialized, within two to three years the company would have to build up 10 or more plants near ports of entry throughout the country. VOA in the meanwhile advised they had presented the proposal to the president of Volkswagenwerk, A.G., for approval. If Volkswagenwerk approved, the Adventure company was expected to negotiate and enter into an intermediate term agreement with VOA.

However, Adventure intends to expand geographically by the end of the next fiscal year to four additional plants near ports of entry throughout the southern and eastern United States. The company's plans call for one new production facility during fiscal 1973 and three additional facilities during 1974. These will be accomplished through agreements either with VOA or with VW distributors located throughout the United States.

The expansion program is to be carried out through the establishment of installation plants at points either near ports of entry or VW distributor storage yards. The functions performed at the installation plants will be limited to installation of components that will be preassembled and stripped from the existing manufacturing plant in Southern California. Initial cost of each installation plant will cover equipment, tools, and start-up costs, estimated at $24,000 total.

The Sylmar plant, responsible for cabinet work and subassemblies, will "drop ship" major components to the installation point.

Adventure employed 85 persons during the peak season but now has 52

---

employees. Eight of these employees are members of the International Association of Machinists and Aerospace Workers Union, which represents certain employees of the San Leandro plant also.

MERCEDES BENZ PROGRAM

The company anticipates substantial expansion through the product diversification represented by the Mercedes Benz program. By June 1973 the company expects a prototype of an improved Mercedes Benz airport bus, which is scheduled for a motor home conversion by September 1973. Mercedes Benz has agreed to consign one or more of the prototypes for the purpose. On completion of the prototype conversion, Mercedes proposes to sponsor a national conference of their dealers to introduce the motor home. They will also support a tour of the motor home to the Mercedes Benz dealers throughout the country. If all were to proceed on schedule, the company would expect to start production of the Mercedes Benz motor home in late 1973. The 1974 fiscal projection, however, does not include revenues from the Mercedes Benz program. The 1974 projections for the company are shown in Exhibit 6.

OPERATING RESULTS

In Fiscal 1970 and 1971 Adventure Campers, Inc., enjoyed a growth in sales from $575,000 to $900,000 and reported pretax incomes of $69,000 and $68,000 respectively. However, the company's management, lacking depth, failed to keep control of operations and could not keep pace with the increased sales volume. When Recreation acquired the company in April 1972 they installed a new top management team. Although this team brought to Recreation's attention the opportunities Adventure had, they were not able to establish the necessary operational control to capitalize on these opportunities.

There was a total lack of inventory control, bottlenecks resulting from shortage of key parts, large increase in the number of employees, and lack of a meaningful financial reporting system. This lack caused an unnecessary buildup of inventory and in some major items amounted to 6 to 12 months of supply.

The situation was further complicated by a 1½ month delay in delivery of the 1973 model van. The problem became acute when a large unsold supply of 1972 Westphalia models were stuck in the hands of the distributors and dealers, particularly in northern California. The result was that sales dropped to $94,000 for the first quarter of fiscal 1973 as against $213,000 for the same period in the previous year. The quarter also saw a pretax loss of $114,600; however, because of the poor financial reporting system, management was not aware of this information until long after the fact.

In December 1972 Angus W. McBain became president and chief executive officer. Since then a number of steps have been taken to improve the company's position. As a consequence, sales for the second quarter ended February 28, 1973, were $290,000 compared to $140,000 of actual sales and $140,000 of consignment sales for comparable periods in fiscal 1972. Sales for March 1973 are expected to exceed March 1972 sales by 70 percent. In December 1972 the employee force was reduced by 30 percent to bring it in line with actual requirements. Other cost controls also were instituted.

Production management has been improved significantly with the addition of Edward Ord—formerly a general manager of Kit Manufacturing, an American Stock Exchange manufacturer of mobile homes and travel trailers—and Lance Rich, formerly a production control supervisor with Beckman Instruments and a senior industrial engineer with Chrysler Corporation. Key personnel responsible for inventory control and sales have also been added. The company expects to hire a well-qualified chief financial officer within the next few weeks.

As of January 31, 1973, the net book value of Recreation was $0.56 per share and included $531,000 of intangible assets, $515,000 for goodwill, and $16,000 for organization expense. Upon offering 60,000 shares at $5 each, the net book value of the common stock will increase to $1.58 per share, with the entire increase attributable to the cash payments made by the purchasers of the common stock sold by Recreation. Consequently all purchasers will absorb a dilution of $3.42 per share in their purchase price.

PLANNED EXPANSION

As of January 31, 1973, Adventure Campers, Inc., had current assets of $253,349 and current liabilities of $404,520, resulting in a working capital deficit of $151,171. Of the $300,000 management expected to get from the offering, they had tentatively earmarked $23,000 for capital improvement of their California operation. Another $64,000 would go towards the new plant in New Jersey, which would include $24,000 for equipment and start-up costs, and $40,000 for working capital. The remaining $213,000 Adventure expected to utilize as working capital for their existing business. Of this, $100,000 would be used to retire an 8 percent short-term note, leaving them approximately $113,000 for accounts payable and inventory financing.

To accomplish its other expansion programs and meet its capital needs, Recreation intends to apply to the Small Business Administration (SBA) for a $200,000 loan. With the proceeds of this loan, management plans to open their installation plant in Ohio (estimated cost $64,000) in close proximity to Midvo, their VW distributors for Ohio and Kentucky. They were also thinking of opening two additional installation plants, one near Jacksonville, Florida, and the other at New Orleans. Normally SBA loans of this kind mature in 10 years and carry an interest rate of approximately 8¾ percent.

When Angus W. McBain became the president and chief executive officer of Adventure Campers in December 1972, he focused all his attention on finding remedies for existing operating difficulties and on hiring capable managers. Now three months later he felt he had to leave the "fire-fighting chores" to his subordinates and to concentrate more on the future direction of the company and on strategic planning. He wondered whether the planned expansion was feasible and desirable.

EXHIBIT 1. Recreation Capital Corporation

Consolidated Balance Sheet
January 31, 1973
(Unaudited)

Assets

Current Assets

Cash	$ 10,536	
Accounts receivable	82,677	
Other receivables	1,663	
Inventories	130,787	
Prepaid expenses	15,212	240,875

Fixed Assets

Machinery & equipment	72,212	
Automotive equipment	41,853	
Office furniture & fixtures	11,880	
Leasehold improvements	27,823	
	153,768	
Less: accumulated depreciation	53,378	100,390

Other Assets

Research & development	74,667	
Deposits & other	7,459	
Federal & state income tax refund	59,300	
Organization expenses	16,162	
Excess of cost over net assets of subsidiary	514,806	672,394
Total Assets		$1,013,659

Liabilities

Current Liabilities

Contracts payable	$ 36,496	
Current portion of long-term debt	50,000	
Notes payable—bank	72,000	
Notes payable—shareholder	110,000	
Accounts payable	137,698	
Accrued liabilities	54,467	
Reserve for warranties	20,900	481,561

Long-term debt, 7% due in
installments to 8/31/75   420,000

Shareholders' Equity

Common stock—$1 par value	200,000	
Retained earnings—8/31/72	(11,094)	
Net loss—5 mos. ended 1/31/73	(76,808)	112,098
Total Liabilities & Stockholders' Equity		$1,013,659

EXHIBIT 2. Recreation Capital Corporation

Adventure Campers, Inc.
(A wholly owned subsidiary of Recreation Capital Corporation)
Balance Sheet—August 31, 1972

Assets

Current Assets

Cash		$ 28,297
Receivables, less reserve of $700		92,384
Inventories, at the lower of cost (first in, first out) or market		
Raw materials and purchased parts	$ 94,453	
Work in process	75,256	169,709
Prepaid expenses		32,548
Total current assets		322,938

Equipment and Leasehold Improvements, at cost

Machinery and equipment	71,121	
Automotive equipment	48,622	
Office furniture and fixtures	10,641	
Leasehold improvements	23,089	
	153,473	
Less—Accumulated depreciation and amortization	36,342	117,131

Other Assets

Research and development	30,437	
Due from parent company	12,074	
Deposits and other	8,172	50,683
		$490,752

Liabilities

Current Liabilities

Equipment purchase contracts		$ 42,400
Unsecured note payable to bank		50,000
Accounts payable		191,879
Accrued liabilities		29,258
Reserve for warranty repairs		20,000
Total current liabilities		333,537

Equipment purchase Contracts,

collateralized by equipment costing $60,849	$ 48,976	
Less—Current portion shown above	42,400	6,576

Commitments and Contingencies

Shareholder's Investment

Common stock, $5 par value—		
Authorized—200,000 shares		
Outstanding—7,336 shares	36,680	
Retained earnings		
Balance, beginning of year	108,514	
Net income for the year	5,445	150,639
		$490,752

EXHIBIT 2. Recreation Capital Corporation, continued

Adventure Campers, Inc.
(A wholly owned subsidiary of Recreation Capital Corporation)
Statement of Income
for the Year Ended August 31, 1972

Net Sales		$1,183,516
Cost of Sales		955,228
		228,288
Operating Expenses		
Selling	$ 58,359	
General and administrative	163,234	221,593
Income from operations		6,695
Other Income, net, including interest expense of $5,890		950
Income before provision for income taxes		7,645
Provision for Income Taxes		2,200
Net Income		$ 5,445
Net Income per Common Share, based on the weighted average number of common shares outstanding during the year		$0.74

Adventure Campers, Inc.
(A wholly owned subsidiary of Recreation Capital Corporation)
Statement of Changes in Financial Position
for the Year Ended August 31, 1972

Source of Cash		
Net income for the year		$ 5,445
Noncash charges to income for depreciation and amortization		39,856
		45,301
Increase in:		
Notes and contracts payable	$ 83,194	
Accounts payable	136,075	
Accrued liabilities	11,936	
Reserve for warranty repairs	3,500	
Retirement of equipment and leasehold improvements, net	17,214	251,919
		297,220
Application of Cash		
Increase in:		
Cash	5,526	
Receivables	58,918	
Inventories	62,771	
Prepaid expenses	22,070	
Purchase of equipment and leasehold improvements	80,621	
Increase in other assets	36,309	
Decrease in income taxes payable	31,005	297,220

EXHIBIT 2 (continued)

Increase in Cash	5,526
Cash Balance, beginning of year	22,771
Cash Balance, end of year	$ 28,297

EXHIBIT 3. Recreation Capital Corporation

Adventure Campers, Inc.
Balance Sheet
January 31, 1973
(Unaudited)

Assets
Current Assets

Cash	$ 10,536	
Accounts receivable	82,677	
Due from parent	12,474	
Other receivables	1,663	
Inventories	130,787	
Prepaid expenses	15,212	253,349

Fixed Assets

Machinery & equipment	72,212	
Automotive equipment	41,853	
Office furniture & fixtures	11,880	
Leasehold improvements	27,823	
	153,768	
Less: accumulated depreciation	53,378	100,390

Other Assets

Research & development	74,667	
Deposits & other	7,459	
Federal & state income tax refund	59,300	141,426
Total Assets		$495,165

Liabilities
Current Liabilities

Contracts payable	$ 36,496	
Notes payable—bank	72,000	
Notes payable—other	110,000	
Accounts payable	137,698	
Accrued liabilities	27,426	
Reserve for warranties	20,900	404,520

Shareholders' Equity

Common stock	36,680	
Retained earnings—beginning	113,959	
Net loss—5 mos. ended 1/31/73	(59,994)	90,645
Total Liabilities & Stockholders' Equity		$495,165

EXHIBIT 4. Recreation Capital Corporation

Adventure Campers, Inc.
1973 Statement of Income
(Unaudited)

	Three Mos. Ended 11/30/72	Two Mos. Ended 1/31/73	Five Mos. Ended 1/31/73
Sales	$ 94,356	$207,180	$301,536
Less: returns & allowances	2,330	4,450	6,780
Net Sales	92,026	202,730	294,756
Cost of Sales			
Materials	37,742	82,872	120,614
Direct labor	39,927	27,615	67,542
Contract services	1,095	53	1,148
Warranty expense—net	300	600	900
Other direct costs	673	851	1,524
	79,737	111,991	191,728
Indirect Costs			
Factory supplies & tools	2,207	1,326	3,533
Shop supervision	12,283	6,322	18,605
Indirect labor	12,145	10,932	23,077
Payroll taxes	7,120	6,330	13,450
Employee benefits	4,452	4,040	8,492
Rent	8,258	6,014	14,272
Depreciation	11,837	7,892	19,729
Equipment rental	2,455	1,470	3,925
Taxes & licenses	2,031	1,694	3,725
Travel expense	1,320	961	2,281
Repairs & maintenance	668	437	1,105
Utilities	1,001	726	1,727
Other indirect costs	2,259	1,007	3,266
	68,036	49,151	117,187
Total Manufacturing Costs	147,773	161,142	308,915
Less: manufacturing costs allocated to capitalized items	(19,958)	(5,383)	(25,341)
	127,815	155,859	283,674
Gross Profit (Loss)	(35,789)	46,871	11,082
Selling Expenses			
Salaries	$ 16,288	$ 7,969	$ 24,257
Advertising	4,928	2,892	7,820
Telephone	3,223	3,901	7,124
Show expenses	4,007	—	4,007
Travel expenses	1,446	409	1,855
Other sales expenses	3,283	2,298	5,581
	33,175	17,649	50,644

EXHIBIT 4 (continued)

General & Administrative Expenses			
Officers' salaries	12,975	13,885	26,860
Office salaries	11,579	6,791	18,370
Insurance	6,222	3,124	9,346
Legal & accounting	5,695	3,877	9,572
Equipment rental	1,329	1,237	2,566
Telephone	652	979	1,631
Travel & entertainment	804	113	917
Taxes & licenses	204	638	842
Other administrative expenses	3,523	604	4,127
	42,983	31,248	74,231
Interest Expense	2,663	2,838	5,501
Income (loss) before income taxes	(114,610)	(4,684)	(119,294)
Income tax refund—loss carryback to prior periods	57,000	2,300	59,300
Net Income (Loss)	$ (57,610)	$ (2,384)	$ (59,994)

EXHIBIT 5. Recreation Capital Corporation

Summary of Historical Results of Operations and Projections
(including operations of Adventure Campers, Inc., prior to acquisition by RCC)

	Year Ended 8/31/70[a]	Year Ended 8/31/71[a]	Year Ended 8/31/72[b]	Year Ended 8/31/73[c]	Year Ended 8/31/74[c]
Net sales	$575,425	$900,637	$1,183,516	$1,926,008	$4,965,000
Pretax income	69,129	67,970	7,645	199,323	1,127,000
Federal income taxes[d]	28,150	25,267	2,200	81,100	487,000
State income taxes	9,606	5,738	—	14,100	76,300
	37,756	31,005	2,200	95,200	563,300
Net income (loss) of Adventure Campers	31,373	36,965	5,445	104,123	563,700
parent company expenses	—	—	16,539	40,356	36,858
Net income (loss)	$ 31,373	$ 36,965	$ (11,094)	$ 63,767	$ 526,842
Net income (loss) per share	$ 0.16	$ 0.18	$ (0.06)	$ 0.29	$ 2.03
Average shares outstanding	200,000	200,000	200,000	223,000	260,000

[a]Amounts based on federal and state income tax returns filed for fiscal 1970 and 1971.
[b]Financial statements of Adventure Campers, Inc., for the year ended August 31, 1972, have been audited by Arthur Andersen & Co.
[c]Estimated.
[d]Assumes filing of consolidated income tax returns.

EXHIBIT 6. Recreation Capital Corporation

Adventure Campers, Inc.
Operating Projection
Fiscal Year Ending August 31, 1974

	California, Midvo, Worldwide	Three New Regions	Combined	
Sales	$3,049,200	$1,966,200	$5,015,400	
Less returns and allowances	30,492	19,662	50,154	
Net sales	3,018,708	1,946,538	4,965,246	
Cost of sales				
Materials	1,280,664	825,804	2,106,468	
Direct labor	365,904	235,944	601,848	
Other manufacturing expenses	311,018	200,552	511,570	
Freight	35,000	43,000	78,000	
	1,992,586	1,305,300	3,297,886	
Gross profit	1,026,122	641,238	1,667,360	(33.2%)
Selling expenses	99,617	64,236	163,853	(3.3%)
General & Administrative expenses	208,291	134,311	342,602	(6.8%)
Interest expense	22,300	11,200	33,500	(0.7%)
Pretax income	$ 695,914	$ 431,491	$1,127,405	(22.4%)

Union Food Company

The Union Food Company (UFC) is a small food processing firm, in business since the 1930s. The firm has recently experienced rapid change caused by its conversion to a federally inspected manufacturing facility able to ship its products in interstate commerce. Changes in ownership and management have created both opportunities and problems for this food processing firm.

Government Inspection

In 1970, conversion from State of California Department of Agriculture inspection to United States Department of Agriculture (USDA) inspection opened wide new markets to UFC. The company now was able to ship its products, which contained meat, outside the State of California into such areas as Nevada, Oregon, and Arizona. It should be noted that firms within the State of California that are themselves USDA inspected companies can accept shipments only from other USDA inspected companies. The step to federal inspection was almost a necessity for UFC's continuation in business.

Change of Ownership

Over the years ownership of UFC had passed through several hands. The most recent changes occurred in 1971 when William Haut, the current owner, acquired all of the outstanding shares of the company. Mr. Haut, young and well-educated, believed the firm was a good investment for several reasons and could be profitable. First, Mr. Haut and his family had been involved successfully in the food industry for many years. Mr. Haut therefore had an excellent working knowledge of the industry and could launch a rapid expansion of the firm's market penetration. Second, UFC was a processor of Mexican foods such as tamales, burritos, tortillas, and taco shells. Mexican food was and is still the fastest growing segment of a rapidly expanding ethnic food industry in the United States. The growth potential according to all projections is far from exhausted. Third, Mr. haut believed financing through a Small Business Administration guaranteed loan would be available for needed capital improvements and equipment purchases. Fourth, Mr. Haut's father, a retired food executive, agreed to come out of retirement to be general manager.

This case was prepared by Edward Poll.

Immediately after acquisition, the Hauts successfully improved the firm's position; it became a profitable producer of Mexican food products. The Hauts' knowledge of the industry led to important cost savings very quickly. Sales then rose to approximately $400,000 per year.

Sales Force

At the time of purchase most of the firm's sales were obtained through brokers. One brokerage firm, which accounted for more than 50 percent of UFC's sales, was owned one-third by the former owner of UFC. This brokerage company had fifteen men in the field and covered store-level as well as buying offices. Because of the close relationship between the two organizations, the sales effort of the brokerage firm had been more concentrated on UFC's account than would otherwise have been the case for an account of this size.

After his purchase of UFC, Mr. Haut, however, became convinced that the sales effort of the brokerage company would decrease significantly. Although sales did not decrease, new accounts were acquired only through UFC's own efforts. The broker was apprised of Mr. Haut's concerns but failed to increase sales. Mr. Haut dismissed the broker six months after he bought the company. No adverse effect on sales followed this action.

The savings that resulted from releasing the broker were used to hire Mr. Al Jackson, a hard-working salesman in his early forties, who had been in the food industry, concentrating on Mexican food sales for ten years in Southern California prior to joining UFC. Sales for UFC have since increased to a level of $480,000 per year.

Financing

Shortly after he acquired the company Mr. Haut completed arrangements through a local bank for a government (SBA) guaranteed loan of $140,000, which was to be repaid over ten years. Of this sum, $65,000 was used to retire an existing 5-year promissory note and deed of trust on the property on which the plant is located. The balance of the funds was used for purchase of equipment, construction of a freezer-cooler, installation of tile on the walls of the manufacturing area, and working capital. The new construction lowered costs by easing clean-up and maintenance tasks and eliminating the need for public cold storage facilities. Prior to these improvements the firm spent over $10,000 per year for these services. Another important result of the improvements was the decreased bacteria count, which improved the quality and increased the shelf-life of the product. The on-premises cooler eliminated one step in the channel of distribution and extended shelf life further. The product now arrives at its destination in much shorter time than before.

Markets

The firm now caters to several markets. They are: 1) the refrigerated, self-service section of the supermarket, more commonly known as the delicatessen; 2) the dry, self-service of either the grocery or delicatessen section of the supermarket, depending on which department purchases taco shells; 3) the frozen, institutional food distributor; 4) the institutional customer, such as schools and the military, who purchases by bid.

The firm's products are currently sold primarily in Southern California, the biggest market in the immediate geographical area. That this is a very large market is shown by the 3 million corn tortillas sold here every day. Even a small share of this market would produce a relatively large dollar volume. However, this area is also the most competitive. Although seeking greater market penetration in Southern California, UFC has also sought to expand into Northern California, Nevada, Arizona, and Utah, areas of volume consumption at higher profit levels.

Products

UFC currently produces 69 products; variations in packaging size are counted as separate products. The firm's primary emphasis was previously on tamales. Mr. Haut has now expanded the line to include burritos (several varieties), pizzas, taco shells, tostado shells, enchiladas, and flour and corn tortillas. Including private label production, tamales still account for 60 percent of UFC's sales.

Competition

UFC now experiences competition from several sources. Capital requirements for production of tortillas and shells are quite small. Many firms, therefore, are competing for these sales, which causes pricing to be a dominant factor in sales. Supermarkets, however, one of the significant avenues of distribution, are not inordinately price conscious. Because they can readily pass their cost increases on to the consumer, they are more concerned with brand recognition and quality. UFC products rate well in these factors.

UFC's other products, such as tamales, experience more limited competition. Capital requirements are higher and technological ability more demanding when dealing with meat products. There is therefore less competition in fresh food manufacturing.

Frozen food manufacturers present another source of competition. However, Mr. Haut and Mr. Jackson both believed they could establish UFC products firmly in their various markets without great competition from frozen food manufacturers. UFC is capable of adapting quickly to more extensive frozen food production if desirable in the future.

Physical Facility

The UFC plant is located in a picturesque community near the Los Angeles metropolitan area and is centrally located on the freeway system. The plant is located on about 25,000 square feet of land, most of it occupied by manufacturing warehouse and office facilities.

It was recently decided to convert a small part of the warehouse into a production area. Drains are being installed and plaster and tile will be installed soon. On receiving USDA approval, UFC will have additional production capacity for projected growth.

Mr. Haut estimated that UFC is currently operating at only 40 percent of production capacity. In assessing this output, Mr. Haut realized that UFC's storage capacity is limited and the company is forced to ship soon after production. This fits advantageously with his policy of delivering the freshest possible product to the consumer.

Financial Statements

Mr. Haut has been able to operate the company profitably since taking over. However, financial returns show that profits have not been as great as anticipated. For the sake of comparison, Exhibit 1 shows the percentage returned by a competitor's taco shell operation. Mr. Haut believes the differences are explainable as follows: First, UFC is privately managed and therefore has different accounting objectives; second, UFC manufactures many items, not all of whose profit margins are equally high; third, UFC's marketing expense is higher because of its greater dispersion of customers.

EXHIBIT 1. Union Food Company

Competitor Mexican Food Products
Income Statement
(Year ended February 29, 1972, unaudited)

	% of sales
Sales	100.0
Cost of sales	
Materials	37.8
Direct labor	27.8
Contract labor	0.2
Total direct costs	65.8
Plant overhead	
Operating supplies	0.6
Utilities	4.1
Repairs and maintenance	0.8
Depreciation—building and equipment	1.7
Insurance	4.2
Taxes and licenses	0.9
Payroll taxes	2.1
Linen	0.8
Total plant overhead	15.2
Cost of goods produced	81.0
Less, increase in inventories	2.9
Cost of sales	78.1
Gross profit	21.9
General and administrative expenses	
Travel and entertainment	—
Commissions	1.8
Auto and truck expense	0.9
Office expense	0.2
Professional services	5.2
Advertising	0.1
Depreciation—furniture and fixtures	0.1
Depreciation—motor vehicles	1.1
Miscellaneous	0.3
Total general and administrative expenses	9.7
Operating profit	12.2
Other expenses	
Interest	1.3
Sales discounts	1.1
Total other expenses	2.4
Net Income	9.8

The financial statement for the fiscal year ended April 30, 1972, the first year under new ownership, showed a current ratio of 2.2 to 1.0 and a debt to equity (plus subordinated debt) ratio of 1.37 to 1.0 (see Exhibit 2).

Acquisition of Tony's Taco Shell Corporation

Mr. Haut recently acquired Tony's Taco Shell Corporation (Tony's) to supplement the product line and the sales of UFC. Tony's manufactured only taco shells and tostado shells at acquisition. Sales were approximately $250,000, half of which were from contracts with local school districts. A statement of the financial condition of Tony's Taco Shell Corporation, October 31, 1972, is given in Exhibit 3.

Mr. Haut saved Tony's from going into bankruptcy by making arrangements with most of the creditors prior to the acquisition. (In most cases creditors settled for 25 percent of their claims.) By doing this, Mr. Haut was able to save Tony's contracts and retain the company's other business, which otherwise would have gone to competitors of UFC. The only creditor who was not approached for settlement was the SBA, which has a lien on Tony's assets and is well-secured. Mr. Haut believes that current negotiations with the SBA will result in satisfactory financial arrangements.

EXHIBIT 2. Union Food Company

Statement of Financial Condition
April 30, 1972

Current Assets			
Cash in bank		$ 11,766	
Accounts receivable		32,207	
Inventory			
Finished goods	$ 5,101		
Food products	6,529		
Packaging	19,956		
Total Inventories		31,586	
Employee advances		40	
Prepaid expenses		2,077	
Total Current Assets			$ 77,676
Current Liabilities			
Accounts payable		$ 15,243	
Contracts payable—current portion		3,003	
S.B.A. loan—current portion (Note 1)		13,167	
Accrued commissions		355	
Accrued wages		2,070	
Accrued payroll taxes		1,933	
Total Current Liabilities			35,771
Working Capital			$ 41,905

EXHIBIT 2 (continued

Property Assets

	Cost	Depreciation	Depreciated Value
Depreciable Assets			
Plant	$ 67,070	$ 560	$ 66,510
Plant improvements	41,965	13,538	28,427
Plant equipment	84,007	14,226	69,781
Office fixtures and equipment	1,612	875	737
Truck	2,900	54	2,846
Total	$197,554	$29,253	$168,301
Land			25,000
Total Property Assets			$193,301

Other Assets

Savings account (Note 2)	$ 420	
Deposits	1,052	
Reorganization costs (net)	326	
Lease rights—truck (net) (Note 3)	5,459	
Loan receivable	5,045	12,302
Total Property and Other Assets		205,603
Total		$247,508

Long-Term Liabilities

Contracts payable (due after one year)	$ 1,250	
S.B.A. loan (Note 1)	126,833	
Total Long-Term Liabilities		$128,083

Other Liabilities

Purchase Money Deed of Trust (Note 4)	26,000	
Total Long-Term and Other Liabilities		154,083
Net Assets—Equity		$ 93,425

Analysis of Equity

Paid-In Equity

Capital stock—authorized 50,000 shares; $10 par value. Issued and outstanding 6,400 shares	$ 64,000	
Contributed capital	26,000	
Total Paid-In Equity	$ 90,000	

Earned Equity

Retained earnings—May 1, 1971	$ 2,375	
Earnings for the year	1,050	
Total Earned Equity	3,425	
Total Equity—as above		$ 93,425
Earnings per Share		$0.16

EXHIBIT 2. Union Food Company, continued

Statement of Operations
for the Year Ended April 30, 1972

Sales		$404,339	
Fees: Sales discounts		4,462	
Net Sales		$399,877	100.00%
Cost of Sales		315,252	78.84
Gross Profit on Sales		$ 84,625	21.16%
Expenses			
Marketing Expenses			
Commissions	$ 8,561		
Advertising	7,072		
Sales salaries	2,471		
Freight and delivery	6,726		
Sales promotion	2,898		
Truck and auto	5,892		
Distributors' allowance	4,811		
Total Marketing Expense		$ 38,431	9.61
Administrative Expenses			
General manager	$12,750		
Office wages	17,144		
Legal and audit	4,490		
Office supplies	857		
Telephone and telegraph	2,553		
Taxes and licenses	2,708		
Payroll taxes	3,071		
Interest expense	4,612		
Dues and subscriptions	242		
Amortization of lease rights	1,460		
Amortization of organization costs	103		
Bad debts	449		
Miscellaneous expense	1,811		
Total Administrative Expenses		52,250	13.07
Total Expenses		90,681	22.68%
Operating Income or (Loss)		$ (6,056)	(1.52)%
Other Income			
Expense recovery	$ 572		
Interest income	206		
Rental income	3,000		
Consulting fees	1,800		
Purchase discounts	478		
Miscellaneous income	1,050		
Total Other Income		7,106	1.78
Pretax Income		$ 1,050	.26%
Federal tax on income	$ 231		
Less: Investment credit applied	231		
Net Earnings		$ 1,050	.26%

EXHIBIT 2 (continued)

Cost of Sales
for the Year Ended April 30, 1972

			Production Percentages
Beginning inventory—Finished Goods		$ 11,248	
Production Costs			
Food Products Cost			
Inventory—Beginning	$ 4,458		
Purchases	126,007		
Total	$130,465		
Less: Inventory—			
ending	6,529		
Food Products Used		$123,936	40.10%
Packaging Costs			
Inventory—beginning	$ 14,174		
Purchases	43,863		
Total	$ 58,037		
Less: Inventory—			
ending	19,956		
Packaging Costs		38,081	12.32
Production Wages		67,144	21.72
Other Production Costs			
Rent	$ 20,200		
Storage	2,642		
Product development	352		
Payroll taxes	5,672		
Compensation insurance	2,014		
Other insurance	6,282		
Depreciation	10,238		
Supplies	4,196		
Maintenance and repairs	9,779		
Utilities	6,924		
Inspection	376		
Spoiled goods	5,374		
Equipment lease	757		
Expense allowance	5,138		
Total Other Costs		79,944	25.86
Total Production Costs		309,105	100.0%
Total Food Costs		$320,353	
Ending Inventory—Finished Goods		5,101	
Cost of Sales		$315,252	

Statement of Changes in Financial Position
for the Year Ended April 30, 1972

Current Assets Increased	
Cash in bank	$ 4,805
Accounts receivable	19,941

EXHIBIT 2 (continued)

Inventory		1,706	
Other current assets		208	
Increase in Current Assets			$ 26,660
Current Liabilities Decreased			
Decreased			
Accounts payable	$ 702		
Contracts payable	3,343		
Accrued expenses	583		
Loans payable	14,300		
Federal income taxes payable	257	$ 19,185	
Increased—S.B.A. loan		13,167	
Decrease in Current Liabilities			6,018
Working Capital Increased			$ 32,678
Property Assets Increased			
Plant	$ 67,070		
Plant improvements	9,620		
Plant equipment	55,552		
Truck	2,900		
Land	25,000		
Increase in Property Assets		$160,142	
Depreciation Allowance Increased			
Depreciation expense during year		10,238	
Net Increase in Property Assets		$149,904	
Other Assets Decreased			
Decrease in loan receivable—			
stockholder	$ 10,000		
Increase in other assets	4,299		
Decrease in other Assets		5,701	
Increase in Property and Other Assets			144,203
Long-Term Liabilities Increased			
Increase in S.B.A. loan	$126,833		
Decrease in contracts payable	3,002		
Increase in Long-Term Liabilities		123,831	
Other Liabilities Increased			
Purchase Money Deed of Trust		26,000	
Increase in Long-Term and other Liabilities			149,831
Net Increase in Equity			$ 27,050
Equity Change			
Equity—end of year		$ 93,425	
Equity—beginning of year		66,375	
Increase in Equity			$ 27,050

EXHIBIT 2. Union Food Company, continued

Notes to Financial Statement
April 30, 1972

Note 1. Small Business Administration Loan—S.B.A. loan $140,000
Period: 120 months—first payment due 6/25/72
          Current portion—11 months at $1,197   13,167
          Long-term portion   126,833
Interest: The rate is subject to semi-annual adjustments up or down de-
          pending upon the current "Normal" rate on June 30 and De-
          cember 31 of each year beginning June 30, 1972. The current rate
          until June 30, 1972 is to be 8¾% simple.
Collateral Pledged
        a. A first lien on the company's machinery and equipment.
        b. A lien on the company's accounts receivable, inventory, chattel, and general
          intangibles.
        c. A first trust deed on the commercial property.
Note 2. Savings account
Beginning on March 15, 1972 an amount of $210 will be transferred to this impounds
account monthly for payment of real estate taxes.
Note 3. Lease rights—Truck
Lease of refrigerated truck is in essence a purchase contract as at the end of the 36-month
lease period the truck can be purcased for $1.
Note 4. Purchase Money Deed of Trust
Note payable due on or before 10 years. Interest at 10% to be paid at maturity. This note
matures subsequent to the final maturity of S.B.A. loan, and is fully subordinate to S.B.A.
loan.

EXHIBIT 3. Union Food Company

Tony's Taco Shell Corporation
Statement of Financial Condition
October 31, 1972
(Unaudited)

Current Assets		
Cash in bank and on hand	$ 669	
Accounts receivable	17,273	
Employee advances	331	
Inventory	12,793	
Prepaid expenses	1,628	
Total Current Assets		$ 32,694
Current Liabilities		
Accounts payable	$ 44,735	
Contracts payable—current portion	2,473	
Notes payable—current portion	11,560	
Accrued payroll taxes	2,049	
Accrued commissions	86	
Accrued wages	990	
Total Current Liabilities		61,893
Working Capital		$ (29,199)

EXHIBIT 3 (continued)

Property Assets

Depreciable Assets	Cost	Accumulated Depreciation	Depreciated Value
Plant	$ 69,943	$ 18,002	$ 51,941
Machinery and equipment	77,877	65,358	12,519
Mills	3,923	2,492	1,431
Trucks	18,303	14,023	4,280
Office furniture and equipment	5,764	5,032	732
Total	$175,810	$104,907	$ 70,903
Land			18,677
Total Property Assets			$ 89,580

Other Assets			
Organization costs		$ 300	
Deposits		1,157	
Loan costs		1,083	
Total Other Assets		2,540	
Total Property and Other Assets			92,120
Long-Term Liabilities			
Contracts payable—due after one year		$ 1,749	
Notes payable—due after one year		71,730	
Total Long-Term Liabilities		$ 73,479	
Other Liabilities			
Advances		$ 4,554	
Notes payable—prior stockholder		3,600	
Total Other Liabilities		8,154	
Total Long-Term and Other Liabilities			81,633
Net Assets—Equity			$ (18,712)

Analysis of Equity		
Paid-In Equity		
Capital Stock—issued and outstanding	$ 3,000	
Contributed capital	17,455	
Total Paid-In Equity	$ 20,455	
Earned Equity		
Retained earnings or (deficit)— March 31, 1972	$ (23,512)	
Loss for seven-month period	(14,155)	
Total Earned Equity or (Deficit)— October 31, 1972	(37,667)	
Total		(17,212)
Less: Treasury stock		1,500
Total Equity—(as shown above)		$ (18,712)

Mr. Haut is now considering whether to merge Tony's sales into the new UFC addition under construction or to inject additional sales immediately into Tony's 10,000-square-foot plant so as to operate at acceptable efficiency. He sees one of these two approaches necessary in order to operate Tony's profitably.

Management

In June 1972, Mr. Haut's father left UFC once more to retire. Mr. Haut has been directing the internal operations since then. Assisting Mr. Haut have been Mr. Jackson, the salesman, and Mr. Ben Lewis, the plant foreman. Mr. Lewis, 36, is a man without formal education who has taught himself several skills. Mr. Haut was impressed with his aggressiveness and willingness to learn. However, Mr. Lewis has had no managerial experience and would find it difficult to take over UFC in the absence of Mr. Haut.

Recent events have required Mr. Haut to spend more time elsewhere. To replace himself, he sought a capable individual, knowledgeable in the food industry and familiar with Mexican-Spanish food. The alternative of operating UFC and Tony's jointly with present personnel proved after trial to be less than satisfactory. Mr. Haut found that the growth of sales and profits he desired could not be achieved without direct, capable management.

Mr. Haut believes he has found the right person to fill the existing void in Mr. Richard Jones, a man in his fifties, a capable marketing manager and former general manager of snack food and Mexican food subsidiaries for several major companies. One of Mr. Jones's former employers is a competitor of UFC. Mr. Jones has agreed to take a reduced salary in exchange for a stock position. If he meets mutually agreed upon objectives, a percentage of the outstanding stock will be transferred to him without cost; he also will have an option to buy additional stock.

ISSUES TO BE MANAGED

The major issues facing the UFC organization are:

- Channels of distribution and geographic coverage
- Product mix
- Pricing strategy
- Integration of Union Food Company (UFC) and Tony's Taco Shell Corporation (Tony's).

Channels of Distribution and Geographic Coverage

UFC is now distributing its products through a variety of channels. The firm utilizes brokers for some of its current sales outside of the metropolitan Los Angeles area. Mr. Haut estimates that approximately 10 percent of the combined sales are derived in this fashion. As mentioned earlier, the severe competition in the local community reduces the profit margin per unit sale and limits the practical use of brokers. However, the ability of a company to sell in other areas such as Arizona, Nevada, Northern California, and in states east of the Rocky Mountains is specifically dependent on local salesmen. UFC is faced with a choice of either employing their own sales personnel or using the services of local brokers. Because of the small size of UFC-Tony's, employment of sales personnel in outlying areas is not feasible. Therefore, UFC must seek additional brokerage relationships if it desires to expand its sales in other geographic areas.

Sales derived from outlying geographic areas would be of value to UFC for several reasons. First, swings in the economic climate of the Southern California community would be less important to UFC only at such time as its sales come from more than the one geographic area. Second, the profit margin on the firm's products should be higher outside the battle field of local competition. This is true in spite of the higher costs of transportation. Third, use of various brokers throughout the Far West would lessen the company's dependence on any one source of sales or channel of distribution.

Mr. Haut estimates that 40 percent of UFC's sales come from distributors, another channel of distribution. Distributors are independent business people who resell UFC's products to outlets such as retail supermarkets, self-service liquor stores, and in-plant feeding facilities. These distributors sell both fresh and frozen products, depending upon their consumer. Included in this category are private label distributors who purchase merchandise packaged under their own brand names. UFC tries to ensure that no single distributor obtains more than 10 percent of its sales. Failure in this regard would increase the firm's vulnerability as the percentage of sales to that distributor increased. Although such sales might be easier, Mr. Haut believes that care should be exercised to achieve a well-balanced growth pattern.

Another channel of distribution, sales to cooperative warehouses, accounts for approximately 10 percent of the firm's sales. These cooperatives include Certified Grocers of California, A. M. Lewis, and others. Sales through this channel could be increased because the cooperative itself is not the ultimate consumer. The retail chain, which is the cooperative's customer, is the ultimate consumer. Additional sales through this channel usually mean wider distribution to more retail markets with a fixed transportation cost.

Unfortunately, the cooperative usually does not do selling and promoting. UFC must seek additional sales through this channel by having Mr. Jackson spend additional time on the accounts of the cooperative, both at their buying offices and at the store level.

Retail warehouses, as opposed to the cooperative warehouse, and military and school institutions account for an additional 35 percent of the firm's sales. Selling directly to retail stores increases UFC's independence when dealing with a buyer for a cooperative warehouse.

School and military sales are important to UFC. These sales are by bid and contract and are therefore less predictable and tend to be less profitable than retail sales. They do, however, provide increased sales growth.

An additional 5 percent of UFC's sales derives from distribution directly to individual retail outlets. This is the least profitable method of distribution. The firm is considering obtaining an established local distributor who could readily absorb these sales. In this way UFC would reduce its distribution cost; it would give only a negotiated, fixed percentage to the individual distributors. It would stimulate sales by special promotional effort with both distributor and retailer.

Product Mix

Mr. Haut earlier indicated that there were some 69 products making up the firm's mix. Because each different size and each different brand was counted as a separate product, the number of products actually available must be reconsidered. The firm now produces tamales, enchiladas, burritos (several varieties), cheese pizza, meat pizza, chile con carne, tortillas (corn and flour), taco shells and tostado shells. Currently the tortilla products (corn and flour tortillas, taco shells and tostado shells) account for approximately 30 percent of the sales volume. Sales of tamales account for another 60 percent, with the remaining products making up the balance. Mr. Haut indicated that the firm has recently obtained the account of a distributor who wants UFC to manufacture tamales under the distributor's own label. This distributor is out of state and would not compete with UFC. Additional sales from this source would approximate $100,000 per year. Another account that is obtainable, given favorable circumstances, is a frozen food manufacturer and distributor of national repute that currently has its private label tamale produced by another firm, a competitor of UFC. Sales from this source alone would approximate $400,000. Mr. Haut indicated that a capital investment of approximately $20,000 for machinery would be required to obtain this account; however, the machinery would also be usable by UFC in the manufacture of its own products.

If both new accounts are obtained and this volume is then added to the current sales volume of UFC, the production of tamales becomes of even greater importance to UFC than its other products. Mr. Haut has indicated that one of UFC's competitors manufactures only burritos and has obtained a sales volume in excess of $5,000,000. It would appear, and Mr. Haut conceded, that no insurmountable effort would be required to produce burritos in greater volume. Sales efforts directed toward this objective could prove beneficial. Capturing 5 percent of the competitor's business would add at least $250,000 in annual sales. Not only would this strengthen the product mix for UFC, but it probably would not even be missed by the competitor—no price war need result from UFC's activities. UFC could then expand further into the existing market for burritos; this market is larger than just the one competitor's present sales volume.

Items such as enchiladas that are easily frozen and transportable are ideal products for military and other institutional sales. They can be produced, frozen, and shipped quickly to their point of destination without extended periods of storage on the premises of UFC. By adding this kind of product, UFC could increase its sales volume without overburdening its present physical facility, which should be able to handle 2 to 3 million dollars in sales volume before further expansion would be needed.

A very important consideration in developing UFC's product mix must be its physical facility. Products that require a large cold storage or freezer capacity may overburden the firm's limited facilities. In such case, public storage would be required, with correspondingly increasing costs. Frozen food sales have traditionally been very competitive; additional costs might cause UFC to be overpriced. One of the factors in determining the firm's ultimate product mix would be the firm's plans about combining UFC's and Tony's physical facilities.

The items that present the greatest opportunity for national distribution to UFC are its tortilla products, specifically taco shells and tostado shells. Such products are being shipped to the eastern states from California. The profit margin is sufficiently high to compensate for the additional transportation charge. Not only can these products be marketed under the firm's own brand name(s) but they also can be packaged for snack food divisions of the major corporations that do not have their own packaging capability. It is estimated that these tortilla products could account for an additional $1 million in sales annually within the next 12 months. This estimate is further justified after considering the industry's estimated sales of 3 million tortillas daily in the Southern California community alone.

Other products are available for manufacture in the Mexican food line. Considering the firm a snack food manufacturer opens still wider vistas. Advantage should be taken of these rapidly expanding markets for Mexican foods and snack food. Exploitation of existing channels of distribution used by the firm should permit sales expansion with only modest increases in sales expense.

Pricing Strategy

Mr. Haut indicated that the former management had no formal pricing strategy. Through lack of attention and controls the price of UFC's products was 20 to 30 percent below the prices of its competitors. Mr. Haut did not believe it was appropriate to drastically alter the previous pricing levels because of recent wage-price controls. However, prices were increased somewhat so that the differential is not now as great as in the past.

To increase profit and to stimulate sales, Mr. Haut introduced a second brand, which was to be a quality product. The pricing strategy on this product was such that there was very little differential between UFC's tamales, for example, and those of its major competitors. UFC has been successful in this approach although its major line is still the original brand.

The ultimate consumer of retail, packaged Mexican food products is, generally speaking, a lower- to middle-income, blue-collar worker. Price, therefore, is particularly important and UFC must be careful not to price itself out of the market. A firm may obtain the lion's share of the market, but excessively high-priced products may cause the total market to diminish. A firm the size of UFC usually is not concerned immediately with such problems. However, because of the rapidly changing nature of the retail supermarket and the large number of new products introduced each year, UFC must not violate sound pricing strategy in its long-range planning.

UFC should use periodic promotions and trade discount rather than newspaper and other media advertising despite their reducing the price of the product somewhat. The budget available to UFC for mass advertising, as is usually the case with a small business, is nonexistent. This is evidenced by Exhibit 2. Limited funds would better be employed for additional capital equipment and plant improvements. External growth by way of acquisition may also be a better use of limited funds.

Integration of Union Food Company and Tony's Taco Shell Corporation

A small company the size of UFC has a great deal of room within which to grow, to expand its sales volume and its profits. An existing business such as UFC, generally speaking, need not concern itself initially with finding a consumer need and catering to that need. In this case demand exists and firms compete on the basis of "making a better mousetrap." In the case at hand, dollar volume in the fresh Mexican food market is many millions of dollars; frozen Mexican foods represent an even larger market, and snack foods show a market larger than either of these. In considering the prospects for UFC, there need not be concern with future demand. The immediate need is for expansion of sales through the efforts of existing personnel, including Mr. Jones. Assuming that Mr. Jones can be successful in obtaining immediate sales, Mr. Haut must answer the question of how best to integrate the activities of UFC and Tony's.

The two most practical alternatives available are: 1) to retain the two existing physical facilities, producing all meat products in UFC's facility and producing all nonmeat, tortilla-based products at Tony's facility; 2) to take production away from Tony's and move it into the area being converted for food processing at UFC, and to sell Tony's facility and liquidate the corporation.

The advantages in the first alternative are that: 1) UFC would have 35,000 square feet of production area instead of 25,000. Expansion into a larger facility could therefore be delayed until such time as the capital structure of UFC were better able to handle such a move; 2) United States Department of Agriculture requirements for nonmeat products are not so stringent and, therefore, the cost of production would be reduced; sanitation standards could be maintained at far less cost for nonmeat items such as tortillas and shells; and 3) keeping the facilities separate would retain the pay-out schedule of the Small Business Administration loan now outstanding on Tony's books, which would permit keeping the property rather than selling it to pay the loan.

The benefits of combining the facilities are: 1) direct supervision would be possible, which would in turn provide for cost savings and improved quality control; 2) liquidating the corporation after merging the physical facilities would force the settlement of remaining debts; 3) the monthly payment required on the SBA loan would be saved, thereby improving the firm's cash flow. Should another facility be rented because of limited physical capacity, the monthly payment would very likely be less than that now made to the SBA. Payment of rent would be an expense, but the current payment to the SBA is part interest and part equity.

Although management could continue to operate both facilities separately, a decision about which approach is to be used must be made soon. If Tony's facility is to be kept, greater emphasis must be placed on acquiring additional tortilla-based sales to improve efficiency of operation. Alternatively, if Tony's current production is to be combined with that of UFC, greater emphasis should be placed on increasing the sales volume of meat-related products because of the greater capacity to produce these products at UFC.

PROJECTED GOALS—CONCLUSION

Mr. Haut and Mr. Jones have agreed that sales volume for the coming fiscal year should exceed $875,000, with net income before taxes no less than $42,000. Projections for the succeeding fiscal year were placed at $1,050,000 sales and $60,000 net income before taxes. These goals are considerably lower than Mr. Haut believes Mr. Jones will reach. Improved marketing effort and external expansion by acquisition could be used to help meet the specified goals. Management, however, must have firm control of its current operations before expanding into diverse areas.

The Potter's Wheel Pottery Studio

INTRODUCTION: THOR GABLE AND THE POTTER'S WHEEL

Thor Gable is a sculptor, potter, carver in wood and stone, and printer of fine fabrics. He has demonstrated the art of pottery making on several television shows, and also in educational films. He also demonstrates and exhibits his art at fairs, art shows, conventions, and other special events. Thor has won over 30 first place prizes for his art work at major art fairs in New York and in California. He continues to gain broader recognition; he recently won first place at a national art show in Chicago.

Thor established The Potter's Wheel pottery studio and gallery in 1968 in Santa Fe, New Mexico. He offered classes in pottery, sculpture, macrame, tie-dye, and batik. In April, 1971, The Potter's Wheel moved to larger facilities.

The Potter's Wheel provides area residents with a pottery shop offering stoneware, sculpture, and non-loom weaving gifts; it also provides a school. Presently, over 100 students take classes in pottery, sculpture, macrame, and non-loom weaving. Besides classroom and work space, the studio features four galleries exhibiting the work of Thor and his students: the Sculpture Deck, Hanging Planter Deck, Non-Loom Weaving Display, and Family House (displaying household wares made of clay). The planter and non-loom weaving products are particularly in vogue.

THE ENVIRONMENT

Internal Environment

Location and Facilities The Potter's Wheel is located on a standard city lot (50 x 130 feet) fronting a main boulevard, Los Altos Boulevard. The studio sits back from Los Altos approximately 20 feet. It is bordered on both sides by motels, which obscure motorists' view of The Potter's Wheel.

The facilities consist of display areas, classrooms, wheel room, office area,

This case was prepared by Andrew Caddes and Lance Thompson under the direction of Hans Schollhammer and Arthur H. Kuriloff.

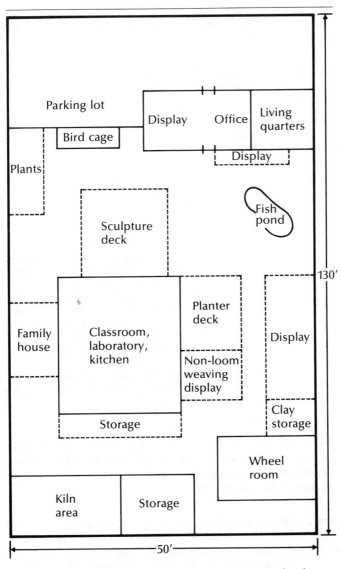

APPENDIX A. Layout of Facilities at the Potter's Wheel

living quarters, storage cabinets, and a small workshop. (See Appendix A for size and layout of facilities.) The major outside displays are along a partially covered walkway encircling the classroom. Bird cages, a dog house, and a fish pond add variety to the outside area. The atmosphere is warm and interesting for students, but for a newcomer it is at first hard to find one's bearings. The main equipment of The Potter's Wheel consists of ten electric potter's wheels (average age three years), guaranteed for a life of five years, and two kilns, one a 20 cubic foot kiln and the other an eight cubic foot kiln. No major additions to facilities and equipment are projected for the next two years.

Operations and Products (Sources of Income) The following four operations and products contribute nearly all revenue:

% of Total Revenue 1972	% of Total Revenue 1973	
57.0	50.5	1) *Classes.* Twelve-week classes begin in winter, spring, and fall. A six-week session is offered in June/July and a four-week session in August. Beginning and advanced classes for men and women of all ages in pottery, sculpture, weaving, and macrame.
20.1	21.7	2) *Pottery Sales.* The Potter's Wheel offers a complete price range of pottery created by Thor Gable and his students. The Potter's Wheel receives a 30 to 40 percent commission on the sale of student pottery.
7.1	8.4	3) *Pottery Supplies.* Nine types of clay and over fifty glazes sold to students and non-students (outsiders).
15.8	19.4	4) *Firing.* The Potter's Wheel fires the work of students and non-students for a fee.

Mr. Gable would like slowly to change the character of his business. He hopes to be able to cut back on his classes and to emphasize the creation and sale of his own work. With a growing reputation as an artist, he hopes to sell more of his high-quality sculpture.

Management and Personnel Thor Gable is owner, manager, artist, and teacher at The Potter's Wheel. He is assisted by 1) a part-time bookkeeper who handles the record-keeping and other office work two days a week, and 2) a part-time assistant who, in addition to artistic assistance, makes minor repairs and is responsible for the general upkeep of the studio. At The Potter's Wheel 43 advanced working students create pottery sold in the studio. Thirteen of these students assist Thor in teaching classes. Many help with maintenance tasks in exchange for instruction. In April, 1974, a new membership program will begin; working students will have to pay a fixed amount annually for use of the facilities. Thor anticipates that this changed policy will reduce the number of working students to approximately 10, giving each individual a greater opportunity to teach classes and more freedom to use the facilities to create pottery.

The Potter's Wheel has a nine person Board of Advisors composed of businesspersons, producers, artists, and housewives. The Potter's Wheel also uses the professional services of a Certified Public Accountant and an attorney.

Expenses The main expenses of The Potter's Wheel can be divided into eight categories:

% Income 1972[a]	% Income 1973	
10.7	34.8	1) *Commissions and Casual Labor.* Part-time employees, teachers, and working students are all paid for services provided on a commission basis. Commissions are also paid on all student pottery sold.
18.5	17.1	2) *Studio Supplies.* Supplies needed to produce pottery, such as glaze, clay, and pottery tools.
8.2	9.7	3) *Rent.* The present lease expires in March, 1975.
4.3	3.7	4) *Office Supplies.* Expenses for record-keeping books, pencils, pens, paper, etc.
7.4	6.7	5) *Utilities.* Telephone, gas, water and power.
4.7	4.9	6) *Repairs and Maintenance.* Repair of kilns required three times yearly. Other expenses for general maintenance of the facilities.
1.6	4.0	7) *Advertising and Promotion.* Includes newspaper ads, printing of pamphlets, show fees, etc.
14.6	5.5	8) *Other Miscellaneous Expenses.* Auto expenses (car is leased), health and car insurance, legal and accounting expenses, taxes and license fees.

Marketing During 1973, the main marketing activities of The Potter's Wheel consisted of monthly directory advertising in the Yellow Pages of the Santa Fe Telephone Directory, two ads run in the Sunday *Santa Fe Sun* and the *Valley Pinksheet* (a throw-away), and printing of a pamphlet describing the studio and classes. Thor (and, to a lesser extent, his students) also attends many art shows, sidewalk crafts shows, and art conventions.

Thor considers his classes a major marketing tool, through "word-of-mouth advertising." He finds that most customers are either former students or people referred to The Potter's Wheel by former students. Thor shows personal interest in all his students; he spends time helping and talking to them. This seems to account for the fact that about 65% of his students stay for at least one year.

[a]Records are questionable for 1972 because of lack of completeness. Accountant handling such records has been replaced by a Certified Public Accountant.

External Environment

Market The Potter's Wheel is located in an affluent section of Santa Fe. It is easily accessible via main streets. Many creative people with the time and money to take pottery classes live in the area. Pottery making is a leisure time activity that is self-actualizing. The Potter's Wheel fills the need for "a studio where you can have freedom of EXPRESSION."[1]

Thor estimates that his customers and students can be classified by annual income as:

50%	High Income	$20,000 or more annually
35%	Middle Income	$20,000–$10,000 annually
15%	Low Income	$10,000 or less annually

These customers and students come from all parts of Santa Fe and the surrounding area. Loyal students come from as far away as Albuquerque and Taos. The energy crisis has affected the attendance of students located in outlying areas. Thor realizes this problem and is trying to arrange sign-ups for car pools.

Competition The Potter's Wheel is a unique studio and gallery. It is the largest pottery school in the Southwest. Unlike other schools, working students are always available to help students. Many other studios lease space to potters; Thor Gable allows his working students to use the facilities, but does not lease permanent work areas. In pottery sales, The Potter's Wheel competes directly with other galleries.

Only one major pottery school is within driving distance of The Potter's Wheel. That school, at Taos, is a complete arts and crafts school at which pottery is only one specialty.

The Potter's Wheel provides a warm, supportive environment that contrasts with what we observed to be a quiet atmosphere of solitary workers at the Taos studio.

The closest retail pottery shop is the Enciso Gallery, located one block west of The Potter's Wheel. It is run by one of Thor Gable's former students.

PROBLEMS IDENTIFIED—SOLUTIONS AND RECOMMENDATIONS

Marketing

Problems Identified—Marketing A study of the revenue trends for The Potter's Wheel over the years 1972 and 1973 indicates problems with lack of growth of the business:

---

[1] Quotation taken from The Potter's Wheel advertising.

Sources of Income	1972	1973	Growth Rate 1972–1973
Clay	$ 3,572	$ 3,711	3.9%
Firing	7,912	9,755	23.3%
Classes	28,551	26,500	− 7.2%
Pottery Sales	10,094	9,426	− 6.6%
Total	$50,129	$49,442	− 1.4%

As shown in the above table, revenues for clay and firing were the only sources of income that increased from 1972 to 1973. Revenues from classes and pottery sales, historically the major sources of income, declined during the same period. Total revenue for the business decreased 1.4 percent.

A breakdown of the monthly revenue trends for these four main sources of income appears in Appendix D. It can be seen that there are few similarities or consistencies over the years 1972 and 1973. The only consistency is that clay and firing revenues appear to be directly related to each other. Other sources of income fluctuate widely without any discernible pattern.

Recommendations—Marketing In order to increase class sign-ups, pottery sales, and eventually total income and profit, we recommend the following:

1. The Potter's Wheel advertised twice in newspapers in 1973. Although advertisements in the *Santa Fe Sun* may be too expensive for The Potter's Wheel, given the size of its operations, small seasonal ads in the *Valley Pinksheet* would not add much cost to the total advertising budget and would reach the right audience. In both 1972 and 1973, January and summer classes produced the greatest revenue. Likewise, summer and the Christmas season were the periods of greatest pottery sales. Since both classes and pottery sales seem to do best in similar periods, both classes and pottery sales could be advertised simultaneously. Besides summer and Christmas, spot ads could be useful before the beginning of each twelve-week session and around holidays when gifts are given.

2. The Potter's Wheel maintains attendance records of all students. Currently, there are over 1500 names that could be used as a mailing list. The mailer should be timed either to correspond with periods of increased income or periods when sales need stimulation. Since Thor develops excellent rapport with his students, the mailer could serve as a type of newsletter telling when classes are being offered, what new displays are being shown, and any interesting information about developments at The Potter's Wheel. To implement this suggestion, it would be desirable to update the mailing lists, removing names of those who have moved and cannot be traced.

3. Awards won at art shows should be publicized in local newspapers. The specific first place ribbon won by Thor at the national art show in Chicago is an ideal example of such an award. By sending copy to the local newspapers, The Potter's Wheel could receive publicity, which is essentially free advertising.

4. Thor should continue to give demonstrations, lectures, and television appearances to spread his reputation and promote The Potter's Wheel.

5. We agree with Thor's idea of displaying students' wares or his pottery periodically in the parking lot in front of the studio. These shows will help to attract the attention of people passing by. They may be drawn by curiosity to see what is inside.

6. A Potter's Wheel brochure should be designed and distributed. The brochure should focus upon what classes are offered and when they meet. It should be aimed at getting new students and informing potential customers about the studio. A suggested design is shown in Appendix B.

7. The Potter's Wheel runs a 1 x 2 inch advertisement in the Yellow Pages of the Santa Fe Telephone Directory. Most students enroll on the recommendation of former students. The ad should be a smaller two line ad to reduce advertising costs.

8. A large central sign in front of the studio reads, "Thor Gable's Potter's Wheel." Fences on either side of the parking lot display signs in smaller letters, which identify the studio's business. These signs by the fence should be replaced by new signs that identify The Potter's Wheel in large letters as POTTERY or POTTERY GALLERY AND SCHOOL.

9. Mark-down sales of pottery items should be continued in times of poor sales. A visible sign in the parking lot should advertise such sales. The latest mark-down of 40 percent may be more drastic than necessary. A 25 percent mark-down should be tried to see if this is sufficiently attractive to bargain hunters while still allowing The Potter's Wheel a decent margin.

10. Customer relations. Teachers of The Potter's Wheel have excellent relationships with the students. Thor and the other teachers are always willing to take time to help and talk with the students. Sometimes, this results in inadvertent neglect of customers. Customers should be treated with special interest, even to the point of occasional neglect of students.

11. Part of The Potter's Wheel parking lot should be reserved for customers (as opposed to regular students). Los Altos is a heavily traveled boulevard and parking on the street is often difficult to find.

12. The Potter's Wheel should continue to offer a product line representative of all price ranges. It should ensure that it has inexpensive pottery as well as high-quality sculpture/pottery/art items, so that it serves the needs of customers, among them many tourists, looking for inexpensive gifts.

13. The pottery items of the different artists should be separated when displayed for sale. Thor Gable, in particular, should clearly identify his items. This will allow customers to perceive his pottery as of better workmanship than that of his students. It must be seen as special if customers are to build loyalty to his work, and eventually trade up to his expensive sculpture items.

Financial Management

Problem Identified—Financial The Potter's Wheel currently does little financial analysis, financial planning, or financial control. Complete financial analysis of the studio is not possible because of the lack of complete information prior to 1973. However, financial statements are available for 1973. Appendices C, D, and E present an analysis of the 1973 financial statements. Opportunities exist for improvement of working capital (cash) management. Analysis of the 1973 balance sheet indicates that working capital is low, inventory turnover (of pottery items) is slow, and the current ratio ($\frac{\text{current assets}}{\text{current liabilities}}$) is low enough to leave The Potter's Wheel in a less favorable financial position than might be hoped for.

Recommendations The revenues and expenses for 1972 and 1973 were determined as accurately as possible and broken down into main categories (Appendix D). Cash flows were then graphed (Appendix E), showing that six out of the last 24 months were periods when cash outflow exceeded inflow. (Note: Cash flow analysis taken from accounting figures, which are on cash basis.)

To correct the main problems identified, a cash projection form was developed. Each month the expected income and expenses should be projected as accurately as possible (Appendix F). At the end of the month, the actual values can be entered and compared with what was forecast. Comparison can be made also to the same month of 1972 and 1973 from data shown in Appendix D. By consistently and conscientiously filling in this report monthly, Thor Gable will gain familiarity with the primary financial factors of The Potter's Wheel. Specifically:

1. Cash management will be improved. The cash inflows are clearly shown on the chart.
2. Financial planning will be instituted.
3. Financial control will result by showing the main revenue/expense items that were not anticipated to deviate from forecast. This will focus upon problem areas.
4. Consistent records will be kept for financial analysis in the future.

Grants

Thor Gable would like grants from government agencies. Most grants require non-profit corporate status and are thus inapplicable to his situation. We recommend that Mr. Gable apply for the Craftsmen's Fellowship Program of the National Endowment for the Arts. The deadline for Fiscal 1974 was December 15, but Thor may apply for Fiscal 1975 this coming fall. This grant meets Thor's needs well as its purpose is "to enable craftsmen to set aside time, to aid in purchasing materials and for other purposes that would enable them to advance their careers."[2]

STRATEGY CHANGES AND CONCLUSION

Thor Gable wishes to spend more of his time furthering his career as an artist. To do this, he must free more time to create works and to build his reputation in the art world. This means reducing pottery classes, his main source of revenue, or turning over more instruction time to assistants. There is a definite risk involved, but there are higher potential monetary and intrinsic rewards from the sale of his best work than he likely can hope for through teaching. He

---

[2]National Endowment for the Arts, *Visual Arts Program Guidelines,* Fiscal Year 1974, p. 6.

also is not prevented from returning to full-time teaching in the event that his new direction is less profitable than anticipated.

If Thor were to continue his business as he currently operates it, he should do all he could to increase the number of classes offered and the total enrollment in those classes. Given his fixed costs, he could increase his profits from classes by 285 percent by increasing class enrollment about 66 percent (See Appendix G).

Along with improved marketing methods, classes might be increased by offering four-week sessions for beginners. This would serve as an introduction to pottery making for those unsure of their ability or continuing interest, who might be unwilling to enroll for a full 12-week session.

Given Thor Gable's desired change in emphasis, here are some possible avenues he can pursue. Ms. Thelma Rodriguez of the County Art Museum suggests that he send slides of his best work to museum curators; she says that he can find which curators would have an interest in his type of art work from the Art Museum Association's *Directory for Museums*. If a museum exhibits his work, art connoiseurs will see it; they would be more likely to buy more expensive work than casual visitors to Thor's shop. Ms. Rodriguez specifically recommends contacting the Curator of California Design, Pasadena Museum of Modern Art, who is putting together a Southwest design exhibit for next fall.

Ms. Rodriguez also suggests that Thor concentrate on competing in "juried" art shows, placing less emphasis on art fairs and local exhibits. These juried shows are more prestigious and offer more exposure to art experts and art buyers. The shows are announced in *Art Week* magazine.

Ms. Michele Tessier, who has worked at the Whitney Museum in New York, believes that Thor would benefit if he found a dealer with clientele likely to purchase expensive works of sculpture. She states that an art dealer might be found through the Art Dealer's Association.

Thor Gable is a talented, imaginative, and aggressive man. Despite any problems we have seen, we cannot help thinking that his business will be basically sound so long as he is intimately involved in it.

APPENDIX B. Suggested Redesigned Pamphlet

POTTERY   SCULPTURE
WEAVING & MACRAME
THOR GABLE'S, THE POTTER'S WHEEL
A STUDIO WHERE YOU CAN HAVE FREEDOM OF EXPRESSION
OUR PHILOSOPHY: "CREATIVITY IN SELF-EXPRESSION"

First you must accept your self, only then can you accept what you create. This is the basic philosophy from which we teach pottery. The road to understanding and practicing this philosophy is through patience, which is the key to learning. "Patience is a measure of time, to be attained through love and understanding."

APPENDIX B (continued)

BEGINNING & ADVANCED CLASSES

Children pottery   12 Lessons
    Use of tools/glazes & 1 bag of clay

$56.00 class
 8.00 lab
$64.00 total

Adult & Teen pottery   12 Lessons
    Use of tools/glazes & 1 bag of clay

$65.00 class
 15.00 lab
$80.00 total

Family Night (Couples only, Friday) for two people
    4 lessons each; use of tools/glazes & 2 bags clay

$40.00 class
 10.00 lab
$50.00 total

CO-OP pottery   12 Lessons (Call Potter's Wheel for fee)
    Advance requirements—3 sets of 12 lessons
    ASK ABOUT OUR CO-OP MEMBERSHIP
Weaving & Macrame   4 Lessons

$24.00 total

SIGN UP NOW!
Maximum 15 students per Class
DEPOSIT OF $40.00 for all classes required as registration fee;
REMAINDER paid in second week of class
ATTENDANCE: You have 15 weeks in which to take 12 lessons

NO REFUND AFTER 3RD WEEK
SALE OF CLAY & FIRING
    Student $2.92/25 pounds of clay   FIRING 2c/sq. in.
    Non-student $4.08/25 pounds of clay   FIRING 2c/sq. in.
    PORCELAIN CLAY $4.24/25 pounds of clay for everyone

APPENDIX C. Financial Statements

Growth Trend	Dec. 30, 1972	Dec. 31, 1973	1972–1973
Capital	$5,101.35	$6,935.45	+ 36%

Working Capital, Dec. 31, 1973	$2,337.49
Current Ratio, Dec. 31, 1973	$8,494/$6,156 = 1.38
Inventory Dec. 31, 1973	$7,500
Monthly Sales, 1973	$4,170
Tax Reserve	$ 130.80

APPENDIX C (continued)

		% Total Income		% Total Income
	1972	1972	1973	1973
Income				
Classes	$28,551	57.0	$25,277	50.5
Firing	7,912	15.8	9,746	19.4
Pottery sales	10,094	20.1	10,360	20.7
Clay sales	3,572	7.1	3,711	7.4
Other			953	1.9
Total Income	50,129		50,046	
Expense				
Commissions, casual labor	$ 5,379	10.7	17,427	34.8
Studio supplies	9,294	18.5	8,537	17.1
Rent	4,097	8.2	4,845	9.7
Utilities	3,752	7.4	3,374	6.7
Repairs and maintenance	2,376	4.7	2,458	4.9
Office supplies	2,157	4.3	1,847	3.7
Advertising	809	1.6	2,011	4.0
Miscellaneous	7,324	14.6	3,949	5.5
Total Expense	35,188		44,447	
Net Profit	$14,941		$ 5,599	

Table title: Income Statement Analysis 1972–1973

Note: Records for 1972 are of questionable accuracy due to incompleteness of the books. The accountant handling the books for 1972 has been released.

APPENDIX D. Revenues

	Clay	Firing	Classes	Pottery Sales	Total
Revenues 1973 ($)					
Jan.	393	514	4,164	312	5,383
Feb.	366	693	1,495	642	3,196
Mar.	401	593	2,626	691	4,501
Apr.	358	960	2,126	794	4,238
May	579	1,226	2,093	585	4,482
June	145	979	2,778	612	4,514
July	186	702	1,648	831	3,367
Aug.	283	773	2,121	910	4,087
Sept.	103	418	2,977	902	4,400
Oct.	324	870	1,753	331	3,278
Nov.	328	1,153	962	907	3,351
Dec.	244	878	1,756	1,907	4,794
Revenues 1972 ($)					
Jan.	176	303	2,640	929	4,048
Feb.	304	554	2,123	161	3,143
Mar.	248	519	1,833	186	2,785
Apr.	154	563	1,968	647	3,331
May	297	458	2,031	1,173	3,959
June	288	535	1,944	675	3,442
July	652	969	3,103	1,070	5,794
Aug.	327	935	3,206	923	5,391
Sept.	96	368	2,995	602	4,061
Oct.	213	715	2,842	696	4,467
Nov.	467	1,140	1,915	1,118	4,639
Dec.	349	853	1,949	1,915	5,066

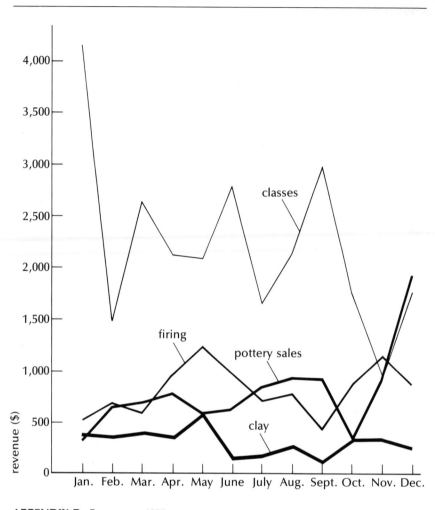

APPENDIX D. Revenues 1973

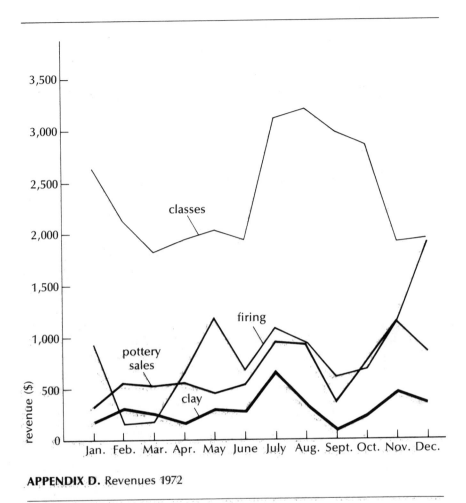

APPENDIX D. Revenues 1972

APPENDIX D (continued)

Expenses 1973 ($)

	Commissions, Labor	Studio Supplies	Rent	Utilities	Repairs, Maintenance	Office Supplies	Advertising	Miscellaneous	Total
Jan.	867	743	375	403	147	122	98	1,009	3,764
Feb.	709	281	375	144	56	22	2	796	2,351
Mar.	1,138	674	375	651	141	371	114	837	4,301
Apr.	1,249	778	450	281	230	16	169	1,135	4,308
May	689	648	450	246	89	77	211	1,257	3,667
June	609	448	450	304	77	186	249	2,301	4,625
July	736	281	200	169	131	189	124	1,572	3,402
Aug.	797	584	720	97	127	27	363	1,496	4,219
Sept.	614	986	450	339	132	160	15	1,571	4,291
Oct.	1,651	761	450	265	83	94	120	535	3,939
Nov.	781	707	450	294	715	12	204	679	3,709
Dec.	794	937	100	180	753	117	260	1,198	4,051

Expenses 1972 ($)

	Commissions, Labor	Studio Supplies	Rent	Utilities	Repairs, Maintenance	Office Supplies	Advertising	Miscellaneous	Total
Jan.	76	403	300	246	341	102	—	527	2,187
Feb.	213	1,141	300	295	201	178	—	727	3,002
Mar.	318	971	121	261	215	202	107	270	2,620
Apr.	313	363	375	102	268	216	112	1,182	3,137
May	349	729	375	717	169	255	255	579	4,065
June	544	1,152	376	267	68	208	28	638	3,972
July	490	386	375	617	41	44	—	629	2,823
Aug.	538	679	375	241	229	141	210	853	3,547
Sept.	493	607	375	308	270	83	—	783	3,120
Oct.	857	1,151	375	221	214	212	97	378	3,563
Nov.	721	1,066	375	—	345	170	—	745	3,465
Dec.	467	646	375	477	14	344	—	14	2,637

APPENDIX D (continued)

	Studio Supplies ($) June 1972–June 1973		
	Tools	Clay	Glazes	Total
1972				
June	47	133	101	281
July	61	343	—	404
Aug.	27	366	9	402
Sept.	69	223	90	382
Oct.	34	432	68	534
Nov.	39	454	35	528
Dec.	29	395	156	580
1973				
Jan.	52	681	53	786
Feb.	45	338	16	299
Mar.	90	272	38	400
Apr.	44	224	3	271
May	32	598	103	733
June	16	214	82	312

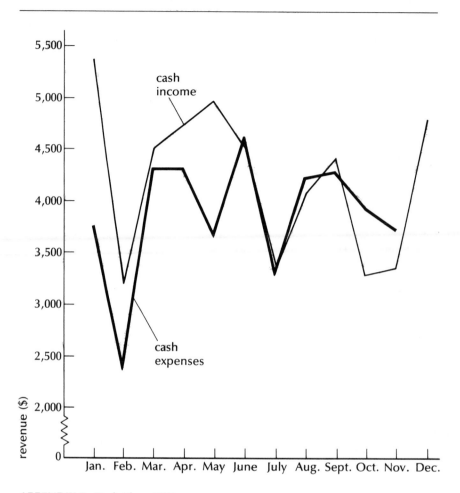

APPENDIX E. Cash Flow 1973

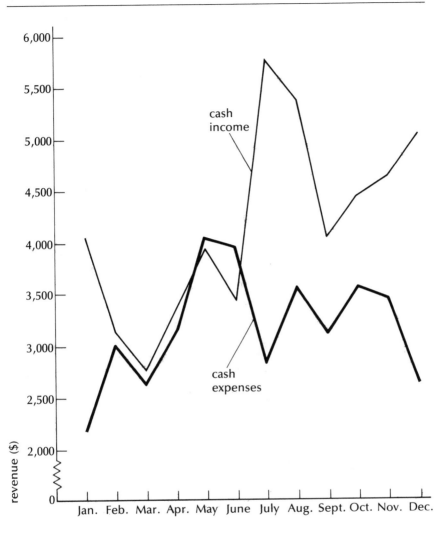

APPENDIX E. Cash Flow 1972

APPENDIX F. Suggested Financial Management Form

	Forecast $/%	Actual $/%	1 Year Ago $/%	2 Years Ago $/%	Forecast—Actual $
Income					
Classes					
Beginning					
Intermediate & advanced					
Children					
Teen					
Couple					
Weaving					
Pottery Sales					
Firing					
Student					
Outside					
Clay sales					
Show sales					
Miscellaneous					
Total Income					
Expenses					
Commissions, labor					
Part-time					
Teachers					
Commissions, sales					
Studio supplies					
Clay					
Glazes					
Tools					
Rent					
Utilities					
Gas					
Phone					
Water & power					
Repairs & maintenance					
Kilns					
Lumber					
Smocks					
Office supplies					
Advertising					
Telephone directory					
Paper					
Miscellaneous					
Auto					
Insurance, legal, accounting					
Total Expenses					
Net Profit,					
Income − Expenses					

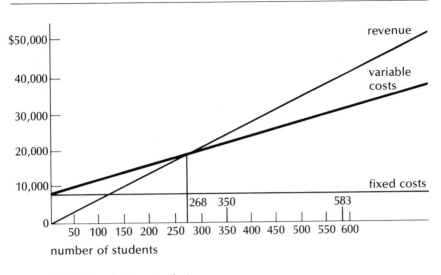

APPENDIX G. Break-Even Analysis

This analysis is only a rough estimation. We suspect that it understates the probable increase in costs; however, we believe it does generally reveal the possibility of improved profits while maintaining the present character of the business.

Taking as fixed costs all but labor and studio supplies, apportioning cost in relation to income because it is impossible to separate more clearly, then 50.5% of costs relate to classes.

50.5% of fixed costs = $9,334 as fixed cost of classes

There are presently three regular 12-week class sessions in a year and a 6-week and a 4-week session in the summer. There are approximately 8.3 students per class and 11 classes per 12-week session. This makes for about 350 full quarter equivalent students. (For the 6-week and 4-week sessions, it is assumed that costs and prices are proportional to 12-week sessions.)

Taking the variable cost of $13,112 and dividing by 350 students gives a variable cost per student of $37.46. Dividing 350 students into the total class revenue of $25,287 gives an average revenue of $72.25 per student.

Break-even point:

$$9,334 + 37.46X = 72.25X,$$
$$34.79X = 9,334,$$
$$X = 268 \text{ students.}$$

Next year Thor is cutting back to ten classes and wants to increase the average number per class. At 15 people per class with ten classes per session, three full sessions and two summer sessions, the maximum number of full time equivalent students is 583.

At that level profit would equal:

$$(34.79) \times (583) - 9,334 = \$10,949$$

This compares with the current profit of:

$(34.79) \times (350) - 9{,}334 = \$2{,}843$, which is 50.5% of $5,630, total profit.

When enrollment is increased to 583, this constitutes a 285% increase in profits for a 66% increase in students.

There is the assumption here that the costs other than labor and studio supplies are fixed. This is not strictly true; they are semivariable. Rent is fixed but utilities, office supplies, etc., will go up with more students. However, matching these will be increases in clay sales and firing revenue, which are positively related to increased numbers of students. (Also in order to service a much larger volume of students, it might be necessary to make a fixed investment in another kiln.)

Not yet taken into account are the marketing costs involved in bringing in new students. Presently ads and promotion are at $2,000 a year. If this analysis is approximately correct, Thor could spend up to the after tax quantity resulting from $8,106 additional profit and still be better off than now. The after tax amount depends on his tax bracket.

Beau Brummel, Inc.

BACKGROUND OF THE OWNER

Mr. Thomas Rogers, owner of Beau Brummel, Inc., is 30 years old. His personality is outgoing; he is articulate and markedly sales-oriented. In addition, we were impressed by his apparent honesty and personal integrity.

Mr. Rogers started in the men's retail clothing business as a youngster, fifteen years ago. He worked for seven years for the owner of a men's clothing store at 1105 Seaview Boulevard. Here he gained a wide experience in the business.

Upon the death of the owner and the settlement of his estate, Mr. Rogers took over the empty store. He acquired the fixtures for $1,000, which came from his personal savings. He was able to obtain $3,000 worth of merchandise on credit from suppliers who had come to know him during the seven years he had worked in the store.

He and his wife ran the store together for the first three years. They sold about $100,000 worth of merchandise during the first year. Mr. Rogers drew $50 per week from the business during the first six months of operation. He was able to raise this to $125 per week during the second half of the year. In the following year, he increased his drawing to $200 per week. It would appear that he operated his business with due care and practiced good husbandry in managing his resources.

Mr. Rogers reports that the neighborhood deteriorated in subsequent years. He states that he suffered from robberies at an increasing rate, ultimately two to three times a month. The result was the cancellation of his insurance coverage. He then decided to move to a more desirable location.

CHARACTERISTICS OF THE NEW LOCATION

Mr. Rogers ultimately settled on his present location in the Montgomery Ward mall, at 121 Lombard Street, between the main east and west thoroughfares of Pine and Northern Boulevards. The neighborhood appears to be a middle- and lower-middle-class area. It now exhibits a predominantly white population but is shifting from white to black. Mr. Rogers estimates that the existing ratio is about 70 percent Caucasian to 30 percent black. In his opinion, this situation will change to show a predominantly black population in about three years, as blacks move in to displace the whites. He believes his business will prosper as this change takes place, assuming positive steps are taken to rectify the present poor marketing situation and practices under which he suffers—and that he can survive during the interim.

CHARACTERISTICS OF PRESENT LOCATION

Beau Brummel, Inc., is located on the ground floor of a two-story portion of the mall, approximately as shown in the attached sketch. The store has a frontage of 16 feet and is about 200 feet in depth. The store front faces on the interior passageway of the ground floor across from an escalator that leads up to the second floor stores and a second floor entrance to Montgomery Ward. Beau Brummel, Inc., is therefore not visible from the parking area that occupies the major portion of the mall (see Exhibit 1).

There are twelve stores on each of the two floors on the south side of the building. Montgomery Ward occupies both floors on the north side of the building.

Of the stores on the ground floor, only five are now occupied, and on the second floor, above Beau Brummel, only four are occupied. Several retail businesses that previously were open on these floors are now out of business. The location of the mall itself and its entrance are such that they do not readily draw the attention of prospective shoppers. In addition, the desolate appearance of the corridors inside the mall lessens the chance of attracting prospective customers.

Casual inspection of the adjacent Montgomery Ward premises on two separate occasions, one in the late morning and one in mid-afternoon during the middle of the week, showed a very light sprinkling of customers, a much sparser trade than customarily may be observed in similar stores, such as Sears or Penney's on nearby Pine Boulevard. A tentative conclusion may be drawn that the proximity of Montgomery Ward does little to stimulate trade in Beau Brummel.

APPEARANCE OF BEAU BRUMMEL, INC.

Mr. Rogers's store presents an attractive appearance. It is colorful, modern in fixture design, and well arranged with ample open space for customers to walk around and see the merchandise. The design of the store was submitted to the owners and approved by them before the installation of fixtures.

LEASING AGREEMENT AND DIFFICULTIES

Mr. Rogers leased the property for a ten-year term from Lee Enterprises, which owns the mall. By the terms of the lease, Mr. Rogers is obliged to pay his portion of the prorated taxes on the property. He states that he has been overcharged for taxes, and that several of the retail store owners who are in financial difficulty have been forgiven their share of the tax payments. As an aside, Mr. Rogers reports that some tenants who have been forced to close their doors for lack of sales have been allowed to terminate their leases.

Mr. Rogers further states that Lee Enterprises agreed in writing to open the mall with a well-advertised public grand opening. They were further to identify

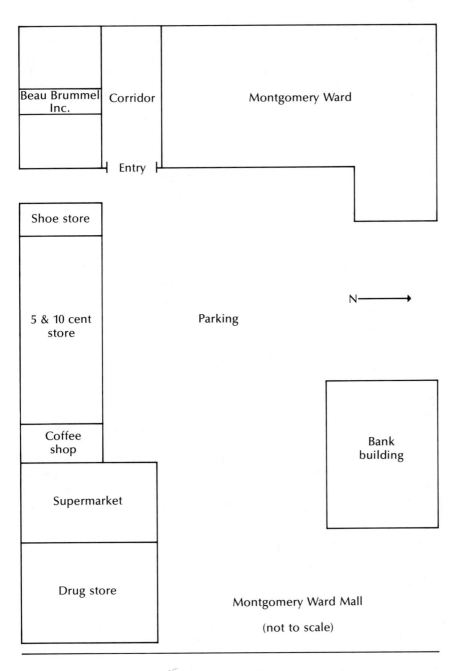

Montgomery Ward Mall

(not to scale)

EXHIBIT 1

the businesses occupying the mall with appropriate signs on the Lombard frontage of the parking lot. Neither of these acts have been performed.

One concession Mr. Rogers has had from the owner is a reduction in rent. For the last year, he has been paying 6 percent of his gross sales in lieu of the $1,000 per month rent originally stipulated in his lease. Rent for this period has been $200 to $300 per month as a consequence.

Mr. Rogers attempted to get a sign installed on the front of the building he occupies. He states that he has Montgomery Ward's approval of the design but has been unable to get the owner to consent to its installation.

FINANCIAL PROBLEMS OF THE BUSINESS

Starting with about $35,000 of his own, Mr. Rogers secured an additional $25,000 through a bank loan co-signed by a well-to-do relative. The latter amount he used to pay for the store fixtures and their installation.

He encountered a seven-month delay in opening his business in the mall because of delay in construction. This delay he attributes to pressure from Montgomery Ward on the owner to complete their portion of the premises so they could open for the Christmas trade in 1969. The construction work force was thereupon shifted from the stores to the Montgomery Ward section. Instead of opening in November as he had planned, Mr. Rogers was forced to delay opening until April 1970. Mr. Rogers says he had no income during this period. He had closed down his previous business and had stored some $50,000 worth of merchandise in boxes at the back of his old store. This delay diminished the attractiveness of his stock, which is highly influenced by current fashion. This factor is critical in his business, since he aims at a market segment comprised of young men in the 25- to 35-year bracket, a style conscious population.

Mr. Rogers estimates his break-even point at $10,000 per month. He indicates he is now doing about half that.

He is currently four months in arrears in meeting his payments to the bank of $750 per month. He has worked out arrangements with his creditors, paying them off at the rate of $400 per month. He says he will do everything in his power to avoid declaring bankruptcy. He is now about $18,000 total in arrears in meeting his business obligations.

INDENTIFICATION OF MAJOR PROBLEMS

A major problem facing Mr. Rogers at this time is obviously one of inadequate cash flow. His relationship with his suppliers seems to be viable enough to enable him to negotiate a holding action pending the solution of his marketing problem.

He faces the allied problem of updating his stock, which he cannot accomplish until there is significant improvement in his financial position.

The solution to his problem of lack of sales lies in bringing in customers. Mr. Rogers states that he does have some established clientele but that he is not getting enough black trade, which he sees as his major source of new customers. He believes black customers won't cross Lombard Street, a dividing line between predominantly black and predominantly white neighborhoods at present. In addition, blacks are not drawn to the Montgomery Ward store from areas east and south of his location. He attributes this to Montgomery Ward's lack of advertising in media that cover those areas. If they were to stimulate black trade by so doing, Mr. Rogers believes his trade would increase with theirs, which seems quite logical.

In summary, Mr. Rogers's serious financial problem could be solved by building his sales. He has wide experience in the business and, in the consultants' opinion, a record of good husbandry and enough business acumen to be successful.

Peak Electronics

Donald Peak had been a manufacturer's representative selling electronic components, primarily miniature insulators, in the greater Southwestern United States during the early 1960s. He had observed in this experience that no manufacturer of insulators was adequately satisfying the experimental and pilot-run needs of either small or large users. Although Mr. Peak had no formal training as an engineer, he was technically competent and had a flair for design. After he conducted extensive market surveys, he decided to abandon his job as manufacturer's representative and start his own business. He formed a sole proprietorship to manufacture miniature insulators by a unique technical process he originated.

He developed a basic marketing strategy for providing full prototype and pilot-run service to all customers. His company now offered both an off-the-shelf product line of high quality insulators, and the special capability of satisfying the short-run needs of small and large manufacturers quickly and at low cost.

COMPANY BACKGROUND

The company started with three employees in Mr. Peak's garage. Within four years the company experienced such growth that it moved to a 12,000-square-foot facility and employed 45 persons. It was incorporated as Peak Electronics in 1968. With an expanding market and Mr. Peak's ingenuity and drive, the company added capacitors and precision delay lines to its products. Sales reached $300,000 in 1970 and doubled during the next two years. Mr. Peak projected the 1975 volume to be at least $2,000,000.

Donald Peak attributed the success of the company to four major factors. First, the sound technical design of products was reflected in the acceptance given the products by the company's many customers and the repeat business the company enjoys. Second, the company's technical strategy, and marketing strategy and segmentation give it the ability to provide short-run or pilot production quantities quickly and economically. (The minimum order is 275

This case was prepared by Arthur H. Kuriloff and John Hemphill, copyright © 1977.

pieces.) The company builds and controls its own tooling; therefore it can meet special design requirements in short order. Third, the company maintains a strong financial position through sound fiscal practice: Peak employs a stringent credit and collection policy. Fourth, an important factor in the success of the company is the loyalty of key personnel, who have worked hard and long to ensure productive output. Many key people in the company view their loyalty as being to the President, Donald Peak, personally.

ORGANIZATION STRUCTURE

Personnel in 1973 comprised 70 operators and assemblers, and 12 persons serving in supervisory or staff positions. Although positions and reporting relationships were loosely defined, the organization appeared to be as shown in the accompanying organization chart.

Most employees in supervisory or staff positions had started with the company as soon as they had completed high school. A few, including Dennis Thompson, Tom Wacker, and Stan Sanders, were taking evening courses toward a college degree. Howard Warner had worked with the company since it had operated in Mr. Peak's garage. He was appointed Vice President in 1969. Close family ties were ubiquitous in the organization. For example, John Peak was the son of Donald Peak, Jim Hill was the son-in-law of Donald Peak, Dennis Fritz was the son of Sylvia Fritz, and Bob Carnes was married to the daughter of Bonnie Parks. Several family relationships existed at the operator and assembler level.

The clerical group took care of phone-in order-taking activities and secretarial duties. The production section, the largest operating unit, manufactured miniature insulators and was headed by Jim Hill. Dennis Fritz and Tom Wacker shared supervision and training duties with Jim Hill, while Fran Stills assisted in supervising and working in the secondary operations activities: primarily filing, drilling, and deburring the insulators.

As indicated on the organization chart, all supervisors and staff persons reported to Donald Peak and Howard Warner. Linda Moore in shipping, however, reported only to Mr. Warner.

Stan Sanders had the responsibility for "100 per cent testing" of all products. Linda Moore, like Hill, Fritz, Sanders, Levy, and several others, had been with the company over five years. She received raw material shipments and prepared Peak Electronics' products for delivery. Fred Levy prepared precision tools and molds for production.

The Delay Line and Capacitor assembly sections were relatively new, having been formed in 1970. Donald Peak hired Bob Carnes away from a competitor because his technical expertise would help the company get into the manufacturing of delay lines and capacitors. Mr. Carnes trained John Peak, the President's son, to supervise the capacitor unit. The Lead Women trained new workers for their unit and provided coordination assistance in addition to their assembly tasks.

OUTSIDE ADVICE IS ENLISTED

In September, 1973, Donald Peak asked two management consultants to analyze the company and help him to redesign the organization. It was learned

Peak Electronics, Inc.
Organization Chart

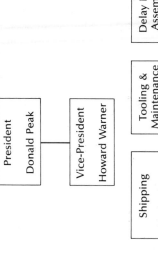

President
Donald Peak

Vice-President
Howard Warner

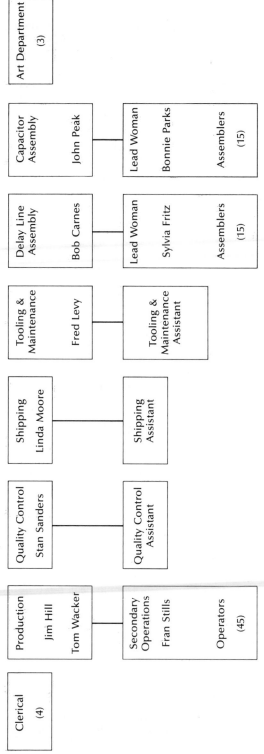

Clerical
(4)

Production
Jim Hill
Tom Wacker

Secondary
Operations
Fran Stills

Operators
(45)

Quality Control
Stan Sanders

Quality Control
Assistant

Shipping
Linda Moore

Shipping
Assistant

Tooling &
Maintenance
Fred Levy

Tooling &
Maintenance
Assistant

Delay Line
Assembly
Bob Carnes

Lead Woman
Sylvia Fritz

Assemblers
(15)

Capacitor
Assembly
John Peak

Lead Woman
Bonnie Parks

Assemblers
(15)

Art Department
(3)

that the company would move to a new location in the northern part of the state and begin operations there in January, 1974. Mr. Peak gave as reasons for the move the need for a larger and more stable pool of labor, an expanded and more modern facility, and easier access to customers. In redesigning the organization, Mr. Peak emphasized his desire to devote more of his attention to the marketing aspect of the business and to spend more time pursuing other business interests and leisure activities.

He stated that he was considering the implementation of the four-day work week in the company. He asked the consultants to determine the feasibility of such action and to provide their conclusions in the final report. He summarized by saying to the consultants, "I want to clean up all the problems before we move into our new plant."

INTERVIEWS PROVIDE RAW DATA

After the consultants became familiar with operational aspects of Peak Electronics, they conducted several depth interviews. Data were obtained from all supervisory and staff personnel and from a sample of operators and assemblers. The interviewees seemed to welcome the opportunity to discuss internal aspects of the company with the consultants. Although the interviews were anticipated to last 30–40 minutes, many continued for more than an hour, and some lasted twice that long. Several interviews were conducted to obtain additional data and to check for reliability.

The data were grouped into six categories and a content analysis was conducted. Responses from the interviewees are reproduced below for each category. The comments were selected on the basis of frequency of mention. The last category, morale, includes data that either overlap or tend to clarify data in other categories.

Interpersonal Relations

"Talking among ourselves while working used to be outlawed, but now it's tolerated."

"There is a mismatch of personnel and positions, especially at the Supervisory level."

"Bob Carnes is after Howard Warner's job and everybody knows it."

"Mr. Peak is moody, unfair, and unpredictable; you can't get his undivided attention."

"We need more direct communication in this company, and less gossip."

"People don't view Howard Warner as a vice president; he's just one of the boys."

"Family squabbles tend to interfere with the work sometimes."

Compensation Policy

"It pays to lay low and keep quiet in the company. If you don't make waves, you get the same raise as everyone else regardless of how hard you work."

"Superior work isn't rewarded."

"We need a sick leave and overtime policy for salaried people."

"It's a complete mystery to most people around here as to how they are evaluated."

"Mr. Peak has always insisted on hiring people at the minimum wage and only grants raises after a one-month trial period."

Working Conditions

"The place needs a janitor; it's dirty all the time."

"I wish we could have music. It would help pass the time."

"Our work is dull, hot, and dirty."

"Even the hourly people are sick and tired of working six days every week. We know orders need to be filled, but nine months of this is long enough."

Turnover and Absenteeism

"John Peak's capacitor group supposedly has 8 to 10 jobs, but only 5 or 6 people usually show up."

"Absenteeism sometimes runs as high as 50 percent. I think most people think up some excuse to get two days off each week."

"Turnover in assemblers has caused a 'rat-race' for the past couple of years."

"I'll bet 60 percent of the assemblers and operators quit each year."

Management Succession

"Mr. Peak can't handle the tremendous work load—he should delegate more."

"Howard Warner is just a high-priced delivery boy and messenger."

"I don't see any evidence of planning or thinking ahead."

"Dennis Fritz is viewed as the most likely replacement for Howard Warner."

Morale

"During Mr. Peak's month-long vacation, the company had an extraordinary volume. When he returned, you couldn't tell whether he was pleased or not."

"It would help if Mr. Peak were interested in you as a person—he used to be!"

"We need clarification of jobs around here."

"It will be difficult to get respect for supervisors who have been drones."

"Mr. Peak should stop touring the departments. He disregards supervisors and mostly criticizes as he goes—it disrupts people unnecessarily."

"I think Mr. Peak likes to see people capitulate."

"The Peak family causes problems. John gets paid more than any employee and he doesn't do anything—people don't know what he does."

"Mr. Peak leads people by fear and intimidation."

"Mr. Peak doesn't compliment anyone, and his demands are excessive."

"I didn't know I was a supervisor until I was informed of this interview."

"Nobody has defined authority and responsibility in the company."

"People go to Dennis Fritz with problems; Jim Hill and Tom Wacker yell at them too much."

"There's some clannishness, and confrontation between families causes problems."

"Turnover is extremely high, and the operators are unhappy across the board."

"The company runs smoother and people feel more relaxed when Mr. Peak is gone."

"I'm tired of being yelled at every day; supervisors show no respect for their people."

"Too many people overlap in their work."

PEAK REACTS TO THE DATA

The consultants summarized the data so as to assure anonymity of the speakers. They then reviewed their findings with Mr. Peak. After hearing some of the comments related to compensation, he said, "I just informed people of their raises a month ago and told them why they got what they did. I think they're just bickering." One of the consultants replied that, "perceptions tend to form an individual's view of reality." As the review continued, Peak asked a few questions for clarification and listened quietly.

The consultants then proceeded to prepare their final report.

NAME INDEX

SUBJECT INDEX